FEDERALISM IN AMERICA

FEDERALISM IN AMERICA

AN ENCYCLOPEDIA ❖ VOLUME ONE ❖ A–J

Edited by Joseph R. Marbach, Ellis Katz, and Troy E. Smith

GREENWOOD PRESS
Westport, Connecticut • London

Library of Congress Cataloging-in-Publication Data

Federalism in America : an encyclopedia / edited by Joseph R. Marbach, Ellis Katz, and Troy E. Smith.
    p. cm.
   Includes bibliographical references and index.
    ISBN 0–313–32947–8 (set : alk. paper)—ISBN 0–313–32948–6 (v. 1 : alk. paper)—ISBN 0–313–32949–4 (v. 2 : alk. paper) 1. Federal government—United States—Encyclopedias. I. Marbach, Joseph R. II. Katz, Ellis. III. Smith, Troy E., 1967–
JK311.F434   2006
320.473'049'03—dc22   2005019213

British Library Cataloguing in Publication Data is available.

Library of Congress Catalog Card Number: 2005019213
ISBN: 0–313–32947–8 (set)
    0–313–32948–6 (vol. I)
    0–313–32949–4 (vol. II)

First published in 2006

Greenwood Press, 88 Post Road West, Westport, CT 06881
An imprint of Greenwood Publishing Group, Inc.
www.greenwood.com

Printed in the United States of America

The paper used in this book complies with the Permanent Paper Standard issued by the National Information Standards Organization (Z39.48–1984)

10 9 8 7 6 5 4 3 2 1

CONTENTS

ALPHABETICAL LIST OF ENTRIES

Topical List of Entries

PREFACE

Our colleague, John Kincaid of Lafayette College, was initially approached about the possibility of editing an encyclopedia dedicated to American federalism. Recognizing the value of such a volume and the fact that prior commitments would prevent him from solely editing it, John invited the three of us to discuss the feasibility of such an undertaking. After agreeing to take on this project and dividing up the workload, we set off on this endeavor.

Our first task was to establish an editorial advisory board of scholars working on the various aspects of federalism that we could turn to for advice and guidance. Next we drew up a preliminary list of the subjects that should be included. This was done by surveying the literature on American federalism and soliciting input from the editorial board, members of the American Political Science Association's Section on Federalism and Intergovernmental Relations, and other scholars who answered our call for authors.

Federalism is one of the essential organizing principles of the U.S. Constitution, and has been a deep and enduring force shaping American politics and public policy. Federalism is the American founders' unique and remarkable contribution to government and political science. While federal structures have spread around the globe alongside democracy, American government remains an important example of how a federal system can be structured, how it evolves, and how it affects government, politics, and policies. Spanning from the drafting of the U.S. Constitution, the Nullification crisis, secession and the Civil War, and the post-war amendments to the New Deal, the Second Reconstruction, various New Federalisms, Devolution, and the new national security initiatives, the history of American federalism is one of contentious battles over the centralization or decentralization of political power and sovereignty, with profound effects for public policy.

Unlike most other nations' governments, U.S. federal, state, and local governments have been partners in shaping domestic policy. At essence, federalism is the debate over the proper role of government in society, seeking to answer the questions arising over which is the proper government to perform these functions. Thus, nearly every major policy area has been affected by federalism. Additionally, every major political institution has had and continues to have some influence on this dynamic relationship. And yet, no major encyclopedic reference has ever been produced on this bedrock principle underlying American political institutions.

In over 400 entries, this reference work offers a comprehensive listing of the theories, concepts, and terms describing American federalism since its inception. The range of entries covers the key constitutional provisions, historical eras and periods, political figures and ideologies, legislation, federal court cases, fiscal arrangements, policy instruments, policy domains, patterns of intergovernmental relations, and other topics relevant to federalism in the United States.

The entries appear in alphabetical order and mingle long interpretive essays with shorter ones. When appropriate, we have included side bars, especially the provisions of the Constitution that are described by various entries. We have also included photographs and maps to illustrate the individuals and events that have shaped the development of American federalism.

We have attempted to identify the most significant terms, concepts, individuals, and court decisions associated with the development of American federalism that would be relevant to our primary audience—undergraduate students receiving their first exposure to this field of study. Some entries that may not have been included are the casualties of both time and space constraints that a project of this type naturally imposes. We also made the editorial decision not to include entries on individual scholars, living or deceased. Rather, we have identified their theoretical contributions to the field and have recognized them in this way.

All the entries were assigned to specific authors. In editing these entries, we were careful to maintain the voice and interpretation of each author, and the views and opinions, when expressed, are those of the author and not of any organization with which he or she may be affiliated.

There are many individuals to whom we owe a debt of gratitude. Our editorial advisory board reviewed and revised the list of entries, suggested potential contributors, and in several instances wrote entries. We are also indebted to the many contributors who wrote this book. These individuals are among some of the most accomplished and respected scholars in the field. Throughout the process, Steven Vetrano of Greenwood Publishing has provided timely advice, assistance in dealing with our authors, and an attention to detail that has made this a better book.

We also thank our families, particularly our wives, for their indulgence and encouragement throughout this process.

J.R.M.
E.K.
T.E.S.

TIMELINE OF AMERICAN FEDERALISM

1754 Albany Plan

1776 Declaration of Independence

1777 Articles of Confederation drafted

1781 Articles of Confederation ratified

1786 Annapolis Convention

1787 Constitutional Convention convened in Philadelphia
The Federalist Papers written

1789 U.S. Constitution takes effect

1791 First ten amendments (Bill of Rights) added to the Constitution
First Bank of the United States established

1798 Alien and Sedition Acts
Kentucky and Virginia Resolutions passed

1810 Supreme Court renders *Fletcher v. Peck* decision

1814 Hartford Convention

1819 Supreme Court renders *McCulloch v. Maryland* and *Dartmouth College v. Woodward* decisions

1824 Supreme Court rules in *Gibbons v. Ogden*

1828 John Calhoun writes *South Carolina Exposition* arguing for the theory of nullification

1830	Webster-Hayne debates
1831	John Calhoun delivers Fort Hill Address
1837	Supreme Court renders *Charles River Bridge Company v. Warren Bridge Company* decision
1842	Supreme Court renders *Prigg v. Pennsylvania* decision
1850	Congress passes Compromise of 1850 and Fugitive Slave Acts
1857	Supreme Court renders *Dred Scott v. Sandford* decision
1861–65	American Civil War
1863	President Abraham Lincoln issues Emancipation Proclamation
1865	Thirteenth Amendment ratified
1866	First Civil Rights Act passed
1868	Fourteenth Amendment ratified
1870	Fifteenth Amendment ratified
1873	Supreme Court renders Slaughterhouse Cases decision
1875	Fourth post–Civil War Civil Rights Act passed
1887	Congress passes Interstate Commerce Commission Act
1890	Congress enacts the Sherman Antitrust Act
1896	Supreme Court renders *Plessy v. Ferguson* decision
1913	Sixteenth Amendment ratified
1925	Supreme Court renders *Gitlow v. New York*
1933–39	Franklin D. Roosevelt's New Deal program enacted
1937	Supreme Court renders *National Labor Relations Board v. Jones and Laughlin Steel Corporation* and *West Coast Hotel Co. v. Parrish* decisions
1941	Supreme Court renders *United States v. Darby* decision
1953	Kestnbaum Commission established by Congress

1954   Supreme Court renders *Brown v. Board of Education of Topeka* decision

1959   U.S. Advisory Commission on Intergovernmental Relations (ACIR) established

1962   Supreme Court renders *Baker v. Carr* decision

1964   Lyndon B. Johnson initiates the Great Society program
Civil Rights Act enacted by Congress

1965   Voting Rights, Medicare, and Medicaid Acts passed by Congress
Supreme Court renders *Griswold v. Connecticut* decision

1970   Richard M. Nixon introduces New Federalism
Environmental Protection Act passed by Congress

1972   Revenue Sharing Act passed by Congress

1973   Supreme Court renders *Roe v. Wade* decision

1976   Supreme Court renders *National League of Cities v. Usery* decision

1977   Jimmy Carter introduces New Partnership program

1981   Ronald Reagan introduces New Federalism

1985   Supreme Court renders *Garcia v. San Antonio Metropolitan Transit Authority* decision

1986   General Revenue Sharing program abolished

1987   Supreme Court renders *South Carolina v. Baker* and *South Dakota v. Dole* decisions

1991   Intermodal Surface Transportation Act enacted

1995   Congressional Republicans implement Contract with America provisions

1996   Supreme Court renders *United States v. Lopez* and *Seminole Tribe of Florida v. Florida* decisions
Advisory Commision on Intergovernmental Relations abolished

1998   Transportation Equity Act for the Twenty-first Century enacted

2000   Supreme Court renders *Bush v. Gore* decision

2001   No Child Left Behind Act enacted
USA PATRIOT Act enacted

Abortion   Abortion is the termination of a pregnancy prior to birth, resulting in the destruction of the fetus. Such termination may arise from spontaneous abortion (termed "miscarriage"), where the fetus is delivered due to underlying fetal or maternal factors. It may also be caused by purposeful conduct including self-induced abortion, or surgical or medical abortion, where the embryo or fetus is removed through the use of instruments or drugs due to medical concerns or a discretionary decision to end the pregnancy. Induced abortion has been practiced throughout history by ancient, medieval, and contemporary societies. Public opinion regarding the propriety of such elective abortion has varied, influenced by religion, philosophy, medicine, and culture. In 1973 the abortion issue was addressed by the U.S. Supreme Court in the landmark decision of *Roe v. Wade*, in which the Court asserted that the Constitution, pursuant to the Fourteenth Amendment due process clause, affords a woman the right to choose abortion, within the context of permissible state regulations that reflect the state's interest in the life of the fetus and the health of the woman. While the Court undeniably reinforced its support of the constitutional core of *Roe* in 1992's *Planned Parenthood v. Casey*, it also provided greater opportunity for state legislatures to regulate the manner in which abortions will be conducted.

Many commentators anticipated that *Roe* would serve to balance the competing interests of the woman, the fetus, and the state and bring resolution to the issue. Instead, abortion has become one of the most divisive and politicized issues in the nation in a variety of contexts. Those conflicts include the morality of aborting a "person" as stated by opponents of abortion called "pro-life" versus the contention by "pro-choice" groups that a woman has a constitutional right to reproductive freedom. The interests of the state and federal government in regulating abortions conflict with the woman's ability to exercise her right of choice in a manner that is not unduly burdened. Further, a jurisprudential conflict exists as to whether the Supreme Court via *Roe* and its progeny violates the tenets of federalism, and whether Congress in issuing legislation like the Partial Birth Abortion Act of 2003 violates the Tenth Amendment reservation of powers to the states to handle those issues, such as family matters, to which the federal government traditionally does not assert jurisdiction. So strongly do these interests permeate the societal landscape that judicial nominees and elected officials are often exposed to a litmus test with regard to their abortion views.

HISTORICAL PERSPECTIVES

A historical review suggests that neither ancient nor contemporary society has exhibited a uniform attitude toward abortion. Instead, there has existed a complex interplay of a variety of religious, legal, medical, and philosophical viewpoints on when life begins and the morality of abortion. Restrictive criminal abortion laws in the United States, which prohibited abortion at any time except to spare the life of the mother, emanated from the latter part of the nineteenth century. Notably, these laws had no precedent in either ancient or common law experience. What is clear is that throughout all historical periods, women have sought abortions for a variety of reasons, abortion has been practiced, and such practice was never universally condemned by society.

Ancient Greeks and Romans appear to have rather freely practiced abortion, with neither the law nor religion posing significant impediments to abortion. Philosophical and religious positions adopted with regard to the commencement of life served to support the acceptance of abortion, at least in the early stages of gestation. Aristotle, for example, who reportedly approved of abortion, espoused a theory of life in which the fetus did not become infused with a soul or attain "animation" until a later stage of development, and did not achieve "rationality" until after live birth. Departures from this approving stance were evident. Notably, the Hippocratic Oath specifically prohibited doctors from providing abortive remedies. Commentators suggest, however, that the oath was not uniformly accepted in the Greek and Roman eras, and that support for abortion was prevalent.

Early Christian philosophers and theologians adopted a view similar to that of the Greeks, and asserted that life for a fetus did not begin until forty days after conception for a male and eighty days for a female. St. Augustine distinguished between the early fetus, which had not yet been infused with a soul, and the later fetus, which had been so endowed. While there existed no concurrence regarding the exact point at which the person was formed or animation occurred, the sentiment prevailed that abortion in the early stages of a pregnancy was not criminal. Thus, even under Christianity in the early eras, abortion prior to animation was not deemed murder. That position eventually altered through a combination of papal edicts, resulting in the current posture of the Roman Catholic Church, which is to regard conception as the beginning of human life, thus rendering any abortion violative of church doctrine.

The significance afforded stages of a pregnancy persisted in English common law. The notion of animation was replaced by the term "quickening," which indicated that point in a pregnancy when the mother could recognize movement of the fetus in the womb. The quickening concept was utilized in common law by seventeenth- and eighteenth-century commentators such as Lord Edward Coke and Sir William Blackstone to denote that abortion performed prior to quickening was not an indictable crime. Commentators suggest that abortion performed subsequent to quickening was deemed a criminal offense, although there exists some dispute as to whether the crime was regarded as a homicide or a high misdemeanor, or whether any consensus developed as to the criminality of postquickening abortion.

This English common law tradition was incorporated into the established common law of the United States. Pursuant to that law, women in the American colonies and later the states were afforded broad discretion to terminate a pregnancy. It was not until the early nineteenth century that a few states, beginning with Connecticut in 1821, adopted criminal legislation to prohibit abortion postquickening. By the latter part of the nineteenth century, many states adopted statutes criminalizing abortion that departed from the quickening distinction, making all abortions illegal and increasing the penalties for offenses. Some commentators assert that the laws primarily protected women from ill-trained quacks; others contend that physicians sought strict regulation in order to control the profession. This anti-abortion campaign succeeded in rendering all abortion illegal in the majority of states unless it was performed by a physician to preserve the life of the mother. In 1873 the federal government entered the movement to oppose abortion when Congress passed the Comstock Law, which made mailing, importing, or transporting information on birth control and abortion a criminal offense.

TWENTIETH-CENTURY ABORTION DEVELOPMENTS

Through the 1950s the state statutory law with regard to abortion remained constant, with a majority of the states continuing to ban abortions, although some afforded exceptions for the health or life of the mother. After World War II, doctors increasingly espoused the notion of therapeutic abortions for those women seeking to terminate abortions. Under this rubric, a hospital abortion board would determine if the health of a woman were threatened by a pregnancy, thereby entitling her to an abortion. The 1960s witnessed a more liberal attitude toward abortion, with both the American Medical Association and the American Law Institute supporting the liberalization of abortion laws. It was the U.S. Supreme Court decision of *Griswold v. Connecticut* in 1965 that provided the crucial underpinnings for the assertion that the right to an abortion was a constitutionally protected right. In *Griswold*, the Court nullified a Connecticut statute that had prohibited the use of contraceptives by married couples by holding that it violated the couple's constitutional right to marital privacy. Such a privacy right, the Court contended, although not specifically enumerated in the Constitution, could be found in the emanations from the Bill of Rights. *Griswold*, coupled with the feminist movement of the 1960s and the activism of Planned Parenthood, a successor organization to the American Birth Control League founded in 1921 by Margaret Sanger, propelled 4 states—New York, Hawaii, Alaska, and Washington—to repeal their criminal abortion statutes.

In a decision regarded by many as the landmark case of the twentieth century, the U.S. Supreme Court in its 1973 ruling, *Roe v. Wade*, invalidated a Texas statute first enacted in 1854 that criminalized abortion, and held that a woman has the fundamental right to choose an abortion based on that privacy provided in the Fourteenth Amendment's due process concept of personal liberty. Establishing a trimester framework that focused on fetal viability, the Court held that during the first trimester, a woman could make an abortion decision with her physician; in the second, the states can establish limitations on that right to protect the health of the woman; and in the third, states can render abortion illegal due to their compelling interest in protecting potential life. *Roe* engendered criticism from both the pro-life groups who assert all abortion is criminal, and those adherents to the principles of federalism who urge that the federal government usurped the states' power to determine the regulation or prohibition of abortion. Subsequent to *Roe*, the states and Congress passed restrictive legislation regarding the exercise of abortion rights. In 1977 Congress enacted the Hyde Amendment, which prohibited the use of Medicaid funds for abortion and which was upheld by the Supreme Court. Further, Congress unsuccessfully endeavored to pass a "human life" bill and a constitutional amendment that would establish personhood at conception in an effort to overturn *Roe*. The Supreme Court, in a series of decisions, continued to uphold challenges against *Roe*, invalidating state restrictions that it deemed inconsistent with this fundamental right, as in *Thornburgh v. American College of Obstetrics and Gynecology* (1986). In other cases, however, while the Court reaffirmed *Roe*, it also permitted strict state prohibitions against abortions in public hospitals in *Webster v. Reproductive Health Services* (1989) and a federal "gag rule" prohibition against the discussion of abortion in federally funded clinics in *Rust v. Sullivan* (1991).

The most significant case to be decided since *Roe* by the Supreme Court is the 1992 decision of *Planned Parenthood v. Casey*, which reasserted the constitutional core of its predecessor while limiting its expanse. Rejecting a surrender to political pressure on the "intensely divisive" issue, the Court adhered to stare decisis and refused to overrule *Roe*. It did, however, replace the trimester framework with a point of viability test, which refers to the time at which the fetus is capable of life outside the womb. States are permitted to regulate standards for abortions prior to that point as long as the restrictions do not impose an "undue burden" upon a woman's fundamental liberty interests. After viability, the state may proscribe abortion except if the mother's health is endangered. Thus, *Casey*, which affords more weight to the state's interest in protecting the fetus before viability, upheld Pennsylvania's statute with regard to both a twenty-four-hour waiting period, and parental notification by adolescents or a judicial hearing known as a bypass option where a judge must decide a minor's maturity and capability of giving informed consent. *Casey* did, however, nullify the spousal notification requirement of the Pennsylvania Abortion Control Act as an unconstitutional provision.

Pursuant to the authority of *Casey* and its "undue burden" standard, many states have enacted restrictions on abortion, which typically include parental consent with a judicial bypass option or parental notification requirements, and mandatory waiting periods. Critics note that if judges are unprepared or unwilling to support the right to an abortion, adolescents are exposed to an undue burden. Other commentators urge that all parental notification statutes constitute an undue burden in that minors, in attempting to avoid such involvement, delay abortions or cross state lines to jurisdictions that contain no such parental requirement. Other laws imposing stricter licensing, building, and safety requirements upon the clinics or doctors' offices performing abortion epitomize the restrictions invoked by the states subsequent to *Casey*.

Partial birth abortion bans enacted by states and Congress illustrate further attempts to restrict access to abortion and raise the issue of federalism. Partial birth abortion legislation, so named by abortion opponents, addresses the infrequently used late-term method of abortion known in medical parlance as dilation and extraction, or D&X. The procedure involves the partial removal of the fetus and the collapse of the skull. More than 30 states have enacted partial birth bans, although most have been struck down in the courts as unconstitutional. In 2000, the Supreme Court in *Stenberg v. Carhart* overturned the Nebraska partial birth ban as unconstitutional because it lacked an exception to protect the mother's health, thus placing an undue burden on women's right to choose. Congress twice attempted to enact similar legislation, but President Bill Clinton vetoed the act. In 2003, however, the federal Partial Birth Abortion Ban Act, which closely duplicates the Nebraska statute, was signed by President George W. Bush. Opponents of this legislation, which represents the first federal law banning a specific abortion procedure since *Roe*, challenge it as a further encroachment on a woman's constitutional right to terminate her pregnancy. Other commentators, raising the issue of federalism, query whether Congress should draft legislation that ordinarily would be within the purview of the state legislators.

During the late 1980s and through the early 1990s, anti-abortion protestors engaged in a range of activities intended to deter abortion practice, including clinic bombings and blockades, assault, arson, bioterrorism, harassment, and the murder of several abortion providers. Opponents of abortion established Web sites that detailed personal information regarding abortion providers accompanied by language some regarded as threatening. The incidents of violence during the years 1986 to 2000 numbered more than 3,000. In 2003, Florida executed Paul Hill, an anti-abortion activist who killed a doctor and his escort in 1994.

The Freedom of Access to Clinic Entrances Act (FACE) was enacted by Congress in 1994 to address the violence engendered by the abortion conflict. FACE, which prohibits the use of force, threats of force, and physical obstruction of clinic entrances, markedly reduced the violent attacks on clinics, although such attacks persist. Constitutional challenges to FACE have not proved successful, as the courts reason that the First Amendment does not afford protection to those acts prohibited by FACE. Efforts to balance the right of legitimate protest against abortion versus an individual's right to obtain medical treatment and counseling resulted in some state legislative enactment of buffer zones. In the 2000 decision of *Hill v. Colorado*, the Supreme Court upheld a Colorado statute that made it a crime at a health care facility for an individual to come within eight feet of another without consent, for purposes of counseling and protest with regard to abortion. The statute was not deemed an unlawful restraint of freedom of speech.

Another vehicle that abortion supporters hoped to utilize in the effort to deter violent or obstructionist protests was the Racketeer Influenced and Corrupt Organizations Act (RICO), a federal statute intended to address organized crime. In 1994 the Supreme Court had ruled that RICO could be utilized to civilly sue and obtain injunctive relief and damages against those who conspired to commit abortion clinic violence. But in the 2003 decision of *Scheidler v. National Organization for Women, Inc.*, the Court held that the activities of the abortion opponents, which deprived persons of the right to a legal abortion by compelling the closing of the clinics, did not satisfy the requisites of extortion necessary for RICO to be invoked. Since the protestors had obtained no property of the clinic through their threats, their coercion alone was not sufficient to justify the application of RICO.

With the Food and Drug Administration's approval in 2000 of the early abortion pill RU-486 (mifepristone), women have been provided with a medical, rather than surgical, form of abortion. It affords them a more private vehicle for abortion, removed from the politics of violence and protests associated with the clinic. The potential exists that Congress or the states could ban medical abortions, with the courts determining if such a ban poses an undue burden on a woman's right as defined by *Casey*.

FEDERALISM AND ABORTION

The federalism issue as applied to abortion relates to the division of power between federal and state government and whether it is appropriate for the federal government to act in this particular sphere. Traditionally states determine their stance on public policy issues such as family matters and medical care through their elected legislature, and such positions are not invalidated by federal courts or the federal legislature. The roots of the federalism issue in this particular context are found in *Griswold* and *Roe*, where some commentators urge that the Supreme Court violated the limitations imposed by federalism by using privacy law to invalidate state legislation regarding contraceptives and abortion. Proponents of federalism opine that the Partial Birth Abortion Ban enacted by Congress also violates the constitutional division of powers. It is argued that Congress is restricted to the powers enumerated in the Constitution, and that such late-term abortion activity has no substantial effect on interstate commerce, the clause in the Constitution that empowers Congress to legislate regarding issues of national import. Other commentators contend that the decisions of *Roe* and *Casey* do comport with the principles of federalism as the Court, in deference to states' rights, protects the constitutional role of the states by affording them the opportunity to regulate abortion before viability of the fetus and even ban it post viability within constitutionally imposed restrictions protecting a woman's fundamental right to an abortion.

The divisive nature of the abortion issue will continue to foment conflict among those who regard abortion as immoral and as violative of the right to life of the fetus, and those who regard abortion as the right of a woman to reproductive freedom, with such right superceding that of a fetus that has not attained personhood. The thirty-first anniversary of the *Roe* decision on January 22, 2004, epitomized the continuing conflict, as abortion opponents held a "March for Life" rally whose aim was to seek support to overturn *Roe*, and to enact further restrictions of the exercise of the abortion right. On that same date, advocates of abortion introduced a measure entitled the Freedom of Choice Act in Congress that would establish a federal statutory right to choose, thus prohibiting the government from interfering with reproductive rights, and invalidating any state and federal restrictions on abortion and family planning services that interfere with a woman's fundamental right to choose. *SEE ALSO:* Bill of Rights; Federal Courts; Fourteenth Amendment; Health Care Policy; Interstate Commerce; Medicaid; Morality Policy; Reagan, Ronald; *Roe v. Wade*; State Government; Tenth Amendment

BIBLIOGRAPHY: Neal E. Devins, *Shaping Constitutional Values: Elected Government, the Supreme Court and the Abortion Debate* (Baltimore: Johns Hopkins University Press, 1996); David J. Garrow, "Abortion before and after *Roe v. Wade*: An Historical Perspective," *Albany Law Review* 62 (1999): 833–852; Leslie J. Reagan, *When Abortion Was a Crime: Women, Medicine, and Law in the United States, 1867–1973* (Berkeley: University of California Press, 1998); and Laurence H. Tribe, *Abortion: The Clash of Absolutes* (New York: W.W. Norton, 1992).

AUDREY WOLFSON LATOURETTE

Abstention   "Abstention" in the American legal culture occurs when a federal court abstains from exercising jurisdiction in either of two circumstances. First, a federal court may abstain from deciding a case otherwise properly before it when a constitutional issue may be affected by an unsettled interpretation of state law. This application of abstention is really a deferral of federal jurisdiction based upon the premise that the federal courts should not prematurely resolve the constitutionality of a state statute. The second application, following the deferral approach to abstention, relates to when a federal court should defer exercising its jurisdiction where a state court has previously initiated a judicial proceeding. In such a case, the state proceeding should be allowed to conclude as both a matter of "our federalism" and comity. Hence, both of the preceding concepts of the doctrine of abstention seek to both promote comity between the federal and state systems in the United States and respect the spheres of judicial influences of both the federal and state judicial systems. *SEE ALSO:* Comity; *Michigan v. Long*; New Judicial Federalism; *Younger v. Harris*

CHARLES D. COLE

Adams, John   Among the founders who were serious students of politics, none wrote less about federalism than John Adams (1735–1826). In his major political treatise, the *Defence of the Constitutions of Government of the United States*, Adams reflected that "to collect together the ancient and modern leagues . . . which have been found to answer the purposes both of government and liberty; to compare them all, with the circumstances, the situation, the geography, the commerce, the population, and the forms of government . . . and consider what further federal powers are wanted, and may be safely given, would be a useful work" (Adams 1787, 364). Yet Adams never wrote such a volume. His writings explored checks and balances within governments, not among governments in a federal union.

In general, Adams held that a confederation was little more than an alliance. In the *Defence*, he said that the Articles of Confederation created a "diplomatic assembly." Because each state retained veto power over all significant laws, and because the Confederation lacked any real power to compel the states to comply with its resolutions, it was not truly a government. In effect, Adams thought the Confederation was an expression of intent to coordinate the conduct of foreign affairs among the discrete states. After defeating the British, the Confederation often failed to do even that, making Adams's diplomatic work very difficult. It was hard to negotiate on behalf of a union that lacked the power to enforce the treaties it signed.

When he first saw the United States' federal Constitution, Adams approved of it since it followed the model he had drafted for Massachusetts and defended in his writings, featuring an executive with a veto, a

John Adams. Library of Congress, Prints and Photographs Division.

bicameral legislature, and separation among the legislative, executive, and judicial branches. Adams made few comments on the federal aspect of the Constitution. The key element of his theory of government was that balance could only be achieved in government if there were three bodies contending for power. When the House, Senate, and president (armed with a veto) squared off against each other, no one institution would achieve a final victory because whenever one grew large the other two would gang up to restrain it. Speaking federally, however, there were only two powers—the central government and the states. Adams thought that either the states or the national government would ultimately have the last word in lawmaking. Although the people could in principle delegate some powers to the states and others to the federal government, they failed to create an institutional mechanism to secure that balance once the Constitution went into effect.

The American's union, Adams thought, was a federal republic, so he referred to the nation in the plural as "these states." Moreover, Adams thought it was wise and good to make laws as local as possible. The people of Virginia, of Ohio, and of Massachusetts needed different sets of laws in order to function. Adams nonetheless thought that the general government was in more need of support in his own day than were those of the states. The people had been obeying the laws of their local governments since the colonial era, but the federal government was a novelty to them.

During his presidency, Adams supported and signed, though he had not proposed, the Alien and Sedition Acts. Adams's support for the Alien Acts grew from the logic of the union. Since the federal government existed to manage the foreign affairs of the union, it certainly had the right to regulate which foreigners may and may not reside in the boundaries of the several states. His support of the Sedition Acts grew from the logic of government. Governments, like individuals, had the right to defend themselves against men who printed vicious and false information about them. Such a right inhered in the definition of government. It was a right that governments had always had in the past, and that they would have in the future.

In sum, Adams believed that the American union was a federation, but, having felt the union suffer from the weakness of the Confederation during his diplomatic tour, his biases were in favor of strengthening the federal power at the expense of that of the states. Moreover, he suspected that in the long run, federalism would prove to be an aspiration rather than an institutional reality. *SEE ALSO:* Alien and Sedition Acts; Articles of Confederation; Continental Congress

RICHARD SAMUELSON

Adamson v. California   Admiral Dewey Adamson was convicted of first-degree murder by the State of California and sentenced to death. During the course of his trial, the prosecutor pointed out to the jury that Adamson had failed to take the witness stand and refute the evidence that the state had adduced against him. This practice was authorized by California's "comment law" allowing prosecutors to comment on the failure of a defendant to testify on his or her own behalf. Over the objection of Adamson's counsel that such comment penalized the defendant's right to be free of compulsory self-incrimination (which includes a defendant's right not to testify at trial), the California courts upheld Adamson's conviction and an appeal was taken to the U.S. Supreme Court.

Almost forty years earlier, in *Twining v. New Jersey* (1908), the Supreme Court had held that the Self-incrimination Clause of the Fifth Amendment of the Bill of Rights was not applicable in state criminal proceedings and that comment on the failure of a defendant to testify did not violate the Due Process Clause of the Fourteenth Amendment. Relying largely on the *Twining* case, the majority of the Supreme Court affirmed Dewey Adamson's conviction and rejected the argument of his counsel that the Self-incrimination Clause applied to the states via the Due Process Clause and rendered comment laws unconstitutional.

Dissenting from the Court's decision, Justice Hugo Black argued that it had been the intent of the framers of the Fourteenth Amendment to make all of the rights in the Bill of Rights applicable to the states (the "total incorporation" theory), including the Self-incrimination Clause of the Fifth Amendment, and that Adamson's conviction should have been reversed. Black's dissent was joined by Justices William O. Douglas, Wiley Rutledge, and Frank Murphy, while Justice Felix Frankfurter attacked Black's "total incorporation" position, arguing that the Due Process Clause of the Fourteenth Amendment guaranteed only the right to a fair trial in state criminal proceedings and thus protected only some rights similar but not identical to some of those in the Bill of Rights.

The *Adamson* case was the high-water mark of the total incorporation position, since it there received more votes in its favor than either before or since, and the position was never adopted by a majority of the Supreme Court. The Court did subsequently, however, adopt the selective incorporation position, holding that most but not all of the rights in the Bill of Rights applied as restrictions on the states via the Due Process Clause of the Fourteenth Amendment. Applying that approach, the Court ultimately reversed *Adamson v. California*, ruling in 1964 that the Self-incrimination Clause of the Fifth Amendment did in fact apply in state criminal proceedings, and in 1965 further ruling that comment laws were unconstitutional because they penalized a defendant's right to be free from compulsory self-incrimination. Admiral Dewey Adamson, however, had been executed by the State of California on December 9, 1949. *SEE ALSO:* Fourteenth Amendment; Incorporation (Nationalization) of the Bill of Rights; *Palko v. Connecticut*

RICHARD C. CORTNER

Admission of New States Under the Articles of Confederation, the original 13 states were "admitted" to the union based on what historian Peter Onuf calls the "doctrine of state succession." That is, these new states formed in confederation with one another would succeed the colonies, largely maintaining the territorial boundaries that had existed prior to the American Revolution as well as the existing laws and authority of the colonies. Beyond the original thirteen states, the ability to admit new states belongs to the U.S. Congress and the federal government as is spelled out in the U.S. Constitution.

As a practical matter, however, the Constitution is vague as to the criteria for admission. Given this, Congress would rely on the preconstitutional precedents for statehood admission set forth in the 1787 Northwest Ordinance. Defining guidelines for the admission of the territories of the Northwest as states, the Ordinance declared that new states were to be admitted on equal footing as existing states, allowed for the formation of governed territories, and provided that upon reaching the population threshold of 60,000 free people, a territory could submit a state constitution to the Congress for approval and statehood admission. Although the ordinance says little about the economic situation of the territory, it became an important criterion for potential states; Congress expected the potential state to be not only

---

ARTICLE IV, SECTION 3, CLAUSE 1

New States may be admitted by the Congress into this Union; but no new State shall be formed or erected within the Jurisdiction of any other State; nor any State be formed by the Junction of two or more States, or Parts of States, without the Consent of the Legislatures of the States concerned as well as of the Congress.

STATE	DATE OF ADMISSION
Delaware	December 7, 1787
Pennsylvania	December 12, 1787
New Jersey	December 18, 1787
Georgia	January 2, 1788
Connecticut	January 9, 1788
Massachusetts	February 6, 1788
Maryland	April 28, 1788
South Carolina	May 23, 1788
New Hampshire	June 21, 1788
Virginia	June 25, 1788
New York	July 26, 1788
North Carolina	November 21, 1789
Rhode Island	May 29, 1790
Vermont	March 4, 1791
Kentucky	June 1, 1792
Tennessee	June 1, 1796
Ohio	March 1, 1803
Louisiana	April 30, 1812
Indiana	December 11, 1816
Mississippi	December 10, 1817
Illinois	December 3, 1818
Alabama	December 14, 1819
Maine	March 15, 1820
Missouri	August 10, 1821
Arkansas	June 15, 1836
Michigan	January 26, 1837
Florida	March 3, 1845
Texas	December 29, 1845
Iowa	December 28, 1846
Wisconsin	May 29, 1848
California	September 9, 1850
Minnesota	May 11, 1858
Oregon	February 14, 1859
Kansas	January 29, 1861
West Virginia	June 20, 1863
Nevada	October 31, 1864
Nebraska	March 1, 1867
Colorado	August 1, 1876
North Dakota	November 2, 1889
South Dakota	November 2, 1889
Montana	November 8, 1889
Washington	November 11, 1889
Idaho	July 3, 1890
Wyoming	July 10, 1890

Continued on next page

independent and prosperous, but also beneficial to the country. The Northwest Ordinance not only governed the admission of states of the Northwest, but also served as the precedent for future statehood decisions.

As the United States underwent efforts at territorial expansion under its policy of Manifest Destiny, the governing of new territories and the admission of new states would continue to occupy the national government. Moreover, given that statehood brings with it at least one seat in the House of Representatives, two seats in the Senate, and at least three votes in the Electoral College, strategic partisan calculations have played key roles in statehood decisions. Indeed, after more or less consensus-oriented statehood admission decisions in the first decade of the republic, critics noted that the regional and partisan motivations of the Louisiana Purchase were laid bare by Thomas Jefferson's extraordinary move.

Such partisan and especially regional motivations came to dominate national statehood decisions. With slavery increasingly dividing the United States' North and South, and with neither southern nor northern interests wanting to cede representational and Electoral College advantages to the other side, statehood admission politics boiled down to a system of interregional compromise whereby one free state would be admitted alongside one slave state. Free state Indiana's admission in 1816 was closely followed by Mississippi's admission in 1817, and Illinois's and Alabama's were paired for admission in 1818 and 1819 respectively. And, when Missouri sought admission, the free state of Maine was carved out of Massachusetts in order to offset any southern advantage.

As regional tensions heightened from the eve of the Civil War to Reconstruction, the potential for interregional compromise was limited. Emerging as early as California's admission in 1850, a new pattern of seeking regional and partisan advantage took hold. From 1850 to the end of reconstruction in 1876, Republicans succeeded in admitting eight new states. Often assessing the party composition of a candidate for statehood admission, Republicans used their advantages and the lack of Democratic and southern voices in Congress

Continued from previous page	
STATE	DATE OF ADMISSION
Utah	*January 4, 1896*
Oklahoma	*November 16, 1907*
New Mexico	*January 6, 1912*
Arizona	*February 14, 1912*
Alaska	*January 3, 1959*
Hawaii	*August 21, 1959*

to admit even those states that had not yet met the population requirements of the Northwest Ordinance. This pattern was maintained throughout state admissions politics of the nineteenth century as Republicans turned an Electoral College victory, as well as a narrow House majority and an expanded Senate majority, into six new states admitted in 1889 and 1890 alone.

Statehood admission in the twentieth century returned to the compromise pattern of the pre–Civil War era although the basis of the compromise is the expected partisanship of the state, as one presumed Democratic state will be paired with one presumed Republican state. This pattern does not portend well for Washington, D.C.'s contemporary campaign for statehood, as this largely Democratic state suffers opposition for lack of a Republican pair.

That Congress could create and admit new states conveyed a supremacy of the national government over both the new states as well as the old. As historian Peter Onuf observed, "If new states were equal to the old states, old states would be equal to the new, and thus share in their diminutive character. Statehood defined in these terms was not only compatible with a stronger union: it demanded one" (Onuf 1982, 459). *SEE ALSO:* Northwest Ordinance of 1784; Northwest Ordinance of 1787

BIBLIOGRAPHY: Nolan McCarty, Keith T. Poole, and Howard Rosenthal, "Congress and the Territorial Expansion of the United States," in *Party, Process and Political Change in Congress: New Perspectives on the History of Congress*, ed. David W. Brady and Mathew D. McCubbins, 392–451 (Stanford, CA: Stanford University Press, 2002); Peter S. Onuf, "From Colony to Territory: Changing Concepts of Statehood in Revolutionary America," *Political Science Quarterly* 97, no. 3 (Fall 1982): 447–59; and Charles Stewart III and Barry R. Weingast, "Stacking the Senate, Changing the Nation: Republican Rotten Boroughs, Statehood Politics and American Political Development," *Studies in American Political Development* 6 (1992): 223–71.

MARGARET M. BUTLER AND DOUGLAS B. HARRIS

Advisory Commission on Intergovernmental Relations   The Advisory Commission on Intergovernmental Relations (ACIR) was established by Congress on September 14, 1959 (P.L. 86-380). A permanent, independent, bipartisan body, the Commission's charge included convening federal, state, and local representatives to consider common problems; serving as a forum for discussing administration and coordination of federal grant programs, including conditions and controls; providing technical assistance to the federal executive and legislative branches to determine the effects of proposed legislation on the federal system; identifying and studying emerging issues or problems confronting federal system partners; recommending the most desirable allocation of governmental functions, responsibilities, and revenues; and suggesting ways to simplify and coordinate tax laws and administrative practices to reduce intergovernmental competition and taxpayer compliance burdens.

EVOLUTION AND RATIONALE

ACIR was an outgrowth of the work of three temporary bodies. In 1949 the first Hoover Commission recommended the creation of a continuing agency to study and guide federal-state relations and to develop budgetary control systems for federal grants. In 1953 Congress created the Commission on Intergovernmental Relations at the request of President Dwight D. Eisenhower, who was concerned about the growth of federal grants-in-aid and regulations. In 1955 the Commission issued a series of research reports ranging from agriculture to welfare, and recommended the establishment of a "permanent center" in the executive branch to give continuing attention to problems in interlevel relationships. Its successor, the Joint Federal-State Action Committee, worked from 1957 to 1959 to identify functions and revenue sources that could be turned back to the states, but was unsuccessful in gaining congressional support. The Committee endorsed its predecessor's recommendation for the establishment of a focal point in the federal executive branch to deal with interlevel problems.

Following hearings on the need for a permanent institution to pay attention to federal-state-local relations, in May 1959 legislation was introduced in both Houses of Congress to create ACIR. Senator Edmund S. Muskie from Maine and Representative L. H. Fountain from North Carolina were champions of this effort. Both served as charter members.

A unique feature was the Commission's twenty-six-member composition. The president appointed twenty members; three represented the federal executive branch, and three the private sector. The remaining were state and local elected officials—four governors, three state legislators, four mayors, and three county officials—nominated by their respective national association. The leadership of the House and Senate appointed three members to represent each body.

This intergovernmental "prism" was a powerful vehicle for looking at problems and issues that transcended boundary, level, and sector. Congress's rationale was that recommendations made by a body with this diverse composition were likely to be administratively and financially practical and politically feasible.

ACTIVITIES

With a budget ranging from $1 million to $2 million annually and a staff from twelve to fifty over the years, the Commission was one of the smallest federal agencies in Washington, D.C. Over its lifespan, the Commission produced 130 reports with recommendations. Major studies were released on fiscal balance in the federal system, urban and rural growth policy, substate and multistate regionalism, law enforcement and criminal justice administration, transportation, citizen participation, local government discretionary authority, the federal government's role in the federal system, the design of federal categorical and block grants, and regulatory federalism. Another 196 information reports containing no recommendations were also released by the Commission.

Beginning in 1972 the Commission sponsored an annual public opinion poll of citizen attitudes toward taxing and spending. Another popular annual volume was statistical compilations of *Significant Features of Fiscal Federalism*. Also popular was the Commission's quarterly magazine, *Intergovernmental Perspective*, which carried summaries of research work, updates on federal-state-local developments, and news about ACIR members and professional staff. Occasionally the Commission would sponsor conferences and convene meetings of state-level ACIRs, to collaborate on intergovernmental issues, developments, and trends.

INFLUENCE

ACIR reports were widely distributed to practitioners and scholars, and used in many college classrooms. The Commission's recommendations were advanced through model legislation, testimony before Congress and state legislatures, and collaboration with the "Big Seven" public interest groups and state associations of local officials. For most of its thirty-seven years, the Commission's work was influential. ACIR played a significant role in the legislative processes resulting in the Intergovernmental Cooperation Act of 1968, Uniform Relocation and Real Property Acquisition Act of 1970, Intergovernmental Personnel Act of 1970, and State and Local Fiscal Assistance Act of 1972 (General Revenue Sharing).

Other pioneering ACIR research and recommendations included the Representative Tax System (comparative state fiscal capacities), payments in lieu of taxes, property tax relief, indexation of personal income taxes, interstate sales taxes, and unfunded mandates reform.

In the early 1990s, during a period of rising concern over the federal deficit, Congress decided to terminate appropriations to support ACIR. The Commission's funding base had become diversified through state contributions, congressionally mandated studies, federal agency contracts, and publications sales, but congressional appropriations accounted for most of ACIR's budget. The Commission's case for continuation was weakened by the steady erosion of Big Seven support for its work, as its recommendations were perceived as increasingly partisan. An unpopular draft report calling for federal mandate relief on state and local governments aroused strong opposition from special interest stakeholders like organized labor and environmentalists. Offending potential liberal supporters, including those in the Clinton administration, while remaining a target for congressional budget cutters, made ACIR vulnerable.

On September 30, 1996, the Commission's doors were closed, and a significant era for intergovernmental relations ended. No similar body has replaced it. *SEE ALSO:* County Government; Criminal Justice; Eisenhower, Dwight D.; Fiscal Federalism; Grants-in-Aid; Intergovernmental Relations; Local Government; Public Administration; Revenue Sharing; Transportation Policy; Unfunded Mandates; Welfare Policy

BIBLIOGRAPHY: Advisory Commission on Intergovernmental Relations, "ACIR and the Federal System 1959–1989," *Intergovernmental Perspective* 15, no. 4 (Fall 1989); David Brunori, "Advice to the New Congress: Bring back the ACIR," *State Tax Notes* (January 15, 2001): 189–91; Bruce McDowell, "Advisory Commission on Intergovernmental Relations in 1996: The End of an Era," *Publius* 27, no. 2 (Spring 1997): 111–28;

and Deil S. Wright, "The Advisory Commission on Intergovernmental Relations: Unique Features and Policy Orientation," *Public Administration Review* 25, no. 2 (June 1965): 193–202.

CARL W. STENBERG

Affirmative Action Affirmative action had its beginnings in March 1961, less than two months after President John F. Kennedy assumed office. It began when Kennedy issued Executive Order 10925, which created the President's Committee on Equal Employment Opportunity. The order mandated that every federal contract include the vow that "the Contractor will not discriminate against any employee or applicant for employment because of race, creed, color, or national origin. The Contractor will take affirmative action, to ensure that applicants are employed, and the employees are treated during employment, without regard to their race, creed, color, or national origin." This term "affirmative action" meant taking the correct steps to curb unfair employment practices and ensure that race, creed, color, and/or national origin are ignored in the process of hiring and retaining employees.

The Civil Rights Act of 1964 installed by President Lyndon B. Johnson after Kennedy's assassination took the concept of equal opportunity employment to the national level. The Act stated in an identical manner to Executive Order 10925 a vow that "[no] person in the United States shall, on the ground of race, color, or national origin, be excluded from participation in, be denied the benefits of, or be subjected to discrimination under any program or activity receiving federal financial assistance." This act, while helpful, was greatly disputed. Within a year, Johnson believed that it was working to level the playing field of employment, since many minorities had long been hobbled by racism and racist practices.

In 1965 President Johnson issued Executive Order 11246, which stated, "It is the policy of the Government of the United States to provide equal opportunity in federal employment for all qualified persons, to prohibit discrimination in employment because of race, creed, color or national origin, and to promote the full realization of equal employment opportunity through a positive, continuing program in each department and agency." This act was later amended to include sex, and all together it further established affirmative actions policies.

Richard Nixon issued a Revised Order No. 4 in 1971, which further refined the definitions of minority groups and implied the requirement of flexible quotas to fill, although with the conclusion of the case of *California v. Bakke* in 1978, the Supreme Court found quotas to be unlawful, but race was upheld as a valid deciding factor in choosing a diverse student body. *SEE ALSO:* Civil Rights Act of 1964; Johnson, Lyndon B.

> BIBLIOGRAPHY: Stephen Cahn, "Stephen Cahn on the History of Affirmative Action (1995)," http://aad.english.ucsb.edu/docs/Cahn.html; and Marquita Sykes, "The Origins of Affirmative Action," http://www.now.org/nnt/08-95/affirmhs.html.

ARTHUR HOLST

Age Discrimination Age discrimination is like other forms of discrimination (e.g., race, gender, and class) that lead to differential treatment of individuals. Age bias is based on negative stereotypes associated with chronological age, especially old age, but it can apply to other stages of the lifespan. For example, the elderly often have prejudices against the young, particularly teenagers, in terms of their dress, language, and behavior.

In relation to the elderly, age bias is also known as ageism, which has been described by Butler as "a process of systematic stereotyping of and discrimination against people just because they are old," (Butler 2001) similar to racism based on skin color or sexism based on gender. This is perpetuated by the belief that with age comes disability, isolation, and loneliness. In American society, with its emphasis on youth and beauty, ageism is often triggered by the fear and dread of aging. Being old is equated with senility, inflexibility, a lack of productivity, a loss of sexuality, ugliness, ill health, and often poverty. Negative images of aging abound in cartoons, jokes, greeting cards, and epithets such as "crock" or "geezer." The mass media play a major role in promoting stereotypes about the elderly who, for example, appear far less often in prime-time television programs than their prevalence in the U.S. population.

Age as a personal characteristic is different from race and sex because nearly all persons will grow old. Americans are now living longer, with an average life expectancy at birth of nearly 77 years compared to 47 years at the beginning of the twentieth century. Average longevity is now 74 years for men and nearly 80 years for women. Those aged 85 and over, with higher levels of morbidity, are the fastest-growing age group in the United States. Because disability also can occur at younger ages, age discrimination is more akin to discrimination against persons with physical disabilities.

All forms of discrimination have become the province of public policy at both the federal and state levels, especially in housing and employment. Age discrimination has triggered two responses. One is "compassionate ageism" that has sought to ameliorate some of the economic downsides of aging, such as loss of income and inadequate access to health care due to retirement, and the lack of social services (e.g., nutrition programs and transportation) tailored to the needs of senior citizens. This led to the enactment of Social Security, Medicare, Medicaid, senior housing programs, and the Older Americans Act. The other response has centered on ensuring that age biases are not permitted in any program or activity receiving federal funds, the major objective of the Age Discrimination Act of 1975 (ADA), or as a barrier to the issuance of driver's licenses.

Unlike policies designed to reduce discrimination against other groups, policies for the elderly have generally not been viewed as reverse discrimination or as associated with affirmative action. During the 1980s, "greedy geezers" were seen by some as getting more than their fair share of government benefits, but public opinion polls have consistently shown strong support for these programs, especially Social Security and Medicare. More recently, age-segregated housing has raised concerns, leading to calls for "elder-friendly" communities that are inclusive for all age groups. Even when the proportion of persons aged 65+ rises to a projected 20 percent of the U.S. population, age discrimination is likely to persist due to the social attitudes described above. *SEE ALSO:* Age Discrimination in Employment Act of 1967

BIBLIOGRAPHY: R. H. Butler, "Ageism," in *The Encyclopedia of Aging*, 3rd ed., ed. G. L. Maddox (New York: Springer Publishing Company, 2001).

PHOEBE LIEBIG

Age Discrimination in Employment Act of 1967   The federal Age Discrimination in Employment Act (ADEA–P.L. 90-202) was enacted in 1967 to protect workers against discrimination based exclusively on their age. Age discrimination (AD) in the workplace is based on several assumptions and stereotypes about older workers: that they should appropriately step aside and make room for younger workers who need to support their families, are rigid and unable to learn new skills, and are less productive than their younger counterparts. AD has several negative effects on older employees: loss of wages and benefits, emotional distress, and greater difficulty in finding another job compared to younger workers. The ADEA, however, was not the first law designed to combat AD in employment; the states enacted such laws earlier. Both federal and state laws were designed to ensure that older workers would receive the same employment protections as younger workers, while at the same time enjoying preferential treatment due to their unique circumstances. The issues addressed in these several laws included the types of prohibited practices, entities to which the legislation applied, age limits, exclusions and exemptions, penalties, and enforcement.

STATE INITIATIVES, 1903–PRESENT

State AD laws predate the ADEA by nearly sixty-five years. In 1903, Colorado was the first state to enact any law banning AD; employees aged 18–60 could not be fired due to their age by any person, firm, corporation, or association doing business in the state. As of 1934, Louisiana disallowed age as a standard in hiring and firing for persons aged 50+, while Massachusetts protected persons aged 45–65 against discrimination in hiring and firing. Many state laws were enacted during the 1950s and mid-1960s: 10 states and Puerto Rico amended existing antidiscrimination laws to include age. Seven passed separate laws barring such discrimination, while seven incorporated AD into their Fair Employment Practices Acts. By 1967, 24 states had some form of prohibition against age bias in the workplace.

The states continued to innovate even after the ADEA was passed. By 1972, only the District of Columbia and 19 states (the majority in the South and the Rocky Mountain regions) lacked AD laws. Characteristically, state laws applied to employers, labor organizations, and employment agencies; state and local employees were not always included. Age limits varied, but half of the states defined the protected group as between 40 and 65, the same standard as the ADEA. Exemptions included small employers, with the number of employees ranging from three to twenty-four; domestic workers; and family employees. In 3 states, public safety employees were excluded. Prohibited practices in state laws always covered AD in hiring, and nearly all covered firing, with a majority prohibiting discrimination in compensation and the conditions and privileges of employment as well. Slightly more than half made it illegal to advertise or classify jobs by age. Twenty-six of the 31 states with AD laws had penalties consisting of fines, generally ranging from $100 to $500; days in jail ranging from 30 to 365; or both fines and imprisonment.

Although 11 states and the District of Columbia still had no AD statutes as of 1976, the states continued to exercise leadership. Florida abolished mandatory retirement in 1976 for all public employees, while California eliminated virtually all mandatory retirement for public and private employees in 1977. The ADEA was amended in 1978 to include this provision; it also allowed employees to choose between federal and state protection, whichever was most favorable. A Supreme Court decision in 1979 held that plaintiffs must file initially at the state level and sixty days later at the federal level. As of 1990, 49 states and 3 U.S. territories had enacted AD laws. Ten years later, all 50 states had AD laws with widely varying provisions; 35 have laws that are applicable to employers with fewer than fifteen employees, thereby extending protections to employees working for small firms beyond federal requirements. Still, many states (e.g., California and Utah) have large proportions of very small employers, the employees of which are not protected by either state laws or the ADEA.

FEDERAL INITIATIVES, 1956–PRESENT

Although the ADEA was not passed until 1967, federal efforts predate that effort. In 1956, the U.S. Civil Service eliminated AD in hiring federal employees. Eight years later, Executive Order 11141 created a policy against AD among federal contractors. AD also was considered by Congress during debates on Title VII of the Civil Rights Act in 1964. Although age was excluded from that Act's provisions, a Department of Labor study was mandated. In 1965, the Department of Labor report identified arbitrary discrimination as a major older worker problem and determined that a national policy was needed to provide protection for persons in states without AD laws and to fill the gaps in existing state laws. The goals of the resulting legislative proposal were to eliminate arbitrary AD in employment, adjust institutional arrangements detrimental to older workers, increase the availability of work for older workers, and educate employers about older worker abilities and needs, as well as the pitfalls of continued discrimination.

Unlike the Civil Rights Act on which it was modeled, the ADEA was enacted with little controversy. The law provided that individuals age 40–65 cannot be limited, segregated, or classified in any way that would restrict employment opportunities or otherwise adversely affect their status as employees. Age per se cannot be used in decisions about hiring, firing, advancement and training practices, compensation, layoffs, or demotions, or in advertising jobs. Exceptions included the Bona Fide Occupational Qualification (BFOQ): AD is appropriate in instances where such discrimination is reasonably necessary for the normal operations of a particular business, for example, airline pilots. Other exceptions included following the terms of a bona fide seniority system, of particular concern to labor unions, or a bona fide benefit plan, for example retirement and insurance. In addition, executives in major leadership or policy-making positions with sizeable pension benefits can be required to retire. The Department of Labor's Wage and Hour Division was responsible for ADEA enforcement. However, the role of states with their own AD statutes was explicitly recognized, with enforcement generally first deferred to the state agency responsible for enforcing antidiscrimination laws, usually the department of labor or employment, human/civil rights commission, or state labor commissioner. The number of AD complaints rose quickly to 1,000 in 1969 and five times that amount in the mid-1970s.

Initially the ADEA did not apply to all older workers. In 1974, AD protection was extended to employers with a minimum of twenty employees and to all federal, state, and local government employees. In 1978, occasioned by a Supreme Court ruling that ADEA did not prohibit mandatory retirement, the law was amended to raise the upper age limit to age 70, eliminate mandatory retirement for most federal employees, and prohibit benefit plans requiring or permitting involuntary retirement. The right to a jury trial was granted, as were delaying the higher mandatory retirement age until 1982 for tenured faculty and allowing mandatory retirement at ages 65–69 for persons in high executive positions. In 1979, ADEA enforcement was given to the Equal Employment Opportunity Commission.

ADEA provisions continued to be changed in the 1980s and 1990s by Congress and the courts. In 1986, the age 70 cap for mandatory retirement was removed, although not for high-ranking executives. Congress also granted temporary exceptions for police, firefighters, and tenured faculty until the end of 1993; the last exemption was subsequently eliminated. In 1987, ADEA provisions were changed to address the age-based treatment of employee benefit plans; and in 1988 and 1990, Congress extended the statute of limitations on filing claims due to EEOC problems in processing claims on a timely basis. Also in 1990, Congress enacted the Older Workers Benefit Protection Act, negating yet another Supreme Court decision permitting employers to provide different employee benefits on the basis of age. In 1996, Congress reenacted ADEA exemptions for police and firefighters that had expired in 1993, permitting state and local governments to impose certain maximum hiring ages and mandatory retirement ages for individuals in those occupations. In addition, apprenticeship programs were no longer permitted to impose age limits on participation.

Studies have shown that AD federal and state laws boost employment of older workers, especially those age 60+, and reduce retirement of older individuals. Yet, AD in the workplace still exists, as revealed by the numbers of complaints and lawsuits filed in the areas of discharge and employee benefits. AD in hiring practices is harder to prove and lawsuits have been less effective in increasing the hiring of older workers, particularly those under the age of 60. Employers have been able to restructure defined benefit pension plans to induce retirement at a desired age; early retirement incentive plans that are offered for a specific time period have been a favored mechanism. By contrast, defined contribution plans, combined with the elimination of mandatory retirement, do lead to later retirement. The continued growth of those plans, plus indications that the baby boomer generation intends to work longer, may lead to more delayed retirements in the future.

Finally, the courts are likely to continue their role in refining and applying the ADEA. However, the impact of these rulings is not all positive for older workers. For example, a Supreme Court ruling in 2000 held that state employees are not authorized to sue states under the ADEA. Lawsuits for age-based dismissals against major corporations, such as Lucent and Ford, have been successful; however, success rates are usually less than 5 percent. On the whole, AD laws have been an important way to ensure that most older workers have greater choices in determining the timing of their retirement. *SEE ALSO:* Age Discrimination

BIBLIOGRAPHY: D. Neumark, "Age Discrimination Legislation in the United States," working paper 8152 (Cambridge, MA: National Bureau of Economic Research, 2001).

PHOEBE LIEBIG

Agricultural Adjustment Act of 1933   The Agricultural Adjustment Act (AAA) represented the first significant effort by the federal government to directly improve the earnings of American farmers. Enacted on May 12, 1933, as part of Franklin D. Roosevelt's New Deal, the AAA marked a turning point in federal agricultural policy. The

AAA regulated agricultural production using the constitutional authority to tax and spend. It, along with other New Deal programs, also signified a new responsibility of the federal government in promoting economic welfare.

After consulting with farm leaders, Henry Wallace, Roosevelt's secretary of agriculture, drafted the act, which established the Agricultural Adjustment Administration. Its purpose was to enter into agreements with farmers to reduce production in return for benefit payments. In addition, the AAA imposed marketing restrictions and levied a tax on the middlemen in order to fund benefit payments. Basic farm goods included in the program were cotton, corn, tobacco, rice, wheat, hogs, and dairy products. The AAA sought to restore parity—that is, the farmers' purchasing power—to what it was during the period of 1910–14, when farm commodity prices were in balance with the price of goods and services. During the 1920s and early 1930s, farmers overproduced because of advances in farm equipment and an increase in acreage due to foreign demand during World War I. After the war, the European market no longer needed American farm commodities, causing an agricultural depression a decade before the Great Depression.

By the time the AAA passed Congress, American farmers had already planted their year's crops. To prevent an additional year of overproduction, Wallace ordered farmers to destroy millions of acres of young corn, cotton, and wheat, and to butcher millions of baby hogs, in order to qualify for subsidy payments. The cost of improving the economic situation for U.S. farmers meant higher prices for the public at a time when unemployment was severe. The justification for this was that the restoration of the farmers' purchasing power would allow them to buy enough industrial goods to stimulate industrial production and provide jobs for urban labor. This was the first time that the federal government paid farmers to restrict production and marketing, an approach that continued in the post-Depression United States.

The AAA was not entirely successful in reaching its goals. Despite the reduction of acreage by 25 percent, farmers still produced more in 1933 than they had in 1932. In 1934, changes made to the act, along with a severe drought, helped reduce production significantly. Even though 1935 farm prices rose 52 percent from their 1932 average, they would never achieve parity.

The 1936 Supreme Court case *United States v. Butler* declared the AAA unconstitutional by a 6–3 vote. The Court ruled it unconstitutional because of the discriminatory processing tax. In reaction, Congress passed the Agricultural Adjustment Act of 1938, which eliminated the tax on processors. The AAA legislation represented only one of many ways that federal authority increased during the Great Depression. *SEE ALSO:* Dairy Compacts; New Deal

BIBLIOGRAPHY: Berta Asch and A. R. Mangus, *Farmers on Relief and Rehabilitation* (New York: Da Capo Press, 1937); James T. Patterson, *The New Deal and the States: Federalism in Transition* (Princeton, NJ: Princeton University Press, 1969); and Van L. Perkins, *Crisis in Agriculture: The Agricultural Adjustment Administration and the New Deal, 1933* (Berkeley: University of California Press, 1969).

STACI L. GATES

Albany Plan The Albany Congress was held in 1754 to bring the colonies together to coordinate with one another and with Britain and Indian allies in the impending

French and Indian War. Its major initiative was a Plan of Union of the Colonies, prepared primarily by Benjamin Franklin and adopted by the Congress. While the plan was never ratified by a single colony, nor by Britain, its elaboration and adoption by the Congress were remarkable feats, and gave the colonies the first serious introduction to the idea of their Union. During debates over the federal Constitution of 1787, Franklin republished it as a proof that the goal of a strong union was no hasty idea.

The Albany Plan's text is brief, fitting on three pages. It provides for a "general government" of the colonies, to be "administered by a President-General, to be appointed and supported by the crown; and a Grand Council, to be chosen by the representatives of the people of the several Colonies met in their respective assemblies." The executive and legislature were given means of balancing each other in the appointment and legislative processes. Each colony got a specified number of votes in the Council, with two for the smallest and seven for the largest colonies. Individual colonies would retain their existing governments and military forces. The union would have authority over all Indian affairs, including war and treaties; over new territories; over a joint army and navy; and to make laws and taxes needed for these purposes, using duties and imposts as well as requisitions on colonial governments.

Franklin in his autobiography remarked that the plan was not ratified because to the Crown it seemed too democratic and to the colonies it seemed too much flavored with the king's prerogative. More prosaically, colonial legislatures feared giving up part of their autonomy; England feared any union of the colonies, lest they become collectively separatist. In later years Franklin proposed to solve the latter danger through representation of Americans in the British Parliament, to enable joint management of the decisions and burdens of the empire.

With neither form of union—Albany or Imperial—adopted, the issue of American payments for the French and Indian War was left unresolved. Individual colonial legislatures procrastinated; Parliament eventually imposed taxes unilaterally on the colonies. This led to resistance and new congresses of the colonies; a union gradually developed de facto against the Crown. As Revolution neared under the slogan "No taxation without representation," Britain began to think about giving representation in Parliament, but Americans were unwilling: they had grown sensitive to Britain's intention of extracting taxes, and to the inferiority of numbers they would suffer in a pan-Britannic Parliament, a status they felt unbearable in light of their growing sense of a divergence of interests.

There remained the issue of uniting the emerging states. The Articles of Confederation did this in a weak fashion, with "one state, one vote" and no coherent executive. The 1787 Constitution did it on a par of strength with the Albany Plan, but in far more sophisticated form.

The Albany Plan was later remembered as a precursor of the Constitution, and also as a lost opportunity for the British Empire. In the 1800s, faced with rebellion in Canada, the British pursued two tracks of reform: greater autonomy for colonial governments, and federations of neighboring groups of colonies (to form Canada, Australia, and South Africa) along with an attempt at federation of the empire as a whole. The first responded to the lessons of 1776; the second, to the lessons of the Albany Plan and the Constitution.

The Albany Plan and Franklin's Imperial Parliament idea were idealized in the late 1800s by the Imperial Federation League and the movement for English-Speaking Union; it was said that Franklin lived to see the continental part of his plan realized in the Constitution, and bequeated the transatlantic half to posterity. Neither movement succeeded in its goal of an intercontinental federation, but both fostered confederal growth, the former in the Imperial Conference and Commonwealth, the latter in the Atlantic Alliance. The subsequent fostering of a European Union within the Atlantic Alliance paralleled in practice Franklin's duality of conception, a continental Union embedded within a looser transatlantic one. *SEE ALSO:* Articles of Confederation; Franklin, Benjamin

IRA STRAUS

Alien and Sedition Acts   From June 18 to July 14, 1798, the Federalist Party in Congress passed four acts regulating the press and controlling the activities of aliens, collectively known as the Alien and Sedition Acts. These were the Naturalization Act, the Alien Act, the Alien Enemies Act, and the Sedition Act. Because of the scandalous treatment of U.S. ministers in France, dubbed the XYZ affair, anti-French sentiment reached a level not seen since the French and Indian War (1756–63), and military conflict with the United States' former ally of the Revolution now seemed likely. With these new laws, Federalists would have the power to deport immigrants who were too prominent in Republican causes and prosecute Republican newspaper editors for seditious libel.

President John Adams, Jefferson's onetime compatriot and friend in the War for Independence, was disturbed by the radicalism of revolutionary France and concurred with the Gazette of the United States that "[s]urely we need a sedition law to keep our own rogues from cutting our throats, and an alien law to prevent the invasion by a host of foreign rogues to assist them." But to Republicans like Jefferson and Madison, the sedition laws were a flagrant violation of the First Amendment's prohibition of any congressional law "abridging the freedom of speech, or of the press." More troubling still, the acts appeared to undermine the Federalists' own original argument that a popular government was a government of delegated powers only. Now Federalists asserted by implication "legislative supremacy" to enact any law deemed necessary to the public safety: "The Government is bound not to deceive the people, and it is equally bound not to suffer them to be deceived. Delusion leads to insurrection and rebellion, which it is the duty of the Government to prevent. This they cannot prevent unless they have a power to punish those who with wicked designs attempt to mislead the people." The Republican response was to invoke the countervailing force of the states, an early test of American federalism.

Congressman Madison and Vice President Jefferson worked in secret to prompt the states to assert responsibility to uphold the Constitution and awaken a popular response to the acts. Secrecy was essential because both men could have been charged under the very acts they were opposing. It was also critical that their actions be recognized as the official statements of state legislatures. It would be far more difficult to prosecute the states of Virginia and Kentucky than particular government officials. Madison prepared the Virginia Resolution while Jefferson worked on Kentucky's protest. Both statements argued in favor of the mediating role of states in the partly federal structure of the union, and reminded Congress that powers not delegated to it were reserved to the states. The Kentucky Resolution was the most radical, actually negating the acts, or declaring them to be "unauthoritative, void, and of no force." The general government was explicitly denied the power to legislate on freedom of speech, press, or religion.

Such matters were explicitly left to the states "to retain to themselves the right of judging how far the licentiousness of speech and of the press may be abridged."

The resolutions incurred their own strong opposition, and it appears that popularly, people were just as much troubled by the prospects of disunion as they were of oppression by the general government. The Federalists were able to rescue the alien and sedition laws from two nearly successful Republican campaigns to repeal them. In the end, however, the controversial laws were simply allowed to expire after Jefferson's assumption of the presidency in 1800.

Though some historians consider the acts to have been relatively mild, especially by comparison with later wartime measures (only ten convictions were brought under the Sedition Act and only one deportation under the Alien Act), these laws marked the first time the federal government attempted to craft and implement legislation for managing a national security emergency. As such, the acts raised fundamental questions about the nature of the U.S. Constitution and the role of the states in defending the rights and liberties of their inhabitants. The political and popular reaction was owing to their innovation and obvious tension with the First Amendment to the Constitution.

Ultimately, the acts did not serve Federalist ambitions very well. Rather than quelling debate, the Republican papers were emboldened to make harsher attacks on Federalists. Popular opinion eventually tipped just enough to ensure a Republican Congress and Jefferson's election to the presidency. *SEE ALSO:* Adams, John; Federalists; Jefferson, Thomas; Kentucky and Virginia Resolutions; Madison, James; National Security; Supremacy Clause: Article VI, Clause 2

BIBLIOGRAPHY: Lance Banning, *The Sacred Fire of Liberty* (Ithaca, NY: Cornell University Press, 1995), 387–95; Bruce Frohnen, ed., *The American Republic: Primary Sources* (Indianapolis: Liberty Fund, 2002); David N. Mayer, *The Constitutional Thought of Thomas Jefferson* (Charlottesville: University Press of Virginia, 1994); John C. Miller, *Crisis in Freedom: The Alien and Sedition Acts* (Boston: Little, Brown and Company, 1952); and James Morton Smith, *Freedom's Fetters* (Ithaca, NY: Cornell University Press, 1966).

HANS L. EICHOLZ

Amendment Process   The Constitution of the United States, as originally written, contained only 7,000 words. However, the authors recognized the necessity of amending the document. The Articles of Confederation, the governing document that preceded the Constitution, required the approval of all states, which complicated the amending of the Articles and ultimately led to the writing of the Constitution.

The Constitution provides for three processes of amendment. The most common procedure requires the amendment to be approved by two-thirds of Congress, meaning both the House of Representatives and the Senate. Then the amendment must be ratified by three-fourths of the state legislatures. At this point, it becomes part of the Constitution and the supreme law of the land. This course of action has resulted in twenty-six of the twenty-seven amendments. In the instance of the repeal of the Prohibition Amendment, the second process is used and the amendment was approved by two-thirds of Congress, but ratified by three-fourths of the states by convention of the people. The third option put forward in the Constitution requires the amendment to be approved by a convention of all states and then ratification either by state legislature or state conventions. This alternative has never been used; the last convention of the states resulted in the elimination of the Articles of Confederation and the writing of the current Constitution of the United States.

The Bill of Rights, the first ten amendments to the Constitution, was approved during the first Congress. To appease the Anti-Federalists, James Madison proposed seventeen possible amendments. Twelve of these were approved by Congress, and ten were ratified by the states and became the Bill of Rights. One of the two denied ratification in the 1790s became the Twenty-seventh Amendment (Congressional Pay) in 1992. The difficulty of passing amendments to the Constitution can be seen as only seventeen amendments have been added in the more than 200 years since the Bill of

---

ARTICLE V

The Congress, whenever two thirds of both Houses shall deem it necessary, shall propose Amendments to this Constitution, or, on the Application of the Legislatures of two thirds of the several States, shall call a Convention for proposing Amendments, which, in either Case, shall be valid to all Intents and Purposes, as Part of this Constitution, when ratified by the Legislatures of three fourths of the several States, or by Conventions in three fourths thereof, as the one or the other Mode of Ratification may be proposed by the Congress; Provided that no Amendment which may be made prior to the Year One thousand eight hundred and eight shall in any Manner affect the first and fourth Clauses in the Ninth Section of the first Article; and that no State, without its Consent, shall be deprived of its equal Suffrage in the Senate.

Rights was added. Since 1919, amendments are proposed with a specific time limit that further increases the difficulty of changing the Constitution. However, this complexity also reduces the possible number of amendments that would permanently alter the Constitution.

The Constitution can be informally changed by a variety of methods. Congress has used the "Elastic Clauses," particularly the Commerce Clause and the Necessary and Proper Clause, to expand the power of legislation. The presidency has also expanded its power through executive agreements. And the Supreme Court, through the power of judicial review, can create a more flexible Constitution or declare legislative or executive action unconstitutional.

Although the process of amending the Constitution of the United States is infrequently accomplished, most of those passed have given Americans greater rights and ability to participate in government. *SEE ALSO:* Articles of Confederation; Bill of Rights; U.S. Constitution

BIBLIOGRAPHY: Barbara A. Bardes et al., *American Government and Politics Today: The Essentials*, 2004–5 ed. (Belmont, CA: Thomson Learning Inc., 2004); and Robert J. Spitzer et al., *Essentials of American Politics* (New York: W.W. Norton and Company, 2002).

SARAH MILLER

American Indians and Federalism   A common definition of federalism, contained in the majority of American government, state and local politics, and public administration texts, is the division of power between the national and state governments. This system, developed as a compromise during the second Constitutional Convention, created a strong central government without stripping states of their inherent sovereignty.

When created, however, the Constitution was largely silent with regard to a third set of sovereign governments operating within what would be called the United States—American Indian nations. The relationships among local, state, and federal governments, while constantly evolving, are much more clearly defined than the relationships between any of these entities and indigenous nations. Relations among First Nations, the federal government, and the states have been something of a shifting target, and the deep legal historical roots that have continually changed, and are still changing, have made it extremely difficult to properly place Indian nations within the federal system of government. For instance, the federal government has recognized tribes as international sovereigns, domestic dependent nations, wards that require protection, and quasi-sovereign governments. Thus federal policies have fluctuated from treating native nations as separate political entities with a status requiring treaties, to an attempt to assimilate native people into the general society by refusing to recognize sovereignty at all.

Lost in the vacillation is the idea that First Nations and their relations to other governments within the federal system are unique in that their position relative to both the states and the federal government is not derived from the Constitution; rather, tribal governments derive their powers from an inherent right of self-government. This inherent right and the unique relationship of the tribal governments to the federal government have created special problems in trying to define the role of tribal governments in the federal system. For instance, local governments, through Dillon's Rule, are creatures of the state and derive their power from the state. Therefore, the place of local governments is outlined. The states, like tribal governments, are in a perpetual process of defining their relationship with the federal government over state sovereignty and federal supremacy. However, the U.S. Constitution clearly establishes the supremacy of federal law through the Supremacy Clause and provides for a much clearer resolution of conflicts between state and federal government. Rules exist that were developed by the judicial system, which determine when state powers are preempted. In this sense, the place of states is somewhat settled—they are sovereign, but their laws can be preempted by the national government. The legal status and the relationship between the tribal and the federal government are quite different in that the policy pendulum has historically swung back and forth between federal trusteeship and tribal self-determination. There has been no Dillon's Rule or consistently applied constitutional clause to clarify the position of tribal governments within the federal system as there has been for the states and local governments. As a result, federal Indian policies have been administered unevenly through different federal administrations, and state governments have never fully understood how they are to relate to tribal nations. Uneven interpretation, implementation, and shifting of Indian policy can be attributed to the fact that Indian nations have historically been in a state of flux. From international equals, toward of the state, and most recently as quasi-sovereigns viewed as states, the placement of Indian nations within the U.S. system of federalism has been continuously changing and evolving.

EARLY PERIOD

Prior to independence and the founding of the United States under the Articles of Confederation, foreign nations such as Spain, France, and England dealt with Indian nations as international sovereigns and more than 500 treaties were signed between these European powers and the various tribal governments in North America. All of these treaties were recognized under international law and established that tribal governments were sovereigns in their own right. The fact that these superpowers would negotiate an agreement is evidence that tribes were viewed as independent governments.

After the war for independence, the newly established U.S. government continued to follow the lead of its colonial predecessors by dealing with tribes via treaties rather than through conquest. The exclusive relationship between the federal government and the various tribal nations was reinforced through several acts of Congress, including the Northwest Ordinance of 1787 and the Trade and Intercourse Act of 1790. The Northwest Ordinance basically provided that Indian land would not be taken and that Indian rights and liberties would always be protected and preserved. The Trade and Intercourse Act dictated that Indian land could not be purchased by states or individual citizens—that only the federal government could enter into agreements to purchase land from tribal nations. Thus we see early on that tribal nations were viewed to be at least on an equal level to states, if not provided an elevated status via the treaty-making process that was normally reserved for foreign governments.

From the mid-1820s through the early part of the twentieth century, perceptions of Indians and the status of tribal nations within our system of federalism would be dramatically changed. Rather than continue to view these unique enclaves as foreign states, moves were made by the U.S. Supreme Court and Congress to move tribal governments to a less prominent position relative to the national government, but there was a continuation of the status of tribes as more than states—albeit with diminished sovereignty.

Despite laws designed to protect Indians from white encroachment (such as the Northwest Ordinance and the Trade and Intercourse Act), the United States was rapidly growing and citizens often looked toward Indian lands as a way to ease migration and settlement. Both Congress and the Supreme Court responded through laws and rulings that shifted the position of Indian nations from that of foreign states to domestic dependent nations that were subject to the plenary power of Congress. *Johnson v. McIntosh* (1823), *Cherokee Nation v. Georgia* (1831), and *Worcester v. Georgia* (1832) are three cases often referred to as the "Marshall Trilogy" after the chief justice at the time, John Marshall. These three cases began to change the position of tribal governments within the American system and clarify where tribal nations stood in relation to both the federal government and various state governments. In *Johnson*, the Court ruled that tribal nations did not own the land on which they resided but were, instead, more like tenants with a right to occupy land owned by the United States. In *Cherokee Nation v. Georgia*, the Court went further by noting that while the tribal nations enjoyed the right to occupy land (set forth in *Johnson*), they could not be accurately defined as foreign nations. Instead, the Court explicitly stated that tribal governments were "domestic dependent nations" and that the relationship between the United States and tribal nations was that of "a ward to its guardian." In other words, the Court ruled that tribal sovereignty was secondary to the power of the United States—the Court-appointed guardian established to protect the well-being of the domestic dependent tribes. While sovereignty relative to the federal government was diminished in both *Johnson* and *Cherokee Nation v. Georgia*, the placement of tribal governments relative to state governments was established in *Worcester*. Here the Court established that state law has no force within Indian borders and that all interactions with tribes are "vested in the government of the United States."

Like the Court, Congress also acted to change the relationship of tribal governments in relation to the United States from that of foreign states to domestic dependent nations. In the Indian Appropriations Act of 1871, a rider was attached that prohibited further treaty making between the U.S. government and tribal governments. Since the very nature of a treaty indicates the recognition of sovereignty and equal position, this act was a clear sign that the relationship was changing and that the placement of first nations within the federal system was changing too. This became evident with the passage of the Land in Severalty Act of 1887 (General Allotment Act or the Dawes Act). This act opened up Indian land for white settlement under the guise of guardianship. White philanthropists believed that assimilation into general society was in the best interest of Indians and that breaking up tribal lands would be the quickest way in achieving this. In the words of Theodore Roosevelt, the Allotment Act was a "mighty pulverizing engine to break up the tribal mass." Indeed it was, as tribal governments saw a drastic reduction in the amount of land they were able to occupy. While the act was challenged by tribal nations as a clear violation of the trust responsibility held by the federal government, the Supreme Court made yet another decision that clarified the status of tribal nations.

In *Lone Wolf v. Hitchcock* (1903), the virtually unquestioned power of Congress over the tribes was upheld by the Court. In this ruling, the Court was asked to determine whether Congress was acting in the best interest of the tribes and whether tribal leaders had been deceived in the process leading up to the General Allotment Act (the Dawes Act). In ruling, the Court essentially stated that dealings with the tribes were the power of Congress and Congress alone, and that political questions were beyond the scope of the Court's power. According to the opinion delivered by Justice Edward D. White,

> Plenary authority over the tribal relations of the Indians has been exercised by Congress from the beginning, and the power has always been deemed a political one, not subject to be controlled by the judicial department of government. We must presume that Congress acted in perfect good faith in the dealings of which complaint is made, and that the legislative branch of the government exercised their best judgment in the premises. In any event, Congress possessed full power in the matter. (187 U.S. 553)

Together, the three doctrines—treaties, the trust relationship, and plenary power—established that Indian tribes, although their inherent internal powers were diminished over reservation territory and affairs, still retained some degree of internal sovereignty; that the United States has trust responsibility for Indian tribes; and that Congress has and exercises an almost unquestioned legislative plenary authority over matters that concern Indian tribes. It is within this changing and evolving framework that we must view American Indian policy and the idea of American Indian federalism, and the related set of rules for states, tribal nations, and the federal government to follow.

MODERN ERA

The 1960s witnessed a cultural awakening in which the plight of many oppressed people was brought to the attention of the general public. From the Civil Rights movement to President Lyndon Johnson's War on Poverty, policies, and legislative acts were put in place to better equalize society. Included in this movement was a renewed interest in the sovereign rights of First Nations. Johnson, for example, devolved some power from the Bureau of Indian Affairs directly to tribal governments as part of his War on Poverty. The idea was that the people most immediately impacted by programs would be in the best position to run them—in other words, they should be allowed a measure of self-rule. The major shift in the position of First Nations within the U.S. system of federalism, however, came under President Richard Nixon. Nixon put forth two separate policies that would eventually place greater emphasis on tribal authority, autonomy, and inherent sovereignty that had been slowly eroded over time. Nixon's "New Federalism" and policy of tribal self-determination would place First Nations on a path toward both greater independence and fuller participation within the political system.

New Federalism

In 1972 President Nixon sought to decentralize the administration of fiscal sources and grants. Nixon's New Federalism was advocated in response to fears that the national government had grown too large and intrusive. It was felt that state and local governments should be given more discretion to deal with state-local needs. Likewise, with the Reagan administration's New Federalism, there was an emphasis on the separation of national and state functions. The administration favored a decentralization of power and policy control to states and local governments such as giving responsibilities in social programs to the states (e.g., Medicaid, food stamps, and AFDC). Although all of President Ronald Reagan's specific proposals were not adopted, the basic idea was that there would be a swap in responsibilities with the federal government and the states and a return of power to the states.

President George Bush extended Reagan's agenda, and President Bill Clinton continued the push for state and local governments to be innovative. Clinton went even further by encouraging the establishment of partnerships among the federal, state, local, and tribal governments under the Reinventing Government movement.

On April 29, 1994, Clinton and his cabinet members met with 300 Native American leaders to express his commitment to "consult with and work with tribal governments within the framework of a government-to-government relationship" (Clinton 1994). For the first time in the nation's history, a president of the United States and all members of his cabinet had met with representatives of Indian nations. Under the Clinton framework, tribes were being viewed as sovereigns and were treated in a manner similar to the relationship between the federal government and the states with regard to the administration of federal regulations. He told tribal leaders gathered in Washington that "together, we can open the greatest era of cooperative understanding and respect among our people ever." Clinton followed through with his promise by issuing numerous executive orders that directed federal agencies to treat tribal nations on a government-to-government basis. In other words, First Nations were once again being viewed as independent and sovereign nations within the larger system rather than simply as wards of the state operating under total control of the federal government.

Self-determination

In 1970 President Nixon announced in his presidential address the official federal Indian policy of self-determination. In this address, Nixon also announced that "the time has come to break decisively with the past and to create the conditions for a new era in which the Indian future is determined by Indian acts and decisions." Contemporary Indian policy and relations are predicated on the philosophical foundation laid by Nixon. On January 4, 1975, Congress implemented the Indian Self-determination and Education Assistance Act of 1975, which permits tribes to assume control and operation of many federal programs on Indian reservations. The act gives express authority to the secretaries of interior and health and human services to contract with, and make grants to, Indian tribes and other Indian organizations for the delivery of federal services. The act reflects a fundamental philosophical change concerning the administration of Indian affairs. Tribal programs are funded by the federal government, but the programs shall be controlled and operated by the tribes themselves. The Indian Financing Act, also passed in 1974, provided grants and loans to help Native Americans utilize and manage their own financial resources for reservation development. Cultural integrity was taken into consideration with the passage of the Indian Religious Freedom Act of 1978.

Beginning in the early 1980s, Indian policy, and therefore the placement of tribal nations within the federal system, began to shift once again. A number of legislative acts, such as the Tribal Self-government Act of 1988 and the Indian Tribal Economic Development and Contract Encouragement Act of 2000, appeared to have been pushing the era of self-determination to new heights and were aimed at an era of true self-government. At the same time, however, other congressional actions and court rulings were inconsistent with the idea of self-governance and actually took away tribal authority—especially relative to state governments. For example, the Indian Gaming Regulatory Act (IGRA) of 1988 allowed for casino-type gaming operations on tribal lands after the signing of a gaming compact with the state. Tribal governments were allowed the flexibility to operate casinos if they wanted, but only if they could convince the state to negotiate a compact—a stark departure from the traditional separation of tribes and states established under *Worcester* in 1832. While one provision of the IGRA allowed tribes to sue states that failed to negotiate in good faith, this provision was ruled unconstitutional by the Supreme Court in *Seminole Tribe of Florida v. Florida* (1996). Thus tribes were left at the mercy of state governments if they wanted to engage in gaming on their own land. Other rulings have tended to support state sovereignty over tribal sovereignty when the two have been at odds. Such decisions have led leading Indian scholar David Wilkins to note that

> the policy ambivalence evident in the conflicting goals of sometimes recognizing tribal self-determination and sometimes seeking to terminate that governing status has lessened only slightly over time. Tribal Nations and their citizens find that their efforts to exercise inherent sovereignty are rarely unchallenged. (Wilkins 2002, 118)

Thus, the uncertainty that has historically defined the position of First Nations within the broader American federal system remains.

The U.S. federal system of government consists of three primary parts—the national, state, and local governments. Governmental authority and relations for each of the three are enumerated in and are based on charters, constitutions, and court decisions. Tribal governments, however, were originally not part of this system. As a result, they were initially dealt with on the basis of international law. Formal government relations were established through treaty and agreements. Because of their changing legal and political status, Indian nations have been treated as international sovereigns, domestic dependent nations, and quasi-sovereign governments. In the course of defining the parameters of the legal and political status of these unique enclaves within the U.S. political system, federal Indian relations have evolved through protectorate and guardianship, and now are a trust relationship—albeit a less dictatorial relationship than the original concept of a trust relationship developed via the Marshall Trilogy. The modern trust relationship is based on a combination of international law, treaties, federal judicial decisions, legislation, and presidential decrees. The modern trust relationship, when coupled with the push for self-determination and New Federalism, relies more heavily upon tribal autonomy. At the same time, paternalistic tendencies have been very much a part of dealings with tribal nations from the very beginning of our nation. The interesting combination of the federal trust relationship, paternalism, and tribal self-government forms a complex backdrop for examining American Indians within the U.S. system of federalism and ensures that the ever-changing status of First Nations will continue to evolve. *SEE ALSO:* Native Americans; New Federalism (Nixon); *Seminole Tribe of Florida v. Florida*

BIBLIOGRAPHY: William J. Clinton, "Government-to-Government Relations with Native American Tribal Governments," Memorandum of April 29, 1994 (FR Doc 94-10877); David H. Getches, Charles F. Wilkinson, and Robert A. Williams, *Federal Indian Law*, 4th ed. (St. Paul, MN: West Publishing, 1998); Sharon O'Brien, *American Indian Tribal Governments* (Norman: University of Oklahoma Press, 1989); and David E. Wilkins, *American Indian Politics and the American Political System* (New York: Rowman & Littlefield, 2002).

JEFFREY S. ASHLEY

American System   The American System was an economic development program that was actuated by Henry Clay of Kentucky. The American System became the cornerstone of the Whig Party platform in the nineteenth century. The American System had three essential components: federal aid for internal improvements, a protective tariff for industry, and a national bank. The American System provided an urbanist model of economic growth that contrasted with the rural model of Jeffersonians. The Whigs advocated a system of internal improvements to facilitate commercial development combined with mercantilist economic policy centered around protective tariffs. As Arthur Schlesinger remarked on Clay's leadership, "He made federalism a living vision, replacing the dry logical prose of Hamilton with thrilling pictures of a glorious future.... [U]nder Clay's solicitous care, this rebaptized federalism slowly won its way to the inner councils of government" (Schlesinger 1945, 12).

Henry Clay and the Whigs formalized this economic model and termed it the American System, as distinct from the hegemonic British System of laissez-faire economic development. The economic policy theory behind it promoted policy nationalism and centralization at the expense of states' rights. Ultimately, Clay's system of "distribution," or intergovernmental revenue sharing, provided a means of building cooperation between levels of government through fiscal policy.

The American System established the constitutional foundation of modern economic development policy and defined strong national government powers as essential for securing the economic prosperity of strong national commercial enterprises. As noted historian Daniel Walker Howe, "Most of the Whig's economic platform was enacted by their successors: the Republican Party firmly established a protective tariff and subsidized business enterprise, and the Democrats under Wilson finally organized a nationwide banking system" (Howe 1979, 22). As American international economic hegemony displaced Britain, the protectionist aspect diminished, but internal improvements, intergovernmental grants, and nationally directed monetary policy based upon central banking remain enduring cornerstones of the American System. *SEE ALSO:* Civil War; Clay, Henry; Economic Development; Internal Improvements; Jackson, Andrew; Rural Policy; Urban Policy

BIBLIOGRAPHY: Maurice G. Baxter, *Henry Clay and the American System* (Lexington: University Press of Kentucky, 1995); Henry Clay, "The American System," in *Speeches of the Hon. Henry Clay, of the Congress of the United States*, ed. Richard Chambers (Cincinnati: Shepard & Stearns, 1842); Daniel Walker Howe, *The Political Culture of the American Whigs* (Chicago: University of Chicago Press, 1979); Robert V. Remini, *Andrew Jackson and the Bank War* (New York: W.W. Norton, 1967); and Arthur M. Schlesinger Jr., *The Age of Jackson* (Boston: Little, Brown, 1945).

Michael W. Hail

Americans with Disabilities Act of 1990   The Americans with Disabilities Act (ADA) was enacted in 1990 "to establish a clear and comprehensive prohibition of discrimination on the basis of disability." The ADA drew on the Civil Rights Act of 1964 (which did not cover people with disabilities) and the Rehabilitation Act of 1973 (which prohibited discrimination against any otherwise qualified person with handicaps in any program receiving federal funding). During the 1970s, many states enacted nondiscrimination laws for the handicapped; by 1990, every state had a law requiring public building accessibility. State and municipal offices and commissions on disability were created. The Education for All Handicapped Children Act of 1975 and the Fair Housing Amendments of 1988 that added persons with disabilities as a protected class also were precursors of the ADA.

The ADA extended the reach of these earlier laws to encompass the private sector and state and local governments not receiving federal funding. It prohibits discrimination against persons with disabilities in employment (Title I), public services and public transportation (Title II), public accommodations and services operated by private entities (Title III), and telecommunications (Title IV). States and localities are required to prohibit discrimination in all services, programs, or activities, including employment. Under Title V, religious communities and private clubs are exempted from the act. In addition, consistent with the principles of federalism, the ADA does not preempt state and local laws that provide equal or greater protections; however, the Eleventh Amendment does not protect states from federal law suits for violations of the ADA.

The ADA is administered by the Equal Employment Opportunity Commission, Department of Justice, Department of Transportation, and Federal Communications Commission. The National Institute of Disability and Rehabilitation Research of the Department of Education provides technical assistance. States and localities are not required to enforce Title III provisions, but must ensure that their codes meet minimum ADA standards. The act has been amended several times since its enactment in 1990 and is undergoing continuous challenges and interpretation in the courts. *SEE ALSO:* Age Discrimination; Civil Rights Act of 1964

BIBLIOGRAPHY: Bureau of National Affairs, Inc., *The Americans with Disabilities Act* (Washington, DC: Author, 1990); Kathryn S. McCarty, *Complying with the Americans with Disabilities Act* (Washington, DC: National League of Cities, 1991); and U.S. Department of Justice, Civil Rights Division, *The Americans with Disabilities Act: Title II Technical Assistance Manual* (Washington, DC: Author, 1993).

PHOEBE LIEBIG

Annapolis Convention of 1786   The Annapolis Convention of 1786 was the first major meeting held to discuss the shortcomings of the Articles of Confederation. Five states attended to discuss the topic of trade agreements that would lay the foundations for the Constitutional Convention to follow a year later. From the establishment of the United States under the Articles of Confederation in 1781, difficulties had arisen in the federal government's management of the confederation of individual state legislatures. Grown out of a loose alliance meant to govern in a time of war, Congress soon became incapable of solving the domestic problems that emerged in a new nation. Central to these problems were state trade disputes and competing claims to territory in the move of westward expansion. After many states bordering the frontier simultaneously claimed land tracts in the West, as well as in the face of rising objections of coastal states on their inability to respond in kind, Congress recognized the need to settle the issue of westward expansion. The passage of the Northwest Ordinance of 1784 designated great tracts of land as territories subject to federal government rule. However, there existed no system of federal courts under the Articles of Confederation to hear conflicting disputes between states regarding unclaimed federal land. Instead, there existed only a complicated system of arbitration by Congress. Realizing that the expansion of territory was of national concern, Congress authorized a limited regular army to occupy the frontier, but state claims to the land prevented further extension of the national government westward.

Recognizing these conflicts in regard to their own borders, Virginia and Maryland embarked on a series of meetings to discuss mutually beneficial solutions. These series of meetings would eventually lead to the Annapolis Convention of 1786. In December 1784, James Madison of Virginia succeeded in setting up a meeting in Annapolis between the two states to discuss the mutual development of the Potomac River, which bordered both states, in an effort to promote the river as a gateway to the West. The result was the creation of the Patowmack Company, formed in 1785 to encourage development on the Potomac and to arbitrate claims of river use. A second conference occurred in Alexandria, Virginia, in March 1785 to discuss commercial issues regarding the Chesapeake Bay. Upon the conclusion of that meeting, it was decided that a larger meeting discussing broader national commercial interests be held the following year with all states attending. In January 1786, Virginia invited the 13 states to attend a convention in Annapolis in September.

The Annapolis Convention began on September 11, 1786. Though all 13 states had been invited, in attendance were delegates from only five: Delaware, New York, New Jersey, Pennsylvania, and Virginia. New Hampshire, Massachusetts, Rhode Island, and North Carolina had appointed commissioners, but these commissioners did not arrive in time for the meeting. Connecticut, Maryland, South Carolina, and Georgia had not appointed commissioners. Formal proceedings began on September 11 when John Dickinson of Delaware, the author of the Articles of the Confederation, was appointed chairman. The 5 states proceeded to discuss problems of trade and commerce for the following three days with very similar objectives. The legislatures of all 5 states in attendance had empowered their commissioners to discuss a uniform system of trade and regulation that would then be presented to the states for ratification. Upon ratification, Congress would be authorized to act to promote and regulate this system. However, the commissioners soon foresaw that other complications would arise regarding larger political issues. These larger complications, which the commissioners were not authorized to discuss, as well as the absence of 8 of the 13 states, convinced the participating states that a larger convention would be necessary.

The major accomplishment of the Annapolis Convention was the call for a federal convention to be attended by all states the following year to address broader problems of governance under the Articles of Confederation. The draft of "Proceedings of Commissioners to Remedy Defects of the Federal Government," the report of the Annapolis Convention commissioners, was written by Alexander Hamilton of New York on September 14, 1786, and a copy of the finished text was carried back to the states' legislatures, as well as Congress, for consideration. This report called on all states to commit themselves to a nationwide convention the following year with delegates from all 13 states in attendance. On September 19, 1786, the *Maryland Journal* printed the first report on the Annapolis Convention and approved of its findings. On February 21, 1787, Congress endorsed the commissioners' call for a federal convention to meet in Philadelphia in May 1787. This convention in Philadelphia would become the Constitutional Convention in which the Articles were not reformed, but rather abandoned in favor of the creation of an entirely new government. *SEE ALSO:* Constitutional Convention of 1787; Madison, James; Northwest Ordinance of 1784

BIBLIOGRAPHY: Gaillard Hunt, *The Life of James Madison* (New York: Russell and Russell, 1968); Jack N. Rakove, *Original Meanings: Politics and Ideas in the Making of the Constitution* (New York: Vintage Books, 1997); and U.S. Department of State, *Documentary History of the Constitution of the United States of America*, vol. 1 (Littleton, CO: Fred B. Rothman & Company, 1998).

MEREDITH BINTZ

Anti-Federalists "Anti-Federalist" describes the philosophical and political position of individuals who, during the Constitutional Convention of 1787 and the subsequent state ratification debates (1787–89), generally opposed the constitution proposed to replace the Articles of Confederation. After ratification of the new Constitution and after the Washington administration took office, the Anti-Federalists formed a political party that was the first opposition party within the American political system. The Anti-Federalist Party evolved over time into the Democratic-Republican Party and ultimately into the Democratic party. Anti-Federalist leaders included individuals such as Patrick Henry of Virginia and Samuel Adams of Massachusetts. Though brief in existence, the Anti-Federalist movement (1787–89) and the Anti-Federalist Party (1789–1800) exerted a profound and lasting effect on American politics.

The Anti-Federalist position referred both to a philosophy about government, as well as to a preferred structure for government and manner in which society ought to be arranged. Anti-Federalist thought cannot be fully and properly understood absent consideration of the larger context, in which one of the paramount concerns of the colonists precipitant of the late Revolution was opposition to a strong central government. As such, the Anti-Federalist paradigm stood in contrast to a number of fundamental assumptions held by proponents ("Federalists") of the proposed constitution. The underpinning objection of the Anti-Federalists was the nature and degree of power (particularly compared to the arrangement existing under the Articles of Confederation) that the proposed new national government would be granted.

Consider the words of the Anti-Federalists in the "Dissent of the Pennsylvania Minority": "[The people of the United States are asked] to consider of a constitution proposed by a convention of the United States, who were not appointed for the purpose of framing a new form of government, but whose powers were expressly confined to altering and amending the present Articles of Confederation. . . . [And furthermore], that the new government will not be a confederacy of states, as it ought, but one consolidated government, founded upon the destruction of the several governments of the states" (*Pennsylvania Packet* 1787).

Consequently, the Anti-Federalist position developed in response to and reflected concerns about the possible perils that the adoption of a more powerful central government could instigate, whether deliberately or inadvertently. Chief among these included too great of a distance, both geographically and politically, between the rulers and the ruled; encroachments on the freedom of individuals; and the undermining of state sovereignty.

To Anti-Federalists, central government meant distant government. Government at a distance was regarded as (1) ineffective because it would not and/or could not be properly attentive to the needs and wishes of the citizenry, and (2) easily corrupted because the people could not particularly monitor or control those in power. In sum, the existence of strong central government was perceived as being generally antithetical to encouraging genuine self-government on the part of a citizenry.

Despite the negative connotation embedded in the label "Anti," it should be pointed out that adherents of the Anti-Federalist position did stand "for" certain propositions. The Anti-Federalists envisioned an American society composed of a collection of small republics. Among other implications, small republics were envisioned as entrusting political power and decision making at the local and state levels. In general, the Anti-Federalists expected that people could and would be self-reliant and self-sufficient in their communities, and that the best instrument for this purpose is some form of limited republican government.

The Anti-Federalists considered the Federalists to overstress devising governing structures that best control people and their potential worst impulses. By contrast, Anti-Federalist philosophy stressed that small self-governing republics served as natural fonts of virtue, and the abundance of virtue would exert sufficient control on individuals.

To the Anti-Federalists, concentrating power at the local and state levels (consistent with the precepts of small republics) creates societies in which people are freer, more virtuous, and, perhaps most critically, more trusting of government and more willing to allow government to undertake certain activities for the public good. The latter in particular is made possible because all citizens, both philosophically and practically, feel themselves a part of government and the decisions being made. Given all the foregoing, then, the Anti-Federalists did not view any need for a stronger central government.

The Anti-Federalists did not prevail in the ratification debates and political contests of their time, as the states eventually approved passage of what became the U.S. Constitution. Nevertheless, the Anti-Federalists did have significant victories that shaped the Constitution, and the legacy of their thought and actions can be discerned today in the contemporary U.S. federal system.

The most significant and far-reaching accomplishment of the Anti-Federalists is that the Bill of Rights (the first ten amendments to the U.S. Constitution) was drafted and passed in large measure to satisfy objections that the Anti-Federalists raised about the proposed constitution. However, as Herbert Storing noted (1981), the Anti-Federalists divided their proposed amendments into two categories, one with protections for individual freedoms and the other with changes in political institutions. The amendments proposed by the Federalists drew almost exclusively from the protection of individual liberties and hardly at all from the changes Anti-Federalists advocated for institutions (i.e., one-year terms for senators and prohibition of direct federal taxation). Nonetheless, the Anti-Federalist legacy is substantially reflected in the Bill of Rights, which has become the exemplar, not just in the United States but indeed around the world, of freedom and civil rights and the need for their vigilant protection.

The Anti-Federalist philosophy contributed an enduring perspective that remains relevant to discussions in contemporary times about the American federal system and the proper balance of power among the various levels and units therein. The Anti-Federalist perspective is the historical and philosophical legacy for those who most emphasize the important role of state and local government within the federal system, the ideal of self-government for and by a citizenry, and the principle of strict construction in interpreting the U.S. Constitution. Indeed, any discussion today about the appropriate policy scope of the federal government is perpetuation of a debate the Anti-Federalists initiated at the time the Constitution was first proposed, and in many respects has continued ever since. *SEE ALSO:* American System; Articles of Confederation; Bill of Rights; Constitutional Convention of 1787; Cooperative Federalism; Creative Federalism; Federalists; Fiscal Federalism; Hamilton, Alexander; Jefferson, Thomas; Local Government; Sovereignty

BIBLIOGRAPHY: W. B. Allen and Gordon Lloyd, eds., *The Essential Anti-Federalist* (Lanham, MD: Rowman & Littlefield, 2002); Allan Bloom, ed., *Confronting the Constitution* (Washington, DC: AEI Press, 1990); Martin Diamond, "What the Framers Meant by Federalism," in *From a Nation of States* (Chicago: Rand McNally, 1974); *Pennsylvania Packet and Daily Advertiser*, December 18, 1787; and Herbert J. Storing, ed., *The Complete Anti-Federalist*, 7 vols. (Chicago: University of Chicago Press, 1981).

DUANE D. MILNE AND MICHAEL W. HAIL

Articles of Confederation   The Articles of Confederation together with the Declaration of Independence formed the first national compact of the United States of America. Following ratification of the Articles by the states on March 1, 1781, Congress assembled for the first time under a formal constitution. Although the plan of confederation proved inadequate to continental governance after independence, the Articles established in law several of the main provisions of American federalism retained and strengthened in the U.S. Constitution of 1787.

The Second Continental Congress proposed drafting articles of confederation on June 11, 1776, just before a plurality of the states adopted the Declaration of Independence. The Congress approved thirteen articles on November 15, 1777, sending a document to the states for ratification on June 26, 1778. Eight states immediately agreed to "The Articles of Confederation and perpetual Union between the states of New Hampshire, Massachusetts-bay Rhode Island and Providence Plantations, Connecticut, New York, New Jersey, Delaware, Maryland, Virginia, North Carolina, South Carolina, and Georgia," as the proposal was officially titled. On March 1, 1781, Maryland became the last to ratify and the first continental constitution took effect. On the next day, the *Journals of the Continental Congress, 1774–89* opened with the words "The United States in Congress Assembled," recognizing the completion of the ratification process and the new relationship among the states. As the *Journal* shows, the following days and months found Congress focused on the prosecution of the War for Independence until hostilities with Great Britain officially ceased with the Treaty of Paris, signed September 3, 1783, and ratified by Congress on July 14, 1784.

The institutional deficiencies of government under the Articles became increasingly clear in peacetime, as catalogued most famously by Alexander Hamilton in *The Federalist* Nos. 9, 15, 20, 21, and 23. According to the Articles, the unicameral Congress could address none of its legislative action directly to individual citizens, nor, indeed, could it enforce any laws pertaining to its proper sphere of authority, the collective choices made by its member states. During the war, the states had pledged to share the burdens of raising troops, but when some failed to follow through with their agreements, Congress lacked the power to sanction them. The Articles granted Congress the power to borrow money, but offered no reliable mechanism to secure funds to repay such debts. Congress could apportion federal expenses, but could not force the states to pay their shares. Congress could make, but not enforce, treaties. The Articles also gave Congress the power to set standards for striking and valuing coinage, fixing weights and measures, and establishing and regulating post offices and postage, but not the ability to sanction its noncompliant members, Congress could use none of these important powers to regulate interstate and foreign commerce. Following the War of Independence, many states erected barriers to trade with tariffs and custom duties that advanced transitory local interests at the expense of national economic development. Rhode Island took considerable advantage of such weaknesses in the Articles by printing paper currency to use for repaying its debts (often devaluing these notes following the exchange), while accepting only specie from its debtors. As Hamilton noted in *The Federalist* No. 9, a body without enforcement powers could not function effectively as a government. The resulting "government of governments," he insisted, had not secured the mutual benefits of association to its member states and was unlikely to remain intact, since member states could not be penalized for pursuing their particular advantage at the expense of the whole. As representatives from the states to the Congress increasingly learned, the defects of the Articles could be summed up in the compact's provisions for remedying these problems—an amendment process that reinforced Congress's dependence on the state legislatures and disconnection from the citizens of the states.

The idea for an amendment procedure was arguably one of the most innovative aspects of the Articles. Although some American colonial governing documents had specifically provided for amendment (e.g., Article XXXIX of the Charter of Liberties and Frame of Government of the Province of Pennsylvania in America, 1682) and many colonial communities offered some method of revisiting and revising their collective choices, formal amendment procedures remained relatively rare in eighteenth-century constitutional designs. The architects of the Articles not only anticipated the need for correction and improvement, but also designed an amendment process that distinguished such constitutional choices from ordinary acts of legislation. By conceiving constitutional decision making as a separate activity, requiring different processes to show a more extensive degree of consent than would be needed for ordinary collective choices, they significantly advanced the theory and practice of representative, constitutional government. Yet, the amendment procedures described in the Articles seemed unable to address the confederacy's defects. Article XIII empowered Congress to propose amendments, which would only become effective if they were ratified by all of the state legislatures. Every attempt to alter the Articles failed to achieve the required unanimous agreement of the states.

The aim of unanimous consent is not as unrealistic as it may sound. Colonial experience with covenants and compacts that required profound processes of deliberation and collective choice often produced broad consensus from diverse interests. Well into the nineteenth century, many American institutions were predicated on the idea that interested parties might be expected to discern their community's long-term common interests and set aside narrow interests when the good of the whole required. The belief that the general government should only address itself to the states as corporate bodies also had federal colonial antecedents. For many architects of the Articles, it would have been difficult to envision an "individual" who was wholly separable from the community; even for those who looked to the more abstract conception of individual rights, actual liberties and obligations as well as more mundane notions of the individual good were secured in the reality of communities. Accordingly, it often only made sense for government to act upon the community; if the states could be considered communities, then a general government could, in fact, destroy them by circumventing the whole to patronize or punish individuals directly. In the view of many, such had been the experience of the colonial communities in relation to Great Britain. The inadequacies of the Articles and its amendment process suggested the limitations of these views, however. Often, the legislatures represented neither communities nor majority interests; amendments, in view of many critics, often failed because an oligarchic legislature shielded narrow interests at the expense of their states.

For many statesmen, including James Madison, the requirement of unanimity only underscored more serious flaws in the confederacy's design. In Madison's view, even unanimous ratification of an amendment by the state legislatures would not change the basic problem that the people might neither secure republican government for their states nor maintain a union of the states, since a violation of the Articles by any state could justify the others in dissolving the entire compact. Only by rethinking the nature of the compact could the "firm league of friendship" described in the Articles develop into a "more perfect Union," as later envisioned by the U.S. Constitution. When such rethinking occurred in 1787, amendment brought forth a new form of government. What remained, however, was the national compact composed of the Declaration of Independence and the U.S. Constitution. It was the compact basis of the confederation that allowed amendment of the amendment procedure under the Articles, ensured uninterrupted rule of law, and preserved constitutional continuity during a period of revolutionary institutional change.

PROVISIONS OF THE ARTICLES OF CONFEDERATION

The form of institutional relationships formed by the Articles of Confederation reflected its framers' experiences and expectations of existing colonial agreements. Article I described a confederacy of "The United States of America," using a phrase that first for the first time in American documentary history. In the Articles, the states entered into their perpetual union, establishing "a firm league of friendship" to "perpetuate mutual friendship and intercourse," as the preamble and Articles III and IV announce. Such language echoes the description of "a firm and perpetual league of friendship" found in the Articles of Confederation (1643) joining the governments of Massachusetts-bay, New Plymouth, Connecticut, and New Haven as the United Colonies of New England. According to Article II of the 1781 agreement, each state was to retain its "sovereignty, freedom and independence" as well as its powers, rights, and jurisdiction except as it expressly delegated such authority "to the United States, in Congress assembled." Article V detailed methods of representation (no less than two and no more than seven delegates to be appointed annually according to procedures designed by each state's legislature), term limits (no member could serve for more than three years in a six-year period), and a "one state, one vote" rule that also drew on colonial practice and early efforts toward a colonywide confederation, including Joseph Galloway's Plan of Union (1774), the Albany Plan of Union (1754), and William Penn's Plan of Union (1697). Like many of the existing state constitutions, the Articles called for a weak executive. When in session, a single president, chosen annually by the delegates, presided. When out of session, the executive was a Committee of the States, composed of one delegate from each state. Also as in many colonial and state legislatures, the court was under the direct congressional control. In these and other provisions, colonial experience shaped the Articles. The colonial legislatures had represented the ever-present expectations of local liberty under the charter governments of British North America in counterpoise to the governors who embodied the authority of the Crown. In gaining independence, conditions no longer dictated legislative preeminence, but existing institutions and assumptions prevailed.

In the new institutional environment, which lacked the counterbalancing authority of the Crown, formerly beneficial aspects of the legislatures' dominance became liabilities. Various flaws in the institutional design represented by Articles VI, VII, VIII, IX, and XII (regarding congressional powers to borrow money, make treaties, raise troops, levy taxes, and regulate commerce) have already been noted. Yet, also within these Articles were several provisions of significant import to the U.S. Constitution as framers sought a new balance among the powers of government as well as the governments of the new nation. Article IV supplied concepts and wording for "full faith and credit" as well as "privileges and immunities" that each free inhabitant would enjoy when traveling or trading across state borders. As a basic expression of federalism, such language indicated that citizenship in the United States exceeded the boundaries of citizenship in a given state. Although the meaning of the Privileges and Immunities Clause was not yet what it would become, the nascent orientation to dual citizenship is to be found in the Articles. Similarly, Article IX suggests the basis for a general court system in which Congress was empowered to adjudicate boundary, jurisdictional, and other disputes between the states. In all, more than half of the provisions and wording of the Articles found their way into the U.S. Constitution, where their authority was given effect by the increase in enforcement powers of the federal government. In 1787, the constitution of a "general government" did not mean a central or unitary government, however; independence from the Crown did not bring about parliamentary government in the American case. The confederal experience had revealed the most basic feature of federation as *shared* authority. The Articles had captured the conditions of limited, distributed, shared constitutional authority in the critical concept of dual citizenship, with the broader implication that citizens must be directly subject to the laws of Congress as well as the laws of their state legislatures. The result of carrying such provisions into the new constitution was a new institutional form—an extended and compound republic—that lay between the extremes of unitary government and a league of sovereign states.

FEDERAL THEORY AND PRACTICE

The Articles contributed to the theory and practice of federalism in several important ways. The Articles provided the institutional basis for an extended republic. By advancing the compact conception of government, the Articles facilitated an amendment process that eventually produced the compound republic of the multiple local, regional, state, and federal governments comprising modern American federalism. Together, the ideas of an extended and compound republic enabled the union of diverse political associations without destroying the integrity of their existing institutions or their peoples' identities.

The primary elements of the extended republic are found in Article XI, which enabled the addition of new states to the confederation upon the approval of 9 member states. The potential addition of new states as the equals of the existing confederation members (itself an unusual provision for the times) supplied one condition for a continental republic. The supermajority requirement for approving new state admissions thwarted any expansionist aspirations of the existing states and provided that republican government would be extended by deliberation and negotiation. The Articles make use of various voting rules to achieve legislative ends. Although a simple majority of 7 states sufficed to enact most matters, Article IX listed several serious matters, including declarations of war, treaties, appropriations, that required a majority of 9 states. This supermajority requirement had several effects, including the refinement of legislative proposals so that they would be attractive to at least 3 of the large states and their adjacent, regional constituencies. In this way, the 9-state rule performed much as Madison would later envision representation in the extended republic. In *The Federalist* No.10, he considered the problems and benefits of small and large republics, concluding that the scope and scale of representation could be designed to refine diverse, contested interests and define their common ground. Elements of such thinking and its institutional expression are already apparent in the Articles. What remained to complete the Madisonian vision was a way for Congress to affect the citizens within the states directly. That institutional transformation turned on the possibility of understanding the Articles as a partial expression of the more fundamental aims set forth in the Declaration of Independence. By interpreting the Articles as part of a compact, these aims were more fully realized in the "amendment" and ratification processes resulting in the U.S. Constitution.

As with every other attempt at amendment, Article XIII appeared to pose an immediate problem to ratification of the new constitution. The Declaration offered a principled way to rethink the basis of union and the amendment process through its doctrine of popular sovereignty. If governments derive "their just powers from the consent of the governed," as the Declaration said, then it followed that amendments to the Articles must be submitted for ratification to the people of the several states in their capacities as citizens of the states. According the Articles (and a basic supposition of federalism), the people could not vote (or be represented) in an amendment process as the "American People," taken as a whole, because that would amount to the people of one state amending a document that would change the constitution of another state. To fulfill the conditions of popular sovereignty and federalism simultaneously, the voters within each state would choose delegates who would convene for the sole purpose of deciding whether to ratify the new constitution. Using the tested 9-state supermajority, the process provided that if 9 states approved the new Constitution, it would become binding upon them; other states would be free to join or remain separate from this new union. In this way, membership continued to be based on unanimous consent, constitutional choice remained distinct from ordinary legislation, and popular sovereignty and re-publicanism were maintained along with federalism as the basic principles of American government. To meet the requirements of the Articles, the framers submitted the proposed constitution to Congress, requesting that Congress send it to the state legis-latures who were requested to call a "Convention of Delegates, chosen in each state by the People thereof." The first step in amending the flaws in the Articles, thus, amounted to amending the amendment procedure to constitute a direct relationship between the general government and the citizens of the several states. The first remedy, thereby, also opened the way for a new relationship between the general government and the people as a whole, completing the initial revolution in American federal theory and practice. This compact enabled a new form of government to emerge from the confederal ex-perience, taking shape as the institutions described by the 1787 U.S. Constitution. *SEE ALSO:* Appendix 2; Covenant; Declaration of Independence; Federalism; U.S. Consti-tution

BIBLIOGRAPHY: Worthington C. Ford et al., eds. *Journals of the Continental Con-gress, 1774–1789* (Washington, DC, 1904–37); Merrill Jensen, *The Articles of Confeder-ation: An Interpretation of the Social-Constitutional History of the American Revolution, 1774–1781* (1940; reprint, Madison: University of Wisconsin Press, 1970); Donald S. Lutz, *The Origins of American Constitutionalism* (Baton Rouge: Louisiana State Univer-sity Press, 1988); Vincent Ostrom, *The Meaning of American Federalism: Constituting a Self-governing Society* (San Francisco: Institute for Contemporary Studies, 1994); and Stephen L. Schechter, ed., *Roots of the Republic: American Founding Documents Inter-preted* (Madison, WI: Madison House Publishers, 1990).

BARBARA ALLEN

B

Bailey v. Drexel Furniture Company   In *Hammer v. Dagenhart* (1918), the Supreme Court invalidated the federal Keating-Owen Child Labor Act, which had forbidden the shipment of goods made by child labor in interstate commerce, on the grounds that this ostensible regulation of commerce was really a regulation of production in violation of the Tenth Amendment. In reaction, Congress enacted the present law, which imposed a 10 percent tax on goods made by child labor. The validity of this tax was contested in *Bailey v. Drexel Furniture Company* in 1922.

Speaking for the Court, Chief Justice William Howard Taft found that the present law, like its predecessor invalidated in *Hammer v. Dagenhart*, extended federal powers too far and invaded the powers reserved to the states by the Tenth Amendment. The fact that it was called a tax rather than a regulation could not save it. "To give such magic to the word tax," Taft wrote, would extend federal power beyond its constitutional limits and would threaten "the sovereignty of the states." *SEE ALSO: Hammer v. Dagenhart*; Taxing and Spending Power; Tenth Amendment

ELLIS KATZ

Baker v. Carr   *Baker v. Carr* (1962) is a landmark case credited with legally establishing the noted principle of "one person, one vote" and with condemning legislative malapportionment. "Malapportionment" refers to the underrepresentation of the population that arises when one legislative district is considerably more populated than another. As some states allocated senators along county lines, urban populations were typically underrepresented in state legislatures. For instance, in New Jersey in 1962, one rural senator represented 49,000 residents, while one urban senator represented 924,000 residents.

However, the setting that catapulted this issue to the Supreme Court's doorstep came about in Tennessee. The disparity in the House district population ranged from 2,340 citizens in one county to 42,298 citizens in another county. Mr. Charles Baker and others filed a lawsuit in U.S. District Court claiming that the malapportionment of the state legislature violated the Equal Protection Clause of the Fourteenth Amendment to the U.S. Constitution. The federal district court applied the precedent from *Colegrove v. Green* (1946) and dismissed the complaint, finding that it was powerless to make a determination of the issue, as it was a political question to be resolved by the political branches of the government.

Baker appealed to the U.S. Supreme Court, which decided to rule on the case, noting that the Political Question Doctrine is "a tool of maintenance of governmental order" and should not be used as a constraint upon the judiciary to examine the legislature's actions. After reargument, the Court rendered a 6–2 decision in favor of Baker. Justice Brennan wrote the majority opinion, establishing that the plaintiffs had legal standing to challenge the state apportionment statutes. The Political Question Doctrine had been redefined, thus opening the window for "judicial resolution of reapportionment cases." However, this decision was most significant because it established that states should possess population equality across legislative districts, thus protecting the concept of one person, one vote. The *Baker* decision also motivated a sweeping reapportionment movement across the nation that culminated in the redrawing of legislative districts in every state and greater representation for both urban areas and African Americans. *SEE ALSO: Colegrove v. Green*; Reapportionment; *Reynolds v. Sims*

BIBLIOGRAPHY: Stephen Ansolabehere and Samuel Issacharoff, "Baker v. Carr in Context: 1946–1964," in *Constitutional Law Stories*, ed. Michael C. Dorf (New York: Foundation Press, 2003): 297–323; *Baker v. Carr*, 369 U.S. 186, 254 (1962); Ann O'M. Bowman and Richard C. Kearney, *State and Local Government*, 3rd ed. (Boston: Houghton Mifflin, 1996); and Lee Epstein and Thomas G. Walker, *Constitutional Law for a Changing America: Institutional Powers and Constraints*, 4th ed. (Washington, DC: Congressional Quarterly, 2001).

JOSEPH N. PATTEN

Baldwin v. Montana Fish and Game Commission In *Baldwin v. Montana Fish and Game Commission* (1978), the U.S. Supreme Court upheld Montana's substantially higher elk-hunting license fee for nonresidents over objections that it violated the Privileges and Immunities Clause of Article IV, which requires that "the Citizens of each State shall be entitled to all Privileges and Immunities of Citizens in the several States." According to the Court, this clause requires a state to treat residents and nonresidents equally only with regard to those privileges and immunities "bearing upon the vitality of the Nation as a single entity." Elk hunting, according to the Court, does not fit into that category. The decision is also interesting because it rejects the doctrine articulated in *Toomer v. Witsell* (1948) that the discrimination against nonresidents must bear some relationship to the problem that the state is attempting to address. *SEE ALSO: Corfield v. Coryell*; Privileges and Immunities Clause: Article IV; *Toomer v. Witsell*

ELLIS KATZ

Banking The American banking system has a tumultuous history of federalist compromise, devolution of authority, and federal preemption. The very conception and proposal of such an instrument of governmental and agency authority were met with debate and opposition as far back as our nation's founding. Originally the brainchild of Alexander Hamilton, the idea of a central bank was a point of contention among many of the founders, especially Thomas Jefferson, who satirically commented that banking institutions were more dangerous than standing armies. Beginning with the Constitution, the history of banking is one of compromise between the federal and state governments. It is essentially a conflict over the devolution of authority and the definition of the role of federal and state policy makers.

The historical roots of the debate began with the Continental Congress and the founding of our nation. Unlike Alexander Hamilton and other Federalists favoring loose construction of the Constitution, Jeffersonians from agrarian backgrounds envisioned simplicity and strict construction, and argued that augmenting federal authority through the centralization of a financial institution ran contrary to the Tenth Amendment. This assertion of states' rights and protest against centralization was countered by Hamiltonians who invoked the Elastic Clause, which authorizes Congress to use whatever means it deems necessary and proper to effectuate the use of any of its enumerated powers including, but not limited to, the power to coin money, lend money, and borrow money from foreign entities.

To the disappointment of Jefferson and other strict constructionists, the First Bank of the United States was established in 1791, but was short-lived. The bank was established primarily as a depository of funds and to assume the national debt. The nation's first attempt at centralizing its banking operations failed because of the emerging role of states and localities vying for competitive positions in the field. When the time came, the First Bank's charter was not renewed, and later a second attempt at centralization was made with the founding of the Second National Bank. The Second Bank was created to manage the debts incurred from the War of 1812 and to restore some measure of economic and monetary stability to the nation. Public sentiment favored centralization, which was legitimized by the landmark decision handed down by Chief Justice John Marshall in the case of *McCulloch v. Maryland*.

This landmark decision favored federal preemption and national supremacy. In this case, the State of Maryland attempted to tax a federal bank branch located within its borders, effectively endeavoring to destroy it and assert state authority. Federalists achieved a major victory with the Marshall's decision that upheld the supremacy of the federal government in instances where state law conflicted with the federal exercise of power. *McCulloch v. Maryland* also laid the framework for a dual banking system.

A dual banking system, a curious relationship of both defined yet intertwined spheres of influence regulated by the federal and state governments, has been the prevailing arrangement in the area of banking from *McCulloch v. Maryland* to present day. This relationship has been marked by constant challenges to federal authority with calls for devolution of authority, answered in the majority of cases with federal preemption. The 1820s under President Andrew Jackson saw a move toward the strengthening of the states and a decentralization of federal authority in the banking sector with the establishment of various pet banks. Decentralization during this period led to the Panics of 1837 and 1847, which called for recentralization to establish uniformity and stability. Accordingly, various pieces of legislation were passed in an effort to achieve the stability and uniformity sought, including, but not limited to, the Independent Treasury Act of 1840, the Federal Income Tax Act, the Legal Tender Act of 1862, the National Currency Act of 1863, and the National Bank Act of 1864. In addition, the Office of the Comptroller of the Currency was created to establish and supervise national banks, as well as to stabilize our currency and economy. Throughout this emergence of a dual banking system, Federalist principles prevailed with power being firmly held in the hands of the national government, resulting in the establishment of uniform standards, rules, and national currency. *SEE ALSO: McCulloch v. Maryland*

VINCENZO M. MOGAVERO

Barron v. Baltimore During the course of paving streets and performing other civic improvements, the City of Baltimore diverted streams so that they emptied into the city's harbor in the vicinity of John Barron's deep-water dock. The area around the dock subsequently became filled with silt, resulting in the virtual destruction of the dock's economic value. This action by the City of Baltimore, Barron argued, violated the Just Compensation Clause of the Fifth Amendment of the Bill of Rights, which forbids the taking of private property for public uses without just compensation. Barron therefore sued the City of Baltimore demanding the compensation to which he believed he was entitled under the Just Compensation Clause. Having ultimately lost his suit in the Maryland courts, Barron then appealed his case to the U.S. Supreme Court.

In *Barron v. Baltimore* (1833), Chief Justice John Marshall, writing for a unanimous Court, noted that the issue raised in Barron's case was "of great importance, but not of much difficulty." This was so, he said, because it was well understood that the Bill of Rights had been added to the U.S. Constitution in 1791 because of fears that the national government would encroach upon basic liberties of the people. The rights in the Bill of Rights, including the Just Compensation Clause of the Fifth Amendment, Marshall continued, were therefore restrictions of the power of the national government alone, and were not applicable as restrictions of the powers of the state and local governments. Since under this interpretation, none of the rights in the Bill of Rights, including the Just Compensation Clause, were restrictive of the powers of the City of Baltimore or the State of Maryland, Barron's case was dismissed by the Court for lack of jurisdiction.

As a result of the decision in *Barron v. Baltimore*, prior to the Civil War the rights in the Bill of Rights could only be validly invoked in challenges to exercises of power by the national government, and not exercises of power by state and local governments. Following the Civil War and the ratification of the Fourteenth Amendment to the Constitution, however, the decision in *Barron v. Baltimore* was modified, since the Supreme Court between 1897 and 1969 interpreted the Due Process Clause of the Fourteenth Amendment to apply most, but not all, of the rights in the Bill of Rights as restrictions of the powers of state and local governments. Among the rights made so applicable to the states is the right to just compensation for private property taken for public uses, which the Supreme Court held to be guaranteed by the Due Process Clause of the Fourteenth Amendment in 1897. *SEE ALSO:* Fourteenth Amendment; Incorporation (Nationalization) of the Bill of Rights; Marshall, John; *Slaughterhouse Cases*; Takings Clause: Fifth Amndment

RICHARD C. CORTNER

Benton v. Maryland *See* Incorporation of the Bill of Rights

Bill of Rights The first draft of the first amendments to the Constitution of the United States was the work of James Madison, who moved his proposed amendments in an historic speech to the House of Representatives in the first session of the First Congress on June 8, 1789.

Madison's fellow congressmen were not receptive to the idea of amending the Constitution so soon, especially when they had before them what they considered the more urgent business of getting the new government up and running. But, however reluctantly, with much grumbling and many delays, congressmen did debate the proposed amendments, heatedly and carefully, over several months, editing and revising and then passing twelve amendments by the required two-thirds majority of both houses, and sending them to the state legislatures for ratification on September 24, 1789.

More than two years later, in a letter addressed to the governors dated March 1, 1792, Secretary of State Thomas Jefferson was finally able to inform them that three-fourths of the state legislatures had ratified ten of the twelve amendments. Those ten articles, the Bill of Rights, thus became "valid to all Intents and Purposes, as part of this Constitution."

The legislative process that resulted in adoption of the Bill of Rights is best understood as a continuation of the controversies that flourished during the many months it took to achieve ratification of the Constitution itself. Events had moved quickly and impressively after the Constitution was ratified. Elections were held for the House of Representatives, and the state legislatures selected their U.S. senators. Presidential electors were chosen, and they in turn elected George Washington president. All seemed to be running smoothly.

But the ratification process had been bitterly contested, and although the necessary number of states had all ratified unconditionally, the margin of victory in the constitutional conventions had been dangerously close in three key states—19 votes out of 355 in Massachusetts, 10 votes out of 168 in Virginia, and only 3 votes out of 57 in New York. All 3 states had attached to their ratification long lists of amendments they expected to be considered favorably, either by Congress or, preferably, by a new constitutional convention. And in fact, first Virginia and then New York, early in May

---

THE BILL OF RIGHTS

Amendment I—Freedom of religion, press, expression. *Congress shall make no law respecting an establishment of religion, or prohibiting the free exercise thereof; or abridging the freedom of speech, or of the press; or the right of the people peaceably to assemble, and to petition the Government for a redress of grievances.*

Amendment II—Right to bear arms. *A well regulated Militia, being necessary to the security of a free State, the right of the people to keep and bear Arms, shall not be infringed.*

Amendment III—Quartering of soldiers. *No Soldier shall, in time of peace be quartered in any house, without the consent of the Owner, nor in time of war, but in a manner to be prescribed by law.*

Amendment IV—Search and seizure. *The right of the people to be secure in their persons, houses, papers, and effects, against unreasonable searches and seizures, shall not be violated, and no Warrants shall issue, but upon probable cause, supported by Oath or affirmation, and particularly describing the place to be searched, and the persons or things to be seized.*

Amendment V—Trial and punishment, compensation for takings. *No person shall be held to answer for a capital, or otherwise infamous crime, unless on a presentment or indictment of a Grand Jury, except in cases arising in the land or naval forces, or in the Militia, when in actual service in time of War or public danger; nor shall any person be subject for the same offense to be twice put in jeopardy of life or limb; nor shall be compelled in any criminal case to be a witness against himself, nor be deprived of life, liberty, or property, without due process of law; nor shall private property be taken for public use, without just compensation.*

Continued on next page

Continued from previous page

Amendment VI—Right to speedy trial, confrontation of witnesses. *In all criminal prosecutions, the accused shall enjoy the right to a speedy and public trial, by an impartial jury of the State and district wherein the crime shall have been committed, which district shall have been previously ascertained by law, and to be informed of the nature and cause of the accusation; to be confronted with the witnesses against him; to have compulsory process for obtaining witnesses in his favor, and to have the Assistance of Counsel for his defence.*

Amendment VII—Trial by jury in civil cases. *In Suits at common law, where the value in controversy shall exceed twenty dollars, the right of trial by jury shall be preserved, and no fact tried by a jury, shall be otherwise re-examined in any Court of the United States, than according to the rules of the common law.*

Amendment VIII—Cruel and unusual punishment. *Excessive bail shall not be required, nor excessive fines imposed, nor cruel and unusual punishments inflicted.*

Amendment IX—Construction of Constitution. *The enumeration in the Constitution, of certain rights, shall not be construed to deny or disparage others retained by the people.*

Amendment X—Powers of the states and people. *The powers not delegated to the United States by the Constitution, nor prohibited by it to the States, are reserved to the States respectively, or to the people.*

1789, submitted applications to Congress to "call a Convention for proposing Amendments," as provided for in Article V of the Constitution. In short, although the branches of government were established and functioning, the Constitution was not yet safe from determined constitutional efforts to revise it drastically. Conflicts from the ratification struggle persisted, conflicts that had to do primarily with the distribution of powers between the states and the government of the United States under the provisions of the new Constitution.

The several state constitutional conventions had proposed over 100 different amendments, and Madison had the full collection of them before him. Almost all of them fell into one of two categories, those having to do with the federal structure and those dealing with rights. Many of the New York proposals having to do with rights, for example, were adopted by Madison almost unchanged and included in his own proposals—"that in time of peace no soldier ought to be quartered in any house without the consent of the owner," "that no person ought to be put twice in jeopardy of life or limb for one and the same offence," "that excessive bail ought not to be required . . . nor cruel or unusual punishments inflicted," and several more.

But the numerous structural amendments proposed by several states were almost completely ignored by Madison, and this led to strenuous complaints in the First Congress by the Anti-Federalists, those who had insisted that the Constitution be amended prior to ratification. They complained that "all the important amendments were omitted" from the deliberations in the House, and they insisted that their "solid and substantial amendments" were the ones the people expect. It fell to Representative Thomas Tudor Tucker of South Carolina to present these structural amendments to the House, drawn from many state ratifying conventions. Tucker's proposed amendments dealt with such matters as the length of terms of office for representatives, senators, and the president; control of congressional elections; congressional powers of taxation; and structure of the federal judiciary. All of these proposals had one aim: to transfer power from the federal government back to the states.

For example, Tucker proposed that "the election of Senators for each State shall be annual." (Senators in the original Constitution were chosen by their state legislatures for six-year terms.) One-year appointments would mean that a senator would be little more than a messenger and mouthpiece for his state legislature, subject to prompt replacement if he did anything other than what the legislature instructed him to do. The Senate would not be a deliberative body, but a gathering of spokesmen for their respective state legislatures.

Article I, Section 5, of the Constitution provides, "Each House shall be the judge of the elections, returns and qualifications of its own Members." Tucker proposed to amend it to read, "Each State shall be the judge (according to its own laws) of the election of its Senators and Representatives."

Tucker also proposed to eliminate most of the federal judiciary. Article I, Section 8, grants Congress the power "to constitute tribunals inferior to the Supreme Court." Tucker proposed to delete mention of inferior tribunals and substitute "courts of admiralty." In addition, he proposed the same demolition in Article III, Section 1, striking out the words "inferior courts" and substituting "courts of admiralty," thus eliminating the presence of federal courts within the states.

As for the presidency, he proposed stripping the president of the title of "commander in chief" of the armed forces. He proposed instead, "The president shall have power to direct (agreeable to law) the operations of the Army and Navy of the United States." This would give the Congress, and especially the Senate, an early and continuing control over matters relating to war and peace.

Tucker proposed many more amendments, seventeen in all, but none of them was approved by the members of the House. There was no discussion of them prior to voting them down.

There were two other significant efforts to strengthen state powers. One was to add to "the right of the people peaceably to assemble," in what is now the First Amendment, the words "to instruct their representatives." There was much disagreement about whether elected officials would be bound by their instructions, but it seemed clear that the intention was to limit the independence of representatives, making sure that they adhered to focusing on local interests.

Another goal unsuccessfully pursued was to insert the word "expressly" in what is now the Tenth Amendment, to make it read, "The powers not expressly delegated to the United States . . . are reserved to the States respectively, or to the people." Both sides in Congress understood that this one-word addition was intended severely to limit the powers delegated to the federal government by denying implied powers. Madison argued the impracticality of such a provision, stating that "there must necessarily be admitted powers by implication, unless the constitution descended to recount every minutia."

Madison won on that issue, but he lost on another that he considered of the greatest importance. One of his proposed amendments would have had a powerful effect on the relations of the state governments and the federal government; it read, "No state shall infringe the right of trial by jury in criminal cases, nor the rights of conscience, nor the freedom of speech, or of the press." This was the only amendment dealing with the actions or laws of states, and seemed aimed at all branches of state government, executive, legislative, and judicial. It was not clear whether it was to be enforced by Congress or the federal judiciary, but it was clear that it was a sweeping provision, corresponding with Madison's view, expressed in a letter to Jefferson, that action to oversee state legislatures was required "to secure individuals agst. encroachment on their rights." Madison went on to identify the states as the source of grave danger. "The mutability of the laws of the States is found to be a serious evil. The injustice of them has been so frequent and so flagrant as to alarm the most steadfast friends of Republicanism." The House had approved this amendment, but the Senate deleted it, for reasons unknown, since the debates of the Senate in those early days were not made public and were not recorded. Madison was said to take this defeat very much to heart, for he considered it "the most valuable amendment on the whole list."

Adoption of the Bill of Rights was a severe defeat for the Anti-Federalists. They expressed their displeasure by voting against the amendments in every recorded vote, including the final vote in Congress. Passage of the Bill of Rights, additions to the Constitution that did not alter one word of the original text, marked the end of any prospect for the passage of the structural amendments.

But it did not end the controversies over the allocation of powers between the states and the federal government, controversies that have persisted down through the centuries, suggesting that these issues, and these struggles, are inherent, ineradicable characteristics of a federal republic. *SEE ALSO:* Anti-Federalists; Incorporation (Nationalization) of the Bill of Rights

BIBLIOGRAPHY: Robert A. Goldwin, *From Parchment to Power: How James Madison Used the Bill of Rights to Save the Constitution* (Washington, DC: AEI Press, 1997); Bernard Schwartz, ed., *The Roots of the Bill of Rights* (New York: Chelsea House Publishers, 1971); Herbert J. Storing, "The Constitution and the Bill of Rights," in *Toward a More Perfect Union: Writings of Herbert J. Storing,* ed. Joseph Bessette (Washington, DC: AEI Press, 1995); and Helen E. Veit, Kenneth R. Bowling, and Charlene Bangs Bickford, eds., *Creating the Bill of Rights: The Documentary Record from the First Federal Congress* (Baltimore: Johns Hopkins University Press, 1991).

ROBERT A. GOLDWIN

Bingham, John A.   John A. Bingham (1815–1900) was a Republican congressman from Ohio who served eight terms between 1855 and 1873, but with an interruption of two years that followed defeat in the election of 1862. After the Civil War he served on the Joint Committee on Reconstruction (1865–69) and from that position became instrumental in drafting the Fourteenth Amendment to the Constitution.

When Congress was considering the Civil Rights Act of 1866, which purported to extend civil rights to freed slaves, Bingham objected that the bill lacked a constitutional foundation. Congress had no power to enact such a law because "the care of the property, the liberty, and the life of the citizen, under the . . . Federal Constitution, is in the States, and not in the Federal Government." Congress passed the bill over President Andrew Johnson's veto, while Bingham undertook the framing of a constitutional amendment that would legitimate the enactment and guarantee federal protection of the civil rights of the Negro.

An early draft, which the Joint Committee reported to both houses, was framed as a grant of power to Congress: "The Congress shall have power to make all laws which shall be necessary and proper to secure to the citizens of each state all privileges and immunities of citizens in the several States [Article IV, Section 2]; and to all persons in the several States equal protection in the rights of life, liberty and property [Fifth Amendment]." This failed to secure support in Congress.

The Joint Committee then resumed consideration of an amendment, and Bingham proposed a different approach, constructed as a prohibition on the states: "No state shall make or enforce any law which shall abridge the privileges or immunities of citizens of the United States; nor shall any state deprive any person of life, liberty or property without due process of law, nor deny to any person within its jurisdiction the equal protection of the laws." This became the core of Section 1 of the Fourteenth Amendment, the meaning of which would depend on judicial interpretation, although a concluding section of the amendment provides, "The Congress shall have power to enforce, by appropriate legislation, the provisions of this article."

Whether Bingham and other sponsors of the amendment intended it to incorporate the first eight articles of the Bill of Rights and apply them to the states became a topic of controversy among jurists and other students of constitutional law. Remarks by Bingham on the floor of the House in 1871 indicated that he intended incorporation, but what he and others said in 1866, when the amendment was under consideration, was less clear. Justice Hugo Black, in a notable dissent in *Adamson v. California* (1947), asserted categorically that the sponsors of the amendment intended incorporation, but the Supreme Court was not persuaded, and adopted instead a practice of selective incorporation of rights deemed fundamental. *SEE ALSO: Adamson v. California*; Bill of Rights; Civil Rights Act of 1875; Civil War; Fourteenth Amendment; Incorporation (Nationalization) of the Bill of Rights; Reconstruction

BIBLIOGRAPHY: Richard L. Aynes, "On Misreading John Bingham and the Fourteenth Amendment," *Yale Law Journal* 103 (October 1993): 57–104; Erving E. Beauregard, *Bingham of the Hills: Politician and Diplomat Extraordinary* (New York: Peter Lang, 1989); and Joseph B. James, *Ratification of the 14th Amendment* (Macon, GA: Mercer University Press, 1984).

MARTHA DERTHICK

Black Codes The term "Black Codes" refers to bodies of laws passed by southern legislatures during the era of Presidential Reconstruction (1865–66) that sought to delineate the social, economic, and political rights of the former slaves. While some of these statutes offered African Americans rights formerly denied to them under slavery, the bulk of these laws were designed to severely restrict black freedom. Accordingly, the Black Codes appeared to many Northerners as an effort at best to reaffirm white supremacy and at worst to reinstitute a system of race relations that would closely resemble slavery.

In mid-1865, President Andrew Johnson detailed his stipulations for readmitting the former Confederate states to the Union. He called on Southerners to form state legislatures and for those bodies to quickly move to repudiate Confederate-era debt, reject secession, and outlaw slavery. By the fall of 1865, southern legislators had begun to take up the thorniest of these issues: the legal status of the former slaves. The Mississippi and South Carolina legislatures were the first to address this issue. Ostensibly written to smooth the transition from slavery to freedom, Black Codes of these states were particularly harsh in character. In an effort to assure that the freedmen would remain under the control of their former masters, Mississippi mandated that all African Americans have written documentation of employment at the beginning of each year or face arrest. Freedmen could also be punished for owning firearms or for offering "insulting gestures, language or acts." South Carolina produced a code that offered similar restrictions. It forced African American artisans and mechanics to pay a steep license fee to practice their craft and banned other freedmen from taking up such trades. In effect, it forced the vast majority of former slaves to remain in their roles as agricultural laborers. South Carolina's code also assessed harsh punishments for petty crimes, including fines up to $1,000, incarceration up to ten years, and corporal punishment for stealing a hog. After the leadership of the Freedman's Bureau and many prominent Republicans reacted unfavorably to these first two codes, the other southern states passed Black Codes in 1866 that, comparatively speaking, were much less punitive and overtly racist in character. Regardless, the Freedman's Bureau and the U.S. Army would move in early 1866 to nullify the aspects of the Black Codes that treated black Southerners differently from white Southerners.

In effect, then, the Black Codes had little lasting impact on African American life in the South. Yet the discriminatory character of these laws convinced many Republicans in Congress that the white South was not ready for self-government and that President Johnson's plan for Reconstruction was doing little to modify the worst aspects of southern society and in effect, was probably perpetuating them. As a result, congressional Republicans moved in 1866 to draw up the legislative blueprints for Radical Reconstruction, a program that saw the federal government undertake an unprecedented effort to transform the character of American life on the state and local level. *SEE ALSO:* Reconstruction; Secession; Slavery

BIBLIOGRAPHY: Eric Foner, *Reconstruction: America's Unfinished Revolution 1863–1877* (New York: Harper & Row, 1988); and Theodore Brantner Wilson, *The Black Codes of the South* (Montgomery: University of Alabama Press, 1965).

GREGORY J. RENOFF

Hugo L. Black. Library of Congress, Prints and Photographs Division.

Black, Hugo L. Hugo L. Black (1886–1971), a native of rural Alabama, was elected to the Senate in 1926, reelected in 1932, and appointed to the Supreme Court in 1937. A strong supporter of the New Deal and an aggressive critic of big business, he was President Franklin Roosevelt's first appointee to the Court. The appointment became controversial when opponents were able to show that Black had belonged to the Ku Klux Klan, a white supremacist organization, in the early 1920s. He was confirmed 63–16 and in thirty-four years on the Court built an imposing record in defense of civil liberties.

Black would have interpreted the first section of the Fourteenth Amendment to have wholly incorporated the Bill of Rights, thereby binding the state governments. He set forth this position at length in a dissent to *Adamson v. California*

(1947). Although the Court did not embrace this view, it arrived by increments at a similar result.

Black was deeply involved in the Court's development of constitutional law on race relations and legislative apportionment, both of which had profound effects on American federalism. He wrote the opinion in *Griffin v. County School Board of Prince Edward County* (1964), which held illegal the action of a local school board in Virginia that had closed its public schools to resist integration and thereafter contributed to the support of private segregated schools. "The time for mere 'deliberate speed' has run out," he said, "and that phrase can no longer justify denying these Prince Edward County school children their constitutional rights to an education equal to that afforded by the public schools in the other parts of Virginia."

He had strongly dissented in *Colegrove v. Green* (1946), in which the Court had held legislative districting to be a political question over which it lacked jurisdiction. After the Court repudiated that decision in *Baker v. Carr* (1962), he joined in the opinion in *Reynolds v. Sims* (1964), which held that representation in state legislatures must be based on population, and he wrote the opinion in *Wesberry v. Sanders* (1964), a case originating in Georgia's Fifth Congressional District that applied the same principle ("equal representation for equal numbers of people") to the U.S. House of Representatives.

Black died one week after retiring from the Court in 1971. *SEE ALSO: Adamson v. California; Baker v. Carr;* Bill of Rights; *Colegrove v. Green;* Fourteenth Amendment; New Deal; *Reynolds v. Sims;* U.S. Supreme Court

BIBLIOGRAPHY: Roger K. Newman, *Hugo Black: A Biography* (New York: Fordham University Press, 1997).

MARTHA DERTHICK

Block Grants   Block grants are an intergovernmental reform that gained momentum in the 1970s during the Nixon administration as a strategy for dealing with the fragmentation and incoherence brought about by the proliferation of grant-in-aid programs during the 1960s, when both the number and the dollar amount of federal grants tripled. The vast majority of these new grant programs were categorical grants, which limited spending to a very narrow program category. Critics, of whom the most vocal were mayors and other local government officials, contended that despite the growth in federal assistance there was no "system" to speak of. Their most frequent concern was that the duplication and overlap of grant programs (multiple programs for the same purpose in multiple federal agencies) confounded their efforts at planning and coordination. Second, they felt federal grant programs distorted local priorities as the lack of uniformity in matching rates across programs tended to steer local budgets toward the "easy money" and away from local priorities they might otherwise prefer. For example, to deal with the problem of traffic congestion in the 1960s state and local officials faced the choice of building more freeways (federal aid would pay for 90 percent of the cost of highway construction) or investing in mass transit (federal aid would only pay 50 percent of the cost of purchasing transit buses or constructing a rapid rail line). Third, local officials were concerned about the timing and uncertainty of grant awards as well as the manner in which funds were allocated. Many officials felt federal funds were more likely to be allocated based on the grantsmanship abilities of local governments (especially the biggest cities) rather than the relative merits and needs of applicant communities.

Although the idea of grant consolidation had surfaced in the 1940s and 1950s, Congress never gave such proposals serious consideration because many members of Congress believed block grants were simply a guise for spending cuts, and that block grants would lessen congressional control over federal programs. In 1966, Congress adopted the Partnership for Health Act, which consolidated sixteen categorical programs into a single block grant for health. Two years later a block grant for law enforcement assistance was passed. In his first major address on domestic policy issues, President Richard Nixon called for a "New Federalism" in "which power, funds, and responsibility will flow from Washington to the States and to the people." Central to Nixon's New Federalism was the enactment of General Revenue Sharing and six special revenue-sharing programs that would consolidate about one-third of the existing categorical grant programs in the areas of education, transportation, community development, job training, and law enforcement. General Revenue Sharing was enacted in 1972, and block grants for job training and community development followed in 1973 and 1974.

The next wave of block granting took place during the first year of the Reagan administration. The Omnibus Budget Reconciliation Act of 1981 created nine new block grants by consolidating more than fifty categorical grants and two existing block grants. A third wave of block grant reforms were proposed by Republicans in the 104th Congress following the 1994 elections, which gave Republicans control of both houses of Congress. The Republican leadership proposed creating over a dozen new block grant programs that would consolidate more than 300 existing grant programs totaling $125 billion. Funding for the new block grant programs as well as existing block grant programs would be considerably smaller with many existing block grants slated for budget cuts ranging from 20 to 50 percent. Though most of the new block grants proposed failed to pass Congress or the president vetoed those that did, most noteworthy was the creation of a new block grant program for welfare, Temporary Assistance to Needy Families (TANF). The TANF program terminated the Aid to Families with Dependent Children (AFDC) program, an open-ended entitlement program that provided cash assistance to needy families and children, and replaced it with a capped block grant to the states. Similar proposals to convert entitlement programs for Medicaid and food stamps into block grants were vetoed by President Bill Clinton.

According to the Advisory Commission on Intergovernmental Relations, five features distinguish block grants from categorical grants: (1) aid is provided for a wide range of activities within a broadly defined functional area; (2) recipient jurisdictions are given broad discretion in defining problems, designing local programs, and allocating resources to support specific projects and activities; (3) federal monitoring and oversight are reduced to the minimum level needed to insure that national goals and objectives are being met; (4) recipient jurisdictions are granted entitlement status (i.e., guaranteed funding), and the amount of funding is determined by a statutory formula as opposed to the discretion of federal administrative agency officials; and (5) the initial recipients of block grants funds tend to be general purpose government officials (e.g., city or state governments) as opposed to specialized government agencies such as urban renewal authorities.

A 1995 report by the U.S. General Accounting Office noted that there were three lessons that could be learned from the experience of the 1981 block grants that should serve as a guide for future congressional action regarding the creation of new block grants. First, there is a need to pay more attention to accountability as Congress frequently added additional conditions that limited state flexibility and in essence "recategorized" some of the new block grants. Second, the tendency to rely on distributions under previous categorical programs as a guide for allocating funds under block grants may not be equitable as such prior distributions generally do not conform well to need, fiscal capacity, or variations in the cost of service provision. Third, though states handled reasonably well the transition to block grants in 1981, the programs being considered for consolidation are often of a fundamentally different nature than the types of programs previously consolidated into block grants (e.g., Medicaid and food stamps).

Presently, there are about two dozen federal block grant programs, which accounted for about 18 percent of federal grant outlays in fiscal 1997. The largest federal block is TANF ($16.5 billion in fiscal year 2005). Other major block grants include Community Development Block Grants ($3 billion), the Child Care and Child Development block grant ($2.1 billion), and the Social Services Block Grant ($1.7 billion). *SEE ALSO:* Categorical Grants; Devolution; Education; Elections; Intergovernmental Relations; Local Government; Medicaid; Nixon, Richard M.; Reagan, Ronald; Revenue Sharing; Transportation Policy; Welfare Policy

BIBLIOGRAPHY: Timothy Conlan, *From New Federalism to Devolution: Twenty-five Years of Intergovernmental Reform* (Washington, DC: Brookings Institution, 1998); Richard P. Nathan, Fred C. Doolittle, and Associates, *Reagan and the States* (Princeton, NJ: Princeton University Press, 1987); George E. Peterson et al., *The Reagan Block Grants* (Washington, DC: Urban Institute, 1986); U.S. Advisory Commission on Intergovernmental Relations, *Block Grants: A Comparative Analysis*, ACIR Report A-60 (Washington, DC: U.S. Government Printing Office, 1977); and U.S. General Accounting Office, *Lessons Learned from Past Block Grants*, GAO Report IPE-82-8, September 23 (Washington, DC: U.S. General Accounting Office, 1982).

MICHAEL J. RICH

Brandeis, Louis D. Louis D. Brandeis was born on November 13, 1856, in Louisville, Kentucky. He studied at Harvard Law School and later began a law practice in Cambridge, Massachusetts, with Samuel Warren. He became a proponent of labor unions and did much pro bono work for various public causes. He married Alice Goldmark in 1891, and they had two daughters.

Brandeis became famous in legal circles with the so-called Brandeis brief. It occurred in 1908 when he argued before the Supreme Court in *Muller v. Oregon* (1908) in behalf of Oregon's maximum hours law for women. Since there were not many precedent cases, and the few that there were generally went against those type of laws, Brandeis devoted only two pages in his brief to legal precedent, but devoted over 100 pages of data showing the bad effects on women of working too many hours. When the Court unanimously upheld the law, it paid tribute to Brandeis's arguments and, even today, briefs that cite extensive social science data are called "Brandeis briefs."

Brandeis helped President Woodrow Wilson formulate his antitrust program. In 1914, Brandeis was the leader of the American Zionist movement. In 1916, an opening arose on the Supreme Court, and Wilson nominated Brandeis, who was confirmed by a vote

Lewis D. Brandeis. Library of Congress, Prints and Photographs Division.

of forty-seven to twenty-two, becoming the first person of the Jewish faith to serve on the Court. During his years on the Court, Brandeis was a firm believer in the First Amendment rights, but a majority of the Court was more conservative than he was in cases involving freedom of speech, and he often dissented in those cases along with Justice Oliver Wendell Holmes Jr. The issue in contention was Holmes's clear and present danger doctrine, with Brandeis and Holmes often finding that the defendants did not create such a danger.

Brandeis also wrote an impassioned dissent in *Olmstead v. United States* (1928). The majority upheld wiretapping but Brandeis dissented, arguing that wiretapping and other forms of surveillance constituted an unreasonable search and seizure in violation of the Fourth Amendment. It was important, Brandeis maintained, for the Fourth Amendment's protection of privacy to keep pace with modern technology or else it would not mean much in the future.

Brandeis, while a supporter of Franklin Roosevelt's New Deal, opposed the president's court-packing plan. He was often a defender of federalism. In *Erie Railroad v. Tompkins* (1938), he held that federal courts could not use federal common law to decide a case; it must use the law of the state involved in the case, either statutory or common. And in *New State Ice Company v. Liebmann* (1932), he referred to the states as the "laboratories of democracy."

Brandeis retired from the Court in 1939 and died of a heart attack on October 5, 1941. Due largely to his zeal for First Amendment rights and the right of privacy, he is rightly considered one of the greatest justices to ever serve on the Court. *SEE ALSO: Erie Railroad Co. v. Tompkins*; *New State Ice Company v. Liebmann*

BIBLIOGRAPHY: Alpheus T. Mason, *Brandeis: A Free Man's Life* (New York: Viking Press, 1946); Philippa Strum, "Louis D. Brandeis," in *Supreme Court Justices: Illustrated Biographies, 1789–1993*, ed. Clare Cushman (Washington, DC: Congressional Quarterly Inc., 1993); and Philippa Strum, *Louis D. Brandeis*: *Justice for the People* (New York: Shocken Books, 1984).

ROBERT W. LANGRAN

Brennan, William J., Jr.   Justice William J. Brennan Jr. served on the U.S. Supreme Court from 1956 to 1990, and during his tenure he influenced federalism in a number of important ways. He was a leading voice for the expansive role of federal courts interpreting the U.S. Constitution to protect individual rights from interference by the states. Yet he also was a leading proponent of state courts relying on their own state constitutions to provide greater protection for individual rights than what was found in the U.S. Constitution.

The connection between these two positions was Brennan's view that the paramount goal of the Constitution was not simply to create a functional government structure but rather to create a system of governance that would advance the human dignity and individual rights of all. To that end, for Brennan federalism was never a goal unto itself; instead, federalism was a distribution of powers that must ebb and flow with the need to protect individual rights.

When Brennan joined the Court, he quickly picked up the mantle of incorporation—the effort to make the provisions of the Bill of Rights apply as limits on the power of the states, not just the federal government. In other decisions, he urged federal courts to step into state reapportionment disputes (*Baker v. Carr* 1962), called for more vigorous federal habeas corpus review of state criminal convictions (*Fay v. Noia* 1963), brought the libel law of all 50 states under the purview of the First Amendment (*New York Times v. Sullivan* 1964), and in dissenting opinions took a dim view of state sovereign immunity in lawsuits by citizens against their own state (*Yeomans v. Kentucky* 1975).

Some of Brennan's positions expanding the role of federal courts angered officials in the states, especially the reapportionment and habeas corpus rulings. In 1964 he spoke in New York to the Conference of [State] Chief Justices. In a speech entitled "Some Aspects of Federalism," he tried to downplay the state-federal rift, saying that "in performing our respective tasks in cases where both our courts function, there can be no reason for contest, not even for petty quarrel." But he also said, "Resolution of these conflicts between state and federal authority has been said to be the most essential of the tasks entrusted to our Court."

The federalism issues that Brennan confronted throughout the Warren Court involved substantive questions of individual rights. But in the Burger Court, Brennan faced a new breed of federalism cases in which the allocation of power to the states and away from Congress was its own end; this was a position pushed largely by Justice William H. Rehnquist in *National League of Cities v. Usery* (1976), holding that Congress lacked the power to apply minimum wage and hour standards to state employees. Brennan vigorously dissented, accusing the majority of "the startling restructuring of our federal system" and warning of "an ominous portent of disruption of our constitutional structure." Rehnquist's decision was later overruled by *Garcia v. San Antonio Metropolitan Transit Authority* (1985), but this exchange of rulings was a precursor of federalism developments that occurred in the 1990s after Brennan left the Court.

Brennan made another significant and

William J. Brennan Jr. Library of Congress, Prints and Photographs Division.

lasting contribution to federalism in 1977 in the form of an article in the *Harvard Law Review*, entitled "State Constitutions and the Protection of Individual Rights." Originally delivered as a speech to the New Jersey Bar Association, the published version urged state courts to remember their own laws and state constitutions as sources for the protection of individual rights. This exhortation came at a time when Brennan perceived that the Supreme Court was cutting back on the availability of federal courts to hear civil liberties and civil rights claims. "The legal revolution which has brought federal law to the fore must not be allowed to inhibit the independent protective force of state law—for without it, the full realizations of our liberties cannot be guaranteed," Brennan wrote. He excoriated the Supreme Court for invoking federalism as a reason for condoning "both isolated and systematic violations of civil liberties," and said the rulings do not "properly understand the nature of federalism." The Court, Brennan said, "has forgotten that one of the strengths of our federal system is that it provides a double source of protection for the rights of our citizens. Federalism is not served when the federal half of that protection is crippled." *SEE ALSO: Garcia v. San Antonio Metropolitan Transit Authority*; *Michigan v. Long*; *National League of Cities v. Usery*; New Judicial Federalism

> BIBLIOGRAPHY: William J. Brennan Jr., "Some Aspects of Federalism," *New York University Law Review* 39 (1964): 945; William J. Brennan Jr., "State Constitutions and the Protection of Individual Rights," *Harvard Law Review* 90 (1977): 489; and Robert C. Post, "Justice Brennan and Federalism," *Constitutional Commentary* 7 (1990): 227.

STEPHEN J. WERMIEL

Bronson v. Kinzie   *Bronson v. Kinzie* (1843) involved an 1825 Illinois law under which property owners could redeem land they sold within twelve months by repaying the purchase price plus interest. In 1841 the legislature made the law retroactively applicable to foreclosed mortgages. The U.S. Supreme Court, speaking through Chief Justice Roger Brooke Taney, invalidated the retroactive provisions of the two 1841 changes. According to Taney, the first of the new laws placed new conditions on the contract injurious and unjust to the mortgage holder. The second one deprived the mortgage holder of the preexisting right to foreclose by a sale of the premises and imposed conditions that would frequently render any sale impossible. Thus the retroactive features of the 1841 laws constituted an impairment of the obligation of contracts in violation of the U.S. Constitution. Future contracts, however, were bound by the new laws. *SEE ALSO: Charles River Bridge Company v. Warren Bridge Company*; Contract Clause; *Dartmouth College v. Woodward*; *Fletcher v. Peck*; *Home Building and Loan v. Blaisdell*; *United States Trust Company v. New Jersey*

ROBERT W. LANGRAN

Brown v. Board of Education   *Brown v. Board of Education of Topeka, Kansas*, the landmark 1954 Supreme Court case that pronounced state-mandated segregation in public schools unconstitutional, was a consolidation of six cases that challenged legally mandated school segregation in Delaware, the District of Columbia, South Carolina, Virginia, and Topeka, Kansas. *Brown* would prove to be a pivotal case in the Supreme Court's history. It reversed the Court's earlier "separate but equal" position in *Plessy* *v. Ferguson* (1896). The decision served as a catalyst for the modern Civil Rights movement. *Brown* was the first decision authored by new Chief Justice Earl Warren and presaged a more activist era in the Court's history.

Brown must be understood within the broader context of the history of race relations in the United States, particularly the history of Jim Crow in the southern states. The Civil War and Reconstruction had brought considerable political, social, and legal change to the nation, particularly the South. The Constitution had been amended to forbid slavery (Thirteenth Amendment), establish black citizenship and the equal treatment of people before the law (Fourteenth Amendment), and provide equal voting rights for men of different races (Fifteenth Amendment). From the late 1860s through the 1890s, there was widespread voting on the part of black men in the South. A number of African American men also held political office in the region.

By the turn of the century, the relatively egalitarian atmosphere of the post–Civil War era was beginning to radically change. Spurred on in part by the withdrawal of federal troops and federal civil rights enforcement from the South, southern states toward the end of the nineteenth century began passing increasingly discriminatory legislation aimed at blacks. The legislation took two forms. The first was legislation aimed at disenfranchising blacks. Because of the Fifteenth Amendment, this had to be done indirectly through such means as literacy tests, grandfather clauses, and other devices. The second type of legislation was Jim Crow legislation, aimed at the separation of blacks and whites in virtually every public venue, seats on trains and street cars, park benches, water fountains, restrooms, and bibles for witnesses in court. Southern (and other) states also maintained segregated public schools.

The U.S. Supreme Court would give its sanction to this system of Jim Crow. It considered the issue in *Plessy v. Ferguson*. That case, involving an 1890 Louisiana statute mandating segregation on railroad cars, became the occasion for the Court to declare that legally enforced segregation was constitutional despite the Fourteenth Amendment's guarantee of equal protection under the law. A key issue in *Plessy* was whether state-mandated segregation stigmatized blacks as inferior. The majority opinion authored by Justice Henry Billings Brown rejected the claim that segregation was stigmatizing and a violation of the Fourteenth Amendment. The opinion by Justice Brown upheld the doctrine of separate but equal, maintaining that as long as the facilities provided for people of different races were equal, there was no constitutional harm in segregation. The majority opinion in *Plessy* was the object of a vigorous lone dissent by Justice John Marshall Harlan.

In the era before World War I, the Supreme Court showed little inclination to seriously consider constitutional challenges to either Jim Crow or disenfranchisement. The Court sustained a Kentucky statute prohibiting integration in private colleges in *Berea College v. Commonwealth of Kentucky* (1905). The Court also rejected a number of challenges against discriminatory regulations that essentially disenfranchised African Americans in many states. The early twentieth century was a period when the federal government essentially provided little or no protection for the civil rights of black citizens. Disenfranchisement and Jim Crow were often accompanied by severe racial violence. Lynching and race riots frequently occurred, often with the acquiescence (and sometimes the participation) of state and local officials.

It was in this bleak atmosphere that the National Association for the Advancement of Colored People (NAACP) was founded. Founded in 1909 by, among others, African

American scholar and civil rights activist W.E.B. DuBois, the NAACP was organized to fight the evils of Jim Crow, disenfranchisement, and lynching. The organization turned to litigation as a primary tool in the fight against racial discrimination early in its history. One of the organization's earliest victories came in the 1917 case *Buchanan v. Warley*. In that case, the NAACP had filed an amicus brief in a challenge to a Kentucky statute that prohibited whites from selling residential property to blacks in majority white neighborhoods. The Supreme Court struck down the statute because it violated freedom of contract.

Buchanan was a small step; nonetheless, it indicated that despite an unsympathetic judicial atmosphere, the Constitution and carefully prepared litigation might be enlisted in the fight against racial discrimination. The idea of using these tools in the fight against Jim Crow was further refined in the 1930s by NAACP attorney Charles Hamilton Houston. Houston was appointed vice dean of the Howard University Law School in 1929. He transformed the predominately black law school, upgrading its quality and giving the institution a new mission—the development and practice of civil rights law. Houston's most important student at Howard was Thurgood Marshall. Marshall, barred from the state law school in his home state of Maryland because he was black, attended Howard and absorbed Houston's lessons on civil rights advocacy.

In the 1930s, the NAACP began to develop its strategy to attack segregated education. Realizing that a frontal assault on segregation as such would stand little chance of success, the civil rights organization decided on a two-pronged strategy to tackle segregation in state-sponsored education. The first prong of this strategy was to attempt force state governments and the courts to treat seriously *Plessy*'s requirement that separate facilities had to be equal. This would be an important and difficult effort because spending, teaching resources, and physical facilities for black schools were significantly below those for white schools in the states that practiced legal segregation. The second prong of the NAACP strategy was to focus litigation efforts on graduate and professional schools in southern states. This was done, in part, because attacking discrimination in graduate and professional education was seen as posing fewer political and social difficulties than attacking segregation in elementary and secondary education.

An early success of this strategy came in 1936 in the case of *Pearson v. Murray*. In *Pearson,* the NAACP successfully brought suit on behalf of Donald Murray, a black resident of Baltimore. Murray had been denied admission to the University of Maryland Law School. Maryland's policy was to provide scholarships to African Americans to study law in out-of-state law schools. Houston and Marshall represented Murray. They convinced the Maryland Court of Appeals that an out-of-state legal education was not equal to one provided at the state university's law school. The Court ordered Murray admitted to the University of Maryland.

The victory in *Pearson* set the stage for other litigation attacking segregation in state graduate and professional schools. In *State ex rel v. Gaines* (1938), Houston successfully argued that Missouri's exclusion of blacks from the state law school was unconstitutional even though the state was willing to pay tuition for black students to attend law school out of state. The U.S. Supreme Court held that an out-of-state legal education was not the equal of attending the state law school. Following *Gaines*, the NAACP had similar successes in the federal courts attacking segregated professional education in Oklahoma and Texas.

While the precedents that were being developed in the professional school segregation cases were important, changing racial attitudes undoubtedly played an even more important role in the decision in *Brown*. World War II brought about significant changes in the racial attitudes of white Americans. The war brought about a new assertiveness on the part of African Americans, many of whom left the rural South and traditional patterns of racial domination for the armed forces and the industrial cities of the North and West. The fight against Nazi racism also caused many white Americans to question traditional racial attitudes. The social sciences were also increasingly calling established racial prejudices into question. The publication in 1944 of Swedish social scientist Gunnar Myrdal's *An American Dilemma: The Negro Problem and Modern Democracy* also had a significant impact, causing many university-educated people to question the practice of segregation.

The change in racial atmosphere in the postwar United States led to a new willingness on the part of the NAACP to confront legally mandated segregation. The organization had more victories in its fight against segregated professional education. There were other important victories in the legal struggle against discrimination. In *Shelly v. Kramer* (1948), the Supreme Court declared that courts could not enforce restrictive covenants barring minorities from certain residential properties, indicating that the Court might be willing to give the Fourteenth Amendment a broader reading than it had in the past. Many in the NAACP believed that the time was right for a frontal assault on segregated education.

Between 1950 and 1952, the NAACP began preparation for the six cases that would collectively come to be known as *Brown v. Board of Education*. The case included one case from South Carolina, *Briggs v. Elliott*; two cases from Delaware, *Gebhart et al. v. Belton* and *Gebhart v. Bulah*; a Virginia case, *Davis v. County School Board of Prince Edward County*; and a case from the District of Columbia, *Bolling v. Sharpe*. The case by which the litigation is known arose in Topeka, Kansas. While Kansas did not have statewide segregation, it gave localities the option to have segregated schools. Topeka's elementary schools were segregated and Oliver Brown, a black resident of Topeka, filed suit in order to allow his daughter to attend a school reserved for whites that both was nearer to his home and had better facilities.

The litigation effort was led by Thurgood Marshall. Marshall assembled a team of rising legal stars in the postwar United States including Jack Greenberg, Constance Baker Motley, Robert L. Carter, Charles Black, Louis Redding, and Spottswood Robinson. Marshall also enlisted the aid of social science experts whose research supported the argument that segregation tended to stigmatize African Americans. One of these social scientists was black psychologist Kenneth Clark, who had done research on the effects of segregation on the self-esteem of black children.

In 1952, the Supreme Court consolidated the six different desegregation cases. The first set of oral arguments was heard by the Court in December of that year. Later, in June 1953, the Court asked for a second set of oral arguments designed to specifically address the issue of whether or not the Fourteenth Amendment was meant to ban school segregation. As that issue was being researched, Chief Justice Fred Vinson died in September 1953. He was replaced by Earl Warren. Most observers agree that Vinson would not have supported the desegregation that the NAACP asked for in *Brown*. The second set of oral arguments was held in December 1953.

It would not be until May 17, 1954, that the Court finally rendered its decision. Between the oral arguments in December and the final decision in May, there was considerable behind-the-scenes drama involving *Brown*. New Chief Justice Earl Warren and Justice Felix Frankfurter were particularly concerned with getting a unanimous decision supporting desegregation. Both justices feared that anything less than unanimity would invite doubt and resistance to the decision. The final decision authored by Chief Justice Warren was unanimous. It declared separate schools to be inherently unequal. The Warren decision was based in part on the importance of education in modern society and also in part on social science evidence showing the damaging nature of segregation.

Although the Warren opinion declared segregated education unconstitutional, *Brown v. Board of Education* did not prescribe any means of implementing the desegregation of schools. This was left to a second *Brown v. Board of Education* decision, frequently referred to as *Brown II*. The latter case was decided the following year in 1955. *Brown II* called for the implementation of desegregation with "all deliberate speed." The actual process of implementing desegregation and dismantling segregated school systems was handled by federal district courts. The process was slow and often painful, and took decades.

Brown provoked considerable controversy when first decided. It was fiercely resisted by many state and local officials who attempted, often with extralegal and sometimes violent means, to nullify the decision. Many commentators also initially criticized the decision for being grounded more in social science evidence than the Constitution. As racial attitudes have changed, so have attitudes toward the 1954 decision. The decision has now become an icon of Supreme Court jurisprudence. As fewer people in public life in recent decades have been willing to defend Jim Crow, the criticisms of *Brown* have become less frequent. More recently, modern commentators have criticized the decision as having been too conservative. Modern critics contend that while the case ended de jure segregation, it did not solve the problems of de facto segregation and inequality. Despite these criticisms, *Brown* had a far-reaching impact on American race relations. The case put the moral authority of the Constitution and the Supreme Court squarely behind the fight against Jim Crow. *SEE ALSO:* Equal Protection of the Laws; Fourteenth Amendment; *Plessy v. Ferguson*

BIBLIOGRAPHY: Robert J. Cottrol, Raymond T. Diamond, and Leland B. Ware, *Brown v. Board of Education: Caste, Culture and the Constitution* (Lawrence: University of Kansas Press, 2003).

ROBERT J. COTTROL

Burbank v. Lockheed Air Terminal *Burbank v. Lockheed Air Terminal* (1973) concerns an ordinance passed by the City of Burbank, California, prohibiting jet aircraft from taking off from the city's airport between the hours of eleven P.M. and seven A.M. The city enacted the legislation to protect its residents from unwanted noise. A closely divided Supreme Court held the ordinance invalid because Congress had preempted state and local control over aircraft noise by its passage of the 1958 Federal Aviation Act (giving the national government sovereignty over airspace) and the 1972 Noise Control Act (which sets noise emission standards for a wide variety of product categories, and specifically targets aircraft noise and sonic booms). According to Justice William O. Douglas, curfews such as the one enacted by the City of Burbank increase airport congestion, cause a loss of efficiency, and aggravate the noise problem. Therefore, because there is need for efficient control of air traffic, only the Federal Aviation Administration, in conjunction with the Environmental Protection Agency, may regulate the subject of aircraft noise. The pervasive nature of the scheme of federal regulation of aircraft leaves no room for state or local regulation. *SEE ALSO:* Commerce among the States; *Hines v. Davidowitz*; *Pennsylvania v. Nelson*; Preemption; *Southern Railway Company v. Reid*; Supremacy Clause: Article VI, Clause 2.

ROBERT W. LANGRAN

Burger, Warren Earl   Warren Earl Burger was born on September 17, 1907, in St. Paul, Minnesota. He graduated from St. Paul College of Law (now called the William Mitchell College of Law) in 1931. He taught there and had a private practice. He married Elvera Stromberg in 1933, and they had a son and daughter. Future Supreme Court Justice Harry Blackmun was best man. In 1953 President Dwight D. Eisenhower appointed him assistant attorney general for the Civil Division at the Justice Department, and two years later appointed him to the Court of Appeals for the District of Columbia. In 1969 President Richard M. Nixon, who had campaigned for president promising to appoint "strict constructionists" to the Supreme Court, nominated Burger to be chief justice. He was confirmed by the Senate by a vote of 74–3.

Burger's decisions cannot be easily classified as liberal or conservative. Despite the widespread expectation that he would attempt to undo, or at least limit, many of the Warren Court's far-reaching liberal decisions, in some areas, he led the Court far beyond what the Warren Court had done. The Burger Court, for example, upheld busing as a remedy for school segregation, gave new meaning to the Equal Protection Clause in striking down a state law that discriminated against women, and held that women have a right to abortion as part of a right of privacy guaranteed by the Due Process Clause of the Fourteenth Amendment.

Burger's concern for federalism shows up in several areas. He attempted to limit the application of the exclusionary rule announced in *Mapp v. Ohio* (1961), as well as the reach of the *Miranda* warnings. He was also successful in limiting access to the federal courts to appeal state court convictions. In *Miller v. California* (1973), he held that local or state, rather than national, community standards should be used in obscenity cases.

In perhaps his most stunning opinion, Burger held in *United States v. Nixon* (1974) that President Nixon (who had appointed him) had to turn over audiotapes needed in the Watergate criminal investigation. The tapes showed presidential involvement in a cover-up, and the Nixon resigned the presidency.

Burger retired from the Court in 1986 to chair the Bicentennial Commission, which oversaw the festivities dealing with the Constitution the following year. He died on June 25, 1995. *SEE ALSO:* Exclusionary Rule; *Mapp v. Ohio*; *Miranda v. Arizona*; *Reed v. Reed*; *Roe v. Wade*

BIBLIOGRAPHY: Burnett Anderson, "Warren E. Burger," in *The Supreme Court Justices: Illustrated Biographies, 1789–1993*, ed. Clare Cushman (Washington, DC: Congressional Quarterly Inc., 1993); Warren E. Burger, *Delivery of Justice* (St. Paul, MN: West Publishing Co., 1990); and Earl M. Maltz, *The Chief Justiceship of Warren Burger, 1969–1986* (Columbia: University of South Carolina Press, 2000).

ROBERT W. LANGRAN

Bush v. Gore In 2000, the U.S. Supreme Court through its decision in *Bush v. Gore* ended the uncertainty surrounding which candidate had actually won the presidential election of that year. Because of the Supreme Court's extremely complicated decision in this case, George W. Bush was declared the winner of the presidential election. The ruling also indicated that the U.S. Constitution and federal statutes can supersede state election laws and decisions of state supreme courts interpreting those state laws.

The 2000 presidential race was extremely close, with the candidate who carried Florida's twenty-five electoral votes ultimately being able to gain the majority of the electors voting in the Electoral College. Florida awarded all of its electoral votes to the candidate who got the most votes for president in the state. The candidate who receives the majority of the Electoral College votes wins the presidential election, regardless of who wins the most popular votes nationwide. On election night in 2000, it became clear that the initial vote count in Florida made that state too close to call. After a few days, eventually the state's Republican secretary of state certified the Republican candidate, George W. Bush, as the winner of that state and its electoral votes. Al Gore, the Democratic candidate, then sued in various Florida state courts for recounts to take place, but only in specific counties in Florida.

The tradition in Florida was that local election boards determined the standards for recounting ballots in their own counties. After a series of decisions by lower state courts, the Florida Supreme Court ruled that the selective recounts should continue in the presidential race, without establishing any statewide standards for counting disputed ballots. To further complicate matters, Florida counties used a wide variety of types of ballots in that election, including the so-called butterfly ballot and paper punch ballots that often left so-called pregnant or hanging chads. These chads were the small pieces of paper that often remained attached to punch ballots if the voter was not careful to make sure that they had punched the ballot correctly.

Before the U.S. Supreme Court accepted the case, most legal commentators said that the Court would not hear the case because there were no federal issues in the dispute. They said this because, traditionally, state election laws had been left to state courts to interpret. However, the U.S. Supreme Court did accept the appeal from the Florida Supreme Court's decision in this case, citing both federal statutory and federal constitutional issues. The U.S. Supreme Court's ruling, handed down on December 12, 2000, revealed that this was an extremely complex case with many federal legal questions. The ruling also revealed that the justices were split into four separate blocs on this decision. Justices John Paul Stevens and Ruth Bader Ginsburg formed one bloc, Justices David Souter and Stephen Breyer formed a second group, Justices Sandra Day O'Connor and Anthony Kennedy formed a third bloc, and finally Chief Justice William Rehnquist and Justices Antonin Scalia and Clarence Thomas formed a fourth group in this case.

The first legal question in this case was whether the Florida Supreme Court could overrule the decision of the Florida secretary of state, which had certified Bush to be the winner of the state, and thus allow the selective recounts to continue. The U.S. Supreme Court's ruling was 6–3 on this issue (with Justices Rehnquist, Scalia, and Thomas in dissent), stating that the Florida Supreme Court had acted properly when it ordered that the recounts should continue. The second legal question revolved around whether the lack of statewide standards for counting disputed ballots violated the Equal Protection Clause of the U.S. Constitution. The Court ruled 7–2 (with Justices Stevens and Ginsburg in dissent) that the Florida Supreme Court was incorrect in not requiring statewide standards for counting the disputed ballots. The third legal question was whether a federal statute required that the recounts had to be completed by December 12, 2000, the day that the U.S. Supreme Court handed down its decision. By a vote of 5–4 (with Justices Stevens, Ginsburg, Souter, and Breyer dissenting), the Court ruled that the federal statute required that the recounts had to end by December 12. Since it was impossible for the recounts to continue, the Court ruled that the secretary of state's decision that George W. Bush had won the most votes in the state would stand. Thus, the U.S. Supreme Court ended the confusion around who would win the majority of the Electoral College. For future elections, it became clear that the federal Constitution requires that states must use uniform statewide standards for recounting disputed ballots within their states. *SEE ALSO:* Elections

BIBLIOGRAPHY: E. J. Dionne and William Kristol, eds., *Bush v Gore: The Court Cases and the Commentary* (Washington, DC: Brookings Institution, 2001); Ronald Dworkin, ed., *A Badly Flawed Election: Debating Bush v. Gore, the Supreme Court and American Democracy* (New York: New Press, 2002); Howard Gillman, *The Votes That Counted: How the Court Decided the 2000 Presidential Election* (Chicago: University of Chicago Press, 2001); and Cass R. Sunstein and Richard A. Epstein, eds., *The Vote: Bush, Gore & the Supreme Court* (Chicago: University of Chicago Press, 2001).

MARK C. MILLER

C

Calhoun, John C. As a politician and political philosopher of constitution, federalism, and state sovereignty, John Caldwell Calhoun (1782–1850) was the most preeminent spokesperson for the antebellum South. Born near Calhoun Mills, Abbeville District (presently Mount Carmel, McCormick County), in the South Carolina upcountry on March 18, 1782, Calhoun graduated from Yale College in 1804. After his education in the North, Calhoun returned home, practiced law, and served as a member of the South Carolina House of Representatives from 1808 to 1809.

At the age of 28, Calhoun entered the national political arena and represented South Carolina in the U.S. House of Representatives from 1811 to 1817, when he resigned to become the secretary of war. An ardent nationalist during this early period of his political career, Calhoun distinguished himself as one of the "War Hawks." Using his influence as acting chair of the House Committee on Foreign Relations, Calhoun urged the War of 1812 with Great Britain to redeem the honor of his country in the face of Britain's disregard of American neutral rights. After the war, Calhoun proposed several reconstruction measures in support of Representative Henry Clay's nation-building program known as the American System. He advocated chartering the Second Bank of the United States to stabilize the necessary currency and encouraged federal spending for internal improvements to build a nationwide network of roads and canals. Calhoun also supported the Tariff of 1816 to eliminate the increased national debt due to the war and to protect his country's fledgling industry. Though unknown to Calhoun then, the tariff issue was soon to ignite an inflammatory controversy.

Having served as secretary of war under President James Monroe's administration from 1817 to 1825, Calhoun became vice president of the United States in 1825 under the administration of President John Quincy Adams. It was during his first term as vice president when the tariff issue eventually came to the forefront, exposing the emerging economic conflicts between the North and the South. The cotton planters throughout South Carolina and the rest of the agrarian South, who detested a protective tariff to ensure their staple exportation overseas, began to perceive that a series of federal tariff policies was only designed to protect the industrial interests in the North at the expense of the cotton-producing southern states. When the Tariff of 1828, which became widely known as the Tariff of Abominations, was enacted, the tariff issue was no longer an economic issue alone. It now also encompassed the old debate as to the extent of federal power in the young union. Calhoun's nationalist sentiments were gradually strained, and he turned himself into a states' rights advocate and sectionalist.

Responding to his constituents' rising criticism of the federal tariff policies and also sensing the bleak prospect of disunion advanced in his native state, Calhoun anonymously penned the *South Carolina Exposition and Protest* for the state legislature during the summer and fall of 1828. While finding himself in the grave dilemma of privately thwarting the tariff measure enacted by the administration that he was a part of as vice president, Calhoun looked for a constitutional alternative to possible revolutionary action. Resurrecting the compact theory embodied in the language of the 1798 Kentucky and Virginia Resolutions fathered by Thomas Jefferson and James

John C. Calhoun. National Portrait Gallery, Smithsonian Institution.

Madison respectively, Calhoun advanced the doctrine of nullification. In the *South Carolina Exposition*, Calhoun argued that the U.S. Constitution was a compact among the states and that each state could not only interpose (that is, block) its authority between the citizens of that state and the laws of the United States, but also nullify (that is, overrule) such laws and actions as being unconstitutional and inoperative in the state. Calhoun's *Exposition* thus became a standard of revolt against the American System of protective tariffs and a clarion call for devising constitutional safeguards to protect the South's impinged minority interests from the abuse of federal power.

In 1828, Calhoun was reelected vice president with President Andrew Jackson. To the dismay of Calhoun and southern cotton planters, Congress failed to reduce the tariff rate under the new administration. When some South Carolinians became restless and threatened to vindicate the doctrine of nullification, Calhoun issued an open letter entitled "On the Relation which the States and General Government Bear to Each Other," more popularly known as the "Fort Hill Address," in the summer of 1831. Using the words "interposition," "veto," and "nullification" interchangeably, Calhoun, no longer anonymously, warned that unless some constitutional checks were administered, the sectional conflicts would become interminable, leading eventually to "the dissolution of the Union itself." When the new Tariff of 1832 provided for reduced tariff revenues but retained the approximately 50 percent rate on cotton and woolen clothing, a special convention of the South Carolina legislature finally formulated its "South Carolina Ordinance of Nullification" in November 1832, proclaiming that the tariff was "null" and "void" within the state. In response, President Jackson denounced nullification as unconstitutional and asked Congress in the following month to enact a "Force Bill" to enforce tariff collections in South Carolina by sending federal troops.

In late December 1832, Calhoun resigned as vice president during South Carolina's

Nullification crisis. Immediately after he left the Jackson administration, Calhoun took a seat as a U.S. senator to defend his state's position and continually served in that capacity until his death in 1850, except for a brief period when he was appointed as secretary of state. By then, the slavery controversy—an entangling issue with the South's slave-plantation economy—had become a predominant concern for Calhoun. It was in his 1837 address to the Senate entitled "Speech on the Reception of Abolition Petitions" that Calhoun contributed to the development of the South's proslavery argument, terming slavery as "a positive good." As the secretary of state under President John Tyler's administration from 1844 to 1845, Calhoun negotiated the annexation of Texas and justified it as a means to expand the area open to slavery. Back to the Senate, Calhoun denounced the proposed Compromise of 1850 on the ground that the measure would not adequately protect the South's slavery interests. Calhoun prepared his last address to the Senate in the midst of the debate over this compromise sponsored by Senator Henry Clay. On March 4, 1850, Calhoun, too ill to deliver the address himself, asked Senator James M. Mason from Virginia to read it for him. Sensing that the union was now "lying dangerously ill," the dying senator made his final plea that the responsibility of saving the union rested on the North. Only four weeks later, on March 31, 1850, Calhoun passed away in Washington, D.C., at the age of 68.

The essence of Calhoun's last address was his proposition for restoration of the sectional equilibrium within the union. To achieve this end, Calhoun propounded that each sectional majority (that is, the North or the South) or each major-interest majority (that is, the manufacturing interests or the agricultural interests) should be given the constitutional power to veto on the acts of the federal government, which represented numerical majority. This doctrine of concurrent majority had been expounded in his *Disquisition on Government*, presenting the case for minority rights within the framework of majority rule. The theory also led Calhoun to conclude that the only adequate means to protect the slavery interests of the South would be the invention of a dual presidency with a northern president and a southern one, each acting concurrently and possessing the definitive veto power. Advancing the doctrine of concurrent majority, Calhoun's *Disquisition* later served as an introduction to his much larger *Discourse on the Constitution and Government of the United States*.

Though history dictates that he was the foremost intellectual figure who influenced the southern secessionists of 1860 to 1861 on the verge of the Civil War, Calhoun never sought that solution. While protecting his region's interest, Calhoun disparately grappled with what Alexander Hamilton, James Madison, and John Jay had repeatedly pondered in penning *The Federalist Papers*—"the nature of the Union." But his final tragedy lies in the fact that his theory of nullification and his defense of the South's morally indefensible institution of human bondage eventually led the way to the destruction of the union that he had so dearly loved. *SEE ALSO:* Civil War; Interposition; Nullification

BIBLIOGRAPHY: Jesse T. Carpenter, *The South as a Conscious Minority, 1789–1861: A Study in Political Thought* (New York: New York University Press, 1930; reprint, Columbia: University of South Carolina Press, 1990); Margaret L. Coit, *John C. Calhoun: American Portrait* (Boston: Houghton Mifflin, 1950; reprint, Columbia: University of South Carolina Press, 1991); William W. Freehling, *Prelude to Civil War: The Nullification Controversy in South Carolina, 1816–1836* (New York: Harper and Row, 1965; reprint, New York: Oxford University Press, 1992); John Niven, *John C. Calhoun and the Price of Union: A Biography* (Baton Rouge: Louisiana State University Press, 1988); Merrill D. Peterson, *The Great Triumvirate: Webster, Clay, and Calhoun* (New York: Oxford University Press, 1987); and Clyde N. Wilson, ed., *The Essential Calhoun: Selections from Writings, Speeches, and Letters* (New Brunswick, NJ: Transaction, 1992).

YASUHIRO KATAGIRI

Cantwell v. Connecticut *See* Incorporation (Nationalization) of the Bill of Rights

Capital Punishment   The United States occupies an unusual position with respect to the death penalty. In its early history, the United States was at the forefront of death penalty reform. Almost immediately after the Constitution was ratified, many states sought to limit the perceived excesses of capital punishment, with several states pursuing the path of abolition by the mid-nineteenth century. Over the past quarter century, though, the United States has become an outlier among democratic countries in its retention of the death penalty. Indeed, the United States' extensive use of the death penalty during this period—especially its application against persons with mental retardation and juveniles—has generated extensive criticism from traditional American allies abroad. The broader history of the American death penalty reflects a deep ambivalence about the wisdom and role of the death penalty, and the two centuries separating early amelioration and modern robustness were punctuated by waves of reform and retrenchment.

Generalizations about the "American" death penalty are hazardous, though, because few areas of American law and practice better illustrate American federalism. The death penalty in the United States is virtually entirely confined to the states (the numbers of federally sentenced death row inmates and federal executions are trivial in relation to the numbers of inmates and executions at the state level), and states vary widely in both their laws concerning the availability of the death penalty and the manner in which they actually administer it.

Capital punishment has been a feature of the American criminal justice system from the time of the founding. In colonial times, the death penalty was available for numerous crimes, mirroring in many respects the English model. However, just as there were some distinctive features of colonial capital punishment practices, the American death penalty departed from its English roots soon after independence. By the early nineteenth century, states generally reduced the number of crimes punishable by death to a handful of crimes whereas England recognized over 200 capital offenses. Indeed, several states actually abolished capital punishment for all crimes other than murder and treason. The reduction of capital offenses was made possible in part by the introduction of penitentiaries and the option of long-term imprisonment in the late eighteenth and early nineteenth centuries.

The reformist impulse was also manifest in states' efforts to limit the automatic application of the death penalty for murder. First, many states developed a hierarchy of murder, distinguishing between "degrees" of the crime: only "first-degree" murder could generate a capital sentence. Later, states gravitated toward discretionary sentencing even with respect to those defendants convicted of murder in the first degree. By the mid-twentieth century, virtually all American jurisdictions retaining the death penalty afforded jurors substantial discretion to withhold the punishment based on the circumstances of the offense and the offender.

Regional variances in death penalty practices date back to the colonial era. The northern colonies were more inclined to punish based on religious imperatives, authorizing the death penalty for such crimes as sodomy, adultery, and blasphemy. The southern colonies, following English law, were more likely to punish property offenses, even minor ones, with death. In addition, slavery generated its own list of capital crimes, such as the offenses of slave revolt and aiding runaway slaves. By the mid-nineteenth century, southern criminal codes openly distinguished by race (and not merely slave status), making numerous offenses capital when committed by black offenders (even "free" blacks) but not capital when committed by whites. Not surprisingly, southern executions disproportionately involved black offenders.

Even within particular states, death penalty practices diverged significantly, with county officials administering executions during the colonial period and throughout much of the nineteenth century. By the end of the nineteenth century, though, executions increasingly were conducted under state rather than local authority. The trend toward state rather than local executions began earlier in the northern states but eventually spread to southern jurisdictions as well.

State-conducted executions peaked during the Depression and declined significantly in the ensuing three decades, with over 1,500 executions conducted nationwide during the 1930s and less than 200 during the 1960s. Executions in the South significantly exceeded executions in other parts of the country over this period, both in absolute numbers and in relation to population size. Nonetheless, nonsouthern states conducted substantial numbers of executions between 1930 and 1965, with Ohio, Pennsylvania, New York, and California joining six southern states (North Carolina, South Carolina, Georgia, Florida, Mississippi, and Texas) as the leading ten states in absolute execution numbers.

LEGAL REGULATION OF THE DEATH PENALTY

Throughout much of American history, courts placed very few restrictions on state capital punishment practices. Some of the more prominent legal challenges focused not on states' ability to execute but rather on the manner in which death sentences were to be carried out. Indeed, much of the history of the American death penalty involves the struggle to "humanize" capital punishment by implementing less painful (or less unseemly) methods of execution. Hanging was the common form of execution during colonial times and throughout the eighteenth century. Hangings, though, often resulted in prolonged death, and numerous "botched" executions led states to seek less gruesome modes of execution. The development of the electric chair in the late eighteenth century, and its promise of quick and painless death, led many states to prescribe electrocution as the sole means of execution. However, even electrocutions could fail, and the U.S. Supreme Court on one occasion was forced to decide whether a Louisianan inmate who survived after a mechanical failure could be forced to endure another attempted electrocution. The Court, noting that "[a]ccidents happen for which no man is to blame," permitted the state to go forward. In the modern era, concerns about (and litigation targeting) electrocution ultimately led to the near-universal adoption of lethal injection as the exclusive means of execution. Changes in the modes of execution reflect the movement toward private, centralized, medicalized executions and away from the public ceremonial executions characteristic of the colonial and early American systems.

The limited legal regulation of the death penalty during the country's first 150 years was attributable largely to a crucial aspect of American federalism: the core protections for criminal defendants in the Bill of Rights were originally designed and interpreted to constrain only federal actors. Whereas federal defendants could assert claims under a variety of constitutional clauses, including the Fourth Amendment's guarantee against unreasonable searches and seizures, the Fifth Amendment's guarantees against compulsory self-incrimination and double jeopardy, the Sixth Amendment's rights to counsel and jury trial, and the Eighth Amendment's prohibition of cruel and unusual punishment, state criminal defendants were forced to frame their legal challenges within the Fourteenth Amendment's general assurance of "due process of law." Accordingly, the federal courts rarely intervened in state criminal matters, including state death penalty practices.

Manifest injustice in some states' systems, though, particularly in the South, led the U.S. Supreme Court to gradually recognize broader federal protections in state trials. The infamous Scottsboro boys litigation in Alabama during the 1930s (*Powell v. Alabama* 1932) led to the Court's recognition of the right to competent counsel in state capital proceedings. The Court reversed another conviction obtained in the *Scottsboro* case because it refused to credit state explanations for the racially disparate selection of jurors. Ultimately, by the late 1960s, virtually of the protections afforded federal prisoners were extended to state prisoners as well. The decisions incorporating the guarantees of the Bill of Rights via the Fourteenth Amendment's Due Process Clause and applying them in state criminal proceedings provided the framework for subsequent federal constitutional regulation of the death penalty.

The growth of protections for state prisoners occurred at the same time that national popular support for the death penalty was waning. The Civil Rights movement had caused many to regard the death penalty—particularly as applied to those convicted of rape—as a legacy of racial discrimination. Indeed, in a brief dissent from a decision declining review in 1963, three justices on the U.S. Supreme Court had astonishingly suggested, without mentioning race, that the death penalty might be excessive and unconstitutional as applied to defendants convicted of rape. Other social developments, including the general upheaval of the 1960s and the disillusionment wrought by the Vietnam War, likewise appeared to contribute to the diminished support for capital punishment. In 1966, public opinion polls revealed for the first time greater public opposition than support for the death penalty.

Emboldened by these legal and social changes, the Legal Defense Fund of the NAACP embarked on a "moratorium" strategy to bring the American death penalty to a halt. The strategy involved challenging death verdicts as vigorously as possible in light of newly recognized rights, especially as defendants approached execution dates. By 1968, executions in the United States had ceased (after one execution nationwide in 1966 and two in 1967). The U.S. Supreme Court then agreed to decide whether the American death penalty remained consistent with the Eighth Amendment's prohibition of cruel and unusual punishments.

The Court's resulting decision in *Furman v. Georgia* (1972) remains the most significant articulation of the constitutional status of the American death penalty. The decision reflected deep divisions on the Court as all nine justices wrote separate opinions supporting their views, with a bare majority (5–4) voting to strike down all then-existing capital statutes. Although two justices urged the Court to abolish the death penalty altogether as inconsistent with evolving standards of decency, the majority's opinion focused on states' administration of the penalty rather than the harshness or cruelty of the penalty itself.

The justices in the majority were united in their concern about the arbitrariness of prevailing sentencing practices. In particular, the majority condemned the unbridled discretion afforded capital punishment decision makers. State capital punishment statutes uniformly failed to specify what factors justified imposing or withholding the death penalty, and the justices in the majority expressed skepticism that the few offenders selected for death from the vast pool of death-eligible defendants truly constituted the "worst" offenders. In response to the Court's decision, states revamped their statutes to address the problem of standardless discretion. A substantial number of states sought to combat the problem of arbitrariness by enacting mandatory death penalty schemes, but the Court rejected this extreme as well, insisting that sentencers must be afforded an opportunity to consider mitigating factors regarding an offender's background and character, and the circumstances of the offense. Other states sought to cabin sentencer discretion by requiring sentencers to find the existence of at least one enumerated aggravating factor before imposing a sentence of death. Having rejected the extremes of standardless discretion and the mandatory death penalty, the Court embraced this middle course of "guided discretion" statutes.

Following the ten-year hiatus in executions, the modern death penalty era was inaugurated with the resumption of executions in 1977. The ensuing quarter century saw extensive litigation concerning various aspects of state death penalty schemes. The Court invalidated the death penalty for the crime of rape (of an adult victim) and found capital punishment excessive as applied to persons with mental retardation. At the same time, the Court rejected broader challenges to the death penalty, such as claims based on statistical evidence highlighting the significance of race (particularly the race of the victim) in capital decision making.

Regional disparities in the modern era have been more pronounced than those of any other era in American history. Although 38 states make the death penalty available for murder, executions are overwhelming confined to the American South and its borders. In the three decades following *Furman v. Georgia*, 11 southern and border states carried out close to 90 percent of the executions nationwide. Southern states executed more inmates than other regions in the period between 1930 and 1960, but states in the Northeast and West actually performed more executions per homicide than the South during that period. Moreover, at least some of the gap between executions in the South and its borders, on the one hand, and the rest of the country, on the other, was attributable to southern exceptionalism with regard to the death penalty for the crime of rape: all of the 455 executions for rape after 1930 in the United States occurred in southern states, border states, and the District of Columbia.

The enormous disparity in execution rates among the 38 states retaining the death penalty is not attributable to significant differences in death-sentencing rates. Indeed, the death-sentencing rates of some states outside of the South are relatively high, with Ohio and Pennsylvania, for example, producing more death verdicts per homicide than Texas and Virginia, the 2 states leading in sheer numbers of executions. As a result, the death row populations outside of the South rival those of the active execution states, with Ohio, Pennsylvania, and California housing more death row inmates at the beginning of the twenty-first century than the 4 states leading in executions in the modern era (Texas, Virginia, Missouri, and Oklahoma).

The modern era has thus seen the creation of three sorts of death penalty jurisdictions: states without the death penalty by law (abolitionist states), states with the death penalty but insignificant numbers of executions (symbolic states), and states with both the death penalty by law and in practice—states actively carrying out executions (executing states).

Most of the scholarly and popular attention to the execution gap between the South and the rest of the country attempts to identify those aspects of southern politics and culture that account for that region's continued robust use of the death penalty. Many explanations have been offered, including those that emphasize the connection between the death penalty and racial fear and oppression, those that point to higher levels of violence generally in the South (including homicide rates), those that highlight the prevalence of fundamentalist religious beliefs (the near-perfect overlap of the "Bible belt" and the "death belt"), and those that focus on the long-standing inadequacies of criminal defense representation in southern jurisdictions.

The long-ignored and perhaps more apt question concerns the rest of the country's decision neither to abandon the death penalty nor to carry out executions. It remains puzzling that the death penalty exists as "law" but not as practice in virtually all of the death penalty jurisdictions outside of the South and its borders. Although there are some modest differences in procedures (method for setting execution dates, structure and timing of state court review, and mechanism for appointment of defense counsel to indigent defendants) among death penalty jurisdictions, such differences are far too minor to explain their extraordinary divergence in practice. In the end, the presence or absence of political will is likely responsible for the divide between symbolic and executing states. The lack of political will can affect the process at many points in the capital punishment system, but primarily in the lengthy processing of cases in state courts and the reluctance to set execution dates in cases that have managed to move through the system.

Overall, the modern era seems to carry forward the historic pattern of reform and retrenchment in the American capital punishment system. The U.S. Supreme Court's decision invalidating standardless discretion schemes was followed by the enthusiastic efforts of states to redraft their capital statutes. After a relative paucity of executions in the 1960s and 1970s, executions became commonplace by the 1990s, reaching a yearly nationwide total in 1999 (ninety-eight) that had not been matched since 1951. At the same time, concerns about the death penalty's reliability and fairness have subsequently intensified the public debate over the death penalty and spawned some significant reforms. The discovery of numerous wrongful convictions involving death-sentenced Illinois prisoners led to a comprehensive study of the Illinois system and ultimately to the decision by the Illinois governor George Ryan in 2003 to commute the death sentences of the entire death row (167 inmates). Other states, influenced by technological advances in the testing of genetic material, have likewise sought to minimize the risk of wrongful convictions and executions by liberalizing indigent defendants' access to pre- and posttrial testing of DNA evidence.

The American death penalty system exemplifies the paradoxes of the larger American criminal justice system. Procedurally, the United States places vastly more restrictions on the investigation and prosecution of crime than other countries. On the substantive side, the United States has adopted an unusually punitive approach in sentencing, reflected in the adoption of mandatory minimum sentences for a host of crimes, including nonviolent (mainly drug) offenses, and "three strikes" laws with severe consequences for recidivists. The modern death penalty carries forward both of these dimensions: the death penalty remains an available punishment throughout most of the country, and yet extensive litigation, particularly in symbolic states, constrains the ultimate implementation of capital sentences.

The central question for the future is whether the course of the modern era is a stable one. As the death rows in symbolic states continue to grow, political pressure is likely to mount from both sides either to proceed with executions or to remove inmates from death row who face no realistic prospect of execution. National abolition of the death penalty through the legislative process is an exceedingly remote—perhaps unthinkable—possibility both because of the absence of the support necessary for such congressional regulation and because of genuine doubts about congressional power to so regulate. Judicial abolition, on the other hand, remains a real possibility, especially if the extreme regionalization of executions persists and the gap between those sentenced to death and those actually executed causes the Court to acknowledge a new form of intolerable arbitrariness. *SEE ALSO:* Fourteenth Amendment; *Furman v. Georgia*; *Gregg v. Georgia*; Incorporation (Nationalization) of the Bill of Rights

BIBLIOGRAPHY: James R. Acker, Robert M. Bohm, and Charles S. Lanier, eds., *America's Experiment with Capital Punishment: Reflections on the Past, Present and Future of the Ultimate Sanction*, 2nd ed. (Durham, NC: Carolina Academic Press, 2003); Stuart Banner, *The Death Penalty: An American History* (Cambridge, MA: Harvard University Press, 2000); Michael Meltsner, *Cruel and Unusual: The United States Supreme Court and Capital Punishment* (New York: Random House, 1973); and Carol S. Steiker and Jordan M. Steiker, "Sober Second Thoughts: Reflections on Two Decades of Constitutional Regulation of Capital Punishment," *Harvard Law Review* 109 (December 1995): 355–438.

JORDAN M. STEIKER

Carter v. Carter Coal Company   This Supreme Court case deals with two very different conceptions of federalism and the scope of Congress's commerce powers. The first conception is dual federalism and assumes that the state and national governments are coequal and have sovereignty over distinct spheres. The second conception is national supremacy or cooperative federalism. In this latter conception, the national government is supreme and is not forbidden from using its powers to affect the constitutional space reserved to the states. In effect, the federal government and the states are junior partners in a cooperative effort to establish policies. The more broadly the commerce clause is read, the more the national government can affect the states. The *Carter* case is a good example of these competing views of federalism.

In 1935 Congress passed the Bituminous Coal Conservation Act in an attempt to bring stability in the coal industry, which was plagued by overproduction, poor wages, and unsafe working conditions. The act required that boards be established that would promulgate regulations on wages, hours, labor relations, and coal production. Producers were encouraged to participate in the program through a tax rebate incentive. A tax of 15 percent was assessed on the value of all coal produced. If a producer participated in the program, they received 90 percent of the tax back in the form of a rebate. Congress stated that it had the authority to pass the act pursuant to its power to regulate interstate commerce. The Carter Coal Company decided that it could not afford to opt out of the program. However, some of its shareholders felt differently and sued the company in an attempt to stop its participation.

Justice George Sutherland's majority opinion in *Carter* advocated a strong dual federalism position. He emphasized that the states existed before the Constitution, and that the Constitution only conferred limited powers to the national government. Therefore,

Congress's powers must be interpreted narrowly; otherwise, the states could be reduced "to little more than geographical subdivisions of the national domain." Sutherland interpreted interstate commerce very narrowly. He argued that coal mining is production, a purely local activity that precedes commerce. If coal mining affects interstate commerce, it is an indirect effect and therefore beyond the reach of the Commerce Clause. Federal regulatory power only attaches when the commodities are in transit; therefore, the Bituminous Coal Conservation Act was unconstitutional.

The *Carter* case marked the apex of the Court's dual federalism jurisprudence and is credited with triggering Franklin Roosevelt's court-packing scheme. The following year, 1937, the Court changed directions and supported the national supremacy view of federalism. *SEE ALSO:* Commerce among the States; *Hammer v. Dagenhart*; *Heart of Atlanta Motel v. United States*; *National Labor Relations Board v. Jones and Laughlin Steel Corporation*; *Schechter Poultry Corporation v. United States*; Tenth Amendment; *United States v. E. C. Knight Company*; *Wickard v. Filburn*

BIBLIOGRAPHY: Lee Epstein and Thomas G. Walker, *Constitutional Law for a Changing America: Institutional Powers and Constraints*, 4th ed. (Washington, DC: CQ Press, 2001); and Kermit L. Hall, ed., *The Oxford Companion to the Supreme Court of the United States* (New York: Oxford University Press, 1992).

BARRY SWEET

Categorical Grants Categorical grants comprise the bulk of activity in the federal grant-in-aid system, both in terms of the number of programs and the amount of funding. Categorical grants derive their name from the fact that their uses are limited to a narrowly defined category of activities that generally are specified in the authorizing legislation.

There are four different types of categorical grants: formula grants, project grants, formula-project grants, and open-ended reimbursement grants. Formula grants are distributed to jurisdictions entitled to funds by the authorizing statute on the basis of a numeric formula that takes into account the relative need of the recipient jurisdiction compared to all other entitlement jurisdictions. Examples of formula elements include population, poverty, per capita income, unemployment, enrollment in public schools, and the like. The formula factors and the weight assigned to each are either prescribed in the authorizing legislation or determined by administrative officials.

Project grants are awarded on a competitive basis by the administering agency, generally following the review of a grant application. Formula-project categorical grants involve a two-stage grant distribution: first a formula grant is used to apportion funding among the states, and then project grants are awarded by state officials to state and local government agencies.

Under open-ended reimbursement grants, the federal government agrees to reimburse a certain percentage of state and local program costs for a prescribed activity or set of activities. Hence, the total amount of the federal grant is open-ended and dependent on the amount of spending incurred by state and local jurisdictions—the more a state spends, the larger its federal grant. Medicaid is an example of an open-ended reimbursement grant, with a state's grant determined by its federal reimbursement rate (which varies from a minimum of 50 percent in several states to a maximum of 77 percent in Mississippi) and the amount of a state's spending for Medicaid-eligible services.

The origins of federal categorical grants can be traced to the Morrill Act of 1862, in which Congress authorized the distribution of public lands to state governments and instructed the states to use the proceeds from the sale of that land to support institutions of higher education (i.e., the "land grant" universities). This aid also came with an additional requirement—the colleges and universities that received assistance were required to provide military instruction. States were also required to submit annual reports to Congress on program expenditures.

The Federal Aid Highway Act of 1916 was the next development milestone in the evolution of the federal grant system. This program was the federal government's first large-scale assistance program and also expanded the federal role by establishing a number of conditions and controls (e.g., project applications, progress reports, expenditure audits, and project closeout) designed to insure that state governments adhered to federal goals and objectives in their use of grant funds.

The most expansive period of growth for categorical grants occurred during the 1960s in response to President Johnson's call for a Great Society. By the end of the decade the number of grant programs had increased from about 150 to nearly 400, funding more than doubled, and the federal government became an important player in several policy areas where it had no previous involvement.

Though successive waves of New Federalism during the Nixon and Reagan administrations sought to consolidate dozens of categorical grant programs into a small number of block grants, the growth of categorical programs continued. Today, there are about 600 grant-in-aid programs, and categorical grants account for about 95 percent of the programs and more than 80 percent of total grant outlays.

The most important fact about categorical grants is their extensive variability. Though on the surface the design features of categorical grants may appear to be technical issues, the decisions made regarding the key design elements of a categorical grant program are political ones and reflect the relative balance of power and influence among federal, state, and local governments. *SEE ALSO:* Block Grants; Categorical Grants; Crosscutting Requirements; Crossover Sanctions; Fiscal Federalism; Formula Grants; Grants-in-Aid; Project Grants; Rural Policy; Supremacy Clause: Article VI, Clause 2; Unfunded Mandates; Urban Policy

BIBLIOGRAPHY: Lawrence D. Brown, James W. Fossett, and Kenneth T. Palmer, *The Changing Politics of Federal Grants* (Washington, DC: Brookings Institution, 1984); Martha Derthick, *The Influence of Federal Grants* (Cambridge, MA: MIT Press, 1970); Robert Jay Dilger, *National Intergovernmental Programs* (Englewood Cliffs, NJ: Prentice Hall, 1989); and U.S. Advisory Commission on Intergovernmental Relations, *Categorical Grants: Their Role and Design*, ACIR Report A-52 (Washington, DC: U.S. Government Printing Office, 1977).

MICHAEL J. RICH

Champion v. Ames In *Champion v. Ames* (1903), the U.S. Supreme Court sustained a federal statute that made it illegal to transport lottery tickets in interstate commerce. Speaking for the five-member majority, Justice John Marshall Harlan claimed that Congress "may . . . exclude from commerce among the states any article . . . it may choose." The Tenth Amendment, according to Harlan, was not a limit on Congress's Commerce Clause power to exclude goods from shipment in interstate commerce, a power "expressly delegated to Congress." Speaking for the dissenters, Chief Justice Melville W. Fuller disagreed and expressed their fear of creating "a centralized government" if the Tenth Amendment did not serve as an effective limit on Congress's power.

In later cases, the Court upheld the power of Congress to enact the Pure Food and Drug Act (*Hipolite Egg Company v. United States* 1911), and the Mann Act (*Hoke v. United States* 1913)—both of which banned the shipment of noxious goods in interstate commerce—but denied congressional authority to ban the shipment of goods made by child labor (*Hammer v. Dagenhart* 1918). *SEE ALSO:* Commerce among the States; *Hammer v. Dagenhart*; *Hipolite Egg Company v. United States*; Tenth Amendment

ELLIS KATZ

Charles River Bridge Company v. Warren Bridge Company   The original U.S. Constitution contained few restrictions on how the states could treat their own citizens. One exception is the Contract Clause—Article I, Section 10, of the Constitution—providing that no state shall pass any law "impairing the obligation of contracts." Under the leadership of Chief Justice John Marshall, the U.S. Supreme Court interpreted the Contract Clause broadly to include public charters as well as private contracts between individuals.

Charles River Bridge Company v. Warren Bridge Company (1837) gave Marshall's successor, Roger Brooke Taney, his first opportunity to interpret the Contract Clause. In 1785, the Commonwealth of Massachusetts issued a charter to the Charles River Bridge Company to build and operate a bridge over the Charles River linking Boston and Charlestown. Commerce flourished, and in 1823 the Massachusetts legislature issued a charter to the Warren Bridge Company for the construction of a second bridge. The older Charles River Bridge Company, fearing the competition from the newer bridge, brought suit, claiming that its 1785 charter constituted a contract within the meaning of the Contract Clause that was now being unconstitutionally interfered with.

Chief Justice Taney, however, in his first major opinion, disagreed, maintaining that public charters must be construed narrowly, so as to protect the public interest and not unduly limit the state's police power. Thus, unless the 1785 charter specifically gave the Charles River Bridge Company an exclusive privilege to operate a bridge over the Charles River, none could be implied.

The *Charles River Bridge* case marks the beginning of the end of the use of the Contract Clause as a limitation on state police powers. *SEE ALSO:* Contract Clause; *Dartmouth College v. Woodward*; *Fletcher v. Peck*; *Home Building and Loan v. Blaisdell*; Marshall, John; Taney, Roger Brooke; *United States Trust Company v. New Jersey*

ROBERT W. LANGRAN

Chisholm v. Georgia   *Chisholm v. Georgia* (1793) is the first case involving a constitutional issue ever decided by the U.S. Supreme Court. Chisholm, a citizen of South Carolina, brought suit in the U.S. Supreme Court against the State of Georgia to recover land the state had seized from his Tory client during the Revolutionary War. The suit was brought in the Supreme Court because Article III of the Constitution extends federal jurisdiction to "controversies between a State and citizens of another State" and specifies that the Supreme Court shall have original jurisdiction in cases in which a state shall be a party.

During the debate over ratification of the Constitution, some Anti-Federalists saw this provision of Article III as an attack on state sovereignty, but Alexander Hamilton in *The Federalist* No. 81 tried to assuage their fears by claiming that the federal courts could hear such cases only if a state gave its consent and waived its sovereign immunity, or if the state itself had originated the suit. The Court, however, disagreed with Hamilton and held that it had jurisdiction in such cases whether or not the state had given its consent to be sued. The decision raised a furor in the states, and in 1798 the Eleventh Amendment was added to the Constitution to provide that "the Judicial Power of the United States shall not be construed to extend to any suit in law or equity, commenced or prosecuted against one of the United States by citizens of another State, or by citizens or subjects of a foreign State." *SEE ALSO:* Eleventh Amendment

ELLIS KATZ

Citizenship   In the United States, citizenship is based upon Enlightenment principles and was developed in the course of the American Revolution (1775–83) and the framing of the U.S. Constitution (1787). Its central characteristic, unique for its time, is the idea of consent. The leaders of the founding generation subscribed to the "social contract" theory of government articulated by the English philosopher John Locke (1632–1704). According to this theory, government derives its authority from a contractual agreement with the governed to which they give their consent. Rather than passively accept the government's right to rule as "subjects," "citizens" actively consent to be ruled and, when their consent has been betrayed, they may withdraw it. Thus, the founding generation asserted that it was "their right" and "their duty" to "throw off such Government" in the Declaration of Independence (1776). The words "We the people" that begin the U.S. Constitution likewise portray an active citizenry consenting to the government it creates.

Although the qualifications for American citizenship were not explicitly defined in the original Constitution, they were gleaned from several of its provisions. Members of the House of Representatives must have "been seven Years a Citizen of the United States" (Article I, Section 2), while members of the Senate must meet the same standard for "nine Years" (Article I, Section 3). The president must be a "natural-born citizen" or a citizen at the time the Constitution was ratified (Article II, Section 1). Additionally, Congress had been delegated the power to "Establish a uniform rule of Naturalization" (Article I, Section 8). Finally, representation in the House would be based upon a formula by which a state's population would "be determined by adding to the whole number of free persons . . . three fifths of all other persons" (Article I, Section 2). These provisions were understood to mean that a "citizen" was an active member of the founding generation and/or had been born on American soil or, finally, had been naturalized. In *Dred Scott v. Sandford* (1857), the Supreme Court declared that slaves, even if they had been freed, were not included as part of "We the people" because they were only "three-fifths" of a person and hence not whole enough to be citizens.

State governments played a major role in shaping and administering citizenship policy until the early twentieth century. They followed English common law in applying the principle of citizenship by place of birth (jus soli), at least to free white males, and by descent (jus sanguinis) for children born to citizens not on U.S. soil. As the Articles of Confederation (1781–89) made no provision for congressional control over citizenship by naturalization, such policies were controlled entirely by the states until the Constitution became effective (1789). The resultant chaos stemming from so many conflicting policies among the states prompted the First Congress to enact a naturalization law in 1790 under its Article I power to provide a "uniform rule." Nevertheless, the states remained responsible for the administration of naturalization policy so that with limited congressional guidance, the states were effectively conferring the rights and obligations of both state and national citizenship. For the most part, however, the courts of the each state upheld the rights of national citizenship conferred by the others.

The ratification of the Fourteenth Amendment to the Constitution (1868) deprived the states, as well as Congress, of the ability to selectively apply the doctrines of jus soli and jus sanguinis to whites only. Its declaration that "[a]ll persons born or naturalized in the United States, and subject to the jurisdiction thereof, are citizens of the United States and of the State wherein they reside," effectively overruled the *Dred Scott* decision's interpretation of the Constitution and made those of African descent just as eligible for citizenship by these means as whites. The Fifteenth Amendment's (1870) de jure (in law) guarantee of the right to vote without regard to race, a fundamental privilege of citizenship, was significantly weakened de facto (in fact) by state "Jim Crow" laws that followed the end of Reconstruction in the 1870s. Women, who had traditionally qualified for birthright citizenship, would not have a similar guarantee of the right to vote until the ratification of the Nineteenth Amendment (1920). Although Native Americans were granted U.S. citizenship under the Indian Citizenship Act (1924), full voting rights in many of the states were denied them until after World War II.

The confluence of urbanization and industrialization that followed the Civil War gave rise to enormous waves of immigration that further tested American citizenship policy and led eventually to a permanent alteration of the states' roles. Like naturalization, immigration policy had been the prerogative of the individual states dating from the colonial period. They attempted variously to restrict and encourage immigration depending upon their internal socioeconomic circumstances. Competition among the states for immigrants and the costs of administering to them gave rise to contradictory policies and heightened interstate conflict. Especially controversial were "head taxes" charged by the states to cover the costs of processing the newcomers. The Supreme Court put an end to the chaos by declaring in an 1876 decision (*Henderson v. New York*) that state immigration laws interfered with the federal government's plenary power to regulate foreign commerce (Article 1, Section 8). One important consequence of this decision was the federal effort to limit the applicability of jus soli citizenship in the United States by prohibiting the children of Chinese immigrants who were born in the United States from becoming citizens as guaranteed by the Fourteenth Amendment. This limitation was overturned by the Supreme Court in 1893 (*United States v. Wong Kim Ark*).

Although the states could no longer regulate immigration, they continued to play a major role in the implementation of naturalization policy. Again, their internal socioeconomic circumstances produced significant policy problems. In short, the grant of citizenship became the tool of urban political machines and their industrial clients who converted, almost literally, boatloads of immigrants into citizens in time to vote in local and state elections. Congress addressed these irregularities and abuses in the Naturalization Act of 1906.

During the twentieth century, the rights of U.S. citizenship were strengthened by constitutional amendments (the Nineteenth, Twenty-third, Twenty-fourth, and Twenty-sixth), laws such as the Civil Rights Act (1964) and Voting Rights Act (1965), and Supreme Court decisions such as *Brown v. Board of Education* (1954) and *Baker v. Carr* (1962). In most of these instances, primacy was given to national citizenship over state discretion to administer it. But as the century drew to a close, new controversies arose concerning the discretion of states in distributing benefits, primarily economic, to resident aliens, indigents, and citizens of other states. *SEE ALSO:* Dual Citizenship; Fourteenth Amendment

> *BIBLIOGRAPHY:* Derek Heater, *What Is Citizenship?* (Malden, MA: Polity Press, 1999); Judith N. Shklar, *American Citizenship: The Quest for Inclusion* (Cambridge, MA: Harvard University Press, 1991); Peter H. Shuck, *Citizens, Strangers, and In-betweens: Essays on Immigration and Citizenship* (Boulder, CO: Westview Press, 1998); and Rogers M. Smith, *Civic Ideals: Conflicting Visions of Citizenship in U.S. History* (New Haven, CT: Yale University Press, 1997).

GORDON P. HENDERSON

City of Boerne v. Flores This significant federalism case (1997) had its origins in a long-standing dispute within the Supreme Court, and then between the Supreme Court and Congress, over the proper meaning of the Free Exercise Clause of the First Amendment. From *Reynolds v. United States* in 1878 through *Braunfeld v. Brown* in 1961, the Court held that the Free Exercise Clause did not require that religious nonconformists be exempted from otherwise valid secular regulations. But in 1963, Justice William Brennan, who had dissented strongly two years before in *Braunfeld*, wrote for the Court in *Sherbert v. Verner*. Here it was held that government could refuse an exemption to the law for a religious nonconformist only if a "compelling state interest" justified such a refusal.

In the years after *Sherbert*, the Court sometimes found a compelling state interest, and sometimes it did not. But in 1990, in *Employment Division v. Smith*, Justice Antonin Scalia wrote an opinion for the Court that appeared to turn Free Exercise jurisprudence back toward the pre-*Sherbert* orthodoxy. The political reaction to the *Smith* decision was immediate and intense. In 1993 Congress passed, and President William Clinton signed, the Religious Freedom Restoration Act (RFRA), which sought, in effect, to overrule *Smith* and restore the compelling state interest test. This set the stage for the collision between Congress and the Court in *Flores*.

Here Justice Anthony Kennedy wrote for the Court and found the Religious Freedom Restoration Act unconstitutional because it was beyond the power of Congress to enact. Since the Free Exercise Clause of the First Amendment applied to the states through the Fourteenth Amendment (*Cantwell v. Connecticut* 1940), Congress, in enacting the RFRA, was acting under its authority conferred by Section 5 of the Fourteenth Amendment to enforce "this article" by appropriate legislation. While not questioning congressional power to enforce the Fourteenth Amendment, Kennedy's opinion made it clear that it was the exclusive province of the Court to decide what the substantive requirements of the Fourteenth Amendment were. In other words, Congress could enforce only what the Court found to be the requirements to be "this article."

The legislative power of Congress under Section 5, Justice Kennedy concluded, was remedial in nature; it did not extend to declaring the substance of what the Fourteenth Amendment requires. Furthermore, Justice Kennedy's opinion established a judicial test for determining when Congress is properly legislating in a remedial mode under Section 5. While admitting that it was not always easy to distinguish between a "remedy" and a newly coined substantive right, the Court said that "the distinction exists and must be observed." To that end the majority held that "there must be a congruence and proportionality between the injury to be prevented or remedied and the means adopted to that end." And the Court, of course, will be the judge of congruence and proportionality.

The federalism dimension of *Flores* constitutes a potentially important limitation on the legislative power of Congress and should be seen in the context of such other federalism decisions as *United States v. Lopez* and *United States v. Morrison*. *SEE ALSO: United States v. Lopez*; *United States v. Morrison*

> BIBLIOGRAPHY: *Braunfeld v. Braun*, 366 U.S. 599 (1961); *Cantwell v. Connecticut*, 310 U.S. 296 (1940); *City of Boerne v. Flores*, 521 U.S. 507 (1997); *Employment Division v. Smith*, 494 U.S. 872 (1990); *Reynolds v. United States*, 98 U.S. 145 (1878); and *Sherbert v. Verner*, 374 U.S. 398 (1963).

RICHARD MORGAN

Civil Rights   *See* Civil Rights Act of 1875; Civil Rights Act of 1964

Civil Rights Act of 1875   The Civil Rights Act of 1875 stated that "all persons within the jurisdiction of the United States shall be entitled to the full and equal enjoyment of the accommodations, advantages, facilities, and privileges of inns, public conveyances on land or water, theaters, and other places of public amusement." It was the fourth of a series of post–Civil War acts (1866, 1870, 1871, and 1875) passed to extend civil rights to African Americans, including the enjoyment of equal rights, liberty, property ownership, and protection from threat and intimidation. In spite of the Thirteenth Amendment, the Fourteenth Amendment, and the Fifteenth Amendment, injustice, discrimination, and violence persisted against former slaves in all levels of American society.

The Civil Rights Acts of 1875 was initially introduced to Congress in 1870 by Massachusetts Senator Charles Sumner and Massachusetts Representative Benjamin F. Butler (Democrat) seeking to end discrimination and segregation in public facilities, establishments, and conveyances. In its preamble, the Act reaffirmed equality and justice for all as stipulated in the Declaration of Independence. The Act contained three main points: first, it outlawed segregation and discrimination in public places on the basis of "nativity, race, color, or persuasion, religious or political." Second, it prohibited disqualifying any citizen for grand or petit jury in state or federal courts "on account of race, color, or previous condition of servitude." Third, it mandated the prosecution of "all crimes and offenses against, and violations of, the provisions of this act" in federal courts and made all cases arising from the violation of the provisions of the act reviewable by the Supreme Court of the United States.

In 1883, the Supreme Court declared the 1875 Act unconstitutional on the ground that, to cite part of the ruling, "the denial of equal accommodations in inns, public conveyances and places of public amusement . . . imposes no badge of slavery or involuntary servitude upon the party, but at most, infringes rights which are protected from State aggression by the XIVth Amendment." The majority decision claimed that discrimination did not go against the spirit of the Thirteenth Amendment and that any infringement of the Fourteenth Amendment should be dealt with by states, not by the federal government. Judge John Harlan disagreed, arguing that discrimination was indeed a badge of servitude and thus Congress had the power to enact legislation to enforce the provisions of the Thirteenth Amendment.

With this ruling, the Supreme Court sanctioned segregation, further reinforced by another Supreme Court decision in 1896 known as *Plessy v. Ferguson*, which upheld the doctrine of "separate but equal" accommodations, facilities, and conveyances for blacks and whites. A Supreme Court ruling in 1954, *Brown v. Board of Education of Topeka*, ended segregation in schools. In 1964, Congress passed a civil rights law in the spirit of the Civil Rights Act of 1875, against discrimination in places of public accommodation. SEE ALSO: *Brown v. Board of Education*; Civil Rights Act of 1964; Declaration of Independence; Fifteenth Amendment; Fourteenth Amendment; *Plessy v. Ferguson*

BIBLIOGRAPHY: Milton R. Konvitz and Theodore Leskes, *A Century of Civil Rights* (New York: Columbia University Press, 1961).

AIMABLE TWAGILIMANA

Civil Rights Act of 1964   President Lyndon B. Johnson signed the Civil Rights Act of 1964 into law on July 2, 1964. It was the first substantial civil rights legislation after Reconstruction following the American Civil War. Composed of eleven titles, the law desegregated public accommodations, authorized the federal government to sue to desegregate public facilities and schools, extended and strengthened the federal Civil Rights Commission, required companies and unions to allow equal employment opportunities, and authorized the U.S. attorney general to intervene in lawsuits where persons alleged denial of equal protection of the laws under the Fourteenth Amendment to the U.S. Constitution.

Although candidate John F. Kennedy campaigned for enlarging civil rights, after the election the issue's controversial nature got low priority on his New Frontier agenda. However, in 1963 civil rights demonstrations and boycotts, widely supported especially by young blacks and whites, prompted the president to action. He proposed the initial bill (H.R. 7152) in a nationwide televised address on June 11, 1963. The basic elements of the bill passed the House Judiciary Committee in October, but by the time of Kennedy's assassination (November 22, 1963), it was buried in the House Rules Committee. No action had been taken on it in the Senate by that time. Both House and Senate opponents sought to delay the bill to death.

Within a week of succeeding to the presidency, Lyndon Johnson made the civil rights bill a priority item for Congress and an issue of "honor to President Kennedy's memory." With Johnson's prodding, the bill cleared the House Rules Committee on January 30, 1964. Despite an extended debate between January 31 and February 10, it passed with a large majority of Democrats and Republicans, 290 to 130. Almost all the opponents were from the southern states.

Despite passage in the House, the power of a filibuster in the Senate led many observers to believe that southern senators could talk the bill to death. Supporters of the bill avoided the southern-dominated Judiciary Committee by putting the bill on the Senate's calendar. After that, nineteen southern senators maintained a filibuster for fifty-seven days until June 10. The substantive matters "most obnoxious" to the Southerners were the fair employment requirements and provisions to cut off federal funds to political entities, such as states (including state schools), for discriminatory practices.

History was made when the Senate broke the filibuster with a cloture vote that cut off debate on the bill. Cloture required 67 votes to pass. It carried with 71 in favor (Democrat, 44; Republican, 27) to 29 against it (Democrat, 23; Republican 6). The bill finally passed in the Senate June 19 by a 73–27 roll call. Among 6 Republicans voting with 21 Democrats against the bill was Barry Goldwater (R-AZ). Shortly after the bill passed, he won nomination as the Republican candidate for president opposing Lyndon Johnson.

The legislation and its enforcement were an issue in the 1964 presidential campaign. Barry Goldwater questioned the bill's constitutionality and the extent to which it should be enforced. Lyndon Johnson pledged full enforcement, and his landslide victory gave impetus to vigorous enforcement of the bill's provisions by his administration. *SEE ALSO:* Great Society; Johnson, Lyndon B.

BIBLIOGRAPHY: Congress and the Nation (Washington, DC: Congressional Quarterly Inc., 1965).

JACK R. VAN DER SLIK

Civil War   The experience of the Civil War compelled citizens to make significant changes in the structure of American federalism, but these changes emerged in unexpected and often unlikely ways. Secession itself posed a direct challenge to the very idea of a federal union, and the repudiation of secession enshrined both the permanence of the federal union and the supremacy of the nation-state. The process of emancipation during the war forced the national government to assume powers that few Americans would have granted it before the conflict. Ensuring freedom in the postwar period required still greater expansions of federal authority, mostly under the auspices of new civil rights legislation. The longevity and intensity of the conflict bolstered the national government at the expense of the states as well. The federal government organized state militia units into a huge national army; established close relationships with the railroads, munitions manufacturers, and other military suppliers; and initiated long-sought legislative changes to create a truly integrated national economy. None of these changes was established easily. The era was marked by conflicts between advocates of expanded federal authority and those who sought to protect the prerogatives of the states. Nor were these changes established with perfect foresight. The necessities of war demanded new policies and new institutional arrangements, but the chaos and uncertainty of war blurred the nature of those changes.

Civil War

POLITICAL AND MILITARY CHALLENGES IN THE NORTH

The most public conflicts in the North over the extension of federal power revolved around Lincoln's suspension of habeas corpus and the jailing of political prisoners. The issue erupted as soon as the war began. Lincoln suspended habeas corpus before Congress came into session in 1861 and periodically throughout the war. The first test of the president's authority to suspend habeas corpus came with the arrest of a Marylander in 1861. John Merryman, a pro-Confederate saboteur, blew up several bridges in Baltimore County to prevent the movement of Union troops. In April, Lincoln had suspended habeas corpus for the area stretching from Washington, D.C., to Philadelphia in order to facilitate the movement of troops into the capital. Merryman was arrested by the military and held in Fort McHenry. Military authorities refused to recognize the writ of habeas corpus issued by Merryman's lawyers to move the case to civilian courts. Merryman was released after seven weeks and later indicted for treason in civil courts, but never tried. The national consequences of his case came in the decision *Ex Parte Merryman*. The U.S. Supreme Court Chief Justice Roger Taney, sitting as circuit court judge in Baltimore, issued a writ for Merryman's release and denied Lincoln's authority to suspend habeas corpus. Lincoln ignored the order, citing Article I, Section 9, of the Constitution, which permits the suspension of the writ "when in Cases of Rebellion or Invasion the public Safety may require it." Taney argued that only Congress could suspend it, but since Lincoln controlled the military he could refuse to release Merryman upon Taney's writ. Lincoln's victory in this dispute, dependent as it was upon his ability to use the army to enforce his decisions, was indicative of how conditional the changes to national authority were during the war.

Conflicts over the extent of executive power continued through the war, as Democrats and civil libertarians in the North protested the suspension of habeas corpus. Lincoln's opponents also took aim at the arrests of political prisoners. The State Department possessed control over internal security at the war's start and under Secretary William Seward's aggressive leadership, hundreds of people, mostly in the border states, were arrested and detained without trial. In February 1862, the War Department assumed control over security and Secretary Edwin Stanton reduced arrests and established commissions to examine the cases of those still in prison. Most were released upon taking the loyalty oath. Arrests rose again in late 1862, as draft opponents demonstrated against the expansion of federal power embodied in the national draft. Union authorities arrested at least 15,000 people during the war, many of which were legitimate arrests of people actively encouraging desertion or draft resistance. But many also were editors, politicians, and others who criticized the administration's policies. Lincoln himself admitted to preferring to err on the side of too many arrests rather than too few, since civil courts prosecuted crimes slowly and people awaiting trial could continue their treasonable activities. Most of the arrests occurred within the border South, which constituted a sort of war zone throughout the conflict. Though Lincoln's opponents attacked both the principle upon which he justified the imposition of martial law and the particular cases where he exercised it, Lincoln's actions were more restrained than the sedition laws enacted during World War I and the mass arrests and detention of Japanese Americans during World War II. Lincoln also made it clear that he did not consider his actions any kind of precedent for future presidents; the decisions he made were taken in the midst of war only to prevent the immediate dissolution of the nation.

The most famous case in the North revolved around the Democratic politician Clement Vallandigham, who was arrested in Ohio in the spring of 1863 for his inflammatory speeches. Charged with disloyal activities, a military court convicted Vallandigham and sentenced him to imprisonment for the duration of the conflict. Despite the furious opposition of Democrats and many moderate Republicans, the local federal judge refused to issue a writ for his release. Seeking to exploit the situation, Ohio Democrats nominated him for governor. Lincoln came under intense pressure to overrule the conviction, but instead he sidestepped the issue and commuted Vallandigham's sentence to banishment to the Confederacy. Vallandigham escaped the South on a blockade runner to Canada and continued his gubernatorial campaign from there, though without success. Vallandigham appealed his case from abroad, arguing that civilians could not be tried by military courts if civilian courts were functioning, but the U.S. Supreme Court refused to hear it. Like Congress, the Court sanctioned the wartime expansions of the president's authority.

More consequential than either the suspension of habeas corpus or the arrest of political prisoners was Lincoln's decision to issue the Emancipation Proclamation. Though rarely framed in terms of its impact on federalism, Lincoln's decision represented a significant shift in authority on one of the most divisive issues in American history. Although the U.S. Constitution did not use the word "slavery," it sanctioned the institution—in the Fugitive Slave Clause and the Three-Fifths Rule—and federal courts had always recognized the constitutionality of slavery in states that sanctioned the institution. When emancipation occurred before the Civil War, it was due to state officials revising their constitutions. During the 1860 presidential campaign, Lincoln repeatedly pledged himself both unwilling and unable to interfere with slavery in those states where it already existed. He maintained this position well into the war, as demonstrated by his efforts to convince border state officials to enact emancipation on their own. The longevity of the conflict, the process of self-emancipation by slaves escaping to Union Army camps, and the necessity of keeping Great Britain and France out of the conflict all drove Lincoln to reconsider his position on whether he possessed the power to enact emancipation. When he did finally issue the Emancipation Proclamation, he did so with the careful language of a lawyer conditioning and justifying his decision. It was undertaken, Lincoln declared, "by virtue of the power in me vested as Commander-in-Chief . . . in time of actual armed rebellion against authority and government of the United States, and as a fit and necessary war measure for suppressing said rebellion." Lincoln knew that his decision would be condemned by those who saw it as an unconstitutional violation of the balance of federal powers, but he argued that without such an action there would soon be no federal government at all.

ECONOMIC AND ADMINISTRATIVE CHANGES IN THE NORTH

The Lincoln administration expanded federal capacities in a number of nonmilitary areas as well. With southern Democrats absent from both chambers, Republicans were able to pass a sequence of long-sought legislative initiatives that elaborated the national market system that emerged in the antebellum period. All of these bills drew on federal authority with regard to land, economic development, and market regulation. The Homestead Act, passed in March 1862, was long-sought legislation that gave 160 acres of land to anyone who remained on it for five years. Under its auspices, 80 million acres were given away in 500,000 parcels, broadly expanding access to the western territories. The Land Grant College Act gave each state 30,000 acres per electoral vote to

Civil War

create agricultural and mechanical colleges. In February 1863, Congress passed the National Bank Act, which authorized the creation of new national banks founded on holdings of U.S. bonds. Congress later imposed a 10 percent tax on state bank notes, effectively ending the independent state bank system. The Legal Tender Act introduced national banknotes, helping to stabilize the northern economy and generating a precedent for the federal government's issuance of paper money. Last, Republicans finally enacted a Pacific Railroad bill, ending a long prewar dispute over the route of the nation's first transcontinental railroad line. In order to pay for the building of the line, the federal government granted 6,400 acres of public land for each mile of track to the Union Pacific and Central Pacific Railroad Companies. This land was then sold by the companies to generate the revenue to build the railroad itself. All of these elements demonstrated the deeply Whiggish outlook that the Republicans had inherited from their predecessors. They all used the federal government to develop and organize the national economy and infrastructure. Northern Democrats, for their part, opposed virtually all of these legislative initiatives, arguing that they were unconstitutional expansions of federal authority and unwise public policies.

THE CONFEDERATE EXPERIENCE

Perhaps surprisingly, given the emphasis placed on states' rights as a justification for war in the postwar period, the Confederacy experienced a growth of national authority similar to what occurred in the United States. Because the Confederate constitution enshrined the principles of state sovereignty, Confederates faced a more contradictory situation, but the war demanded centralization and a strong government. Most of the significant policy initiatives were undertaken by Jefferson Davis, with the Confederate Congress occasionally obstructing but usually sanctioning his actions. Governors emerged as the most vocal opponents of Davis's measures, though his vice president, Alexander Stephens, became a vociferous critic of the administration as well. Governor Joseph Brown of Georgia, in particular, frustrated Davis's efforts to solidify national control over manpower and resources in the Confederacy. The Confederacy never organized its Supreme Court, so there was no final arbiter to decide the merits of the arguments between Davis, Brown, and others.

Just as in the North, the issue of the suspension of habeas corpus animated critics of federal authority. In 1861, some Confederate commanders arrested civilians for disloyal activities and refused to respond to writs issued by civilian courts. Davis did not interfere, in effect sanctioning their actions. In February 1862, the Confederate Congress authorized Davis to suspend habeas corpus in advance of Union General George McClellan's attack on the Richmond Peninsula. Davis was consequently granted the authority to impose martial law in several places, though each time the power was tailored narrowly to meet the situation. These actions brought the wrath of civil libertarians down on him, even though he used the power more sparingly than did Lincoln. The battle between nationalists and libertarians in the Confederacy raged throughout the war, but Davis's aggressive pursuit of expanded federal authority should not necessarily be read as a complete abdication of the prewar southern tradition. Like Lincoln, Davis sought to respond to the situations with which he was confronted; he argued that unless he used federal power to protect the Confederacy, the Confederacy would not last.

Through the course of the war, the Davis administration responded progressively to pressures placed on the new nation by the war. In the face of a severe manpower dilemma in early 1862, the Confederacy imposed the first national draft in American history, one part of which automatically reenlisted for three years all those men who had signed up for one-year terms of service. The draft was vigorously opposed by soldiers and civilians alike, who regarded it as an illegal usurpation of authority by the national government. In September 1862, amendments to the draft were passed that included carefully crafted rules for exemptions. These exemptions gave the federal government enormous control over the shape of the civilian workforce. In effect, the Confederate government controlled all of nation's manpower by the end of 1862. Conflicts also developed around the tax-in-kind, a 10 percent tax in key foodstuffs adopted in early 1863, which hit yeomen very hard. The law angered states' rights advocates still more because the foodstuffs obtained by the Confederate government were redistributed to poor families, putting the Confederacy in the business of dispensing welfare, something that even local governments had eschewed in the prewar South. Another piece of centralizing legislation that clearly broke with prewar traditions was impressment. Adopted in late 1863, this law gave the government and the army the authority to seize needed supplies and reimburse people in the rapidly depreciating Confederate scrip. Like the tax-in-kind, this measure was deemed necessary to maintain the war, though it drew the ire of states' rights activists around the Confederacy. Governor Brown of Georgia engaged in a long correspondence with Davis, protesting the constitutionality of a variety of measures that Davis advocated. Unlike governors in the North, Brown went so far as to obstruct the ability of federal agents to carry out laws such as conscription and impressment.

PUBLIC PERCEPTIONS OF WARTIME CHANGES

The similarities in governance between the North and the South were mirrored in the reactions of citizens of each section to the changes undertaken by their respective governments. Most civilians complained bitterly about the expansion of national authority, but most accepted it as the price for winning the war. Within each section, a die-hard political opposition did not accept the changes as legitimate and spent much of the war articulating its opposition to the policies of centralization. In the North, Democrats formed the main body of opposition to the Republicans' legislative initiatives. They had opposed Whigs' efforts before the war to use the government on behalf of business, and they saw little improvement in the cozy relationship between Washington and the railroad companies during the war. Their opposition was both principled and political. They sincerely preferred a federal system with balanced national and state authority, and they condemned the way that Republicans used new federal powers to build their constituency.

Conservative Northerners strongly opposed the draft, which passed after the Confederate version but was similar in most respects. The high point of opposition came in the infamous New York City Draft Riots of 1863, when gangs of white laborers attacked and murdered dozens of the city's black residents. Alongside the principled policy opposition to the draft made by politicians was a deep anger among conservatives at the notion that white men were being forced to fight a war for black freedom. Thus, in the North more of the anger toward the draft came from its racial implications than from the change it constituted in federal-state relations. Confederates articulated their opposition to the draft in more principled terms than Northerners but opposed it just as strongly. Likewise, they denounced the tax-in-kind, impressment, and various other centralizing measures as violations of the new Confederate constitution. Still, a majority of residents in both sections sanctioned the governments that passed these laws, especially in their willingness to send men to fight and die in the armies. Accepting the necessity of wartime measures did not mean that civilians in either section anticipated that the centralizing elements would make a substantive difference in how their governments functioned after the war. The notable exception is the category of northern economic legislation, which was strongly supported by well-connected and powerful communities across the North. The reluctance that attended most of the changes in governance should discourage any easy assumption that the Civil War was an inevitable stop on the path to a "modern" United States. Federalism advanced in the shadow of war, which was impossible to predict or direct. The repudiation of secession guaranteed the supremacy and permanence of the federal government, and the Union's endorsement of emancipation obligated it to devise the mostly federal structures that would ensure it lasted, but Republicans did not completely abandon their antebellum orientation. In general, Republicans, and most Northerners, remained committed to preserving state power as a balance to federal authority. The North did not engage in the type of broad centralization of power that accompanied nationalist movements in Europe at the time. Indeed, the history of the era following Reconstruction reveals the limits to Republicans' vision, as new reformers felt compelled to organized themselves to combat the corporate autonomy and influence that had been so central to northern victory in the war. *SEE ALSO:* Economic Development; Federal Courts; Governors and Federalism; Homestead Act of 1862; Jefferson, Thomas; Reconstruction; Secession; Slavery; Sovereignty; Taney, Roger Brooke; Welfare Policy

BIBLIOGRAPHY: Herman Belz, *Emancipation and Equal Rights: Politics and Constitutionalism in the Civil War Era* (New York: Norton, 1978); Richard Bensel, *Yankee Leviathan: The Origins of Central State Authority in America, 1859–1877* (Cambridge: Cambridge University Press, 1990); Harold Hyman and William M. Wiecek, *Equal Justice under Law: Constitutional Development, 1835–1875* (New York: Harper & Row, 1982); Mark E. Neely, *The Fate of Liberty: Abraham Lincoln and Civil Liberties* (New York: Oxford University Press, 1991); Mark E. Neely, *Southern Rights: Political Prisoners and the Myth of Confederate Constitutionalism* (Charlottesville: University Press of Virginia, 1999); and George C. Rable, *The Confederate Republic: A Revolution against Politics* (Chapel Hill: University of North Carolina Press, 1994).

AARON SHEEHAN-DEAN

Clay, Henry   Henry Clay, of Lexington, Kentucky, was a national leader who was one of the founding fathers of the Whig Party and also known as the "Sage of Ashland" and the "Great Compromiser." Member of the Kentucky General Assembly, five-term U.S. senator, and six-term member of the U.S. House of Representatives, of which he served as speaker of the House from 1811 to 1820 and from 1823 to 1825, he was also a candidate for president in 1824 and 1832 for the Federalist and National Republicans, and in 1844 for the Whigs. Clay was also U.S. secretary of state from 1825 to 1829. His extensive public service positioned him in key leadership roles during the development of the early republic, and Clay impacted the development of federalism in two important policy areas, economic development and states' rights. Despite the enduring legacy of Henry Clay's economic plan, termed the American System, his political leadership placed him in difficult circumstances to win the presidency and build the national consensus he desired for his Whig program.

Clay was the primary architect of the American System. The American System had three essential components: federal aid for internal improvements, a protective tariff for industry, and a national bank. The American System provided an urbanist model of economic growth that contrasted with the rural model of Jeffersonians, and the economic policy theory behind it promoted nationalism at the expense of states' rights. Clay's American System established the foundation of modern economic development policy and defined strong national government powers as essential for securing the economic prosperity of strong national commercial enterprises.

Henry Clay was known as the Great Compromiser because of his role in mitigating the increasing conflict in the federal system between slave and free states. This was a critical role Clay played when Missouri's application for statehood created a federalism crisis. Clay supported a compromise: allowing slavery to continue in Missouri but otherwise prohibiting it North of the 36 degree 30 minute latitude. When the controversy again erupted over Missouri's attempt to prohibit the movement of free blacks, Clay emerged in 1821 as the leader of the second Missouri Compromise, whereby Missouri agreed not to deprive a citizen from another state of equal rights and privileges. After the Mexican War, which Clay opposed, he was elected to the U.S. Senate from Kentucky and introduced the Compromise of 1850 to deal with the crisis over the extension of slavery into the areas of California and New Mexico acquired from Mexico. Clay's death in 1852 left a void in national leadership that contributed to the ultimate crisis of federalism in 1860. *SEE ALSO:* American System; Civil War; Compromise of 1850; Internal Improvements; Jackson, Andrew; Missouri Compromise of 1820; Secession; Slavery

Henry Clay. National Portrait Gallery, Smithsonian Institution.

BIBLIOGRAPHY: Maurice G. Baxter, *Henry Clay and the American System* (Lexington: University Press of Kentucky, 1995); Richard Chambers, *Speeches of the Hon. Henry Clay, of the Congress of the United States* (Cincinnati, OH: Shepard & Stearns, 1842); Robert V. Remini, *Henry Clay: Statesman for the Union* (New York: W.W. Norton, 1991); and Kimberly C. Shankman, *Compromise and the Constitution: The Political Thought of Henry Clay* (Lanham, MD: Lexington Books, 1999).

MICHAEL W. HAIL

Coastal Zone Management Act of 1972   Congress enacted the Coastal Zone Management Act of 1972 (CZMA) to protect natural resources in coastal areas, including aquatic life, coastal waters, and adjacent lands (16 U.S.C. §1451 et seq.). This includes islands, transitional and intertidal areas, salt marshes, wetlands, and beaches. The CZMA's primary goal is to protect, improve, and restore the quality of coastal waters by encouraging and assisting states in managing coastal zones "through the development and implementation of management programs to achieve wise use of the land and water resources of the coastal zone, giving full consideration to ecological, cultural, historic, and esthetic values as well as the needs for compatible economic development" (Id. §1452[1]–[2]).

Congress observed that about 75 percent of Americans lived in coastal states, and recognized, from two important studies on the health of coastal waters, that development in coastal watersheds was leading to problems of estuarine pollution and degradation of coastal waters and adjacent wetlands (S. Rep. 92-753, at 4777 [1972]). In response to these indicators, congressional delegates introduced several bills in the Ninety-first Congress and held many hearings. Although none of the bills was enacted during that term, Congress adjourned with a consensus that a state management approach was preferable, due in part to pressure from 22 coastal states, and indeed several states adopted their own programs without waiting for final action on the proposed CZMA. The congressional legislators recognized that "the ultimate success of a coastal management program [would] depend on the effective cooperation of federal, state, regional, and local agencies" (S. Rep. 92-753 at 4778 [1972]). Eventually, the CZMA became law on October 27, 1972, and has been amended several times since.

Congress incorporated a system of "cooperative federalism" into the CZMA by encouraging coordination and cooperation between appropriate federal, state, and local agencies. The cooperative nature of the act is apparent in nearly all its aspects, including collecting and analyzing data, preparing management plans and programs, and implementing these plans and programs. Management plans and programs are to be developed consistent with federal rules and regulations, and notice must be given to afford "opportunity of full participation by relevant Federal agencies, State agencies, local governments," and other interested parties. The act sets aside a state fund for assisting and encouraging programs that provide for protections of the natural resources within the coastal zone, the management of coastal development, public recreation places in coastal zones, assistance in redeveloping deteriorating coastal zones, consultation with federal agencies, and planning and studying coastal zones and ecosystems. In addition to cooperation between the states and the federal government, the act requires federal interagency cooperation and also requires any federal action taken in coastal areas to be consistent with state management programs (Id. §1456).

As mentioned above, the act has been amended many times since its inception. In 1975, minor revisions were made to the administration of the grant program. In 1976, the Coastal Energy Impact Program was established in order to make coastal zones more self-sufficient in terms of energy. Also in 1976, an amendment created an Interstate Grants Program and a research and technical assistance grant program, called for the expansion of the estuarine sanctuary program to include public spaces, and established a national system for evaluating the performance of state management activities. Another amendment set up a new system of Resource Management Improvement Grants in 1980, which preserved certain coastal areas, redeveloped urban waterfronts, and worked to improve public access to beaches.

The act has incentive programs to promote coastal zone awareness, security, and purity. It provides for the Walter B. Jones Excellence in Coastal Management Awards, which are given to individuals outside the federal government whose contribution to the field of coastal zone management has been significant, including five local governments that made the most progress, and up to ten graduate students whose academic study promises to contribute to the field in particular.

To ensure that everything completed is accounted for the person in charge of enforcing the CZMA at the U.S. Environmental Protection Agency (EPA) is required to submit a biennial report to Congress. This report contains detailed information on the various CZMA-, state-, and federally-sponsored programs that deal with coastal zone management. Also, states and regions that are doing all that they can to manage their coastal zones correctly are labeled, in order to attract their attention and garner support for coastal zone management. *SEE ALSO:* Devolution; Environmental Policy

BIBLIOGRAPHY: "Coastal Zone Management Act," 61C Am. Jur. 2d Pollution Control §§1132, 1133; John A. Duff, "The Coastal Zone Management Act: Reverse Pre-emption or Contractual Federalism?" *Ocean & Coastal Law Journal* 6 (2001): 109–17; Lieutenant Patrick J. Gibbons, JAGC, USN, "Too Much of a Good Thing? Federal Supremacy and the Devolution of Regulatory Power: The Case of the Coastal Zone Management Act," *Naval Law Review* 48 (2001): 84; and David R. Godschalk, "Implementing Coastal Zone Management: 1972–1990," *Coastal Management* 20 (1992): 93.

VAUGHN PICKELL AND ARTHUR HOLST

Coercive Federalism   Coercive federalism is a period of American federalism that began in the late 1960s. It is characterized by substantial growth in the power of the federal government relative to the states and by the ability of the federal government to override state powers and impose policies on the states. Coercive federalism has ten significant characteristics. One has been an unprecedented increase of policy conditions attached to grants-in-aid, conditions that enable the federal government to achieve national objectives that lie beyond Congress's constitutionally enumerated powers and also to extract more spending on federal objectives from state and local governments. An example is the 21-year-old drinking age condition attached to federal highway aid in 1984. The No Child Left Behind Act (NCLB) of 2002 is another example, which became a cause célèbre for the states because of its costly testing and performance requirements.

Second, there has been a sharp rise in congressional earmarking of specific projects in grants-in-aid, thus denying discretion to state and local officials. The number of earmarks increased from under 2,000 in 1998 to 9,362 by 2003. Third, federal aid has shifted substantially from places to persons; that is, almost two-thirds of federal aid is now dedicated for payments to individuals (i.e., social welfare). For example, Medicaid alone now accounts for almost 45 percent of all federal aid. As a result, place-oriented aid for such functions as infrastructure, economic development, and education has declined steeply, and increased aid for social welfare has locked state budgets into programs subject to rising federal regulation and matching state costs.

Mandates are a fourth characteristic of coercive federalism. Congress enacted one major mandate in 1931, one in 1940, none during 1941–63, nine during 1964–69, twenty-five during the 1970s, and twenty-seven in the 1980s. The Unfunded Mandates Reform Act of 1995 cut new mandate enactments sharply, but did not eliminate standing mandates. Fifth, federal preemptions of state powers have risen to historically unprecedented levels. Of 439 explicit preemptions passed by Congress from 1789 to 1991, 233 (or 53 percent) were enacted only from 1969 to 1991. No post-1991 count is available, but most observers agree that Congress continues to enact large numbers of preemptions. In turn, preemptions are frequently upheld by the U.S. Supreme Court. A sixth feature of coercive federalism has been federal constraints on state taxation and borrowing, beginning especially with the enactment of limits on tax-exempt private activity bonds in 1984. Federal judicial and statutory prohibitions of state taxation of Internet services and sales are among the most prominent, current constraints. In November 2004, Congress extended its Internet tax ban (i.e., the Internet Tax Nondiscrimination Act) to November 2007.

A seventh characteristic has been the federalization of state criminal law. There are now some 3,500 federal criminal offenses, nearly half of which have been enacted since the mid-1960s. The number of federal prisoners increased from about 20,000 in 1981 to nearly 175,000 in 2004, and the number of federal prosecutors jumped from 1,500 in 1981 to more than 7,000. Generally, federal criminal laws (e.g., drug laws) are tougher than comparable state laws and make prosecutions and convictions easier than under state laws.

Coercive federalism has been marked, as well, by the demise of executive and congressional intergovernmental institutions established during the era of cooperative federalism to enhance cooperation. Most notable was the death of the U.S. Advisory Commission on Intergovernmental Relations (ACIR) in 1996 after thirty-seven years of operation. Ninth, there has been a decline in federal-state cooperation in major grant programs such as Medicaid and surface transportation, with Congress earmarking and altering programs more in response to national and regional interest groups than to elected state and local officials.

Tenth, coercive federalism has been marked by unprecedented numbers of federal court orders and large numbers of lawsuits filed against state and local governments in federal courts. Although federal court orders dictating major and costly changes in such institutions as schools, prisons, and mental health facilities have declined since the early 1990s, state and local governments are subject to high levels of litigation in federal courts, with various interests often trying to block major state policy initiatives through litigation. The U.S. Supreme Court resurrected the Eleventh Amendment in the 1990s to restrain some types of such litigation, but the Court's decisions have been quite limited. *SEE ALSO:* Cooperative Federalism; Economic Development; Education; Enumerated Powers of the U.S. Constitution; Federal Courts; Housing; Intergovernmental Relations; Medicaid; No Child Left Behind Act; Preemption; Transportation Policy; Unfunded Mandates; Welfare Policy

BIBLIOGRAPHY: John Kincaid, "From Cooperation to Coercion in American Federalism: Housing, Fragmentation, and Preemption, 1780–1992," *Journal of Law and Politics* 9 (Winter 1993): 333–433; and John Kincaid, "From Cooperative to Coercive Federalism," *Annals of the American Academy of Political and Social Science* 509 (May 1990): 139–52.

JOHN KINCAID

Cohens v. Virginia   The power the Supreme Court possesses to decide cases in which a state is a party conventionally dates from *Cohens v. Virginia* (1821). This case was an appeal from a state court decision fining Philip and Mendes Cohen $100 for selling out-of-state lottery tickets in violation of state law. When the Supreme Court announced that argument would be held on the validity of the conviction, the Virginia legislature took the unusual step of instructing state lawyers to argue only the jurisdictional point, and that the Supreme Court could not adjudicate appeals in cases when a state was a party. Such a practice, in effect, would immunize state criminal trials from federal review.

John Marshall's opinion for the Court rejected Virginia's jurisdictional pretenses, concluding that states enjoy no sovereign immunity from federal judicial processes. "[A] case arising under the constitution or laws of the United States," the chief justice asserted, "is cognizable in the Courts of the Union, whoever may be the parties to that case." A literal reading of Article III, Section 2, did suggest that the Supreme Court was limited to exercising original jurisdiction over cases in which a state was a party. Nevertheless, the justices rejected that claim and Virginia's further claim that the Eleventh Amendment prohibited federal courts from adjudicating an appeal from two citizens of Maryland who were convicted of a criminal offense by a Virginia court. The constitutional ban on extending "the Judicial power of the United States . . . to any suit in law or equity, commenced or prosecuted against one of the United States by Citizens of another State," Marshall stated, did not bar federal jurisdiction when a state initiated a suit or criminal prosecution against a citizen of another state. *Cohens* reaffirmed the judicial power to declare state laws unconstitutional that Justice Joseph Story had previously defended in *Martin v. Hunter's Lessee* (1816). Letting localities resolve constitutional controversies for themselves, Marshall asserted, "would prostrate . . . the government and its laws at the feet of every state" by giving "each member . . . a veto on the will of the whole."

Common claims that *Cohens* and *Martin v. Hunter's Lessee* established federal judicial power to declare state laws unconstitutional and reverse state appellate courts need some revision. The Marshall Court did assert these powers in those opinions. The justices in *Cohens*, however, avoided open conflict with Virginia by ruling that, although they had the power to reverse a state criminal conviction, state criminal convention in the case before the justices was valid. When antebellum federal courts decided against states, the judicial ruling was frequently ignored. The Civil War probably did more than any judicial decision to establish federal power over state governments. *SEE ALSO:* Marshall, John; *Martin v. Hunter's Lessee*

BIBLIOGRAPHY: Mark Graber, "The Passive-Aggressive Virtues: *Cohens v. Virginia* and the Problematic Establishment of Judicial Review," *Constitutional Commentary* 12 (1995): 67; and G. Edward White, *The Marshall Court and Cultural Change, 1815–1835,* abridged ed. (New York: Oxford University Press, 1991).

MARK A. GRABER

Cole v. Arkansas   *See* Incorporation (Nationalization) of the Bill of Rights

Colegrove v. Green   Until it was overruled by *Baker v. Carr* in 1962, *Colegrove v. Green* (1946) was the leading precedent on legislative apportionment, holding that apportionment was a "political question" and therefore not within the power of courts to decide.

The case itself involved a challenge to Illinois' congressional elections. According to the petitioner, the districts from which Illinois' members of the U.S. House of Representatives were elected were so unequal in population as to violate the Constitution. Justice Felix Frankfurter, writing for the majority, refused to consider Colegrove's contention, maintaining that "authority for dealing with such problems resides elsewhere. The Constitution [Article I, Section 4] has conferred upon Congress exclusive authority to secure fair representation by the States in the [House of Representatives]." "Courts," according to Frankfurter, "ought not to enter this political thicket." *SEE ALSO: Baker v. Carr*; Reapportionment; *Reynolds v. Sims*

ELLIS KATZ

Comity   "Comity" is generally recognized as a courtesy or privilege extended as a matter of deference and good will rather than as a matter of right. The concept of comity is recognized in the American legal culture between nations and states of the United States. Comity between nations is generally defined as the body of rules that nations observe toward one another as a matter of courtesy or mutual convenience even though the rules do not form part of international law. Nations extending comity to other nations do, as a matter of practice, expect the same courtesy for its citizens within the jurisdiction of the nation to which comity is extended. The intranational comity between states of the United States is generally defined as the practice by which the courts of one state follow the decisions of another even though not bound by the law to do so. True comity is not a rule of law, statutorily or constitutionally. The comity concept is one of practice that has a value in securing uniformity of decision and discouraging repeated litigation of the same question. *SEE ALSO:* Abstention; *Michigan v. Long*; New Judicial Federalism; *Younger v. Harris*

CHARLES D. COLE

Commerce among the States   A national power to regulate commerce, along with the closely connected need for national revenues, was the most immediate cause of the Philadelphia Convention that drafted the Constitution. Three attempts had been made to give Congress this power under the Articles of Confederation, and the 1786 Annapolis Convention that proposed the Philadelphia Convention was itself an outgrowth of commercial disputes among the states bordering the Chesapeake Bay. By 1787 many felt that the commercial plight of the nation was bad and deteriorating. The single biggest issue was the largely unexpected exclusion of Americans from most trade with the British Caribbean resulting from the Order in Council of July 2, 1783, which cut off the United States from its largest and most profitable export market. Americans depended on the island trade for profits with which to pay for British manufactured goods. Without this trade, Americans ran up a large trade deficit because of a flood of British manufactured imports as soon as the war was over, which also undercut infant American manufactures. Britain's policy was seen by many, especially Madison, as an attempt to keep the former colonies commercially dependent on the former mother country. In addition, as Madison bluntly adverted to in his *Vices of the Political Sys-*

tem of the United States, written on the eve of the Convention, the states were injuring their commerce with each other as well as foreign commerce by taxing and discriminating against each other's trade, violating treaty obligations, and other measures. The power to regulate commerce, therefore, grew out of recognition of the need to create a national economic unit that could bargain as a whole with Britain, while eliminating internal barriers and discrimination.

Achieving a power over commerce required complicated compromises. Not only would this power have to be taken from the states, but also having this power at the national level would itself unleash complex new dynamics. In particular, the slave states, especially North Carolina, South Carolina, and Georgia, deeply feared that the power over commerce might be exercised by a northern majority to endanger slavery. The commercially weaker states, such as New Jersey, Connecticut, Delaware, Maryland, North Carolina, and Georgia, all depended on the ports of neighboring larger states for their imports and exports, and therefore demanded an end to import, export and other fees and discrimination by their stronger neighbors. They also feared that their more populous neighbors would use the national power over commerce to continue to exploit them. Thus the delegates debated long over whether the power over commerce should require a supermajority, which the South wanted, or be exercised by simple majority, and they surrounded it with a constellation of clauses limiting state and federal power that both prohibited exploitation and promoted an open internal market, and still allowed for a state role, such as those dealing with no federal export taxes, no state import or export duties, no state tonnage or inspection duties or fees, no port preferences, protections of slavery, and others. Most of their attention was on foreign trade, with little discussion of commerce among the states. The power that emerged was a power to regulate three kinds of commerce: commerce among the states, foreign commerce, and commerce with the Indian tribes.

Because so much time was spent on limits on the power over commerce, virtually no time was spent in the Philadelphia Convention or in the state ratifying conventions discussing the extent of the power to regulate commerce itself, or on differences between its branches, making it difficult to discern the actual intent of the framers. In addition, naming these three branches of commerce under a single power to regulate implied that a fourth category of commerce existed, generally called the domestic, internal, or intrastate commerce power, which was also not discussed. In addition, as the nation's economy shifted away from dependence on foreign trade during the 1780s to one largely oriented to developing a vast internal market a few decades later, as the economy became more fully monetized and as local markets became more fully integrated nationally, as a tiny manufacturing sector grew to a dominant one a century later, as technology produced new goods, as dominant theories of national wealth production changed from mercantilism to laissez-faire to a somewhat more socially oriented government, and as federalism itself changed, the challenge of defining the regulation of commerce in connection with maintaining the federal system seemed to became ever more complex and difficult to connect to the framers.

EARLY INTERPRETATIONS

Until the passage of the 1887 Interstate Commerce Act regulating railroads, Congress exercised the power over commerce infrequently and narrowly, primarily over navigation and customs, so that the Court dealt largely with state laws that seemed to interfere with commerce among the states rather than evaluating federal laws *Gibbons v.*

Ogden (1824) was the Marshall Court's first and main opportunity to define the power over commerce. The State of New York had granted a monopoly of steamboat transportation to Robert Fulton and his successor, Aaron Ogden. In retaliation, New Jersey and Connecticut imposed fines on anyone sailing under protection of such a monopoly. To Marshall, this "threatened to revive all the defects of the Confederation" and was precisely the kind of situation that the power over commerce was designed to prevent. Marshall struck down the monopoly as being preempted by the federal Coastal Licensing Act, which licensed Thomas Gibbons's boat. The decision established that the federal power over commerce among the states certainly applied to transportation, including new technologies such as steam, but that it included buying and selling and more, "the commercial intercourse between nations, and parts of nations, in all its branches." Rejecting the argument that the power over commerce among the states could regulate only on the border between states, Marshall said that "among" meant "intermingled with" and could reach inside a state where necessary, and that the national power was complete in itself, like the power wielded by a unitary government. He acknowledged a sphere of state internal powers including powers over commercial objects, but argued that the national government could regulate local activities when they affected commerce among the states. While popular, broad, and nationalist, the decision did not clearly resolve issues such as precisely what activities were considered to be commercial, whether in the absence of a clear conflict with federal statutes a state could continue to exercise a concurrent state power over commerce or whether the federal power was exclusive, and how far activities not commercial in themselves might be regulated in order to regulate commerce among the states. In large part, these issues still occupy the Court.

In *Willson v. Black-Bird Creek Marsh Co.* (1829), where Delaware had authorized the damming of a navigable stream, Marshall accepted under the circumstances of that case the right of states to regulate activities that might affect commerce among the states, where the congressional power over commerce was in "its dormant state," meaning that when Congress had not legislated in a particular area, the power over commerce as interpreted by the Court would not necessarily preempt state law that otherwise seemed to interfere with commerce among the states.

A few years later, with Marshall gone, the country rapidly growing internally aided and regulated largely by state and local government, and the slavery issue increasingly polarizing political life, the court moved under Chief Justice Roger Brooke Taney's leadership to a position more explicitly favorable to state freedom to pass laws that affected commerce where there was no congressional statute involved, an attempt to avoid any possible entanglements over slavery. In *New York v. Miln* (1837), the Court found that a New York law imposing bonds and fines on ship captains who brought pauper immigrants into the city did not interfere with the power over commerce because people were not articles of commerce, and instead was an exercise of the state police power, the first time this power was used to allow states to regulate the content of vessels moving among the states. Decisions over the next few years were generally pro-state though often unclear as to why, as the Court tried to avoid decisions that might imply a federal power to regulate slavery, the *License Cases* (1847) and the *Passenger Cases* (1849) being good examples. In *Cooley v. Board of Wardens* (1852), involving the right of the Port of Philadelphia to impose charges on ships entering the port but not hiring local pilots, the Court formulated a rule of "selective exclusiveness" whereby matters that were "in their nature national, or admit only of one uniform system," would preempt state action even without congressional action, while other types of state actions might not necessarily be prohibited by the Court. This doctrine seemed to reinforce the dualistic interpretation of the Tenth Amendment, but unfortunately the Court did not provide much guidance on how to tell what was "national" and what was not.

THE POST–CIVIL WAR AND THE GROWTH OF THE NATIONAL ECONOMY ERA

After the Civil War the economy became increasingly manufacturing based, with national enterprises and railroads. In 1886 the court struck down state regulation of railroads under *Cooley* if the railroads were interstate in *Wabash, St. Louis & Pacific Railway Co. v. Illinois*. This left the (by now largely national) railroad network unregulated, but also impelled Congress to pass the Interstate Commerce Act the next year, and the Court now began to interpret how far federal law could go under the power over commerce. In the *Shreveport Rate Cases* (1914), the court upheld regulation of railroads inside states under this act as a necessary adjunct of interstate regulation. Chief Justice Charles Hughes wrote that the intrastate activities of carriers "having a close and substantial relation to interstate traffic" were subject to national regulation, "not because Congress possesses the authority to regulate the internal commerce of a State, as such, but that it does possess the power to foster and protect interstate commerce."

In addition to railroads, the Court also allowed some expansion of federal power over commerce into the previously untouched areas of morals or social activities, creating a federal police power that might compete with that of the states. In *Champion v. Ames* (the Lottery Case; 1903), the Court upheld against Tenth Amendment challenges a national law prohibiting the transportation across state lines of lottery tickets because the tickets as articles of commerce were bad in themselves, and followed in *Hipolite Egg Company v. United States* (1911) by upholding the Pure Food and Drug Act's bans on interstate transportation of dangerous food and in *Hoke v. United States* (1913) with a validation of the Mann Act prohibiting the transportation of women across state lines for immoral purposes.

Otherwise, however, the court was not very favorable to federal legislation. For example, in *United States v. E. C. Knight Company* (1895), the case whose name stands for the Court's restrictive policies toward national legislation during this era, the Court eviscerated the new Sherman Antitrust Act by declaring that even though a monopoly of manufacturing—98 percent of the nation's sugar refining capacity—was proven, Congress could not regulate it or break it up because manufacturing itself was not commerce, and its regulation was reserved to the Tenth Amendment police powers of the states. Chief Justice Melville Fuller dismissed Harlan's strong dissent, which pointed to the practical fact that manufacturing was an integral part of national commerce, by holding that manufacturing only indirectly affected commerce, a distinction widely felt to be artificial. As a result, when manufacturing was involved, the commerce-prohibiting power upheld in the morals and police power cases would not allow Congress to prohibit, for example, the products of child labor. In *Hammer v. Dagenhart* (the Child Labor Case; 1918), the Court narrowly overturned a law prohibiting the interstate transportation of goods made by child labor. However, in *Swift & Company v. United States* (1905) the Court did approve Sherman Act prohibitions of price fixing in meat dealing, finding that even though individual transactions involving cattle going to market were largely inside states, the whole business was part of a single national "current of commerce" that could be nationally regulated.

While the Court often struck down federal laws based on deference to federalism, it was not particularly supportive of state regulation of commerce either. In *Lochner v. New York* (1905), for example, the Court overturned New York's restrictions on hours and conditions of bakery workers as exceeding the state police powers and as violating Fourteenth Amendment due process–based "freedom of contract" limits on state power. *Lochner*'s restrictions on state policies combined with court restrictions on federal laws such as *Knight* created the sense that the court's defense of the states against the federal power over commerce was secondary to its interest in laissez-faire.

THE NEW DEAL ERA

Thus the status of the power over commerce among the states versus federalism was a complicated one as the nation entered the Great Depression. As Franklin D. Roosevelt took office in 1933 with an unprecedentedly broad agenda to stop the effects of the Depression as well as to create the rudiments of a national welfare system and broadly promote economic development, a major confrontation with the Court began. The Court struck down many, though not all, of Roosevelt's early programs under the power over commerce, often citing federalism as the reason, though many felt that the Court's ideological commitment to laissez-faire was as much if not more the explanation. In *Schechter Poultry Corporation v. United States* (1935), the Court applied the *Knight* direct-indirect, commerce versus production distinction, as well as the argument that Congress had wrongly delegated its own legislative power, striking down the National Industrial Recovery Act, a key New Deal law that regulated wages, hours, and industry practices, for intruding on "intrastate business." The next year in *Carter v. Carter Coal Co.*, the Court applied the same logic to strike down the Bituminous Coal Conservation Act setting wage and hour controls for coal mining. After his massive 1936 electoral victory, a frustrated Roosevelt proposed his "court-packing" plan to save his domestic programs. While Congress was still debating the plan, however, in April 1937 the Court made a momentous change of direction. In *NLRB v. Jones and Laughlin Steel Corporation*, which challenged new federal rules requiring corporations to recognize and deal with unions, the Court by 5–4 explicitly abandoned the rigid and impractical *Knight* approach, and instead reverted to the practical approach of *Shreveport* and *Swift*, looking less to artificial distinctions than to how something affected commerce among the states. In upholding the 1935 Wagner Act, the Court recognized that it "is the effect upon commerce, not the source of the injury, which is the criterion." In *United States v. Darby* (1941), the Court relied on *Shreveport* to uphold wage and hour restrictions under the 1938 Fair Labor Standards Act, and specifically overruled *Hammer v. Dagenhart* in upholding the act's ban on the shipment of goods made without complying with the law. Justice Harlan Stone took specific aim at the Tenth Amendment, asserting it was but "a truism that all is retained which has not been surrendered," ending for decades the idea that certain areas of commercial activity or state activities that affected commerce were inherently left to the states.

The broadest application of the power over commerce came in *Wickard v. Filburn* (1942). Roscoe Filburn was fined for growing wheat in excess of the quota allowed under the Agricultural Adjustment Act, which tried to help raised depressed farm prices by limiting the supply of grain. He argued that because the excess wheat he grew was for his personal consumption and use, it was local and noncommercial activity and not under the power over commerce among the states. The Court found that "even if [Filburn's] activity be local and though it may not be regarded as commerce, it may still, whatever its nature, be reached by Congress if it exerts a substantial economic effect on interstate commerce." Moreover, "That [Filburn's] own contribution to the demand for wheat may be trivial by itself is not enough to remove him from the scope of federal regulation where, as here, his contribution, taken together with that of many others similarly situated, if far from trivial." Thus trivial, local, noncommercial activity could trigger federal regulation if it affected commerce in the "aggregate."

For nearly seventy years, the Court deferred almost totally to ever broader regulation by Congress under the power over commerce. In the vitally important cases *Katzenbach v. McClung* (1964) and *Heart of Atlanta Motel v. United States* (1964), the Court resoundingly endorsed the use of the affecting commerce test as well as the aggregation test of *Wickard* to sustain the public accommodations sections of the landmark 1964 Civil Rights Act. In both cases the Court endorsed reaching inside a state to regulate activities such as renting hotel rooms and restaurant service that, while commercial, might be only marginally interstate in themselves, on the grounds that the activities collectively affected commerce among the states. A federal police power was strengthened based on the *Wickard* rationale in 1971 in *Perez v. United States*, which upheld a federal criminal law against loan sharking. In 1981 the court similarly upheld an environmental law regulating strip mining in *Hodel v. Virginia Surface Mining and Reclamation Association*. Little seemed to stand in the way of Congress using the power over commerce for virtually any regulation of the economy, or of social matters that only affected economics.

However, directly regulating states themselves as economic actors gave the Court more difficulty. In *National League of Cities v. Usery* (1976), Justice William Rehnquist, writing for a closely divided Court, did try to set a limit by protecting "traditional" and "integral governmental functions" of state and local government from application to them as employers of the Fair Labor Standards Act provisions on hours and wages. To be sure, the Court had always noted that there were limits to the power over commerce, as it did even in *Wickard*. The *Usery* test proved unworkable, however, and was rejected in 1985 in *Garcia v. San Antonio Metropolitan Transit Authority*. *Garcia* adopted Herbert Wechsler's "political safeguards of federalism" doctrine—meaning that the electorate's hold over Congress and the president should be the main check on the power over commerce where it impinged on state and local government.

LOPEZ V. UNITED STATES

But the Court was still closely divided over federalism and the regulation of commerce. In 1992, in *New York v. United States*, the court struck down part of a federal commerce power-based law requiring New York to take title to nuclear waste, with Justice Sandra Day O'Conner finding that the national government could not simply "commandeer" state governments to follow federal directives on something as fundamental as taking title to property. The anticommandeering principle again was employed in *Printz v. United States* (1997), where the Court struck down part of the Brady Gun Control Bill requiring local police to do background checks on gun purchasers.

But the Court's most significant decision limiting the power over commerce among the states since 1937 came in *Lopez v. United States* (1995). Finding that the Gun-Free School Zone Act of 1990 went too far by making it a federal crime to possess a gun within 500 feet of a school, an activity neither commercial nor among the states, the Court posed some new limits on Congress's power to regulate commerce in order to prevent the power over commerce becoming "a general police power of the sort retained by the States." Writing for the five-member majority, Chief Justice Rehnquist addressed the question of whether things affecting commerce needed to substantially or significantly affect commerce, choosing "substantially." The Court also posed the additional requirement that the power over commerce among the states could only apply to things that were economic in nature. Rehnquist's majority and the concurring opinions by Justices Anthony Kennedy and O'Conner focused heavily on the need to protect federalism from limitless federal power, while Justice Clarence Thomas's concurrence urged a return to what he asserted was the framers' intent that the power over commerce only regulate buying, selling, barter, and transportation.

The only major case explicitly based on *Lopez* so far has been *U.S. v. Morrison* (2000), which struck down the Violence against Women Act as exceeding the power over commerce among the states. However, following the path of *New York v. United States* and expanding notions of inherent state sovereignty, since *Lopez* the same five justices have struck down parts of the Age Discrimination in Employment Act, *Kimel v. Florida Board of Regents* (2000), the Fair Labor Standards Act, *Alden v. Maine* (1999), and other acts granting citizens rights to sue states for violation of these laws under federal laws passed under the power to regulate commerce among the states. The Court has used similar logic to weaken the power over Indian commerce. Though these decisions are based on the Court's desire to give greater scope to the inherent sovereignty or dignity of the states, the practical effect of these "state sovereignty" and "anticommandeering" decisions is to further limit the reach of the power to regulate commerce among the states, since most of the laws struck down were passed under the power over commerce.

THE DORMANT COMMERCE CLAUSE AND PREEMPTION

As mentioned above, before the Court began addressing the validity of positive legislation by Congress in the late 1880s, most of the Court's concern with the power over commerce concerned limits on state action implicit in the national power over commerce, the court-created dormant Commerce Clause doctrine. In some ways this power protects federalism by keeping states from exploiting each other or injuring the national market from which ultimately they themselves benefit, though it may also stifle creative policies. The Court's approach now focuses on striking down state laws that either facially discriminate against commerce, laws that are facially neutral but that in fact have a protectionist purpose or effect, and those that are facially neutral but still burden commerce. The first category is exemplified by *Philadelphia v. New Jersey* (1978), where the latter state's law against out-of-state trash was struck down as overt discrimination. However, in *Maine v. Taylor* (1986), the court allowed Maine to ban out-of-state baitfish to protect its own stock from disease. In *Camps Newfound/Owatonna, Inc. v. Town of Harrison* (1997), the court struck down as facially discriminatory a state exemption from property tax for in-state nonprofit corporations, but not those of out of state. The second category is perhaps best exemplified by *H. P. Hood & Sons v. Du Mond* (1949), where the court struck New York's denial of a license for a milk-receiving depot in New York for a Boston milk distributor on the grounds that it would lead to "destructive competition in a market already adequately served." The Court found that this seemingly neutral purpose masked a desire to protect local depots from out-of-state competition. The last category was given its modern formulation in *Pike v. Bruce Church, Inc.* (1970), where the court said a "legitimate local interest" that burdens commerce incidentally might be upheld depending on the purpose and whether less burdensome means are available to promote the local purpose.

An exception to the dormant Commerce Clause is the "market participant" doctrine, which allows states and localities to provide goods and services in the marketplace and prefer their own citizens as consumers or providers. The most recent consideration of this doctrine, however, disallowed Alaska's requirement that lumber cut there must also be partially processed there, in *South-Central Timber Development, Inc. v. Wunnicke* (1984).

While some of the Court's attention has focused on how the dormant Commerce Clause and varying meanings of the power over commerce affect federalism, courts are often called upon to decide whether states are preempted by federal law. This doctrine too has varied somewhat over time, but now includes three situations: (1) where Congress has expressly preempted state law, which is normally relatively easy to determine; (2) where Congress has displayed an intent to occupy the field, called "field preemption"; and (3) implied preclusions. Naturally the latter two categories are heavily fact dependent. A controversial finding of federal preemption under the foreign affairs powers is *Crosby v. National Foreign Trade Council* (2000), discussed under the power over foreign trade. *SEE ALSO: Cooley v. Board of Wardens*; Commerce with the Indian Tribes; Commerce with Foreign Nations; Eleventh Amendment; *Gibbons v. Ogden*; Marshall, John; O'Connor, Sandra Day; Preemption; Rehnquist, William; Taney, Roger Brooke

BIBLIOGRAPHY: Edward S. Corwin, *The Commerce Power versus States Rights* (Gloucester, MA: Peter Smith, 1962); Felix Frankfurter, *The Commerce Clause under Marshall, Taney and Waite* (Chicago: Quadrangle Books, 1964); Kathleen M. Sullivan and Gerald Gunther, *Constitutional Law*, 14th ed. (New York: Foundation Press, 2001); and Laurence H. Tribe, *American Constitutional Law*, 3rd ed. (New York: Foundation Press, 2000).

CONRAD J. WEILER JR.

Commerce with Foreign Nations   The Article I, Section 8, power to regulate foreign commerce, the particular power that in many ways brought about the Constitution, has not caused the Court to deal with the definitional problems, controversy, or direct conflict with state regulations that the power over commerce among the states has generated. Also, even though the language of the Constitution places all three aspects of commerce—among the states, foreign, and with the Indian tribes—under the same extent of regulatory power, a point that James Madison himself conceded, and even though the power over foreign commerce operates under somewhat similar doctrines of "dormant foreign commerce power" and preemption where Congress has acted, in recent years, especially, the federal power over foreign commerce has been construed more broadly and with less deference to federalism than its domestic analogue.

Like the power over commerce among the states, the Court did not rule on the extent of the power over foreign commerce for decades after the Constitution went into effect, the first test coming in 1827 in *Brown v. Maryland*, and like other commerce cases until the late 1880s, this too involved less the definition of federal power than the Court enforced dormant Foreign Commerce Clause. *Brown* in-

ARTICLE I, SECTION 8, CLAUSE 3

To regulate Commerce with foreign Nations, and among the several States, and with the Indian Tribes.

volved a Maryland license required of importers of goods from abroad. Chief Justice John Marshall sustained challenges to the law based both on the ban on state import duties in Article I, Section 10, and as an interference with foreign commerce. Marshall's opinion stated that while goods from abroad were still in their "original packet," they could not be taxed by a state. Marshall's implication that the original packet doctrine applied to goods imported from sister states as well was explicitly rejected in 1869 in *Woodruff v. Parham*, the Court ruling that a local tax on all goods that did not discriminate against commerce among the states was acceptable. The dormant foreign commerce power, like its domestic counterpart, both drew upon some cases involving foreign commerce, and continued to be invoked with similar results regarding state laws.

Since the great changes in the nation's involvement in international affairs resulting from World War II and the extraordinary dangers of the Cold War, the Court has given more deference to the power over foreign commerce as well as sometimes joined it with a new implied foreign affairs power when state interests are involved. *Zschernig v. Miller* (1968) introduced this latter doctrine into federalism concerns. There, an Oregon inheritance law prohibiting aliens from inheriting property if their own country did not allow Americans the same right, a law aimed at Communist countries, was overturned by the Court as interfering in foreign affairs because it had "great potential for disruption or embarassment." This decision had deep roots in cases such as *Missouri v. Holland* (1920), where Justice Oliver Wendell Holmes wrote in upholding a treaty protecting migratory birds from hunting, which Missouri argued was a power reserved to it, and that the Tenth Amendment had no bearing on foreign affairs. Another source of *Zschernig* was the Court's ruling in 1936 in *United States v. Curtiss-Wright Export Corp.* on the need for unity with the president as the "sole organ" of the government in foreign affairs.

Following this general trend of elevating foreign affairs above domestic considerations, the Court's criteria for federal preemption of state law include additional considerations than under the power over commerce among the states. The rules for evaluating state taxes affecting interstate commerce were set out in *Complete Auto Transit, Inc. v. Brady* (1977) and include "whether the tax is applied to an activity with a substantial nexus with the taxing state, is fairly apportioned, does not discriminate against interstate commerce, and is fairly related to the services provided by the State." In *Japan Line, Ltd. v. Los Angeles County* (1979), however, the Court applied these and added two more to overturn a local tax on Japanese shipping containers. The court held regarding foreign commerce that this tax might lead to double taxation if Japan also taxed the containers and that it would also disrupt the need for national uniformity in foreign commerce. To be sure, in *Barclay's Bank PLC v. Franchise Tax Board* (1994) the Supreme Court rejected a challenge to California's method for allocating, for tax purposes, the income earned by multinational corporations. Although California's allocation formula differed from that used by most other jurisdictions, California applied the same method to all corporations, foreign and domestic. The Court held that even though it placed incidental burdens on foreign commerce, the state statute did not discriminate against foreign commerce. However, the Court did ask whether the California statute impaired the federal government's ability to speak with "one voice" in foreign affairs.

The Court will uphold preemption outside of tax if Congress expresses an intent to preempt, if an intent to occupy a field can be implied, or if state law conflicts with federal. *Pacific Gas & Elec. Co. v. State Energy Resources Conservation & Development*

Comm'n (1983). The Court found conflict with the implied foreign affairs power to preempt a state law in *Crosby v. National Foreign Trade Council* (2000). Here, the same Court that a few years earlier divided over narrowing the domestic commerce power in *Lopez* unanimously avoided the federalism issues that had motivated *Lopez* when businesses challenged a Massachusetts law prohibiting the state from purchasing goods or services from companies doing business in Myanmar (Burma), reflecting widespread disapproval of the despotic regime there. Later, Congress passed a law empowering the president to prevent American investment in Myanmar and to try to secure better treatment of human rights. Though this law was passed in part under the power to regulate foreign commerce, the Court framed the issue as one of foreign policy, and struck down the Massachusetts law because it was an "obstacle" to the president's ability to "speak for the United States" in the conduct of foreign policy.

Potential challenges for federalism are presented by multilateral trade agreements such as the North American Free Trade Agreement (NAFTA) and the World Trade Organization (WTO) passed under the foreign commerce power. These agreements subject state laws to a wide range of international standards and sanctions, such as the Agreement on Government Procurement that was partly at issue in *Crosby*, and the threat made by the European Union in 2003 to target the products of individual states after winning a dispute before the WTO over President Bush's steel tariffs. Though the framers intended to protect states by requiring that major agreements with other countries be approved by two-thirds of the Senate as treaties, not by congressional majority under the power over foreign commerce, the loss of this distinction has been accepted. In general, the power to regulate foreign commerce today is not subject to the same federalistic limits as the power over commerce among the states. *SEE ALSO:* Commerce with the Indian Tribes; *Crosby v. National Foreign Trade Council*; *Missouri v. Holland*; Preemption

BIBLIOGRAPHY: Louis Henkin, *Foreign Affairs and the Constitution*, 2nd ed. (Oxford: Clarendon Press, 1996); Peter J. Spiro, "The Role of the States in Foreign Affairs: Foreign Relations Federalism," *University Colorado Law Review* 70 (1999): 1223; and Kathleen M. Sullivan and Gerald Gunther, *Constitutional Law*, 14th ed. (New York: Foundation Press, 2001).

CONRAD J. WEILER JR.

Commerce with the Indian Tribes   The power to regulate commerce with the Indian Tribes was placed in the Constitution to clarify and continue a power over Indian commerce and to generally manage Indian affairs, a power that was already in the Articles of Confederation but had not stopped some states from dealings with Indians in ways detrimental to the national interest. As a means to give the federal government power to deal with the then–still numerous and powerful prior inhabitants of the land, in addition to the treaty and military powers and the power to dispose of and make rules for federal territory, this power was seen primarily as a limit on the states. By placing the Indian tribes on the same level as foreign nations and the states, this power is thought to recognize the tribes as semisovereign—as "third sovereigns" in our system. It is sometimes difficult to separate the different constitutional sources of power over the Indians underlying policy, but the power over Indian commerce is very important, especially after 1871, when the United States ceased making treaties with the Indians.

The power over Indian commerce, including a dormant component and the capacity to preempt state law even in the absence of congressional legislation, then assumed greater importance after 1871, and is now the main way that the national government exerts its sovereignty over the Indians. This branch of the power over commerce has a broader reach than the other two, especially the power over commerce among the states. Unlike that power, which is limited in a number of ways in favor of state sovereignty, the Indian commerce power has long been regarded as a source of absolute control over all manner of Indian affairs, not limited by any narrow definition of commerce or limits that the Tenth Amendment may place on commerce among the states.

The foundational concepts supporting federal power over Indians were laid down in a trilogy of decisions by Chief Justice John Marshall. In *Johnson v. McIntosh* (1823), *Cherokee Nation v. Georgia* (1831), and *Worcester v. Georgia* (1832), Marshall designated the Indians as "domestic dependent nations," something akin to wards of the federal government, which also controlled the land they were on, but remaining a distinct people with the right to rule themselves within the larger framework of federal law, free from interference from the states. Over the years there have been numerous changes in the direction of what have often been detrimental policies toward the Indians, but the basic constitutional framework and assumptions laid down by Marshall have remained, at least until recently.

By the New Deal, an attempt to give some meaningful recognition to Indian independence and self-governance began, but recent years have seen an increase of state power relative to that of both the Indian tribes and the power of Congress to regulate them, especially under the Rehnquist Court's federalism jurisprudence, which has asserted the power of the Court over application of the Indian commerce power. In *Seminole Tribe of Florida v. Florida* (1995), the Court ruled that Congress's Indian Commerce Clause power does not extend to infringing the inherent sovereignty of the states by forcing them to negotiate in good faith with Indians over Indian gambling enterprises, an emerging area of great activity for Indian tribes that Congress had tried to structure in a balanced way. This decision had far broader effects than merely on the regulation of Indian commerce, becoming a basis of the emerging Eleventh Amendment inherent state sovereignty decisions of the Court, which have also limited the reach of the power over commerce among the states and the Section 5 enforcement power of the Fourteenth Amendment. *SEE ALSO:* American Indians and Federalism; Eleventh Amendment; Foreign Policy; Native American Sovereignty; *Seminole Tribe of Florida v. Florida*

BIBLIOGRAPHY: Robert N. Clinton, "Sovereignty and the Native American Nation: The Dormant Indian Commerce Clause," *Connecticut Law Review* 27 (1995): 1055; "Native Americans," in *The Oxford Companion to the Supreme Court of the United States*, ed. Kermit Hall (New York: Oxford University Press, 1992), 577–81; and Alex Tallchief Skibine, "The Dialogic of Federalism in Federal Indian Law and the Rehnquist Court: The Need for Coherence and Integration," *Texas Forum on Civil Liberties & Civil Rights* 8 (2003): 1.

CONRAD J. WEILER JR.

Community Development Block Grants The Community Development Block Grant (CDBG) program, initially authorized by the Housing and Community Development Act of 1974, was one of the centerpieces of President Richard Nixon's New Federalism reforms designed to decentralize decision-making responsibilities to state and local governments. The CDBG program consolidated seven existing categorical grant programs—including urban renewal and Model Cities—into a block grant for community development, with funding distributed on an annual basis to eligible jurisdictions.

The statute established two categories of funding under CDBG—metropolitan (entitlement) and nonmetropolitan (discretionary). Entitlement jurisdictions, which included all central cities, all cities with populations of 50,000 or more, and urban counties with a population of at least 200,000 that were also authorized by their state governments to undertake housing and community development activities, were guaranteed block grant funds on an annual basis as determined by a formula. Communities that did not qualify for entitlement status were permitted to apply for discretionary funding under the Small Cities component of the program.

In an effort to direct a greater share of CDBG funding to needier jurisdictions, Congress added a second formula when the program was reauthorized in 1977. Funding for entitlement jurisdictions is distributed through a dual formula system, with communities receiving their grant based on one of two formulas: formula A, which is based on population, overcrowded housing, and poverty; or formula B, which is based on growth lag, age of housing, and poverty. Entitlement communities receive their grant through whichever formula yields the larger grant, though all grants are prorated down to insure that total funding falls within the amount appropriated by Congress.

The proposal that President Nixon sent to Congress initially conceived of CDBG as a special revenue-sharing program, whereas the Congress called its proposal a "block grant." These differences in perception were more than just semantics. At the core was the question of how much control the federal government would have over recipient jurisdictions—particularly on the front-end or application review stage—and the extent to which communities should be guided by federal goals and objectives in determining how they would use their block grant funds. While the legislation that was signed into law involved compromises on both sides, the program that emerged was much closer to the ideal type of a block grant than revenue sharing. The legislation called for a detailed annual application and front-end review by federal officials and also required each entitlement jurisdiction to develop a community development program that was consistent with national objectives. Section 104(b)(2) of the legislation identified three primary objectives for the CDBG program: to (1) "give maximum feasible priority to activities which will benefit low- or moderate-income families," (2) "aid in the prevention or elimination of slums or blight," and (3) "meet other community development needs having a particular urgency."

Interpretation of the meaning of those objectives and the relative importance of them (i.e., should one objective be more important than the others?) was the source of considerable tension between Congress, the executive branch, and select entitlement jurisdictions during the early years of the program. Generally, Republican administrations (such as Ford and Reagan) took a "hands-off" interpretation of the legislation and gave entitlement communities broad discretion in the design and administration of their community development programs. When President Jimmy Carter took office in 1977, HUD moved quickly to tighten the social and geographic targeting objectives of the CDBG program, placing strong emphasis on insuring that CDBG funds were being directed to activities that would primarily benefit low and moderate-income families. Following the election of Ronald Reagan in 1980, HUD moved quickly to substantially relax the application and front-end review requirements and also shifted its position on the three national objectives, choosing to treat them as "coequal" objectives rather than give primary importance to the objective of primarily benefiting low- and moderate-income families.

The Reagan administration also succeeded in changing the nature of the discretionary portion of the CDBG program, transferring control over the distribution of funds to nonentitlement cities from the federal government to the states through the creation of a state-administered Small Cities Community Development Block Grant program.

In fiscal 2005, $2.9 billion in CDBG funds were awarded to more than 1,100 entitlement jurisdictions, including 614 central cities, 332 suburban cities, and 165 urban counties. The largest grants were awarded to New York City ($207 million), Chicago ($95 million), and Los Angeles ($83 million). Overall, 13 cities received block grants of $20 million or more.

CDBG funds are used for a wide variety of purposes by recipient jurisdictions. In fiscal 2004, one-third of the $4.7 billion spent by all CDBG recipients were used for public facilities and improvements, 24 percent was spent on housing activities, 11 percent for public services, 9 percent for economic development, and 14 percent for planning and administration. The single largest program use among entitlement cities was housing (27 percent), predominantly the rehabilitation of owner-occupied housing, followed closely by public improvements (24 percent). More than half of the funds spent through the state-administered portion of the CDBG program for nonentitlement communities was awarded for public improvements and facilities (56 percent) followed by housing (16 percent) and economic development (15 percent) activities. *SEE ALSO:* Block Grants; Economic Development; Housing; Johnson, Lyndon B.; Nixon, Richard M.; Reagan, Ronald W.; Revenue Sharing

BIBLIOGRAPHY: Paul R. Dommel and Associates, *Decentralizing Community Development* (Washington, DC: Brookings Institution, 1982); Edward T. Jennings Jr., Dale Krane, Alex N. Pattakos, and B. J. Reed, *From Nation to States: The Small Cities Community Development Block Grant Program* (Albany: State University of New York Press, 1986); Michael J. Rich, *Federal Policymaking and the Poor: National Goals, Local Choices, and Distributional Outcomes* (Princeton, NJ: Princeton University Press, 1993); Christopher Walker, Paul R. Dommel, Harry P. Hatry, Amy Bogdon, and Patrick Boxall, *Federal Funds, Local Choices: An Evaluation of the Community Development Block Grant Program* (Washington, DC: Urban Institute, 1994); and Christopher Walker, Christopher Hayes, George Galster, Patrick Boxall, and Jennifer E. H. Johnson, *The Impact of CDBG Spending on Urban Neighborhoods* (Washington, DC: Urban Institute, 2002).

MICHAEL J. RICH

Competitive Federalism   "Competitive federalism" refers to the existence and desirability of competition among governments and jurisdictions in a federal political system. Competition among governments can be defined as rivalry whereby each government attempts to obtain some scarce benefit or resource (e.g., foreign investment) or to avoid a certain cost (e.g., a large welfare population). Such competition is likely to occur in a federal system characterized by noncentralization, by substantial self-governing authority on the part of the system's constituent governments (e.g., states or provinces) as well as the national government, and by population mobility between the system's constituent governments (e.g., many individuals moving from one state to another). Competition is likely to be stifled when a federal system is highly centralized, constituent governments enjoy little power, and population mobility is low.

Generally, there are two types of competition among governments in a federal system: intergovernmental and interjurisdictional.

Intergovernmental competition, called vertical competition by some observers, entails competition among different orders of government having different powers, such as competition between the national government and state governments, competition between state governments and local governments, competition between a county and other local governments within its territory, and competition between general-purpose and special-purpose local governments. A principal cause of intergovernmental competition is forum shopping, namely, the tendency of voters and interest groups to seek redress of grievances by going from one government forum to another—federal, state, and local—seeking the best response. In addition, federal, state, and local officials compete to some extent with each other for voter affections. As James Madison argued in *The Federalist* No. 46, "If . . . the people should in future become more partial to the federal than State governments, the change can only result from such manifest and irresistible proofs of a better administration, as will overcome all their antecedent propensities."

Interjurisdictional competition, called horizontal competition by some observers, encompasses competition between governments having comparable powers in a federal system, such as competition among states (i.e., interstate competition) and competition among municipalities (i.e., interlocal competition). A principal cause of interjurisdictional competition is population mobility. That is, people and business firms "vote with their feet" by moving from one state or locality to another, thus putting pressure on state and local governments to compete with one another in order to retain and to attract residents and businesses.

Governments use fiscal tools (e.g., taxes and spending) as well as regulatory powers to compete with each other. A state government might, for example, seek to improve its comparative attractiveness for business investment by reducing certain taxes and improving its transportation infrastructure. The national government might compete with state governments by offering better services or superior protections of individual rights.

An advantage of intergovernmental competition is that it can sustain a sufficient balance of power in a federal system to prevent either the disintegration of the system into its constituent parts or the centralization of the system into monopolistic tyranny while, at the same time, improving responsiveness to citizens. A disadvantage of intergovernmental competition is that it can deteriorate into excessive spending and corruption as national and state officials compete for voter affections.

A common criticism of interjurisdictional competition is that state and local governments waste resources and race to the bottom in seeking to attract residents and businesses. That is, they offer wasteful tax incentives; spend tax money on needless projects; reduce important regulations, such as environmental regulation; and reduce certain types of spending, such as welfare spending, so as to attract certain residents and businesses and repel others, such as poor people. Advantages commonly attributed to interjurisdictional competition include greater fiscal discipline, better efficiency, more innovation, and races to the top as governments seek to attract and retain residents and businesses. *SEE ALSO:* Coercive Federalism; Cooperative Federalism; Dual Federalism

BIBLIOGRAPHY: Daphne A. Kenyon and John Kincaid, eds., *Competition among States and Local Governments: Efficiency and Equity in American Federalism* (Washington, DC: Urban Institute Press, 1991).

JOHN KINCAID

Comprehensive Employment and Training Act   The Comprehensive Employment and Training Act (CETA) represented an ambitious federal undertaking to decentralize government employment and training programs stemming from President Richard Nixon's "New Federalism" proposals. State and local labor market conditions varied greatly across the nation, as did target populations needing assistance. Local communities were thought best able to determine their own needs, resolve problems, and improve the conditions of those economically disadvantaged, unemployed, or underemployed. First enacted in 1973 by Congress, CETA was reauthorized in 1978 but was eventually replaced by the Job Training Partnership Act in 1982.

CETA programs spanned the service of four presidents—Nixon, Ford, Carter, and Reagan—and were often controversial. U.S. Department of Labor (USDOL) spending for employment and training during the Carter years totaled $34 billion, more than 2.5 times the amount during 1973–76, with about 4 million eligible individuals receiving training or public service jobs each year. Enormous expenditures, coupled with the decentralized nature of job creation and training efforts, brought allegations of fraud, waste, and abuse. Sometimes those who enrolled did not meet federally set eligibility criteria. Sometimes the temporary jobs filled by eligible individuals within state and local government agencies were ones originally paid for from local tax resources, so that the result was impermissible federal funds substitution and no net job creation. Lastly, job training for eligible individuals frequently did not lead to hoped-for permanent jobs.

Another controversy involved a lack of coordination with and bypassing of some state and local officials. CETA "prime sponsors" eligible to receive USDOL grants were cities and counties of more than 100,000 population, with governors responsible for operating "balance-of-state" programs covering largely rural areas only; thus, most federal block grant funds bypassed state governments. Discretionary funds made available to governors for statewide programs, including the operation of state employment and training councils, were intended to help coordinate the efforts of all prime sponsors and subcontractors, but did not result in such statewide cooperation. Moreover, USDOL grants made directly to Native Americans, migrants, and others bypassed all prime sponsors. State legislators, city council members, and others having appropriations and policy responsibilities felt left out of the CETA executive branch–centered process. So did the vocational education community, and local school board members whose schools were receiving CETA funds from prime sponsors.

Accordingly, CETA represents both noble federalism intentions and compassion in assisting those truly needing job training and employment, but also a lack of program effectiveness and governmental accountability. *SEE ALSO:* New Federalism (Nixon)

BIBLIOGRAPHY: Advisory Commission on Intergovernmental Relations, *The Comprehensive Employment and Training Act: Early Readings from a Hybrid Block Grant* (Washington, DC: ACIR, 1977); Illinois General Assembly, *The Comprehensive Employment and Training Act (CETA): A Critical Issue in Intergovernmental Relations* (Springfield: Illinois Commission on Intergovernmental Cooperation, 1979); William Mirengoff and Lester Rindler, *CETA: Manpower Programs under Local Control* (Washington, DC: National Academy of Sciences, 1978); and Bonnie B. Snedeker and David M. Snedeker, *CETA: Decentralization on Trial* (Salt Lake City, UT: Olympus Publishing Company, 1978).

ROBERT P. GOSS

Compromise of 1850   The sectional conflict that led to the Missouri Compromise of 1820 again came to a head after the Mexican War. Two issues aroused bitter debate in Congress: distributing new land in a way that would appease both the North and the South, and developing a more rigorous system for capturing and prosecuting fugitive slaves. The eventual answer was the Compromise of 1850. California was admitted as a free state, while New Mexico and Utah were allowed to choose their positions on slavery, both chose to be free. New Mexico received additional land from Texas, while the federal government agreed to pay Texas's war debt. In perhaps its most controversial move, Congress also passed a new Fugitive Slave Act that forced citizens to help capture slaves, waived fugitive slaves' right to a jury trial, and set up a new system of federal enforcement. Finally, the slave trade in Washington, D.C., was abolished.

The Compromise of 1850 was the result of one of the most infamous congressional battles in American history. Senator Henry Clay of Kentucky originally wanted to pass the provisions as a single, or omnibus, bill. But Clay's plan met resistance from both northern and southern congressmen. New York Senator William Seward argued against any expansion of slavery, claiming it was prohibited by a "higher law than the Constitution." Conversely, John C. Calhoun of South Carolina claimed that attacking slavery cut "the cords which bind these states together." When the omnibus bill came before Congress, it failed.

Senator Stephen A. Douglas of Illinois, an ardent supporter of the compromise, intervened with a new plan. He broke the omnibus bill into individual bills, sensing that the ideas of passing them as one had created unnecessary political dispute. His strategy worked, as the series of bills passed Congress. Again, a complicated compromise had succeeded at cooling the dispute between the North and South over the existence, enforcement, and expansion of the "peculiar institution." But the issue would not go away, and tensions continued to build over slavery, culminating in the Civil War only eleven years later. *SEE ALSO:* Admission of New States; Calhoun, John C.; Civil War; Clay, Henry; Fugitive Slave Acts; Missouri Compromise of 1820; Slavery; States' Rights

ROBERT HEINRICH

Concurrent Powers   The federal government is a government of delegated powers, meaning that it has only those powers delegated to it by the Constitution. All other powers, the Tenth Amendment reads, "are reserved to the states . . . or to the people." The powers delegated to the federal government may be exclusive, meaning that they may be exercised only by the federal government, or they may be concurrent, meaning that they can be exercised by both the federal and state governments. While the term "concurrent" is used only in the Eighteenth Amendment, granting both the federal government and the states concurrent authority to enforce Prohibition, other powers may be concurrent if they are not granted exclusively to the federal government by the explicit language of the Constitution, or if the exercise of state authority in the same domain is not incompatible with the exercise of national power.

Deciding which powers are exclusive and which are concurrent is a difficult and continuing undertaking. In the modern period, the issue is usually framed in the context of preemption, and the U.S. Supreme Court has played an important role in determining whether the federal government has "occupied the field" to such an extent that state action in a given area is precluded, effectively making federal authority exclusive. *SEE ALSO:* Concurrent Powers; Preemption; Reserved Powers

ELLIS KATZ

Conditional Grants Conditional grants are monetary transfers from one level of government to another, either through competitive project grants or through more general block grants, which place conditions on the use of the transferred funds by the recipient government. The conditions may be either financial or substantive in nature. In other words, the grantor uses these grants to induce certain reactions on the part of the grantee in order to bring the lower-level government into line with the higher-level government's policy objectives. The greater the conditions placed upon the grant, the less flexible is the program for the recipient government. Financial conditions usually entail matching requirements, and they are typically stated as a percentage of the grant amount or as a percentage of total project costs, and financial matching requirements must come from local revenues. On the other hand, substantive requirements reflect the nature of uses to which the recipient may apply the federal money. Many grant programs are for very specific uses, and therefore states may or may not elect to compete for them, based on their local needs and policy priorities.

As the federal grants-in-aid system evolved in the second half of the twentieth century, conditions on federal transfers grew in prominence. As James Sundquist (Sundquist and Davis 1969) noted, the grant conditions, matching requirements, and allocation formulas of early grants "reflected a good deal of federal deference" to state and local governments. But by the 1970s, Martha Derthick (1996) commented that the national government had made state and local governments "agents of its purposes through aggressive use of grant-in-aid conditions and partial preemptions." The shift from land grants to monetary grants in the nineteenth century gave way to a shift within monetary grants in the twentieth century toward greater specificity and, in particular, an increase in block grants (which were categorical in purpose) and project grants (which are specific in purpose). Given the inclusion of increased conditions on federal monies, intergovernmental transfers became less flexible for the recipient governments. While states are free to choose whether or not to compete for such grants, state reactions to fiscal pressure during times of recession and shrinking budgets include an increased dependence on the federal government for financial assistance. As a result, states often turned to federal programs to maintain programs and current service levels.

Through the combination of increased conditions on grants and the increased dependence by states on federal revenue, many came to fear that national policy objectives would displace state and local policy preferences. In other words, federal policy causes local discretionary revenue to be displaced from programs of local choice and expended on programs for which federal grant funds are available. The result is that state and local governments have established long-standing programs tailored to fit federal grant requirements. In most cases, the recipient government increases program spending by an amount less than that of the grant, but by more than would be expected from the same increase from local revenue; this response has been labeled the "flypaper effect." *SEE ALSO:* Block Grants; Categorical Grants; Crosscutting Requirements; Crossover Sanctions; Formula Grants; Grants-in-Aid; Project Grants; Rural Policy; Supremacy Clause: Article VI, Clause 2; Unfunded Mandates; Urban Policy

BIBLIOGRAPHY: Martha Derthick, "Crossing Thresholds: Federalism in the 1960s," *Journal of Policy History* 8 (1996): 64–80; Daniel J. Elazar, *American Federalism: A View from the States*, 2nd ed. (New York: Thomas Y. Crowell Company, 1972); George E. Hale and Marian Lief Palley, *The Politics of Federal Grants* (Washington, DC: CQ Press, 1981); Michael J. Rich, "Distributive Politics and the Allocation of Federal Grants," *American Political Science Review* 83, no. 1 (March 1989): 193; James L. Sundquist and David W. Davis, *Making Federalism Work* (Washington, DC: Brookings Institution, 1969); and Craig Volden, "Asymmetric Effects of Intergovernmental Grants: Analysis and Implication for U.S. Welfare Policy," *Publius* 29, no. 3 (Summer 1999): 51.

JEREMY L. HALL AND MICHAEL W. HAIL

Confederate States of America The Confederate States of America (CSA) had two constitutions, a Provisional Constitution that was in effect from February 8, 1861, to February 18, 1862, until the Permanent Constitution, ratified March 1861, became operational. The Provisional Constitution was expeditiously adopted in order to establish a provisional national government. It was modeled after the U.S. Constitution, with the notable exceptions of a unicameral legislature with each state having one vote and the president being elected by the Congress to serve one six-year term.

During the transition from the U.S. to the CSA Constitutions, U.S. statutes and case law remained in force unless repealed by the CSA Congress or overturned by CSA courts. The CSA Constitution was firmly grounded in American constitutionalism. The CSA's constitutional innovations reflected the southern states' preference for states' rights and not rejection of unionism per se. They were very much convinced of the utility of membership in a voluntary union consisting of other states acting in concert for their collective interests. They were also convinced that the Union from which they recently seceded provided a constitutional blueprint from which to structure a reformed union geared toward the collective interests of its member states.

Although much of the CSA Constitution is a word-for-word copy of the U.S. Constitution, it includes significant structural changes (e.g., incorporating the first ten amendments into the text of the constitution) and linguistic modifications (e.g., removing the general welfare clauses) from the U.S. Constitution. Those modifications were designed to shift the balance of governmental powers to the states. For example, it was well known by southern statesmen that U.S. Supreme Court justices have pedantically scoured the structure and wording of the U.S. Constitution to determine the power relations between the national and state governments. Changes to be found in the CSA Constitution substantively alter mostly CSA legislative, and to a lesser extent

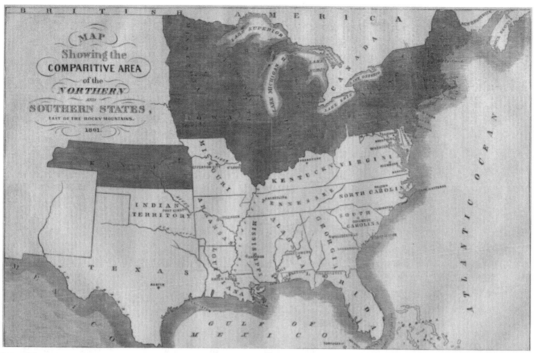

Map showing the Confederate States of America. Courtesy of Son of the South (www.sonofthesouth.net).

executive and juridical, policy prerogatives over the states. An overview of the CSA Constitution makes this clear.

The CSA preamble affirms that the people of the Confederacy ordained and established the CSA Constitution through their respective states, "each State acting in its sovereign and independent character." A national constitution ordained and established by the people of the nation places the national unit as the principal and the states as its agents, whereas a national constitution with the states as the principals and the national government as their agent alters the power relations between the national and state governments. Accordingly, if a state is not the source of authority (i.e., a principal), it cannot withdraw that authority from the national government when its interests dictate that it should. The CSA preamble clarifies that it was the individual states, not the collective national will of the people, that are the principals. Moreover, the CSA framers deleted the phrases "provide for the common defense" and "promote the general Welfare" in the attempt to particularize the document's application to the states, in contradistinction to a general application to the people of the CSA. This is closer to the commitment to states' rights found in Article II of the Articles of Confederation: "Each State retains its sovereignty, freedom and independence, and every Power, Jurisdiction and rights, which is not by this confederation expressly delegated to the United States, in Congress assembled."

The purpose of the CSA Constitution was to form a "permanent federal government," not a "more perfect Union." In his late antebellum statements, President Lincoln put the southern states on notice that "if destruction of the Union, by one, or by a part only, of the States, be lawfully possible, the Union is *less* perfect than before;

the Constitution having lost the vital element of perpetuity." As the Confederate framers insisted, a perfect union is one that is based upon the consent of its members, the states. Accordingly, the permanent CSA federal government stemmed from the CSA union. If the latter ceased to exist—that is, it being dissolved by the states, either individually within the borders of a particular state or collectively among all the states—the federal government would by default cease to exist. The CSA logic is (1) the states individually and voluntarily acceded to the CSA union delegated powers to realize certain common policy objectives shared with the other states, (2) states are subject to the jurisdiction of the CSA government's delegated powers while members of the CSA union, and (3) a state's secession from the CSA union placed the seceded state outside the jurisdiction of the CSA's delegated powers. In other words, the states do not exist for the union, but the union exists for the states. The "perfection" of the union is contingent upon its capacity to serve the interests of its member states, and not a perpetuity held coercively intact. This is why the framers of the CSA Constitution considered including a secession clause, but decided that such a clause would be superfluous in a voluntary union based upon the active consent of its member states.

The CSA Constitution also lacks the "general Welfare" clause as an objective of the union or the Congress. Removal of this phrase prevented the CSA Congress from exercising a general police power and intruding upon the police powers of the states.

The preamble invokes "the favor and guidance of Almighty God." Incorporating this transcendental order directly into the CSA Constitution made God the guarantor of its terms and the Constitution more than a legal document; it was a covenant among the states contingent upon their willingness to morally and ethically interact with one another.

In contrast to the U.S. Constitution, the CSA Constitution's vestment clause (Article I, Section 1) "delegates" rather than "grants" all legislative power to a Congress. The significance of this word change was made clear in the landmark case *McCulloch v. Maryland* (1819), through which Chief Justice John Marshall conferred on the national government granted legislative powers that, unlike delegated powers, may not be recalled by a state or states, but only collectively by the American people.

The CSA's preference for the states is reaffirmed in the reserved state powers, or Tenth Amendment. The CSA Tenth Amendment reads, "The powers not delegated to the Confederate States by the Constitution, nor prohibited by it to the States, are reserved to the States, respectively, or to the people thereof." Except for the last word, this is a duplicate of the U.S. Constitution's Tenth Amendment. The word "thereof" in the CSA Constitution neutralizes the prospects that the American people constitute an alternative repository of power to the states. Indeed, CSA powers are exercised directly on the Confederate people, but with states as the guardians as to how those powers are to be exercised. The addition of this word was intended to resolve uncertainties between the national and state governments over delegated and reserved powers.

Anticipating a deluge of immigration from northern states and abroad as the Confederacy commercially prospered, the Constitution disqualified foreign-born citizens from voting in elections for members of the House of Representatives (Article I, Section 2, Clause 1). By essentially disenfranchising nonindigenous Southerners, CSA framers manifest an appreciation of a southern community and attempted to prevent any relocated northern or western interests from percolating upward. However, new states were admitted to the Confederacy upon a two-thirds vote in the House and Senate (with the Senate voting by state; Article IV, Section 3). So, nonsouthern interests could have a voice in CSA politics, but only as a state—and such a state could only be admitted by two-thirds vote, whereas in the U.S. Constitution admission to the union requires only a majority vote.

State preeminence over the national government was affirmed by authorizing states to impeach federal judges and officers by a two-thirds vote of both branches of that state's legislature (Article I, Section 2). The CSA Congress could circumvent this state impeachment power by assigning CSA judicial and other federal officers beyond the limits of any one state. But such circumvention was unlikely, given the strong states' rights mindset of the Confederacy. The provision is a strong indication that the states were not to be subservient to CSA judges and bureaucrats, but the two-thirds vote requirement made that accountability judicially respectable.

Unlike the U.S. government, the CSA Constitution allowed executive officials a seat in both chambers of Congress to discuss measures pertaining to their department (Article I, Section 6, Clause 2). Unlike a committee hearing where executive department heads are questioned by legislators, this innovation was a nod toward cabinet government, through which cooperation between the two branches of government was to be enhanced, especially in light of the president being limited to a nonreeligible six-year term (Article II, Section 1).

The CSA Constitution authorized the president to line-item veto appropriations (Article I, Section 7, Clause 2). This provision provided the president with the means to thwart regional majorities from gaining the legislative advantage over regional minorities, a prominent concern of the southern states as they watched their influence in legislative politics decline.

Congress's appropriation power was constitutionally limited. These limitations included prohibitions against protectionist tariffs, internal improvements (except those paid by the users of and expended in those ports where paid to cover operational expenses), discharging debts through bankruptcy, and privatizing the CSA post office in 1863. Furthermore, Congress had to specify exact dollar amounts; it had to limit all bills and laws to one subject, noted in the title; and export duties and appropriation bills required a two-thirds majority vote (Article I, Sections 8 and 9).

The CSA Constitution's slave-related provisions acknowledged the slave issue to be of national importance and intentionally curtailed states' rights to import slaves from outside the Confederacy (Article I, Section 9, Clauses 1 and 2). The CSA Constitution let states determine whether to be slave or free, but, reflecting the *Dred Scott* U.S. Supreme Court decision, protected the right of owners to transit with their slaves through the CSA's states and territories (Article IV, Sections 2 and 3). However, strong consensus regarding slavery was likely guaranteed by prohibiting nonnative Southerners from voting for federal officials and by the two-thirds vote of the House and Senate required to admit new states, free or slave, into the Confederacy.

In the attempt to shore up states' rights in the event of the more mundane checks and balances breaking down, 3 states could convene a constitutional convention to address the concerns of a small minority of states (Article V, Section 1). Proposed constitutional amendments were ratified by a two-thirds approval of either state legislatures or state conventions. Technically, this could tie up the CSA government for long periods of time. But consensus of all member states, and not national governmental efficiency, was the objective. This clause was designed to procure the former.

The common thread that held these states together under the compact of the CSA Constitution was their commitment to states' rights, a commitment that has its origins in the American Anti-Federalist and Jeffersonian traditions of American federalism. The exigencies of war led the CSA to exercise powers that rankled states' rights advocates, such as national conscription and impressment policies. But, as noted above, the CSA Constitution equipped the states to reclaim the policy prerogatives of states' rights by constraining the legislative powers of the CSA Congress, limiting the CSA president to a onetime six-year term, empowering the states to impeach CSA officials, lowering the bar to convene constitutional conventions, and, if all else fails, seceding from the CSA. This was a form of American federalism much more resistant to the centralization of policy prerogatives at the national level and predicated upon the consent of all the states to a much greater extent than the U.S. Union. *SEE ALSO:* Articles of Confederation; Civil War; Constitutional Convention of 1787; Covenant; Welfare Policy; Internal Improvements; Lincoln, Abraham; Police Power; Reconstruction; Reserved Powers; Secession; Slavery; Sovereignty

BIBLIOGRAPHY: Marshall DeRosa, *The Confederate Constitution of 1861: An Inquiry into American Constitutionalism* (Columbia: University of Missouri Press, 1991); Daniel J. Elazar, *Building toward Civil War: Generational Rhythms in American Politics* (New York: Madison Books, 1992); Charles Lee, *The Confederate Constitutions* (Chapel Hill: University of North Carolina Press, 1963); Forrest McDonald, *States' Rights and Union: Imperium in Imperio* (Lawrence: University Press of Kansas, 2000); and George C. Rable, *The Confederate Republic: A Revolution against Politics* (Chapel Hill: University of North Carolina Press, 1994).

MARSHALL DeROSA

Connecticut Compromise   The Connecticut Compromise was a proposal in the Constitutional Convention of 1787 to create a bicameral legislature composed of a Senate, with equal representation of the states, and a House of Representatives apportioned according to population. This proposal helped solved the difficult dispute over whether the character of the national government should be confederal or national and how representation in Congress should be allocated. Representatives from the more populous states generally wanted representation to be based on population, as presented in the Virginia Plan. Representatives from the small states generally preferred a confederal approach where states enjoy equal representation in the legislature, as expressed in the New Jersey Plan. The Connecticut Compromise drew from each to create the bicameral U.S. Congress. The result is a national government that is neither wholly confederal nor wholly national, but a hybrid of federal and confederal elements never before seen in government.

The Connecticut Compromise created a distinct form of federal government. A confederal government is a federation with limited powers to direct the participating, sovereign states and no authority over the individual states' citizens. A national government consolidates the states into a single government with authority over the states and their citizens. A federal system of government mixes these two distinct forms of government. The founders considered various versions of a federal system at the Constitutional Convention. The Virginia Plan proposed a federal system that divided and separated the powers and operations of the national and state governments so that the national government was of a purely national character, but states retained authority and responsibility over specific issues that the national government could not contravene. The Connecticut Compromise interjected federal elements (the equal representation of the states) into the national government and paved the way for other federal elements (such as the Electoral College) to be added as well (Zuckert 1986).

By giving the states equal representation in the Senate, the Connecticut Compromise appeared to give the states a significant role in checking and balancing power in the national government. Yet other constitutional provisions released senators from state control to act independently. Unlike representatives under the Articles of Confederation and Constitutional Convention, the Constitution requires that senators be paid by the national government, serve six-year terms (the longest of any elected federal official), and vote individually rather than as a state bloc. These three constitutional elements gave senators a certain independence from the state legislatures that elected them to deliberate with other senators and vote according to what they thought would benefit the states as members of the union. In other words, the structure of the Senate is federal, but the operations of the Senate are national (Malbin 1987).

Largely as a result of the Connecticut Compromise, the United States' federal system has been referred to by some scholars and jurists as "a bundle of compromises." Yet, the United States' federal system of government is more than a bundle of compromises. Many of those attending the Constitutional Convention came away thinking that the federal system created by the Constitution was a "singular and remarkable" feat of achievement. John Dickenson, who proposed the Connecticut Compromise, wrote, "There is another improvement equally deserving regard, and that is, the varied representation of sovereignties and people in the constitution now proposed. It has been said, that this representation was a mere compromise. It was not a mere compromise. The equal representation of each state in one branch of the legislature, was an original substantive proposition." The two strongest opponents of inserting federal elements into the national government, James Madison and James Wilson, later viewed this change positively. James Madison referred to the federal system as "a system without a precedent ancient or modern, a system founded on popular rights, and so combining a federal form with the forms of individual Republics, as may enable each to supply the defects of the other and obtain the advantages of both." And James Wilson of Pennsylvania remarked, "I will confess that in the organization of this body a compromise between contending interests is discernible; and when we reflect how various the laws, commerce, habits, population and extent of the confederated States, this evidence of mutual concession and accommodation ought rather to command a generous applause, than to excite jealousy and reproach. For my part, my admiration can only be equaled by my astonishment in beholding so perfect a system formed from such heterogeneous materials."

Without the Connecticut Compromise, it is very likely that the Constitutional Convention would have foundered. The Connecticut Compromise provided a means out of the impasse by conceiving of a unique form of government that mixed federal elements into a national government. By combining confederal and national government elements, the founders crafted a unique form of government that has become known as "federal government." *SEE ALSO:* Articles of Confederation; Constitutional Convention of 1787; Electoral College; *The Federalist Papers*; Hamilton, Alexander; Madison, James; Seventeenth Amendment; State Legislatures; U.S. Congress; Virginia Plan

BIBLIOGRAPHY: Alexander Hamilton, James Madison, and John Jay, "39," in *The Federalist Papers*, ed. Clinton Rossiter (New York: New American Library, 1961); Michael J.

Malbin, "Congress during the Convention and Ratification," in *The Framing and Ratification of the Constitution*, ed. Leonard W. Levy and Dennis J. Mahoney, 185–208 (New York: Macmillan, 1987); and Michael Zuckert, "Federalism and the Founding: Toward a Reinterpretation of the Constitutional Convention," *Review of Politics* 48 (1986): 166–210.

TROY E. SMITH

Constitutional Convention of 1787　The Constitutional Convention was a signal event in the history of federalism for it was there that the American style of federalism originated. The innovations in theory and design introduced in American federalism have in turn revolutionized the practice of federalism worldwide.

The Convention was the gathering of delegates from 12 of the new American states—Rhode Island never did participate—that wrote the Constitution for the union. The meeting, originally scheduled to open in Philadelphia on May 14, 1787, did not actually begin until May 25, when a sufficient number of delegations finally arrived to make it possible to conduct deliberations. The Convention ended on September 17, when the delegates signed the draft constitution they had prepared.

The proposed constitution was to replace the Articles of Confederation, the constitution of the American union in force when the Convention met. Even though the Articles had been formally in place only since 1781, the Constitutional Convention was the fruit of many years' efforts throughout America to revise the existing confederal union. Those efforts, largely frustrated by the requirement of unanimous consent by all states to any changes in the Articles, had reached a peak of sorts in the Annapolis Convention of 1786. That meeting had been called to discuss commercial matters of mutual interest to the states, matters over which the government under the Articles had no power. The Annapolis Convention fell far short of success, however, for delegates from only 5 states appeared by the time the conference was scheduled to begin. One reason why attendance was so sparse was the prevailing conviction that more than commercial reform was needed to invigorate the governance of the union. In line with that thought, the delegates who did come to Annapolis, rather than concede the failure of their assembly, took the occasion to call for a general convention to meet in Philadelphia the following year "to take into consideration the situation of the United States, [and] to devise such further provisions as shall appear to them to render the constitution of the Federal Government adequate to the exigencies of the Union." The states responded with greater alacrity to this invitation, which then encouraged Congress under the Articles to add its endorsement to a convention in February 1787. One reason for the better response to this second call for a general gathering was the outbreak of Shays's Rebellion in western Massachusetts in August 1786. This rebellion was the result of an economic downturn coupled with the effort by Massachusetts to pay off its war debt quickly through heavy taxes, the results of which were a spate of farm foreclosures and the emergence of a group of angry and desperate farmers who took up arms to attempt to ease their situation. The Massachusetts militia was able to handle the uprising, but a wave of concern was felt throughout the union, for the Articles government had once again proved its feebleness when it was unable to contribute any significant aid to the effort to put down the insurrection.

At one time or another, 55 delegates from the 12 participating states took part in the Convention, but there was fluctuation at the fringes as some delegates came and went. At one point, for example, New York was completely unrepresented, for the majority of its delegates, quite unsympathetic to the direction in which the Convention was moving, just went home. The delegates were for the most part among the most distinguished men in the United States, including George Washington and Benjamin Franklin, probably the two best-known figures in the United States. All the delegates were prominent in the politics of their home states and many, like James Madison, had been active in the Government of the Confederation during and after the Revolution. Thirty-nine of the fifty-five had served in the Confederation Congress. Important figures were absent as well. Thomas Jefferson and John Adams were in Europe as diplomats. Moreover, some well-known leaders, like Patrick Henry of Virginia, suspicious of the intentions of those supporting the Convention, declined to attend. Some of these men, like Henry and fellow Virginian Richard Henry Lee, became leaders of the movement to oppose ratification of the new constitution after the Convention concluded its work.

After the resounding failure of previous efforts to reform the Articles, the success of the Convention is all the more remarkable. Three factors seem especially significant. First, the situation facing the American union was increasingly recognized as rather desperate. In addition to the scare of Shays's Rebellion, the government under the Articles faced financial insolvency, ineffectiveness in foreign relations, and weakness at home. A consensus had grown that some change was necessary if the union was to survive. Secondly, some of the delegates had begun to think about the problems of union in a more than ad hoc fashion. Previous efforts at reform had been narrowly focused on particular problems as they emerged. During the year between the Annapolis and Philadelphia gatherings, James Madison in particular had been thinking about the needs of federal governance in a broader perspective. The problem of the Articles, he concluded, derived not from this or that particular defect, but from more fundamental errors of theory and design. The approach to both federal union and republican governance needed a major overhaul. The broader perspectives that Madison and others brought to Philadelphia helped break through the various stalemates that had dominated politics pre-1787.

The rules of procedure adopted by the Convention at its opening also helped greatly. The most important, probably, was the decision to maintain secrecy for the proceedings, a resolve that was remarkably well kept to. The secrecy of the Convention's deliberations gave delegates insulation from immediate scrutiny, which allowed them to consider the rather radical reforms that were immediately laid before them, and which eventually evolved into the Constitution. Since their work was, at the end of the day, to face public scrutiny and consent or rejection, there was nothing undemocratic or inappropriate about the secrecy of the proceedings. Also important was the selection of George Washington as presiding officer of the Convention. His unrivaled prestige and gravity of character lent authority to the proceedings for those in Philadelphia and to the final result for those in the country at large.

More controversial than either of the above two initial decisions, and more ambiguous in its contribution to a successful outcome, was the adoption of the rule that state delegations would each possess one vote in the Convention, the same rule that prevailed in the Articles Congress. Delegates from larger states sought a weighted voting system in which states like Virginia, large and wealthy, would have more voting power than, say, tiny Delaware. The equal voting rule gave the smaller states much more power to influence the outcome than would have been the case under the other system and on occasion led to tense moments when the smaller states were able to stymie the larger states. Nonetheless, on balance the equal voting rule also probably contributed to the

Convention's success by encouraging accommodation and compromise, which led to a document that all the states could more readily agree to accept.

From the point of view of federalism, the Convention conveniently divides into two large units. The dividing point is the so-called Connecticut Compromise, which put in place the main features of the federal system. Almost at the very beginning of the Convention, Governor Edmund Randolph of Virginia rose to offer a constitutional plan on behalf of his state's delegation. This plan, known to history as the Virginia Plan, was in the main the result of Madison's constitutional thinking in the period before the Convention met. While most Americans expected the Convention to come up with some sort of revision of the Articles of Confederation, the Virginia Plan took an entirely different tack right at the outset. It did not begin with the Articles, but in effect scrapped them and began afresh with a completely new outline for the government of the union.

Since the Convention had been called to revise the Articles, many delegates and later many in the country were concerned that the Convention stepped outside the bounds of its mandate when it took up the revolutionary Virginia Plan. Madison had concluded that a complete departure from the Articles was required because on the two key constitutional issues—federalism and republicanism—the Articles were radically deficient. In order to be effective, the government of the union had to be able to execute its own laws directly on its own citizens. The government of the union therefore had to have its own instrumentalities of action, an executive and a judiciary, and could not persist as a merely rule-recommending body as was the case under the Articles. This insight produced the revolutionary element of American federalism: instead of serving as a corporate entity relating to other corporate entities, its member states, the government of the union would have a direct legal and political relationship with the citizens of the entire union, who would be its citizens as well as citizens of their respective states. Each level of government would have a sphere of action, or objects, or powers in which it would act on its citizens. Since the government of the union would operate directly on its own citizens, the citizens would have to have a hand in selecting the officers of the union government. The principles of the Revolution as expressed in the Declaration of Independence required no less. Thus, at least some parts of the union government must be selected by and responsible to the citizenry via direct elections; the Articles system according to which delegates to the Articles Congress were selected by the governments of the states had to be scrapped.

The union required a proper government, that is, a government with its own legislative, executive, and judicial agencies. According to American theories of legitimacy this government, like all governments, had to be a properly republican government. That theory of legitimacy had stood in the way of constructing a strong union in the past because Americans tended to believe that only relatively small republics were possible. Only in a small republic, they believed, could the necessary popular controls and political responsibility be imposed. Madison's studies led him to conclude that these American theories about republicanism were also false and that a different kind of republican institution could be at once legitimate according to the true principles of political right, could be implemented at the union level, and would be more effective overall as a governing institution. His Virginia Plan thus constituted a major new departure with respect to the principles for constructing a federal union and for constructing a republic.

Among other innovations in the Virginia Plan, two were particularly significant for the course of the Convention it its first phase. The principle of representation in the legislature was to shift entirely away from equal state representation to a system that would apportion representation in proportion to population, or wealth, or some composite measure of state power and significance. Proportional representation was to prevail in both houses of the proposed legislature.

The second innovation concerned the mode of selection of union officers. According to Madison's thinking, it was crucial to exclude agencies of the state government from having any role in selecting the officers under the new constitution. Thus, the Virginia Plan proposed that the people directly elect the lower house and that the lower house select the upper house. The two houses together would select the executive. The states as political entities would have no part.

The Convention was remarkably receptive at first to the very radical departures from precedent contained in the Virginia Plan. As the result of a clause-by-clause consideration of the plan, the Convention tentatively adopted its general principles and most of its specific features as well. There were, however, some reservations and hesitations expressed over matters such as the complete exclusion of the states and the rigorous application of the principle of proportional representation throughout the government. These reservations came to a head in mid-June when William Paterson of New Jersey, which was considered one of the "small states," introduced an alternative plan to that of Virginia. It was considerably less radical than the Virginia Plan, but also went well beyond the Articles of Confederation, testifying to the degree of consensus that had emerged around the proposition that significant change was required. The New Jersey Plan accepted the Madisonian idea that the government of the union required its own agencies of action, and it thus proposed (rather weak) executive and judicial organs. It also provided (limited) independent financial resources and military powers to the union government. At the same time, it reverted to the Articles scheme of a unicameral legislature with equal state representation, selected by the state governments.

The Convention treated the New Jersey proposals much less kindly than the Virginia resolutions and after a few days' debate voted them down, 7 states to 3 (with 1 divided). Nonetheless, the hesitations about the Virginia Plan remained. Part of the reservations came from the smaller states, which saw that the shift to the Virginia system of representation would lead to a large loss of power and influence in the councils of the union compared to what they had in the past. Joined to that were fears of a government as large, powerful, distant, and separate from the state governments as the Virginia Plan proposed. It was not enough, however, for the Convention to adopt one plan or another by majority vote, for all the states would have to individually accept the new constitution in order to become members of the union. Those with reservations made a stand on the principle of representation and debate in the weeks following rejection of the New Jersey Plan often became harsh, with some delegates even threatening to break up the Convention. Although there were "dead enders" on both sides, cool, centrist heads pushed toward an accommodation with those who opposed the representation formula in the Virginia Plan. The result was the Connecticut Compromise of early July, so named because members of the Connecticut delegation took a leading hand in working it out. The compromise introduced the famous formula of American federalism: proportional representation in the lower house, and equal representation by states in the upper house. The latter provision reinforced the earlier decision to allow the states a hand in the selection of the representatives to the upper house. The system as a whole thus has been plausibly described as a composite, in part constituting a union of the people of the United States, in part a union of the states.

Once the difficult issue of representation was worked out, the second phase of the

Convention went much more smoothly. This is not to say there were no difficult tasks to be accomplished. The Convention had a particularly difficult time constituting the executive branch, in part because of lingering fears of strong executive power; many considered a strong executive "the fetus of monarchy," and they wished to avoid that at all costs. The Connecticut Compromise provided part of the key to the solution of the conundrum regarding the executive, for the process for selecting the president attempted to combine national and federal elements as the Connecticut principle did.

The second phase of the Convention also produced two features of the U.S. Constitution particularly relevant for federalism. The Virginia Plan had contained a very general provision for legislative power in the new Congress, but the principle of the new federalism required a more determinate division of spheres of authority between the states and the general government. The Convention worked out the enumeration of powers contained in Article I, Section 8, during this second phase.

The other important federalism-related issue of the second phase involved the relations between the different levels of government. The enumeration of powers outlined separate spheres but left inevitable boundary issues. How would the borders between the two levels of government be policed, and how would encroachments by one or the other be dealt with? The New Jersey Plan provided a key part of the solution. It had contained a provision declaring the supremacy of laws of the general government over those of states. This solution was taken into the new constitution as Article VI and in effect given to the new judiciary to enforce. Thus, the Supreme Court became "the umpire of the federal system."

So successful had the Convention been that when, in mid-September, it finally came up with a reasonably complete draft (lacking, most notably, only a bill of rights), that draft was able to gain the consent of all the states present. That is not to say that every individual delegate approved or signed the U.S. Constitution, for some of the most prominent, like George Mason of Virginia, refused to sign. But the draft Constitution emerged from the convention with the signatures of a majority from each state and the support of Washington, Franklin, Madison, and a bevy of other prestigious leaders. It needed ratification by 9 states in order to go into operation. That such a radical break with the past could have occurred on the basis of a deliberative assembly and a series of popular ratification conventions justifies the description frequently given of the proceedings of the Convention—it was indeed "the miracle at Philadelphia." *SEE ALSO:* Annapolis Convention of 1786; Anti-Federalists; Articles of Confederation; Connecticut Compromise; Federalists; U.S. Constitution

BIBLIOGRAPHY: Catherine Drinker Bowen, *Miracle at Philadelphia: The Story of the Constitutional Convention* (Boston: Little, Brown, 1966); Max Farrand, ed., *The Records of the Federal Convention of 1787* (New Haven, CT: Yale University Press, 1966); Calvin C. Jillson, *Constitution Making: Conflict and Consensus in the Federal Convention of 1787* (New York: Agathon Press, 1988); Clinton Rossiter, *1787: The Grand Convention* (New York: Macmillan, 1966); and Michael Zuckert, "Federalism and the Founding," *Review of Politics* 48 (1986): 166–210.

MICHAEL ZUCKERT

Continental Congress   Following the Boston Tea Party in December 1773, the British government closed the Boston port, placed a British general in charge of Massachusetts's government, and prohibited Massachusetts from trying any British officer. Rather than comply, the people of Boston chose to resist. People throughout the colonies rallied to their cause and established committees of correspondence to learn what was happening in Boston. By the summer, the colonies had agreed to congress to coordinate their efforts. In September 1774, 12 of the 13 colonies sent delegates to Philadelphia to participate in the First Continental Congress. This was the first official assembly of the colonies since 9 colonies had convened for the Stamp Act Congress of 1765.

The First Continental Congress decided to stand in solidarity with Boston. It created the Continental Association, which called for a boycott of British trade, for internal discipline and sacrifice, and for committees in each community to publish the names of merchants violating the boycott, confiscate contraband, and encourage public discipline and sacrifice. Edward Countryman wrote that this decision "may have been the most important single step in the transformation of the American movement from one of resistance to one of revolution" (Countryman 1985, 5). The First Continental Congress adjourned in October after agreeing to meet the next year in order to assess the effectiveness of the association.

Before the Second Continental Congress convened, open hostilities between British soldiers and colonial minutemen had broken out in Lexington and Concord. The battle of Bunker Hill and the American capture of Fort Ticonderoga soon followed. All 13 colonies sent delegates to the Second Continental Congress; included in attendance were Benjamin Franklin and Thomas Jefferson. The Second Continental Congress lacked legal authority but assumed responsibility to govern. It appointed George Washington to head the army located outside Boston, authorized printing paper certificates to help pay for the war, and ratified the Declaration of Independence that formally dissolved the colonies' ties to Britain.

Between 1776 and 1781, the Continental Congress was the de facto government of the 13 colonies. Lacking the power to compel the states, it passed nonbinding resolutions for the states to provide money, supplies, and troops to support the war effort. Those states proximate to the fighting were most likely to heed the Continental Congress's resolutions. Recognizing the need for a stronger national government, the Continental Congress drafted, approved, and sent to the states for ratification the Articles of Confederation. Upon final ratification of the Articles of Confederation in 1781, the Continental Congress was retired. *SEE ALSO:* Articles of Confederation; Declaration of Independence; Jefferson, Thomas

BIBLIOGRAPHY: Edward Countryman, *The American Revolution* (New York: Hill and Wang, 1985); and Gordon S. Wood, *The Creation of the American Republic, 1776–1787* (New York: W.W. Norton, 1969).

TROY E. SMITH

Contract Clause   Article I, Section 10, of the Constitution provides, "No state shall . . . pass any law impairing the Obligation of Contracts." Often overlooked today, the Contract Clause occupied a pivotal place in constitutional law until the early twentieth century and served as a key protection for property rights. The clause evidenced the commitment of the framers to private economic ordering.

Following the American Revolution, state legislatures regularly intervened in debtor-creditor relations with laws designed to impede the collection of debts. The Contract Clause was little discussed at the Constitutional Convention, but the provision was clearly intended to curb state debtor relief laws that undermined the sanctity of private agreements and threatened to disrupt credit relationships. The clause was modeled after a similar provision in the Northwest Ordinance of 1787 that barred legislative interference with private contracts. It bears emphasis that the framers selected broader language that seemingly covered all types of public as well as private contracts. Many state constitutions also included language forbidding the impairment of contracts.

The Contract Clause early assumed a major role in constitutional development. In 1792 a federal circuit court struck down a state debtor relief law as an impairment of contract. During the tenure of John Marshall as chief justice (1801–35), the Contract Clause was the principal vehicle by which the Supreme Court vindicated the rights of property owners against state abridgement. A champion of private property, business enterprise, and the national market, Marshall viewed skeptically state interference with private economic arrangements.

ARTICLE I, SECTION 10, CLAUSE 1

No State shall enter into any Treaty, Alliance, or Confederation; grant Letters of Marque and Reprisal; coin Money; emit Bills of Credit; make any Thing but gold and silver Coin a Tender in Payment of Debts; pass any Bill of Attainder, ex post facto Law, or Law impairing the Obligation of Contracts, or grant any Title of Nobility.

In the landmark case of *Fletcher v. Peck* (1810), Marshall ruled that the Contract Clause covered every type of contract and prevented a state from breaching its own agreements. Consequently, the Georgia legislature could not rescind a land grant despite allegations of bribery in the original sale. In *Fletcher*, Marshall tellingly characterized the Contract Clause as a "bill of rights for the people of each state." Thereafter the Marshall Court applied the Contract Clause to a variety of public contracts, including state tax exemptions to business. More importantly, the Court in *Dartmouth College v. Woodward* (1819) concluded that the grant of a corporate charter was a constitutionally protected contract, and that legislative alterations of the charter violated the Contract Clause. This decision encouraged the growth of corporate enterprise by affording constitutional safeguards against legislative abridgement of charters of incorporation.

In the absence of a national bankruptcy law, the states continued to enact debt relief legislation. In *Sturges v. Crowninshield* (1819), Marshall held that New York's bankruptcy law was invalid because it relieved debtors of the obligation to pay debts contracted before the measure was passed. On the other hand, in *Ogden v. Sanders* (1827), over a rare dissent by Marshall, the Court maintained that the Contract Clause did not operate prospectively. Hence, state laws could reach debts incurred after the date of enactment.

Despite differences in outlook between Marshall and his successor as chief justice, Roger B. Taney (1835–64), the Supreme Court continued to apply the Contract Clause vigorously. To be sure, Taney was inclined to give the states greater latitude in fashioning economic policy. In *Charles River Bridge v. Warren Bridge* (1837), for example, Taney insisted that state grants and charters must be strictly construed to facilitate economic growth, and he rejected the notion that implied corporate privileges were protected by the Contract Clause. Yet the Court under Taney strictly enforced the Contract

Clause in cases involving debtor relief laws and grants of tax exemption. In the leading case of *Bronson v. Kinzie* (1843), the justices found two Illinois statutes that retroactively limited the foreclosure rights of mortgagees to be an unconstitutional abrogation of contractual obligations.

The attempted repudiation of bonded debt by localities in the late nineteenth century was repeatedly challenged as a violation of the Contract Clause. Drawing upon principles derived from the Contract Clause, in *Gelpche v. City of Dubuque* (1864) the Taney Court protected the legitimate expectation of bondholders from a subsequent state court decision that previously sustained that bonds were invalid under state law. In effect, the Court decided that a state court could not divest the rights of bondholders by a retroactive change in the law. Thereafter, the Waite and Fuller Courts repeatedly invoked the Contract Clause to uphold local government bonds in the hands of creditors against repudiation.

Despite the high regard shown for the sanctity of contract manifest in these decisions, the Contract Clause gradually waned in importance during the late nineteenth and early twentieth centuries. In part this was because other constitutional provisions, such as the Due Process and Taking Clauses, emerged as stronger guarantees of property rights. But other factors were also at work. By its terms, the Contract Clause applied just to the states and afforded no protection from federal interference with contractual arrangements. Moreover, the clause precluded only retroactive impairment of existing contracts, leaving the states free to regulate the terms of future contracts.

Of greater significance was recognition by the Supreme Court of exceptions to the Contract Clause. In *Stone v. Mississippi* (1880), the justices concluded that a state could outlaw the sale of lottery tickets despite the fact that a charter had previously granted the right to operate a lottery. The Supreme Court reasoned that a state legislature could not bargain away its authority to guard the health, safety, and morals of the public. The concept of an alienable police power opened the door for state legislatures to modify or revoke public contracts.

Still, the Supreme Court in the early twentieth century continued to rely on the Contract Clause to strike down debt relief laws and measures designed to frustrate the payment of state bonds. The eclipse of the Contract Clause is linked with *Home Building and Loan Association v. Blaisdell* (1934). At issue was the validity of a state mortgage moratorium statute enacted during the Great Depression. Although this was the very type of law that appeared to fall within the purview of the Contract Clause, a sharply divided Supreme Court upheld the statute as a reasonable response to emergency economic conditions. The Court in *Blaisdell* did not intend to wound the Contract Clause fatally, and in fact, the justices applied the clause several times to invalidate state debtor relief laws in the late 1930s. But after the constitutional revolution of 1937, the Supreme Court ceased to scrutinize economic regulations meaningfully, and the once potent Contract Clause was neglected for decades.

It would be premature, however, to dismiss the Contract Clause as a dead letter. In the 1970s the Supreme Court revived the clause to a limited extent, invalidating state laws in *United States Trust Co. v. New Jersey* (1977) and in *Allied Structural Steel Co. v. Spannaus* (1978). Some lower federal and state courts have also invoked the Contract Clause to curb state legislative interference with private and public contractual arrangements. The Contract Clause therefore retains a modest degree of vitality as a safeguard for economic rights. *SEE ALSO: Bronson v. Kinzie; Charles River Bridge Company v. Warren Bridge Company; Dartmouth College v. Woodward; Fletcher v.*

Peck; *Home Building and Loan v. Blaisdell*; Marshall, John; *Stone v. Mississippi*; Substantive Due Process; Taney, Roger Brooke; *United States Trust Company v. New Jersey*

BIBLIOGRAPHY: James W. Ely Jr., *The Guardian of Every Other Right: A Constitutional History of Property Rights*, 2nd ed. (New York: Oxford University Press, 1998); James W. Ely Jr., ed., *Property Rights in American History: The Contract Clause in American History* (New York: Garland Publishing, 1997); Samuel R. Olken, "Charles Evans Hughes and the Blaisdell Decision: A Historical Study of Contract Clause Jurisprudence," *Oregon Law Review* 72 (Fall 1993): 513–602; and Benjamin F. Wright, *The Contract Clause of the Constitution* (Cambridge, MA: Harvard University Press, 1938).

JAMES W. ELY JR.

Contract with America   The Contract with America and its chief architect, House Speaker Newt Gingrich of Georgia, became guiding forces for the 104th Congress when Republicans took majority control of the House of Representatives for the first time in forty years after the 1994 elections. Although it was essentially a campaign document, the "contract" promised that Republicans would institute procedural reforms in the House and would hold floor votes on ten legislative provisions with public opinion poll–tested titles such as the "American Dream Restoration Act," "Fiscal Responsibility Act," "Common Sense Legal Reform Act," "Personal Responsibility Act," and "Taking Back Our Streets Act."

Inasmuch as the contract portended important changes in all manner of fiscal, social, and defense policies, it also offered the potential for a significantly new direction in the federal balance of power between the national government and the states. The contract marked an important moment in Republicans' continued efforts to implement a "New Federalism" by shrinking the national government and devolving discretion over myriad policy areas to state and local government officials. House Republicans' commitment to reducing the size of the federal government found expression in contract provisions that sought a constitutional amendment requiring a balanced federal budget, legislation to give the president the line-item veto power, and the Unfunded Mandate Reform Act, which limited the national government's ability to impose policy mandates on states without providing federal funds for implementation.

Perhaps the most striking examples of the contract's efforts at devolution were its welfare and crime provisions. On welfare, Republicans replaced Aid to Families with Dependent Children (AFDC), a long-standing federal entitlement program, with Temporary Assistance for Needy Families (TANF), a block grant program that allowed state governments to tailor their welfare programs and restrictions on recipients to meet their own policy and political goals. On crime, Republicans replaced President Bill Clinton's 1994 crime bill, which provided grants to state and local governments to administer crime control and social programs (some of which were as specific as establishing inner-city "midnight basketball" programs), with block grants allowing state and local officials greater flexibility in how to spend federal dollars.

Nevertheless, Republicans were not averse to the use of federal power. Although, on the whole, the contract devolved policy discretion to the states, critics charge that these devolution efforts also transferred significant financial burdens to state and local governments seeking to compensate for cuts in federal spending. Moreover, if Republicans were willing to give greater discretion to the states in most instances, they also evinced a willingness to use the tactics of "coercive federalism" whereby the national government withholds funding from states who fail to comply with national officeholders' policy goals. For example, one of the contract's crime proposals, eventually passed as the Violent Criminal Incarceration Act, required that states strengthen their criminal sentencing guidelines in order to be eligible for $10.5 billion in federal block grants to states for the purposes of prison construction and administration. *SEE ALSO:* Coercive Federalism; New Federalism (Reagan)

> *BIBLIOGRAPHY:* Ed Gillespie and Bob Schellhas, eds., *Contract with America: The Bold Plan by Rep. Newt Gingrich, Rep. Dick Armey, and the House Republicans to Change the Nation* (New York: Random House, 1994); and James G. Gimpel, *Legislating the Revolution: The Contract with America in Its First 100 Days* (Boston: Allyn and Bacon, 1996).

DOUGLAS B. HARRIS

Cooley v. Board of Wardens In *Cooley v. Board of Wardens* (1852), the U.S. Supreme Court, by a vote of 7–2, upheld the constitutionality of a Pennsylvania law that required all ships entering or leaving the Port of Philadelphia to hire a local pilot. States may regulate interstate commerce, said the Court in an opinion authored by Justice Benjamin Curtis, as long as there is no prohibition in federal law and the subject on which the state is legislating does not require a uniform national policy. This so-called Cooley Rule has stood the test of time and guides state and federal courts today.

Article I, Section 8, Clause 3, of the U.S. Constitution grants to Congress the power "to regulate commerce with foreign nations, and among the several states." During the First Congress (1789–91), two interpretations of the nature of this power were put forward. Some members of Congress expressed the view that the federal commerce power was exclusive. It was a prohibition on state regulation of interstate and foreign commerce. Another example of an exclusive federal power is Congress's authority to make laws for the seat of the national government, currently the District of Columbia. Those who made this argument feared that local and state laws would interfere with the free flow of commerce, as they had under the Articles of Confederation (1781–88), and render impossible the achievement of a single, national, common market, on which the country's economic growth and prosperity depended. Other members of the First Congress considered the commerce power analogous to the taxing power. They are concurrent powers, with both the states and the federal government enjoying authority to impose taxes and regulate interstate and foreign commerce. Those who supported this reading feared interference with the autonomy retained by the states under the Constitution over their local affairs.

The Supreme Court first addressed the question of the nature of the commerce power in *Gibbons v. Ogden* (1824). The Court found a New York law granting a monopoly over the operation of steamboats between New York and New Jersey unconstitutional because it conflicted with an Act of Congress regulating navigation of the coastal waters of the United States. Speaking for a unanimous Court, Chief Justice John Marshall held that the commerce power was neither exclusive nor concurrent. The states were free to make laws governing their internal commerce and to exercise their police power, the authority to protect the health, safety, welfare, and morals of their people. The congressional power to regulate interstate commerce, however, is supreme when exercised and all conflicting state laws are void. Marshall, however, did not say whether states could regulate interstate commerce in the absence of federal legislation.

The Supreme Court addressed the question of the extent of state power when the federal commerce authority lies in its "dormant," or negative, state in *Cooley*. Justice Benjamin Curtis acknowledged that under its commerce power, Congress can regulate all aspects of navigation, including the hiring of pilots. Whether ship captains can safely enter and leave a port without turning their ship over to a local pilot varies from port to port. Rather than pass a uniform law on this question, Congress in 1789 adopted the state pilotage laws, thus giving them the force of federal legislation. The Pennsylvania law challenged in *Cooley*, however, was not passed until 1803. The majority, nevertheless, considered the law valid because the subject of engaging pilots lends itself to diverse legislation at the local level. The silence of Congress expresses that body's intent to leave pilot laws up to the states. Justice Curtis, however, said that the states are not free to regulate all aspects of interstate commerce when Congress is silent. Some subjects of interstate commerce require a uniform system of regulation throughout the nation. On these subjects, the commerce power is exclusive and only Congress can legislate. *Cooley*, however, provided no guidance on which subjects required a single national rule.

Justice John McLean in his dissenting opinion quoted from Marshall's opinion in *Gibbons v. Ogden*. Marshall said that after the adoption of the Constitution, the states lost their power to regulate the conduct of pilots. These state laws would have been of no effect if the First Congress had not in 1789 adopted them and made them federal law. McLean insisted that Marshall considered the regulation of pilots to be part of the exclusive power of Congress to regulate interstate and foreign commerce. McLean said that the decision of the majority in *Cooley* would adversely affect the commercial prosperity of the country.

Justice Curtis's majority opinion in favor of the challenged state law in *Cooley* was consistent with the pattern of the Court under Chief Justice Roger Taney. The Taney Court (1836–64) was considerably more sympathetic to the claims of state power than the Marshall Court (1801–35) had been. *Cooley* enlarged the reserved powers of the states, recognizing a power in them to regulate interstate and foreign commerce in the absence of congressional prohibitions.

The *Cooley* rule led to a significant increase in judicial power because the courts had to decide in a series of subsequent cases whether a particular subject of interstate commerce required a uniform national rule. An alternative reading of the commerce power is that Congress is the proper judge of whether a state law burdens interstate commerce. After all, the Constitution grants to Congress, not the courts, the power to regulate commerce among the states. Under this interpretation, congressional silence implies congressional acquiescence in what the states are doing. The *Cooley* precedent led to cases such as *Southern Pacific Company v. State of Arizona* (1945). For safety reasons, Arizona, exercising its police power, limited the number of railroad cars per train that could pass through the state. Although there was no congressional prohibition on such laws, the Supreme Court invalidated the Arizona limitation as an excessive burden on interstate commerce. Chief Justice Harlan Stone (1941–46) asserted that Congress had left it to the courts to formulate rules interpreting the Commerce Clause because of the danger that the states posed to the commerce of the nation and the fact that judges had proven themselves capable of determining the facts necessary to render an informed judgment.

These cases, in which the Court balances the benefits to the local jurisdiction of a particular regulation of interstate commerce against the costs to the national economy, were to Justice Hugo Black unacceptable instances of judicial activism. Dissenting in the *Arizona* case, Justice Black advocated judicial abstention in negative Commerce Clause cases. The local law, he said, was the will of the people of Arizona. Congress's silence represents the will of the American people that train-length limitations that vary from state to state are acceptable. The *Cooley* rule, he concluded, violates the democratic principle. The Court, he claimed, had made itself into a superlegislature and was making factual determinations and policy decisions that it was not suited to make. The rule, however, stands, and state and local governments remain free to pass laws affecting interstate commerce that are valid as long as Congress takes no action to nullify them. One reason for the *Cooley* rule's longevity is that both liberal and conservative justices find it attractive. Conservative judges do not hesitate to exercise judicial review to strike down state and municipal laws that impose unacceptable costs on business. Examples include environmental and health and safety laws. Liberal judges, on the other hand, support such state legislation and want to protect it even in the absence of congressional action. *SEE ALSO:* Black, Hugo L.; Commerce among the States; Concurrent Powers; Exclusive Powers; *Gibbons v. Ogden*; Marshall, John; Police Power; Taney, Roger Brooke

BIBLIOGRAPHY: Jacob W. Landynski and Saul K. Padover, *The Living U.S. Constitution: Historical Background, Landmark Supreme Court Decisions* (New York: Meridian, 1995); Bernard Schwartz, *A History of the Supreme Court* (New York: Oxford University Press, 1995); John R. Vile, *A Companion to the United States Constitution and Its Amendments* (Westport, CT: Praeger, 2001); and William M. Wiecek and Stanley L. Kutler, *Liberty under Law: The Supreme Court in American Life* (Baltimore: Johns Hopkins University Press, 1988).

KENNETH M. HOLLAND

Cooperative Federalism   Cooperative federalism is a model of intergovernmental relations that recognizes the overlapping functions of the national and state governments. This model can be contrasted with the model of dual federalism, which maintains that the national and state governments have distinct and separate government functions.

In general, cooperative federalism asserts that governmental power is not concentrated at any governmental level or in any agency. Instead, the national and state governments share power. For instance, bureaucratic agencies at the national and state level normally carry out governmental programs jointly. Because the governments' responsibilities are split between many levels of government, citizens and organized interests have many access points to influence public policy.

The constitutional foundations of the cooperative model of federalism are threefold. First, the proponents of cooperative federalism rely on a broad interpretation of the Supremacy Clause (Article VI) of the Constitution. Second, they contend that the Necessary and Proper Clause (Article 1, Section 8), also known as the Elastic Clause, allows the national government to make laws that are essential to carrying out the government's inherent powers. Finally, they hold a narrow interpretation of the Tenth Amendment.

Although the term "cooperative federalism" was originated in the 1930s, the roots of cooperative federalism reach back to the administration of Thomas Jefferson. During the nineteenth century, the national government used land grants to support a variety of state governmental programs such as higher education, veterans' benefits, and transportation infrastructure. The Swamp Lands Acts of 1849, 1850, and 1860 are a prime example of this strategy. Under the various versions of this law, Congress ceded millions of acres of federal wetlands to 15 interior and coastal states. The acreage was "reclaimed" (i.e., drained) by the states and sold, with the profits being used to fund flood control. This strategy was later used in the Morrill Act of 1862, which gave land grants to the states to help fund the creation of state colleges.

The model of cooperative federalism was expanded during Franklin D. Roosevelt's New Deal. The influence of the national government over social welfare policies continued after World War II and into the 1960s when Lyndon B. Johnson declared his War on Poverty. Johnson's efforts to expand this safety net are often referred to as "creative federalism."

A "rights revolution" during the late 1960s and 1970s extended the idea of cooperative federalism as the national government became involved in issues such as the environment, job safety, mental health, education, and the rights of disabled individuals. As the national government shaped new public policies to deal with these issues, it relied on the states to implement a wide array of federally imposed mandates.

The modern view of cooperative federalism is very different than the model used in the nineteenth century. In the 1970s, federal mandates became more exacting and binding, and no longer emphasize unconditional assistance to the states. The national government also provided deadlines for compliance and could penalize the states for failing to meet them.

Some political scientists have a stricter interpretation of cooperative federalism. John Kincaid, for instance, has designated the time period of 1954–78 as the time frame for cooperative federalism in the United States. Since the late 1970s, there has been a swing toward the model of dual federalism, especially during Ronald Reagan's administration. *SEE ALSO:* Coercive Federalism; Creative Federalism; Dual Federalism; Marble Cake Federalism; New Federalism (Reagan)

BIBLIOGRAPHY: Russell Hanson, "Intergovernmental Relations," in *Politics in the American States: A Comparative Analysis*, 7th ed., ed. Virginia Gray, Russell L. Hanson, and Herbert Jacob (Washington, DC: CQ Press, 1999); John Kincaid, "From Cooperative to Coercive Federalism," *Annals of the American Academy of Political and Social Science* 509 (May 1990): 139–52; and Marc Landy and Sidney M. Milkis, *American Government: Balancing Democracy and Rights* (Boston: McGraw-Hill Higher Education, 2004).

MARY HALLOCK MORRIS

Corfield v. Coryell   Article IV, Section 2, Clause 1, of the Constitution provides, "The citizens of each state shall be entitled to all Privileges and Immunities of Citizens in the several states," a provision sometimes known as the interstate Privilege and Immunities Clause. *Corfield v. Coryell* (1823) was apparently the first and remains a leading federal case interpreting this clause. *Corfield* was not a Supreme Court case, but was decided by Justice Bushrod Washington serving as Circuit Court judge. The case involved a New Jersey law limiting the gathering of oysters within the state to "actual inhabitants or residents of the state." The law was challenged as discriminating against citizens of other states and thus as in violation of Article IV, Section 2, Clause 1. The question implicit in the case was whether that constitutional provision prohibited states from all discrimination between their own citizens and citizens of other states of the union, or merely prohibited discrimination over a narrower range of rights. Justice Washington concluded the law was constitutional, for Article IV, Section 2, protects only "those privileges and immunities which are, in their nature, fundamental; which belong, of right, to the citizens of all free governments; and which have, at all times, been enjoyed by the citizens of the several states which compose this Union, from the time of their becoming free, independent, and sovereign." The right to gather oysters, he concluded, was not among these fundamental rights. *SEE ALSO: Baldwin v. Montana Fish and Game Commission*; Privileges and Immunities Clause: Article IV; *Toomer v. Witsell*

BIBLIOGRAPHY: David S. Bogern, *Privileges and Immunities* (Westport, CT: Praeger, 2003).

MICHAEL ZUCKERT

Council of State Governments   The Council of State Governments (CSG) was established in 1933 as a nonprofit umbrella organization for all state officials. Core responsibilities have been information collection and dissemination, interstate cooperation and problem-solving promotion, trend and emerging issue identification, and state administration and management improvement.

SERVICES

CSG serves all branches of state government. Headquartered in Lexington, Kentucky, services include research studies, an information clearinghouse, inquiry responses, innovations reports, suggested legislation, secretariat support, leadership development and training, and conferences. While promoting state sovereignty, CSG does not lobby.

The Council's "signature" publication is the annual *Book of the States*, containing statistical compilations and analyses of constitutional amendments; trends in the executive, legislative, and judicial branches; summaries of developments in elections, finances, management, and major policy areas; overviews of federalism and state-local relations; and background information on each state. CSG publishes a monthly magazine, *State News*; a quarterly on best practices and solutions, *Spectrum*; an annual volume of *Suggested State Legislation*; and periodic rosters of state officials.

GOVERNANCE AND FUNDING

CSG is a regionally based national organization. Four regional offices (Atlanta; Sacramento; Lombard, Illinois; and New York City) each support a legislative conference (southern, western, midwestern, and eastern). CSG also supports two regional governors' associations (southern and midwestern). These offices receive move than half of the Council's budget to provide regionally focused research, training, technical assistance, and conferences.

CSG's Governing Board, composed of all governors, two legislators from each state, and constituent organization representatives, meets annually to review programs, activities, and finances. From this group, an Executive Committee of about thirty-five members provides direction and oversight between the annual meetings. Typically a governor is president of CSG's Governing Board and a legislator is chair of the Executive Committee.

The Council's chief funding sources are state appropriations, based on population. Other sources include dues assessments for secretariat services to groups of officials such as lieutenant governors, publications sales, and grants from federal agencies and foundations. Since the 1980s, private contributions through a Corporate Associates program have supplemented the Council's budget.

Beginning in the late 1970s, the governors, legislators, attorneys general, and budget directors chose to establish separate offices in Washington, D.C. They desired dedicated staff, direct access to Washington policy makers and regulators, and a lobbying agenda. Later the auditors, comptrollers, and treasurers and secretaries of state followed suit. To facilitate collaboration and help monitor the status of federal legislation, regulations, and programs, CSG maintains a small Washington office in the Hall of the States.

While a smaller umbrella organization than it was seventy years ago, CSG still plays a valuable role in collecting and disseminating information and insights on best practices, innovations, and solutions to the problems that state officials experience, nationally and regionally. It remains the only organization spanning all three branches of state government. *SEE ALSO:* Intergovernmental Lobbying

BIBLIOGRAPHY: Council of State Governments, "The Council of State Governments," in *The Book of the States 1984–85* (Lexington, KY: Council of State Governments, 1984); and *State Government News* 26, no. 12 (December 1983).

CARL W. STENBERG

Councils of Governments   A Council of Governments (COG) is a voluntary association of local governments, situated in either a metropolitan or rural area, designed to promote discussion and intergovernmental cooperation among its members concerning common and regional problems, and to engage in planning on a multijurisdictional basis. Their chief elected official (i.e., mayor or chairperson of the county board) usually represents a member of a council of governments. A council of governments is not a government, and it does not have the authority to levy taxes, pass ordinances, or regulate local governments. The revenues of a council of governments are derived from membership fees, and state and federal sources. Characteristically, a council of governments has a relatively small staff, composed of an executive director, several physical and social planners, and supporting personnel, although the staff of councils of governments situated in metropolitan areas are typically significantly larger.

HISTORICAL OVERVIEW

Although a few regional councils of locally elected officials existed as early as the 1930s, the first modern-day council of governments, sometimes referred to as a regional council, was the Supervisors' Inter-County Committee (SICC), composed of six member counties, organized in the Detroit metropolitan area in 1954. The Southeast Michigan Council of Governments (SEMCOG) eventually succeeded this body on January 1, 1968. SEMCOG is a much more inclusive organization involving counties, cities, townships, villages, and school districts. The Metropolitan Regional Council was organized in 1956 in the New York City region, but it failed to achieve significant cooperation among and between the local governments in the area because various suburban jurisdictions feared domination by New York City. In contrast, early successful examples of council of governments bodies include the Metropolitan Washington Council of Governments (Washington, D.C.) formed in 1957, along with the Puget Sound Governmental Conference (Seattle) established in the same year, and the Association of Bay Area Governments organized in 1961. It should be noted that these early councils of governments were largely the product of local initiative, and enjoyed only a limited amount of federal support and virtually no support from their respective states.

Although, over the years, state statutory and financial support for the establishment of councils of governments has been decidedly uneven, the initiation in the mid-1960s of strong federal support for the council of governments movement resulted in a spectacular increase in the number of these bodies during the era from 1965 to1980. By the latter year there were approximately 660 councils of governments established throughout all the regions of the United States. Federal planning incentives and metropolitan areawide review requirements commencing in 1965 strongly encouraged and, indeed, required the formation of a council of governments in each of our metropolitan areas. Congress approved direct support for these bodies through Section 701(g) of the 1965 Housing Act, for underwriting two-thirds of the costs of studies, the collection of data, and the preparation of regional plans and programs. Section 204 of the Demonstration Cities and Metropolitan Development Act of 1966 further stimulated the establishment of councils of governments by requiring that all local applications for federal funding, involving forty grant and loan programs, be reviewed and commented upon by a council of governments. This areawide review requirement was considerably enhanced by the passage of the Intergovernmental Cooperation Act of 1968. Acting on the basis of this legislation, the Bureau of the Budget, which later evolved into the Office of Management and Budget (OMB), issued Circular A-95, which expanded the areawide review function of councils to include over 150 federally assisted programs. These review requirements encouraged councils of governments, in order to receive maximum federal funding, to devote a large amount of attention to the matters of low-income housing, water and sewer development, citizen participation, and recreation planning.

Congressional legislation passed in the 1970s reinforced the stature and role of councils of governments in the intergovernmental management system. This legislation included the Water Pollution Control Act (1972), considerably strengthened by various amendments in 1976; the Coastal Zone Management Act (1972); and the Rural Development Act (1972). Additional congressional action in the policy areas of air pollution, solid waste management, mass transportation, health planning, and economic development enhanced the role of councils of governments in the intergovernmental system. By 1976, thirty-two federal assistance programs were of a decided regional orientation, compared with only twenty-four similar programs in 1972.

However, President Ronald Reagan's administration and Congress substantially reversed in the early 1980s the federal government's long-term trend of providing financial, intergovernmental management, and statutory support for councils of governments. It drastically reduced "701" funding for councils, which had constituted a major source of general fiscal support for these organizations. Even more critically, the Reagan administration, favoring the deregulation and devolution of powers in the federal system, terminated through an executive order the A-95 review process in favor of a new approach, which encouraged the states to develop their own regional review process. These actions provoked a "shakedown" or sorting-out era for councils of governments. In short, those councils of governments that were heavily dependent on the federal largesse and that lacked a strong base of local—and, to a somewhat lesser degree, state—support simply vanished from the metropolitan and rural landscape. As a result of these developments, by 1990 the number of councils of governments declined to about 500. Viable councils, seeking to maintain their organizational semblance, became much more responsive to the pragmatic needs of their local members and more involved in brokering or entrepreneurial activities, such as establishing joint purchasing programs, and conducting physical and social planning endeavors, on a contract basis, for their member units.

In a twist of fate, congressional legislation passed in the 1990s once again emphasized the importance of regional planning and the role of councils of governments in the intergovernmental management system. This legislation includes the Intermodal Surface Transportation Efficiency Act (ISTEA) of 1991 and the Clean Air Act Amendments (CAA) enacted by Congress in 1990. In order for communities and regions to secure federal funding, ISTEA requires the designation of a metropolitan planning organization (MPO) in each area—often, this is an existing council of governments or some other metropolitan planning body—to be responsible for the development of a comprehensive and balanced regional transportation plan. The CAA requires that metropolitan areas develop and implement satisfactory regional air quality standards or risk losing federal funds for transportation projects.

ORGANIZATIONAL STRUCTURE

Larger council of governments, in terms of membership, have a rather elaborate organizational structure. The basic representational body of a council of governments is the general assembly. Its chief elected official usually represents each local governmental member. While many councils provide equal voting rights to their members in the general assembly, some apportion votes according to the population of each member unit, while others make use of some other kind of standard to determine member-voting privileges. In addition to chief elected local officials, some councils provide membership in their general assembly for other public officials, including state legislators elected from districts in the region, and/or appropriate state administrative officials.

The general membership of each council of governments usually convenes twice a year, although some council assemblies meet as often as six times a year, while other councils hold a single annual meeting. At these meetings the representatives, either meeting in a body or in subject-oriented workshops, discuss and debate the various problems confronting the region. Also, they consider and act upon general policy recommendations brought before them by the council leadership and, usually, annually elect the officers of the organization.

Except in those instances where councils have a limited membership, the functions of specific policy making and program development are vested in the body of the executive committee or board; further, most councils hold the executive committee responsible for the expenditure of council funds. By design, the size of executive committees is relatively small in number; the average size of an executive committee is about eleven members, although some committees have as many as thirty-five, while others have as few as three. The members of the executive committee are usually elected by the delegates of the general assembly, although many council bylaws ensure representation on these bodies to a certain type or combination of members. Invariably, councils guarantee core cities representation on the executive committee. While some councils provide members of the executive board with equal voting privileges, others distribute voting strength on the basis of population or some other standard. The members of the executive committee usually meet once a month to transact council business. For the day-to-day operation of the council, the executive committee retains, in most cases, a full-time executive director who serves at their pleasure; in turn, the executive director hires supporting staff.

Councils establish various policy committees for setting priorities and developing work programs. These committees are composed primarily of representatives of the general assembly, although often individuals with demonstrated professional and technical expertise, who are not council representatives, are also appointed to these committees. The functional concerns of these bodies include, but are not limited to, such matters as (1) land use and growth, (2) criminal justice, (3) economic development, (4) highways and mass transportation, (5) natural resources and open space, and (6) human resources. In addition, some councils establish advisory technical committees, composed of professional council staff that provide technical assistance to the policy committees.

In reality, it is neither the general assembly nor the executive committee of the council, but rather the executive director and her or his staff, who are primarily involved in program development and implementation. The overwhelming majority of executive directors of councils of governments have been trained as planners, although a fair proportion have academic backgrounds in the social sciences. Most executive directors were affiliated with another council or served as a municipal or metropolitan planner before assuming their present position. A considerable number of executive directors have been drawn from the ranks of the city or county management profession. Generally, besides administering the council, executive directors are responsible for agenda formulation, project development, budget development, and maintaining contact with appropriate local, state, and federal officials. They share the responsibilities of policy formation and citizen public relations with members of the executive board. Crucially, the success of a council depends to a substantial degree on the competence of the executive director and her or his dedicated commitment to the organization and to the concept of regionalism.

Similar to executive directors, most of the professional staff of councils are planners, although a considerable number have academic backgrounds in public administration, civil engineering, economics, sociology, and law enforcement planning. A significant amount of staff time is spent on developing regional plans, with the balance of time allocated primarily to providing technical assistance to member governments, assisting local governments in preparing applications for state and federal grants, and providing various and important services to member governments.

FUNCTIONAL ACTIVITIES

The most salient function of a council of governments is that of serving as a forum of discussion where chief elected officials (i.e., mayors and board chairpersons) can periodically come together to discuss common and regional problems. Council meetings perform the very important function of acquainting and familiarizing elected public officials with their counterparts throughout the region. Rather than the initial meetings of councils constituting a gathering of friends, they are in reality arenas composed of relative strangers. Council deliberations serve to enhance communication among local officials, stimulate and improve general local governmental coordination and coopera-tion, and generate new ideas about local problems. Importantly, council meetings serve to promote a significant measure of "social capital" or trust among the council repre-sentatives, enabling them to better discuss common and regional problems, and pos-sible policy responses to these problems.

Second, councils of governments have long been involved in various general and specific regional planning endeavors. At minimum, virtually all councils are involved in comprehensive land-use planning, with an increasing emphasis of these plans de-voted to social needs and human concerns. Councils have conducted a considerable amount of specific functional planning, involving economic development, highways and mass transportation, law enforcement, air and water pollution, sewers, solid waste and water, and open space and recreation. In addition, commencing in the 1980s, and reflective of their increasing entrepreneurial orientation, councils have engaged in a sig-nificant amount of local comprehensive planning, on a contract basis, especially for their governmental members of a limited population.

Commencing in the mid-1960s and until the advent of the Reagan administration, most councils of governments served as the federal areawide regional review agency for their area. As noted previously, Section 204 of the 1966 Demonstration Cities and Metropolitan Development Act required applications for federal assistance for a large number of programs to be reviewed by an areawide agency, to determine their con-gruency and compatibility with regional needs. The Bureau of the Budget significantly expanded this review power of councils to include virtually all federal assistance for local programs with its issuance of the A-95 Circular. However, the Reagan adminis-tration rescinded Circular A-95 and terminated the federal areawide review role of councils in the early 1980s; from that era forward, the areawide review role of coun-cils was determined and, if applicable, incorporated by their respective states into their system of intergovernmental management.

Finally, with their diminished role as regional review agencies, councils of govern-ments have placed an increasing emphasis on serving the needs of their member gov-ernments. Practically all councils serve as a data collection, repository, and dissemination agency for their region. Many councils have established joint purchas-ing programs for the benefit of their members. In addition, the leadership of many coun-cils have accepted the responsibility of testifying before state legislative committees on matters of concern to their region.

CRITICISMS

Councils of governments have been criticized on a number of grounds. First, a rather steady criticism of councils since their inception is that they have generally not dealt with the serious socioeconomic problems of their regions. Due to their organizational need to operate on the basis of membership consensus, councils have not usually been in the forefront in confronting and solving difficult issues relating to poverty, racism, education, housing, and crime. Second, councils have been criticized for the often lack-luster involvement of many of the representatives of their member governments; on this score, it has been argued that most of the work of councils is done by the mem-bers of the executive committee and council staff. In addition, councils have been charged with failing to gain a higher degree of saliency on the local political landscape and in relating to the citizenry, with the result that relatively few citizens are aware of councils and their functional role and activities. And, finally, especially the so-called academic consolidationists have charged that councils have impeded and delayed the needed implementation of metropolitan governmental structures.

Councils of governments have not served as a panacea for dealing with or alleviating all of the difficult problems of the regions they serve. On the other hand, councils have served as vehicles of incremental political change, both of a structural and attitudinal nature. Councils have provided an arena where like elected local officials have been able to familiarize themselves with each other, engendering "social capital" and a greater sense of areawide trust. This has allowed them to more earnestly and openly discuss mutual and regional problems, and the possible policy options to be adopted to alleviate these problems. Councils have facilitated, promoted, and carried out a range of specific, functional, and comprehensive regional planning efforts. Councils have provided a wide range of various services for their members, including the collection and dissemination of data and the establishment of joint purchasing programs. They have stimulated not only greater local horizontal intergovernmental cooperation, but also governmental cooperation of a vertical nature, involving the local, state, and federal levels of government. Perhaps, the most significant contribution of councils is that they have furthered the concept of areawide and metropolitan regionalism. Reflective of this, the sort of metropolitan leadership and regional statesmanship that were so lacking in American urban and rural areas at the middle of the last century have become more prominent features on the governmental and political landscape. *SEE ALSO:* Deregulation; Devolution; Economic Development; Education; Housing; Land Use; Metropolitan Planning Organizations; Reagan, Ronald; School Districts; Transportation Policy

BIBLIOGRAPHY: William R. Dodge, *Regional Excellence: Governing Together to Compete Globally and Flourish Locally* (Washington, DC: National League of Cities, 1996); Melvin B. Mogulof, *Governing Metropolitan Areas: A Critical Review of Councils of Governments and the Federal Role* (Washington, DC: Urban Institute, 1971); Myron Orfield, *Metropolitics: A Regional Agenda for Community and Stability* (Washington, DC: Brookings Institution Press, 1997); and Nelson Wikstrom, *Councils of Governments: A Study of Political Incrementalism* (Chicago: Nelson-Hall, 1977).

NELSON WIKSTROM

County Government   There are over 3,000 county governmental units in the United States employing over 2.5 million employees. Traditionally counties have overseen such functions as road construction, hospital and health services, social welfare programs, public safety and corrections, and parks and recreation facilities. These functions often place counties directly in the mix between federal and state programs. Increasingly, counties find themselves competing with the overall interests of large metropolitan areas that overlap county and often state lines, thus creating complicated jurisdictional issues concerning taxation, service delivery, and economic development activities. Yet in rural areas, county governments are increasingly becoming the sole provider of services for larger and larger areas as populations continue to decrease. *SEE ALSO:* Economic Development; Intergovernmental Management; International City/County Management Association; State-Local Relations; Welfare Policy

BIBLIOGRAPHY: U.S. Census Bureau, *Statistical Abstract of the United States: 2002* (Washington, DC: Department of Commerce, U.S. Census Bureau).

DAVID R. CONNELLY

Covenant   A covenant is a morally informed, perpetual, consent-based agreement that depends primarily on the efforts of the covenanting parties themselves for monitoring and enforcement. In this way, covenants differ from the related concepts of contract and compact in their greater emphasis on the moral, as distinct from the legal claims and obligations of the parties involved. In the New England colonial context, covenant or *foederal* theology (*foedus*, Latin for covenant) inspired social and political beliefs that informed federations of church and civil communities.

Like conceptions of natural law and right, the covenant idea reflects a people's beliefs about the origins and proper constitution of political society, giving meaning to ideas such as justice and liberty. From a political perspective, citizens bound by covenant were obliged to exceed the narrow specifications of an agreement, realizing the spirit as well as the letter of the law in their daily activities. The covenantal emphasis on voluntarism rendered individuals responsible to judge and be judged under the conditions of their pact. Several characteristics of covenanting emerge from the New England archetype: an emphasis on self-control as a part of self-rule, the primacy of commitments based in consent, the telos of a partnership with God, a resulting reorientation of authority among moral equals, and the prominence of deliberation and collective choice arrangements.

Covenants are related to other consent-based arrangements, including compacts and contracts, but each type uses different proportions of moral, ethical, and legal constraint to secure compliance. A covenant's moral and ontological dimensions are primary. Compacts also reflect moral concerns, but its legal compulsions equal its moral claims. The legal dimension of a contract predominates. As a result, these agreements' duration, scope, and means of enforcement also differ. Contracts are of limited duration, for limited purposes, and with limited liabilities, and are enforced by a third party.

Covenants and compacts are formal agreements witnessed by the highest relevant authority, religious or civil, respectively, suggesting a distinction between their "secular" and "sacred" qualities. In practice, however, secular and sacred agreements coexisted under the same covenantal rubric. Covenants and compacts did not always enjoy the status of law; nevertheless, they often acted as founding documents influencing a community's public activity, including the establishment of a "due form of government."

AMERICAN EXAMPLES

The "Agreement between the Settlers at New Plymouth" (the Mayflower Compact), November 11, 1620, is the oldest political covenant in the New World. It is considered a covenant because it invokes God as witness to the agreement. The Salem Covenant (1629) and Enlarged Salem Covenant (1636) articulate beliefs that informed developing civil and church communities. The Dedham Covenant (1636) founded a town government. The Cambridge Platform (1648) established the congregational system of covenanted churches in New England, setting the pattern for later civil and church federations. The Declaration of Independence (1776) follows the covenant form and, when linked to the frame of government supplied by either the Articles of Confederation (1781) or the U.S. Constitution (1787), established a national compact in the federal tradition. *SEE ALSO:* Articles of Confederation; Declaration of Independence; U.S. Constitution

BIBLIOGRAPHY: Barbara Allen, "Martin Luther King's Civil Disobedience and the American Covenant Tradition," *Publius: The Journal of Federalism* 30, no. 4 (Fall 2000): 71–113; Daniel J. Elazar, *The Covenant Tradition in Politics*, 4 vols. (New Brunswick, NJ: Transaction Publishers, 1995–98); and Donald S. Lutz, *The Origins of American Constitutionalism* (Baton Rouge: Louisiana State University Press, 1988).

BARBARA ALLEN

Craig v. Boren *See* Equal Protection of the Laws; Equal Rights Amendment; Gender and Federalism

Creative Federalism   Beginning in the late 1950s and lasting through the late 1960s, federalism went through a creative phase that saw a flurry of new programs and a greater linkage of the federal, state, and local governments. The creative phase achieved its zenith during the administration of President Lyndon Johnson (1963–69), who coined the term in a famous commencement address at the University of Michigan in 1964. In fact, the creative phase is closely identified with Johnson's Great Society series of programs and policies as well as his administration's views of intergovernmental relationships, which focused on increased cooperation between levels of governments, enhancing the role of local governments and citizens, and identifying innovative, or "creative," ways of tackling policy problems, particularly poverty and racial injustice. Overall, during the 1960s, the federal system, as David Walker put it, became bigger in dollars and programs, broader in the range of governmental functions affected, deeper regarding grant conditions and the expanding number of recipient local governments and nonprofit organizations involved in implementing programs, and more complicated.

Specifically, three key features of federalism emerged in the creative phase: a proliferation of categorical project grants, enhanced program planning and a greater focus on administration, and increased citizen and interest group participation in intergovernmental affairs.

During the creative phase, the federal government increasingly created categorical project grants that sought to help state and local governments address policy problems and further certain federal goals in nearly every policy area, such as health, social welfare, the environment, transportation, and crime and justice. For example, federal grant outlays increased from $4.9 billion in 1959 to $23.9 billion in 1970, and in just a two-year period of time (1964–66) over 100 project grants were approved. These grants had the effect of the federal government increasingly driving the policy priorities of state and local affairs, as most of the grants narrowly defined the ways the funds could be used, defined targeted populations or geographic areas, and contained reporting requirements. In addition, many grants had matching requirements that make states or localities fund a certain share of the program and supplement the federal funding—thereby increasing the federal role in state and local allocation of fiscal resources.

During this period, the federal government also created intergovernmental programs that had significant planning and administrative requirements attached to them. The federal administrative requirements focused on requiring state and localities to stipulate how the money would be used to address the goals outlined by Congress or a federal agency. In fact, many federal grant programs required states and localities to submit elaborate proposals or requests before federal funds were approved. Applying for and administering these grants required extensive administrative skills and substantial resources. In fact, during the creative phase, securing and administering federal grants became an increasingly important activity for governors, mayors, program professions, and other state and local officials. Due to differences in the fiscal administrative resources, not all governments were equally able to tap into the new flood of federal money. However, in many cases program administrators at the state and local levels had a great deal of flexibility to use the federal grant funds, once they were approved.

A third key feature of the creative phase was the increasing participation of citizens and interest groups in the federal system. Many Great Society programs attempted to achieve maximum citizen participation at the local level and were aimed at increasing opportunities for minorities and the economically disadvantaged to have a say in how they were governed. In fact, creative phase categorical grants often bypassed state governments and were provided directly to local governments in order to provide support to those closest to the citizenry. For example, some new federal programs encouraged or even required state and local governments to involve clients of the programs in operating them and making administrative and policy decisions. The promotion of community action agencies in the War on Poverty—with the intention of empowering local citizens and advocates to become more involved in their own affairs—exemplified this approach. However, this approach often led to clashes between citizens and advocates on one side and elected officials and program professionals on the other side. In addition, interest groups also became a more significant part of the intergovernmental system during the creative phase. For example, some cities began using lobbyists and private consultants to push for, identify, secure, and even help manage federal grants.

During the creative phase, the federal government also implemented a series of far-reaching new programs and laws that have had a fundamental impact on federalism. Most of these were established in a brief period of time as part of the Great Society efforts of the mid-1960s. These new programs and legislation included Medicaid, Project Head Start, Model Cities, the Water Quality Act, the Elementary and Secondary Education Act, the Voting Rights Act, and the Older Americans Act. This period also saw the creation of a number of new federal agencies that further helped the federal government to extend its reach into state and local affairs, including the Departments of Transportation and of Housing and Urban Development.

As government officials and citizens gained more experience with the programs and policies of the creative phase, several problems emerged. For one, there were often gaps between high expectations and performance or results, which contributed to the citizen disenchantment of the late 1960s. In 1975, the Government Accounting Office released a comprehensive evaluation of federal aid programs created during this era and summarized a number of other problems that are commonly associated with the creative phase. For example, the report noted that the federal government lacked mechanisms for disseminating information needed by state and local governments to adequately identify and manage grant programs; state and local government experienced difficulties in identifying sources of federal aid, as well as applying for and administering it; and the federal grant system was highly fragmented with similar programs being administered by different federal agencies, fostering complex and varying application and administrative processes and requirements that created obstacles to meeting citizen and client needs. Accordingly, during the 1970s there were heightened calls for consolidating categorical grants into broader block grants, simplifying application and implementation requirements, and increasing state and local flexibility in administering grant programs. *SEE ALSO:* Categorical Grants; Cooperative Federalism; Great Society; Johnson, Lyndon B.; Project Grants

BIBLIOGRAPHY: U.S. General Accounting Office, *Fundamental Changes Are Needed in Federal Assistance to State and Local Governments*, GAO/GGD-75-75 (Washington, DC: GAO, 1975); David Walker, *The Rebirth of Federalism*, 2nd ed. (New York: Chatham House, 1999); and Deil S. Wright, *Understanding Intergovernmental Relations* (Pacific Grove, CA: Brooks/Cole Publishing, 1988).

THOMAS YATSCO

Criminal Justice The United States has fifty-one separate criminal justice systems—each of the 50 states and of the federal government. Criminal laws vary substantially across these different jurisdictions. Perhaps the most significant example is the variation in the death penalty, in which 38 states and the federal government have statutes allowing for executions and 12 states do not. Thus, a person convicted of first-degree murder in Florida, in Pennsylvania, or in federal court, for example, may be put to death, while someone convicted of the same crime in West Virginia or Iowa cannot.

Other differences between states, and between the states and the federal government, are less dramatic but nonetheless important. For example, some states allow for the use of marijuana to treat certain medical conditions while other states and the federal government prohibit its use entirely. There is also substantial variation in the manner in which sanctions are imposed and in the length of incarceration for similar crimes. The federal government and some states, for example, operate under sentencing guidelines that require judges to impose a sentence within a narrow range established by statute. In other states, judges are given wide latitude in determining sentencing outcomes. Similarly, the federal government generally imposes longer sentences for gun and drug offenses than many state governments.

For most of the country's history, criminal justice was almost exclusively the province of state and local governments. State governments created criminal laws, and local police and prosecutors executed those laws. In the early years of the republic, the federal government handled primarily cases that were uniquely federal concerns, such as piracy, counterfeiting, and smuggling.

Several developments in the twentieth century contributed to the creation of new federal crimes, as well as the growth of federal jurisdiction over what had traditionally been state crimes. The invention of the automobile, for example, resulted in the National Motor Vehicle Act in 1919 (also known as the Dyer Act), which prohibited driving stolen cars across state lines. Moral crusades led to the passage of the Eighteenth Amendment, also known as the Volstead Act or Prohibition, which outlawed the production and sale of alcohol (the amendment was later repealed with the adoption of the Twenty-first Amendment in 1933).

In the latter half of the twentieth century, the lines between federal and state criminal jurisdiction have further blurred as Congress has made gun and drug possession, carjacking, and fraud federal offenses. There is now little distinction between state and federal criminal jurisdiction in terms of substantive laws.

However, federal authority to prosecute criminals far surpasses the resources provided to federal investigative agencies and prosecutors. Thus, the vast majority of criminal defendants are still arrested, charged, and sentenced in state courts. *SEE ALSO:* State Courts; USA PATRIOT Act of 2001

BIBLIOGRAPHY: Lawrence M. Friedman, *Crime and Punishment in American History* (New York: Basic Books, 1993); Herbert Jacob, *Justice in America: Courts,*

Lawyers and the Judicial Process (Boston: Little, Brown 1984); and Daniel Richman, "The Changing Boundaries Between Federal and Local Law Enforcement," in *Boundary Changes in Criminal Justice*, vol. 2 (Washington, DC: Office of Justice Programs, 2000).

LISA L. MILLER

Crosby v. National Foreign Trade Council The *Crosby* case (2000) represents perhaps the Rehnquist Court's most important encounter with the intersection between federalism, separation of powers, and foreign affairs. The case arose out of an attempt by the Commonwealth of Massachusetts to protest human rights abuses by the military regime in Burma (renamed Myanmar after the junta's 1988 coup). In June 1996, the Commonwealth enacted a law that generally barred state entities from purchasing goods or services from persons or corporations doing business in Burma. (Exceptions written into the statute meant that companies doing business in Burma could compete for state contracts but suffered a 10 percent penalty to their bids.) The National Foreign Trade Council, a group representing companies engaged in foreign commerce, brought a federal lawsuit to enjoin enforcement of the Commonwealth's Burma Law on three grounds: (1) that the law infringed the federal government's exclusive foreign affairs power, (2) that it violated the dormant Foreign Commerce Clause, and (3) that the state law was preempted by sanctions on Burma enacted at the federal level three months after the state measure.

The federal district court enjoined enforcement of the law based on the first of these claims, and the U.S. Court of Appeals for the First Circuit affirmed by accepting all three theories. The Supreme Court likewise upheld the injunction, but on much narrower grounds. Refusing to reach the exclusive foreign affairs power and dormant foreign commerce arguments, Justice David Souter's opinion for a unanimous court held that the state law was preempted by the federal statute providing for national sanctions. Although nothing in the federal statute expressly preempted state or local measures, the Court found a conflict between the Massachusetts law and three distinct aspects of the federal statute. First, the federal law conferred discretion upon the president either to expand the range of federal sanctions against Burma or to terminate those sanctions, either because they were detrimental to national security or upon finding that Burma had made significant progress in human rights. Presuming that state-level sanctions would not be subject to presidential control, the Court held that the state law unduly narrowed the flexibility that Congress meant to give the president. Second, the Court noted that the Massachusetts sanctions went further than the federal law, penalizing private activities in Burma that Congress had elected not to reach under the federal law. Noting that "[s]anctions are drawn not only to bar what they prohibit but to allow what they permit," Justice Souter concluded that "the inconsistency of sanctions here undermines the congressional calibration of force." Third, the Court found Massachusetts' effort to chart its own course with respect to Burma inconsistent with Congress's statutory mandate that the president work with other countries to develop a "comprehensive, multilateral strategy to bring democracy to and improve human rights practices and the quality of life in Burma." Relying on statements by midlevel State Department officials that the Massachusetts law interfered with U.S. diplomacy, as well as on protests by foreign governments (including a formal proceeding initiated by Japan and the European Union before the World Trade Organization), the Court found that the state law thwarted Congress's intent for the nation to speak with "one voice" on Burma policy.

The second of these arguments is a fairly conventional point in the Court's preemption jurisprudence; state law often regulates private activity more strictly than federal law, and courts must make difficult judgment calls as to whether such state regulation is a welcome supplement to federal measures or an invalid attempt to reach conduct that Congress meant to exempt. The first and third points, however, are more unusual in that they give preemptive force to Congress's delegation of authority to the president, even though the president had taken no formal action pursuant to that authority that could be pointed to as preempting the state measure. That aspect of the Court's opinion has led some commentators to suggest that the Court is applying a more stringent preemption analysis in foreign affairs cases than it does in domestic preemption litigation. Other scholars have questioned whether the "one voice" paradigm is a realistic picture of American government, given the sharing of foreign affairs authority between the president and a multimember Congress, as well as frequent and public divisions of opinion within the executive branch. Still other observers, however, have suggested that *Crosby* should be viewed as less a case about federalism than one about separation of powers: by foreclosing state efforts to conduct their own foreign policies even where Congress may lack the political will to preempt those policies expressly, the decision protects the president's primacy in foreign affairs. Yet by tying the analysis closely to the specific provisions of the federal Burma statute, Justice Souter's opinion left the precise limits of state activities affecting foreign affairs to be worked out in future decisions. *SEE ALSO:* Commerce with Foreign Nations; Preemption

BIBLIOGRAPHY: American Insurance Association v. Garamendi, 539 U.S. 396 (2003); Sarah H. Cleveland, "*Crosby* and the 'One-Voice' Myth in U.S. Foreign Relations," *Villanova Law Review* 46 (2001): 975; Jack Goldsmith, "Statutory Foreign Affairs Preemption," *Supreme Court Review* (2000): 175; and Ernest A. Young, "Dual Federalism, Concurrent Jurisdiction, and the Foreign Affairs Exception," *George Washington Law Review* 69 (2001): 139.

ERNEST A. YOUNG

Crosscutting Requirements   Crosscutting requirements are a specific type of mandate. They impose requirements or conditions on all grants and programs involving federal money. These requirements apply "horizontally" to all federal agencies and programs, as well as "vertically" to all state and local governments and agencies receiving or passing through federal funds. An example of a crosscutting requirement is the nondiscrimination provision in the Civil Rights Act of 1964, which requires, "No person in the United States shall, on the ground of race, color, or national origin, be excluded from participation in, be denied the benefits of, or be subjected to discrimination under any program receiving Federal financial assistance." Since the passage of that requirement, Congress has approved many more crosscutting requirements. Generally, crosscutting requirements are sorted into the general categories of nondiscrimination, health and safety, and environmental protection. Crosscutting requirements have also included such things as historical preservation and animal welfare and relocation assistance. Congress often approves crosscutting requirements without providing funding to cover the consequent costs of the requirements. *SEE ALSO:* Civil Rights Act of

1964; Crossover Sanctions; Environmental Policy; Fiscal Federalism; Pass through Requirements; Unfunded Mandates

BIBLIOGRAPHY: Advisory Commission on Intergovernmental Relations (ACIR), *Regulatory Federalism: Policy, Process, Impact and Reform*, A-95, February (Washington, DC: ACIR, 1984), 7–11; and David B. Walker, *The Rebirth of Federalism*, 2nd ed. (New York: Chatham House Publishers, 1999).

TROY E. SMITH

Crossover Sanctions Crossover sanctions are fiscal sanctions applied to one government program in order to influence policy in another program area. Because the sanction withholds money in a program separate from the one where the change is desired, the sanction is said to "cross over." Crossover sanctions are most common in federal programs where Congress wants to induce change in state policy but lacks the authority to preempt the states in that particular area. These coercive sanctions are based on Congress's constitutional authority to spend for the general welfare.

Crossover sanctions began with the Hatch Act of 1939, which sanctioned federal grants-in-aid programs if states failed to use merit principles in selecting and promoting state personnel financed with federal funds. In 1965, after states failed to respond to a federal bonus program and regulate billboard advertising along new interstate highways, Congress added a crossover sanction to the Highway Beautification Act to withhold 10 percent of a state's highway construction funds if the state failed to comply with the new federal billboard control requirements. In the Emergency Highway Energy Conservation Act of 1974, Congress stopped all federal funds for highway construction projects in any state with a speed limit greater than 55 mph. This provision was repealed in 1995, and 33 states immediately raised their speed limits. Congress applied the threat of withholding federal highway funds again in 1984 to persuade states to raise their minimum alcohol drinking age to 21.

Crossover sanctions are one means by which Congress uses federal aid to influence state and local policies over which it has no constitutional authority, legal oversight, or enforcement mechanisms. *SEE ALSO:* Crosscutting Requirements; Fiscal Federalism; Grants-in-Aid; Intergovernmental Relations; Preemption; Welfare Policy

BIBLIOGRAPHY: Advisory Commission on Intergovernmental Relations (ACIR), *Regulatory Federalism: Policy, Process, Impact and Reform*, A-95, February (Washington, DC: ACIR, 1984), 7–11; and Joseph F. Zimmerman, "National-State Relations: Cooperative Federalism in the Twentieth Century," *Publius: The Journal of Federalism* 31, no. 2 (Spring 2001): 15–30.

TROY E. SMITH

Cruzan v. Missouri Department of Health *Cruzan v. Missouri Department of Health* (1990) was a Supreme Court case concerning the so-called right to die. Nancy Cruzan was a 32-year-old woman who was incompetent due to having received severe injuries in an automobile accident seven-and-one-half years earlier. Her parents wanted to terminate her artificial nutrition and hydration, but the hospital refused. Missouri requires evidence of the incompetent's wishes to be clear and convincing, and they did not find that in Nancy's case. Chief Justice William Rehnquist, in a 5–4 decision, upheld the state. He balanced liberty against relevant state interests and thought that Nancy's observation that she did not want to live life as a "vegetable" was not enough evidence. He thought there was no substantial proof that her parents' views reflected hers. The dissenters, on the other hand, thought that Nancy was entitled to die with dignity. She had the right to be free from unwanted medical intervention, and the control should be in the hands of persons who have her best interest at heart, not the state legislature. One of the outcomes of the case was that most states now have living will laws that allow individuals to make their wishes about medical treatment known in advance of a crisis that may render them unable to speak. *SEE ALSO: Washington v. Glucksberg*

ROBERT W. LANGRAN

$\Leftrightarrow$ **D**

Dairy Compacts   A dairy compact is a legally binding agreement among states to set the minimum price for milk paid by milk processors to dairy farmers in the compact's member states. State legislatures in several regions of the country have shown interest in dairy compacts, but the U.S. Congress has only approved the Northeast Interstate Dairy Compact (NIDC), in the 1996 Farm Bill. Connecticut, Massachusetts, Maine, New Hampshire, Rhode Island, and Vermont were members of the Compact. NIDC's authorization expired in 2002.

The dairy compact was constitutionally significant because Congress granted the power to regulate aspects of interstate trade to a state organization rather than a federal agency. In Article I, Section 10, the U.S. Constitution permits states to enter into an "agreement or compact" with other states, subject to Congress's review or approval.

Proponents of the NIDC argued that existing Federal Milk Marketing Orders (FMMOs), the federal milk-pricing system since the Agricultural Marketing Agreement Act of 1937, ill-served northeastern dairy farmers by undervaluing production costs. They also argued that FMMOs did not incorporate the environmental or land-use benefits that smaller dairy farms in the Northeast might provide. Likewise, supporters argued that raising the milk price would maintain the number, or at least slow the loss, of dairy farms.

Opponents of the NIDC, largely from the upper Midwest and from dairy product processors, argued that the compact erected unconstitutional trade barriers between states. They argued that if the price that milk processors paid to farmers were higher inside the compact—which was true for thirty-six of the fifty months the NIDC was in operation—farmers would sell milk only to processors inside the region. They also argued that increased milk prices would raise the cost of federal low-income food programs like the school-lunch program and Women, Infants, and Children. While the NIDC was drafted to offset any increase in price for these programs, state policy was dictating federal spending, critics said.

A controversial aspect of the NIDC was its influence on consumer milk prices and on the prices for dairy farmers outside compact states. Economic analyses of both have been mixed. Estimates on the increase in the milk price to consumers in the NIDC ranged from 2 cents to 27 cents per gallon. Estimates on the change in price paid to

145

farmers by processors in the NIDC ranged from 53 cents more per hundredweight (100 pounds) of milk to 5 cents less. Outside the compact, research suggested that prices to farmers fell between 3 cents and 14 cents per hundredweight.

The price for milk is heavily regulated because milk is highly perishable and must be taken from the farm to a processor at least every other day, or the milk will spoil. As a result, in the short term, milk production is not sensitive to supply and demand, nor can dairy farmers wait for better prices.

BIBLIOGRAPHY: Daniel A. Lass, Mawunyo Adanu, and P. Geoffrey Allen, "Impacts of the Northeast Dairy Compact on New England Retail Prices," *Agricultural and Resource Economics Review* 30, no. 1 (2001): 83–92; Alden C. Manchester and Don P. Blayney, "Milk Pricing in the United States," *Agriculture Information Bulletin*, no. 761 (Washington, DC: U.S. Department of Agriculture, 2001); Office of Management and Budget, "The Economic Effects of the Northeast Interstate Dairy Compact" (Washington, DC: U.S. Office of Management and Budget, 1998).

ARNOLD SHOBER

Darby Lumber Company v. United States In *Darby Lumber Company v. United States* (1941), the U.S. Supreme Court sustained the constitutionality of the federal Fair Labor Standards Act (FLSA), which set minimum wages and other working conditions for employees in all businesses (including manufacturing) engaged in interstate commerce. In its decision, the Court explicitly overruled *Hammer v. Dagenhart* (1918) and dismissed arguments that the FLSA invaded powers reserved to the states by the Tenth Amendment, referring to that amendment as "but a truism." *SEE ALSO: Hammer v. Dagenhart*; Tenth Amendment

ELLIS KATZ

Dartmouth College v. Woodward Dartmouth College had been granted a charter by the Crown during the colonial period. After independence, the State of New Hampshire created a new board of trustees who attempted to take control of the college. The secretary and treasurer of the college would not turn over to the new board of trustees the college's papers and seal, and the board sued. In his 1819 decision, Chief Justice John Marshall made three major points. First, he made clear that the college was a private institution, not a public one, thus limiting the legislature's control over it. Second, he held that public charters were contracts within the meaning of the Constitution. His final point was that the state, by its creation of a new board of trustees in violation of the old charter, had enacted a law "impairing the obligation of contracts" in violation of Article I, Section 10, of the Constitution—the Contract Clause. *SEE ALSO:* Contract Clause; *Fletcher v. Peck*; *Home Building and Loan v. Blaisdell*; *Stone v. Mississippi*; *United States Trust Company v. New Jersey*

ROBERT W. LANGRAN

De Jonge v. Oregon *See* Incorporation (Nationalization) of the Bill of Rights

Decentralization "Decentralization" is a widely used term that lacks a precise definition. Generally, decentralization refers to the transfer of specific types of decision-making authority from a central or higher-level entity to subordinate field, regional, and/or local entities. That is, a national government or central government might transfer, constitutionally or legislatively, certain decision-making authority to regional (e.g., provincial) or local (e.g., municipal) governments. Similarly, agencies of a national or central government might transfer certain decision-making authority to their own field offices or to agencies of regional or local governments. Decision-making authority might be transferred, as well, to special regional or functional authorities or to public corporations and enterprises. Within the private sector, decentralization refers to transfers of decision-making authority from a firm's headquarters to a firm's divisions or subsidiaries. Hence, decentralization ordinarily involves transfers of decision-making authority to geographically dispersed entities that are presumably closer to, more knowledgeable about, and more responsive to citizens, voters, clients, customers, or suppliers. Some observers also define decentralization as including transfers of decision-making authority from government to private organizations (e.g., for-profit and nonprofit corporations, nongovernmental organizations, and civic associations). However, such transfers are more often referred to as the privatization of public functions. Privatization may or may not involve decentralization, depending on the degree of monopolization or cartelization that exists within the market of the privatized function.

Usually, decentralization entails explicit transfers of decision-making authority that are limited to specific programs and functions; consequently, the subordinate entities are not entitled to make independent decisions outside of their realms of decentralized authority. Decentralization also implies that the central or higher-level entity that decentralized authority can also unilaterally take back, or recentralize, that authority at any time.

One can also distinguish subjects of decentralization. In *Democracy in America* (1835), for example, Alexis de Tocqueville argued that modern democracies should be politically centralized but administratively decentralized. That is, authority to make all policy decisions should reside in the national government subject to majority rule, but the administration and implementation of policy should reside with regional and local governments. Similarly, while authority to mandate the provision of public services (e.g., education) and standards for those services might belong to the national or central government, authority for the actual production of those services (e.g., local schools) might be decentralized to regional or local governments.

Decentralization also might entail structural, functional, fiscal, and/or personnel matters. "Structural decentralization" refers to the authority of regional or local governments to establish their own form of government (e.g., home rule in U.S. states) or, in the case of field agencies, to structure their own operations. "Functional decentralization" refers to the authority of regional or local governments to make independent decisions about specific policy and service functions (e.g., fire, police, sanitation, and welfare). "Fiscal decentralization" involves the extent to which regional or local governments can independently (1) adopt and collect their own sources of revenue (e.g., levy sales, income, or property taxes), (2) set their own tax rules and rates, (3) borrow funds, and (4) expend their revenues on locally determined programs and projects. Decentralization with respect to personnel refers to the extent to which regional or local governments can independently decide such matters as public employment levels, employment rules, remuneration rates, employment conditions, fringe benefits, and collective bargaining. *SEE ALSO:* Devolution; Noncentralization

BIBLIOGRAPHY: Dennis A. Rondinelli, "Government Decentralization in Comparative Perspective: Theory and Practice in Developing Countries," *International Review of Administrative Sciences* 47, no. 2 (June 1981): 133–45; U.S. Advisory Commission on Intergovernmental Relations, *Measuring Local Discretionary Authority* (Washington, DC: U.S. Government Printing Office, 1981), M131; and U.S. Advisory Commission on Intergovernmental Relations, *State Laws Governing Local Government Structure and Administration* (Washington, DC: U.S. Advisory Commission on Intergovernmental Relations, 1993), M186.

JOHN KINCAID

Declaration of Independence   The Declaration of Independence is an act adopted by the Second Continental Congress in Philadelphia on July 4, 1776, proclaiming American independence from Great Britain. The committee members charged with drafting the Declaration were Thomas Jefferson of Virginia, John Adams of Massachusetts, Benjamin Franklin of Pennsylvania, Roger Sherman of Connecticut, and Robert R. Livingston of New York. Because of his reputation as a good writer, Thomas Jefferson was asked by the other members to draft the Declaration. In his writing, he drew on commonplace philosophical and political ideas already articulated by himself and others, including *A Summary View of the Rights of British America* (1774); a congressional pamphlet he had helped to write in 1775 titled *A Declaration of the Causes and Necessity of Taking Up Arms; The Virginia Declaration of Rights* (1776), drafted by James Mason and Thomas Ludwell Lee; Thomas Jefferson's own drafts of the *Virginia Constitution*; Thomas Paine's *Common Sense* (1776); the English Declaration of Rights (1688–89); and John Locke's *Second Treatise of Government* (1690). Thomas Jefferson turned familiar expressions, phrases, and ideas from these different texts into a rhetorical and elegant tour de force affirming natural rights, portraying King George III of Great Britain as a tyrant, justifying a change of government, and declaring the United States a new nation.

   The text can be divided into four parts: the introduction (the first paragraph), the preamble, the indictment of King George III and the condemnation of the British people, and the actual declaration (the last paragraph). The introduction solemnly declares the opportunity of the act, asserting that this is an inescapable moment in the history of the colonies when these need to form an independent nation to secure "the Laws of Nature and Nature's God." The invocation of these rights connects secular government to Christian, Calvinist theology, essentially arguing that for human laws and governments to succeed they need to conform to God's law. Certain of God's special dispensation, the Declaration invokes him twice in the actual proclamation of independence "for the Rectitude of our Intentions" and "with a firm Reliance on the Protection of divine Providence."

   The preamble invokes the "self-evident" truths, including equality and the God-given rights of "Life, Liberty and the Pursuit of Happiness." The Declaration then discusses an idea that is at the heart of American democracy, that is, power comes from the consent of the governed, and government is established to secure the God-given rights. When governments fail to protect these rights, the people are justified in altering their government and putting in place a new one that will function to their satisfaction.

The idea of equality reflects John Locke's sense of political equality: all men are created equal as members of the human race with the same faculty and the same advantages from nature. This view rejects birth-earned authority and instead establishes the idea that only the consent of equals should determine who has power and how it is shared by different structures of government.

The other "self-evident" truths were adapted from John Locke's expression "Life, Liberty and the Pursuit of Property" in *Second Treatise of Government*. Locke posited that humans naturally compete for possessions and status, and conflict in this competition is only averted by the "Law of Nature" that requires respect for the rights and property of others. Because some people do not play fairly, the government must protect the natural rights of everybody.

After the introductory phrase of the preamble, "We hold these truths to be self-evident," we have three clauses that have the same structure: "that all men are created equal," "that they are endowed by their Creator with certain unalienable rights," and "that among these are Life, Liberty and the Pursuit of Happiness." Within the last part, there is another balanced structure, also with three elements: "Life, Liberty and the Pursuit of Happiness." The Declaration is a revolutionary document that calls for a drastic act—altering government—with great potential of violence. In using an orderly, formulaic structure (called "membrum" in rhetoric), the text conveys revolutionary ideas in a nonthreatening, reassuring way in an unjust and chaotic world created by King George III. The use of this well-established rhetorical strategy throughout the text (including within the last sentence—"we mutually pledge to each other our Lives, our Fortunes and our sacred Honor") imposes a sense of order, harmony, and dignity to a grave situation while, at the same time, it radically alters the course of history.

The preamble ends with an appeal to the unbiased, just, "candid world" to consider the articles of indictment of King George III. The phrase "To prove this" prepares the audience for a long list of facts that leave no doubt in the mind of the "Whole Mankind" and the "Candid World" about the "repeated injuries and usurpations" of King George III.

The indictment consists of a list of twenty-eight grievances that condemn King George III for his abuse of power, his conspiracy against the American people, his use of violence and cruelty, and his failure to respond to "repeated injury" in spite of "repeated petitions." The grievances against the king are followed by a paragraph denouncing "the British Brethren" for their failure to disavow the policies of their king and their legislature.

The last paragraph declares the independence of the United States of America as an inescapable conclusion. With these words a new nation is born, with full power to do all the things that other nations of the world do, such as levying war, concluding peace treaties and alliances, and establishing trade relations with other nations. Again, this is done in the name of the people and with the certitude of divine protection.

The Declaration of Independence is the most important founding document in that it provided the founding principles for the republic and its Constitution and influenced the legislative checks and balances, different state constitutions, and local government texts. The same principles were embraced by many nations and have inspired subsequent generations of American leaders dealing with critical national problems such as Abraham Lincoln during the Civil War (1861–65) and Martin Luther King Jr. during the Civil Rights movement of the 1950s and 1960s. *SEE ALSO:* Continental Congress; Covenant; Jefferson, Thomas

BIBLIOGRAPHY: Scott Douglas Gerber, ed., *The Declaration of Independence: Origins and Impact* (Washington, DC: CQ Press, 2002); and Allen Jayne, *Jefferson's Declaration of Independence: Origins, Philosophy and Theology* (Lexington: University Press of Kentucky, 1998).

Aimable Twagilimana

Deregulation   "Deregulation" refers to the trend that began in the late 1970s and early 1980s to reduce national government control of industries including air travel, trucking, railroads, and telecommunications. The perceived success of such initiatives in cutting consumer costs has led to further deregulation at all levels of the federal system. Concurrent efforts to shift policy responsibilities from the federal to the state level have reinforced the move toward national-level deregulation, but have had somewhat disparate consequences for state-level regulation.

Traditionally, government regulation takes three basic forms: social regulation that protects the safety and health of consumers, antitrust regulation to prevent monopolies, and the regulation of so-called natural monopolies. The latter are industries with high fixed costs who operate more efficiently as a monopoly, but whose prices are regulated. Public utilities are a classic example. At the federal level, regulation in all three areas began in the late 1800s and early 1900s with the creation of agencies such as the Federal Trade Commission, Antitrust Division of the Justice Department, Interstate Commerce Commission, and Food and Drug Administration. State regulation in social and antitrust areas emerged prior to (and, in some cases, paved the way for) federal action. For example, the 1877 Supreme Court case *Munn v. Illinois* gave states the power to regulate prices of firms with monopolistic tendencies before the creation of federal regulators.

The trend toward deregulation focused initially on industries that had been previously considered natural monopolies. Shifts in economic theory led policy elites to conclude that reducing regulations would benefit consumers. National political leaders then seized on deregulation as a way to deal with major public concerns of the time, such as inflation.

The successful federal deregulation of airlines, trucking, railroads, and telecommunications led many states and even local governments to alter their approaches to regulation. Two basic patterns emerged. In social and antitrust regulation arenas, federal deregulation often led to more aggressive state efforts to fill the perceived vacuum. For instance, state attorneys general took on the tobacco industry, leading to a landmark $206 billion financial settlement in 1998. State efforts to implement "patients' bills of rights" or to impose more stringent emissions requirements on cars are other examples of state social regulation that occurred due to federal inactivity in an era of "devolution." In the realm of antitrust policy, state initiatives to break up the monopoly power of the Microsoft Corporation after the U.S. Justice Department settled its case (*United States v. Microsoft Corporation*) illustrate a similar pattern.

Concerning natural monopoly regulation, by contrast, states have emulated the federal trend toward deregulation, most prominently in the realm of electric power. As was the case in other areas discussed above, electricity deregulation stemmed in part from changing economic theories, especially the insight that electricity generation (as opposed to transmission and distribution) was not a natural monopoly. The development of regional transmission grids that precluded every utility from having to have enough capacity to supply all the power in its service area in times of high usage reinforced this belief. Political pressure from large industrial users of power also fostered deregulation. As a result, most states have adopted some form of deregulation that allows electricity companies to compete for customers in the area of power generation, but not the transmission or distribution through power lines, which remain a monopoly.

A few general points about deregulation in the context of federalism are worth noting. First, deregulation illustrates the often-noted tendency of federal systems to promote experimentation and policy learning. The success of early federal efforts at deregulating industries formerly considered natural monopolies led Congress and the Federal Energy Regulatory Commission to encourage state utility regulators to relax their rules on generated power. States have also learned from each other how to implement deregulation effectively. For example, Pennsylvania is widely regarded as an effective model of electricity deregulation, while California is seen as a failure. The increasing importance of international accords such as the North American Free Trade Agreement may hamper experimentation by limiting how much subnational regulatory practices may vary.

Second, the nuances of deregulation depend on the level of government that is responsible. There is some consensus that federal deregulation has been proconsumer. The power of business in state politics makes it less certain that the average citizen will benefit, however, as the locus of deregulation shifts. For example, most states prohibit residential electricity customers from negotiating as a group for lower rates, leaving them less likely to reap the benefits of decontrol than industrial users. On the other hand, in some cases of social and antitrust regulation, especially those affecting industries that are not large local employers, state regulation is likely to be more stringent.

Third, states institutions vary, thereby increasing the inconsistency of both regulation and deregulation across jurisdictions. For example, state utility boards differ in their capability to oversee deregulation. More representative boards, which are often elected, tend to deregulate in a way that protects politically powerful interests, limiting how broad the impact will be. Appointed utility commissioners tend to be better educated and may have the technical expertise to support deregulation and to implement it effectively. *SEE ALSO:* Devolution; Electric Industry Restructuring; Environmental Policy; Interstate Commerce

BIBLIOGRAPHY: Martha Derthick and Paul Quirk, *The Politics of Deregulation* (Washington, DC: Brookings Institution, 1985); Timothy Schiller, "Rewiring the System: The Changing Structure of the Electric Power Industry," *Federal Reserve Bank of Philadelphia Business Review*, no. 1 (2000): 26–33; and Bruce A. Williams, "Economic Regulation and Environmental Protection," in *Politics in the American States*, ed. Virginia Gray, Russell L. Hanson, and Herbert Jacob (Washington, DC: CQ Press, 1999), 434–73.

KEITH BOECKELMAN

Devolution "Devolution" is a widely used term that lacks a precise definition and is often used interchangeably with "decentralization." Decentralization, however, entails explicit transfers of decision-making authority that are limited to specific programs or functions. Such transfers from a central or higher-level entity to subordinate field, regional, and/or local entities do not ordinarily give the subordinate entities rights of autonomous self-government. Decentralization also implies that the central or higher-level entity can unilaterally recentralize authority.

Devolution, which can be instituted constitutionally or legislatively, implies a transfer of substantial, or even complete, power and authority for a range of important governmental functions from a national or central government to subordinate regional governments (e.g., provinces or states) or local governments (e.g., municipalities or metropolitan entities) such that the regional or local governments are invested with substantial rights of autonomous self-government. A key power in devolution crucial for self-government is the authority of a regional or local government to (1) adopt and collect its own sources of revenue (e.g., levy sales, income, or property taxes), (2) set its own tax rules and rates, (3) borrow funds, and (4) expend its revenues for locally determined purposes.

A leading example of devolution was the delegation in 1998 and 1999 of substantial powers and authority in the United Kingdom to Scotland, Wales, and Northern Ireland. The reopening under devolution of Scotland's parliament after a more than 300-year hiatus symbolized the restoration of significant autonomous self-government for Scotland. There have also been substantial devolutions of power from Spain's central government to such regions as the Basque Country, Catalonia, and Galicia. These examples indicate that devolution can be asymmetrical; that is, some regions or localities are granted, or entitled to receive, more powers than other regions. These examples indicate, as well, that devolution is sometimes a response to demands for autonomy by territorially based ethnic, national, religious, linguistic, and/or religious groups.

Usually, devolution, like decentralization, implies that the national or central government can unilaterally revoke acts of devolution and, thus, take back devolved powers. This happened in the United Kingdom in 1972 when Britain abolished Northern Ireland's parliament. In some cases, however, there are constitutional guarantees of devolution that protect against revocation; in other cases, the political imperatives of devolution might be sufficient to prevent revocation.

In the United States, the term "devolution" gained some currency when, in 1953, the American Municipal Association proposed a devolution-of-powers approach to municipal home rule. Under this approach, adopted by about 12 states, a state government devolves all powers capable of delegation to local governments for purposes of autonomous self-government. A local government is thereby free to exercise any appropriate power that is not expressly limited or prohibited by the state's constitution, the local government's charter, or a general state statute. For example, the Missouri and Pennsylvania Constitutions state that "a municipality which has a home-rule charter may exercise any power or perform any function not denied by this Constitution, by its home-rule charter, or by the General Assembly at any time." Under this approach, the state legislature is the principal determinant of the degree of autonomous local self-government because the legislature retains complete statutory authority to adjust the boundary between state and local powers.

The term "devolution" gained wider currency during the 1980s and 1990s when various observers used the term to describe developments that seemed to suggest a revolution in state-federal relations entailing substantial devolutions of power from the U.S. federal government to the states. President Richard M. Nixon's New Federalism was termed devolutionary because General Revenue Sharing (GRS) and the block grants advocated by Nixon provided greater discretion and flexibility for state and local governments than traditional categorical and project grants. Nixon also decentralized various grant-in-aid and regulatory functions to federal regional offices. However, GRS, enacted in 1972, was terminated for states in 1980 and for local governments in 1986.

In addition, GRS and block grants together never accounted for more than 18 percent of all federal aid to state and local governments. Some observers also described President Ronald Reagan's New Federalism as devolutionary, but his major New Federalism proposals were not enacted, he abolished the functions of federal regional offices established by Nixon, and he supported the final termination of GRS in 1986. Although Reagan convinced Congress to enact new block grants (i.e., nine new block grants in 1981), block grants again never accounted for more than 18 percent of all federal aid. Meanwhile, Reagan signed more bills preempting state powers than any previous president; he also approved major conditions attached to aid, such as the 21-year-old drinking age condition attached to federal highway aid in 1984. In the mid-1980s, the U.S. Advisory Commission on Intergovernmental Relations proposed devolving various programs to state and local governments; however, the Commission referred to its proposals as "turnbacks," namely, restorations to state and local governments of functions for which those governments were once entirely responsible prior to federal intervention. None of the proposed programs were turned back to states and localities.

The 1996 welfare reform law—the Personal Responsibility and Work Opportunity Reconciliation Act (PRWORA)—enacted during Bill Clinton's presidency was deemed devolutionary by some observers because PRWORA created a new block grant, Temporary Assistance for Needy Families (TANF), and allowed states considerable discretion in implementing PRWORA. However, PRWORA is encumbered with conditions; states must achieve very specific federal objectives; states face fiscal and civil penalties for failures to meet the federal objectives; and TANF's funding is dwarfed by other categorical grant welfare programs, especially Medicaid, a highly conditioned categorical grant program that accounts for nearly 45 percent of all federal aid to state and local governments. Congress's failure to reauthorize PRWORA in 2002 and for several years thereafter because of disagreements over policy objectives further indicated that PRWORA is not an example of devolution but merely of federal delegation of administrative discretion to the states to select the means by which they achieve mandated federal objectives.

Strictly speaking, there can be no devolution of powers from the U.S. federal government to the states without constitutional change because the federal government possesses only those powers delegated to it by the people of the states through the U.S. Constitution. All other powers are reserved to the states or to the people (see the Tenth Amendment to the U.S. Constitution). Hence, the states are sovereign in their own right, and they derive their self-governing powers from their own people, not from the U.S. government or the people of the United States. However, each U.S. state government is a unitary government possessing inherent and plenary residual powers, whereas in the case of local governments there is no inherent or sovereign right of self-government. Consequently, it is possible to devolve powers from a state government to local governments. *SEE ALSO:* Decentralization; Noncentralization

BIBLIOGRAPHY: Timothy Conlan, *From New Federalism to Devolution: Twenty-five Years of Intergovernmental Reform* (Washington, DC: Brookings Institution, 1988); John Kincaid, "De Facto Devolution and Urban Defunding: The Priority of Persons over Places," *Journal of Urban Affairs* 21, no. 2 (Summer): 135–67; U.S. Advisory Commission on Intergovernmental Relations, *Devolving Federal Program Responsibilities and Revenue Sources to State and Local Governments*, A-104 (Washington, DC: U.S. Government Printing Office, 1986); and U.S. Advisory Commission on Intergovernmental Relations, *Devolving Selected Federal-Aid Highway Programs and Revenue Bases: A Critical Appraisal*, A-108 (Washington, DC: U.S. Government Printing Office, 1987).

JOHN KINCAID

Dillon's Rule Named after nineteenth-century Ohio Judge John Forrest Dillon, who famously expounded the principle, Dillon's Rule is a strict construction of the authority of local governments in the United States. The dictum builds on their legal foundation as "creatures" of their state governments, thus claiming a world of limited autonomy for municipalities and other local governments. Local powers thus are restricted to what state legislatures and constitutions expressly grant, what is necessary or implied by these delegated powers, and what is essential to the purposes of a municipal corporation. Any doubt as to what is permissible is to be resolved by the courts against local governments and in favor of state control. Local governments, according to Dillon, are "the mere tenants at will of their legislature" (*City of Clinton v. Cedar Rapids and Missouri River Railroad*, 24 Iowa 455, 475 [1868]).

Judge Dillon expressed what was the conventional legal wisdom in the nineteenth century, reflecting also the assertion of state legislative powers in many areas and the widespread distrust of the competence and honesty of municipal governments. His comprehensive and forceful formulation appeared in the five editions of his *Commentaries on the Law of Municipal Corporations* (first published in 1872) and influenced generations of attorneys and courts. Dillon's Rule became a metaphor for the paternalism of state government over local issues, in which state legislatures operated as the effective governing bodies for localities. With little if any discretion to set their own course, local governments continually went to their state capitals as supplicants, seeking legislation for changes both ordinary and extraordinary—for example, to increase city council and municipal officer salaries, collect certain fees, and reorganize departments.

Another well-known midwestern judge in the nineteenth century, Thomas McIntyre Cooley of Michigan, expounded a contrary view of municipal authority and hence the state-local relationship. Cooley wrote that localities had an inherent right to self-government, one that could be traced to Anglo-Saxon traditions and that appeared in the governance of some of the colonial communities during the English settlement of the country. As compared to Dillon's strictly legalistic and state-oriented interpretation, Cooley's theory was based on extraconstitutional elements of popular sovereignty and the grassroots foundations of American democracy. Although cited by courts in a number of states, Cooley's doctrine never reached the level of acceptance and application achieved by Dillon's Rule.

The grasp of Dillon's Rule was gradually relaxed over the years as many states delegated varying degrees of discretionary authority to their municipal and county governments, including the ability to adopt home rule charters with structural flexibility. Still, Dillon's Rule continues to outline the basic state-local legal relationship: state governments are the ultimate source of local authority, whether restricted or expansive. *SEE ALSO:* Home Rule

BIBLIOGRAPHY: John Forest Dillon, *Commentaries on the Law of Municipal Corporations*, vol. 1, 2nd ed. (Boston: Little, Brown and Company, 1873).

ALVIN D. SOKOLOW

Direct Election of Senators   *See* Seventeenth Amendment

Diversity of Citizenship Jurisdiction   Article III, Section 2, of the U.S. Constitution provides that the judicial power of the United States shall extend to controversies "between citizen of different states" as well as controversies "between a state, or the citizens thereof, and foreign states, citizens or subjects." The authority of federal courts to hear the second category of controversies is sometimes described as "alienage jurisdiction," although federal court power over both of these two categories falls under the umbrella term "diversity jurisdiction."

Congress first authorized federal courts to exercise diversity jurisdiction in the Judiciary Act of 1789. Although the constitutional and legislative history is not altogether clear, courts and scholars generally agree that the 1789 legislation and the constitutional grant in Article III were motivated by the fear that a federal forum was needed to hear diversity cases because state courts would be prejudiced against out-of-state parties. Federal court jurisdiction was thought necessary to provide a neutral, impartial forum for resolution of the lawsuits.

Modern requirements governing diversity cases appear in federal law (28 U.S.C. §1332), which provides that federal district courts have original jurisdiction over diversity cases in which the amount in controversy exceeds $75,000. In order for a federal court to have jurisdiction to adjudicate cases under this statute, the lawsuit must be a civil action and must be between (1) citizens of different states of the United States; (2) citizens of a state of the United States and citizens or subjects of a foreign state; or (3) citizens of different states of the United States, in which citizens or subjects of a foreign state are additional parties.

> **ARTICLE III, SECTION 2, CLAUSE 1**
>
> *The judicial Power shall extend to all Cases, in Law and Equity, arising under this Constitution, the Laws of the United States, and Treaties made, or which shall be made, under their Authority;—to all Cases affecting Ambassadors, other public Ministers and Consuls;—to all Cases of admiralty and maritime Jurisdiction;—to Controversies to which the United States shall be a Party;—to Controversies between two or more States;—between a State and Citizens of another State;—between Citizens of different States, between Citizens of the same State claiming Lands under Grants of different States, and between a State, or the Citizens thereof, and foreign States, Citizens or Subjects.*

Courts have interpreted this section of the law strictly so as not to expand federal court power at the expense of state court power. For example, the U.S. Supreme Court has interpreted the law to require "complete diversity," and has therefore prohibited diversity jurisdiction where any parties on opposing sides of litigation share common citizenship. Citizenship is determined as of the time that the plaintiff commences the suit. Where a question is present about whether diversity jurisdiction exists in a case, courts resolve all doubt against finding jurisdiction. Consistent with the strict approach to applying this law, federal courts are not bound by the alignment of the parties in the pleadings and may make their own determination about which parties are truly opposing each other. Moreover, parties can neither confer jurisdiction by consent nor waive jurisdictional defects.

Section 1332 lacks any specification about the subject matter of cases for which federal courts may exercise diversity jurisdiction. Nevertheless, the federal courts have long held that they lack jurisdiction in most domestic relations and probate matters, even though the parties are diverse. The law governing in diversity actions is state law, although federal law can be applied to procedural matters. *SEE ALSO:* Citizenship

BIBLIOGRAPHY: Robert N. Clinton, "A Mandatory View of Federal Court Jurisdiction: A Guided Quest for the Original Understanding of Article III," *University of Pennsylvania Law Review* 132 (1984): 741; Henry J. Friendly, "The Historic Basis of Diversity Jurisdiction," *Harvard Law Review* 41 (1928): 483; and James W. Moore et al., *Moore's Federal Practice*, 3rd ed. (New York: Matthew Bender, 1997).

LAURA E. LITTLE

Dred Scott v. Sandford The *Dred Scott* case (1857) vaulted the Supreme Court into the midst of the swirling controversy over slavery that erupted into the Civil War in a few brief years. There can be little doubt the case contributed to raising the level of conflict and thus contributed to the coming of the war. The case raised two very important constitutional questions, which in the given context were also important political questions: does Congress have the power to prohibit slavery in the territories of the United States? Can black persons be citizens of the United States? The Court, speaking through Chief Justice Roger B. Taney, answered in the negative to both questions. The first issue arose because Dred Scott, a slave, had been taken into a federal territory where, under provisions of the Missouri Compromise Law (1820), slavery was forbidden. He sued for his freedom in federal court, but Taney ruled that since slavery is expressly affirmed in the Constitution, Congress lacks the power to prohibit it. This part of the ruling was politically important, because the Republican Party had recently formed around the policy of reenacting and extending the prohibition of slavery in the territories. Taney also ruled that blacks could not be citizens of the United States, and thus could not sue in federal courts or appeal to other federal constitutional protections, for they were not part of the "people of the United States" who adopted the

Dred Scott. Library of Congress, Prints and Photographs Division.

Constitution. Taney went so far as to proclaim that the founders considered blacks "a subordinate and inferior class of beings, who . . . had no rights or privileges but such as those who held the power and government might choose to grant them." *SEE ALSO:* Slavery; Taney, Roger Brooke

BIBLIOGRAPHY: Dan E. Fehrenbacher, *The Dred Scott Case: Its Significance in American Law and Politics* (New York: Oxford University Press, 1978); and Paul Finkelman, *Dred Scott v. Sandford: A Brief History with Documents* (New York: Bedford/St. Martin's, 1997).

MICHAEL ZUCKERT

Dual Citizenship In federal systems such as the United States, the term "dual citizenship" can have several meanings. One is a citizen of one's nation and then again a citizen of one's constituent unit and again of one's local place(s) of residence. One can also be a citizen of two, or even more, nations. Finally, one can be a citizen of an indigenous group such as Native American tribes. In many respects, then, many people are more accurately said to occupy "multiple" citizenships.

In the United States, the original Constitution (1787) established a dual national-state citizenship in several of its provisions. A national citizenship, for instance, was recognized in the requirements that eligibility for election to the House of Representatives and the U.S. Senate depended in part on having been a "citizen of the United States" for a specific period of years (Article I, Sections 2 and 3) and that the president must be a "natural born citizen" of the United States (Article II, Section 1). Likewise, a state citizenship is codified in Article IV, Section 2: "The citizens of each state shall be entitled to the privileges and immunities of citizens in the several states"; and in the extension of federal court jurisdiction to disputes between "citizens of different states" (Article III, Section 2).

Although the framers of the Constitution formalized the existence of two distinct citizenships, they did so without clearly defining the relative parameters of each or the relationship between them. As with most policy areas prior to the Civil War (1861–65), citizenship policy was made in accordance with a dual federalist model. Each level of government made policy to apply within its particular jurisdiction. Thus, the national government codified regulations for national citizenship in the Naturalization Act of 1790, while the states were free to establish rules for citizenship within their respective borders. Interestingly, states were largely responsible for implementing the 1790 Act, and there were variations of definitions, rights, and obligations. For the most part, however, the courts of each state upheld the rights of national citizenship conferred by the others.

The Fourteenth Amendment (1868) to the Constitution specifically defined national and state citizenship and seemingly removed any contradiction between the two. The Amendment declares that "[a]ll persons born or naturalized in the United States, and subject to the jurisdiction thereof, are citizens of the United States and of the State wherein they reside." It further declares that individual states may not deprive U.S. citizens of the "privileges and immunities" stemming from that citizenship or deprive their own citizens of "life, liberty, or property without due process of law." Additionally, each state must afford all of its citizens the "equal protection of the laws." The intent and long-term effect of the Fourteenth Amendment was to establish in law and in practice that national citizenship takes primacy over state citizenship and that state citizenship must conform to certain national standards.

As with so many policy areas in American intergovernmental relations, citizenship under the Fourteenth Amendment is the product of numerous political and legal struggles. Although the constitutional rule stated a comity between national and state (and local) citizenship, the statutes and practices putting it into effect differed widely among the states and were a persistent source of national conflict. Many states developed laws that created, in fact, two classes of citizenship. The right to vote, a sine qua non of citizenship, was guaranteed without regard to race by the Fifteenth Amendment (1870), but black citizens in particular were routinely prevented from exercising the franchise in their respective states by the "Jim Crow" laws that followed the end of Reconstruction in 1876. Women were not guaranteed the vote until 1920 by the Nineteenth Amendment. For Native Americans, the rights of citizenship conferred by the Indian Citizenship Act (1924) did not include the right to vote in many state elections until after World War II. The "separate but equal" doctrine articulated by the Supreme Court in *Plessy v. Ferguson* (1896) meant that black citizens and citizens from other categories could exercise their rights "equally," but separately, from whites. Many of these discrepancies were corrected by the Supreme Court in decisions on equal protection (*Brown v. Board of Education* 1954) and voting rights (*Baker v. Carr* 1962) and by the Congress in the Civil Rights Act of 1964 and Voting Rights Act of 1965.

Despite this de jure and de facto primacy of national citizenship, each state retains wide discretion in the distribution of citizen rights and obligations within its borders. For instance, each state's constitution can grant its citizens as many civil rights and liberties as it wishes, as long as they are no less than those conferred by the national government. States can determine for themselves what legal remedies its citizens shall have, what legal relationships it will endorse (e.g., marriage), and what benefits they are entitled to receive. States can even endorse substate citizenships in the local governments they charter, and allow the citizens of those smaller communities to determine some of these questions for themselves. But through all of this, each citizen must be treated in accordance with the Fourteenth Amendment's general requirements and the congressional acts that implement them.

When "dual citizenship" refers not to the federal relationship but rather to American citizens who hold citizenship in other countries, the issues are quite different. All persons born on U.S. soil are American citizens. Such "jus soli" (of the soil) citizenship raises the possibility that non-Americans will journey to the United States to bear their children on U.S. soil without intending to stay. Likewise, all persons born to U.S. citizens when not on U.S. soil are automatically U.S. citizens. This "jus sanguinis" (of the blood) citizenship can produce citizens who have not and never will set foot on U.S. soil. Although there have been several attempts by Congress and by individual states to place limitations on citizenship acquired through jus soli, the Supreme Court continues to uphold its 1893 decision (*United States v. Wong Kim Ark*) prohibiting all such limitations. Congress has placed residency requirements on the parents of jus sanguinis children. Naturalized American citizens are required to renounce allegiance to their former national citizenship. This is difficult to implement, as witnessed by the many dual citizens who regularly vote in American and in foreign national elections. Underlying such regulations is the assumption that a decision to join the American polity through the naturalization process is tantamount to consent to the American ideology, a consent that is noticeably absent in the jus soli and jus sanguinis means of acquiring American citizenship. *SEE ALSO: Brown v. Board of Education*; Citizenship; *Plessy v. Ferguson*

BIBLIOGRAPHY: Derek Heater, *What Is Citizenship?* (Malden, MA: Polity Press, 1999); Vicki C. Jackson, "Citizenship and Federalism," in *Citizenship Today: Global Perspectives and Practices*, ed. T. Alexander Aleinikoff and Douglas Klusmeyer, (Washington, DC: Carnegie Endowment for International Peace [Brookings Institution Press], 2001); David Jacobson, *Rights across Borders: Immigration and the Decline of Citizenship* (Baltimore: Johns Hopkins University Press, 1996); and Peter H. Shuck, *Citizens, Strangers, and In-betweens: Essays on Immigration and Citizenship* (Boulder, CO: Westview Press, 1998).

GORDON P. HENDERSON

Dual Federalism   Dual federalism is both a theory of how a federal system should allocate governmental powers, responsibilities, and resources and an era of American political history. As a theory, dual federalism holds that the federal and state governments both have power over individuals but that power is limited to separate and distinct spheres of authority, and each government is neither subordinate to nor liable to be deprived of its authority by the other. A government organized according to the theory of dual federalism is often compared to a layer cake where each layer represents a different level of government and the powers, responsibilities, and resources of each layer remain separate and distinct from the others.

Dual federalism appears consistent with a narrow reading of the U.S. Constitution. Such a reading must narrowly interpret the Commerce Clause, Necessary and Proper Clause, Supremacy Clause, and Tenth Amendment. A dual federalism reading of the Constitution limits the federal government's authority to foreign affairs, military affairs, and commerce with foreign nations, between the states, and with the Indian tribes. The national government's authority over interstate commerce includes responsibility for currency, weights and measures, patents and copyrights, and bankruptcy laws. All other powers not defined in the Constitution or prohibited to the states, according to the Tenth Amendment, are reserved to the states. These state powers, often called the police powers, include responsibility for the public's health, safety, and welfare. Dual federalism was the predominant theory for interpreting the Constitution from 1789 to 1901.

The era of dual federalism refers to the period of American political history when the Constitution was interpreted as creating separate and distinct spheres of authority between the federal and state governments. The practice of dual federalism was considerably messier than the theory of dual federalism. Morton Grodzins and Daniel Elazar demonstrated that during the era of dual federalism some overlap, cooperation, and resource sharing between the federal and state governments occurred. These instances of overlap and sharing were more often exceptions than the rule. More importantly, a dual federalism interpretation of the Constitution cannot exactly define the proper jurisdictions of the federal and state governments and prevent one from invading the jurisdiction of the other.

Prior to the Civil War, many conflicts erupted over the proper authority and jurisdiction of the national and state governments. Thomas Jefferson encouraged a version of dual federalism in his unsuccessful effort to prevent President Washington from creating a national bank and later in his support for the Kentucky and Virginia Resolutions. The Supreme Court dealt with conflicts between the national and state governments in many cases, including *McCulloch v. Maryland* (1819), *Gibbons v. Ogden* (1824), *Barron v. Baltimore* (1833), and *Dred Scott v. Sandford* (1856). At the Hartford Convention of 1814, New England representatives approved the idea that states exist as sovereign entities with rights that could not be violated by the national government. John C. Calhoun, building on the idea of states' rights, articulated a theory authorizing states to nullify federal laws. In 1832, the South Carolina legislature, believing that the national tariffs of 1828 and 1832 unfairly harmed southern interests, drew on Calhoun's ideas to pass a law declaring the tariffs null and void. President Andrew Jackson declared South Carolina's action tantamount to treason and prepared for military action to force compliance with the tariff. Congress supported the president with passage of the Force Act, but military action was allayed when Congress passed the 1833 tariff, which incrementally reduced the tariff over the next decade. While the period prior to the Civil War saw varied opinions of what the Constitution authorized and prohibited, most were consistent with a theory of dual federalism.

The theory of dual federalism survived the Civil War but was seriously challenged by the Industrial Revolution. The Civil War expanded the national government's sphere of authority, and confirmed the supremacy of federal laws and the inviolability of the union, but the national government, consistent with a theory of dual federalism, refrained from regulating the domestic affairs and intrastate commerce of the states. Dual federalism faced a fatal challenge with the Industrial Revolution. The Industrial Revolution allowed firms to amass great wealth and economic power, which some used to exploit workers and markets. Governments appeared to be the only force strong enough to counter these large firms. State governments faced two obstacles to controlling large firms: first, a Supreme Court that favored laissez-faire economic theory over state regulatory powers; and second, a few states that, in exchange for high licensing fees and business taxes, allowed firms to engage in what most other states considered bad business practices. Unable to regulate and control large firms, states were unable to fully protect their citizens and interests, and public opinion slowly turned against the states. Federal authority grew with the passage of the Sherman Antitrust Act (1890), and the Interstate Commerce Commission Act (1887). In 1901 President Theodore Roosevelt argued that national interests had become too decentralized and the nation needed a stronger national government to protect the common man. Roosevelt laid the foundation for ending dual federalism.

Over the next three decades, dual federalism decayed. National government grants to state and local governments inserted federal programs and objectives into state and local governments. By 1920 the federal government oversaw eleven grant programs allocating $30 million. These grants grew significantly during the New Deal. The New Deal also expanded the national government's powers to intervene in intrastate affairs. Also, the Supreme Court supported this shift when it changed from supporting laissez-faire economic policies to supporting national policies regulating intrastate activities. By the end of the second New Deal (1940), the era of dual federalism had clearly ended and the nation had moved into the era of cooperative federalism.

Some claim that the Supreme Court, under the direction of Chief Justice William Rehnquist, is trying to restore dual federalism, particularly in its reading of the Eleventh Amendment. The Rehnquist Court has ruled that the judicial power of the United States does not extend to the states, and therefore workers may not sue states for discrimination under federal age and disability standards and states may not be sued by people who claim the state promoted unfair competition in the marketplace. Most of these rulings were 5–4 decisions, and whether they will stand and be expanded over time is as yet unclear. *SEE ALSO: Barron v. Baltimore*; Civil War; Commerce among the States; Eleventh Amendment; *Gibbons v. Ogden*; Grants-in-Aid; Hartford Convention; Layer Cake Federalism; *McCulloch v. Maryland*; Necessary and Proper Clause; New Deal; Nullification; Police Power; Roosevelt, Theodore; Supremacy Clause: Article VI, Clause 2; Tenth Amendment

BIBLIOGRAPHY: Eugene Boyd, *American Federalism, 1776 to 1997: Significant Events*, http://usinfo.state.gov/usa/infousa/politics/states/federal.htm; and Sandra Osbourn, *Federalism: Key Episodes in the History of the American Federal System*, CRS Report 82-139 GOV (Washington, DC: U.S. Library of Congress, Congressional Research Service, 1982).

TROY E. SMITH

Due Process   *See* Fourteenth Amendment

Duncan v. Louisiana   *See* Incorporation (Nationalization) of the Bill of Rights

Dunn v. Blumstein   In *Dunn v. Blumstein* (1972), the U.S. Supreme Court struck down Tennessee's durational residency requirement to vote. The law required a one-year residency in the state and a thirty-day residency in the county in order to vote. The state had argued that the durational requirement prevented fraud and made the voters knowledgeable, but the Court said that a substantial period of residency failed the strict scrutiny test: there was not an overriding reason to curtail a right as fundamental as voting. The Court pointed out that Congress in the 1970 Voting Rights Act set thirty days of residency in a state to make a person eligible to vote in a presidential election, and that was an ample period for a state to complete whatever administrative tasks that are necessary to prevent fraud. An appropriately defined and uniformly applied requirement of bona fide residence may be necessary for a political community, but the durational requirement in this case abridged not only the right to vote, but also the right to travel, which is protected against state infringement by the Privileges and Immunities Clause of the Fourteenth Amendment. *SEE ALSO: Edwards v. California*; Privileges and Immunities Clause: Fourteenth Amendment

ROBERT W. LANGRAN

E

Economic Development   "Economic development policy" refers to government actions that are intended to affect growth in the economy, either through development (a structural change in production) or growth (an increase in output based on existing production). The role of economic development policy in the development of American federalism has always been inextricably linked to the process of urbanization and industrialization. In the early republic, the Founding Fathers had significant disagreement over the role of government in the economy. The most famous illustration of the two primary schools of thought can be found in the competing letters from members of President Washington's cabinet debating the proposed Bank of the United States.

Thomas Jefferson argues the Anti-Federalist position that the Bank would be unconstitutional, and that such policy devices would undermine the long-term stability of the republic by unbalancing federalism toward nationalist designs. Alexander Hamilton argues the prevailing Federalist position that the Constitution must be interpreted with flexibility and that implied powers existed with the regulation of commerce that made the Bank constitutional, and ultimately, that this nation-directed economic policy was necessary to maintain the republic in the long term. Hamiltonian thinking ultimately prevailed, but not without significant periods of conflict during the period of dual federalism. The fundamental differences between Jeffersonians and Hamiltonians were over the degree of constitutional responsibility for the national government and, more generally, over the proper role of government in the economic development process. The constitutional question centered around the issues of states' rights and property rights. Business interests and urban centers sought government intervention for a variety of economic development needs, among them to provide investment capital, to stabilize currency and markets, to subsidize production costs, and to control competition through tariffs. The goal of the Hamiltonians was to create a national economy by reducing state barriers to competition and utilizing national policy to build domestic industry. Ultimately, the consolidation of regional, state, and substate economies into a national economy was desired by the Hamiltonians, whereas the Jeffersonians sought a self-sufficient economy based primarily on agriculture.

Future debates between Henry Clay and other proponents of the American System advocated by the Whigs, on one hand, and "strict constructionist" Democrats like John C. Calhoun, on the other, would center on the same basic issue of economic development; was it a fundamentally state and local issue, or was it one that was inherently national? Among the most famous presidential vetoes of the first 100 years of U.S. political history centered around these "internal improvements," such as those by James Madison and Andrew Jackson. These "internal improvements" were, and in many instances still remain, the fundamental building blocks of economic development policy at all levels of government. Whether the government had the authority to engage in "internal improvements" by building bridges, roads, utilities, transportation, and general infrastructure was the central question of the period of dual federalism. After the Civil War, the question of national authority for economic development was settled in the Hamiltonian style, and major national involvement in education, railroads and transportation, housing, and infrastructure followed.

In the period following World War II, economic development policy was transformed following the passage of New Deal programs that gave the government responsibility for a range of economic policies (from public works to retirement to a broad range of business regulation). The establishment of the last iteration of the National Bank, the Federal Reserve System, remains a cornerstone of economic development policy today. Cooperative federalism and creative federalism provided new intergovernmental paradigms for the delivery of nationally determined policies in economic development, and new national agencies established an enduring national policy role (examples include the U.S. Department of Housing and Urban Development, the Economic Development Administration, the Rural Electrification Service within the USDA, the Tennessee Valley Authority, and the Appalachian Regional Commission). The New Federalism paradigm developed by Reagan (building on the earlier Nixon New Federalism) sought to return to dual federalism and repudiated the constitutional foundation of the prior nationalist periods of cooperative and creative federalism. Reagan retained a strong responsibility for national government to support and encourage economic development policy, but the means of exercising this power was redirected toward devolution of policy authority to the states.

It is in this period of New Federalism, established by Reagan, that we examine current trends and policy debates in economic development. Major questions in economic development policy today are concerned with the most effective ways for state and local governments to conduct economic development with or without federal assistance. Should states continue to compete individually, or should they develop interstate partnerships? Should states continue traditional incentive programs or develop tertiary quality-of-life programs? Should states target the development of a workforce or recruitment of industries? Should state and local governments control growth through planning and zoning or through market-based incentives? Scholars in the field are divided over the answers to these questions, and no consensus seems likely in the near future. In fact, some have even raised questions over the effectiveness of government doing anything at all to affect the perceived efficient operation of private sector markets. Government has even come to question whether it can effectively manage programs over which it has authority, and the outsourcing of government services to the private sector has risen dramatically in recent years. The erosion of hierarchy, and with it accountability, has witnessed the exponential expansion of what Thomas Anton (1989) called Third Party Federalism. The nongovernmental or pseudo-governmental organizations (private, nonprofit, foundation, special district, and pseudo-public corporations) that constitute the expanding web of intergovernmental organizations in American federalism make the present era one of high complexity, dispersed interdependence, and fragmented conflict.

There are two common types of ranking systems: one looks at typological definitions (the substance of the policies), and the other looks at relative performance (the outcomes of the policies). Martin Saiz (2001) has developed a typological state index of infrastructure programs that measures the commitment of states to various economic development policy types. This measure of economic development policy type utilizes a policy index that takes the policy type as a function of overall state economic development spending. These policy types further reflect the heterogeneity of economic policy making at the state level and underscore the importance of policy leadership and authority relationships distinct from actual policy outcomes or fiscal flows. Saiz's three types are locational, entreprenurial, and infrastructural. Locational policy is an approach with the dominant resources placed in factors that improve relative competition. Infrastructual policy making is a static, low-innovation approach that expresses the more traditional importance for "internal improvements" such as utilities and transportation. Entrepreneurial policy emphasizes the development of intellectual capital and innovation capacity.

While Saiz's work represents the typological ranking, a number of organizations and researchers, including the Southern Growth Policies Board, the Milken Institute, the Progressive Policy Institute, and the Corporation for Enterprise Development, have developed relative state performance rankings tied in particular to new economy development or innovation capacity. These ranking systems attempt to assess which states have been most successful at "new economy" development. Though these performance ratings differ substantially, most aggregate a series of variables to create a single composite index representing state performance. Not particularly useful at informing policy, these indices have recently been improved by the categorization of variables by type of capacity and by separating capacity measures from outcome measures. These indices reflect the ongoing interstate competition for economic growth and development in a changing and uncertain economy, and further highlight the intergovernmental aspects of funding and implementing programs to further economic growth at the local, state, and national level. Despite the increased importance for economic development policy and the growing diversity of approaches and programs, there remain persistent pockets of poverty in urban inner cities as well as in rural areas.

Economic development rankings have become a popular way for media, policy, and academic gatekeepers to communicate the effectiveness of economic development policies. But the quality of the measures that constitute these indices remains highly questionable. The uncertain reliability of ranking indices leaves descriptive statistics (number of jobs or businesses created, average wages, etc.) as objective measures to which politicians at all levels of government continue to perform. The facile association of these measures with traditional "smokestack chasing" economic development strategies leaves advocates of "new economy" or high-tech, science-based business development with a challenging and complex task. The management of intellectual capital at a range of places such as universities, research laboratories, and nonprofits is a complex task and one that requires sophisticated policy tools and effective long-range planning. Thus, the current landscape of economic development policy continues to reflect high complexity, dispersed interdependence, and fragmented conflict, just as does the intergovernmental system that manages it. *SEE ALSO:* American System; Cooperative Federalism; Creative Federalism; Dual Federalism; Fiscal Federalism; Hamilton, Alexander; Internal Improvements; Jefferson, Thomas; New Federalism (Nixon); New Federalism (Reagan); Reagan, Ronald; Roosevelt, Franklin D.

BIBLIOGRAPHY: Thomas J. Anton, *American Federalism and Public Policy* (Philadelphia: Temple University Press, 1989); David R. Beam, "Washington's Regulation of States and Localities: Origins and Issues," *Intergovernmental Perspective* 7, no. 10 (Summer 1981); Timothy Conlan, *New Federalism* (Washington, DC: Brookings Institution, 1988); Marian Lief Palley and Howard Palley, *Urban America and Public Policies* (Lexington, MA: D. C. Heath, 1977); Martin Saiz, "Politics and Economic Development: Why Governments Adopt Different Strategies to Induce Economic Growth," *Policy Studies Journal* 29, no. 2 (2001): 203–14; Martin Saiz and Susan E. Clark, "Economic Development and Infrastructure Policy," in *Politics in the American States: A Comparative Analysis*, ed. Virginia Gray, Russell L. Hanson, and Herbert Jacob (Washington, DC: CQ Press, 1999); and Stephen Skowronek, *Building A New American State: The Expansion of State Administrative Capacities, 1877–1920* (Cambridge: Cambridge University Press, 1982).

MICHAEL W. HAIL AND JEREMY L. HALL

Economic Opportunity Act of 1964   President Lyndon B. Johnson proposed a "War on Poverty" in 1964 that took form in an omnibus poverty bill (S. 2642) that was enacted as the Economic Opportunity Act (EOA, Public Law 88-452). It was the first major policy proposal from the Johnson administration, but it included several elements that had been considered previously by Congress. It established national government programs for job training, adult education, migrant worker assistance, and small-business loans. It resulted in specific entities including Volunteers in Service to America (VISTA), the Job Corps, the Neighborhood Youth Corps, Head Start, and Community Action Agencies (CAAs). The act established the Office of Economic Opportunity (OEO) as a unit in the Executive Office of the President, thereby engaging that institution and the presidency directly in the administration of governmental service programs.

Most congressional Republicans hotly resisted the bill. They condemned the proposal as a hodgepodge of duplicative programs, an enlargement of national government authority at the expense of state and local governments, and wasteful spending for expanded bureaucracy during an election year, but the legislation passed easily. The Senate passed the bill 61–34. In the House, Republicans sought help from southern Democrats to defeat the bill, but the administration accepted a proposal to give state governors a veto power over community action projects, thereby accommodating most of the Southerners. Thus amended, the House passed the bill with support from all 144 northern Democrats and 60 of 100 southern Democrats. The final vote was to 226–185.

By 1968 there were 1,600 CAAs engaged directly in aiding the poor and unemployed. According to the act, the clients of services were to have "maximum feasible participation" in the poverty program planning. Increasingly, such programs came into conflict with state and local agencies and politics.

Under the administrations of Presidents Richard Nixon, Gerald Ford, and Ronald Reagan, parts of the act were reduced in scope and assigned to other departments. In 1974 the Ford administration dismantled the OEO. In 1981 Congress and the Reagan administration rescinded EOA and created a block grant system for poverty assistance that consolidated 200 federal programs and increased the discretion and authority of the states in administering poverty services. Under the U.S. Department of Health and Human Resources, the Office of Community Services provides the Community Services Block Grant. It supports the institutional operations of a state-administered network of 1,100 agencies, predominantly CAAs, which deliver services to low-income Americans. *SEE ALSO:* Great Society; Johnson, Lyndon B.

BIBLIOGRAPHY: Congress and the Nation (Washington DC: Congressional Quarterly Inc., 1965); and Meg Power, Gretchen Knowlton, and Maggie Spade-Aguilar, *Community Services Block Grant Statistical Support FY 2000: Executive Summary*, July (Washington, DC: National Association for Community Block Grant Programs, 2002).

JACK R. VAN DER SLIK

Education   Public education is a shared responsibility in American federalism. The system of educational governance facilitates a division of power and control among the three planes of government, namely, federal, state, and local. Although the federal government has expanded its involvement in educational policy since the 1960s, public education remains the primary responsibility of state and local government.

State control in education is established by its own constitutional framework. In general, states handle a wide range of key educational issues, including compulsory attendance, teacher certification, curriculum standards, the operation of districts, graduation requirements, unions' right to collective bargaining, and school funding. With federal funds accounting for somewhere between 5 and 10 percent of public school revenue in the last several decades, the K–12 budget typical constitutes one-third of the total state and local revenue. Due to the property taxpayers' movement and court decisions on funding disparity among districts, a growing number of states play a primary fiscal role. In 1959, the average state share was only 38 percent of the K–12 budget.

Historically, the federal government has taken a permissive role in education that is consistent with Morton Grodzins's notion of federalism as a "layer cake." Article I, Section 8, of the U.S. Constitution specifies the "enumerated powers" that Congress enjoys, and the Tenth Amendment granted state autonomy in virtually all domestic affairs, including education. The dual structure was further maintained by local customs, practice, and belief. Observing the state-local relations in the New England townships in the mid-nineteenth century, Alexis de Tocqueville in *Democracy in America* wrote, "Thus it is true that the tax is voted by the legislature, but it is the township that apportions and collects it; the existence of a school is imposed, but the township builds it, pays for it, and directs it." The division of power within the federal system was so strong that it continued to preserve state control over its internal affairs, including the de jure segregation of schools, many decades following the Civil War.

Federal involvement in education sharply increased during the Great Society era of the 1960s and the 1970s. Several events converged to shift the federal role from permissiveness to engagement. During the immediate post–World War II period, Congress enacted the G.I. Bill to enable veterans to receive a college education of their choice. The Cold War competition saw the passage of the National Defense Education Act in 1958 shortly after the Soviet Union's satellite, *Sputnik*, successfully orbited Earth. At the same time, the 1954 landmark Supreme Court ruling on *Brown v. Board of Education* and the congressional enactment of the 1964 Civil Rights Act sharpened federal attention to the needs of disadvantaged students. In 1965, Congress enacted the Elementary and Secondary Education Act (ESEA). Despite several revisions and extension, Title I of the ESEA continues to allot federal funds to schools with a high concentration of low-income students for supplemental instructional services. Over the years, federal educational programs have become an important component of the grant-in-aid system, providing supplemental services to economically disadvantaged children, racial and ethnic minorities, students with disabilities, high school dropouts, and English language learners.

As Congress enacted the No Child Left Behind Act of 2001, the federal government further expands its activities to promote educational accountability for all children. The federal law requires annual testing of students at the elementary grades in core subject areas, mandates the hiring of "highly qualified teachers" in classrooms by 2005–6, and grants state and local agencies substantial authority in taking "corrective actions" to turn around failing schools. Further, the law provides school choice to parents to take their children out of failing schools. Equally significant in terms of federal intervention is the legislative intent in closing the achievement gaps among racial/ethnic subgroups as well as income subgroups. These federal expectations are likely to shape the policy and practice at the state and local level.

In response to growing public concerns about school performance, as illuminated with the passage of the No Child Left Behind Act, state government has assumed visibly greater responsibility in driving educational reform. Recent state legislation and gubernatorial actions on educational accountability, choice, and the takeover of districts and schools provide a new empirical basis to rethink the balance of power between state and local government. A hybrid of state authority may have emerged to the effect that one now sees both centralizing and decentralizing tendencies occurring at the same time, often within the same state.

The decentralizing tendency is illuminated by an increasing number of states that rely on market-like competition as the driving force to raise student performance. The charter school reform represents the most extensive state effort to promote choice. Thirty-seven states and the District of Columbia operated a total of over 2,000 charter schools during 2001. Although charter schools are labeled as public schools, their renewable contracts are held accountable for outcome-based performance and are governed by state regulations regarding safety, health, dismissal, and civil rights. In return, charter schools enjoy substantial autonomy in setting teachers' salaries and work conditions. School funding follows students to the charter schools, which are operated on a multiyear renewable contract. Further, only 2 states did not allow for home schooling in 2001. Nationwide, almost 900,000 school-age children are home schooled.

A seemingly centralizing tendency is suggested by the state enactment of takeover legislation over low-performing districts and schools. About half of the states allow state takeover of local school districts, permitting state officials to exert authority over a district in the case of "academic bankruptcy," or woefully low-performing schools. State takeover legislation often enables the mayor to take over the local school system, as shown in Boston, Chicago, Cleveland, Philadelphia, Baltimore, and New York. The effectiveness of mayoral takeover has been facilitated by mayoral vision on outcome-based accountability, broad public dissatisfaction with "a crisis" in school performance over several years, the willingness of the state Republican leadership to work with the mayor, strong business support, and the weakened legitimacy of traditionally powerful unions. *SEE ALSO:* Elementary and Secondary Education Act of 1965; No Child Left Behind Act, School Districts

KENNETH K. WONG

Education Commission of the States   The Education Commission of the States (ECS) was created by an interstate compact in 1965 to strengthen the capacity of the states as a counterbalance to the rapidly expanding federal influence in education during President Johnson's Great Society initiative. With start-up grants from the Carnegie Corporation and the Ford Foundation, Governor Terry Sanford of North Carolina co-founded the ECS and convened its first meeting in Chicago in 1966, when 36 states had formally ratified the compact and chose Denver as its headquarters. By 2004, 40 current and former governors served as the chair of the ECS. To ensure bipartisanship, the chair's position alternates between Republicans and Democrats and the vice chair's position is held by a state legislator.

Recognizing the states' constitutional authority in education, the ECS serves as a strategic consortium of state policy stakeholders in education. It is neither a lobbying organization nor an entity that is narrowly defined in terms of a particular political or policy office (such as the U.S. Conference of the Mayors). It encompasses broad representation across a wide spectrum of educational interests at the state level. In 1995, for example, Republican Governor Tommy Thompson (Wisconsin) was elected to chair both the ECS and the National Governors' Association, thereby strengthening the ties between the two organizations. In 2002, the ECS sided with the National Board for Professional Standards following the release of a critical study on the effectiveness of the national certification standards. In addition to the elected political representatives, the ECS addresses the needs of the K–12 community and the higher education, business, and civic sectors. The ECS's clearinghouse and dissemination functions have provided technical assistance and facilitated interstate and intrastate exchanges of ideas on emerging reform issues.

This network of broad-based stakeholders has enabled the ECS to adapt to the changing policy environment over the last four decades. During the 1970s and the 1980s, when state governments faced numerous constitutional challenges on funding equity, the ECS conducted extensive studies on funding reform issues. With growing public demand for accountability and greater involvement by governors and mayors, the ECS is now actively embarking on research and development in governance reform, charter schools, service learning, and democracy and citizenship. Given the prominence of the 2001 No Child Left Behind Act, the ECS has tracked progress made by every state in meeting the federal standards. In recent years, ECS's task forces and reports challenge the educational establishment to reform the district and state bureaucracy, to rethink the functions and design of the school board, to create a system of chartering schools, and to reassess teacher certification standards. As education remains a top item on state and national agendas, the ECS will continue to evolve in its role as a partner in our "creative federalism." *SEE ALSO:* Education; Interstate Compacts

BIBLIOGRAPHY: http://ecs.org.

K<small>ENNETH</small> K. W<small>ONG</small>

Edwards v. California   In *Edwards v. California* (1941), the U.S. Supreme Court invalidated California's "anti-Okie" law, which had made it a crime to bring an indigent person, who was not a resident of California, into that state. The purpose of the law was to prevent those who had lost everything when severe drought hit the Southwest from coming into California and becoming a drain on the state's resources. A unanimous Court, speaking through Justice James Byrnes, invalidated the law, calling it an unconstitutional obstruction to interstate commerce. Four justices—William Douglas, Hugo Black, Frank Murphy, and Robert Jackson—concurred, agreeing with the outcome but for a different reason. They felt the law abridged the right to move about freely in the country, which is a privilege of U.S. citizenship protected against state infringement by the Privileges and Immunities Clause of the Fourteenth Amendment. *SEE ALSO: Dunn v. Blumstein*; Privileges and Immunities Clause: Fourteenth Amendment

ROBERT W. LANGRAN

Eisenhower, Dwight D. As the first Republican president since Herbert Hoover, Dwight D. Eisenhower (1890–1969) saw it as his responsibility to peel back what he perceived as the negative trend of the accrual of power in the national government under the New Deal and its consequent paternalism and even "creeping socialism." Though a doctrinaire conservative on most questions of federal-state relations, Eisenhower was nevertheless pragmatic enough, both in terms of politics and policy, to recognize the staying power of the New Deal and the potential positive uses of national government power.

Believing that twenty years of Democratic control had established dangerous trends toward the increase of federal power, Eisenhower spent considerable time and official effort questioning the appropriate balance of federal-state power. In a 1953 message to Congress, "Recommending the Establishment of a Commission to Study Federal, State, and Local Relations," Eisenhower argued that given the accrual of power in Washington under the New Deal, "the Federal Government has entered fields which, under our Constitution, are the primary responsibilities of state and local governments." Seeking to rationalize the federal balance of power that had developed in a "piecemeal and often haphazard" way and to study the efficiency and appropriateness of federal grant-in-aid programs, Eisenhower took first steps to control this key centralizing trend of the New Deal. Indeed, these efforts to address and track the development of American federalism led to the creation of the Advisory Commission on Intergovernmental Relations in 1959.

Despite these longheld ideological principles on the proper federal balance of power, one key action of the Eisenhower administration involved significant use of national government power. Eisenhower used national government force in a showdown between the authority of the federal courts and recalcitrant southern state offi-

Dwight D. Eisenhower. Library of Congress, Prints and Photographs Division.

cials over the desegregation of public schools. When Arkansas Governor Orval Faubus defied the U.S. Supreme Court's ruling that schools be integrated and called out the Arkansas National Guard to maintain racial segregation of Little Rock's schools, Eisenhower, who had previously disavowed using federal coercion to enforce court rulings, signed Executive Order 10730, which federalized the Arkansas National Guard and mobilized National Guard and U.S. Army forces to compel Arkansas' compliance with the U.S. Constitution.

Consistent with the political strength of the New Deal and the more general trend toward the expansion of national government power in the twentieth century, for all of his attention to a more traditional role for national, state, and local governments, Eisenhower also expanded the reach of the national government as the use of grants-in-aid expanded during his tenure and the national government's role in providing entitlements solidified. Moreover, Eisenhower's interstate highway system represents one of the largest national government public works programs of the twentieth century. *SEE ALSO:* Cooperative Federalism; National Defense and Interstate Highway Act of 1956

BIBLIOGRAPHY: Robert Frederick Burk, *The Eisenhower Administration and Black Civil Rights* (Knoxville: University of Tennessee Press, 1984); Douglas B. Harris, "Dwight Eisenhower and the New Deal: The Politics of Preemption," *Presidential Studies Quarterly* 27, no. 2 (Spring 1997): 333–42; William E. Leuchtenberg, *In the Shadow of FDR: Harry Truman to George W. Bush*, 3rd rev. and updated ed. (Ithaca, NY: Cornell University Press, 2001); and Gary W. Reichard, *The Reaffirmation of Republicanism* (Knoxville: University of Tennessee Press, 1975).

Douglas B. Harris

Elections The success of a federal system depends to some degree on maintaining the autonomy of its federal and constituent units of governments, and nothing, it seems, could be more threatening to that autonomy than to divest a government of the authority to control its own internal democratic processes. Nevertheless, in a vivid demonstration of the U.S. Constitution's preference for blending rather than strictly dividing power, the American federal system allocates to each level of government considerable authority to regulate elections conducted by the other.

The Constitution's original allocation of regulatory authority over elections reflected the framers' fear that the national government might become dangerously powerful and independent. While taking for granted that states would exercise exclusive control over their own internal democratic processes, the framers provided numerous avenues by which states might indirectly restrain the national government by influencing national political processes. Thus, Article I, Section 2, provides that eligibility to vote in congressional elections is controlled not by federal law, but by state law. Article II, Section 1, authorizes states to determine eligibility to vote for presidential electors, and even permits state legislatures to dispense with popular presidential elections altogether and select the state's presidential electors themselves, as many state legislatures did during the nation's first few decades. Under the original constitutional plan, each state legislature also directly appointed the state's two senators, although the Seventeenth Amendment replaced this system in 1913 with one of direct popular election.

Article I, Section 4, goes even further by providing that the "Times, Places and Manner" of holding congressional elections are to be regulated in the first instance by state law. Although Article I, Section 4, also authorizes Congress to "make or alter" state regulations, Congress has used this authority sparingly. Consequently, virtually every aspect of federal elections has long been regulated principally by detailed state election codes.

Following the Civil War, however, aspects of state electoral processes were regulated increasingly at the national level. Much of the necessary authority was provided in a series of constitutional amendments that restricted states' regulatory discretion while simultaneously granting Congress explicit enforcement authority. These amendments included provisions curtailing the states' discretion to deny the franchise on the basis of race, sex, or failure to pay a poll tax, and to set the age of voting eligibility higher than 18.

The Equal Protection Clause of the Fourteenth Amendment also imposes numerous restraints on the authority of states to structure their internal electoral processes as they see fit. Most importantly, the clause requires states to apportion representation in the state legislature and in Congress according to a principle of one person, one vote. This means that states must draw election districts such that, for any particular elected body, each election district contains roughly equal numbers of people. The clause has also been held to prohibit "vote dilution" through gerrymandering or the use in certain circumstances of at-large voting systems, and to limit the authority of states to impose lengthy residency requirements or property ownership as prerequisites to voting. Following the 2000 presidential election, the Supreme Court ruled that the Equal Protection Clause limits the kinds of procedures that states may use in counting ballots. Furthermore, the First Amendment's protection of free speech severely limits the power of states to regulate political speech, the activities of political parties, age of voting eligibility higher than 18, and the spending and donation of money in political campaigns.

Congress has invoked its constitutional authority to regulate state elections only rarely, but when it has done so its actions sometimes have been powerful and intrusive. By far the strongest of these federal statutes is the Voting Rights Act, enacted by Congress using its power to enforce the Fifteenth Amendment's prohibition on racial discrimination in voting. The act's most invasive provision, Section 5, identifies states and counties with significant histories of racial discrimination in electoral processes and prohibits them from adopting any changes to voting practices and procedures without the prior approval of the federal government.

Although the Constitution thus creates a formal system of substantially intermingled state and national authority over elections, an equally significant blurring of the boundaries of intergovernmental power has occurred outside the formal legal system under the auspices of the national political parties. In a development completely unanticipated by the framers, political parties quickly emerged and then organized themselves not into distinct state and national party systems, but into a single unified system in which the major parties coordinate partisan activity at both the state and national levels for the purpose of contesting offices at all levels. In this system, state and national officeholders are often able, in their capacity as party leaders, to exert significant influence on the way elections are conducted throughout the system, even where the formal allocation of authority might seem to deny them any influence. For example, although Congress has formally left the regulation of congressional apportionment to the states, members of Congress nevertheless typically exert significant influence on the way congressional districts, and even in many cases state legislative districts, are drawn by their state legislatures.

The extensive formal and informal interpenetration of state and national authority over elections has led to a certain degree of uniformity in electoral structures and practices around the nation. Nevertheless, states still possess considerable regulatory independence in certain areas, and have occasionally used this independence to grant their own citizens more extensive rights of political participation than the U.S. Constitution grants to Americans generally. Most prominently, states typically make many more offices elective than does the national government, including state-level cabinet posts, judicial positions, and numerous local offices. Many states provide opportunities for direct democracy through the initiative and referendum, and through requirements for popular approval of state or local fiscal measures. Some states impose tighter controls over elected officials than appear on the national level through the use of term limits, rotation in office requirements, or recall procedures. States have also occasionally introduced reforms such as nonpartisanship, alternative voting systems, innovative formats for primary elections, and remote voting electronically and by mail. *SEE ALSO:* Amendment Process; Civil War; Fourteenth Amendment; Political Parties; Racial Discrimination; Referendum; Seventeenth Amendment; State Legislatures; Voting Rights Act of 1965

BIBLIOGRAPHY: Alexander Keyssar, *The Right to Vote: The Contested History of Democracy in the United States* (New York: Basic Books, 2000); Larry D. Kramer, "Putting the Politics Back into the Political Safeguards of Federalism," *Columbia Law Review* 100 (2000): 215–93; and G. Alan Tarr, *Understanding State Constitutions* (Princeton, NJ: Princeton University Press, 1998).

JAMES A. GARDNER

Electoral College   The Electoral College is the official and definitive election body that selects the president of the United States. The Electoral College was established by the Founding Fathers as a compromise between election of the president by Congress and election by popular vote. The Electoral College was a part of the compromises between large and small states necessary for achieving majority support for the Constitution developed at the Constitutional Convention in Philadelphia. Among those favoring small-state interests was Maryland's attorney general, Luther Martin. Martin was the author of the Electoral College proposal at the Philadelphia convention. His proposal drew on the experience, philosophy, and history of Maryland's colonial constitution, which provided for an electoral college to select its upper house.

The Constitution directs that each state legislature determine the method of selecting that state's electors for the Electoral College. At various times state legislatures have determined that the state legislature, its districts, or the state as a whole would elect that state's electors. Presently, electors in all states are popularly elected on a statewide, winner-take-all ticket except in Nebraska and Maine, where electors are elected by special districts.

Each state's allotment of electors is equal to its number of House members plus two senators. The exception is District of Columbia, which has no voting members in Congress, but the Twenty-third Amendment to the Constitution gave the citizens of the District of Columbia at least three electoral votes. The Electoral College currently consists of 538 electors (one for each of the 435 members of the House of Representatives and

100 senators, and 3 for the District of Columbia). The decennial census is used to reapportion the number of electors allocated among the states, based upon reapportionment of the House of Representatives.

State laws vary on the appointment of electors and the selection process, the regulation of method and place of voting, and the official certification and transmission of results. The slates of electors in each state are generally chosen by the political parties. The electors in all states and the District of Columbia are elected on the Tuesday after the first Monday in November. The states then prepare a list of the slate of electors for the candidate who receives the most popular votes on a Certificate of Ascertainment. The electors meet in each state on the first Monday after the second Wednesday in December to cast their votes for president and vice president. No national constitutional provision or federal law requires electors to vote in accordance with the popular vote in their state, though some states have taken measures to direct electors to vote in accordance with the popular vote in their states. The electors prepare six original Certificates of Vote and annex a Certificate of Ascertainment to each one. Each Certificate of Vote lists all persons voted for as president and the number of electors voting for each person, and separately lists all persons voted for as vice president and the number of electors voting for each person.

The governor of each state prepares seven original Certificates of Ascertainment. The states send one original, along with two authenticated copies or two additional originals, to the archivist of the United States at the National Archives and Records Administration (NARA) by registered mail, which must be received by the first Monday after the second Wednesday in December. The archivist transmits the originals to NARA's Office of the Federal Register (OFR), and OFR forwards one copy to each House of Congress and retains the original.

The votes are officially counted by Congress early in January. The candidate who wins a majority of the votes cast in the Electoral College is elected. Presently, a majority of 270 electoral votes is required to elect the president and vice president. If no presidential candidate wins a majority of electoral votes, the Twelfth Amendment to the Constitution provides for the presidential election to be decided by the House of Representatives. The House would select the president by majority vote, choosing from the three candidates who received the greatest number of electoral votes. The vote would be taken by state, with each state delegation having one vote. If no vice presidential candidate wins a majority of electoral votes, the Senate would select the vice president by majority vote, with each senator choosing from the two candidates who received the greatest number of electoral votes. In both chambers the states are the primary constituency represented, as reflected by voting by state in the House and the assumed state suffrage inherently reflected in state representation in the Senate.

Despite periodic calls for reform, the safeguards of federalism designed by the Founding Fathers that are the foundation of the Electoral College remain intact. The Electoral College provides an intrinsic embodiment of federalism by combining the House (population) and Senate (states) representation methods in determination of the allocation of electors. The design of the Electoral College not only provides incentive for broad, inclusive campaigning across the breadth of the nation, but also minimizes the potential impact of any electoral irregularities by decentralizing the proportion of votes by state. The Electoral College remains one of the most significant and enduring constitutional contributions to the balance of federalism. *SEE ALSO:* Constitutional Convention of 1787; Political Parties; Presidency; Reapportionment; State Legislatures

BIBLIOGRAPHY: George Anastaplo, *The Amendments to the Constitution* (Baltimore: Johns Hopkins University Press, 1995); Allan Bloom, ed., *Confronting the Constitution* (Washington, DC: AEI Press, 1990); M. E. Bradford, *Founding Fathers*, 2nd ed. (Lawrence: University Press of Kansas, 1994); and Martin Diamond, *The Founding of the Democratic Republic* (Itasca, IL: F. E. Peacock, 1981).

MICHAEL W. HAIL AND DUANE D. MILNE

Electric Industry Restructuring   Electric energy is vital to the economic vitality of communities and nations. The regulatory compact that fostered this vital service provided a utility with an exclusive service territory in exchange for the obligation to serve all customers upon demand in a reliable and safe manner. Most of these utilities (whether public and privately owned) were vertically integrated enterprises that bundled the generation, transmission, and distribution functions. Customer rates were regulated to ensure that the utilities received a guaranteed rate of return (i.e., profit margin). These monopoly arrangements conflict with the trend for consumer choice in market transactions.

Because electricity cannot be stored, an extensive system of interconnection provides utilities the opportunity to buy and sell energy from one another in order to gain efficiencies and to enhance reliability. However, this same interstate grid permits a problem in one community to ripple across entire regions.

Based on the Public Utility Holding Company Act of 1935 and the Energy Power Act of 1992, the Federal Energy Regulatory Commission (FERC) controls the resale of electricity (wholesale) but is prohibited from mandating retail competition. Starting in 1996, FERC required electric utilities providing transmission facilities to treat their system as a toll road with posted nondiscriminatory tariffs and, in effect, required all utilities to restructure into separate generation, transmission, and distribution services. The goal was to facilitate the transfer (or "wheeling") of electric energy from a supplier to a bulk-purchase customer over the electric lines owned by a third party without discrimination. While still outside the ambit of FERC, retail competition, in contrast, refers to the use by one energy supplier of another's transmission and/or distribution system to reach the end customer.

Despite opening the wholesale market to competition, Congress has continued to honor state interest in controlling retail competition. States have regulated electric utilities since the early twentieth century. Unraveling the state regulatory structure to introduce customer choice is not easy. Change requires reopening decisions that ensure universal service, provide affordable energy for low-income ratepayers, promote economic development, protect the environment, preserve network reliability, control the siting of energy facilities and power lines, and maintain a flow of tax revenue from one of the largest industries in a state. For example, states have established opaque tax structures with the burden hidden in regulated electric prices. In a violation of tax neutrality, competing energy providers face different tax burdens. State actions to move toward retail competition were active until California's pathbreaking deregulation structure collapsed in 2001.

State-local relations are also affected by electric industry restructuring. Local governments may own and regulate their own electric utility, and use electricity prices to offset general property taxes. These types of city decisions conflict with state-imposed consumer choice. Similarly, state regulatory powers are vulnerable to Congress broadening the scope of national interest in this network economy. *SEE ALSO:* Deregulation

BIBLIOGRAPHY: Richard F. Hirsh, *Power Loss: The Origins of Deregulation and Restructuring in the American Utility System* (Cambridge, MA: MIT Press, 2001); and Bruce Seaman and W. Bartley Hildreth, "Deregulation of Utilities: A Challenge and an Opportunity for State and Local Tax Policy," in *State and Local Finances under Pressure*, ed. David L. Sjoquist (Cheltenham, UK: Edward Elgar, 2003).

W. Bartley Hildreth

Elementary and Secondary Education Act of 1965   This legislation expanded the role of the federal government in matters of education policy. Heretofore education policy was the realm of state and local governments, except for piecemeal federal government assistance beginning with the Morrill Act (1862).

The Elementary and Secondary Education Act (ESEA) constituted a basic part in what President Lyndon B. Johnson articulated as the "Great Society." Previous congressional bills to assist education with funds for school construction and teachers' salaries failed because of controversy about segregated schools and church-state issues regarding parochial schools. However, the Civil Rights Act of 1964 addressed the segregation issue and this proposal focused assistance upon school districts with many children from low-income families rather than on buildings and teachers' salaries.

Much of the credit for the substance and legislative success of the bill went to President Johnson, the "teacher who became president." He requested action on a proposed bill in an education message on January 12, 1965. The bill (H.R. 2362) received swift and favorable action in the House, gaining committee approval on March 8 and passage on a roll call by the whole House on March 26 (263–153). In less than three weeks the Senate approved the bill without changes, adopting it on April 9 with a favorable vote (73–18) as Public Law 89-10.

The law provided $1.1 billion to assist school districts with impoverished children. The provisions of the law were intended to affect schools in over 90 percent of the nation's counties. Federal grants went to states that distributed the money to school districts according to the number of low-income (less than $2,000 per year) families served. Additional provisions of the law authorized grants for textbooks and library material, community educational centers, educational research, and funding to strengthen departments of education in the states.

The act paved the way for the federal government to intrude increasingly in education with Head Start, the Higher Education Act, the Bilingual Education Act, the Native American Education Act, the Education for all Handicapped Children Act (later named the Individuals with Disabilities Act), and the establishment of the Department of Education as a cabinet-level entity.

ESEA continued as the federal government's flagship aid program for disadvantaged students. A significant restructuring of the act occurred in 2001 with the passage of President George Bush's proposed No Child Left Behind Act, which incorporated substantial student testing and accountability requirements into the law. Adopted with compromises by a variety of interests, the reauthorized law received bipartisan support with approval in the House by a 281–41 vote on December 13 and approval less than a week later in the Senate on an 87–10 vote. The president signed the bill on January 8, 2002.

While the federal government plays a significant part in education policy oversight, its fiscal contribution continues to be small. The National Center for Education Statistics estimated in 2003 that states supply 50 percent of funding for elementary and secondary schools, local districts supplied 43 percent, and 7 percent comes from the national government. *SEE ALSO:* Education; Morrill Act of 1862; No Child Left Behind Act

BIBLIOGRAPHY: *Congress and the Nation*, vols. 2, 3 and 4 (Washington, DC: Congressional Quarterly Inc., 1969, 1973, 1977); U.S. Department of Education, National Center for Educational Statistics, "Revenues and Expenditures for Public Elementary and Secondary Education: School Year 2000–2001," NCES 2003-362, May (Washington, DC: U.S. Department of Education, 2003).

JACK R. VAN DER SLIK

Eleventh Amendment   The Eleventh Amendment provides that "the Judicial power of the United States shall not be construed to extend to any suit in law or equity, commenced or prosecuted against one of the United States by Citizens of another State, or by Citizens or Subjects of any Foreign State."

The protection offered states by the Eleventh Amendment is grounded in the doctrine of state sovereignty, a principle establishing that sovereign governments may not be sued without their consent. Although the Supreme Court broadly interpreted the amendment at the outset, it soon created a number of exceptions to the immunity doctrine that vitiated much of its effect. Beginning in the 1990s, however, almost 200 years after the ratification of the amendment, the Supreme Court construed it to expand state sovereignty, declaring states immune from money damages in lawsuits brought against them for violating laws related to unfair labor practices, employment discrimination, patent protection, and unfair trade practices.

The Eleventh Amendment was ratified in 1798 to overturn the U.S. Supreme Court's decision in *Chisholm v. Georgia* (1793), in which the Court was asked to decide whether a citizen of South Car-

> AMENDMENT XI
>
> *The Judicial power of the United States shall not be construed to extend to any suit in law or equity, commenced or prosecuted against one of the United States by Citizens of another State, or by Citizens or Subjects of any Foreign State.*

olina was permitted to sue the State of Georgia for payment of debts owed on Revolutionary War bonds. Although Georgia claimed that it was immune from suit, the Court ruled that the U.S. Constitution allowed the plaintiff to override the state's immunity defense. The nation's reaction was swift and the Eleventh Amendment, quickly approved in Congress and ratified by the states, barred the federal courts from hearing suits brought against a state by citizens of another state.

In *Hans v. Louisiana* (1890), the Supreme Court ruled on another dispute arising out of a state's indebtedness to its bondholders. Although the plain language of the amendment only applies to suits against a state by citizens of another state, the state argued that the federal courts lacked constitutional authority to hear any cases brought by pri-

MAJOR SUPREME COURT CASES DEALING WITH THE ELEVENTH AMENDMENT

Alden v. Maine, *527 U.S. 706 (1999)*

Board of Trustees of University of Alabama v. Garrett, *531 U.S. 356 (2001)*

Chisholm v. Georgia, *2 U.S. (2 Dall.) 419 (1793)*

City of Boerne v. Flores, *521 U.S. 507 (1997)*

Cleburne v. Cleburne Living Center, *473 U.S. 432 (1985)*

College Savings Bank v. Florida Prepaid Postsecondary Education Expense Board, *527 U.S. 666 (1999)*

Ex Parte Young, *209 U.S. 123 (1908)*

Federal Maritime Commission v. South Carolina State Ports Authority, *535 U.S. 743 (2002)*

Fitzpatrick v. Bitzer, *427 U.S. 445 (1976)*

Florida Prepaid Postsecondary Education Expense Board v. College Savings Bank, *527 U.S. 627 (1999)*

Hans v. Louisiana, *134 U.S. 1 (1890)*

Hibbs v. Department of Human Resources, *123 S.Ct. 1972 (2003)*

Kimel v. Florida, *528 U.S. 62 (2000)*

Pennsylvania v. Union Gas Company, *491 U.S. 1 (1989)*

Seminole Tribe of Florida v. Florida, *517 U.S. 441 (1996)*

vate citizens against a state without the consent of the state. The Supreme Court agreed, expanding the concept of state sovereignty by ruling that the Eleventh Amendment also conferred immunity on states in suits brought by their own citizens. Despite the broad statement in *Hans*, however, states were not granted immunity in all cases. Suits may be brought against states by the federal government or by other states; moreover, states may waive their immunity. Additionally, the state's immunity does not extend to its instrumentalities, such as cities or counties, unless they are considered "arms of the state."

In 1908, the Court began to retreat from the principle of state sovereignty established in the Eleventh Amendment and *Hans*. In *Ex Parte Young* (1908), the Court ruled that the amendment does not bar suits for ongoing constitutional violations brought against state officials in their official capacities. *Young* is based on the fiction that a suit against a state officer does not constitute a suit against the state if the suit only seeks an injunction (a court order) to stop the unconstitutional behavior. However, because the amendment bars suits for money damages, individuals may not seek such damages for past violations because those funds would have to be paid from the state treasury.

The Supreme Court created another exception to the Eleventh Amendment in *Fitzpatrick v. Bitzer* (1976). The case was brought by Connecticut employees under Title VII of the 1964 Civil Rights Act, a law originally applying to private employers and extended to the states in 1972; they claimed the state's retirement plan discriminated against them on the basis of sex. The Court restricted the potency of the immunity doctrine by ruling that because the Fourteenth Amendment, arising out of the post–Civil War era, was intended to alter the relationship between the federal government and the states, Congress was permitted to abrogate (revoke) the state's Eleventh Amendment immunity as part of its remedial authority under Section 5 of the Fourteenth Amendment. Section 5, the enforcement provision, gives Congress the authority to enforce the guarantees of the substantive provisions of the Fourteenth Amendment, among them the Equal Protection Clause.

The Court made it clear in *Fitzpatrick* that Congress must clearly indicate its intent to abrogate state sovereign immunity when enacting a statute under the authority of the Fourteenth Amendment.

Then, in *Pennsylvania v. Union Gas Company* (1989), the Court added another exception to the Eleventh Amendment, ruling that Congress had the power to abrogate sovereign immunity under Article I, Section 8, of the Constitution, the Interstate Commerce Clause. However, in *Seminole Tribe of Florida v. Florida* (1996), the Court was asked to reconsider whether the Eleventh Amendment protects states from suits for damages in laws enacted under Congress's authority to regulate commerce. *Seminole Tribe* revolved around a dispute between the Seminole Indians and the State of Florida over a provision of the Indian Gaming Regulatory Act of 1988. The Court overruled *Union Gas*, enlarging the scope of the protection offered states by the Eleventh Amendment by ruling that the Commerce Clauses, in this case, the Indian Commerce Clause, did not authorize Congress to abrogate state immunity. Speaking for the majority, Chief Justice William Rehnquist identified two standards for determining whether Congress had validly abrogated a state's Eleventh Amendment immunity: first, Congress must clearly intend to do so; and second, it must have the power to do so. Although *Seminole Tribe* did not hold that states were excused from complying with federal law, nor that the federal government was barred from bringing an action against an unconsenting state for violating federal law, the Court confirmed that Congress's power to abrogate state immunity was restricted to laws validly enacted under Section 5 of the Fourteenth Amendment.

Following *Seminole Tribe*, the Court made it clear that Congress's power to negate a state's Eleventh Amendment immunity was solely derived from the enabling clause of the Fourteenth Amendment, Section 5. And in *City of Boerne v. Flores* (1997), a case that arose in a challenge to the Religious Freedom Restoration Act of 1993, the Court specified the limits of Congress's enforcement power under Section 5, adopting a rule of "congruence and proportionality." Although not well defined by the Supreme Court, the "congruence and proportionality" test became the standard for determining whether Congress had the proper authority to abrogate the state's Eleventh Amendment immunity in laws enacted under Section 5. To meet this standard, Congress must have evidence that the state had been guilty of unconstitutional conduct and the law must be within Congress's ability to cure the injury by restricting the state's conduct. Although failure to meet the test would not affect the status of the law as applied to private individuals or even states, it would absolve states from damage liability in suits brought by private individuals.

In two 1999 cases arising out of the same set of facts, the Court expanded state immunity by curtailing Congress's authority to hold states accountable in suits for unfair trade practices and patent infringement. In *Florida Prepaid Postsecondary Education Expense Board v. College Savings Bank* (1999), the majority held that Congress exceeded its authority in enacting the Patent and Plant Variety Protection Remedy Clarification Act of 1992—a federal law subjecting states to private suits for patent infringement—because there was insufficient evidence of state infringement on patent rights. In *College Savings Bank v. Florida Prepaid Postsecondary Education Expense Board* (1999), the same majority ruled that the Trademark Remedy Clarification Act of 1992, a law declaring that states engaged in interstate marketing are subject to private suit, was also unconstitutional because it was not aimed at protecting property interests within the scope of the Due Process Clause of the Fourteenth Amendment.

In the third and most important of the 1999 trilogy of cases, *Alden v. Maine* (1999), the Court again raised the bar of state immunity by holding that the Eleventh Amendment protected states from suit in state, as well as federal, court. The decision arose from an action brought by a group of Maine employees who claimed the state violated their rights under the Fair Labor Standards Act of 1938. The Court extended the sovereign immunity doctrine once again by ruling that individuals who are excluded from federal court on the basis of the Eleventh Amendment cannot circumvent the doctrine by suing the state in state court either.

During the next two years, the Supreme Court's interpretation of the Eleventh Amendment jeopardized the effectiveness of two federal equal opportunity employment laws by barring state workers from bringing damage suits against states in their capacity as employers. With almost 5 million state employees nationwide, the consequences for continually expanding state immunity under the Eleventh Amendment immunity would become increasingly important to the labor force in the United States.

The Age Discrimination in Employment Act (ADEA), enacted in 1967 under Congress's authority to regulate interstate commerce, makes it unlawful to make employment decisions on the basis of age. Initially limited to private employers, the law was later amended to include state employers. Although it seemed likely that Congress had intended to allow individuals to sue states for damages in federal court, the law did not expressly abrogate Eleventh Amendment immunity. In January 2000, the Court announced its ruling on state immunity from ADEA suits in *Kimel v. Florida* (2000). A majority of the Court believed that Congress had intended the ADEA to abrogate state immunity, but when it applied the *City of Boerne* standard, it found that Congress had insufficient evidence that states were guilty of unconstitutional discrimination on the basis of age. Moreover, because the Constitution allows states to distinguish among people on age-related grounds as long as these distinctions are reasonable, the law would punish a greater range of behavior than would be considered unconstitutional according to the Equal Protection Clause of the Fourteenth Amendment. Thus, because the law prevented states from making reasonable employment decisions based on age, the Court concluded that it exceeded the bounds of Congress's authority under Section 5.

The Americans with Disabilities Act (ADA) of 1990 was enacted under Congress's authority to regulate interstate commerce as well as to enforce the equal rights guarantees of the Fourteenth Amendment; however, unlike the ADEA, it explicitly deprived states of Eleventh Amendment immunity from suit. But in *Board of Trustees of the University of Alabama v. Garrett* (2001), although the Court acknowledged that Congress had clearly intended to abrogate state immunity, it questioned whether it exceeded its authority under Section 5 in doing so. In applying the "congruence and proportionality" test from *City of Boerne*, the Court cited its ruling on disability rights in *Cleburne v. Cleburne Living Center* (1985) and concluded that states had great latitude in laws based on disability. Although the ADA demanded that employers, including state employers, accommodate the needs of people with disabilities, the Constitution merely required them to act rationally. And, as in *Kimel*, the Court found that Congress had not provided sufficient evidence that states had unlawfully discriminated against people with disabilities. Because the Court determined that the ADA was not "congruent and proportional" to any violation of the Fourteenth Amendment committed by the states under the *City of Boerne* standard, the law exceeded Congress's authority to abrogate state immunity.

The next year, the Supreme Court addressed a related Eleventh Amendment issue in *Federal Maritime Commission v. South Carolina State Ports Authority* (2002). South Carolina Maritime Services filed a complaint with the Federal Maritime Commission, charging the South Carolina Ports Authority with violating the Shipping Act of 1984 by refusing it permission to berth a ship in a Charleston seaport. The high court determined that the barriers to suits for money damages erected by the Eleventh Amendment extend to federal administrative agencies, also preventing them from adjudicating the actions of private individuals against states.

In another case involving a federal law aimed at employment discrimination, *Hibbs v. Department of Human Resources* (2003), the Supreme Court was asked to decide if the Eleventh Amendment granted states immunity from a suit brought under the 1993 Family Medical Leave Act (FMLA). The FMLA, enacted under Congress's authority under the Interstate Commerce Clause and the Fourteenth Amendment, requires employers to allow workers to take up to twelve weeks of unpaid leave because of their own health problems or to care for an ailing family member; it permitted workers to sue their employers, including states, for damages for violating the act. Encouraged by the high court's decisions in the age and disability discrimination suits, states argued they were immune from damages in suits brought under the FMLA.

The controversy in *Hibbs* arose in 1997 when William Hibbs, who had taken time off from work to care for his wife, charged that the state violated the FMLA by firing him. The state argued that the Eleventh Amendment protected it from a suit for damages. The principal issue in the case was whether the FMLA exceeded Congress's authority under the Fourteenth Amendment, thus allowing the state to insulate itself from the suit. Following the principles established in *Seminole Tribe*, the high court confirmed that Congress had clearly indicated its intention that the FMLA abrogated state immunity from suits for money damages. Next, applying the standard set in *City of Boerne*, the Court reiterated that when Congress attempts to revoke a state's immunity, it must demonstrate a "congruence and proportionality" between the injury to be remedied (the state's unconstitutional law or policy) and the federal statute enacted to cure the injury. In assessing whether Congress had acted within its authority under Section 5 of the Fourteenth Amendment, the Court must determine that the state has violated the Fourteenth Amendment and that the law in question merely provides a remedy for the state's unconstitutional conduct without imposing a higher standard on the state than the one imposed by the Fourteenth Amendment.

When it examined the legislative history of the FMLA, the Court determined that it was aimed at addressing the pervasive problem of sex discrimination in the workplace. Congress had indicated its concern that women's family responsibilities for their children or parents had a detrimental effect on their employment status. Unlike *Kimel* and *Garrett*, in which the Court held that states had not violated the Constitution when differentiating among people on the basis of age or disability, the Court cited a long history of state laws restricting women's opportunities in the workplace. Moreover, Congress had found significant evidence that states were continuing to discriminate on the basis of sex, especially in the administration of workers' leave benefits. Policies, such as restricting parental leaves to women, were based on a stereotype that caring for the family is the woman's responsibility; by establishing a gender-neutral leave policy, the FMLA aimed at eradicating the stereotype and reducing the employer's incentive to hire only men. The Court concluded that the state's pattern of discrimination was sufficient to justify this law aimed at remedying its unconstitutional conduct and

Congress was within its authority to abrogate the state's immunity under the Fourteenth Amendment. Thus, *Hibbs* halted, at least temporarily, the Court's policy of immunizing states from damage suits.

Beginning in the 1990s, with the exception of its ruling in *Hibbs*, the Supreme Court has relied on the Eleventh Amendment to expand state sovereignty. It has declared states immune from private damage suits brought under federal employment discrimination laws as well as protected states from suit by private individuals for violation of patent laws and unfair marketing practices. In extending the parameters of state sovereignty through its interpretation of the Eleventh Amendment, the Court has prevented the federal government from providing effective relief to individuals harmed by state violations of federal rights guarantees. Although the Court's rulings have continued to recognize congressional authority to enact federal law in these areas, they have barred suits against states for infringing on these rights. By insulating state governments from private suits, the Court has jeopardized Congress's ability to hold states accountable for violating federal laws and diminished the protection offered individuals under these laws. *SEE ALSO: Seminole Tribe of Florida v. Florida*; States' Rights; Tenth Amendment

BIBLIOGRAPHY: Robert F. Nagel, *The Implosion of American Federalism* (Oxford: Oxford University Press, 2001); and John T. Noonan Jr., *Narrowing the Nation's Power* (Berkeley: University of California Press, 2002).

SUSAN GLUCK MEZEY

Eminent Domain.   *See* Takings Clause: Fifth Amendment

Enumerated Powers of the U.S. Constitution   Instead of a totally unified central government with all legislative power, the U.S. Constitution created a federalist system with power divided between the national government and the states. Unlike the governments of most other countries, therefore, the United States has a national government of limited or "enumerated" powers. Congress can exercise only powers granted it by the Constitution, mostly in Article I, Section 8. Examples among the eighteen powers listed there include the power regulate immigration and naturalization, coin money and regulate the currency, establish post offices, and grant patents and copyrights to promote science and the arts. Also listed, however, are the powers of Congress to tax in order to "pay the Debts and provide for the common Defense and general Welfare of the United States," to regulate interstate and foreign commerce, and to declare war and raise and regulate military forces. These powers are so broad and basic that they have proved very difficult to confine. In addition, Congress has the power to "make all laws which shall be necessary and proper" for executing its specified powers, which is considered a grant of "implied powers." These powers have been so broadly interpreted by Congress, the president, and the Supreme Court that as a practical matter there is very little, if anything, today that Congress cannot regulate if it is determined to do so.

The power to tax, for example, enables Congress to raise almost unlimited amounts of money and effectively control the nation's resources. Congress can then use this money, in the form of conditional grants to the states, to induce the states to enact laws that Congress is not authorized to enact itself. Congress, for example, clearly has no power to regulate the minimum age for the purchase or consumption of alcoholic beverages. Congress has nonetheless effectively set a national minimum drinking age of 21. It was able to do this by simply making it a condition of the grant of highway funds to the states that the states exercise their power to enact the drinking age desired by Congress. Congress can discourage or even effectively prohibit almost any activity, for example, gambling, or product, for example, sawed-off shotguns, by simply placing a high enough tax on it.

Congress's power to regulate interstate commerce has similarly proven to be a means of enabling Congress to regulate almost anything. The power to regulate interstate commerce, the Supreme Court has held, includes the power to regulate things that "affect" interstate commerce, and almost everything, it turns out, affects interstate commerce. Congress has no power, for example, to directly regulate labor relations. But labor relations can affect production and production affects sales, and sales affect interstate commerce. Congress, therefore, can and has created rights of employees to form unions and has set a national minimum wage, all as an exercise of its power to regulate interstate commerce. Congress can prohibit a farmer from growing wheat for his or her own use, the Supreme Court has held, because that forces the farmer to buy the wheat he or she needs, which affects the demand for wheat, which affects the price and therefore sales in interstate commerce.

The power to regulate interstate commerce includes the power to prohibit or place conditions upon the movement of goods or people from state to state. Thus, although Congress has no direct power to regulate in the interest, for example, of health and safety—that is clearly a power (often called the "police power") left exclusively for the states—Congress has passed the Pure Food and Drug Act (1906), prohibiting the interstate ship-

ARTICLE I, SECTION 8

Clause 1: The Congress shall have Power To lay and collect Taxes, Duties, Imposts and Excises, to pay the Debts and provide for the common Defence and general Welfare of the United States; but all Duties, Imposts and Excises shall be uniform throughout the United States;

Clause 2: To borrow Money on the credit of the United States;

Clause 3: To regulate Commerce with foreign Nations, and among the several States, and with the Indian Tribes;

Clause 4: To establish an uniform Rule of Naturalization, and uniform Laws on the subject of Bankruptcies throughout the United States;

Clause 5: To coin Money, regulate the Value thereof, and of foreign Coin, and fix the Standard of Weights and Measures;

Clause 6: To provide for the Punishment of counterfeiting the Securities and current Coin of the United States;

Clause 7: To establish Post Offices and post Roads;

Clause 8: To promote the Progress of Science and useful Arts, by securing for limited Times to Authors and Inventors the exclusive Right to their respective Writings and Discoveries;

Clause 9: To constitute Tribunals inferior to the supreme Court;

Clause 10: To define and punish Piracies and Felonies committed on the high Seas, and Offences against the Law of Nations;

Clause 11: To declare War, grant Letters of Marque and Reprisal, and make Rules concerning Captures on Land and Water;

Clause 12: To raise and support Armies, but no Appropriation of Money to that Use shall be for a longer Term than two Years;

Clause 13: To provide and maintain a Navy;

Continued on next page

Continued from previous page

Clause 14: To make Rules for the Government and Regulation of the land and naval Forces;

Clause 15: To provide for calling forth the Militia to execute the Laws of the Union, suppress Insurrections and repel Invasions;

Clause 16: To provide for organizing, arming, and disciplining, the Militia, and for governing such Part of them as may be employed in the Service of the United States, reserving to the States respectively, the Appointment of the Officers, and the Authority of training the Militia according to the discipline prescribed by Congress;

Clause 17: To exercise exclusive Legislation in all Cases whatsoever, over such District (not exceeding ten Miles square) as may, by Cession of particular States, and the Acceptance of Congress, become the Seat of the Government of the United States, and to exercise like Authority over all Places purchased by the Consent of the Legislature of the State in which the Same shall be, for the Erection of Forts, Magazines, Arsenals, dock-Yards, and other needful Buildings;—And

Clause 18: To make all Laws which shall be necessary and proper for carrying into Execution the foregoing Powers, and all other Powers vested by this Constitution in the Government of the United States, or in any Department or Officer thereof.

ment of adulterated foods or mislabeled drugs, and it prohibits the interstate shipment of automobiles without seat belts. Congress cannot make kidnapping a federal crime, but it can make it a federal crime to carry a kidnapped person across a state line.

The result is that American federalism has become, to a large extent, not a real limit on Congress's power but in effect simply a requirement that Congress do indirectly what it cannot do directly. The reason for this is that although it appears that the American people strongly favor the concept of federalism—limited national power with most matters of domestic social policy left to the states—as an ideal, they also usually favor, inconsistently, a national government able to deal with whatever is seen as a general and widespread problem. Federalism, therefore, almost always gives way to insistent demands for national action on some matter of current concern, even though it might seem to be a local issue—for example, the humane treatment of animals—and the result is a national government of practically unlimited power. *SEE ALSO:* Commerce among the States; Implied Powers of the U.S. Constitution; Military Affairs; Necessary and Proper Clause; Police Power; *United States v. Lopez*

BIBLIOGRAPHY: Raoul Berger, *Federalism: The Founder's Design* (Norman: University of Oklahoma Press, 1987); Lino A. Graglia, "*United States v. Lopez*: Judicial Review under the Commerce Clause," *Texas Law Review* 74 (1996): 719; and Michael W. McConnell, "Federalism: Evaluating the Framers Design," *University of Chicago Law Review* 54 (1987): 1484.

Lino A. Graglia

Environmental Policy   "Environmental policy" is a term that describes a broad set of public policies including, but not restricted to, goals ranging from the protection of human health and safety from air and water pollution to the preservation of culturally important natural landmarks. The responsibility for and authority of environmental policy is most commonly shared among federal, state, and local governments.

The majority of federal statutes considered to be the founding cornerstone of U.S.

environmental policy were first enacted in the 1970s. Prior to this time, the issues associated with the natural environment were considered to be the exclusive domain of the state and local governments. A growing understanding of the impact of pollution and environmental quality on human health, combined with the tendency of these impacts to affect individuals across state borders, led to a change toward a more comprehensive and centralized approach to environmental protection.

Federal environmental statutes have developed as a form of cooperative federalism, where the authority for environmental decision making is divided between the federal and state government. Many of the federal environmental statutes expressly reserve the right for the states to develop more stringent regulatory controls than those imposed by the federal Environmental Protection Agency (EPA). That action by Congress allows the federal government and the states to fashion the necessary working relationships without constant conflict over the appropriate approach to the vast array of environmental problems facing the country. For example, the Clean Air Act (42 USC §7401 et seq.) establishes the ambient air quality standards for over 27,000 of the major stationary sources of air pollutants. The federal government sets primary standards for each of the regulated pollutants, which are based on human health protection. It is also responsible for setting secondary standards to protect other types of concerns, such as aesthetic values, private property values, and the negative impacts of pollution on vegetation. The individual states are in charge of ensuring that minimum quality standards are being met through the development of state implementation plans that determine, among other things, how, why, when, and where the air emissions will be tested. Similarly, division of responsibility arrangements can also be found in other federal environmental statutes such as the Clean Water Act (33 U.S.C. §1251 et seq.) and the Resource Conservation and Recovery Act (42 U.S.C. §6901 et seq.). Although the state and federal government must work together for a common goal, the struggle for control over environmental policy continues to exist within the framework of cooperative federalism.

THE BASIS OF FEDERAL AUTHORITY

The federal authority to regulate environmental issues is derived from the U.S. Constitution. The constitutional authority for federal environmental policy has been grounded, primarily, in what is known as the Commerce Clause. To a lesser extent, the treaty, property, and spending powers have also been used as a basis for federal control.

The Commerce Clause provides the federal government with the power to regulate commerce among the states. Beginning in the 1930s, the courts began an expansion of the exercise of federal powers permitted under the Commerce Clause. Congress has used this broad interpretation to justify a wide array of environmental statutes, including some that have very weak connections to interstate commerce. In 1995, the Supreme Court began to signal a change in the interpretation of the Commerce Clause. In the case of *United States v. Lopez* (514 U.S. 549 [1995]), the Court suggested several limitations to the interpretation of federal authority. In particular, the Court emphasized the need to find an enforceable limit to the application of the Commerce Clause in terms of defining activities that both directly and substantially affected interstate commerce. Even with this interpretation, the Commerce Clause still gives Congress extensive authority to regulate a wide array of environmental issues. For example, pollution control under the Clean Air Act and the Clean Water Act regulates commercial activities that clearly fall under the umbrella of interstate commerce. However, the constitutionality of federal environmental laws that regulate private land use, such as the Endangered Species Act, are more open to question.

The treaty powers of the federal government supersede state laws, and the treaty power has been used to establish federal control over environmental issues that otherwise would belong to the individual states. In 1913, the U.S. Congress passed the Migratory Bird Act, which placed specific hunting limitations on many species of migratory birds. Arrests for violations under the act were argued in court, where it was decided that the law was unconstitutional as the federal statute encroached on state authority. Common law had always held that the power to regulate the taking of wildlife belonged to the states. In 1916, the United States and Great Britain, on behalf of Canada, adopted the Migratory Bird Treaty, and soon thereafter Congress passed the Migratory Bird Treaty Act (16 U.S.C. 703–12) to implement the provisions of the treaty. Challenges to this new Act were upheld on the basis of the federal treaty power. The environmental protection of federal lands as well as private areas surrounding the lands has been successfully defended under the Property Clause. Finally, the spending powers of the federal government have been linked with environmental policy and used in various ways. For example, federal highway funds have been tied to the statewide attainment of ambient air standards, and government subsidy programs have provided funds to private firms for the voluntary adoption of pollution reduction technologies.

THE BASIS FOR STATE AND LOCAL AUTHORITY

The Tenth Amendment of the U.S. Constitution provides each state with all of the powers not specifically delegated to the federal government. This provides the states with broader statutory powers over environmental issues as compared to the federal government. The states have priority of jurisdiction in regard to the regulation of private and public property, with the exception of federal lands. This includes conservation, protection, and land use. Most states, however, typically devolve land-use decisions to the local governments. The states retain police power and the control of fish and wildlife within their own borders. One question that arises is as follows: if the states possess such broad authority over environmental issues, why do we see so much environmental legislation emanating from Congress?

THE JUSTIFICATION FOR FEDERAL CONTROL

Federal authority over environmental policy is often justified solely on the basis of it being best suited to deal with the unique features associated with environmental problems. Of these unique features, three of them tend to be most commonly discussed: (1) the interaction of economic activity and environmental protection, (2) externalities, and (3) the scientific complexity associated with environmental policy. Each of these features is discussed in more detail in the following section.

"Race to the Bottom"

The sources of a majority of the pollution and environmental degradation regulated through environmental policy are engaged in what can be called "socially valuable economic activities." For example, some water pollution is a by-product of food production, and some of the air pollution produced is a by-product of the manufacturing of pharmaceuticals. In addition, there is often some habitat disruption as a by-product of the production of lumber for homes. As a result, environmental policy both affects, and is affected by, many aspects of the economy. Many proponents of centralized environmental policy argue that it will prevent state and local governments from pursuing economic gain to the detriment of the environment. Environmental regulation imposes costs on economic activities. Therefore, an acceptable balance between economic development and environmental protection must be found.

If authority over environmental policy were to rest solely with the states, the potential exists for interstate competition to result in what has been referred to as a "race to the bottom." States seek to entice economic development away from other states by lowering the cost of doing business within their borders. This can be accomplished by reducing regulatory compliance costs through lower environmental standards. Interstate competition for economic development provides an incentive for all other states to follow suit. In the end, each state will have equally poor environmental standards, as well as the inability to entice new economic development through further compliance cost reductions. The race to the bottom is a form of the "prisoner's dilemma" and is a result of noncooperative behavior among states. Although it is in each state's best interest to collectively maintain appropriate environmental standards, individual competition results in each state pursuing an agenda that makes it worse off in terms of being unable to entice new businesses through reduced compliance costs, as well as providing its citizenry with reduced environmental amenities. Federal regulation of environmental policy can avoid this problem by mandating each state to meet a set of minimal environmental standards, removing the potential for using reduced environmental standards as a means of enticing new businesses.

Although the "race to the bottom" argument has commonly been used to justify much of our federal environmental policy, its validity is questionable. Research has yet to show that the requisite incentives for the "race to the bottom" actually exist. However, given the opportunity, very few states have adopted environmental standards more stringent than the federal minimum standards, and perhaps this signals that the potential does exist. Arguments against the "race to the bottom" justification contend that, if the problem does in fact exist, the reliance on federally set minimum standards does not fix it. Instead, it shifts the race to some other area such as worker safety or tax rates.

Externalities

It is obvious that pollution does not respect political boundaries. The problem of acid rain is a classic example. Acid rain damage to lakes and forests in the Adirondack region of New York is the product of sulfur dioxide and nitrogen oxides emitted primarily from coal-fired electric power generators in the Midwest and Mid-Atlantic states. The presence of pollution spillovers means that states with pollution sources will not take all costs into account when formulating their environmental policies. The affected states bear the costs of pollution coming across their borders, but with little or no legislative recourse for addressing the problem. However, federal standards can address spillover effects, requiring the pollution-generating states to bear their own costs of pollution control.

State environmental regulations can also impose externalities on other states in terms of imposing financial costs on out-of-state producers. California's automobile emissions control standards are an example of this. The state implementing the regulation will tend to ignore the compliance costs imposed on manufacturers outside of the state, and the manufacturers pass the increased costs back to the consumers in all of the states. Federal regulations can be justified when state environmental policies impose sizable costs on interstate business.

Scientific Complexity

Environmental policy requires a high level of scientific data collection and analysis. This includes standard setting, but also extends to the monitoring and enforcement of standards. The expenditures for many of the technical aspects of environmental regulation are quite large. Concentrating the processing of these recurrent and technically difficult tasks at the federal level can create cost savings when compared with the costs of having each state perform these tasks individually. For example, the federal government has the resources to effectively perform research linking environmental standards to human health risks in setting policy, and can then apply these finding across all states.

THE WEAKNESSES OF FEDERAL CONTROL

The benefits of federal control of environmental policy come with corresponding costs. When these costs are substantial, the justification of federal authority over environmental policy is questionable. Utilizing a centralized approach has implications in terms of the impact of reliance on uniform standards, as well as the loss of local public participation.

As we have seen, the use of national uniform standards is justified on the grounds of avoiding the "race to the bottom" and interstate externalities, as well as reducing the costs associated with the scientific complexity of environmental regulation. However, these uniform national standards do not reflect the unique costs and benefits of each state. While the federal government can achieve some cost savings by taking advantage of centralized data collection and analysis, each individual state has greater knowledge of the unique attributes of the local community and environment. Each state is also familiar with local preferences, as well as the distinct costs associated with meeting any given standard. This information is important in setting environmental standards that balance the needs of the local community, and therefore must be taken into account. Uniform national standards are unable to incorporate this local information and therefore are likely to be inefficient and poorly representative of the true preferences of the citizens.

Although the potential for a "race to the bottom" is an often-cited justification for federal authority over environmental regulation, the most apparent justification is the presence of interstate externalities and spillover effects. While this justifies a crucial role for federal government oversight in environmental regulation, it does not require any particular form of policy response. Flexibility in terms of the assignment of responsibility among different levels of government, and between the public and private sector, as well as in terms of the type of policy instrument are at the heart of environmental policy success. Cooperative federalism allows for this flexibility in design. *SEE ALSO:* Great Society

BIBLIOGRAPHY: Kirsten Engle and Susan Rose-Ackerman, "Environmental Federalism in the United States: The Risks of Devolution," in *Regulatory Competition and Economic Integration: Comparative Perspectives*, ed. Daniel Esty and Damien Geradin (Oxford: Oxford University Press, 2001); Richard L. Revesz, "Rehabilitating Interstate Competition: Rethinking the 'Race-to-the-Bottom' Rationale for Federal Environmental Regulation," *New York University Law Review* 67 (1992); 1210; Denise Scheberle, *Federalism and Environmental Policy: Trust and the Politics of Implementation* (Washington, DC: Georgetown University Press, 1997); and Richard B. Stewart, "Pyramids of Sacrifice? Problems of Federalism in Mandating State Implementation of National Environmental Policy," *Yale Law Journal* 86 (1977): 1196–272.

MICHAEL A. TAYLOR

Equal Opportunity Employment Commission v. Wyoming   *See* Age Discrimination

Equal Protection of the Laws   One fundamental characteristic of the American constitutional system has been the precept that a law cannot discriminate among individuals who are essentially similar. Americans believe that laws must not distinguish between different groups. The legal challenge raised by equal protection jurisprudence has been to determine when such distinctions are appropriate and constitutional. The primary articulation of this understanding is found in the Fourteenth Amendment to the Constitution, passed in 1868 after the end of the Civil War. While this amendment was designed to ensure that newly freed slaves as well as "free blacks" were granted full citizenship, the Fourteenth Amendment also placed specific responsibilities on the states as to how they must treat their citizens. More specifically, the Fourteenth Amendment prohibits each state from making or enforcing any law "which shall abridge the privileges or immunities of citizens of the United States; . . . deprive any person of life, liberty, or property without due process of law; . . . [or] deny to any person within its jurisdiction the equal protection of the laws." In Section 5 of the Fourteenth Amendment, Congress is empowered to enforce these guarantees through federal legislation. The history of equal protection in the United States has not been one where equality of all citizens has been uniformly valued; in fact, much of our political and legal debate has centered on the questions of what is meant by "equality" and how it best may be secured. One source of these debates is the inherent tension between personal liberty and societal equality—two values equally promised by the Constitution, but guaranteed to be in conflict. Justice Robert Jackson, in his concurrence in *Railway Express Agency v. New York* (1949), underscored the importance of equal protection for citizens and the special role the courts play in its enforcement:

> The framers of the Constitution knew, and we should not forget today, that there is no more effective practical guaranty against arbitrary and unreasonable government than to require that the principles of law which officials would impose upon a minority must be imposed generally. Conversely, nothing opens the door to arbitrary action so effectively as to allow those officials to pick and choose only a few to whom they will apply legislation and thus to escape the political retribution that might be visited upon them if larger numbers were affected. Courts can take no better measure than to assure that laws will be just than to require that laws be equal in operation. (*Railway Express Agency v. New York* 336 U.S. 106)

By guaranteeing equal protection of the laws, the Fourteenth Amendment was designed to prevent states from treating people who were newly freed from slavery differently from other citizens. This amendment has had significance well beyond the eradication of slavery. Equal protection requires that individuals be similarly valued before the law and that personal characteristics such as race, gender, and religion can rarely enter into legislative determinations. However, statutes do not and cannot treat people identically;

consequently, there are certain types of classifications that are considered constitutional under the Equal Protection Clause. For example, truck drivers are often given a lower speed limit because trucks are heavier and need longer stopping distances than cars. Since truck drivers (as opposed to car drivers) are not provided special protection by the Constitution, states can easily make this legal distinction. The Supreme Court and the lower federal courts create tests to determine when laws distinguishing between groups and classes of citizens are constitutional and when they are unconstitutional. One significant and continuing point of conflict has been the identification of characteristics that may be legally considered as having a "protected status" under the law. This status ensures that the courts will look more stringently at laws that treat such designated groups differently from the remainder of the population. Over time, race has been given greater protection while gender has received less protection. Age, poverty, sexual preference, and disability have been granted even fewer protections.

HISTORICAL DEVELOPMENT

In 1869, the State of Louisiana decided to award a single company exclusive rights to slaughter animals for a twenty-five-year period. A lawsuit was filed by an association of New Orleans butchers. These men argued that their equal protection rights, among others, were violated by this state-created monopoly. The Supreme Court first interpreted the Equal Protection Clause in their 1873 decision of The *Slaughterhouse Cases*. The Court determined that the Equal Protection Clause was not designed for the protection of all citizens, limiting the application of the Fourteenth Amendment to primarily protect African Americans. As Justice Samuel Miller in his majority opinion noted, "The existence of laws in the states where the emancipated negroes resided, which discriminated with gross injustice and hardship against them as a class, was the evil to be remedied by this clause, and by it such laws are forbidden." Furthermore, the Court applied this doctrine to African Americans in the 1880 case of *Strauder v. West Virginia*, in which a state law that excluded blacks from jury duty was found to be unconstitutional. Using the powers granted them under Section 5 of the Fourteenth Amendment, the Reconstruction Congress passed numerous laws designed to protect blacks from Ku Klux Klan violence, private and state discrimination, and other forms of harassment. However, the Court quickly indicated that the federal power to protect these new citizens was greatly limited. In the 1883 Civil Rights Cases, the Court deemed unconstitutional the Civil Rights Act of 1875, which "prohibited private persons from violating the rights of other persons to the full and equal enjoyment of public accommodations on the basis of race and color." Through a series of legal renderings, the Court found that many of the federal laws passed by Congress to protect blacks in the South were too broad. The Fourteenth Amendment was not meant to prevent one citizen from harming another; the Court determined that this amendment only protected citizens from state action.

In 1896, the Court extended this reasoning and recognized that state laws distinguishing between races could be constitutional; this decision allowed Jim Crow segregation laws to continue both in the South and in the North. *Plessy v. Ferguson* (1896) determined that the Equal Protection Clause allows legally mandated separate facilities for black and white citizens, as long as these facilities were equal. By "equal," the Court required that black citizens have access to the same type of facilities (e.g., public restrooms, drinking fountains, and public transportations) as whites, but did not re quire that such facilities had to be of the same quality. States were allowed to distinguish on the basis of race; equal protection was interpreted as requiring equal availability, not equal quality. This was deemed "separate but equal."

ORDINARY SCRUTINY

Over time, the Supreme Court has developed several different standards to help determine the constitutionality of state laws under the Equal Protection Clause. Historically, the first standard has come to be known as "ordinary scrutiny." Ordinary scrutiny was initially used for all forms of equal protection litigation. To meet this standard of ordinary scrutiny, the state must simply demonstrate that there is a rational foundation for the discriminatory law. This level of scrutiny is known as the "minimal rationality" standard. Under most circumstances, a state simply had to demonstrate that there was a rational foundation for the distinction between groups. For example, many states fund public school education based on property taxes. The result is that there may be great disparities between school districts in terms of assessed property values and consequently the funds spent per pupil. In *San Antonio Independent School District v. Rodriguez* (1973), a group of Mexican American parents challenged these disparities before the Supreme Court. The Supreme Court, using ordinary scrutiny, found that the state funding system was not based on a discriminatory purpose; instead, it was designed to assure "a basic education for every child in the state" and to permit and encourage "a large measure of participation in and control of each district's school at the local level." The statute therefore bore a rational relationship to a legitimate state purpose. If a state cannot demonstrate a relationship between the state objective and the discrimination required by the statute, then the state law is in violation of the Equal Protection Clause. This approach assumes that state legislation is constitutional, and the burden of proof falls heavily on the litigant challenging the validity of the statute.

STRICT SCRUTINY

It was not until the 1938 case of *United States v. Carolene Products Company* that the Court suggested there might be another way of interpreting the Equal Protection Clause, providing more protection to individuals. Footnote 4 of the majority decision suggested that the Court apply a higher degree of scrutiny to legislation that discriminated against minorities who were deemed "discrete and insular." The Court did not initially define these terms; rather, the determination of which groups were provided this higher level of protection evolved through legislation and litigation. In Footnote 4, the Court was suggesting a "strict scrutiny" test, a means of providing greater protection to "suspect classifications": groups that have immutable or unchangeable characteristics and a history of emotionally based antagonism toward them, which is otherwise known as "invidious discrimination." Suspect classifications included groups of citizens who were separated from other citizens by virtue of being religious, ethnic, or racial minorities. If state legislation identifies such groups for differential treatment, federal courts assume the statute to be unconstitutional—unless the state can demonstrate that the classification is necessary to achieve a permissible state objective. The Court extended this highest standard, called "strict scrutiny," to all laws that violate fundamental freedoms (such as religion, speech, and press), legislation that restricts political rights (such as the right to vote, politically organize, peaceably assemble, or disseminate information), and statutes impacting suspect classes. In *Carolene Products*, the Court introduced a dual approach to the Equal Protection Clause—a more deferential, ordinary scrutiny of legislation regulating economic rights, and a more meticulous, strict scrutiny of statutes limiting civil rights and liberties.

Strict scrutiny of the Equal Protection Clause was considered in the case of *Korematsu v. United States* (1944). In the majority decision, the Court upheld the 1942 Executive Order no. 34 authorizing the creation of "military zones," in which the military could exclude individuals to prevent sabotage and espionage. Justified by claims of national security, tens of thousands of Japanese Americans on the West Coast were given curfews, evacuated, and interned in "relocation camps." Because this law applied only to American citizens of Japanese ancestry, it was challenged as a violation of the Equal Protection Clause of the Fourteenth Amendment. In his majority opinion, Justice Hugo Black stated,

> It should be noted, to begin with, that all legal restrictions which curtail the civil rights of a single racial group are immediately suspect. That is not to say that all such restrictions are unconstitutional. It is to say that courts must subject them to the most rigid [strict] scrutiny. Pressing public necessity may sometimes justify the existence of such restrictions; racial antagonism never can. (*Korematsy v. United States* 324 U.S. 885)

While the Equal Protection Clause was cited in the case, it was not perceived by the Court to be applicable against presidential claims of national security. In later years, the national security claims have been reevaluated, and the Japanese exclusion cases are now perceived to be one of the greater violations of civil rights in U.S. history.

Brown v. Board of Education (1954) is famous because it provided a clear new definition of the Equal Protection Clause and overturned *Plessy v. Ferguson*; equal protection is now understood as meaning that laws mandating segregation are by definition unequal. Attempts to make segregated facilities equal in a qualitative sense could not save legally separated school systems, and by extension, other manifestations of Jim Crow (e.g., water fountains and public restrooms). In the process of deciding *Brown*, the Court also determined that the Equal Protection Clause applies to federal legislation. One of the five school desegregation cases that made up *Brown* was located in Washington, D.C. Because Washington, D.C., is not a state, its citizens receive no protections under the Fourteenth Amendment. In the 1955 case of *Bolling v. Sharpe*, the Supreme Court ruled that inherent within the Fifth Amendment's due process provision is a federal guarantee of the equal protection of the laws. It was in the 1971 case of *Graham v. Richardson* that the Supreme Court also extended strict scrutiny to laws discriminating against aliens or non-U.S. citizens. While several laws that have treated aliens differently in the areas of employment, education, and civil liberties have passed constitutional muster, such legislation must still survive strict scrutiny.

An Emerging New Standard: Intermediate Scrutiny

Ordinary scrutiny has been the benchmark for most equal protection claims. However, the exception carved out by strict scrutiny has provided a new direction for courts considering statutes making racial distinctions. While gender fits many of the attributes inherent in suspect classification—an immutable characteristic and a history of "invidious" discrimination—in most circumstances, the Supreme Court has not considered gender as meeting the required criteria for strict scrutiny.

Historically, gender fell under ordinary scrutiny. In 1961, the U.S. Supreme Court in

Hoyt v. Florida (1961) found that a Florida statute requiring women to register for jury service while men were automatically placed in jury pools was seen as not violating equal protection claims. The Court found a reasonable relationship between the statute and the belief that women are the "center of the home and family life" and thereby warrant different treatment under the law. This was the last case in which the Supreme Court used ordinary scrutiny to evaluate the constitutionality of laws relating to gender distinctions. It was not until *Reed v. Reed* (1971) that sex discrimination would be found unconstitutional under the Equal Protection Clause. After this decision, the Court crafted a new equal protection standard designed solely for gender: intermediate scrutiny. This stricter standard inquires if the challenged classification is "really reasonable"—does it serve an important governmental objective, and is it substantially related to those ends? Despite defining this new standard, not until the 1976 case of *Craig v. Boren* did the Supreme Court recognized its reliance on intermediate, or "semistrict," scrutiny.

While the Supreme Court has never applied strict scrutiny to a gender discrimination case, the Court has slowly heightened the intermediate standard of scrutiny. In the 1996 *United States v. Virginia* case, the Court evaluated the constitutionality of the male-only admissions policy of the Virginia Military Institute (VMI). In her majority opinion, Justice Ruth Bader Ginsburg argued that the state must show "exceedingly persuasive justification" for differential treatment, in this case the exclusion of women from VMI. This is a higher requirement for the state than originally articulated in *Craig v. Boren* and a stronger constitutional protection against gender discrimination.

CONTINUING APPLICATIONS

While women slowly gained protection from statutory discrimination under the Equal Protection Clause, racial minorities saw the clause's meaning change from an articulation of group protections to a perception that the Fourteenth Amendment only prohibited discrimination against individuals. In the 1989 case of *Richmond v. Croson* and the 1995 *Adarand Constructors, Inc. v. Pena* case, the Supreme Court determined that any state legislation considering race would be considered under the requirements of strict scrutiny. Prior to these decisions, statutes designed to incorporate previously excluded groups (such as affirmative action legislation) were understood to be benign forms of discrimination and not included under the strict scrutiny parameters. The Rehnquist Court in these decisions determined that the Fourteenth Amendment required any form of racial consideration in a law, regardless of intent to include or exclude, to be constitutionally questionable. This does not mean that affirmative action plans are unconstitutional, but it does require that all such state legislation demonstrate that the law is as narrowly tailored as possible and necessary for the achievement of a legitimate state objective.

At the beginning of the twenty-first century, equal protection moved beyond the traditional considerations of race and gender. In the 2000 case of *Bush v. Gore*, in which the Supreme Court determined the outcome of the 2000 presidential election, most members of the Court found that the presidential ballot recounting procedures in Florida violated the Equal Protection Clause. Many scholars found this to be a new interpretation and application of the Fourteenth Amendment because the protection of such fundamental rights as voting had rarely been granted equal protection consideration. Other groups, including homosexuals and the disabled, have attempted to heighten the level of scrutiny used by courts in equal protection litigation; they have generally not been successful. In 2001, the U.S. Supreme Court in *University of Alabama v. Garrett* found Section 1 of the 1990 Americans with Disabilities Act to be unconstitutional because it provided a disabled individual the ability to challenge state discrimination in federal court. The Court determined that "disability" was not a suspect classification under the Fourteenth Amendment; consequently, states are permitted to pass legislation and take other actions that may disadvantage disabled people. According to *Garrett*, such action does not violate the Equal Protection Clause, as long as the state can articulate a rational justification for their action and meet the requirements of ordinary scrutiny.

The Court did find in 1996, in the case of *Romer v. Evans*, that a Colorado constitutional amendment banning the inclusion of homosexuals as a protected class was a violation of the Equal Protection Clause. Amendment 2 prevented any Colorado city, town, or county from protecting the rights of homosexuals through legislative, judicial, or executive activity. Justice Anthony Kennedy, in the majority opinion, noted that the law does not merely prevent a group from being granted special rights, but instead "imposes a special disability upon those persons alone. Homosexuals are forbidden the safeguards that others enjoy or may seek without constraint." Kennedy found no need to apply strict scrutiny; in fact, he found that the law could not even pass the lowest level of scrutiny: "Its sheer breadth is so discontinuous with the reasons offered for it that the amendment seems inexplicable by anything but animus toward the class that it affects; it lacks a rational relationship to legitimate state interests."

Similar rulings have been made in the classifications of age and relative wealth. The Court has consistently determined that poverty is not an immutable characteristic; instead, it is subject to change over the course of an individual's life. Consequently, laws that disadvantage the poor are evaluated under ordinary scrutiny, as the *Rodriguez* case revealed. Age is also not found to be a suspect classification, although age discrimination, like discrimination against people with disabilities, has been clearly prohibited by a number of federal laws. In 2000, the Court reinforced this ruling in *Kimel v. Florida Board of Regents*, noting that "[o]ld age . . . does not define a discrete and insular minority because all persons, if they live out normal life spans, will experience it." While questions of who is covered under protected status remain vibrant before the Court, ordinary scrutiny has been consistently applied to most forms of discrimination outside of race, alienage, and gender.

The changing interpretation of the Equal Protection Clause has shaped and will continue to define legal standards in the United States. The reframing of protected classes and the increased coverage of individual rights, as well as the altered federal legal standards, have generally been mirrored by the interpretations of the state equal protection clauses. While states frequently act as "laboratories of democracy" in the extension of personal rights, the Equal Protection Clause and its conceptual equivalents have generally not served the states as strongly as the federal government. *SEE ALSO: Brown v. Board of Education*; Fourteenth Amendment; *Plessy v. Ferguson*; *Reed v. Reed*; *Slaughterhouse Cases*

BIBLIOGRAPHY: Judith A. Baer, *Equality under the Constitution: Reclaiming the Fourteenth Amendment* (Ithaca, NY: Cornell University Press, 1983); Stanley H. Friedelbaum, "State Equal Protection: Its Diverse Guises and Effects," *Albany Law Review* 66 (2003): 599; Pamela S. Karlan, "Equal Protection, Due Process, and the Stereoscopic Fourteenth Amendment," *McGeorge Law Review* 33 (Spring 2002): 473; and Donald G. Nieman,

Promises to Keep: African-Americans and the Constitutional Order, 1776 to the Present (New York: Oxford University Press, 1991).

MICHELLE D. DEARDORFF

Equal Rights Amendment   The Equal Rights Amendment (ERA) was a proposed amendment to the U.S. Constitution to guarantee women's rights and equality under the law. The amendment passed Congress in 1972, but was declared dead in 1982, 3 states short of the required 38 states (three-fourths of the states) needed for adoption of a constitutional amendment. The ERA read, "Equality of rights under the law shall not be denied or abridged by the United States or any State on the basis of sex."

The ERA was first introduced in Congress in December 1923 by Daniel Anthony, a Republican from Kansas who was the nephew of Susan B. Anthony. The original amendment read, "Men and Women shall have equal rights throughout the United States and every place subject to its jurisdiction." The amendment was introduced in every session of Congress from 1923 until it was passed by Congress in 1972.

Women's groups such as the National Organization for Women (NOW) were active in lobbying Congress to pass the ERA, as they believed the amendment was necessary to ensure equal treatment under the law due to the U.S. Supreme Court's interpretation of the Equal Protection Clause of the Fourteenth Amendment prior to 1971. The Court had failed to hold that the clause protects women from some forms of discrimination by the states and the federal government. In 1971 the Supreme Court overturned a state law as unconstitutional under the Equal Protection Clause due to sex discrimination for the first time in *Reed v. Reed*. Further protection against sex discrimination was achieved in *Craig v. Boren* (1976), a case in which the Supreme Court overturned an Oklahoma law requiring males to be older than females to purchase beer as a violation of equal protection. In the *Reed* case the Court used the same standard it uses in scrutinizing laws that do not classify based on sex or race. In the *Craig* case it used a higher standard known as "intermediate scrutiny" for the first time. The standard makes it more difficult for a law making a gender distinction to be upheld than other laws. The Court, however, did not apply the "strict scrutiny" that it uses in race cases as NOW and other women's groups had hoped. Some women argued that the ERA was no longer necessary due to these changes in constitutional law, while others still felt the ERA was necessary for symbolic purposes or to actually ensure gender equality.

Modern opposition to the ERA was led by Phyllis Schlafly of Illinois, who founded the conservative group Eagle Forum, which originally focused on opposition to ERA. Schlafly's movement, known as "Stop ERA," was a grassroots effort that mobilized ordinary women across the United States against the ERA. The major arguments made by the opposition were that protections and privileges granted to women would be lost,

> PROPOSED AMENDMENT
>
> *Section 1. Equality of rights under the law shall not be denied or abridged by the United States or by any state on account of sex.*
>
> *Section 2. The Congress shall have the power to enforce, by appropriate legislation, the provisions of this article.*
>
> *Section 3. This amendment shall take effect two years after the date of ratification.*

such as the exemption from the military draft and the right to financial support from their husbands. To emphasize what the movement saw as a major threat to women and families, activists in the movement dressed their daughters in dresses and pinned signs on them that read, "Don't Draft Me." In Illinois and elsewhere, the military service argument was a major reason why the ERA was not ratified. Also, after the U.S. Supreme Court decision in *Roe v. Wade* (1973) guaranteed the right to abortion, ERA opponents argued that it would guarantee publicly funded abortions on demand. The ERA needed 3 more states for ratification in 1982 when the new limit for ratification set by Congress had expired.

While some argue that the ERA is no longer necessary in light of current laws and court rulings, it has been reintroduced in every session of Congress since 1982. In the 108th (2003–4) Congress, New York Representative Carolyn Maloney sponsored a new ERA in the House of Representatives. Senator Edward Kennedy of Massachusetts sponsored the new ERA in the Senate. If a new ERA passes Congress, it will start the ratification process over again. Many women's organizations support the passage of a new ERA, including NOW, the American Civil Liberties Union (ACLU), the League of Women Voters (LWV), and other groups in the National Council of Women's Organizations.

Also, the Alice Paul Institute has focused on a "three-state strategy" in Illinois, Missouri, and Florida, arguing that Congress can still extend the time limit for ratification on the 1972 ERA given that a different session of Congress extended the deadline once already. Also, they point out that the Twenty-seventh Amendment banning members of Congress from voting themselves a pay raise, which takes effect prior to the next election cycle, was ratified by the required number of states over 200 years after it passed Congress. *SEE ALSO:* Amendment Process; Gender and Federalism; Women's Rights

BIBLIOGRAPHY: Janet K. Boles, *The Politics of the Equal Rights Amendment: Conflict and the Decision Process* (New York: Longman, 1991); and Jane Mansbridge, *Why We Lost the ERA* (Chicago: University of Chicago Press, 1986).

MAUREEN RAND OAKLEY

Erie Railroad Co. v. Tompkins *Erie Railroad Co. v. Tompkins* (1938) overruled *Swift v. Tyson* (1842), a decision that construed Section 34 of the Judiciary Act of 1789, the so-called Rules of Decision Act. The statute provided that "the laws of the several states" were to be the "rules of decision" in the federal courts in cases where federal law did not apply. In an opinion written by Justice Joseph Story, *Swift* held that the word "laws" in the statute referred to state constitutions, statutes, and "long-established local customs" but not to decisions of state courts involving matters of "general" commercial jurisprudence. Thus, under *Swift*, the federal courts were free to ignore state judicial decisions in "general" law cases and to make their own "independent" judgment as to the properly applicable rule of "state" common law. Rejecting the idea that there could be a "general" common law existing independent of the sovereign power of the states, *Erie* held that the word "laws" in Section 34 must be construed to include judicial decisions and that the federal courts were required, when adjudicating issues involving state-created rights, to follow state court decisions in determining the law of the different states.

Justice Louis D. Brandeis wrote for a five-justice majority. His opinion criticized Swift for bringing "injustice and confusion" to the law by allowing the federal courts to ignore the common-law rules applied in the courts of the various states and to apply, instead, their own different rules of "general" common law. The result was that state and federal courts frequently followed conflicting sets of common law rules, a situation that encouraged parties to attempt to manipulate jurisdictional rules involving citizenship, party structure, and the amount in controversy in an effort to navigate their case into the specific court—state or federal—that applied the set of common law rules that was most advantageous to them. Because non-citizens of a forum state were able to exploit that opportunity more commonly and effectively than were citizens of the forum state, the opinion maintained that the Swift doctrine "in practice" unfairly discriminated against citizens of forum states and in favor of those who were non-citizens.

From the moment *Erie* was announced, critics questioned its reasoning. Some charged that its constitutional language was merely dicta because the decision did nothing more than alter the construction of a federal statute. Others argued that the opinion failed to articulate any clear and coherent constitutional theory. Doubt about the opinion's meaning and foundation was so pervasive that the Court itself did not refer to *Erie* as a constitutional decision for almost two decades. By the 1950s, however, commentators were beginning to embrace the view that *Erie* was a constitutional decision and that, by protecting the lawmaking authority of the states, it announced a basic principle of federalism. By the 1980s, after the profession had generally come to accept the idea that *Erie* was a federalism decision, some commentators—and at least two Supreme Court justices (Lewis F. Powell Jr. and William H. Rehnquist)—were advancing the view that *Erie* was based on separation-of-powers principles because it limited the lawmaking authority of the federal judiciary and subordinated that power to the lawmaking primacy of Congress. By the beginning of the twenty-first century, most legal writers accepted *Erie* as a constitutional decision, and a majority seemed to agree that it served the principles of both federalism and the separation of powers.

In spite of continuing disagreements about its constitutional foundation, *Erie* quickly became, and remained, a foundational case in American law. Its importance lies primarily in three areas. First, it inspired the judicial development of "the *Erie* doctrine," a complex set of rules—designed in large part to curb "forum shopping" between state and federal courts—that determine when and to what extent the federal courts must follow state law. One subset of rules, for example, identifies *Erie*'s reach, establishing that it controls whenever federal courts decide issues of state-created rights. Thus, *Erie*'s mandate reaches beyond federal diversity jurisdiction but does not apply when the federal courts adjudicate issues of federal law. Another subset distinguishes between the "substantive" rules of state law that the federal courts must follow and the "procedural" rules of state law that they are not required to apply. It is because "the *Erie* doctrine" does not require federal courts to apply state "procedural" law that they are able to follow the congressionally mandated Federal Rules of Civil Procedure.

Second, in conjunction with *Murdock v. City of Memphis* (1875), *Erie* defines the operative scope of state judicial authority in the nation's federal system. *Murdock* established the principle that the U.S. Supreme Court has no jurisdiction to review judgments of state courts that are properly based on state law grounds, and *Erie* requires the federal judiciary—when adjudicating state-created rights—to follow the substantive rulings of those state courts. Thus, the two decisions together define the area in which the federal judiciary as a whole must honor and enforce the legal rules that state courts establish.

Finally, *Erie* helped underwrite a major reorientation of the federal judiciary. *Swift*'s "general" law had placed the federal courts in a position of ambiguous equality with state courts and—because "general" law was, in theory, "state" law—prevented them from developing judge-made rules that constituted truly "federal" law, that is, rules that were binding on the states under the Supremacy Clause. *Erie* changed matters. By identifying state courts with "local" common law issues, it implicitly identified the federal courts with more important "national" law issues; and by eliminating the "general" law, it gradually turned the federal courts toward using truly "federal" sources of lawmaking authority—the Constitution, treaties, and statutes of the United States—to give their judge-made rules the authority of supreme national law. Thus, as a matter of institutional evolution, though not of the Court's "original intent," *Erie* helped to alter the image of the federal courts, expand their power and prestige, and magnify their role vis-à-vis the state courts.

BIBLIOGRAPHY: Tony Freyer, *Harmony & Dissonance: The* Swift *&* Erie *Cases in American Federalism* (New York: New York University Press, 1981); Edward A. Purcell Jr., *Brandeis and the Progressive Constitution*: Erie, *the Judicial Power, and the Politics of the Federal Courts in the Twentieth Century* (New Haven, CT: Yale University Press, 2000); and Edward A. Purcell Jr., "The Story of *Erie*: How Litigants, Lawyers, Judges, Politics, and Social Change Reshape the Law," in *Civil Procedure Stories*, ed. Kevin M. Clermont (New York: Foundation Press, 2004).

EDWARD A. PURCELL JR.

Everson v. Board of Education *See* Incorporation (Nationalization) of the Bill of Rights

Exclusionary Rule The Fourth Amendment to the U.S. Constitution provides, "The right of the people to be secure in their persons, houses, papers, and effects, against unreasonable searches and seizures, shall not be violated, and no Warrants shall issue, but upon probable cause, supported by Oath or affirmation, and particularly describing the place to be searched, and the person or things to be seized." The unanswered question, however, is what happens to evidence seized due to an unreasonable search or seizure?

The Supreme Court first addressed this issue in the 1914 case of *Weeks v. United States*. William Robert Weeks Jr. was arrested and charged with sending lottery tickets through the mails. His house was then searched without a warrant, and the papers seized were used in his trial to help convict him. The Court, in reversing the opinion, formulated the exclusionary rule, which holds that evidence obtained through an unreasonable search and seizure cannot be used in a federal court. It was not clear, however, if the exclusionary rule was a necessary part of the Fourth Amendment or simply a rule of evidence formulated by the Supreme Court to be followed by all inferior federal courts.

Furthermore, since *Weeks* dealt with federal courts, the Court next had to consider the relationship between the Fourth Amendment's prohibition on unreasonable searches and seizures and the requirements of the Due Process Clause of the Fourteenth Amendment, including the question of the exclusionary rule. In *Wolf v. Colorado* (1947), the

Court held that the right to be free of unreasonable searches and seizures is "fundamental," and thus incorporated by the Fourteenth Amendment's Due Process Clause against infringement by the states, but it refused to incorporate the exclusionary rule. Writing for the Court, Justice Felix Frankfurter maintained that considerations of federalism require that the states be given wide latitude in developing remedies for unreasonable searches and seizures committed by their officials.

One consequence of *Wolf* was that state officials could obtain evidence illegally and then turn it over to federal officials who would use it to convict somebody: the so-called silver platter doctrine. Because the federal authorities had not conducted the illegal search, the evidence was admissible. In the 1960 case of *Elkins v. United States*, however, the Court held that evidence obtained this way was inadmissible as a Fourth Amendment violation.

The following year, in *Mapp v. Ohio*, the Court reversed *Wolf* and held that the Fourth Amendment's exclusionary rule was now applicable against the states by way of the Due Process Clause of the Fourteenth Amendment. The Court's rationale was that it was meaningless to give people the right to be free from unreasonable searches and seizures in their states, but then have the states be able to use that evidence to convict. The exclusionary rule, according to the Court, was the only remedy for illegal searches.

Mapp v. Ohio did not end the debate over the exclusionary rule. The Supreme Court, especially under the leadership of Chief Justice Warren Burger but also under his successor, William Rehnquist, fashioned several modifications that limited the scope of the exclusionary rule. For example, in *Illinois v. Gates* (1983), the Court allowed evidence obtained by a search warrant issued on the basis of an anonymous letter to the police because the police followed the letter with an investigation that supported the information in the letter. The rationale was based on a totality-of-circumstances approach.

In similar fashion, in *United States v. Leon* (1984), the Court allowed evidence to be used when a warrant was issued based on a tip from a confidential informant of unproven reliability, because the magistrate issuing it was detached and neutral, and the exclusionary rule is meant to deter police. In this case, the police had acted in good faith; it was the magistrate who had erred. Likewise, in the companion case of *Massachusetts v. Sheppard*, the Court again allowed the evidence when the wrong search warrant was issued by the magistrate. The rationale was the same: the police acted in good faith, and the magistrate made the mistake.

In *Arizona v. Evans* (1995), the Court allowed evidence to be used even though erroneous information leading to the search resulted from the clerical error of a court employee, who had not deleted a traffic warrant from a computer even though a judge had squelched it. The rationale once more was that the mistake was not made by the police, but by a person who had no stake in the outcome of a particular criminal prosecution.

In *Pennsylvania Board of Probation and Parole v. Scott* (1998), the Court allowed evidence obtained without a warrant to be used for a parole revocation hearing rather than a criminal trial because the state has an overwhelming interest in ensuring that parolees comply with their parole conditions as they are more likely to commit criminal offenses than are average citizens.

Also in 1998, in *Minnesota v. Carter*, the Court allowed evidence to be used based on a warrant that was issued after an officer, acting on a tip, had observed drug activity by looking through a gap in closed blinds. The two people convicted did not live in the apartment, and thus the Court reasoned that they could not expect privacy in a place that was not theirs but was simply a place to do business.

The debate about the exclusionary rule continues. On the one side are those who feel that no evidence obtained unreasonably may ever be used in court. On the other side are those who would like to see the rule eliminated, as it allows the guilty to go free on a "technicality." The end result is a rule that is still in effect but diluted by several decisions of the Supreme Court. *SEE ALSO:* Burger, Warren Earl; Fourteenth Amendment; Incorporation (Nationalization) of the Bill of Rights

BIBLIOGRAPHY: James B. Haddad et al., *Criminal Procedure* (New York: Foundation Press, 1988); Jerold H. Israel, Yale Kamisar, and Wayne R. LaFave, *Criminal Procedure and the Constitution* (St. Paul, MN: Thomson West, 2003); Irving J. Klein and Christopher J. Morse, *Constitutional Law for Criminal Justice Professionals* (New York: Looseleaf Law Publications, 2002); and Lloyd L. Weinreb, ed., *Leading Constitutional Cases on Criminal Justice* (New York: Foundation Press, 2003).

ROBERT W. LANGRAN

Exclusive Powers   The federal government is a government of delegated powers, meaning that it has only those powers delegated to it by the Constitution. All other powers, the Tenth Amendment reads, "are reserved to the states . . . or to the people." The powers delegated to the federal government may be exclusive, meaning that they may be exercised only by the federal government, or they may be concurrent, meaning that they can be exercised by both the federal and state governments. Sometimes it is apparent when a power is exclusive because the Constitution is explicit, such as in Article I, Section 8, when it grants Congress the power to "exercise *exclusive* Legislation" over the nation's capitol. In other places, when delegating a power to the federal government, the Constitution specifically denies the same power to the states. For example, Article I, Section 8, of the Constitution gives Congress the power to "coin money" while Section 10 of the same article specifically prohibits the states from "coin[ing] Money." There may also be instances, as Alexander Hamilton points out in *The Federalist* No. 32, when "a similar authority in the States would be absolutely and totally contradictory and repugnant" to a power vested in the federal government, such as the power of "prescribing rules for naturalization," even though the Constitution does not explicitly deny this power to the states. There are also times when the exercise of federal authority preempts a field and precludes state regulation of the same subject matter, even though the state would be free to exercise its authority over the matter if the federal government had not acted. Finally, there are instances in which courts have held that the exercise of state authority is inconsistent with the grant of the commerce power to the federal government even though the federal government has not exercised its power. This is termed the "dormant power of the Commerce Clause." *SEE ALSO:* Commerce among the States; Concurrent Powers; Preemption; Reserved Powers

ELLIS KATZ

Executive Branch Organizations   The executive branch is organized around the principal of delivering governmental services that have been assigned to the executive either by the federal or state Constitution or by subsequent law. Initially at the federal level, this organization was rather simple as the executive was not required to provide much more than mail services and road and canal construction, and conduct foreign policy. Yet, as the nation matured so did the responsibilities assigned to the executive. By the early part of the twentieth century it became apparent that the executive organizational structure lacked the ability to administer a modern state. Yet a simple tension has always existed between the legislature (Congress and state legislatures) and its lawmaking function and the executive (presidents and governors) and his or her implementing responsibilities. Considerable power is obtained in the administering of the law, and as the complexity of society increased so did the power of executive agencies. Thus, the executive administers and the legislature monitors the implementation to ensure that its intent has been maintained.

By the late 1930s, it had become apparent that the apparatus for governing was inadequate for the demands placed upon the executive. In 1936, the President's Committee on Administrative Management (commonly referred to as the Brownlow Committee after its chairman, Louis Brownlow) was established with the charge of examining the organization of the executive branch and making recommendations concerning reorganizations that would help the executive better govern. This was followed in 1946 by the Administrative Procedures Act, which seeks to standardize federal administrative practices across many agencies. Perhaps the most sweeping of the reform commissions was the Hoover Commissions I and II (1947–49 and 1953–55 respectively) chaired by former President Herbert Hoover. The first Hoover Commission sought to greatly expand the managerial capacities of the president by surrounding him with a highly professional staff, while the second commission sought to address governmental functions by recommending that federal activities that compete with private interests should be curtailed. These executive reorganization activities were also mirrored in the states and larger local governments during the same time frame.

Currently the federal executive branch is organized around four distinct organizational forms. First is the Executive Office of the President. Here can be found such entities as the Office of Management and Budget (OMB), National Security Council, and Council of Economic Advisors. Second are the departments. There are currently fifteen departments: agriculture, commerce, defense, education, energy, health and human services, homeland security, housing and urban development, interior, justice, labor, state, transportation, treasury, and veteran affairs. Each department is headed by a secretary who is approved by the Senate. After the departments come the independent establishments and government corporations. A sampling includes the Central Intelligence Agency (CIA), Environmental Protection Agency (EPA), General Services Administration (GSA), National Aeronautics and Space Administration (NASA), Office of Personnel Management (OPM), Social Security Administration, and U.S. Postal Service. In all, there are fifty-four such entities. Finally, the executive branch has quasi-official agencies, which include the Legal Services Corporation, Smithsonian Institution, State Justice Institute, U.S. Institute of Peace, and several multilateral and bilateral organizations.

Many, if not all, of the executive branch agencies interact with state and local governments, and many have almost identical agencies at the state level. The existence of these similar if not identical state executive branch organizations is often not by accident. Indeed, it is often easy to trace the emergence of a state agency back to the creation of a similar federal entity. Once a federal executive branch agency has been created, it will often use grants to encourage the creation of similar state agencies not only for the purposes of administering the various programs but also for establishing allies at the state level for its continued existence and expansion. Martha Derthick has observed that the state agencies become "the formal recipient of federal funds, the formal channel for federal communication with the state, and a possessor of authority within state government," thus establishing a powerful and highly influential alliance between the agencies that often challenges traditional legislative and executive control mechanisms. This role as the "formal" entry point of federal funds and communications provides the state agency with legitimacy and considerable power within state government structures and generally allies them with their federal counterpart, often at the exclusion of other state-level entities.

It is important to note that in many cases, each federal agency develops its own strategy for dealing with state and local entities based on the type of activity being conducted. Thus, some agencies adopt highly decentralized patterns of interaction and service delivery while others may choose a highly centralized structure. Executive branch agencies also find themselves often serving multiple masters. The final "head" of any executive branch agency is naturally the executive. However, almost all funding for these agencies originates in legislative committees, and with the rise of advocacy groups no executive agency can ignore their role. Typically this relationship has been described as an Iron Triangle, a metaphor describing the world in which policy decisions are made between executive agencies, legislative committees, and interest groups. However, of more recent origin is the term "policy networks," which seems to capture better the nature of executive agencies and the "web" of interest under which they function. This network model also better captures the interaction between federal agencies and their state counterparts as well as the power often exerted by powerful local lobbies on a particular policy of interest.

Several million employees work within executive agencies across all levels of government; these employees are generally well-educated, reasonably well-paid individuals motivated by the policy area in which they are employed. They are people who want to work for the EPA or the CIA and oftentimes plan on continual employment through multiple presidents. This can create difficulties for the executive who has four and maybe eight years with which to deliver on campaign promises. Generally speaking, those who work in executive branch organizations fall under the civil service protection systems (instituted at the federal level with the Pendleton Act in 1883). In essence, this insulates employees from a change in the executive. For the executive this may prove to be problematic since personnel may not always be responsive to policy changes (bureaucratic resistance). As such, one of the biggest changes at the federal level (also at the state level in many instances as well) to come out of the reform movements discussed earlier is the creation of the Senior Executive Service (SES), which allows the president/governor to appoint a certain number of officials within each agency to establish his or her own control, independent of the civil service laws. Indeed this need for the executive to have greater control over agencies and their staff has led to a call for revamping the civil service process and allowing for greater hiring and firing control to be vested in the executive. The first agency to seriously test this new model is the Department of Homeland Security, where the president has the power to remove poor-performing employees and also pay more "market-based" salaries. *SEE ALSO:* Intergovernmental Management; Intergovernmental Relations; Public Administration; Public Officials' Associations; State Government

BIBLIOGRAPHY: Martha Derthick, "Ways of Achieving Federal Objectives," in *American Intergovernmental Relations: Foundations, Perspectives, and Issues*, 3rd ed., ed.

Laurence J. O'Toole Jr. (Washington, DC: CQ Press, 2000); Jay M. Shafritz, Albert C. Hyde, and Sandra J. Parkes, eds., *The Classics of Public Administration*, 5th ed. (Belmont, CA: Wadsworth/Thomson Learning, 2004); and *U.S. Government Manual*, 2003–4 ed. (Washington, DC: U.S. Government Printing Office, 2003–4), http://www.gpoaccess.gov/index.html.

DAVID R. CONNELLY

Executive Orders   The issue of federalism has not always been a high priority for presidents. Few presidents have issued executive orders addressing federalism, let alone executive orders of any import. However, the phrase "getting the government off the people's backs" uttered by President Ronald Reagan and the subsequent declaration that "the era of big government is over" by President Bill Clinton lend a nice backdrop to examine how both presidents addressed federalism through the use of executive orders.

An executive order is supposed to be a clarification of how a law should be implemented, and most executive orders are that. Executive orders, though, do not require congressional action to become effective, but still have the full force of law. As a result, presidents sometimes will use executive orders to implement part of their policy agenda without having to go to Congress to enact legislation—or, in the words of some scholars, to do an end run around Congress.

Ronald Reagan issued the most prominent executive order addressing federalism on October 26, 1987. Executive Order (EO) 12612 expressed Reagan's desire "to restore the division of governmental responsibilities between the national government and the States that was intended by the Framers of the Constitution and to ensure that the principles of federalism . . . guide the Executive departments and agencies in the formulation and implementation of policies." It defined "policies that have federalism implications" as those "regulations, legislative comments or proposed legislation, and other policy statements or actions that have substantial direct effects on the States, on the relationship between the national government and the States, or on the distribution of power and responsibilities among the various levels of government."

Executive Order 12612 contained several directives to federal agencies regarding "policies that have federalism implications." First, it required executive departments, when formulating and implementing such policies, to be guided by nine fundamental federalism principles. Second, agencies also should adhere to a set of four criteria for formulating and implementing policies, including refraining from establishing uniform, national standards and, when such standards are required, consulting with appropriate state-level officials and organizations in developing those standards. Third, the order provided guidelines regarding how to construe regulations with respect to possible preemption of state law. Fourth, executive departments were directed not to submit to Congress legislation that would, for example, regulate the states in certain ways or preempt state law except under certain conditions. Fifth, EO 12612 required executive department heads to designate an official to be responsible for implementing the order. Sixth, the Office of Management and Budget was made responsible for ensuring the federal agencies' compliance with the order. Finally, agencies were directed to identify proposed regulatory and statutory provisions that have significant federalism implications and, when appropriate, to address substantial federalism concerns.

President Bill Clinton's first foray into the issue of federalism via the executive order came in 1993 through EO 12875. This order addressed the processes in which state and

203

local officials provided input into regulatory proposals that contained significant unfunded mandates. It delineated that state and local governments "should have more flexibility to design solutions to the problems faced by citizens in this country without excessive micromanagement and unnecessary regulation from the Federal Government."

EO 12875 would make Clinton appear to support a states' rights position. However, he angered states' rights advocates by issuing Executive Order 13083 in May 1998, to replace EO 12612 and EO 12875. Like Reagan's directive, EO 13083 starts with a set of guiding principles regarding federalism; unlike its predecessor, which focused on a fundamental, philosophical view of the rights afforded to the states under the Constitution, Clinton's order sought a balance between federal and states' rights and addressed the practical benefits that arise when states are afforded the ability to experiment in policy making. EO 13083 also removed the requirement that each department have a designated official overseeing implementation of EO 12612. In addition, departments would not have been required to prepare federalism assessments for policies that have federalism implications. Before EO 13083 became effective, however, Clinton suspended it and later repealed it through other executive orders (EO 13095 and EO 13132, respectively) following concerns raised by the National Governors' Association, among others. As a result, President Reagan's EO 12612 remained in effect.

Both Reagan's issuing of EO 12612 and Clinton's attempt to replace it with EO 13083 reflect what a charged issue federalism can be when a president addresses it through the use of executive orders. The language of both orders reflects the symbolic importance of the issue. But one also should address the question of what practical effect the use of an executive order has on the issue of federalism. At least one major study concludes that the answer is "little."

The General Accounting Office (GAO) reviewed federal agencies' rules issued between April 1, 1996, and December 31, 1998. Among its findings, the GAO determined that of the 11,414 rules promulgated during the study period, only 26 percent mentioned EO 12612 in its preamble. When the GAO narrowed its review only to 117 "major" rules, the preamble of only one indicated that it had federalism implications, even though states' rights supporters claim that nearly all of the major rules had such implications. Finally, the GAO study noted that the OMB, by its own admission, had taken little specific action regarding implementing EO 12612 (although OMB officials did contend that OMB's requirements under the order are considered as part of OMB's regulatory review process). Although the GAO acknowledged certain limitations of its study, its report provides at least some evidence that the relationship between executive orders and federalism may be more about symbolic positioning rather than tangible results. *SEE ALSO:* National Governors' Association; Preemption; Presidency; Reagan, Ronald; Unfunded Mandates; White House Office of Intergovernmental Affairs

BIBLIOGRAPHY: William Clinton, "Presidential Executive Order 13083: Federalism," *Fed. Reg.* 63, no. 27651 (1998); Phillip J. Cooper, *By Order of the President: The Use and Abuse of Executive Direct Action* (Lawrence: University Press of Kansas, 2002); Ronald Reagan, "Presidential Executive Order 12612: Federalism," *Fed. Reg.* 52, no. 41685 (1987); and L. Nye Stevens, "Federalism: Previous Initiatives Have Little Effect on Agency Rulemaking," GAO Report GAO/T-GGD-99-131 (Washington, DC: U.S. General Accounting Office, 1999).

Victoria A. Farrar-Myers

Externalities/Spillovers   Externalities are uncompensated third-party effects result-ing from the production and/or consumption of goods and services. In other words, an externality results from the gap between the private cost or benefit of a good and the social cost or benefit of the good. A spillover is an externality that spills over into areas beyond the authority of the government where the externality is produced. For example, pollution is an *externality*, because the producers of pollution do not bear the full so-cial and environmental costs of that pollution. The acid rain that falls in the eastern states is a *spillover* of the pollution produced by coal-burning electric generators in American midwestern states.

Externalities are a form of market failure and, as such, justify governmental inter-vention to correct. When externalities become spillovers, governments with broader jurisdiction (e.g., state or nation) may be necessary to correct or alleviate the exter-nality/spillover, because such a government may have jurisdiction over where the ex-ternality is produced and where the effects of the externality are felt. Also, these governments often have greater expertise for responding to the externality. Conse-quently, the existence of, or potential for, externalities and spillovers is often used to justify national standards and programs.

Externalities/spillovers may result from interjurisdictional competition. Without state or national standards, local governments may reduce their environmental standards, labor protections, welfare programs, and taxes as a means to attract businesses to move to their locality. Other governments competing for those same businesses may feel pres-sured to respond in kind in order to attract the businesses. This interjurisdictional com-petition may result in a "race to the bottom" as each government seeks a competitive edge by reducing its standards below the other. There is little evidence supporting the interjurisdictional competition or race-to-the-bottom theses, because most businesses' location decisions are based on not just cost but also quality of life issues.

Externalities/spillovers reveal important tradeoffs that occur in a federal system. Ac-cording to Gordon Tullock (1994), the smaller the government, the more likely the gov-ernment will reflect the interests of the citizens, the more likely the small government will produce spillovers that affect others, and the more likely outsiders will produce externalities that spill over and affect those within the small government. This tradeoff establishes a justification for a federal form of government, under which local govern-ments can be responsive to citizens and governments with broader jurisdiction can cor-rect or alleviate externalities and spillovers. *SEE ALSO:* Environmental Policy; Welfare Policy

BIBLIOGRAPHY: Paul E. Peterson, *The Price of Federalism* (Washington, DC: Brook-ings Institution, 1995); Susan Rose-Ackerman, "Does Federalism Matter? Political Choice in a Federal Republic," *Journal of Political Economy* 89 (1981): 152–65; and Gordon Tul-lock, *The New Federalist* (Vancouver: Fraser Institute, 1994).

TROY E. SMITH

Extradition   *See* Interstate Rendition

❖ **F**

Federal Courts Article III of the U.S. Constitution authorizes federal courts when it provides that "the judicial Power of the United States shall be vested in one supreme Court and such inferior Courts as Congress shall from time to time ordain and establish." The federal judicial system so authorized has grown from a 6-member Supreme Court and 13 lower-court federal judges in 11 states and territories in 1789 to a judiciary of about 1,700 judges in 94 district courts (each of which has within it a bankruptcy court), 12 regional and 1 national courts of appeals, and the 9-member Supreme Court of the United States.

The federal district and appellate courts do not constitute all the "courts" created by the federal government. What distinguishes the courts of the judicial branch of government—commonly called "the federal courts"—is that they exercise, to repeat the phrase in Article III, "the judicial power of the United States." Congress has created other courts to help it implement the legislative powers granted it by Article I of the Constitution. Those "Article I courts" include, for example, a court to hear tax cases, courts within the armed services, courts to hear cases involving immigrants, and bodies of "administrative law judges" within federal agencies such as the Social Security Administration. Although these courts may look somewhat like Article III courts, they are not part of the judicial branch. Executive branch officials may review the decisions of some Article I courts, followed in some cases by review by Article III courts. Article III courts review the decisions of other Article I courts directly.

FEDERAL JURISDICTION

Most judicial business in the United States is done, not in the courts established by the federal government, but rather in the courts established by each of the states. At the start of the twenty-first century, compared to the roughly 1,700 federal judges, there were almost 30,000 state judges, a rough indication of the comparative workloads of the federal and state courts. In essence, legal controversies in the United States are the province of state courts unless Congress has vested jurisdiction of those controversies in the federal courts. The Constitution, in Article III, Section 2, tells Congress which disputes it may assign to the federal courts.

Federal jurisdiction is sufficiently complex as to merit its own textbooks, law school courses, and a steady stream of litigation. The following are the basic elements of federal court jurisdiction.

Cases in which the U.S. government is a party: federal courts exercise exclusive jurisdiction over prosecutions under federal criminal statutes, which are brought by attorneys of the U.S. Department of Justice, and civil actions to which the U.S. government is a party.

Civil cases involving provisions of the U.S. Constitution and federal laws and treaties: jurisdiction over civil actions under federal statutes is exclusively federal in some but not all cases. This exclusive jurisdiction includes but is hardly limited to so-called federal specialties, such as bankruptcy, patent and copyright, and admiralty and maritime cases. In some areas, both state and federal courts may hear cases involving federal law. For example, a federal law makes railroads responsible for injuries suffered by their employees while working for the railroad; however, the law permits such employees to claim violation of these federal statutory rights by bringing suit in either state or federal court. As a general rule, if a person sues someone in state court and the suit claims violation of a federal right, the defendant may request that the case be transferred to federal court (in legal parlance, the defendant "removes" the case to federal court).

In all cases—civil and criminal—state courts must observe federal law, such as the rights of criminal defendants established by the U.S. Constitution. Article VI of the Constitution makes clear that the Constitution, laws enacted by Congress, and treaties are "the supreme Law of the Land," and state judges are obliged to follow them notwithstanding any contrary state laws. This does not mean that a court may not enforce a state law that is different in some way from a federal law. The court may enforce the state law as long as that law does not violate the federal law.

Civil cases under state law between citizens of different states or suits where an alien is a part: The federal courts' "diversity of citizenship" jurisdiction allows litigants in civil cases that involve citizens of different states to bring their cases in, or remove them to, federal court, even if they involve no matter of federal law. For example, if a citizen of Wisconsin filed a lawsuit in Wisconsin state court against a citizen of Illinois over the Milwaukee automobile accident in which they were involved, the Illinois citizen might wish to remove the case to federal court under the diversity of citizenship jurisdiction. There are various requirements for invoking that jurisdiction; for example, the amount of money in dispute must exceed a minimum amount set by federal statute.

Disputes between two states: When states sue each other—a rare occurrence—the case goes directly to the U.S. Supreme Court, which usually appoints a "special master" to investigate the matter for it. Such a suit may arise, for example, over disputes over state boundaries and access to water in the disputed land.

The Supreme Court, of course, is the final appellate court for cases involving the federal constitution and federal laws. Litigants in cases presenting federal questions decided either by the federal courts of appeals or the state supreme courts may ask the Supreme Court to review those decisions. Other federal courts may also review state court decisions, however. For example, individuals convicted in state court, with their convictions upheld by the highest court of the state, may, in limited circumstances, file actions in federal trial court, called habeas corpus petitions, asking a federal judge to review the decisions of the state courts. The federal judge's decision may then be appealed to the federal appellate courts.

FEDERAL COURT STRUCTURE

The structure of the federal judiciary is basically a matter for Congress to determine. The Constitution says nothing on the subject other than that there will be a supreme court and may be other federal courts if Congress wishes to create them. In fact, when the Constitution was adopted, there was strong sentiment among many citizens who were leery of the new government that Congress should create no lower federal courts and leave all cases to the state courts.

Over the years, Congress has created a federal judicial system with the following elements. First, it has divided the country into ninety-four federal judicial districts and created in each district a U.S. district court—the chief federal trial court. Trial courts decide the facts in dispute in a case and apply the law to those facts. Most cases are actually resolved after conferences between the lawyers (and sometimes the judge) without the need for a trial.

The judges of the district court are (1) district judges, who exercise full judicial power; (2) bankruptcy judges, who constitute a unit of the district court (the federal bankruptcy court) and decide bankruptcy cases referred to them by the district judges; and (3) magistrate judges, who perform work assigned to them by the district judges, within statutory limits.

No district's boundary crosses state lines (with one small exception—to keep Yellowstone National Park wholly within a single judicial district). For some districts, the boundaries are the state lines; the federal judicial district of New Mexico, for example, is the entire state. Other states have several judicial districts; Congress has divided New York, for example, into four judicial districts. Congress also specifies the number of federal district judgeships in each district (and the number of bankruptcy judgeships as well). The number of district judgeships ranges from two to almost thirty. In the early twenty-first century, federal district courts disposed of around 300,000 cases per year, most of them civil cases.

Each district is within one of twelve regional circuits. Within each circuit is a court of appeals, which hears appeals from the district courts of the circuit. Each circuit but

Map of the eleven regional circuits established in 1981.

one, the District of Columbia circuit, embraces at least 3 states' federal judicial districts. Just as Congress specifies the number of judgeships in each district court, it specifies the number of judgeships for each court of appeals, ranging roughly between ten and thirty. In addition to the twelve regional circuits, Congress has created the federal circuit, whose court of appeals has a nationwide jurisdiction over appeals in certain areas, including charges of patent infringement and disputes over customs appealed to it from a special Article III court, the Court of International Trade. The courts of appeals dispose of well less than 100,000 cases per year.

The nine-member Supreme Court in Washington hears appeals from the federal courts of appeals and from the state supreme courts in cases involving federal law. Congress has provided the Supreme Court, though, great discretion as to the cases it will decide. Each year the Court is asked to hear many more cases than it decides. From the late 1990s into the next decade, the Court was actually deciding well under 100 cases per year, although the number of cases presented to it each year approached 10,000. For the most part, the Court selects for review cases that allow it to resolve conflicting interpretations of federal law by the federal appellate courts or state supreme courts, or to give national resolution to important legal questions (and to important political questions that have a strong legal component).

JUDICIAL SELECTION

The Constitution and federal laws are almost totally silent on the manner of selecting federal district judges, courts of appeals judges, and Supreme Court justices. The Constitution authorizes the president to nominate members of the Supreme Court and, pursuant to a constitutional provision, Congress has directed that the president nominate district judges and courts of appeals judges. If the Senate approves the president's nominees, they are appointed as justices or judges. The selection process for federal judges is overtly dependent on partisan politics; roughly nine out of every ten judges appointed by any president are at least nominal members of the president's political party.

Despite this fact, federal judges are generally regarded as of very high caliber. For one thing, the Justice Department and the White House conduct thorough investigations of potential nominees, and the Senate Judiciary Committee conducts an investigation of the nominee once received from the president. Various other groups, including a committee of the American Bar Association, weigh in with comments on nominees' credentials.

Moreover, judges appointed by the president have very strong job security, which encourages them to decide cases according to the facts and laws rather than to favor those who appointed them. Article III of the Constitution, in order to promote the independent exercise of "the judicial power of the United States," provides that the judges who exercise it may serve "during good Behaviour," which is essentially for life. They may be removed from office only by impeachment in the House of Representatives and conviction in the Senate. In the history of the United States through 2005, the House has impeached thirteen judges; the Senate has convicted seven and acquitted four, and two resigned.

About half the federal judges, however, are not presidentially appointed, life-tenured judges but are instead appointed by other judges for fixed terms. Bankruptcy judges are selected by the courts of appeals of their respective circuits and serve fourteen-year terms. Magistrate judges are selected for eight-year terms by the district judges of their respective districts. These limited terms are not inconsistent with Article III's promise of judicial independence to those who exercise the judicial power of the United States. That is because bankruptcy judges and magistrate judges are not ultimately responsible for the exercise of that power. Instead, these term-limited judges decide matters referred to them by judges who do exercise that power and who may change the term-limited judges' decisions before they become final.

JUDICIAL ADMINISTRATION

In many countries, the executive branch of government is responsible for the administration of the judicial branch. In such countries, the department of justice or its equivalent determines how much money to spend for the courts' operations and how to spend it on personnel, acquire equipment, and similar matters. In the United States, the general view—at least since the middle of the twentieth century—has been that this situation creates inevitable conflicts of interest because while justice department officials are deciding how much money to allocate to judges for administrative support, other officials of that same department are seeking favorable judicial decisions from the judges. That creates a risk either that officials will punish judges for unfavorable decisions or that judges will make decisions favorable to the government to curry favor with those who hold the judicial purse strings. Even if the risk is not great, the appearance of a conflict could be damaging.

To avoid that situation in the federal courts, Congress has created the Judicial Conference of the United States, comprising the chief judges of each federal court of appeals, a district judge elected from each regional circuit, and the chief judge of the Court of International Trade. The chief justice presides over the Conference, which meets twice a year and works through a system of committees to determine how much money to seek each year from Congress and how to administer the funds provided, including attendant matters such as personnel regulations and financial management procedures. The Conference also develops rules of procedure to govern the processing of cases in federal courts, and comments on legislation that may affect the operation of the courts. Although having Congress fund the courts and oversee their operations might also create a conflict of interest, the general view is that, in a republic, it is better for the legislature than the executive to decide these matters. Moreover, it would be impractical and unwise to allow judges to draw as much money from the treasury as they wish—the legislature is the obvious source. The important point, though, is that the judicial branches in the United States deal directly with their respective legislatures for funding rather than relying on the executive branch to do so on their behalf.

The Conference is assisted by the Administrative Office of the U.S. Courts, which carries out its many administrative duties under the Conference's supervision. The Federal Judicial Center, a separate agency within the judicial branch, is responsible for the continuing education of judges and supporting personnel of the courts, and for research on such matters as the impact of new policies and procedures. Congress created both agencies at the request of the Judicial Conference.

In addition to these national bodies, councils of judges in each regional circuit see to administrative matters within the circuit. They also receive complaints from citizens about whether federal judges have engaged in misconduct or are unable to perform their duties.

Substantial administrative discretion resides as well in the individual federal courts across the country. In each district court and court of appeals, the judges are supported by court managers and their staffs who assist in the processing of cases and the management of court personnel. For the roughly 1,700 federal judges nationwide, there are about 30,000 supporting personnel. *SEE ALSO:* Diversity of Citizenship Jurisdiction; State Courts; Suits between States; Supreme Court of the United States

BIBLIOGRAPHY: Administrative Office of the U.S. Courts, http://www.uscourts.gov; Robert Carp and Ronald Stidham, *Judicial Process in America*, 3rd ed. (Washington, DC: Congressional Quarterly, 1996); Federal Judicial Center, http://www.fjc.gov (includes information on federal judicial history and "Inside the Federal Courts"); Richard Posner, *The Federal Courts: Challenge and Reform* (Cambridge, MA: Harvard University Press, 1996); and Edwin Surrency, *History of the Federal Courts*, 2nd ed. (New York: Oceana Press, 2002).

RUSSELL WHEELER

Federal-Local Relations   The belief in states' rights runs deep in American political culture, and a commitment to local control runs deeper still. As a result many public goods and services in the United States are provided locally, with little or no federal participation. Others involve federal agencies only because counties, cities, and special districts accept grants-in-aid for projects of mutual interest to local and national policy makers. Most federal-local relations revolve around these grants and their administration, and the interactions are generally collaborative, if not always amicable.

The federal government does not rely solely on grants to obtain cooperation from local governments, however. Within limits, Congress can require local governments to perform certain functions, and it can prohibit them from acting contrary to national policy. Both forms of compulsion breed resentment at the local level, and if enough areas are affected, the political backlash may force Congress to seek compliance by more cooperative means. This is most likely to happen when governors and legislators ally themselves with local officials, presenting a united front to their elected representatives in Congress.

Some localities are entirely under federal jurisdiction and have no voting representatives in Congress. In these areas, federal agencies act as the local government, or decide how that government is constituted, and by whom. Consider the nation's capital, which occupies most of the federal District of Columbia. For a century after the Civil War, three commissioners appointed by the president governed the City of Washington, subject to the approval of standing committees in Congress. In 1967 the commissioners gave way to a mayor and council appointed by the president, but pressure for greater powers of self-determination led to passage of a Home Rule Act in 1973. The act confers powers on a locally elected council and mayor, but Congress retains control over the district's budget and has the authority to overturn local ordinances. The Senate confirms presidential nominees to the local judiciary, too, fueling demands for voting representation in Congress and even statehood, which Congress has so far refused.

Congressional control over local areas extends far beyond the District of Columbia. During the nineteenth century, land purchases, wars, treaties, and the conquest of native lands greatly expanded the United States. The territories were administered militarily until Congress organized them politically, enacting laws; establishing territorial governments; confirming the appointment of territorial governors, judges, and marshals; and financing administrative operations. As their numbers increased, the people of each territory sought admission to statehood under a constitution of their own making and eventually became full-fledged members of the Union.

Federal control over local affairs did not end when territories became states, however. As the price of admission, Congress frequently reserved large parcels of territorial lands for national use. Military reservations are found everywhere in the United States, and they are controlled by the U.S. Department of Defense, not local governments. This can lead to friction between neighbors, but nearby communities also benefit economically from military bases. Some become so dependent that a decision to close obsolete bases threatens them with economic ruin and triggers resistance from members of Congress whose constituents are affected.

Additionally, there are about 275 federal reservations for Native Americans, most of them in the West. They are controlled by tribal governments, which operate independently of state governments and their subdivisions. However, tribal governments are not independent of Congress, which has the plenary power over "domestic nations," just as it controls insular territories. In the past, Congress used its power to abrogate treaties, dilute tribal ownership of lands, and regulate tribal governance. Recently, Congress has limited the jurisdiction of tribal courts in criminal cases, but it seems more inclined to respect the autonomy of tribes in civil matters.

Finally, large tracts of federal land are reserved for national parks (78 million acres), fish and wildlife management (88 million acres), national forests (191 million acres), and grazing (266 million acres). The lands are managed by the National Park Service, U.S. Fish and Wildlife Service, U.S. Forest Service, and Bureau of Land Management, respectively. These agencies decide who may use federal lands, when, and for what purposes. Their decisions are not subject to local or state control, and are frequently criticized by people who live near the affected areas and want access to public lands.

All told, federal land reservations consume more than half of the total land area of 13 states west of the 105th meridian. Federal lands make up 62 percent of Idaho and Utah, 68 percent of Alaska, and 83 percent of Nevada. Not surprisingly, land-use policy is a persistent source of conflict between federal agencies and western state and local governments. During the late 1970s and early 1980s, resentment of federal regulation of public lands peaked in the western states; the Sagebrush Rebellion, as it was known, culminated in Ronald Reagan's appointment of Colorado's James Watt as secretary of the interior. Every interior secretary since then has come from a western state, and federal policy has become more responsive to local sentiments.

More significant than the acreage of land under federal jurisdiction is the large number of local governments formed under state constitutions. The autonomy of these 85,000 governments varies from state to state, but is generally increasing as legislatures delegate powers and responsibilities to communities. As far as the federal government is concerned, however, local governments are under state control, and this has two important implications.

First, state agencies usually mediate formal relations between federal agencies and local governments. Federal officials rely on state officials to obtain local compliance with program requirements, and state officials seek to coordinate and control interactions between their local governments and federal units. Local governments sometimes forge direct ties with federal agencies, but for the most part they rely on political connections. During the 1960s, for example, big-city mayors were aligned with Democrats in Washington who supported urban redevelopment programs. When Richard

Nixon became president, federal policy shifted in favor of suburban officials, who tended to be Republican. Politics and administration are inevitably conjoined in federal-local relations.

Second, states' rights limit the power of Congress, and those same limits protect local governments insofar as they are constituted by states. Thus, Congress is in no position to order local governments to do its bidding, except when exercising powers exclusively assigned to it by the Constitution. Lacking broad powers of compulsion, Congress ordinarily secures cooperation from state and local governments by offering financial compensation for doing what it wants them to do.

As Tip O'Neill (D-MA), former speaker of the House of Representatives, famously observed, "All politics is local." He was referring to the propensity of elected Representatives to understand national policy in terms of its effects on their constituents, and to view their constituents' concerns as problems requiring national attention. "Pork barrel" legislation is the best-known example of this orientation: representatives and senators bring home the bacon by passing legislation that benefits constituents in their districts and states.

Grants-in-aid are related to pork barrel spending. Such grants provide matching funds for constructing roads, sewage treatment facilities, and other elements of municipal infrastructure, or subsidizing education programs, public housing, social services, public assistance, and a host of community development projects. Many of these grants are awarded on the basis of population or need, and are available to all local governments that qualify. Increasingly, federal grants allow considerable discretion over the use of funds by local authorities, who complain about categorical grants with too many strings attached. These features explain the popularity of grants in city halls and state capitals—and hence Congress's enthusiasm for grants.

Indeed, the number of grants has grown steadily over the years as Congress created more incentives for local governments to fulfill its wishes. There are now several hundred federal grant programs providing more than $300 billion in annual assistance to state and local governments. About 10 percent of that amount flows directly to local governments. The remainder goes to state governments, but much of it is earmarked for local use and must be passed along to counties, cities, and special districts. Thus, local government spending on public goods and services is quite heavily subsidized by the federal government.

The federal subsidy was even larger in the late 1970s and early 1980s, when Congress provided general and special revenue-sharing funds to local governments, in addition to categorical grants-in-aid. Shortfalls in the federal budget led to the elimination of revenue sharing, and constrained the growth of grants-in-aid. Congress turned to more coercive measures, including sanctions, in order to realize its policy objectives. Local policy makers who refused to comply with federal regulations were threatened with loss of funds, and some states lost highway funds because they refused to lower speed limits and reduce the threshold for drunk driving.

Sometimes Congress simply imposes new responsibilities on state and local governments without providing additional funds. State and local officials strongly resent these "unfunded mandates," which override their own policy objectives and political priorities. Indeed, the proliferation of unfunded mandates has led to calls for greater restraint on the part of Congress, but the political incentive to address national concerns without raising federal taxes is very strong, so mandating continues.

Two examples make this point. The Americans with Disabilities Act (ADA) was signed into law with great fanfare in 1990. It prohibits discrimination against persons with disabilities in employment, government services, public accommodations, commercial facilities, and transportation. Many ADA provisions affect businesses, but state and local governments are required to make their facilities accessible to people with disabilities, too. This includes public buses and transit stations, which must be equipped with wheelchair lifts and related equipment. These capital improvements are costly, and they are not covered by federal funds. To comply with the mandate, state and local officials must decide whether to increase taxes or divert resources from programs that are popular with businesses, unions, taxpayers, and other potent interest groups.

Federally mandated environmental protection is even more costly. The Clean Air Act, Clean Water Act, and Safe Drinking Water Acts are administered by the Environmental Protection Agency (EPA), which sets minimum standards of air and water quality for the nation. The EPA also monitors state and local governments' progress in meeting these standards by regulating polluters under their jurisdiction. If progress is not made, the EPA can assume control, depriving states and localities of their traditional role in environmental policy making. Local governments must therefore compel factories and businesses to reduce emissions, and they must insure that municipal power plants also meet EPA standards. They may even have to regulate auto and truck usage or provide alternatives in the form of mass transit, since gasoline-powered engines are a major source of air pollution.

Similarly broad measures are required to meet the EPA's water quality standards. Point-source pollution must be controlled, storm water runoff must be contained, and sewage must be treated—and most of the enforcement and treatment are done by local governments. During the 1970s, Congress made grants-in-aid available for treatment plants and the like, but these have been replaced by loans that must be repaid. Local governments also find it necessary to regulate growth patterns in order to protect watersheds, which brings them into conflict with developers, construction companies, and property rights advocates. Hence local officials bear the political costs, while Congress and other national officials reap credit for protecting the environment.

In both of these examples, local officials (or at least many of them) have the same goals as Congress; they want to make public services accessible to people with disabilities, and they certainly want constituents to enjoy clean air and water. But local officials also want more flexibility when implementing policies that affect them deeply; failing that, they want more money from Congress to carry out its bidding. Congress has its own mandate, however; voters want policy makers in Washington to guarantee their rights and protect them from environmental hazards, without raising income taxes. Federalism allows Congress to satisfy these conflicting desires by delegating responsibility, while retaining control over policy.

The federal government not only compels state and local governments to perform actions favored in Washington, D.C., but also proscribes state and local actions that conflict with national policy. For example, mayors and city councils might want to protect local businesses and their employees from foreign competition and interstate commerce, but the Constitution reserves those powers to Congress. Neither can local governments restrict immigration or enforce laws against illegal immigration in order to limit the demand for public services. Only Congress has the authority to regulate immigration. Here and in other areas, federal law is supreme; it preempts the right to self-determination at the local level.

Political considerations limit the exercise of federal power over local governments;

members of the House of Representatives are elected from local districts, and senators have local roots, too. For this reason, Congress prefers to use grants-in-aid and other means of persuasion to get its way. The Supreme Court does not have this luxury, and some of the most visible examples of federal intervention involve the judicial enforcement of civil rights. Under the U.S. Constitution, individuals are entitled to equal protection under the law. Consequently, state and local governments cannot discriminate on the basis of gender, race, religion, or political creed, even if local or regional sentiment favors disparate treatment of one sort or another.

It was not always so. National guarantees of civil rights were not added until 1868, when the Fourteenth Amendment was ratified. Even then the Supreme Court responded conservatively, construing "equal protection" and "due process" quite narrowly. In *Plessy v. Ferguson* (1896), the Court upheld the constitutionality of a Louisiana law requiring the segregation of races in public transportation. State laws and local ordinances providing "separate but equal" facilities proliferated after the Court's ruling, with particularly pernicious effects in public schools.

In *Brown v. Board of Education* (1954), the Supreme Court overturned *Plessy*, holding, "Separate educational facilities are inherently unequal." The Court subsequently ordered local school systems to desegregate with "all deliberate speed," but state and local authorities in the South resisted the rulings. In September 1957 Governor Orval Faubus ordered the National Guard to surround Central High School in Little Rock, Arkansas, preventing African American students from entering. A federal judge voided the order, but angry whites threatened the safety of anyone who crossed the color line until President Dwight Eisenhower sent troops from the Army's 101st Airborne Division to maintain order.

Desegregation was required in many urban school systems outside the South, too. Federal judges in Boston, Detroit, Denver, and several other cities ordered districts to achieve racial balance within their schools. Busing was mandated, with African American students being transported to schools that were predominantly white and, less commonly, white students being transported to schools that were predominantly black or Hispanic. Tensions erupted, and many white parents either enrolled their children in private schools or fled to the suburban school districts. Judicial activism in this policy area then subsided.

As the enforcement of civil rights shows, federal involvement in local affairs ebbs and flows. The level of federal involvement depends on which party controls Congress, and what domestic policies they pursue. Generally speaking, Democrats use categorical grants-in aid, as well as tough mandates and prohibitions, to assert federal leadership in local affairs. Republicans strive to minimize "coercive federalism," and they prefer less restrictive, though not necessarily smaller, grants-in-aid. Changes in party control at the national level usually produce changes in federal-local relations, in accordance with new ideas about the role of government in our lives. *SEE ALSO:* Americans with Disabilities Act of 1990; *Brown v. Board of Education*; Civil Rights Act of 1964; Coercive Federalism; Crosscutting Requirements; Crossover Sanctions; Eisenhower, Dwight D.; Environmental Policy; Formula Grants; Fourteenth Amendment; Grants-in-Aid; Guarantee Clause; Home Rule; Land Use; Native Americans; Pass through Requirements; *Plessy v. Ferguson*; Public Lands; Revenue Sharing; *Roe v. Wade*; Safe Drinking Water Act of 1974; Sovereignty; Special Districts; State Constitutions; States' Rights; Supremacy Clause: Article VI, Clause 2; Unfunded Mandates; U.S. Territories

BIBLIOGRAPHY: Thomas J. Anton, *American Federalism and Public Policy: How the System Works* (New York: Random House, 1989); R. McGregor Cawley, *Federal Land, Western Anger: The Sagebrush Rebellion and Environmental Politics* (Lawrence: University Press of Kansas, 1996); Timothy Conlan, *From New Federalism to Devolution: Twenty-five Years of Intergovernmental Reform* (Washington, DC: Brookings Institution, 1998); and Deil S. Wright, *Understanding Intergovernmental Relations*, 3rd ed. (Pacific Grove, CA: Brooks/Cole, 1988).

RUSSELL L. HANSON

Federal-State Relations   The federalism literature has traditionally paid considerable attention to the relationship between the federal government and the states. That relationship has many facets, from legal and financial to political, and has varied from cordial to combative. Although the U.S. Constitution provides some structure for the federal-state relationship, some constitutional provisions are not very clear, and some have been the basis for major controversies over the years.

THE CONSTITUTIONAL FRAMEWORK

One important set of constitutional provisions gives the states a number of guarantees. The national government cannot impose a tax or duty on any state's exports, grant preferences to the ports of one state over those of another, or require ships heading toward or away from one state to clear or pay duties at another port (Article I, Section 9). States cannot be divided or merged without the consent of the state legislature(s) involved (Article IV, Section 3), and no state can be deprived of equal representation in the U.S. Senate without the state's consent (Article V).

All states are guaranteed protection against invasion and, at the request of the governor or legislature, against domestic disorder (Article IV, Section 4). The national government apparently has the authority to intervene even without the governor or legislature's request in order to enforce national laws, protect federal property, or protect the country. That same section guarantees each state a republican form of government, a provision that is subject to various interpretations. The federal courts have been reluctant to hear cases regarding that matter since the mid-1800s. Apparently the guarantee of a republican form of government does not prohibit the states from allowing citizens to vote on public policy issues, a practice that more resembles direct democracy than a republic (which usually emphasizes representative democracy).

The Second Amendment to the Constitution protects each state's right to have a militia, a provision that has more usually been discussed in cases regarding gun control laws than cases involving state militias. The Eleventh Amendment gives each state immunity from lawsuits in federal courts if the suit is brought by a resident of another state or country unless the state agrees to the suit. Since the mid-1990s, several Supreme Court rulings overturned suits against state governments, even if the state government had been accused of violating federal law. However, the Court has not been consistent in that view. It was willing to hear cases brought by the George W. Bush campaign during the dispute over the 2000 presidential election in Florida and upheld the right of people to sue state governments regarding violations of the Family and Medical Leave Act (FMLA; see Davis and Peltason 2004, 372–74).

RESTRICTIONS ON STATES

Several constitutional provisions regulate or limit state authority in various ways (see Article I, Section 10). The states may not adopt treaties or other international agreements, although they may work to attract foreign firms to locate or invest in the state and to encourage other countries to permit more imports of the state's products. The states may not tax imports or exports without the approval of Congress, and they may not coin their own money. States are prohibited from impairing the obligations of contracts, but that provision does not ban all types of state regulation of business activity.

Article I, Section 10, also prohibits states from adopting bills of attainder (which punish particular people without a trial) and ex post facto laws (which make an action illegal after it took place). The Reconstruction Amendments (Thirteenth through Fifteenth) had the effect of limiting state authority in a number of ways. The Thirteenth Amendment banned slavery. The Fourteenth Amendment prohibited the states from abridging the privileges and immunities of citizens, and it provided that no state could deprive anyone of life, liberty, or property without due process of law. It also provided that states could not deny anyone equal protection under the law. Those provisions have been the subject of numerous controversies over the years. The Fifteenth Amendment held that the right to vote could not be denied or abridged because of race, color, or previous condition of servitude. After Reconstruction ended, however, the national government conspicuously failed to enforce that amendment for many years. Widespread denial of voting rights of African Americans resulted until the 1960s, when the national government began protecting voting rights more effectively.

Several later amendments also dealt with voting rights. The Nineteenth Amendment gave women the right to vote, and the Twenty-sixth Amendment gave 18-to-20-year-olds the same right. The Twenty-fourth Amendment banned using the poll tax as a requirement for voting in federal elections, and the Supreme Court subsequently extended that protection to voting in all state and local elections, a decision that was based on the equal protection provision of the Fourteenth Amendment.

MUDDYING THE WATERS A BIT

Some constitutional provisions have been sources of major controversies in federal-state relations. Article I, Section 8, gives Congress very broad authority to raise and spend money. Since the 1930s, the courts have generally held that this power enables Congress to attach rules and regulations to federal funds in order to influence state and local government actions, even if Congress does not have the authority to legislate directly to regulate those same actions. Some observers have criticized that broad interpretation, but it has generally prevailed since the mid-1930s.

That same section gives Congress the authority to regulate interstate commerce, but the extent of that authority has provoked considerable debate. The federal courts have sometimes allowed a very broad interpretation of the commerce power by upholding federal law regulating a variety of activities that could affect interstate commerce. However, the courts have sometimes taken a narrower view of the commerce power. In several recent cases, the Supreme Court struck down provisions of federal gun laws and the Violence against Women Act. Part of the justification for those decisions was the assertion that the matters addressed in those laws did not seem adequately related to interstate commerce, although a number of the justices did not agree with those rulings (see Davis and Peltason 2004, 111–14). Some observers felt that the court's actions reflected a growing inclination to protect the powers of the states from federal encroachment. However, an alternative possibility is that the court's actions reflect a lack of support for gun control laws and women's issues.

Additional controversies have erupted over the Necessary and Proper Clause (at the end of Article I, Section 8), which gives Congress the authority to make laws in order to execute the various powers granted to the national government. Some commentators have concluded that the provision should be interpreted narrowly, with "necessary and proper" translated as "essential" or "indispensable." Other analysts prefer a broader interpretation and contend that the provision includes actions that are helpful or convenient for implementing the delegated powers, not just essential actions.

The Constitution's Supremacy Clause (Article VI, Section 2) provides that the Constitution, along with the laws and treaties made under its authority, are the supreme law of the land. Although this provision seems fairly clear at first glance, there have sometimes been disputes over whether specific national government actions have exceeded its constitutional authority. Acts of Congress, for example, are part of the supreme law of the land only if they are consistent with the Constitution. The Tenth Amendment, which states that powers not delegated to the national government and not denied to states belong to the states or to the public, has also provoked controversies. Its meaning depends a great deal on how broadly the national government's powers are interpreted.

THE FEDERAL GOVERNMENT'S ACTIONS

From the mid-1930s through the mid-1990s, the Supreme Court accepted a relatively broad interpretation of the national government's powers. The Court played important leadership roles in establishing national policies regarding racial segregation, the rights of criminal suspects, and abortion. All of those actions provoked criticism that the Court had exceeded its authority, and some critics complained that the Court was promoting national government expansion at the expense of the states. However, this period was also marked by a dramatic expansion of state governments, which became increasingly active in many domestic policy issues, including education, welfare, health care, and transportation.

The White House and Congress also supported expanding the national government's role in domestic policy making, although the nature and extent of that support have varied considerably. Franklin Roosevelt and Lyndon Johnson pushed for greater national involvement in many domestic policies, but many other presidents have also helped to foster more national influence, sometimes on a more selective basis. President George W. Bush, who in many respects is quite conservative, has helped expand the national government's involvement in education and in a variety of programs related to homeland security. He has advocated tighter federal control over some welfare policies, and he has called for a constitutional amendment banning same-sex marriages, in spite of the fact that family law has traditionally been a state responsibility.

CONFLICT WITHIN FEDERAL-STATE RELATIONS

In the history of the American federal system, it is difficult to find a series of events that have tested its fabric more than the fight for racial equality. Looking at the struggle within a historical perspective, from the very beginnings of the nation to the work of the Reverend Dr. Martin Luther King Jr., will show both the abilities and shortcomings of the federal system to address controversies and how changing the scope of conflict can induce changes within the system itself. The scope of conflict includes the size and location of a political conflict, the level(s) of government involved, the branch(es) of government involved, and the political groups involved.

Slavery caused many political conflicts and required a terrible civil war to resolve. Underlying the conflict was the question about which level of government should have the authority over slaves and slave-related issues. From the Constitutional Convention of 1787 to 1860, the southern, proslavery states successfully fought off challenges to shift authority over slavery from the states to the federal government.

During the framing of the Constitution, the question of how the slaves would be counted for the purpose of congressional apportionment and taxing was at the forefront. The slave states wanted slaves to count as full human beings for congressional apportionment, but not to count as part of the state's human population when it came to matters of taxation. In order to secure the approval of the southern states, the Constitution counted each slave as three-fifths of a human being. This gave the slave states greater representation in the House of Representatives.

The slave states won another important battle in Article I, Section 9, of the U.S. Constitution, which prohibited Congress from stopping slave importation until 1808. This allowed the states to determine the regulations and laws overseeing slave importation for two decades. In scope-of-conflict terms, the national government stayed out of the question of slavery in order to secure the approval of the slave states for a new union.

In the following decades, conflict arose over keeping a balance in Congress between free and slave states. This conflict reached a pitch with Missouri's application of admission as a slave state in 1819. If accepted, Missouri would have given the slave states a decided advantage in Congress (see Morison 1965, 138). The Missouri Compromise, which admitted Missouri (as a slave state) and Maine (as a free state), addressed the immediate problem without any true resolution of the issue.

The country remained divided between slave states and free states. The scope of conflict remained primarily within the purview of the states; the legal rights of African Americans depended (for the most part) on the individual actions of the state in question. Later compromises relied in part on local preferences regarding slavery. Territorial governments in Utah and New Mexico were organized without reference to slavery (1850). The Kansas-Nebraska Act also relied on local preferences six years later. This transference from the national to the state government, with the federal government deciding "not to decide," would be the standard solution to the issue of slave versus free state for years to come.

The scope of conflict shifted out of the legislature and into the judiciary when the Supreme Court agreed to hear the case *Dred Scott v. Sandford* (1857). Dred Scott was a slave who had traveled with his "master" through a territory that was governed as a free, nonslave jurisdiction. Years later, Dred Scott claimed his rights to freedom based on that jurisdiction's statute. The Supreme Court decided that the statute establishing the Missouri Compromise was unconstitutional; most of the justices held that Congress did not have the authority to prohibit slavery in U.S. territories and that a segment of human beings were nothing more than property. The Court also ruled that slaves could not be citizens and were not entitled to any constitutional protection of their rights. In scope-of-conflict terms, the battle went from the states to the Supreme Court, who proceeded to send the issue back to the states and territories.

These compromises and court decision ultimately failed, and the issue was fought on the battlefields of the Civil War. As a result, the nation adopted the Thirteenth, Four teenth, and Fifteenth Amendments to the Constitution, which abolished slavery, prohibited the suffrage from being denied based on race, and guaranteed all citizens privileges and immunities and due process of law. These amendments appeared to shift the scope of conflict and give the national government control of these issues. Yet, that is not the case and the scope of conflict continued to be a determining factor in civil rights for nearly a century.

In *Plessy v. Ferguson* (1896), the Supreme Court determined that the Fourteenth Amendment made all equal in the eyes of the law, but not in social situations. Social equality, in the opinion of this Supreme Court, was an entirely different issue. The Court determined that segregation was legal as long as the accommodations (be they schools, restroom facilities, etc.) were "separate, but equal." They were in fact separate, but rarely (if ever) equal. From a scope-of-conflict viewpoint, the Supreme Court decided that the national government would not resolve social inequality and left the matter in the hands of the individual state governments. Whether and how the states implemented "separate, but equal" would be a matter for the states.

States saw a more activist national government with the introduction of the New Deal. As the federal government addressed problems of social inequity, the Supreme Court justices shifted their paradigm and allowed the national government to alleviate suffering from social problems. While the "separate, but equal" concept was not overturned at this time, the question of whether "equal" really meant that the implementation was "equal" (i.e., new textbooks in a white school would mean the same new textbooks at the black school) was looked at, yet major change did not come until the 1950s. In *Brown v. Board of Education* (1954), the Court acknowledged the unfairness found within "separate, but equal." They ruled that racial segregation in educational institutions was in fact unconstitutional and that the process of desegregation was to occur "with all deliberate speed." At this point, the scope of conflict would appear to have shifted from the states to the national government, yet another scope-of-conflict issue arose over what "deliberate" speed really meant. To the southern states, it could take a long time. By 1964, only 2 percent of black children in southern schools were attending an integrated facility.

Voting was another issue. Poll taxes, grandfather clauses, and literacy tests were all used to keep segments of the population from voting. These "implementation problems" were addressed in the Voting Rights Act of 1965, which instructed the U.S. attorney general to abolish literacy tests under certain circumstances and send in national workers to register voters under simplified structures. Even so, certain southern states still found ways to circumvent the intent of the federal legislation.

Southern states found additional ways to thwart efforts to provide equality between the races. Through the process of racial gerrymandering, the State of Mississippi was able to fragment the black voting population in such a way that black majorities were not able to elect a black member of Congress until 1986. This serves as another clear lesson that in a federal system, there are many different levels and institutions where political conflicts may be fought. Who controls the debate and determines the outcome is often determined by where the scope of conflict is located.

COOPERATION WITHIN FEDERAL-STATE RELATIONS

On the other side, there is a continuing and increasing amount of cooperative activities between the planes of government. These acts of cooperation are not necessarily evident in any legislation or constitutional provision, but are implemented through less formal, friendly contacts. Letters of concern, e-mails, and text messages all allow players at different levels and branches of government to express concerns and ideas through an informal network that has the features of flexibility and quickness—elements that are not found as often in more formalistic aspects of the federal-state governments. This communication between actors on different levels and in different branches of government also creates the opportunity for technical assistance throughout the various stages of policy making and implementation. Should one branch or level of government have experience in a certain activity, this knowledge base can be used by less experienced actors.

An example of cooperation between federal-state governments is emergency assistance. During times of disaster (such as floods and earthquakes), the interactions between different levels of government can mean the difference, literally, between life and death. Military forces can be used during times of severe unrest to keep order for short periods of time, forest service resources can be dispatched to local entities during times of fires, and communication equipment can be lent out to localities with less resources. While cooperation can occur between different levels and branches of government, it does not necessarily insure that there will be no conflict. National officials may be hesitant to involve troops when the possibility of injury and death to civilians might bring about negative public opinion—though doing nothing also runs that risk as well (Glendening and Reeves 1984, 115). Another example of cooperation between the different levels of government would be sharing the operations of a governmental venture. While the states have a law enforcement function, the national government has a law enforcement role as well, which can result in joint operations and task forces to reduce crime.

In the legislative arena, supporting legislation is yet another example of cooperation between national and state governments. While a state can make a good or activity illegal within its borders, if the good or activity can easily flow across the border, it makes the law less effective. Using supporting legislation from the national government can extend the reach of the state's law into other jurisdictions, allowing its policies to potentially have more strength. These ventures that have sharing as an element do more than just help efficiency; they also have an important political element.

When a program is implemented by only one level of government, that level of government has all of the responsibility for the success (or failure) of the program. When that implementation is a shared venture and should things take a negative turn, there is an opportunity to share the political blame. In addition, sharing the costs for an expensive program or initiative can make the difference between the success and failure of the program itself.

The federalism literature portrays the relationship between the national government and the states in many different ways. Some observers are impressed by the combative nature of federal-state relations; many discussions of mandates follow that theme. In a related vein, some analysts emphasize the national government's use of coercive measures to pressure state officials to follow national policies.

Other observers see the federal-state relationship as more cooperative, at least most of the time (see Grodzins 1984). When disagreements do arise, they are more likely to be resolved by bargaining and negotiations, not national government commands. To take one recent example, the nationwide 55 miles per hour speed limit initially suggested a national government imposing its will on the states. Before long, however, reports revealed that some states were doing little to enforce the limit. Although national officials initially tried to encourage greater compliance, the limit was progressively watered down and then repealed altogether. The final outcome indicated that the states are far from helpless when disagreements do arise. *SEE ALSO:* Abortion; American System; *Brown v. Board of Education*; Civil Rights Act of 1875; Civil Rights Act of 1964; Civil War; Constitutional Convention of 1787; Crosscutting Requirements; Crossover Sanctions; *Dred Scott v. Sandford*; Education; Elections; Federal Courts; Fifteenth Amendment; Fourteenth Amendment; Health Care Policy; Intergovernmental Relations; Interstate Commerce; Johnson, Lyndon B.; Local Government; Missouri Compromise of 1820; Necessary and Proper Clause; New Deal; *Plessy v. Ferguson*; Privileges and Immunities Clause: Article IV; Privileges and Immunities Clause: Fourteenth Amendment; Reconstruction; Slavery; Supremacy Clause: Article VI, Clause 2; Tenth Amendment; Transportation Policy; Unfunded Mandates; Voting Rights Act of 1965

BIBLIOGRAPHY: Sue Davis and J. W. Peltason, *Understanding the Constitution*, 16th ed. (Belmont, CA: Wadsworth/Thomson Learning, 2004); Paris N. Glendening and Mavis Mann Reeves, *Pragmatic Federalism*, 2nd ed. (Pacific Palisades, CA: Palisades Publishers, 1984). Morton Grodzins, *The American System* (New Brunswick, NJ: Transaction, 1984). Samuel Eliot Morison, *The Oxford History of the American People* (New York: Oxford University Press, 1965); David Nice and Patricia Fredericksen, *The Politics of Intergovernmental Relations*, 2nd ed. (Chicago: Nelson-Hall, 1995); J. Mitchell Pickerill and Cornell W. Clayton, "The Rehnquist Court and the Political Dynamics of Federalism," *Perspectives on Politics* 2, no. 2 (2004): 233–48; C. Herman Prichett, *The American Constitution*, 3rd ed. (New York: McGraw-Hill, 1977); and David Walker, *The Rebirth of Federalism*, 2nd ed. (New York: Chatham House, 1999).

ERIC GRULKE AND DAVID C. NICE

Federalism   Federalism and its kindred terms (e.g., "federal") are used, most broadly, to describe the mode of political organization that unites separate polities into an overarching political system so as to allow each to maintain its fundamental political integrity. Federal systems do this by distributing power among general and constituent governments in a manner designed to protect the existence and authority of all the governments. By requiring that basic policies be made and implemented through negotiation in some form, it enables all to share the system's decision making and decision-making processes.

DIFFERENT CONCEPTIONS

No single definition of federalism has proved satisfactory to all students, primarily because of the difficulties in relating theoretical formulations to the evidence gathered from observing the actual operation of federal systems. Attempts at definition have also foundered on the problems of distinguishing between (1) the federal principle as a broad social concept and federalism as a narrower political device, (2) two classic but different conceptions of federalism, (3) authentically federal systems and political systems that utilize elements of the federal principle, (4) mature and emergent federal systems, and (5) federalism and "intergovernmental relations" as distinct political phenomena.

Social and Political Principle

Federalism, conceived in the broadest social sense, looks to the linkage of people and institutions by mutual consent, without the sacrifice of their individual identities, as the ideal form of social organization. First formulated in the covenant theories of the Bible (Kaufman 1937–48), this conception of federalism was revived by the Bible-centered "federal" theologians of seventeenth-century Britain and New England (Miller [1939] 1961), who coined the term "federal"—derived from the Latin *foedus* (covenant)—in 1645 to describe the system of holy and enduring covenants between God and man that lay the foundation of their worldview. This conception of federalism was given new theoretical form by nineteenth-century French and German social theorists. Closely related to the various theories of social contract, it is characterized by the desire to build society on the basis of coordinative rather than subordinative relationships and by the emphasis on partnership among parties with equal claims to legitimacy who seek to cultivate their diverse integrities within a common social order (Boehm 1931).

As a political device, federalism can be viewed more narrowly as a kind of political order animated by political principles that emphasize the primacy of bargaining and negotiated coordination among several power centers as a prelude to the exercise of power within a single political system, and that stress the value of dispersed power centers as a means for safeguarding individual and local liberties. This means, in effect, that political institutions common to different political systems, when combined within a federal system and animated by federal principles, are effectively endowed with a distinctive character. For example, while political parties are common in modern political systems, parties animated by the federal principle show unique characteristics of fragmentation and a lack of central discipline that increase the power of local groups within the system as a whole (Grodzins 1960a).

Federation and Confederation

Federal ideas have been systematically conceptualized in two different ways. On the one hand, federalism has been conceived as a means to unite a people already linked by bonds of nationality through the distribution of political power among the nation's constituent units. In such cases, the polities that constitute the federal system are unalterably parts of the national whole, and federalism invariably leads to the development of a strong national government operating in direct contact with the people it serves, just as the constituent governments do. On the other hand, federalism has also been conceived as a means to unify diverse peoples for important but limited purposes, without disrupting their primary ties to the individual polities that constitute the federal system. In such cases the federal government is generally limited in its scope and powers, functioning through constituent governments that retain their plenary autonomy, and to a substantial degree is dependent upon them.

Both conceptions of federalism have evolved from early federal experiments. The principles of strong national federalism were first applied by the ancient Israelites, beginning in the thirteenth century B.C., to maintain their national unity through linking their several tribes under a single national constitution and at least quasi-federal political institutions (Bright 1959). Several centuries later, the Greek city-states experimented with federal-style institutions as means for the promotion of intranational harmony and cooperation, primarily for defensive purposes, through associations (e.g., the Achaean League) that came close to what were later defined as confederations

(Freeman [1863] 1893). A modified form of the Greek view was developed by the sixteenth-century theorists (Gierke [1913] 1934). They held that federalism meant a permanent league of states united through a perpetual covenant, binding under international law, in which the constituent states delegated enumerated powers to a general government while retaining full rights of internal sovereignty.

However, when the American system—the prototype of modern federal systems—emerged in the late eighteenth century, its architects developed a conception of federalism much like that of ancient Israel. From the first, American federalism functioned to serve a people with a single national identity and was constituted with a strong national government to serve that people on a national basis, though, as late as 1789, *The Federalist* could describe the new American Constitution as "partly national and partly federal" in deference to the then-accepted views. The successful efforts of the supporters of the Constitution to appropriate the term "federalist" for their own use (Main 1961, ix–xi) restored to common usage the older conception of federalism as a noncentralized national union bound by municipal law, with a general government superior to the governments of the constituent states (Diamond 1963).

Just as the American system became the prototype for other modern federal systems, so the American conception of federalism became the generally accepted one. The other conception was ultimately subsumed under the word "confederation" and its kindred terms. The two systems described by these different conceptions reflect, in part, the distinctions implied in the German *Staatenbund* (confederation) and *Bundesstaat* (federation), terms developed in the mid-nineteenth century (Mogi 1931). A certain degree of confusion remains because the terms invented to describe both systems were used indiscriminately for many years.

Though the American conception of federalism is today almost universally accepted as the most accurate usage, the confederal conception remains a living and legitimate aspect of the federal idea in its largest political sense. Today, the latter is most prominent among certain advocates of limited European union (the Common Market exemplifies a confederal form) and among many so-called world federalists.

Federalism and Related Systems

Federal systems are often confused with four other forms of political order that make use of specific federal principles. The use of some federal principles in multiple monarchies, legislative unions, empires, and decentralized unitary systems can have important consequences similar to those in authentically federal systems. But the fact that such principles do not permeate the four systems makes the distinctions between them and true federations extremely important. Federal systems differ from multiple (or dual) monarchies in two essential ways. The central constitutional characteristic of the multiple monarchy is that union exists only in the person of the sovereign and is maintained only through the exercise of executive power in the sovereign's name. No significant common institutions exist to unite the constituent polities—no common legislatures, no common legal system, and little in the way of a common political substructure. On the contrary, each constituent polity maintains its own political system, which the monarch guarantees to support under the terms of his or her compact with the realm. Multiple monarchies have historically been less than democratic regimes. Even where there have been tendencies toward democratization, the very fact that union exists only by virtue of the common sovereign has tended to elevate the position of the monarch to one of real power. Attempts to transfer sovereignty or the attributes of sovereignty elsewhere, by their very nature, stimulate the division of this kind of association of civil societies into separate polities. Thus, the Austro-Hungarian Empire was held together by the Hapsburg emperors and disintegrated when that family ceased to rule (Sharma 1953, ch. 7). The dual monarchy of Sweden and Norway ceased to function when democratic government was introduced, transferring the attributes of sovereignty from the monarch to the nation(s). In Spain, on the other hand, the inability of the Spaniards to transform a multiple monarchy into a federal system, in a locale that by nature demanded peninsular union of some sort, led to the consolidation of the constituent polities into something approximating a unitary state that remained highly unstable because of the local barriers to consolidation that could be neither accommodated nor eradicated (Elliott 1964).

Multiple monarchies have been transformed into stable and unified polities through legislative union. The United Kingdom is a case in point. The centrifugal tendencies of the seventeenth-century dual monarchy linking England and Scotland were finally eliminated through a legislative union of the two nations in 1707. Legislative union bears very close resemblance to federal union at several crucial points. Though designed to direct public allegiance to a single national authority, the terms of the union encourage the political system to retain certain noncentralizing elements. The government of the nation remains national rather than central in character, since it is created by a perpetual covenant that guarantees the constituent parties their boundaries, representation in the national legislature, and certain local autonomies, such as their own systems of municipal law. Legislative unions usually unite unequal polities. The centralizing tendencies induced by this are somewhat counterbalanced by the residual desire for local self-government in the constituent states. Thus, in the United Kingdom the cabinet has acquired a supremacy not foreseen in 1707, but within the framework of cabinet government Scotland has acquired a national ministry of its own with a separate administrative structure, based in Scotland, for most of its governmental programs (Milne 1957).

Federal systems also differ from empires allowing cultural home rule. Such empires have often been termed "federal"—in some cases because they claim to be. The Roman Empire was the classic example of this kind of political system in the ancient world, and the Soviet Union may well have been its classic modern counterpart. In both cases, highly centralized political authorities possessing a virtual monopoly of power decide, for reasons of policy, to allow local populations with different ethnic or cultural backgrounds to maintain a degree of cultural home rule, provided that they remain politically subservient to the imperial regime. While this often appears to offer a substantial degree of local autonomy, its political effects are purposely kept minimal. Any local efforts to transform cultural home rule into political power are invariably met with suppressive force from the central government, even to the point of revoking cultural rights, as examples from the history of both empires reveal.

Federal systems are clearly different from decentralized unitary states, even though such states may allow local governments considerable autonomy in some ways. In such states, local powers are invariably restricted to local matters, as determined by the central authorities, and are subject to national supervision, restriction, and even withdrawal, though tradition may mitigate against precipitous action by the central government in areas where local privileges have been established. Still, as the English experience has shown, even powerful traditions supporting local autonomy have not stood in the way of great reconcentration of power by democratically elected parliaments when such action has been deemed necessary by a national majority.

Mature and Emergent Federal Systems

Several studies (Macmahon 1955; Wheare [1946] 1964) have attempted to draw distinctions between mature and emergent federal systems. The thrust of their argument is that federalism, when used to unify separate political systems to form a new nation, and federalism as a form of decentralized government in an established nation encourage markedly different kinds of political behavior. In the former case, federalism serves as a means to bring tenuous unity to nations composed of highly autonomous polities, with the locus of power remaining among the constituent units. As federal systems mature, so the argument goes, power is increasingly concentrated at the center, and federalism remains only to promote a certain amount of decentralization within an otherwise highly unified political system. Wheare goes so far as to argue that federalism is a transitional phenomenon useful in promoting progressively larger polities, which are then gradually discarded (in fact, if not in form) as an unnecessary encumbrance. This argument may have some validity in describing the history of nonfederal political systems that have utilized federal principles to promote national unity. For example, it can be used to describe the evolution of the United Kingdom into its present constitutional state. It cannot be applied, however, to any of the three exemplary federal systems—Canada, Switzerland, and the United States. Their national ties existed from the first, and their national governments were granted broad powers at the outset. Nor has federalism declined in importance as those nations have matured. There are undoubtedly differences between mature and emergent federal systems, but those differences are more likely to relate to the character of conflict and negotiation between the general and constituent governments than to their relative strengths.

Federalism and Intergovernmental Relations

Because the study of federalism at its most immediately empirical level heavily stresses the study of intergovernmental relations, the two are often considered to be synonymous. Federalism, however, is something much more than the relationships between governmental units, involving as it does principles that are designed to establish the proper character of those relationships and that must also affect the character of other political institutions within federal systems. As already indicated, federalism concerns the way in which federal principles influence party and electoral systems in federal polities just as much as it concerns the way in which local governments relate to their regional or national ones, or to each other. Moreover, the study of intergovernmental relations exists apart from the study of federalism, since such relationships are to be found in all political systems, federal or otherwise, where there is more than one government extant within a given polity.

CHARACTERISTICS AND OPERATIONAL PRINCIPLES

The most useful way to attempt to understand federalism as a political phenomenon is to under—take a survey of the basic characteristics of federal systems, principles, and processes in order to understand both the manner and the direction of their development.

As a first step, it seems necessary to identify the various federal systems that exist today or have existed in the past; only then can we analyze them as operating political systems. However, identifying federal systems is no simple matter, as we have just seen. The difficulties are heightened by the wide functional differences easily observed in the various political systems that call themselves federal and by the often greater operational similarities between self-styled "federal" and "unitary" systems. Contrast, for example, the political systerns of Australia and the Soviet Union, Canada and Mexico, and Switzerland and Yugoslavia, or compare the United States and Great Britain.

Moreover, federal systems have historically been marked by great internal distinctions between theory and practice, perhaps more so than other political systems. In the United States, the measure of the maintenance of federalism was long considered to be the degree of separation of government activities by level, because it was generally believed that such separation actually existed. In fact, American federalism from the first had been characterized by extensive intergovernmental functional collaboration within the framework of separate governmental structures (Elazar 1962). Similarly, the Canadian federal system has always been described as one in which the federal government is clearly dominant—the repository of all powers not explicitly granted to the provinces. Yet since the brief period of federal supremacy in the years immediately following confederation, the provinces have consistently gained power at federal expense (Smiley 1965). The Russian federal constitution went so far as to grant each Soviet republic the right of secession—a patent impossibility under the realities of the Russian political system.

Nevertheless, some basic characteristics and operational principles common to all truly federal systems can be identified, and can help us to define such systems. These may be divided into three essential elements and a number of supplementary ones.

Written Constitution

First, the federal relationship must be established or confirmed through a perpetual covenant of union, inevitably embodied in a written constitution that outlines, among other things, the terms by which power is divided or shared in the political system and that can be altered only by extraordinary procedures. Every existing federal nation possesses a written constitution, as do most of the other nations incorporating elements of the federal principle. Juridically, federal constitutions are distinctive in that they are not simply compacts between the rulers and the ruled but involve the people, the general government, and the polities constituting the federal union. Moreover, the constituent polities retain local constitution-making rights of their own.

Noncentralization

The political system must reinforce the terms of the constitution through an actual diffusion of power among a number of substantially self-sustaining centers that are generally coincident with the constituent polities established by the federal compact. Such a diffusion of power may be termed "noncentralization." It differs from decentralization—the conditional diffusion of specific powers to subordinate local governments by a central government, subject to recall by unilateral decision. It is also more than devolution—the special grant of powers to a subnational unit by a central government, not normally rescindable. Noncentralization ensures that no matter how certain powers may be shared by the general and constituent governments at any point in time, the authority to participate in exercising them cannot be taken away from either without mutual consent. Constituent polities in federal systems are able to participate as partners in national governmental activities and to act unilaterally with a high degree of autonomy in areas constitutionally open to them—even on crucial questions and, to a degree, in opposition to national policies, because they possess effectively irrevocable powers.

Areal Division of Power

A third element that appears to be essential in any federal system is the internal division of authority and power on an areal basis (Maass 1959), what in the United States has been called "territorial democracy." It is theoretically possible to create a federal system whose constituent units are fixed but not territorially based. There were premodern protofederations of nomadic tribes, and some observers have seen federal elements in nations constitutionally structured to accommodate social and political divisions along ethnic, religious, or even ideological lines. Nevertheless, no authentic federal system has existed without an areal basis for the federal division. Historically, when areal divisions of power have given way to divisions on the basis of functional interest, federalism has been replaced by pluralism. In modern democratic theory the argument between Federalists and Anti-Federalists has frequently revolved around the respective values of areal and functional diffusions of power. Theorists who have argued the obsolescence of federalism while endorsing the values used to justify its existence have generally based their case on the superior utility of pluralism (Mogi 1931, 1059–115). Proponents of the federal-areal division argue that the deficiencies of territorial democracy are greatly overshadowed by the neutrality of areal representation of functional interests, and they argue further that any other system devised for giving power to these interests has proved unable to cope with the complexities and changes of interest endemic in a dynamic age while certainly limiting the advantages for local differentiation inherent in the areal system.

Studies of federal systems indicate the existence of other elements that supplement the three basic ones. While all of them are not always present in every federal system, their near universality leads one to the conclusion that they serve important functions in the maintenance of federalism in each. Similarly, while many of them are found individually in various kinds of political systems, it is their combination within a single system structured around the basic elements that is characteristic of federalism.

Maintaining Union

Generally characteristic of modern federal systems are direct lines of communication between the public and both the general and the constituent governments, which allow the public to exert direct influence on both governments and permit them to exercise direct authority over a common citizenry. The people may (and usually do) elect representatives to all governments that serve them. All of the governments may (and usually do) administer programs so as to serve the individual citizen directly. The courts may serve both levels of government, applying the relevant laws directly.

The existence of those direct lines of communication—one of the major features distinguishing federations from leagues—is usually predicated on the existence of a sense of common nationality binding the constituent polities and peoples of federal nations together, another element requisite for the maintenance of a successful federal system. In some countries this sense has been inherited, but in most it has had to be invented. Federalism in Germany has been based on a common sense of an inherited German nationhood. In the United States, Argentina, and Australia, a sense of nationhood had to be at least partly invented. National consciousness soon became second nature in those countries, since none of their constituent states ever had much more than a partially developed national consciousness of its own. Canada, Switzerland, and Yugoslavia have had to invent a sense of common nationality strong enough to embrace "nationality groups" whose intense national feelings are rooted in the constituent polities. In such newly formed federal systems as India, Malaysia, and Nigeria, the future of federalism is endangered by the absence of a common sense of nationality. Contrary to some theories, federalism has not proved to be a particularly good device for integrating diverse nationalities into a single political system unless it has been accompanied by other factors compelling integration.

Geographic necessity has been a major factor promoting the maintenance of union within federal systems, even in the face of strong pressures toward disunion. The Mississippi Valley in the United States, the Alps in Switzerland, the island character of the Australian continent, and the mountains and jungles surrounding Brazil have served as direct geographic influences promoting unity. More political than "natural," but no less compelling geographically, have been the pressures for Canadian union generated by that country's neighbor to the south or for the federation of the German states generated by their neighbors to the east and west.

Maintaining Noncentralization

It has been well demonstrated that the constituent polities in a federal system must be fairly equal in population and wealth, or at least balanced geographically or numerically in their inequalities, if noncentralization is to be maintained. The United States has been able to overcome its internal inequities because each geographic section has included both great and small states. In Canada, the ethnic differences between the two largest provinces have served to inject balance into the system. The existence of groups of cantons in different size categories has helped maintain Swiss federalism. Similar distributions exist in every other system whose federal character is not in question.

The existence of a large polity dominating smaller states with which it is nominally federated on equal terms has often been one of the major reasons for the failure of federalism. In the German federal empire of the late nineteenth century, Prussia was so obviously dominant that the other states had little opportunity to provide national leadership or even a reasonably strong hedge against the desires of its king and government. Similarly, even without the problem of the Communist Party, the existence of the Russian Soviet Federal Socialist Republic, which occupied three-fourths of the area and contained three-fifths of the population of the Soviet Union, would have severely crippled the possibilities of maintaining authentic federal relationships in that country.

Successful federal systems have also been characterized by the permanence of the boundaries of their constituent units. This does not mean that boundary changes cannot occur, but it does mean that as a matter of constitutional law such changes can be made only with the consent of the polities involved and that, as a matter of political policy, they are avoided except in the most extreme situations. Boundary changes have occurred in the "classic" federal systems—the United States divided Virginia during the Civil War, Canada has enlarged the boundaries of its provinces, and Switzerland has divided cantons—but they have been the exception rather than the rule, and in every case at least the formal consent of the constituent polities was given. Even in weaker federal systems, such as those of Latin America, state boundaries have tended to remain relatively secure. When boundary changes have been made, as in the postwar re-drawing of *Lander* boundaries in West Germany to account for the diminished terri-tory of the Federal Republic and the alteration of state lines to recognize linguistic unities in India, the essential heartlands of the polities involved have been preserved.

In a few very important cases, noncentralization is both reflected and supported through the constitutionally guaranteed existence of different systems of law in the con-stituent polities. Though the differences in those systems are likely to be somewhat eroded over time—the extent of their preservation varying from system to system—their continued existence as separate systems and the national mixture of laws that their existence promotes act as great bulwarks against centralization. In the United States, each state's legal system stems directly and to a certain extent uniquely from English law, while federal law occupies only an interstitial position binding the systems of the 50 states together insofar as necessary. The resulting mixture of laws keeps the ad-ministration of justice, even in federal courts, substantially noncentralized (Macmahon 1955, ch. 11). In Canada, the existence of common law and civil law systems side by side is one constitutional guarantee of French Canadian cultural survival. Noncentral-ized legal systems, a particularly Anglo-American device, are often used in legislative as well as federal unions. They are rare in other political cultures and have become less common in all federal systems established since 1900. More common is the provision for modification of national legal codes by the subnational governments to meet spe-cial local needs, as in Switzerland.

The point is generally well taken that unless the constituent polities have substantial influence over the formal or informal amending process, the federal character of the system is open to question. Since many constitutional changes are made without re-course to formal constitutional amendment, the position of the constituent polities must be additionally protected by a constitution designed so that any serious changes in the political order can be made only by the decision of dispersed majorities that reflect the areal division of powers. This protection, which federal theorists have argued is im-portant for popular government as well as for federalism (Diamond 1963), is a feature of the most truly federal systems.

Noncentralization is strengthened in all federal systems by giving the constituent polities guaranteed representation in the national legislature and, often, by giving them a guaranteed role in the national political process. In some federal systems, notably those of the United States and Switzerland, the latter is guaranteed in the written con-stitution. In others, such as Canada and those in Latin America, certain powers of par-ticipation have been acquired and have become part of the traditional constitution.

Recent studies have shown that the existence of a noncentralized party system is per-haps the most important single element in the maintenance of federal noncentraliza-tion (Macmahon 1955). Noncentralized parties initially develop because of the constitutional arrangements of the federal compact, but once they have come into ex-istence, they tend to be self-perpetuating and to function as decentralizing forces in their own right.

The United States and Canada provide two examples of the different forms that can be assumed by a noncentralized party system. In the United States, where party re-sponsibility is minimal and virtually nonexistent on the national level, a two-party sys-tem has developed, with the parties actually being coalitions of the several state or, in some cases, local party organizations functioning as national units only for the quad-rennial presidential elections or for purposes of organizing the national Congress. Party financing and decision making are functions that are dispersed either among the state organizations or among widely divergent factions operating nationwide. In Canada, on the other hand, the parliamentary form of government, with its concomitant requirement of party responsibility, means that at the national level considerably more party cohesiveness must be maintained simply in order to gain and hold power.

The noncentralized party system in Canada has developed through a fragmentation of the parties along regional or provincial lines. The parties with nationwide bases are still divided internally along provincial lines, with each provincial organization autonomous. Individual provinces are frequently dominated by regional parties that send only a few representatives to the national legislature, adding to the fragmentation of the system. Very often, the party victorious in national elections is the one that is briefly able to expand its base to most nearly national proportions.

European-style federal systems where parliamentary government is the norm follow the Canadian model. Australia and Switzerland come closest to paralleling it, and traces of it can be found in the German Federal Republic. A more centralized variation of the same pattern exists in countries like India, in which the national government is dominated by one very large and diffuse national party that is held together nationally by personal leadership but is quite factionalized in the states where it must share the governing power with other parties.

Federal nations with less developed party systems frequently gain some of the same decentralizing effects through what Latin Americans call *caudillismo*—noncentralized personal leadership systems that diffuse power through strong local leaders operating in the constituent polities. Caudillistic noncentralization is most characteristic of Latin American federal systems but apparently exists in such new federations as Nigeria and Malaysia as well.

The importance to federalism of a noncentralized party system is well illustrated by contrast with those formally federal nations dominated by one highly centralized party, such as the Soviet Union, Yugoslavia, and Mexico. In all three cases, the dominant party has operated to limit the power of the constituent polities in direct proportion to the extent of its dominance.

Ultimately, however, noncentralization is maintained to the extent that there is respect for the federal principle within each federal system. Such respect is necessarily reflected in the immediate recognition by the decision-making publics that the preservation of the constituent polities is as important as the preservation of the nation as a whole. In the words of the American Chief Justice Salmon P. Chase, federalism looks to "an indestructible Union, composed of indestructible States" (*Texas v. White* 1869). This recognition may be based on loyalty to particular constituent polities or on an understanding of the role played by federalism in animating the political system along certain unique lines. Thus, those who value government by conciliation and partnership, with emphasis on local control, are likely to have respect for the federal principle.

Citizens of a federal nation must show that respect in two ways, by showing self-restraint and by cultivating the political art of negotiation. Federalism can exist only where there is considerable tolerance of diversity and willingness to take political action through conciliation even when the power to act unilaterally is available. The usual prerequisite to action in federal systems is the ability to build consensus rather than the power to threaten coercion. Western federal nations can furnish many examples of the exercise of national self-restraint in dealing with difficult federal problems. Even in a federal system as centralized as that of India, the constitutional right of the national government to assume control of the state governments is exercised as little as possible—notably when the Communists win local elections—and is then clearly a temporary action.

The historical record indicates that the dual purpose implied in Chase's dictum has been at least as responsible for the creation of federal systems as has the single interest in political unification. The Canadian confederation came into being not only to create a new nation out of the British North American colonies but also to give Ontario and Quebec autonomous political systems of their own. Similarly, every move toward greater union in the Swiss confederation has been made in order to preserve the independence of the cantons from both outside encroachment and revolutionary centralism (Sharma 1953, 269–75). A good case can be made that similar motivations were important in the creation of Australia, Malaysia, Nigeria, and the United States.

Maintaining the Federal Principle

Several of the devices commonly found in federal systems serve to maintain the federal principle per se and are consequently supportive of both the national government and the constituent polities. Two of these are particularly common and important.

The maintenance of federalism requires that the nation and its constituent polities each have a substantially complete set of governing institutions of their own with the right—within limits set by the compact—to modify those institutions unilaterally. Separate legislative and administrative institutions are both necessary. This does not necessarily mean that all governmental activities must be carried out by separate institutions at each level. It is possible for the agencies of one government to serve as agents of the other by mutual agreement. But each government must have the needed institutions to function independently in the areas of its authority and the structural resources to cooperate freely with the other government's counterpart agencies.

In this regard, the contractual sharing of public responsibilities by all governments in the system appears to be a central characteristic of federalism. Sharing, broadly conceived, includes common involvement in policy making, financing, and administration of government activities. In contemporary federal systems, it is characterized by extensive intergovernmental collaboration. Sharing can be based on highly formal arrangements or informal agreements. In federal systems, it is usually contractual in nature. The contract—politically a limited expression of the compact principle—is used in formal arrangements as a legal device to enable governments responsible to separate polities to engage in joint action while remaining independent entities. Even where government agencies cooperate without formally contracting to do so, the spirit of federalism that pervades ongoing federal systems tends to infuse the participating parties with a sense of contractual obligation.

In any federal system, it is likely that there will be continued tension between the federal government and the constituent polities over the years and that different "balances" between them will develop at different times. The existence of this tension is an integral part of the federal relationship, and its character does much to determine the future of federalism in each system. The question of federal-state relations that it produces is perennially a matter of public concern because virtually all other political issues arising in a federal system are phrased in terms of their implications for federalism. In this way, federalism imposes a way of looking at problems that stands apart from the substantive issues raised by the problems themselves. This is particularly true of those issues that affect the very fabric of society. In the United States, for example, the race question is a problem of federal-state as well as black-white relations, and the same is true of the cultural question in Canada and the linguistic question in India.

The End Product

The very terminology of federalism is characterized by a revealing ambiguity that is indicative of the end product of federal systems. The word "federalize" is used to describe the unification of "sovereign" states into a federal polity and also the permanent devolution of authority and power within a nation to subnational governments. In this ambiguity lies the essence of the federal principle—the perpetuation of both union and noncentralization.

Viewed from the top, the combination of the elements discussed above results in a federal rather than a central government, that is, a government composed of a nation-wide coalition of political institutions, some with predominantly local power bases (such as the national legislature), and others with predominantly national power bases (such as the national bureaucracy). This government, whose power is thus diffused vertically and laterally, functions in cooperation with the constituent polities that it must conciliate in order to act. Decision making is characterized by heavy reliance upon negotiation and bargaining and by minimal reliance upon the exercise of force. Operations are characterized by a measure of disorder, since noncentralization breeds multiple power centers located at or cutting across all levels of government. Each of these centers seeks to keep open routes of access to the others, usually succeeding because it is in the best interests of all to maintain this kind of disorder as part of the "rules of the game."

Viewed locally, a federal system consists of governmental inputs from different sources whose local connections normally serve to fragment local authority. However, because such a system rewards those who actively seek to reconcile the diffuse elements and bind them together for a larger purpose, local political leaders can control these inputs to a great extent. While this may not prevent the national government from exercising great power at any given time or from increasing its total power over time, it does mean that as long as the federal principle remains operative, the public can and almost invariably does limit certain kinds of national government actions or guides such actions into particular channels (often directed toward strengthening the constituent governments) by invoking the terms of the compact.

Viewed theoretically, these patterns of behavior and the arguments advanced to justify them serve to reaffirm the fundamental principles that (1) the strength of a federal polity does not stem from the power of the national government but from the authority vested in the nation as a whole, (2) both the national government and the governments of the constituent polities are possessed of delegated powers only, and (3) all governments are limited by the common national constitution.

All this should make it apparent that federalism is a form of popular government embodying elements of both republicanism and democracy. The federal structures occasionally adopted by nondemocratic systems must generally be considered "window dressing" except insofar as the injection of the federal principle may serve as a democratizing force in itself. In Yugoslavia, for example, the existence of a federal superstructure has proved useful in fostering such decentralization as the Communist Party leadership wished to allow and may even have played a role in stimulating decentralizing tendencies.

EMPIRICAL AND THEORETICAL DEVELOPMENT

Ancient Protofederal Systems

Long before the term "federal" was invented, there were political systems that embodied elements of the federal principle. The Israelite political system was probably the first example in recorded history of a union of constituent polities based on a sense of common nationality, with national and tribal political institutions and some division of functions between the two partly formalized by a written constitution. As a republic it was never able to overcome the problems of national executive leadership and succession and, after some 200 years, revised its constitution to superimpose a limited monarchy on its federal institutions. Still, as many of the seventeenth-century Federalists noted, it came closer to resembling a modern federal system than any comparable premodern nation. Its classic intellectual product, the Bible, was the first book to discuss the problems of a federal polity.

Permanent leagues of independent states united by a sense of common need but without any sense of common nationhood were found in various parts of the Greek world. They were entrusted with certain matters in the realm of foreign affairs and defense but were in every respect accountable to their member states. The classic example of this system was the Achaean League (251–146 B.C.), a protofederal system often erroneously considered to be the first federal polity (Freeman [1863] 1893). The Greeks left some descriptions of their leagues but no theoretical discussions of the league as a political system. Except for Aristotle's criticisms, the great Greek political theorists ignored federalism as a political principle because the very idea contradicted their conception of the small, unified polis as the only basis upon which to build the good regime.

Several of the great ancient empires, notably the Persian, Hellenic, and Roman Empires, structured their political systems around the principle of cultural home rule. Since political life was virtually inseparable from the religious and cultural aspects of society in the ancient world, imperial recognition of local constitutions offered a measure of contractual devolution of political power; however, as in more recent examples of this form of imperialism, such home rule was not a matter of local right but represented a conditional grant subject to unilateral revocation by the imperial rulers.

Medieval Experiments

Elements of the federal principle are foreshadowed in medieval feudalism through its emphasis on essentially immutable contractual relationships that permanently link the contracting parties while guaranteeing their rights. However, the hierarchical character of these relationships, coupled with the lack of practical mechanisms to maintain the terms of the contracts, led to the degeneration of those elements in most feudal societies. Another movement in the direction of federalism grew out of the development of medieval commercial towns in central Europe that formed leagues for mutual defense and assistance following the Greek model. The most important development in this period was the first confederation of Swiss cantons in 1291 for mutual aid in defense of their independence. The success of this effort was in no small measure due to its connection, from the beginning, with quasi-popular government. These embryonic federal experiments all proceeded pragmatically while federal theory was confined to juridical discussions of the corporate relationships between polities in the Holy Roman Empire.

Ultimately a fusion of contractual elements from feudalism with political mechanisms from the commercial confederacies gave rise to the immediate antecedents of modern federalism. The Christian states on the Iberian Peninsula created a political system that in its most advanced stages came very close to authentic federalism. During the years of the Spanish Reconquest, most of the peninsula was reorganized under the *fuero* system, which established local governments with relatively liberal political institutions in order to encourage resettlement. New states were formed through feudal-style contractual relationships designed to protect local rights. Three of these states joined in a quasi-federal arrangement under the Crown of Aragon, each of them (plus several in Italy added later) retaining its own constitution and governing institutions as well as acquiring representation in the overall Aragonese government. The unification of Spain under a multiple monarchy in 1469 left most of these federal elements intact for the next two and a half centuries, but the demands of the monarchy ultimately subverted them, transforming Spain into a precariously centralized state.

In the sixteenth century, certain emergent civil societies, influenced by the Reformation to return to Scripture as a political source, by the Spanish system of political organization, as well as by local necessity, began to apply federal principles for state-building purposes. The Hapsburg heirs to the Spanish crown had applied Iberian principles to the organization of their other European possessions. Their governmental reforms in the Netherlands provided an organizational basis for the federation of the United Provinces in the late sixteenth century. When that country gained its independence, it established a political system that, while unable to solve the most crucial technical problems of federalism, maintained itself in federal style for 200 years, until Napoleon put an end to its existence, leaving a residue of noncentralization that marks the Netherlands today.

The Swiss, in the meantime, were developing their own techniques for combining feudal and commercial elements to create a loose confederation of cantons, which was also influenced by biblical ideas and, perhaps negatively, by contacts with Hapsburg Spain. Achieving full independence in 1648, the Swiss confederation remained loosely leagued for two centuries (except for the Napoleonic interlude), until it adopted a federal constitution in 1848.

First Modern Formulations

The protofederalism of the United Provinces and the Swiss cantons, coming at the outset of the age of nationalism, also stimulated the first serious efforts to formulate federal theories based on modern political ideas. Jean Bodin analyzed the possibilities of federation in light of the problem of sovereignty. Hugo Grotius and Samuel Pufendorf examined federal arrangements as aspects of international law. These theorists all treated federalism as an aspect of international law. Johannes Althusius (1603), analyzing the Dutch and Swiss constitutions, was the first to perceive that federalism was really concerned with problems of national unity. The real father of modern federal theory, he was also the first to connect federalism with popular sovereignty and to distinguish between leagues, multiple monarchies, and confederations. His retention of hierarchical principles and his emphasis on the corporate organization of society both flawed the federal character of his work and reflected the empirical roots of his analysis.

Thus the rise of the nation-state in the sixteenth and seventeenth centuries stimulated federal solutions to the problems of national unification. In all but a few countries on the periphery of western Europe, the application of federal principles foundered on three problems: (1) the conciliation of feudally rooted hierarchies with a system demanding fundamental social equality in order to facilitate the sharing of power, (2) the reconciliation of local autonomy with national energy in an era of political upheaval that required most nations to maintain a state of constant mobilization basically incompatible with the toleration of local differences, and (3) the problem of executive leadership and succession, which is particularly complex in federal systems and was not solved until the United States invented the elected presidency.

Modern Federalism

The rise of modern imperialism also contributed to the emergence of federalism, as indicated by the works of the important prerevolutionary political theorists of the eighteenth century, for example, Montesquieu and Adam Smith. Here, too, the Spanish experience was influential, but it remained for the British to create the requisite popular institutions in their colonization of North America and for the biblically influenced colonists to create the theoretical justification for these institutions. The theoretical ambiguity of those quasi-federal institutions led Americans to assume that their relationship to the British government was federal, while London entertained no such notion (Becker [1922] 1958). The Americans' response to their view of the imperial system helped them develop the federal ideas they were later to use so creatively.

The founders of the United States of America can be said to have transformed and organized the principles of federalism into a practical system of government. They were able to do so partly because their nation developed without the disadvantages that plagued earlier federal systems. As a postfeudal society, the United States had no serious problem of coping with hierarchies. As a relatively isolated nation, external pressures for centralization were not present for nearly 150 years. American political inventiveness took care of the internal problems of applying the federal principle, though not without having to fight a major civil war to resolve some of them. Though the specific forms of American federalism were not widely imitated with success, its basic principles of organization were emulated by almost every other nation attempting the federal solution to the problems of popular government in a pluralistic civil society. The creation of the theoretical framework for those principles was part and parcel of the invention of federalism. Set forth in its basics in the debate over ratification of the U.S. Constitution, that framework had at its core *The Federalist* (Hamilton, Madison, and Jay [1787–88] 1961), the classic formulation of the principles of modern federalism. Equally important to the evolution of federal systems, however, were the arguments of those who wished to preserve even greater state autonomy; many of these arguments were transformed into tools to promote extraconstitutional decentralization during the nineteenth century.

From the first, American contributions to federal theory—even those of the few theorists not actively involved in politics—have been rooted in the practical concerns of maintaining a federal system. Most of these contributions have, accordingly, been formulated as discussions of constitutional law. The courts, particularly the federal Supreme Court, have conducted continuing debate on the meaning and character of federalism through the medium of case law. Leading political figures, such as Albert Gallatin, John Calhoun, Abraham Lincoln, Woodrow Wilson, and Theodore and Franklin D. Roosevelt, have made real contributions through their state papers. The pragmatic orientation of those contributions, however, has tended to obscure their more lasting theoretical importance (Anderson 1955).

The French Revolution, while stimulating the development of popular government, was essentially hostile to the spirit and institutions of federalism. Its immediate heirs tried to destroy federal institutions in western Europe in the name of democracy, and the subsequent bearers of its tradition have proved equally hostile to federal ideas—except insofar as some of them have equated federalism with decentralized government.

In the nineteenth century, several of the new Latin American nations, following the United States' example and also influenced by the federal elements in the Hispanic imperial tradition, experimented with federalism, with distinctly mixed results. Even where federalism survived in theory, the instability of Latin American governments and the frequent recourse to dictatorial regimes hampered its effective operation. Even so, the three largest Latin American nations—Argentina, Brazil, and Mexico—retain federal systems of varying political significance; federal principles are also included in the political systems of Colombia and Venezuela.

In the mid-nineteenth century, European politicians and political theorists, stimulated by necessity, the American example, and the very influential studies of Tocqueville ([1835] 1945), turned to consider federalism as a form of democratic political organization. Though practical applications remained few, numerous works were produced, primarily in the German-speaking countries, where doctrinaire and metaphysical analyses of federalism in relation to the problems of nationalism, sovereignty, and popular consent were in vogue. The most important of these works were the theoretical formulations of Bluntschli (1849–52), based on his observations of federal reorganization in Switzerland, and the historical studies of Gierke ([1913] 1934). In the end, federal principles were used in the unification of Germany, and Switzerland adopted a modern federal constitution. Fully federal solutions were rejected in other nations, but several adopted quasi-federal institutions to meet particular problems of unification and decentralization.

During the late nineteenth century, British interest in imperial federalism was manifested in several ways. Canada and Australia were given federal constitutions and dominion status in 1867 and 1901, respectively, and the foundations were laid for the federal unification of India. British political theorists interested in imperial unity and internal devolution explored contemporary (Bryce [1888] 1909) and historical (Freeman [1863] 1893) federal experiments and presented arguments of their own as to the utility and proper organization of federal systems (Labilliere 1894).

Whereas in the nineteenth century federalism was used to abet ethnic nationalism, in the twentieth it has been used as a means to unify multiethnic nations. Several of the ethnically heterogeneous nations created or reconstructed after World War I, including the Soviet Union and Yugoslavia, formally embraced federalism as a nominal solution to their nationality problems. The United Kingdom added a federal dimension at the same time to accommodate the Irish. The extension of nation-building activities to Asia and Africa, where ethnic diversity is even greater than in Europe, has led to new efforts in the same vein. In nations outside of the totalitarian orbit, such as India and Malaysia, federalism has been used to secure political and cultural rights for the larger ethnolinguistic groups. In Africa, where the survival of separate ethnic groups has been called into question by the native nationalists, federalism has been applied in several nations, including Nigeria and Cameroon, as a device for sharing political power rather than a way to maintain cultural autonomy.

The Contemporary Study of Federalism

The emergence of political science as a discipline in the late nineteenth century stimulated a shift from an explicitly normative to a predominantly empirical interest in federalism. Such noted British scholars as Bryce (1901) and Dicey ([1885] 1961) were the first to study federalism as part of their general interest in political systems. American scholars began their work in the 1870s, as the Civil War generation was passing into history, but their first works still reflected the issues of the war. Thus Burgess (1886) concluded that the utility of the states was dissipated by modern technology just as their power was destroyed by the war, while Wilson ([1885] 1961) accepted the view that the war had wrought great changes but still saw federalism as alive and vital.

Though these men and their colleagues laid the foundations for the empirical study of federal systems with the tools of contemporary political science, federalism as a field of study was neglected for many years. The rise of other problems to attract the attention of scholars, the negation of earlier legalistic and metaphysical approaches, and the decline of normative interest in the federal principle combined to dissuade younger political scientists from examining questions of federal government, except incidentally, until the twentieth century was well advanced.

Renewed interest in the field first developed when American students of public administration found themselves confronted with problems of intergovernmental relations at nearly every turn. The study of intergovernmental relations in the administrative realm brought about significant gains in the understanding of the process of federal government, not the least of which was a growing recognition that the assumptions about federalism underlying their work, borrowed whole from nineteenth-century theorists, needed serious reexamination. Beginning in the 1930s and 1940s, American and British political scientists began to raise fundamental questions about the nature of federal systems and the interrelationships of their governmental components (Anderson 1946). In the 1950s these questions were expanded to include, among others, problems of political influence, the role of political parties, the historical development of federal systems, and the meaning of earlier federal theories (Bachelder and Shaw 1964). By the early 1960s, students of existing federal governments were rediscovering the need to clarify the principles of federalism in order to understand the operation of those governments. Students of comparative government were also becoming increasingly interested in problems of political integration, centralization, and decentralization—all of which stimulated new interest in the systematic study of federalism.

EVALUATION

While many attempts to establish federal systems have ended in failure, such systems, once established, have proved to be most durable. No authentic federal system that has lasted for even fifteen years has ever been abandoned except through revolutionary disruption (as in the case of Germany), and in every such case federalism—showing remarkable resilience—has ultimately been restored. Certain theories to the contrary, there is no evidence that federalism represents a transitional stage on the road to unitary government. No federal system in history has ever "evolved" into a unitary one, nor has any established system been structurally consolidated by internal decision. On the contrary, federal devices to conciliate minority populations have been used in place of force to maintain unity even in consolidated systems. Moreover, federal systems or systems strongly influenced by the federal principle have been among the most stable and long lasting of polities.

At the same time, relatively few cultures have been able to utilize federal principles in government. Anglo-American civil societies have done so most successfully. Even those not fully committed to federalism have, without exception, included elements of the federal principle in whatever systems they have chosen, no doubt because both constitutionalism and noncentralization rate high on the scale of Anglo-American political values.

Of the sixteen formally federal nations that exist in the world today, Australia, Cameroon, Canada, India, Malaysia, Nigeria, and the United States were created under British colonial tutelage. These seven include all the nations established since World War II that have been able to maintain federal systems, and they provide most of the successful examples of federalism in operation. Of the nine remaining federal nations, Argentina, Brazil, and Mexico fall directly within the Hispanic political tradition, and Austria, Germany, and Switzerland, though they follow the Germanic political tradition, were also influenced by Hispanic ideas at some point in their development. Both political traditions have been influential in stimulating federal inclinations in many of the nonfederal nations, but they have been notably less successful in fostering lasting federal institutions; the Hispanic tradition has failed to combine federalism and stability, while the Germanic has tended toward authoritarian centralization. (The three remaining nations, Libya, the former Soviet Union, and former Yugoslavia, are federal in name and formal structure but hardly in any meaningful sense of the term.)

The successful operation of federal systems requires a particular kind of political environment, one that is conducive to popular government and has the strong traditions of political cooperation and self-restraint that are needed to maintain a system that minimizes the use of coercion. Beyond the level of tradition, federal systems operate best in societies with sufficient homogeneity of fundamental interests—or consensus—to allow a great deal of latitude in political operations and to place primary reliance upon voluntary collaboration. The existence of severe strains on the body politic that lead to the use of force to maintain domestic order is even more inimical to the successful maintenance of federal patterns of government than of other forms of popular government. Moreover, federal systems are most successful in civil societies with the human resources to fill many public offices competently and with material resources plentiful enough to allow a measure of economic waste in payment for the luxury of liberty. *SEE ALSO:* Federal-State Relations; Intergovernmental Relations; U.S. Constitution

BIBLIOGRAPHY: Johannes Althusius, *Politica methodice digesta,* ed. Carl J. Friedrich (1603; reprint, Cambridge, MA: Harvard University Press, 1932); American Academy of Political and Social Science, *Intergovernmental Relations in the United States,* Annals, vol. 359, ed. Harry W. Reynolds Jr. (Philadelphia: AAPSS, 1965); William Anderson, *Federalism and Intergovernmental Relations: A Budget of Suggestions for Research* (Chicago: Public Administration Service, 1946); William Anderson, *The Nation and the States: Rivals or Partners?* (Minneapolis: University of Minnesota Press, 1955); Vernon V. Aspaturian, "The Theory and Practice of Soviet Federalism," *Journal of Politics* 12 (1950): 20–51; Glen L. Bachelder and Paul C. Shaw, "Federalism: A Selected Bibliography" (Michigan State University, Institute for Community Development and Services, 1964);

This essay is reprinted from David L. Sills (ed.), *The International Encyclopedia of the Social Sciences* (New York: Macmillan, 1972). Reprinted by permission of the Gale Group.

Carl L. Becker, *The Declaration of Independence: A Study in the History of Political Ideas* (1922; reprint, New York: Vintage, 1958); Anthony H. Birch, *Federalism, Finance and Social Legislation in Canada, Australia, and the United States* (Oxford: Clarendon, 1955); Johann K. Bluntschli, *Geschichte des schweizerischen Bundesrechtes*, 2 vols. (Zurich: Meyer & Zeller, 1849–52); Max H. Boehm, "Federalism," in *Encyclopedia of the Social Sciences*, vol. 6, 169–72 (New York: Macmillan, 1931); Joan Bondurant, *Regionalism vs. Provincialism: A Study in Problems of Indian National Unity*, India Press Digests Monograph Series, no. 4 (Berkeley: University of California Press, 1958); Lionel Brett, ed., *Constitutional Problems of Federalism in Nigeria* (Lagos, Nigeria: Times Press, 1961); John Bright, *A History of Israel* (Philadelphia: Westminster Press, 1959); James Bryce, *The American Commonwealth*, 3rd ed., 2 vols. (1888; reprint, New York and London: Macmillan, 1909); James Bryce, *Studies in History and Jurisprudence* (New York: Oxford University Press, 1901); John W. Burgess, "The American Commonwealth," *Political Science Quarterly* 1 (1886): 9–35; Canada, Royal Commission on Dominion-Provincial Relations, *Report*, 3 vols. (Ottawa: Patenaud, 1940), vol. 1: *Canada: 1867–1939*, vol. 2: *Recommendations*, vol. 3: *Documentation*; Claremont Men's College, Institute for Studies in Federalism, *Essays in Federalism*, ed. George C. S. Benson et al. (Claremont, CA: Claremont Men's College, 1961); George A. Codding, *The Federal Government of Switzerland* (Boston: Houghton Mifflin, 1961); Zehman Cowen, *Federal Jurisdiction in Australia* (New York: Oxford University Press, 1959); Martin Diamond, "*The Federalist*," in *History of Political Philosophy*, ed. Leo Strauss and Joseph Cropsey, 573–93 (Chicago: Rand McNally, 1963); Albert V. Dicey, *Introduction to the Study of the Law of the Constitution*, 10th ed., intro. by E.C.S. Wade (1885; reprint, London: Macmillan; New York: St. Martin's, 1961); Daniel J. Elazar, *The American Partnership: Intergovernmental Cooperation in the Nineteenth-Century United States* (Chicago: University of Chicago Press, 1962); Daniel J. Elazar, *American Federalism: A View from the States* (New York: Crowell, 1966); John H. Elliott, *Imperial Spain: 1469–1716* (New York: St. Martin's, 1964); Edward A. Freeman, *The History of Federal Government in Greece and Italy*, 2nd ed. (1863; reprint, London: Macmillan, 1893); Otto von Gierke, *Natural Law and the Theory of Society: 1500 to 1800* trans. with intro. by Ernst Barker (1913; reprint, Cambridge: Cambridge University Press, 1934); Robert A. Goldwin, ed., *A Nation of States: Essays on the American Federal System* (Chicago: Rand McNally, 1963); W. Brooke Graves, *American Intergovernmental Relations: Their Origins, Historical Development, and Current Status* (New York: Scribner, 1964); Morton Grodzins, "American Political Parties and the American System," *Western Political Quarterly* 13 (1960a): 974–98; Morton Grodzins, "The Federal System," in *U.S. President's Commission on National Goals, Goals for Americans*, 265–82 (Englewood Cliffs, NJ: Prentice-Hall, 1960b); Morton Grodzins, *The American System: A New View of Government in the United States* (Chicago: Rand McNally, 1966); Alexander Hamilton, James Madison, and John Jay, *The Federalist*, ed. with intro. and notes by Jacob E. Cooke (1787–88; reprint, Middletown, CT: Wesleyan University Press, 1961); Ursula K. Hicks et al., *Federalism and Economic Growth in Underdeveloped Countries: A Symposium* (New York: Oxford University Press, 1961); Yerezxel Kaufmann, *The Religion of Israel: From Its Beginnings to the Babylonian Exile* (1937–48; reprint, Chicago: University of Chicago Press, 1960); Francis P. de Labilliere, *Federal Britain: Or, Unity and Federation of the Empire* (London: Low, Marston, 1894); William S. Livingston, ed., *Federalism in the Commonwealth: A Bibliographical Commentary* (London: Cassell, 1963); Arthur Maass, ed. *Area and Power: A Theory of Local Government* (Glencoe, IL: Free Press, 1959); Arthur W. Macmahon, ed., *Federalism: Mature and*

Emergent (1955; reprint, New York: Russell, 1962); Jackson T. Main, *The Anti-Federalists: Critics of the Constitution, 1781–1788* (Chapel Hill: University of North Carolina Press, 1961); Perry Miller, *The New England Mind: The Seventeenth Century* (1939; reprint, Boston: Beacon, 1961); David Milne, *The Scottish Office and Other Scottish Government Departments* (New York: Oxford University Press, 1957); Ssobei Mogi, *The Problem of Federalism: A Study in the History of Political Theory*, 2 vols. (London: Allen & Unwin, 1931); William A. Riker, *Federalism. Origin, Operation, Significance* (Boston: Little, 1964); John R. Schmidhauser, *The Supreme Court as Final Arbiter in Federal-State Relations: 1789–1957* (Chapel Hill: University of North Carolina Press, 1958); Beij M. Sharma, *Federalism in Theory and Practice*, 2 vols. (Chandausi, India: Bhargava, 1953); Donald V. Smiley, "The Rowell-Sirois Report, Provincial Autonomy, and Post-War Canadian Federalism," *Canadian Journal of Economics and Political Science* 28 (1962): 54–69; Donald V. Smiley, "The Two Themes of Canadian Federalism," *Canadian Journal of Economics and Political Science* 31 (1965): 80–97; Alexis de Tocqueville, *Democracy in America*, 2 vols. (1835; reprint, New York: Knopf, 1945); U.S. Commission on Intergovernmental Relations, *A Report to the President for Transmittal to the Congress* (Washington, DC: Government Printing Office, 1955); U.S. Congress, House, Committee on Government Operations, *Intergovernmental Relations in the United States: A Selected Bibliography* (1955; reprint, Washington, DC: Government Printing Office, 1956); Roger H. Wells, *The States in West German Federalism: A Study of Federal-State Relations, 1949–1960* (New York: Bookman, 1961); Kenneth C. Wheare, *Federal Government*, 4th ed. (1946; reprint, New York: Oxford University Press, 1964); and Woodrow Wilson, *Congressional Government: A Study in American Politics* (1885; reprint, New York: Meridian, 1961).

DANIEL J. ELAZAR

Federalism Summit   The States' Federalism Summit was a three-day conference held in October 1995 in Cincinnati, Ohio, to assess the state of American federalism and to consider a set of administrative, statutory, and constitutional proposals to restore a better balance of power between the states and the federal government. The proposals had been developed by a Scholars Advisory Committee consisting of Stewart A. Baker, Charles Cooper, Daniel J. Elazar, A. E. Dick Howard, Jon Felde, Barry Friedman, John Kincaid (committee chair), Deborah Jones Merritt, Charles Rothfeld, and Robert Silvanik. The summit was composed of more than 120 elected state executive and legislative leaders, most of whom were members of the executive committees of the Council of State Governments, National Governors' Association, National Conference of State Legislatures, American Legislative Exchange Council, and State Legislative Leaders' Foundation. These five organizations cosponsored the summit. Leadership for the summit was provided principally by Governor Michael O. Leavitt (R-UT), Governor Ben Nelson (D-NE), and State Senate President Stanley J. Aronoff (R-OH).

The States' Federalism Summit concluded that the following four remedial options merited "further consideration and exploration of opportunities for common action" by state leaders:

1. A federalism statute to be enacted by Congress to enhance the political safeguards of federalism and to give states a more effective voice in congressional deliberations by, among other things, requiring members of Congress to identify the constitutional

sources of their authority to legislate on specific subjects and giving state leaders a larger role in shaping federal rule making

2. A constitutional amendment (labeled the National Reconsideration Amendment) to provide the people of the states, through their legislatures, the power to require the Congress to reconsider laws, specific provisions of laws, or executive regulations that interfere with state authority by allowing two-thirds of the state legislatures to repeal a federal law or regulation, subject to subsequent override by a two-thirds vote of the U.S. House and the U.S. Senate

3. A constitutional amendment to allow three-fourths of the state legislatures to propose amendments to the U.S. Constitution, subject to subsequent ratification by a two-thirds vote of the U.S. House and the U.S. Senate

4. A statute or constitutional amendment to provide states the following kinds of relief from federal regulatory and fiscal burdens:

   a. No state would be obligated, without its consent, to enact or enforce any state law or regulation or to administer any federal regulatory program imposed by a law enacted by the Congress.

   b. No condition (i.e., rule or regulation) imposed by a law enacted by the Congress on federal funds received by the states would be valid unless the condition was stated clearly and did no more than specify the purposes for which, or manner in which, the funds were to be spent by the states.

   c. No obligation imposed on the states by a law enacted by the Congress would be enforceable against the states unless the federal government provided the affected states with the funds needed to pay the states' costs of complying with the federal obligation.

Some critics accused the summit of being a covert attempt to instigate a constitutional convention that could significantly rewrite the U.S. Constitution. The summit's proposals also were opposed by numerous interest groups, such as business, civil rights, and environmental groups that support assertions of federal power over the states. Many local government officials expressed concerns about the summit as well, in part because they believed they should have been invited by the state leaders to participate in the summit. In addition, the urgency of the summit's proposals was weakened by congressional enactment of the Unfunded Mandates Reform Act of 1995, which assuaged the concerns about unfunded federal mandates that had been expressed by many state and local leaders. As a result, even though the summit's state leaders lobbied the Congress and sought to build public support for the summit's proposals, none of the proposals were enacted into law or added to the U.S. Constitution. *SEE ALSO:* States' Rights

BIBLIOGRAPHY: Council of State Governments, *Restoring Balance in the Federal System: A Report of the Intergovernmental Affairs Committee* (Lexington, KY: Council of State Governments, 1989); and Council of State Governments, *Restoring Balance to the American Federal System: A Report of the Proceedings of the 1995 States' Federalism Summit* (Lexington, KY: Council of State Governments, 1996).

JOHN KINCAID

The Federalist Papers *The Federalist Papers* originated as a series of articles in a New York newspaper in 1787–88. Published anonymously under the pen name of "Publius," they were written primarily for instrumental political purposes: to promote ratification of the Constitution and defend it against its critics.

Initiated by Alexander Hamilton, the series came to eighty-five articles, the majority by Hamilton himself, twenty-six by James Madison, and five by John Jay. *The Federalist* was the title under which Hamilton collected the papers for publication as a book.

Despite their polemical origin, the papers are widely viewed as the best work of political philosophy produced in the United States, and as the best expositions of the Constitution to be found amidst all the ratification debates. They are frequently cited for discerning the meaning of the Constitution and the intentions of the founders, although Hamilton's papers are not always reliable as an exposition of his views: in *The Federalist*, Hamilton took care to avoid coming out clearly with his views on either the inadequacies of the Constitution or the potentiality for using it dynamically. Instead, he expressed himself indirectly, arguing that the only real danger would arise from the potential weaknesses of the central government under the Constitution, not from its potentialities for greater strength as charged by its opponents. Despite this, *The Federalist* can be and frequently has been referred to for its exposition of Hamilton's position on executive authority, judicial review, and other institutional aspects of the Constitution.

The Federalist Papers are also admired abroad—sometimes more than in the United States. Hamilton is held in high esteem abroad: while in America his realist style is received with suspicion of undemocratic intentions, abroad it is taken as a reassurance of solidity, and it is the Jeffersonian idealist style that is received with suspicion of hidden intentions. *The Federalist Papers* are studied by jurists and legal scholars and cited for writing other countries' constitutions. In this capacity they have played a significant role in the spread of federal, democratic, and constitutional governments around the world.

MODERN FEDERATION AS EXPOUNDED BY THE FEDERALIST

The Federalist Papers defended a new form of federalism: what it called "federation" as differentiated from "confederation." There were precursors for this usage; *The Federalist Papers* solidified it. All subsequent federalism has been influenced by the example of "federation" in the United States; indeed, the success of it in the United States has led to its being known as "modern federation" in contrast to "classical confederation." In its basic structures and principles, it has served as the model for most subsequent federal unions, as well as for the reform of older confederacies such as Switzerland.

The main distinguishing characteristics of the model of modern federation, elucidated and defended by *The Federalist Papers*, are as follows:

1. The federal government's most important figures, the legislative, are elected largely by the individual citizens, rather than being primarily selected by the governments of member states as in confederation.

2. Conversely, federal law applies directly to individuals, through federal courts and agencies, rather than to member states as in confederation.

3. State citizens become also federal citizens, and naturalization criteria are established federally.

4. The federal Constitution and federal laws and treaties are the supreme law of the land, over and above state constitutions and laws.

5. Federal powers are enumerated, along with what came to be called an "Elastic Clause" (the authority to take measures "necessary and proper" for implementing its enumerated powers); the states keep the vast range of "reserved" powers, that is, the unspecified generality of other potential governmental powers. States cannot act where the federal government is assigned exclusive competence, nor where preempted by lawful federal action; they are specifically excluded from independent foreign relations, from maintaining an army or navy, from interfering with money, and from disrupting contracts or imposing tariffs.

6. Federal and state laws operate in parallel or as "coordinate" powers, each applying directly to individual citizens, rather than acting primarily through or with dependence on one another.

This "coordinate" method applies only to the "vertical" division of powers between federal and state governments, not to the "horizontal" or "functional" division of federal powers into executive, legislative, and judicial branches. The latter "separation of powers" is made in such a form as to deliberately keep the three branches mutually dependent on one another, so that no one of them can step forth—excepting the executive in emergencies—as a full-fledged authority on its own. This mutual functional dependence within the federal level is considered an assurance of steadiness of the rule of law and lack of arbitrariness; by contrast, obstructionism was feared if there were to remain a relation of dependence upon a vertically separate level of government. Thus the turn to "coordinate" powers, with federal and state operations proceeding autonomously from one another, or what came to be called "coordinate federalism." This terminology encapsulated the departure from the old confederalism, in which federal government operations had been heavily dependent on the states.

AMBIGUITIES OF COORDINATE FEDERALISM IN THE FEDERALIST

Despite *The Federalist*'s strong preference for coordinate powers, there are important deviations from it. For example, there are "concurrent" or overlapping powers, such as taxation. This, Hamilton says in *The Federalist* No. 32, necessarily follows from "the division of sovereign power": each level of government needs it in order to function with "full vigor" on its own (thus allowing the celebratory formulation for American federalism, "strong States *and* a strong Federal Government"). Coordinate federalism requires, it turns out, some concurrent powers, not just coordinate powers.

In practice, the deviations from the "coordinate" theory go farther still. For the militia, the state governments have the competence to appoint all the officers and to conduct the training most of the time, but the federal government is authorized to regulate the training and discipline, as well as to place the militia when needed under federal command (a provision defended by Hamilton in *The Federalist* No. 29). For commercial law, the states draw up the detailed codes, but the federal power to regulate interstate commerce opened the door to broad federal interference with state codes in the twentieth century. In these spheres there is state authority, but it is subordinated to federal authority—a situation close to the traditional hierarchical model, not to the matrix model sometimes used for the coordinate ideal.

While the states are reserved the wider range of powers, the federal government is assigned the prime cuts among the powers. Its competences go to what are usually viewed as core areas of sovereignty—foreign relations, military, and currency—as well as to regulation of some state powers when they get too close to high politics or to interstate concerns. It already formally held most of these competences during the Confederation, but now could carry them out independently of state action. *The Federalist Papers* advertise this as being the main point of the Constitution: not a fearsome matter of extending the powers of the federal government into newfangled realms, but the unobjectionable matter of rendering its already agreed-upon powers effective. This effectiveness is achieved by adding the key structural characteristic of the modern sovereign state, elaborated by Hobbes in terms not dissimilar to passages in *The Federalist*: that of penetrating all intermediate levels and reaching down to the individual citizen to derive its authorization and, conversely, to impose its obligations.

In the early years after the Constitution, many federal powers remained dependent de facto on cooperation from the states; *The Federalist*'s authors worried that the states would use this dependence to whittle away federal powers, and defended the Constitution's provisions for federal supremacy as a protection against such whittling away. Later it was the states that became more dependent on federal cooperation. There was an undefined potential for developing the powers of the two levels of government in a cooperative or mutually dependent form; in the twentieth century, the federal government developed this into what came to be called "cooperative federalism," wielding its superior financial resources to influence state policy in the fields of cooperation.

USE AND ABUSE OF THE FEDERALIST

The Federalist Papers have been used with increasing frequency as a guide for interpreting the Constitution. Bernard Bailyn (2003) has counted the frequency and found an almost linear progression: from occasional use by the Supreme Court in the years just after 1789 to more frequent use with every passing stage in American history. Much of this use he regards as abuse of the *Papers*.

The notes of Madison on the Constitutional Convention of 1787 are in principle a better source for discovering intention, but are less often used than *The Federalist*. They are harder to read, are harder to systematize, and have a structure of shifting counterpoint rather than consistent exposition. Moreover, they were just notes of debates where people were thinking out loud, not formal polished documents, and got off to a yawning start: they were kept secret for half a century.

The Federalist Papers, while clearer, are often subjected to questionable interpretation. Taking the *Papers* as gospel shorn from context, the result can be to stand the purpose of the authors on its head.

The crux of the problem is the fact that *The Federalist Papers* were both polemically vigorous and politically prudent. They were intended to promote ratification of a stronger central government as something that could sustain itself, sink deeper roots, and grow higher capabilities over time. In doing so, they often found it expedient to emphasize how weak the Constitution was and portray it as incapable of being stretched in the ways that opponents feared and proponents sometimes quietly wished. They cannot always be taken at face value.

To locate the original intention of the Constitution itself, the place to start would not be *The Federalist Papers*, but—as Madison did in *The Federalist* No. 40—the authorizing resolutions for the Constitutional Convention. There one finds a clear and repeated expression of purpose, namely, to create a stronger federal government, and specifically to "render the federal Constitution adequate to the exigencies of government and the preservation of the Union" (Madison 1788). Next one would have to look at the brief statement of purpose in the preamble of the Constitution. There, the lead purpose is "in Order to form a more perfect Union," followed by a number of more specific functional purposes understood to be bound up with a more perfect union.

The intention of the *wording* of the Constitution would be found by looking at the Committee on Style at the Constitutional Convention, a group dominated by centralizing federalists. It took the hard substance of the constitutional plan that had been agreed upon in the months of debate, and proceeded to rewrite it in a soft cautious language, restoring important symbolic phrases of the old confederation in order to assuage the fears of the Convention's opponents. It helped in ratification, but at the usual cost of PR: obfuscation. Theorists of nullification and secession, such as Calhoun, would later cite the confederal language as proof that each state still retained its sovereignty unchanged.

The original purpose of *The Federalist Papers* is the least in doubt of the entire series of documents: it was to encourage ratification and answer the critics who argued the Constitution was a blueprint for tyranny. As such, it was prone to carry further the diplomatic disguises already introduced by the Committee on Style. The authors, particularly Hamilton, argued repeatedly that, if anything, the government proposed by the Constitution would be too weak, not too strong. They said this with a purpose, not of restraining it further—as would be done by taking their descriptions of its weaknesses as indications of original intent—but of enabling its strengths to come into play and get reinforced by bonds of habit.

Hamilton in practice opposed "strict constructionism" regarding federal enumerated powers; he generally emphasized the Elastic ("necessary and proper") Clause in the 1790s. But in *The Federalist Papers*, Hamilton in No. 33 justifies the Elastic and Supremacy Clauses in cautious, defensive, polemical fashion, denying any elastic intention but only the necessity of defending against what he portrays as the main danger: that of a whittling away of federal power by the states. Madison in No. 44 is slightly more expansive, arguing the necessity of recurrence in any federal constitution to "the doctrine of construction or implication" and warning against the ruinously constrictive construction that the states would end up applying to federal powers in the absence of the Elastic Clause. The logical implication was that either one side or the other—either the federal government or the states—must dominate the process of construing the extent of federal powers, and his preference in 1787–88 was for the federal government to predominate. In *The Federalist*, he warned against continuing dangers of interposition by the states against federal authority; at the Convention, he had advocated a congressional "negative" on state laws, that is, a federal power of interposition against state laws, as the only way of preventing individual states from flying out of the common orbit. While a legislative negative was rejected at the Convention, a judicial negative was later achieved in practice by the establishment of judicial review under a Federalist-led Supreme Court. Hamilton in *The Federalist* Nos. 78 and 80 provided support for judicial review, arguing—in defensive form as ever—that it was needed for preventing state encroachments from reducing the Constitution to naught.

The Elastic Clause was a residuum at the end of the Constitutional Convention flowing from the original pre-Convention resolutions. The resolutions called for powers "adequate to the exigencies of the Union"; the Convention met and enumerated the federal powers and structures that it could specifically agree on, then invested the remainder of its mandate into the Elastic and Supremacy Clauses, in which the Constitution makes itself supreme and grants its government all powers "necessary and proper" for carrying out the functions it specifies. There is a direct historical line in this, extending afterward to Hamilton's broad construction of the Elastic Clause in the 1790s. From beginning to end, the underlying thought is dynamic, to do all that is necessary for union and government. The static, defensive exegesis of the Elastic Clause in *The Federalist Papers*, and in subsequent conceptions of strict construction, is implausible.

THE FEDERALIST *AND THE GLOBAL SPREAD OF MODERN FEDERATION*

The success of the modern federation in the United States after 1789 made it the main norm for subsequent federalism. *The Federalist Papers* provided the template for federation building; Hamilton was celebrated as its greatest evangelist. Switzerland reformed its confederation in 1848 and 1870 along the lines of modern federation. The new Latin American countries also often adopted federal constitutions in this period, although their implementation of federalism, like that of democracy itself, was sketchy.

After 1865, several British emigrant colonies adopted the overall model of modern federation: first the Canadian colonies (despite using the name "confederation"), then the Australian ones (using "commonwealth"), then South Africa (using "union"; there the ideological role of Hamilton and *The Federalist* was enormous, and the result was almost a unitary state). After 1945, several countries emerging out of the British dependent empire, such as India and Nigeria, adopted variants of modern federation. Defeated Germany and Austria also adopted federal constitutions. Later, other European and Third World countries also federalized their formerly unitary states. The process is by no means finished. Enumerating all the countries that had developed federal elements in their governance, Daniel Elazar concluded in the 1980s that a "federal revolution" was in process.

Once modern federation was known as a solution to the limitations of confederation, there has been less tolerance for the inconsistencies of confederation. Confederalism was a compromise between the extremes of separation and a unitary centralized state, splitting the difference; modern federation is more like a synthesis that upgrades both sides. What in previous millennia could be seen in confederalism as a lesser evil and a reasonable price to pay for avoiding the extremes, after 1787 came to seem like a collection of unnecessary contradictions: and if unnecessary, then also intolerable, once compared to what was available through modern federation.

The Federalist Papers have themselves been the strongest propagators of the view that confederalism is an inherently failed system. They made their case forcefully, not as scholars but as debaters for ratifying the Constitution. Their case was one-sided but had substance. They showed that confederation, even when successful, was working on an emergency basis, or else on a basis of special fortunate circumstances or external pressures. They offered in its place a structure that could work well on an ordinary systematic basis, without incessant crises or fears of collapse or dependence on special circumstances.

In recent years, it has been argued that Swiss confederalism was an impressive success, and so in a sense it was, holding together for half a millennium. Yet half a century after modern federation was invented in the United States, the Swiss found their old confederal system a failure and replaced it with one modeled along the lines of the modern federal one. The description of the old Swiss confederation as a failure became a commonplace, it entered into the realm of patriotic Swiss conviction. The judgment looks too harsh when the length of the two historical experiences are viewed side by side, yet has carried conviction in an evolutionary sense, as the cumulative outcome of historical experience. After the Constitution and *The Federalist Papers*, confederalism could not remain as successful in terms of longevity as it had been previously; the historical space for it shrank, while new and larger spaces opened up for modern federation. The advance of technology worked in the same direction, increasing interdependence within national territories and making localities more intertwined.

Despite the shrinkage of space for confederation within national bounds, confederation took on new force on another level. The American Union's survival of the Civil War and consolidation afterwards gave a further impetus to discussion of modern federation, understood not only as a static technique for more sophisticated government within a given space, but also as a dynamic method of uniting people across wider spaces, in order to meet the needs of modern technological progress and the growth of interdependence. International federalist movements emerged after 1865, taking *The Federalist Papers* as their bible. They gained influence in the face of the world wars of the 1900s, feeding into the development of international organizations ranging from very loose and weak ones to integrative alliances and confederations such as NATO and the EU. The missionary ideology of *The Federalist*, used by its proponents for pummeling confederation, led on the international level to new confederations. When some (such as the League of Nations) were viewed as failures, further missionary use of *The Federalist* fed into the formation of still more confederations, often stronger and better conceived but confederations nonetheless, even if (as in the case of the EU) with a genetic plan of evolving into a federation. Federation seemed no less necessary but more difficult than federalist propagandists had suggested. Reflection on this situation led to an academic school of integration theory in the 1950s and 1960s, which treated functionalism and confederation as necessary historical phases in integration; in the neofunctionalist version of the theory it would lead eventually to federation, and in the version of Karl Deutsch it need not move beyond a "pluralistic security-community." The work of Deutsch tied in with the view that confederation had been a greater success historically than was usually credited; to prove the success of the American confederation, Deutsch and his colleagues cited Merrill Jensen, an historian highly critical of *The Federalist* and friendly to the Anti-Federalists or Confederalists. Jensen argued that the Articles of Confederation had been a success, contrary to the American patriotic story that paralleled the Swiss one in condemning the confederalist experience. The relevance of *The Federalist Papers* was seen in this new literature as minimal, except at the final stages of a process that was only beginning and that the *Papers* themselves mystified as a matter of tactical necessity for getting a difficult decision made. Their exaggerations of the defects of confederalism were highlighted; their argument that only federation would "work" was seen as both a mistake and a diversion from the direction that progress would actually need to take in this era. It was only their normative orientation that was seen as helpful. The very success of *The Federalist Papers* had led to their partial eclipse. Nevertheless, their eclipse on the supranational level may not be permanent, and their influence on the level of national constitutionalism has remained enormous throughout. *SEE ALSO:* Anti-Federalists; Federalists; Hamilton, Alexander; Madison, James

BIBLIOGRAPHY: Bernard Bailyn, *To Begin the World Anew: The Genius and Ambiguities of the American Founding* (New York: Knopf, 2003); Madison, James, *The Federal-*

ist Paper 40 (New York Pachet, January 18, 1788); Clinton Rossiter ed., *The Federalist Papers* (New York: Signet, 1999).

IRA STRAUS

Federalists   The Constitutional Convention elaborated what some of its participants already called "federation" in place of "confederation"; subsequently the new system came to be known as a "modern federation." Not everyone embraced it as an improvement within federalism. From a pure and fixed Confederalist standpoint, it was seen as a betrayal of federalism.

Proponents of the Constitution seized for themselves the title of Federalists, using it for *The Federalist Papers* while labeling their opponents "Anti-Federalists." The label seemed unfair since most Anti-Federalists thought of themselves as the "true federalists" and favored at least in principle some strengthening of the federal power, yet was partly fair since many Anti-Federalists in practice opposed any real strengthening of federal power as contrary to their doctrine of the sovereignty of the member states, and since modern federation retained many elements of federalism while giving them a more effective form.

With the victory of the Constitution, the "Federalist" and "Anti-Federalist" labels stuck. A few years later, as parties emerged, one of them, built around Alexander Hamilton and pro–federal government views, called itself the Federalist Party. The opposing Democratic-Republican party, built around Thomas Jefferson and supported by James Madison, included many former Anti-Federalists; having accepted the Constitution once a Bill of Rights was added, they advocated "strict construction" of the Constitution to restrain the growth of federal power. The Federalists built on the first words of the Constitution's preamble and on the Elastic Clause; the Democratic-Republicans built on the last words of Bill of Rights: the Tenth, or states' rights, Amendment.

Despite the linguistic victory of the Federalists in taking over the word, the view widely persisted that the Anti-Federalists were the true federalists. After the union was consolidated and its territorial growth completed, this view was in some respects reinforced: with the success of modern federation, decentralization not unification seemed like the sole remaining activist or ideological business for federalism within the United States. "New federalisms" were proclaimed by presidents in the late 1900s, always with a decentralizing thrust, although movements for international unions also put out publications entitled "New Federalist." Sometimes the term "federalism" has been associated with extreme decentralizing ideologies reintroducing "Anti-Federalist" themes; this is seen in the Federalist Society, an association of lawyers whose membership has overlapped with a less well-known Antifederalist Society.

The validity of the decentralizing trend in usage is as open to question as the centralizing Federalists' earlier seizure of the word. In Europe the term "federalism" remains closely associated with the ideas of *The Federalist* and of forming a continent-wide Union. The original usage of the term "federalism," from the days of classical antiquity to the 1780s, was for bringing several states together into a union: *e pluribus unum*. This was the primary purpose of the Articles of Confederation, the Constitution, *The Federalist Papers*, and the Federalist Party alike. The federal decentralization of unitary states—a sort of *ex uno plura* (out of one, many: the opposite "e pluribus unum" out of many, one)—was an idea that arose later within well-entrenched national states. The reason it arose was due to the success of modern federation in the United States in reconciling federalism with the benefits that other modern nation-states had come to cherish from the sovereignty of their central government. Modern federation having proved itself as a sophisticated form of government at the same time as proving itself an efficient form for uniting people, it could be reapplied in a kind of reverse engineering for decentralizing hitherto unitary states.

The Federalist Party itself, ascendent under Presidents Washington and Adams, suffered from the Adams-Hamilton feud, fell from power with the election of Jefferson to the presidency, suffered a further decline into a New England regional party, and embarrassed its very federalism by resorting to secessionist threats to back up its opposition to the War of 1812. In fairness to the Federalists, it should be acknowledged that the dilemmas they faced, as a party of union within a union torn by the issue of slavery, were well nigh unresolvable: should they proceed as an impatient, northern, antislavery party to push toward a free and homogeneous union, or should they proceed as a party of compromise and wait on history to find a way to make the union work better? They tended toward the first path and faded out.

The Whig Party arose in their place, and subsequently the Republican Party. It followed up on Federalist themes, under Lincoln as the party seeking the elimination of slavery and the consolidation of the Union as a single form of society, and under Theodore Roosevelt as the neo-Hamiltonian party favoring a strong federal government, a unified national economic policy, and alliance with the British Empire on the world stage. In later decades, the Republican and Democratic parties partly switched their Hamiltonian and Jeffersonian themes, the Democrats favoring a larger federal economic role although the Republicans still favoring strong if lean government. *SEE ALSO:* Anti-Federalists; Constitutional Convention of 1787; *The Federalist Papers*

IRA STRAUS

Fifteenth Amendment   Congress approved the Fifteenth Amendment in February 1869, and the required number of states ratified the amendment by March 1870. The amendment prohibited discrimination of voting rights based on "race, color, or previous condition of servitude." While it extended voting rights to African Americans across the nation, it faced a long road to actually being practiced by many states and localities.

The Reconstruction Acts of 1867 extended voting rights to black Americans in former Confederate states only. Three factors motivated Republicans to extend voting rights nationwide. First, many Republicans felt a moral obligation to avoid hypocrisy. Second, Republicans feared a counterattack by whites toward the now-freed slaves and believed that voting rights would enable black Americans to act with political force. Finally, some Republicans believed that giving African Americans the right to vote would give their party a political advantage by creating a broader electorate.

Congress debated three versions of the amendment. The first prohibited vot-

---

AMENDMENT XV

1. *The right of citizens of the United States to vote shall not be denied or abridged by the United States or by any State on account of race, color, or previous condition of servitude.*

2. *The Congress shall have power to enforce this article by appropriate legislation.*

ing discrimination based on race. A second version explicitly prohibited the use of literacy tests, poll taxes, and conditions of birth to discriminate against voters. Finally, the third version simply extended suffrage universally to all men over the age of 21. After much debate, the first version was accepted by Congress and sent to the states for ratification, though some Republicans felt that this version left many avenues open for discrimination.

The amendment faced wide opposition from whites across the United States, especially from former Confederate states. As some Republicans expected, those opposed to the amendment devised strategies that limited or eliminated black suffrage. Those strategies included extralegal means (e.g., physical violence and verbal threats) and "legal" means (e.g., poll taxes and literacy requirements).

The Supreme Court upheld many of the legal means for circumventing the language of the Fifteenth Amendment. In *Williams v. Mississippi* (1898), the Court decided that literacy tests, required by Mississippi's constitution, did not discriminate on account of race. This decision opened the way for other states in the former Confederacy to rewrite their constitutions in an effort to limit black voting. As a result, state governments disenfranchised thousands of black Americans using the Court's decision as justification.

The spirit of the Fifteenth Amendment would not be realized until Congress passed the Voting Rights Act of 1965. This act gave the federal government the power to oversee voter registration and made literacy tests illegal. The act significantly helped to increase both voting by African Americans and the number of African American representatives in Congress. *SEE ALSO:* Civil War; Fourteenth Amendment; Reconstruction; Slavery; Voting Rights Act of 1965

JEREMY BOGGS

Fiscal Federalism   Fiscal federalism is an economic framework for understanding the relationship among federal, state, and local governments that focuses on the division of spending and taxing powers among these governments.

Fiscal federalism is an economic, rather than political, theory of relationships among central and noncentral governments. The primary focus is the division of responsibilities among different types of governments. For example, the traditional theory of fiscal federalism argues that the central government should be responsible for macroeconomic policies but local governments should be primarily responsible for fire protection services. A secondary focus of fiscal federalism is the division of revenue-raising powers among various governments, often referred to as "tax assignment." Here the traditional theory of fiscal federalism argues that taxes on highly mobile entities should be assigned to the central government, and taxes on less mobile entities to state or local governments. Finally, grants-in-aid become an important topic in fiscal federalism because of the potential mismatch between a government's expenditure responsibilities and its tax capacity.

The traditional theory of fiscal federalism sets out principles regarding the proper division of spending responsibilities and taxing powers among types of governments. However, the term "fiscal federalism" is often used in a broader sense that includes a description of the actual division of spending and taxing powers.

Economists often use the term "fiscal federalism" to refer to one part of the field of public finance. Public finance is the economics of government spending and taxation, and when more than one type of government is involved economists apply the label of "fiscal federalism."

There are some differences between fiscal federalism and political theories of federalism. Fiscal federalism applies to any country with both central and decentralized governments, as long as the decentralized governments have some control over spending and taxing policies. This control does not have to be substantial or constitutionally based. Thus fiscal federalism applies to many countries that political scientists would categorize as unitary rather than federal. When applied to the United States, fiscal federalism typically includes local governments in addition to the federal government and state governments. In the fiscal federalism framework, the fact that local government powers are not constitutionally independent is irrelevant.

Fiscal federalism ignores politics, political institutions, and political power. Fiscal federalism must also be distinguished from a second economic theory of federalism, competitive federalism. Competitive federalism focuses on competition among governments, another subject area ignored in fiscal federalism.

DIVISION OF EXPENDITURE RESPONSIBILITIES

Government expenditure responsibilities can be divided into stabilization, distribution, and allocation functions. Fiscal federalism provides general guidelines for dividing these responsibilities among federal, state, and local governments based on the nature of the expenditure function and the relative capabilities of the different types of governments.

The stabilization function entails efforts to impact unemployment and inflation levels and stimulate economic growth. Stabilization tools include fiscal and monetary policies. As no state or local government is big enough to affect the overall level of economic activity, experts agree for the most part that the stabilization function is best left to the federal government.

The distribution function concerns use of government's powers of spending and taxation to redistribute income, in particular by providing assistance to poor households. Experts agree that this function is usually best left to the federal government. State or local efforts to redistribute income can be rendered ineffective because of the small geographic reach of these governments and their mobile populations. For example, efforts to redistribute income from high-income to low-income households could lead to a counterproductive out-migration of high-income households and immigration of low-income households.

The allocation function concerns the production or provision of goods and services, such as national defense, university education, or garbage collection. Whether these functions should be provided by federal, state, or local governments depends upon a number of factors. First, the geographic reach of service benefits must be considered. As the benefits of national defense are national in scope, this service is best left to the federal government. In contrast, the impact of fire protection is local, and can often be best provided by local governments.

Economies of scale (per unit costs of production fall as the scale of production rises) and externalities or spillovers (whereby activities undertaken in one geographic area impact citizens in another area) are factors that tend to make government goods and services best provided by larger units of government such as the federal government or state governments.

Diversity in demand is the most important factor favoring local government provi-

TABLE 1. Percentage of Expenditures on Selected Functions by Type of Government

	Federal (%)	State (%)	Local (%)	Total (%)
Defense	100	0	0	100
Education	6	25	69	100
Health and Hospitals	74	12	14	100
Public Welfare	20	69	11	100
Social Security	100	0	0	100

Source: U.S. Statistical Abstract (2004–5).

sion of government goods and services. Local governments can best tailor services to fit the needs of their citizens. Decentralized provision of government services also facilitates a natural laboratory in which innovations tried and proved successful by one government can be adopted by an entire state or the federal government.

For the most part, the division of expenditure responsibilities in the U.S. federal system follows the pattern suggested in the traditional theory of fiscal federalism. Thus, the federal government provides national defense, state governments provide highways and university education, and local governments provide police and fire protection and K–12 schools.

However, there are some anomalies, such as the large nonfederal role in public welfare, largely a distribution function. In addition, there is some overlap of responsibilities, as in the provision of K–12 education in which state governments and the federal government have been playing an increasing role. Periodically, calls are made to change the division of expenditure responsibilities. Thus, Alice Rivlin (1992), a prominent economist and policy analyst, suggested the federal government eliminate most of its programs in education, housing, highways, social services, economic development, and job training, instead focusing on international issues and taking over full responsibility for health care financing, which it now shares with states in the Medicaid program.

TAX ASSIGNMENT

Once expenditure responsibilities are divided among federal, state, and local governments, it is necessary to ensure that each government has the tools to fulfill its responsibilities. The ability to raise revenues via taxes will be considered first.

Experts have advised that certain types of taxes are most appropriate for central governments and others most appropriate for state and local governments. Taxes that are most appropriate for central governments are taxes on highly mobile factors, taxes used to redistribute income, taxes with unstable revenue patterns, and source-based taxes such as corporation income taxes. Taxes most appropriate for noncentral governments are taxes on immobile factors such as property, and residence-based taxes such as personal income and retail sales taxes.

TABLE 2. Percentage Reliance on Different Tax Sources by U.S. Federal, State, and Local Governments

	Federal (%)	State (%)	Local (%)	Total (%)
Individual Income	84	14	1	100
Corporation Income	87	12	1	100
Sales and Excise	15	69	16	100
Death and Gift	79	21	0	100
Property	0	4	96	100

Source: U.S. Census (2000).

As Table 3 illustrates, the use of taxes in the U.S. system of fiscal federalism closely follows the tax assignment prescription of the experts.

One exception is that state governments collect a significant portion of corporate income tax revenues. This appears to violate the prescription against state and local government reliance on source-based taxes with unstable revenues. Another exception is that state governments raise about one-fifth of death and gift taxes, which violates the principle that state governments should not levy taxes on a mobile base. To some extent, the federal credit against state estate tax payments was a mechanism for allowing states to rely on this mobile tax base without suffering the usual consequence of a declining tax base.

THE ROLE OF INTERGOVERNMENTAL GRANTS

One reason for federal grants to state and local governments (and state grants to local governments) is that revenues of the subcentral governments may not be sufficient to meet their expenditure responsibilities. In other words, the federal government may provide grants to state and local governments when their tax capacities are insufficient. Block grants that do not affect the relative prices of government services can be the appropriate type of grant to respond to this problem.

In some circumstances, matching grants might be the appropriate type of grant. Consider state environmental programs that have positive spillover effects on other states. Without a federal matching grant, no state would have an incentive to take these beneficial spillovers into account when setting expenditure levels. With a matching grant, the federal government could set an appropriate matching rate so that states freely choose the correct level of environmental spending. For example, if 25 percent of the additional benefits of environmental spending by one state spilled over to other states, the federal government could set the federal match of the environmental grant at 25 percent.

Table 3 shows how federal grants to state and local governments have changed from 1960 to 2003. Whether measured as a percentage of total federal outlays, total state and local expenditures, or the national economy (GDP), federal grants to state and local governments grew from 1960 to 1980. The 1980s saw a decline in federal

TABLE 3. Trends in Federal Grants to State and Local Governments

	Federal Grants as a Percentage of:		
	Total Federal Outlays	State and Local Expenditures	Gross Domestic Product (GDP)
1960	7.6	18.2	1.4
1965	9.2	19.1	1.6
1970	12.3	23.0	2.4
1975	15.0	25.7	3.2
1980	15.5	28.5	3.4
1985	11.2	21.7	2.6
1990	10.8	19.0	2.4
1995	14.8	23.2	3.1
2000	15.9	22.8	2.9
2003	17.9	26.1	3.6

Source: Budget of the U.S. Government, FY2005 (2005).

aid to state and local governments as a result of the Reagan administration's policies intended to shrink the role of the federal government and increase the role of states. In the 1990s, largely because of the growth of the Medicaid program, an open-ended matching grant, federal grants to state and local governments began to grow again.

The composition of federal aid to state and local governments has also changed in important ways. The proportion of grants to places, such as grants for capital investment, has shrunk, and the proportion of grants to individuals has increased markedly. In 1960, 35 percent of total federal grants to state and local governments were payments for individuals; by 2003 this percentage had grown to 64 percent. The most important grant to individuals is Medicaid, which has become the single largest federal grant to state and local governments.

OTHER WAYS THAT THE FEDERAL GOVERNMENT AFFECTS STATE AND LOCAL GOVERNMENTS

The federal government affects state and local governments in many other ways. First, indirect forms of federal aid to state and local governments will be discussed.

The federal government provides indirect aid to state and local governments through two provisions of the federal tax code. Individuals can deduct individual income, real estate, and personal property taxes if they itemize deductions on their federal income

TABLE 4. Cost of Major Forms of Aid to State and Local Governments

Type of Aid	Dollars (Billions)	% of Total
Grants	$387.3	77
Tax Deductibility	$71.9	14
Exclusion of Interest on Debt	$44.6	9
Total	$503.8	100

Source: Budget of the U.S. Government, FY2005 (2005).

tax returns. Tax deductibility is considered a "tax expenditure" because it represents a departure from the standard tax base, and without this allowed deduction the existing federal tax code would raise more revenue. This provision of the federal tax code may make it easier for state and local governments to raise taxes and increase spending.

A second form of indirect federal aid to state and local governments is the exemption from federal taxation of interest on state and local debt, which allows state and local governments to issue debt at lower interest rates than they would otherwise be able to.

Table 4 compares the cost of federal grants-in-aid to these two indirect forms of aid. Although federal grants to state and local governments account for about three-fourths of the total cost of federal aid to state and local governments, the cost to the federal government of indirect aid through the tax code is also significant.

The federal government affects state and local governments in four other important ways. State personal and corporate income taxes are often linked to their federal counterparts. For example, some states that impose personal income taxes link their taxes to federal adjusted gross income (AGI). When the federal government changes provisions of the federal tax code that impact the value of AGI, this impacts state tax revenues unless states take explicit action to "decouple" from federal tax policy changes. Increases in federal AGI will tend to increase state income tax revenues; decreases in federal AGI will tend to decrease state income tax revenues.

The federal government also imposes costs on state and local governments through regulatory requirements called mandates. One example is a direct federal order to implement a particular federal standard, such as the requirement that all public transportation systems be fully accessible to handicapped individuals. Problems with measuring the financial burden of federal mandates are considerable.

The federal government also affects state and local governments through the Constitution, court interpretations of the Constitution, and federal law (other than mandates). These can all be considered "rules of the game." For example, federal law relating to sales taxation makes it difficult for states to collect sales taxes from consumers ordering merchandise from mail-order catalogs or making purchases via the Internet.

A final means by which the federal government affects state and local governments is through its management of fiscal and monetary policy. During periods of economic growth, state and local tax revenues tend to rise; during recessions, state and local government expenditure responsibilities tend to increase while revenues fall, straining state and local budgets. *SEE ALSO:* Block Grants; Decentralization; Economic Development; Education; Externalities/Spillovers; Health Care Policy; Local Government; Medicaid; Reagan, Ronald; Unfunded Mandates; Welfare Policy

BIBLIOGRAPHY: Budget of the United States Government, FY 2005 (Washington, DC: Government Printing Office, 2005); Ronald C. Fisher, ed., *Intergovernmental Fiscal Relations* (Boston: Kluwer Academic, 1997); Wallace E. Oates, "An Essay on Fiscal Federalism," *Journal of Economic Literature* 37, no. 3 (September 1999): 1120–49; Wallace E. Oates, *Fiscal Federalism* (New York: Harcourt Brace Jovanovich, 1972); Alice Rivlin, *Reviving the American Dream* (Washington, DC: Brookings Institution, 1992); *Statistical Abstract of the United States 2005* (Washington, DC: Government Printing Office, 2005); and U.S. Census, http://www.census.gov/govs/estimate/01gp00us.html.

DAPHNE A. KENYON

Fletcher v. Peck *Fletcher v. Peck* (1810) was the first time the Supreme Court interpreted the Contract Clause of the Constitution (Article I, Section 10, which prohibits states from passing laws that impair the obligation of contracts). In 1795 the Georgia legislature had sold much of its western land to land companies, who in turn sold it to individuals. It was later discovered that many members of the legislature had been bribed. The new legislature, elected in 1796, repealed the land grant. Since innocent third parties had bought the land, a suit was filed concerning title to the land. Chief Justice John Marshall held that the original land grant was a contract and that the subsequent repeal broke the contract and therefore violated the Constitution. *SEE ALSO:* Contract Clause; *Dartmouth College v. Woodward*; *Home Building and Loan v. Blaisdell*; *Stone v. Mississippi*; *United States Trust Company v. New Jersey*

ROBERT W. LANGRAN

Foreign Policy Federalism has played a major but little-noticed role in U.S. foreign policy. Its greatest successes in this sphere, paradoxically, were in eliminating foreign policy among the founding states of the United States and in removing the territories it subsequently absorbed from the realm of foreign policy. These developments, which came in the early period of the Union, are usually not conceived of as foreign policies; but for Americans who did so conceive of them, they provided models for later applications of federalism in external diplomacy.

The Constitution obviated the need for a foreign policy on the part of the individual states of the union, whether toward other countries or toward one another. The Articles of Confederation had forbidden separate state foreign policies, but the temptation remained; the stronger union after 1787 eliminated the temptation. Similarly, the Constitution, while unable to prevent civil war between the northern and southern regions of the Union with their different forms of society, eliminated the danger of war between individual states—an impressive accomplishment as settlers moved westward where the old colonies had overlapping claims.

Technically, federalism made foreign policy complicated. Under the Confederation, important treaties of the union were disobeyed by states, making diplomacy difficult.

The Constitution resolved this problem but still kept diplomacy difficult. By separating legislature from the executive, it made the ratification of treaties uncertain compared to other countries and weakened the coherence of foreign policy. As a bargain between states that did not always trust each other—Southerners feared treaties might betray their interests in the Mississippi—it imposed a two thirds requirement on Senate ratification of treaties. John Hay, a Neo-Federalist secretary of state more than a century later, called this the irreparable mistake of the Constitution.

However, as a compensating factor, federalism introduced a new simplifying element into foreign policy: the possibility of annexations yielding constitutionally equal states that could homogenize with the others, sparing itself the usual imperial or center-periphery tensions. The Articles of Confederation had provisions for admitting other countries by decision of nine states. The 1787 Constitution enabled a majority of both Houses of Congress to admit a new state, making the admission of a state formally easier than a treaty with a state.

What really made rapid expansion possible, however, was that the Constitution based everyday congressional decision making on simple majorities, and executive implementation no longer dependent on the member states. This enabled the Congress and executive to keep functioning without loss of efficiency when the number of member states increased. Expansion thus occurred without any widening, deepening tension. The 1787 form of federation facilitated expansion in a manner and degree without historical precedent. And expansion was the most important element in the first century of American foreign policy.

In other external diplomacy, Federalist ideals played a smaller role at first. The original generation of Founding Fathers dreamed of wider applications of federalism—Thomas Jefferson dreamed of an Anglo-American-Spanish confederacy, Thomas Paine of an Anglo-American-French one in the early stages of the French Revolution; James Madison and Jefferson noted the absence of any absolute limits on how far modern federalism could be extended; and Benjamin Franklin wrote to a friend in Paris that if the federal Constitution could succeed, there was no reason not to unite Europe in "one Grand Republick and Federal Union." However, none of this went farther than personal speculations, usually private. After the 1790s, it faded away from the comments of national leaders; lesser, if still estimable, figures continued such thoughts.

After 1865, international federalism reemerged as a subject for speculation, this time both among national leaders such as President Ulysses Grant and among leading intellectuals—in Europe as well as the United States. A huge impression was made by the successful consolidation of the American federation following its testing in civil war, and also by the human cost of modern war.

International unions of states were in fact developed in the twentieth century, under the pressure of the wars and the influence of federative movements. They developed on all three levels, European, Atlantic, and global. These unions took the form of confederations: the European Union, the Atlantic alliance structures (NATO, OECD, G-8), and the UN system. Confederalism thereby experienced a revival, thanks in part, paradoxically, to Federalist propaganda imbued with the Anti-Confederalist spirit of *The Federalist Papers.*

The founders of international institutions were in each case a mix of Federalist and Non-Federalist national leaders and officials; the institutional mixes of federal, confederal, and nonfederal elements can be traced to the balance between those who pushed for federalism and those who resisted it. The League of Nations was the child of

Woodrow Wilson, who felt that the ultimate goal was world federalism and the League was the first step; the idea was pioneered by a League to Enforce Peace, a public movement whose guiding spirit, Hamilton Holt, was a world Federalist. NATO was negotiated by Atlantic Federalists such as John Hickerson and Theodore Achilles of the U.S. State Department, and their counterparts in other countries such as Lester Pearson of Canada, as well as by Non-Federalists in the United States and other governments such as Dean Acheson. The European Community (EC) was negotiated overwhelmingly by Federalists, and so was able to include in its founding treaties a Federalist commitment to "an ever closer Union of the European peoples," a goal to which it has increasingly approximated itself, becoming the European Union (EU) in 1992.

The United States played a central role in promoting these international organizations and their federal features. Woodrow Wilson was only the first to do so. The Marshall Plan used its funds to pressure Europeans to form an economic federation; it spawned the Organization for European Economic Cooperation (OEEC), the latter serving as one of the most fertile of international organizations: father-in-law to the EC, direct father to the OECD, and uncle to NATO, which took many of its personnel and practices. The CIA helped finance the European Movement, which in turn spawned the Hague Congress and Council of Europe and backed Jean Monnet in forming the EC.

Monnet himself always worked closely with the United States, starting out in World War I as an organizer of the Atlantic alliance, and forming close liaisons in the interwar years with figures such as William Clayton and John Foster Dulles—both Federalists. Clayton wanted an economic federation of Europe within an Atlantic political federation and a world of free trade leading to eventual world federation. Dulles advocated a complete European federation within an Atlantic confederation or federation, and eventual world federation. Clayton, as undersecretary of state for economic affairs, helped negotiate the Bretton Woods institutions and wrote the memo on the economic collapse of Europe that led to the Marshall Plan. He personally insisted to European leaders that the funds would flow only if they set up a permanent joint organization: thus the birth of OEEC. Dulles guided Senator Arthur Vandenberg, who sponsored the bipartisan resolution laying the ground for NATO, and as secretary of state pushed hard in 1953–54 for the Europeans to form a full federation. His idea of liberation drew on the Federalist nucleus approach. He remains respected in Europe even if usually condemned in the United States on left-right grounds.

These individuals did not operate in a vacuum. They could play pivotal roles because there was a large milieu supporting federalism in American foreign policy thinking. This milieu had grown for nearly a century. Later it shrank in the 1960s, and American federative initiative shrank with it. The primary American role in promoting international organization and federalism was a consequence of American ideals and of the enormous emerging power of the United States—itself credited to its rapid federal expansion, bringing it to the point at which, by 1890, it surpassed all European powers save Russia in population, and had a larger active loyal citizenry than any country anywhere. It entered into the heart of world politics only then, in the 1890s. From the start it sought a moral orientation for the use of its power, looking for something more relevant to an interdependent world than classical realpolitik. Its ideals of democracy and federalism provided its two most important motifs for moralizing foreign policy in the twentieth century.

The two motifs became intertwined. The confederalism of Woodrow Wilson was part of his plan to "make the world safe for democracy"; the federalism of the 1940s was meant to stabilize democracy and avoid new Weimars—in effect, to make democracy safe for the world. Federalism was envisaged as making a success of democracy in central and southern Europe where before it had always been problematic; democracy in turn was a criterion for membership in the federative unions. This combination of roles was applied in the EU as well as NATO. While democracy has been the most vocal of American political exports, federalism has been comparably important in practice.

For nearly all Federalist movements from the 1860s to the 1940s, whether in Europe, the United States, or elsewhere, the inspirational point of reference was the American union and its bible, *The Federalist Papers*. Those *Papers* had argued that the new 1787 form of federation could eliminate rivalry and war between its member states, could free democracy of its traditional penchant for extremism and instability, could overcome the frailties of previous confederations, and could unite the freedom and expanse of federalism with the efficiency of the modern central sovereign state—all matters of greatest importance for international politics. The United States seemed to bear out in practice these happy predictions.

The Civil War, to be sure, served as warning as well as inspiration: warning, in showing that Union does not eliminate all dangers of war; yet inspiration, in showing that the Union, with its strong form of federal entities elected by the people, could grow roots deep enough to endure a rift running straight through its body politic and heal with unusual rapidity. The warning led some Federalists, often called "regionalists," to be cautious; they generally restricted their proposed unions to countries with similar democratic regimes and societies with similar forms and levels of development. Some of them salvaged a hope for ultimate world federation by leaving a door open for others to join after meeting the standards; this was the "nucleus" idea, modeled rhetorically on the United States' expansion from 13 states to 50. World Federalists gave a different answer to the warning, arguing that technology and globalization were rapidly erasing distinctions, and were making interdependence so great and war so costly that the dangers of remaining separate had become greater than the dangers of federation on a global scale.

The UN system reflected the globalist approach; the EU and NATO reflected the regional nucleus approach. NATO included in its founding treaties the provision of leaving a door open to later-emerging democratic states to join; the EC treaty called emotionally upon all free Europeans to join in its project. Realists and neutralists argued that this would only alienate those left out and lead to counterunions like the Warsaw Pact. Nevertheless, the EU and NATO gradually attracted all countries in their neighborhood to wish to join, including by the 1980s their enemies; the prospect of joining played a role in motivating the Soviet bloc countries to abandon communism and to hope to be able to succeed as democracies.

The American Federalist roots of contemporary international confederacies raise a question of whether they have a genetic code of evolving toward modern federation. In the case of the EU, this seems plausible; the trend toward federation has accelerated since 1989. Elsewhere such a telos has been less in evidence; the Atlantic and global institutions have continued to evolve and in some respects deepen, but more slowly and without clear direction. The slowdown correlates to the decline of American support for international federalism since the Vietnam War and the rise of the "small is beautiful" philosophy.

The decline of the goal of federalism in American foreign policy has continued, with ups and downs, for several decades; it may or may not be permanent. The rise of international federalism in American thinking and policy proceeded even longer. It was propelled by pride in the American political innovation and by increases in interdependence, factors that have not disappeared.

In view of the depth of national sovereignty and identity, and the profound differences between national societies with collective corporate achievements to defend, an endpoint of modern federation seems unlikely for most international organizations: what worked for a union of British colonies may not be appropriate for a union of historical nations. Yet in view of ever-accelerating growth of technology and interdependence, it seems that some form of efficient federalism must eventually be achieved. If international federations do emerge, they will come after a process already much lengthier than the Federalist movements had anticipated in their idealization of the U.S. Constitutional Convention, and take forms unique in many respects. Nevertheless they may, like the EU, incorporate some basic principles of the modern national federation pioneered in the United States, such as the direct election of federal representatives and direct legal obligation of citizens to federal authorities. *SEE ALSO:* Commerce with Foreign Nations

IRA STRAUS

Formula Grants   Formula grants, sometimes also called "state-administered grants," are a method by which the federal government distributes more than $400 billion annually to state and local governments to implement federal policies. Formula grant programs include health care for the poor, health insurance for children, special needs and K–12 education, transportation improvement, law enforcement/homeland security, nutrition programs for children and pregnant women, and welfare (Temporary Assistance for Needy Families, or TANF). Combined, more than 175 different formula grants from fourteen different federal government departments total nearly 85 percent of all federal government grants-in-aid to state and local governments.

Unlike other federal grants, state and local governments are not required to compete against each other to receive formula grant funds. Each grant is based on a specific formula established by law or Congress that determines which funds a state or community may be qualified to receive. In the case of matching formula grants, formulas determine what proportion of the total funds the lower government will have to provide to get the federal (matching) funding. In many cases, states with high unemployment, poverty (for health care, education, and nutrition), or highway miles (for transportation); with poorly performing education systems; and so on can qualify to receive several times the state contribution in federal matching funds. Many of these matching formula grants also include minimum floor amounts awarded, giving a funding advantage to smaller, perhaps less affluent states.

The ten most expensive federal formula grant programs as of 2002 in order of decreasing cost are (1) Medicaid; (2) Highway Planning and Construction; (3) Welfare (Family Assistance Grants under TANF); (4) Title I Local Education Grants; (5) Special Needs Education Grants; (6) Head Start, early childhood education; (7) the National School Lunch Program; (8) Title IV-E Foster Care programs; (9) Women, Infant and Children's nutrition program (for low-income pregnant women and infants); and (10) the State Children's Health Insurance Program (SCHIP; Ransdell 2004).

HEALTH AND HUMAN SERVICES FORMULA GRANTS

Medicaid: The Most Expensive Federal Matching Grant

The Department of Health and Human Services (HHS) administers nearly two-thirds of all federal formula grant dollars, and four of the top ten funded programs. This includes the single most expensive federal formula grant program, Medicaid, which is more than five times larger than any other federal formula grant program. It provides long-term medical care for 50 million low-income Americans, including 22.6 million low-income children and 12 million elderly disabled. Passed in 1965 during Lyndon Johnson's Great Society, Medicaid is a matching grant. The federal government pays from 50 to 83 percent of the cost, with the balance paid by the states. The poorest states are able to receive more than four federal dollars funding for each dollar of state funding they contribute. Federal government Medicaid expenditures increased by 149 percent during the 1990s, from $53.3 billion (1991) to $132.7 billion in 2001. The National Governors' Association found Medicaid costs increased on average 12 percent per year, and drug coverage 18 percent a year from 2000 to 2003, resulting in federal government expenditures of more than $275 billion for Medicaid and SCHIP (combined) in fiscal year 2003.

According to a 2001 Kaiser Commission report, Medicaid spending for the poor, for children, and for the disabled consumes an average of 15 percent of state budgets (Smith 2001). Increasing state Medicaid costs now rank second behind the costs of public education as a proportion of state budgets. Since 2001, governors and state legislatures have been forced to limit Medicaid coverage to help balance state budgets and close combined operating budget deficits of between $40 and $50 billion. According to a 2002 National Association of State Budget Officers report, "47 states took steps to reduce Medicaid expenditures in state fiscal years 2002 or 2003. Budget cutting policies included: implementing cost containment programs for pharmaceuticals, freezing or lowering payment rates to hospitals, physicians, HMOs and nursing homes, reducing or eliminating optional Medicaid benefits like dental or vision, increasing beneficiaries' copayments, and scaling back eligibility" (Ku, Ross, and Nathanson 2002). The U.S. House Budget Committee's proposed budget for fiscal year 2006 calls for a total of $15.1 billion to be cut from Medicaid and SCHIP over the next five years.

HHS also administers the third most expensive formula grant program, the Family Assistance Grants under the TANF program. They are part of the 1996 Personal Responsibility and Work Opportunities Act (Public Law 104-193), most commonly known as "welfare reform." As of 2001, the federal government spent $16.5 billion on these grants to states, based on their poverty rates, joblessness rates, and prior AFDC (i.e., welfare grant expenses) from 1992 to 1995. Although "welfare" rolls have dropped by 40 percent since 1996, the federal expenditures for these fixed-sum grants have remained largely stable.

Since 1997, another huge and rapidly expanding HHS-administered formula grant program has been the State Children's Health Insurance Program (SCHIP), also known as Title XXI of the Balanced Budget Act of 1997. The federal government has provided more than $40 billion in matching funds since 1997 for states to implement and administer health care services to its low-income children whose family income ranges up to 200 percent of the federal poverty level. The federal grant to states has a minimum floor, above which it funds based upon 50 percent of the number of low-income children in the state, adjusted for a state cost of living and a cost of health care factor.

DEPARTMENT OF TRANSPORTATION FORMULA GRANTS

The Department of Transportation administers the second most expensive formula grants, known as the TEA-21 grants, which totaled $27.6 billion in 2001. The Highway Planning and Construction Grants are part of the Transportation Efficiency Act for the Twenty-first Century. This grant is computed based on a complex formula involving highway lane miles (excluding interstate highways) and the average miles traveled per capita. This grant program grew by 91 percent in the past decade. These grants are of particular importance to local units of government.

DEPARTMENT OF EDUCATION FORMULA GRANTS

The Department of Education (DOE) administers thirty-seven different formula grant programs, including the fourth (Title I Grants to Local Schools), fifth (Special Needs Education Grants), and sixth (Head Start early childhood education grants) most expensive federal formula grant programs. Title I Grants provide the single largest federal source of funding for local K–12 public education, to help poor disadvantaged children learn. Most of the federal Special Education grants to the states were originally part of the 1997 Individuals with Disabilities Education Act (IDEA, Public Law 101-476). These grants grew from $3 billion in 1997 to $7.4 billion in 2002 to provide assistance, early intervention services, and public education to nearly 6 million disabled children from ages 2 to 21. Head Start grants, started in the mid-1960s, now include $390 million in funding for preschool learning readiness educational grants.

HOMELAND SECURITY FORMULA GRANTS

Although much smaller in dollar amounts, an area of significant fiscal strain for state (and particularly local) units of government law enforcement agencies are the formula grants administered by the Department of Homeland Security, which was established in 2002. Over $3.3 billion in formula grants were established as part of the Homeland Security provisions of the USA PATRIOT Act in 2001 authorized by Congress. Little of that funding has actually been appropriated (paid) to reimburse local governments for increased security and law enforcement expenses. According to the U.S. Conference of Mayors, as of September 2003 90 percent of local governments, and as of 2004 52 percent of local governments, had still received no funding under homeland security formula grant programs. Formula grants currently authorized to be administered by the Department of Homeland Security's Office of Domestic Preparedness Grant Program include the Firefighter Grants Programs ($715 million in 2005), the State Homeland Security Grant Program (SHGP) at $1.1 billion in 2005, the Urban Area Security Initiative grants for terrorism prevention funded at $885 million, Law Enforcement Terrorism Prevention Program grants funded at $400 million, and various Citizen Corps and Emergency Management Planning Grants totaling less than $200 million in 2005. *SEE ALSO:* Education; Great Society; Medicaid; State Legislatures; Transportation Policy; USA PATRIOT Act of 2001; Welfare Policy

BIBLIOGRAPHY: Leighton Ku, Donna Cohen Ross, and Melanie Nathanson, *State Medicaid Cutbacks and the Federal Role in Providing Fiscal Relief to States* (Washington, DC: Center on Budget and Policy Priorities, 2002); Tim Ransdell, ed., *Federal Formula Grants and California* (San Francisco: Public Policy Institute of California, 2004); and Vernon Smith, "Medicaid Budgets Under Stress: Survey Findings for State Fiscal Year 2000, 2001, and 2002" (Kaiser Commission on Medicaid and the Uninsured, October 2001).

ELIZABETH G. WILLIAMS

Fourteenth Amendment The Fourteenth Amendment was one of three articles added to the Constitution in the wake of and in response to the Civil War and the events leading up to the war. The Fourteenth Amendment is the most complex of the three, serving as the receptacle for a number of different concerns of the Republican-dominated thirty-ninth Congress that adopted the amendment.

PROVISIONS OF THE AMENDMENT

Section 1 was and remains the most important part of the amendment, defining U.S. and state citizens, supplying protection for the privileges and immunities of U.S. citizens against abridgment by the states, and forbidding the states from depriving persons of life, liberty, or property without due process of law, or from denying to persons within their jurisdiction the equal protection of the laws.

The second section provides a new formula for representation in Congress to replace the three-fifths clause of Article 1, Section 2, according to which slaves were counted as three-fifths of a person in the calculation of the number of representatives each state was due. Section 2 of the Fourteenth Amendment provides that representation in the House of Representatives is to be calculated on the basis of the total population of the state ("Indians not taxed" excepted, as in the original Article 1 provision). However, the amendment also provides that "the basis" of representation will be reduced "in the proportion" in which males 21 years of age and older are denied the right to vote by the state. Thus Section 2 of the amendment does not require states to extend the suffrage to all males who are of age, but it does penalize states that do not do so. This provision was a response to the emancipation after the war and to the resentment many Northerners had over the representational bonus southern ruling elites had reaped because of their nonvoting slaves. This provision was meant to prevent these elites from garnering an even larger bonus from disenfranchised free blacks, who now were to be counted as whole persons for apportionment purposes.

Section 3 of the amendment rendered ineligible for state or federal public office any person who had served in such offices before the war and, having taken an oath to support the U.S. Constitution, "engaged in insurrection or rebellion." This provision, on its face, had the effect of rendering ineligible for political office nearly the entire prewar southern elite. It did contain an override clause, however, according to which a two-thirds vote in Congress could "remove such disability."

Section 4 prohibited the federal government or any state from paying debts incurred in support of "insurrection or rebellion against the United States," or from compensating any losses resulting from the emancipation of the slaves. Although compensated emancipation had been on the table before the war, the struggle had produced a new consensus that compensation was unmerited. Finally, Section 5 succinctly provided that "the Congress shall have power to enforce, by appropriate legislation, the provisions of this article."

HISTORY OF THE ADOPTION OF THE AMENDMENT

Although to different degrees important at the time, Sections 2–4 have not had the lasting significance of Sections 1 and 5. Section 1 is clearly an effort to supply new constitutional protections for the newly freed slaves, although it must be noted that its language is much broader and more general. At the time of passage of the Thirteenth Amendment, providing for emancipation, it was not contemplated that further amendments such as Section 1 of the Fourteenth, or the Fifteenth Amendment (which dealt with voting rights), would be required. Nonetheless, it soon became apparent that emancipation alone would not be sufficient. The southern states very quickly passed new laws, known as Black Codes, intended to regulate the freedmen and in many cases reduce them to a state of quasi-slavery. These laws imposed many special disabilities and restrictions, including a denial of the right to bear arms, to live where they chose, and to use the courts freely. These Black Codes provoked an immediate reaction in Congress, with two important pieces of legislation introduced early in 1866. One became the Civil Rights Act of 1866, a bill that was intended to protect the freedmen from the state Black Codes by declaring that "there shall be no discrimination in civil rights or immunities among the inhabitants of . . . the United States on account of race, color, or previous condition of servitude," along with a substantial list of specific matters (e.g., the right to make contracts or to sue) about which the states were to provide "the same right" to all persons without regard to race, color, and so on. The law contained enforcement mechanisms and provided penalties for those who, acting under color of law, violated its provisions. The Civil Rights Act passed Congress in March 1866, but was vetoed shortly thereafter by President Andrew Johnson, largely on constitutional grounds. It was repassed over the president's veto, but the constitutional questions raised by the president's veto lent new importance to the second piece of legislation, what ultimately became the first and fifth sections of the Fourteenth Amendment. This legislation was also originally introduced early in 1866, in fact prior to the Civil Rights bill. An early version was cast in very broad language, empowering Congress to protect privileges and immunities and to guarantee equal protection of the rights to life, liberty, and property. This draft was debated in February 1866, met a good deal of resistance, and then was sent back to committee for revision, where it languished while the Civil Rights bill received more attention. Finally in May 1866 a revised draft amendment was introduced in Congress, which passed it on to the states for ratification in June of that year. The amendment was seen as an important part of the Republican Party platform for the congressional elections of 1866, and ratification of it was made a precondition for the rebel states regaining their seats in Congress. In 1868 it received the requisite number of state ratifications, and it became part of the Constitution.

THE MEANING OF THE AMENDMENT

The Fourteenth Amendment has been the most adjudicated part of the Constitution since its adoption, and it has been among the most controversial parts of the Constitution within both the political and scholarly worlds. Two broad sorts of interpretations have emerged. Some have understood the amendment to be transformative of the Constitution, a radical restructuring of the original constitutional order. Others have seen the amendment as working relatively minor changes in the constitutional system. The alternative readings of the amendment emerged in the very first Supreme Court case under it, the *Slaughterhouse Cases* of 1873. In these cases, Justice Samuel Miller, writing for the Court majority, adhered to the minimal change view; in dissent Justice Stephen Field defended the major constitutional revolution position. These alternatives have continued to dominate much of the constitutional scholarship of the next century and a half. The range of opinion is fostered by at least two aspects of the amendment. Its language is broad and apparently vague, leaving readers, it seems, much room for filling in on their own. The other important fact is the history of adoption, in which the amendment was so intertwined with the Civil Rights Act, a fact that has encouraged some to see the amendment as intending, in the main, to constitutionalize the Civil Rights Act. That has led some to interpret the amendment in light of the more concrete provisions of the Civil Rights Act. Others, however, note that the amendment was introduced before the Civil Rights bill, and can hardly have its sole meaning to be the constitutionalization of a bill that did not yet exist. Those who emphasize this part of the history tend to read the amendment as more far-reaching than the Civil Rights bill.

A third view, taking clues from speeches of advocates of the amendment in Congress, attempts to locate the overall intent of the amendment in a realm between the other two. It holds that the amendment aims to "complete the Constitution," that is, to remedy certain basic flaws in the Constitution, some of which had been noted at the time of the drafting of the Constitution by no less a personage than James Madison, main architect of the original Constitution. It was not merely that the Constitution had failed to resolve the problem of slavery on which the Union eventually foundered in 1861, but it had failed to provide adequately against the centrifugal forces characteristic of federal systems, and it had also failed to provide adequately for rights protections in the states. This third theory of the amendment sees it as making substantial changes in the constitutional order, but not revolutionizing the system. It is rather a completion, in that it carries out intuitions of what the Constitution should have been, at least as envisaged by Madison.

Each of the three general and overall views of the amendment has a set of more specific interpretations of the chief clauses of Section 2 to accompany it. All agree that the first clause, defining citizens of the United States and the states, had the chief effect of overruling the notorious *Dred Scott* (1857) case, which had decreed that descendants of slaves could never become citizens of the United States. Instead, the amendment provided that all persons born or naturalized in the United States were citizens of the United States, a definition that brought the former slaves well within its terms. It also provided that such U.S. citizens were also citizens of "the state wherein they reside," a definition that clearly made U.S. citizenship prior in some sense to state citizenship.

The constitutional revolution interpretation, not surprisingly, has the most far-reaching interpretations of the rest of Section 1's provisions. In the form Justice Field gave it in early post-Reconstruction decisions, the amendment protects all "the fundamental rights, privileges, and immunities which belong to [a person] as a freeman and free citizen" (*Slaughterhouse*). The constitutional revolutionists tend not to be very discriminating in discerning different meanings in different parts of Section 1. Thus, when Field's reading of the privileges or immunities provisions was rejected by the court majority, he found the same protections to be contained in the Equal Protection and Due Process Clauses. The implications of this expansive view for the grant of legislative power to Congress in Section 5 are equally immense. Congress is seen to have more or less plenary power to act to protect the basic rights identified in the amendment. One frequent criticism of the constitutional revolution theory is that it ignores the resistance to the original form of the amendment as debated in February 1866, and reads the amendment as if it remained in the language debated then.

At the other extreme, Justice Miller's minor modification approach reads the Privileges and Immunities Clause in a very narrow way, finding in it hardly any more protections than existed prior to the adoption of the amendment. The emphasis is instead placed on the effort to supply additional safeguards for the rights of freedmen contained in the other clauses of Section 1. As became visible in later cases like *Plessy v. Ferguson* (1896), the minimal change view did not find very potent protections for the freedmen in these clauses either. With regard to congressional power under Section 5, the partisans of minimal change tended to hold to "the state action doctrine," that is, the view that Congress may reach only actions by states or state officials and under no circumstances actions by private individuals (*Civil Rights Cases* 1883). As became clear over time, the minimal change view was very solicitous on behalf of the traditional federal system.

The "completing the Constitution" theory takes a more restrained view of what was accomplished by the Privileges and Immunities Clause than the "revolutionists" do. It notices, as does Justice Miller in *Slaughterhouse*, that the amendment identifies two kinds of citizenship, state and U.S., and that Section 1 protects only the privileges and immunities attached to the latter. This theory goes well beyond Miller's view, however, in that it finds new substantive protections in the Privileges or Immunities Clause. Protected are special rights due to citizens of the United States by virtue of the Constitution or the nature of the federal union. Chief among these protections are those mentioned in the Bill of Rights. According to proponents of the "completing the Constitution" view, then, the Bill of Rights is meant to be incorporated against the states by the Privileges or Immunities Clause. Partisans of this theory recognize, however, that the rest of Section 1 refers to "persons" and not to "citizens of the U.S." All persons are protected against state deprivations of life, liberty, and property—the basic natural rights—without due process of law. They are also entitled to equal legal protection of these basic rights by the states. Thus the amendment supplies a new protection to natural or fundamental rights against threats to those rights by the states. A state can threaten rights in two ways: it can directly infringe on them when it seizes the objects of rights (life, liberty, or property) without proper legal authority, or it can infringe them indirectly by failing to provide protection (or equal protection) for these rights. The "completing" theory shares with the revolutionary theory the idea that the amendment does supply protections for the most basic rights, but it differs in that it finds that protection in the Equal Protection and Due Process Clauses, and thus clearly recognizes that the states retain primary custody for the protection of these fundamental rights. The new constitutional right established is a federal right to protection by the states (not Congress) of one's natural or fundamental rights. This theory of the amendment can thus be called "corrective federalism," that is, the states govern, but if they misstep on rights questions the federal government can correct them. In line with the corrective federalism theory, Section 5 is read to provide for a "state failure" empowerment of Congress. This power goes beyond the "state action" doctrine in that if the states systematically fail, either through lack of will or lack of ability, to provide equal legal protection of rights, Congress may step in to provide such protection. Shortly after the adoption of the amendment, Congress acted on this theory in passing laws to protect freedmen against the Ku Klux Klan in the South.

Since the amendment was adopted, the Supreme Court has not consistently adhered to one or another of these theories of the amendment, and that has been responsible for the vacillating and not entirely satisfactory role of the Fourteenth Amendment in American constitutional history. *SEE ALSO:* Equal Protection of the Laws; Incorporation (Nationalization) of the Bill of Rights; *Plessy v. Ferguson*; Privileges and Immunities Clause: Fourteenth Amendment; *Slaughterhouse Cases*

BIBLIOGRAPHY: Akhil Reed Amar, *The Bill of Rights* (New Haven, CT: Yale University Press, 1998); Raoul Berger, *Government by Judiciary: The Transformation of the Fourteenth Amendment*, 2nd ed. (Indianapolis, IN: Liberty Classics, 1997); James E. Bond, *No Easy Walk to Freedom: Reconstruction and the Ratification of the Fourteenth Amendment* (Westport, CT: Praeger, 1997); Michael Kent Curtis, *No State Shall Abridge: The Fourteenth Amendment and the Bill of Rights* (Durham, NC: Duke University Press, 1986); Robert K. Kaczorowski, *The Politics of Judicial Interpretation: The Federal Courts, Department of Justice, and Civil Rights, 1866–1876* (New York: Oceana Publications, 1985); Earl M. Maltz, *Civil Rights, The Constitution, and Congress, 1863–1869* (Lawrence: University Press of Kansas, 1990); Jacobus ten Broek, *Equal under the Law* (New York: Collier, 1965); Michael P. Zuckert, "Completing the Constitution: The Fourteenth Amendment and Constitutional Rights," *Publius* 22, no. 2 (Spring 1993): 69–91; and Michael P. Zuckert, "Congressional Power under the Fourteenth Amendment: The Original Understanding of Section 5," *Constitutional Commentary* 3 (Winter 1986): 123–55.

Michael Zuckert

Frankfurter, Felix   No person rose from more humble beginnings, was more brilliant, and seemed more fully prepared for service on the Supreme Court than Felix Frankfurter. However, his career on the Court, especially on questions of federalism, has sparked debate among scholars and observers. Frankfurter's personal neuroses and frequently enigmatic, conservative judicial posture on many federalism issues surprised, and ultimately disappointed, many of the liberal supporters of the president who appointed him, Franklin D. Roosevelt. In doing so, though, he also established a model for judicial self-restraint, and states' rights–oriented decisions, that won him legions of judicial followers.

Felix Frankfurter arrived in the United States from his native Austria in 1894, at the age of 12, without being able to speak a word of English. Remarkably, just 11 years later he graduated as the valedictorian from Harvard Law School. After stints in a prominent New York City law firm, the U.S. attorney's office in New York, and the War Department as the counsel for the Bureau of Insular Affairs, Frankfurter was asked in 1914 to join the faculty of Harvard Law School. Eventually he would be named the Byrne Professor of Administrative Law, become close friends with self-restraint-oriented Supreme Court Justices Oliver Wendell Holmes and Louis D. Brandeis, and write so many influential law books that he would become recognized as one of the foremost legal scholars in the United States.

Having experienced anti-Semitism in his earlier career, Frankfurter found that his Jewish religion put him at odds once again with the puritanical Brahmin Harvard administration and Boston society. Nevertheless, Frankfurter showed tremendous courage and compassion, supplementing his legal academic work with nonprofit Progressive legal reform work for a variety of causes. Working sometimes at the suggestion and

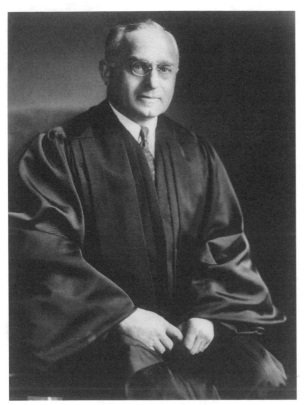

Felix Frankfurter. Library of Congress, Prints and Photographs Division.

with the financial support of then–Supreme Court Justice Louis D. Brandeis, Frankfurter argued the Oregon as well as Washington, D.C., minimum wage law cases before the Court, argued on behalf of accused bomber Tom Mooney to President Woodrow Wilson, joined and then left the religious reformist Zionist Organization, defended law school colleague Zechariah Chafee who was being attacked by conservative Harvard alumni, and argued the appellate case of convicted payroll robbery murderers and anarchists Niccola Sacco and Bartolomeo Vanzetti. Despite all of the controversy surrounding these activities, Frankfurter was offered a seat on the Supreme Judicial Court of Massachusetts, which he declined.

After Franklin D. Roosevelt was elected president, Frankfurter turned down the U.S. solicitor generalship, helped to draft the revolutionary Securities Act, and resisted all other formal government appointments. Instead, he became a powerful informal adviser to the president on both policy and personnel selection. In time, the New Deal was staffed with legions of what were termed "Felix's Happy Hot Dogs," giving Frankfurter even more influence over public policy.

After his appointment to the U.S. Supreme Court in 1939, replacing Benjamin N. Cardozo in what came to be known as the "Jewish Seat" on the Court, Frankfurter seemed poised to take a leadership position that would direct the other justices in a liberal, New Deal direction and possibly even end with his elevation to the chief justiceship. But such was not to be. Frankfurter instead adopted a conservative, states' rights–oriented, self-restraint position on civil liberties issues, which ultimately separated him jurisprudentially from the other liberals on the Court. In addition, his backstage manipulation on the Court separated him from them personally and led to long-term feuds that prevented him from amassing long-term conservative majorities on many of the issues most important to him.

Early on the Court, Frankfurter seemed to be supportive of the state and national government's position in wartime policies, supporting the forced flag salute of public school children over their First Amendment religious objections and the ill-advised Japanese internment policy over due process and equal protection rights claims by litigants. However, when it came to the issue of extending the Bill of Rights' protection to the states, thus enabling the national judiciary to supervise and make more uniform the actions of the state judiciary, Frankfurter developed a more states' rights position. For him, these civil liberties issues were best left to the interpretations of various state judges to define the Fourteenth Amendment's Due Process Clause. Thus, the answers to various political questions were to be left either to the states, the level of government closest to the people serving as what Justice Brandeis called the "laboratories for democracy," or to the elected political branches, rather than the appointed, life-tenured judges. Thus, for him, rather than extend the full protection of the Fourth Amendment's "search and seizure," the Fifth Amendment's "self-incrimination," the Sixth Amendment's "right to counsel," and the Eighth Amendment's "cruel and unusual punishment" provisions to the states, thus protecting defendants' rights, Frankfurter was much more protective under the Fourteenth Amendment's "Due Process Clause" of the state's determination of individuals' rights, barring only government actions that "shocked his conscience." Similarly, when the national government was asked to use the Fourteenth Amendment's Equal Protection Clause to supervise the reapportionment efforts of state legislatures, Frankfurter argued that this was not an area for judicial regulation, but rather was to be decided by a political remedy. While Frankfurter did support the national government's power to desegregate the public schools in the 1954 *Brown v. Board of Education* case, once again he argued behind the scenes for a more limited interpretation of the Fourteenth Amendment's equal protection power. As a result of these and other states' rights decisions, Frankfurter the reformist lawyer came to be seen as Frankfurter the conservative judge. Only after he was compelled to retire from the Court in 1962 after suffering a devastating stroke, and was replaced by a reliable liberal, judicial activist, John F. Kennedy's Secretary of Labor Arthur Goldberg, was the fifth vote added to the liberals on the Court that enabled the revolutionary liberal activist Warren Court to more fully extend the national judicial power to the states.

Frankfurter's legacy on the Court did not end after his death in 1965; rather, he established a constitutional foundation for the states' rights position on federalism issues that continues to influence modern American constitutional law. *SEE ALSO:* Fourteenth Amendment; Incorporation (Nationalization) of the Bill of Rights; U.S. Supreme Court

BIBLIOGRAPHY: H. N. Hirsch, *The Enigma of Felix Frankfurter* (New York: Basic Books, 1981); Joseph P. Lash, *From the Diaries of Felix Frankfurter* (New York: W.W. Norton, 1975); Bruce Allen Murphy, *The Brandeis/Frankfurter Connection: The Secret Political Activities of Two Supreme Court Justices* (New York: Oxford University Press, 1982); and Michael E. Parrish, *Felix Frankfurter and His Times: The Reform Years* (New York: Free Press, 1982).

BRUCE ALLEN MURPHY

Franklin, Benjamin   Benjamin Franklin was the most original and versatile of the founders in his Federalist ideas. Impressed by the nearby Iroquois Confederation and by the success of the Anglo-Scottish parliamentary union of 1707, he advocated federal and parliamentary unions throughout his political career.

Franklin launched the idea of a union of all the colonies in 1754, at the first major Congress of the Colonies in Albany, to strengthen the empire against the French: the idea of union thus arose first out of imperial exuberance, and was prior to the idea of independence. He proposed in the 1760s colonial representation in London, which would have constituted an imperial parliament for managing the common business of the empire. He offered a first draft of the Articles of Confederation to the Continental Congress. He participated actively in the Constitutional Convention of 1787. The Constitution's drafting completed, he urged upon a Parisian friend a united states of Europe. After the Constitution was ratified, he wrote an antislavery treatise; ultimately abolition would prove necessary for deepening the union into one of equally free and mobile citizens, although in the interim the issue spelled division. He died in the next year, on April 17, 1790.

Franklin's Albany Plan was the first to make union of the colonies a serious issue. He published a cartoon, "Join or Die," and later remarked, "We must all hang together or assuredly we shall all hang separately." With time, however, the meaning of the union changed. Initially it was to be a union within the British Empire, for the sake of strengthening it through a two-tiered structure with an American legislative council and an imperial parliament in London. Later, the idea became one of a union of the colonies for resistance to impositions from the British Parliament. In this form, the union came gradually into being.

As the dispute between the colonies and Britain deepened, Americans came to reject the idea of representation in the British Parliament. Franklin, after urging the idea upon the British, belatedly renounced it, leaving it to his old friend Joseph Galloway and those later spurned as Tories. In his mission to France, he worked long and ultimately successfully for an alliance against Britain—the reverse of his plan at Albany for a union against France. His ultimate peace treaty with England largely vitiated the French alliance; his final federalism was American and neutral.

Benjamin Franklin. National Portrait Gallery, Smithsonian Institution; Gift of the Morris and Gwendolyn Cafritz Foundation.

Franklin had a special relation to the Enlightenment. A self-made man born in 1706, he rose from a printer to become a writer, philosopher, inventor, scientist, and political leader. His discoveries on electricity made him famous throughout Europe; his embrace of Voltaire, during his mission to France, was a high point in Enlightenment symbolism.

The liberation of humans and their reconciling for cooperation were the two great themes of Franklin's political life, in this embodying with a unique directness the cause of the Enlightenment philosophies. Thus he focused his key projects on consolidating and expanding what he saw as the empire of freedom. He feared lest the fragile pottery of the British Empire would be cracked, and so it was. His hopes remained for the American half, in which he saw the greater future. Those hopes rested with the new union, itself also fragile.

George Washington remarked, in his first farewell address as commander in chief in 1783, that the United States' success or failure after independence would determine the fate and reputation of freedom for ages to come, and that its success depended on reinforcing the Union. Franklin shared the outlook. It was no longer a matter of union against an external enemy, but to make good on the internal promise of the United States. The hopes of the Enlightenment would rise or fall with this refined American federalism.

At the close of the Constitutional Convention, nearing the close of his life, Franklin said (as recorded by James Madison) that he had often wondered, in the course of the Convention "and the vicissitudes of my hopes and fears as to its issue," whether the Sun of America "was rising or setting: But now at length I have the happiness to know that it is a rising and not a setting Sun." His optimism strengthened, he wrote in October 1787 to a friend in Paris (Ferdinand Grand) that "[i]f (the Constitution) succeeds, I do not see why you might not in Europe carry good Henry the 4th the Project of into Execution, by forming a Federal Union and One Grand Republick." France's King Henry the Fourth envisioned a United Europe dubbed the "Grand Design." One hundred and sixty years later, Americans would pressure Europeans into beginning to do this with the Marshall Plan.

Franklin's cosmopolitanism survived a rough political life; in a letter of December 4, 1789, he wrote (to David Hartley), "God grant, that not only the Love of Liberty, but a thorough Knowledge of the Rights of Man, may pervade all the Nations of the Earth, so that a Philosopher may set his Foot anywhere on its Surface, and say, 'This is my Country.'" *SEE ALSO:* Albany Plan; Constitutional Convention of 1787; Continental Congress

IRA STRAUS

Fugitive Slave Acts   The Fugitive Slave Acts were passed in 1793 and 1850 as attempts to legislate the return of runaway slaves to southern slave owners. The first Fugitive Slave Act was passed by Congress in 1793. The law did not grow from southern anxiety over slaves escaping to the North; rather, it was born from the desire to clarify the rights of the fugitive slave and to determine the judicial process for the return of slaves. Southerners were disappointed with the 1793 law because it set up a system in which the slave owner petitioned the district judge of the state in which the slave was found for the slave's return. However, the law did little to protect the free black citizens of the North. As abolitionist sentiments grew in the North, the enforcement of the Fugitive Slave Law was much opposed by judges and citizens, which led to demands by southern congressmen and southern slaveholders for a stronger law. These Southerners argued that free states ignored their legislative duty to the slave states.

After many attempts to construct a bill with stricter requirements for the return of fugitive slaves, a new Senate bill was introduced in January 1850. The new bill allowed for a slave owner to approach any state official ranging from judge to postmaster to reclaim his slave with sufficient proof, and a federal marshal was able to issue the arrest warrant and could arrest the slave in the same manner as an owner. The new bill applied a $1,000 fine for those who harbored or assisted the fugitive slave. The bill elicited mixed responses from both Southerners and Northerners. Southerners believed that the bill did not extend their "property" rights enough, and Northerners protested that the bill did not provide protection for "free" African Americans residing in the North. In February, Henry Clay, a statesman from Kentucky, proposed the Compromise of 1850, which included this fugitive slave bill. The compromise passed with the new bill, which gave federal authorities power to reclaim slaves as well as provided slave owners with stronger legal power to have their slaves returned. This law, signed by President Millard Fillmore, was the most stringent measure passed regarding fugitive slaves, and it was the only benefit Southerners received from the Compromise. The final Fugitive Slave Act represented a contradiction to the pro–states' rights southern platform because the South accepted federal legislation that eliminated state initiatives to protect fugitive slaves. More importantly, the Fugitive Slave Act of 1850 resonated that fugitive slaves were not safe in the North any longer. *SEE ALSO:* Clay, Henry; Compromise of 1850; States' Rights

BIBLIOGRAPHY: Stanley W. Campbell, *The Slave Catchers: Enforcement of the Fugitive Slave Law, 1850–1860* (Chapel Hill: University of North Carolina Press, 1970); Paul Finkleman, ed., *Slavery and the Law* (Madison, WI: Madison House, 1997); and Glenn M. Linden, ed., *Voices from the Gathering Storm: The Coming of the American Civil War* (Wilmington, DE: Scholarly Resources, 2001).

KELLY J. BAKER

Fugitive Slave Provision: Article IV   Article IV, Section 2, Clause 3, the so-called Fugitive Slave Clause, provides, "No person held to Service or Labour in one state, under the Laws thereof, escaping into another, shall, in Consequence of any Law or Regulation therein, be discharged from such Service or Labour, but shall be delivered up on Claim of the Party to whom such Service or Labour may be due." This provision is one of the bundle of provisions inserted into the Constitution to protect the interests of the slaveholding states as a condition for their entering the new system. Although the clause itself does not specify who has the power or responsibility to "deliver up" escaped slaves, Congress very early passed a Fugitive Slave Act (1793). This law provided that an owner or "his agents or attorney" could apply to a federal judge in any state to which a slave had fled, and upon minimal proof of ownership be given a certificate to return the escapee to the state of servitude. The law also set penalties against those found guilty of aiding fugitive slaves in their efforts to escape. The law was controversial on two grounds at least: the question arose as to whether Congress possessed authority to enforce the Fugitive Slave Clause, and objections were raised about the lack of protection afforded to alleged escaped slaves. Many northern states responded with laws attempting to establish protection for free blacks and, even, to frustrate the reclaiming of fugitives. These actions in turn led to increased demands from the slaveholding states for better enforcement of the Fugitive Slave Clause. Part of the Compromise of 1850 was a new Fugitive Slave Act, providing special federal commissioners and other devices to make it easier for fugitive slaves to be recovered, and striking forcefully against the efforts by states or private individuals to protect free blacks or frustrate the recapture of fugitives. The law proved to be a source of great friction in the years leading up to the war. *SEE ALSO:* Fugitive Slave Acts; Fugitive Slaves and American Federalism

BIBLIOGRAPHY: Don E. Fehrenbacher, *The Slave Holding Republic* (New York: Oxford University Press, 2001).

MICHAEL ZUCKERT

Fugitive Slaves and American Federalism   From the Constitutional Convention of 1787 until the end of the Civil War, slavery undermined American federalism and challenged the very possibility of harmony within the federal union. The challenge to federalism came most directly when slaves were found in free states or free blacks were found in slave states. Slaves in free states could be considered in two categories: slaves in transit and fugitive slaves. The Constitutional Convention did not provide any direct protection for the right of masters to travel with their slaves in free states, and thus issues of slave transit were left entirely to state comity. By the end of the antebellum period, comity had more or less collapsed on this issue, as most northern states refused to allow masters the right to pass through their territory with slaves in transit, and most southern states refused to allow northern free blacks to enter their jurisdictions. Nor would southern states recognize the new status as free people that slaves might have acquired by visiting the North. This issue was constitutionally and legally significant, even though by the 1850s it involved relatively few slaves or free blacks. Few masters took their slaves north, and few northern blacks ventured south. Nevertheless, at the federal level the *Dred Scott v. Sandford* (1857) case made the issue central to the crisis of the Union. Similarly, a case from New York, *Lemmon v. the People* (1860), led to an enormous controversy between New York and Virginia over the right of masters to travel through free states with their slaves. Had the Civil War not started when it did, this case would likely have brought the issues of slavery, comity, and federalism directly before the U.S. Supreme Court.

Controversies over fugitive slaves drew much greater attention from the founding until the end of slavery. In the summer of 1787, the issue arose in both the Articles of Confederation Congress and the Constitutional Convention. In the Northwest Ordinance (1787), the Congress provided,

> There shall be neither slavery nor involuntary servitude in the said territory, otherwise than in the punishment of crimes, whereof the party shall have been duly convicted: provided always, that any person escaping into the same, from whom labour or service is lawfully claimed in any one of the original states, such fugitive may be lawfully reclaimed, and conveyed to the person claiming his or her labour or service as aforesaid.

This was the first fugitive slave provision in federal law. It had very little jurisprudential impact, because the Articles were soon superseded by the Constitution and the Fugitive Slave Clause of Article IV, Section 2, Paragraph 3, of the Constitution superseded the clause in the Northwest Ordinance. Nevertheless, the clause in the Ordinance of 1787 established two principles of federalism: first, that the na-

---

ARTICLE IV, SECTION 2, CLAUSE 3

No Person held to Service or Labour in one State, under the Laws thereof, escaping into another, shall, in Consequence of any Law or Regulation therein, be discharged from such Service or Labour, but shall be delivered up on Claim of the Party to whom such Service or Labour may be due.

---

tional government had some responsibility to protect the slave property of masters; and second, that free states should not be allowed to terminate the master-slave relationship if a slave escaped into a state where slavery was illegal. These principles were in direct conflict with the common law at the time of the Revolution, which held that slaves became free the moment they entered free jurisdictions, even if they did so by running away from their masters.

Near the end of the Constitutional Convention, Pierce Butler of South Carolina proposed what became the Fugitive Slave Clause. There was virtually no debate over the clause or how it was to be implemented, and the next day, without any recorded vote, the Convention adopted the clause. In its final version it provided,

> No person held to Service or Labour in one State, under the Laws thereof, escaping into another, shall, in Consequence of any Law or Regulation therein, be discharged from such Service or Labour, but shall be delivered up on Claim of the Party to whom such Service or Labour may be due.

In *Prigg v. Pennsylvania* (1842), Justice Joseph Story would later assert that this clause was essential to the creation of the Constitution. The historical record suggests otherwise. Rather, it was a last-minute addition to the Constitution that Northerners seemed to lack the energy to analyze or oppose. Thus, the demands of the South for protection of their special property carried the day, setting the stage for constant conflicts over federalism.

In 1793, Congress passed a statute to regulate the return of both fugitives from justice and fugitive slaves. The fugitive slave provision of the statute generated little controversy at the time, although given the wording of the constitutional clause and its location in Article IV, Section 2, of the Constitution, there was some doubt as to whether Congress had the power to pass this legislation. In *Jack v. Martin* (1835), New York's highest court held that the federal law was unconstitutional because Congress lacked the power to regulate the return of fugitive slaves. In the same case, the New York court remanded the fugitive slave, Jack, to his owner on the grounds that New York had a constitutional obligation to enforce the clause in the Constitution.

In the 1820s a number of states passed "personal liberty laws" that were designed to prevent the kidnapping of free blacks or the removal of them under the 1793 law. These laws provided greater procedural protections for alleged fugitive slaves. In *Prigg v. Pennsylvania* (1842), Justice Story, speaking for an 8–1 majority on the Supreme Court, held that all such laws were unconstitutional because they interfered with the absolute right of a master to recover a fugitive slave. The decision callously ignored the rights of free blacks, including at least one and possibly two free black children who had been illegally seized by Edward Prigg and taken from Pennsylvania to Maryland. In a nod toward federalism, Justice Story did say that the states were free to prohibit their officials from taking part in fugitive slave cases, although he emphatically declared that such a result would have violated the spirit of the Constitution. In the next two decades, a number of states did exactly that. In the Fugitive Slave Law of 1850, Congress responded to growing northern noncooperation by providing an elaborate system of federal enforcement of the constitutional provision. The law provided for the appointment of federal commissioners in every county to oversee the return of fugitive slaves and allowed these commissioners to call on federal marshals, the army, and "all good citizens" to enforce their rulings.

The 1850 law in effect negated any notion of federalism in the enforcement of the Constitution's Fugitive Slave Clause. Congress preempted the states and denied them any role in the implementation of the clause. This was the first time in the nation's history that the national government had a law enforcement role and presence at the local level. The results were decidedly mixed. Between 1850 and 1861, federal authorities returned about 370 slaves to their masters, but it is estimated that more than 10,000 slaves escaped to the North in that period and another 10,000 or so probably were already living in the North. At the same time, violent resistance to the law led to spectacular rescues in Boston, Massachusetts; Syracuse, New York; Wellington, Ohio; and Milwaukee, Wisconsin, while in Christiana, Pennsylvania, fugitive slaves fought a gun battle with a federal marshal and a slave catcher before killing the claimant and escaping. In a number of places, local officials indicted slave catchers, masters claiming fugitives, or even federal marshals. The Wisconsin Supreme Court declared the 1850 law unconstitutional, although the U.S. Supreme Court overturned this in *Ableman v. Booth* (1859). Opposition to the return of fugitive slaves led many northern politicians, including Governors William H. Seward of New York and Salmon P. Chase of Ohio, to take a strong states' rights position in their relationship to the federal government. Southerners, meanwhile, demanded a more activist federal government to protect their interests. This led to the ironic decision in *Kentucky v. Dennison* (1861). Two Ohio governors, Chase and William Dennison, refused to remand to Kentucky authorities a free black accused of "stealing" a slave, who he had helped escape to Ohio. A unanimous Supreme Court upheld the states' rights arguments of Governor Dennison, not because Chief Justice Roger Brooke Taney had any sympathy with the free black or the Ohio governors, but because to do otherwise would have given the Lincoln administration the legal power to coerce state governors to support the Constitution. By this time, 7 states had left the Union. Most of the seceding states cited the failure of the North to support the return of fugitive slaves as a reason for leaving the Union. Thus, in the end this provision designed to secure interstate cooperation instead undermined national harmony and federalism. *SEE ALSO: Dred Scott v. Sandford*; *Prigg v. Pennsylvania*

BIBLIOGRAPHY: Stanley Campbell, *The Slave Catchers* (Chapel Hill: University of North Carolina Press, 1968); Paul Finkelman, *An Imperfect Union: Slavery, Comity, and Federalism* (Chapel Hill: University of North Carolina Press, 1981); Paul Finkelman, *Slavery and the Founders: Race and Liberty in the Age of Jefferson*, 2nd ed. (Armonk, NY: M. E. Sharpe, 2001); Paul Finkelman, "Story Telling on the Supreme Court: *Prigg v. Pennsylvania* and Justice Joseph Story's Judicial Nationalism," *Supreme Court Review* 1994 (1995): 247–94; and Thomas D. Morris, *Free Men All: The Personal Liberty Laws of the North, 1780–1861* (Baltimore: Johns Hopkins University Press, 1974).

PAUL FINKELMAN

Full Faith and Credit Clause: Article IV, Section 1   Article IV, Section 1, of the Constitution provides, "Full Faith and Credit shall be given in each State to the public Acts, Records, and judicial Proceedings of every other State; And the Congress may by general Laws prescribe the Manner in which such Acts, Records and Proceedings shall be proved, and the Effect thereof." On its face, the Full Faith and Credit Clause affects the structure of American federalism and interstate relations in two fundamental ways. First, it requires each state within the union to give full faith and credit to the acts, records, and judicial proceedings of the other states. And second, it allows Congress to further effectuate the first clause by clarifying the manner in which out-of-state acts, records, and judicial proceedings are to be proven and the effect they are to be given.

The text of the clause suggests that states are obligated to give full effect to the official actions of other states. For example, if a person obtains a judgment of divorce in Nevada, the plain language of the Full Faith and Credit Clause seemingly requires all other states to recognize and effectuate the legal validity of this decree. But the practical reality is that while states regularly give legal effect to the acts, records, and judgments of other states when they are consistent with the policies and interests of the forum state, they retain substantial discretion to reject full faith and credit to these out-of-state actions when they conflict with the laws or public policy interests of the forum state.

THE ORIGINS OF THE CLAUSE

Many view English common law as the genesis for the Full Faith and Credit Clause, finding the terms "faith" and "credit" to be terms of art developed as part of the discourse between English common law (secular) and ecclesiastical (religious) courts. Court decisions from the end of the sixteenth century reveal that some common law courts gave "faith and credit" to the decisions of ecclesiastical courts and allowed the decisions of these courts to govern disputes under common law. In some cases, the phrase "faith and credit" was used alone, while in others the phrase was modified as "entire faith and credit," "full credit," or "full faith." Some scholars assert that when the modifier "full" or "entire" was used, the phrase meant that the judgment or records from another court would be not only admissible in the forum court but also conclusive as to the truth of the matter asserted.

Evidence suggests, however, that the complete phrase "full faith and credit" was not used until it was incorporated by the United States in the Articles of Confederation. On November 12, 1777, a clause reading, "That full faith and credit shall be given in each of these States to the Records, Acts, and Judicial Proceedings of the Court and Magistrates of every other State," was adopted by the Continental Congress and included in the Articles of Confederation. Records indicate that this provision was approved without any debate. And although the Articles generally afforded the states substantial autonomy and independence, the Full Faith and Credit Clause was one provision where the states were constitutionally obligated to provide some level of cooperation and deference to the official actions of other states.

There are five reported cases addressing the Full Faith and Credit Clause under the Articles of Confederation between 1786 and 1788. In two of these cases, the forum court gave conclusive effect to judgments rendered by out-of-state courts. In the other three cases, the forum court ruled that it was not obligated to give conclusive effect to the extraterritorial judgment, based either on a finding that the out-of-state court lacked jurisdiction to render its initial judgment or that the Full Faith and Credit Clause required only evidentiary consideration, not conclusive effect, to be given to the other state's judgment. Thus, from the inception of the clause, there was debate over its scope and substance. In fact, in addressing the clause as used in the Articles of Confederation, James Madison commented that its meaning was "extremely indeterminate" and of "little importance under any interpretation which it will bear."

Like many other provisions in the Articles of Confederation, the Full Faith and Credit Clause was readopted and included in the Constitution, taken from the last paragraph of Article IV of the Articles and placed in the first provision of Article IV of the Constitution. The members of the Constitutional Convention adopted the Articles' version of the Clause, but made two fundamental modifications. First, the framers extended the clause to include nonjudicial "public" acts because they believed that the acts of state legislatures sometimes served similar purposes to acts of courts. And second, they gave Congress the power to prescribe the manner in which acts, records, and judicial proceedings could be proved and the effect thereof. This second provision was proposed by James Madison, who felt that it was necessary given the "nature of the Union." Others, including Edmund Randolph of Virginia, disagreed with Madison's proposal, claiming that it would allow Congress to impose future limitations on the power of the states, particularly with respect to their ability to consider the effect of out-of-state judgments.

As ratified in 1789, the literal language of the Full Faith and Credit Clause provides for a more hierarchical model of federalism. The first provision requires states to extend full faith and credit to the acts, records, and judicial proceedings of other states, thereby imposing a uniform standard on the states regarding the treatment of official actions of other states. And the second provision gives Congress the authority to further effectuate the manner in which states must receive and treat out-of-state acts, records, and judgments. Both of these provisions reflect a blueprint for hierarchy in federal-state relations, whereby the states are required to abide by a uniform limitation on their sovereignty in interstate legal disputes and the federal government reigns supreme when it comes to further regulation of this area of interstate relations.

THE MEANING OF FULL FAITH AND CREDIT

The Full Faith and Credit Clause, as with most other constitutional provisions, has been the subject of conflicting interpretations, and despite the seemingly clear language of the clause, there appears to be very little consensus regarding the scope and meaning of the text. Constitutional scholars and legal advocates have reviewed the records from English courts, the Continental Congress, and the Constitutional Convention in an effort to understand the original intent of the provision, but this has resulted in conflicting interpretations. These interpretations can be grouped into two general theories—compact theory and national theory.

Compact theory maintains that the Full Faith and Credit Clause was written with the intent of placing few restrictions on states in their consideration of extraterritorial acts, records, and proceedings. Despite the mandatory-sounding language of the clause, compact theorists claim that the words cannot be taken literally, but instead must be read within the historical context and logical intent of the framers. Viewed in this light, compact theory holds that the clause was never intended to remove the states' discretion in deciding which law—their own or another state's—to apply to legal disputes within their own borders. Under this theory, the clause requires states only to admit the relevant acts, records, and judicial proceedings of other states into the evidentiary record of a given legal dispute, and to consider such evidence along with other forms of evidence presented. Compact theorists claim that English common law, the debates among the constitutional framers, and judicial interpretations all suggest that the clause was designed to require only evidentiary consideration of other states' official actions, and not for making extraterritorial acts, records, and judicial proceedings conclusions of law.

National theorists, on the other hand, promote a more literal interpretation of the clause. Under this theory, the clause was designed to form one union out of several independent states by providing a clear national command regarding the manner in which states must interact with each other in interstate legal disputes. National theorists claim that, in most situations, the Full Faith and Credit Clause not only requires states to admit the acts, records, and judgments of other states into evidence, but also requires states to afford these official actions full legal effect as well.

CONGRESSIONAL AND JUDICIAL CONSIDERATION OF THE CLAUSE

Following the ratification of the Constitution, the First Congress did not waste any time exercising its power under the Full Faith and Credit Clause. On February 1, 1790, Congress passed legislation detailing the procedure for authenticating records and judicial proceedings and declaring that, properly authenticated, these records and proceedings would have the same "faith and credit" given to them in every court within the United States, as they have in their originating court. Congress, however, did not include "public acts" in the effects clause of this legislation, and for a considerable time this led to controversy as to whether out-of-state legislative acts were to be afforded full faith and credit. Ultimately, Congress resolved this conflict in 1948 when it amended the 1790 statute to include "acts" in the effects provision ("1948 Act"). Accordingly, under 28 U.S. Code, Section 1738, "Acts, records and judicial proceedings shall have the same full faith and credit in every court within the United States and its Territories and Possessions as they have by law or usage in the courts of such State, Territory, or Possession from which they are taken."

Other examples of congressional action under Article IV include the 1980 Parental Kidnapping Prevention Act, which requires each state to enforce child custody determinations made by other states; the 1994 Full Faith and Credit for Child Support Orders Act, which requires states to enforce child support orders made by the child's home state; and the 1996 Defense of Marriage Act, which provides an exemption to states under the Full Faith and Credit Clause allowing them to refuse recognition to same-sex marriages solemnized in other states.

ARTICLE IV, SECTION 1

Full Faith and Credit shall be given in each State to the public Acts, Records, and judicial Proceedings of every other State. And the Congress may by general Laws prescribe the Manner in which such Acts, Records and Proceedings shall be proved, and the Effect thereof.

But despite this legislation, Congress has remained silent on many other areas of law potentially affected by the Full Faith and Credit Clause. More critically, both state and federal courts have regarded the literal language of the Full Faith and Credit Clause and the 1948 Act to be unmanageable and their resulting effects to be "absurd."

With regard to "public acts," the U.S. Supreme Court ruled in *Alaska Packers Association v. Industrial Accident Commission* (1935) that "a rigid and literal enforcement of the full faith and credit clause [for acts] . . . would lead to the absurd result that, whenever a conflict arises, the statute of each state must be enforced in the courts of the other, but cannot in its own." Given the potential for such illogical results, state courts have not strictly abided by the literal mandates of the Full Faith and Credit Clause or the 1948 Act in cases where a conflict exists between the law of the forum state and that of another state. Instead, states have independently developed elaborate and extraconstitutional rules for resolving interstate conflicts of law. These rules, known as conflict-of-law or choice-of-law rules, vary from state to state, and may be applied differently depending on the nature of the legal dispute (tort law, domestic relations, insurance law, etc.). But overall, these rules are a series of doctrines and laws adopted individually by the states that have largely displaced the Full Faith and Credit Clause and the 1948 Act as the governing principles for many interstate conflicts regarding "public acts."

A similar development occurred with respect to the interstate treatment of records and judgments, as states have applied a less-than-literal application of the clause and the 1948 Act to these extraterritorial actions as well. Instead, under modern theories of full faith and credit, the forum state's public policy interests have become a central factor for determining whether an out-of-state act, record, or judgment will be effectuated. And in cases where the forum state finds that the recognition of an out-of-state record or judgment, such as a marriage certificate or divorce decree, would violate the forum state's public policy, courts have denied full faith and credit to these records and proceedings. This approach to full faith and credit generally has been reinforced by federal courts. As Supreme Court Justice Stanley Reed concluded in *Griffin v. McCoach* (1941), "A state is not required to enforce a law obnoxious to its policy."

This so-called public policy exception to the Full Faith and Credit Clause is not unique to interstate relations in the United States, but was a legal doctrine originally developed in private international law, a body of law dealing with the rights and obligations of individuals in international transactions. Within this area of law, countries are permitted to refuse recognition to the official actions or decrees of another country in private disputes where the extraterritorial action or decree runs afoul of the forum country's policy interests.

THE PRACTICAL EFFECT OF FULL FAITH AND CREDIT

The frequent disregard for and inexact application of the Full Faith and Credit Clause has led some legal scholars to suggest that, in conflict-of-law disputes, the Full Faith and Credit Clause applies only when there is a "compelling need" to use it. As a result, states have enjoyed a considerable amount of discretion in deciding whether to enforce the official action of another state, under a strict interpretation and application of the Full Faith and Credit Clause, or whether to deny full faith and credit because the forum state's interests are better served by applying its own law or public policy. This reality has led some scholars to observe that the Full Faith and Credit Clause means "almost nothing" and that state courts can easily avoid what little it does mean.

In the end, the general disregard for the Full Faith and Credit Clause has resulted in a model of federalism that is far less hierarchical in nature than the text of Article IV would suggest. And those concerned with the expansion of federal authority over the states, which has occurred under the Necessary and Proper, Supremacy, and Commerce Clauses, find an inverted flow of authority under the Full Faith and Credit Clause, where state sovereignty has in most cases reigned supreme. *SEE ALSO:* Citizenship

BIBLIOGRAPHY: Lea Brilmayer, *Conflict of Laws: Foundations and Future Directions* (Boston: Little, Brown, 1991); Robert H. Jackson, *Full Faith and Credit: The Lawyer's Clause of the Constitution* (New York: Columbia University Press, 1945); Douglas Laycock, "Equal Citizens of Equal and Territorial States: The Constitutional Foundations of Choice of Law," *Columbia Law Review* 92 (1992): 249–337; and Russell J. Weintraub, "Who's Afraid of Constitutional Limitations on Choice of Law?" *Hofstra Law Review* 10 (1981): 17.

JOHN P. FELDMEIER

Fundamental Orders of Connecticut   The Fundamental Orders of Connecticut was the first written constitution in the American colonies. In 1639, the three towns that comprised the Connecticut colony, Hartford, Windsor, and Wethersfield, formed a common government based on the federal principle. The form of government provided the basis for the expansion of the colony and eventually became the framework for Connecticut's first state constitution, adopted in 1776 and lasting until 1818.

The Fundamental Orders is a constitution in the sense that it created a new people, laid out the political values of this people, established a new government, and defined its political institutions. The Fundamental Orders created a General Court that was composed of the three branches of government, a governor (the executive); twelve deputies—four from each town (the legislature); and six magistrates (the judiciary). The form was parliamentary in nature, empowering the deputies to elect the governor and the magistrates.

As noted, the Fundamental Orders embodied the federal principle. The towns maintained their own form of government and conducted elections for colonial deputies, who were initially apportioned on the basis of each town rather than by population. Thus, the towns (or constituent units) provided the basis for representation. The powers of the colonial government were specified in Article X (a precursor to the enumerated powers found in the U.S. Constitution). These powers included the ability to levy taxes, make laws for the common good, settle land disputes, and punish crimes. Article X also included a supremacy clause. Finally, the Orders provided for expansion, allowing new towns to be added to the compact.

Some other notable features of the Fundamental Orders include term limits for the governor, who was prohibited from serving two consecutive terms. More significantly, the government established was based on the principle of popular sovereignty, a concept not present in English common law, nor one that had yet been articulated in Liberal political theory. *SEE ALSO:* Articles of Confederation; State Constitutions; U.S. Constitution

BIBLIOGRAPHY: Perry Miller, *Errand in the Wilderness* (Cambridge, MA: Harvard University Press, 1956); and Stephen L. Schechter, *Roots of the Republic: American Founding Documents Interpreted* (Madison, WI: Madison House, 1990).

JOSEPH R. MARBACH

Furman v. Georgia   The Supreme Court has never held that the death penalty, per se, is a violation of the Eighth Amendment's prohibition against cruel and unusual punishment. However, in *Furman v. Georgia* (1972), the Court found that Georgia's death penalty statute was defective because it allowed juries too much discretion in deciding who would receive the death penalty, leading to arbitrary and discriminatory sentencing patterns. In particular the Court was troubled by statistics demonstrating that African Americans were more likely than whites to receive the death penalty for similar types of crimes.

The Court was not unified in its reasoning (nine different opinions were issued in this case). Two justices argued that "evolving standards of decency" had reached the point to where the death penalty was no longer acceptable under any circumstances. The other three justices who constituted the five-member majority were concerned about due process and equal protection violations present in the statutes, but rejected the argument that the death penalty could never be permitted under the Constitution. The dissenters argued that the courts should defer to popular opinion and legislative prerogatives in sentencing decisions, noting that public opinion and a majority of state legislatures favored use of the death penalty. They also argued that the Court had failed to follow precedent.

The ruling in *Furman* effectively ended executions for a number of years. However, most states redrafted their death penalty statutes in an effort to bring them into compliance with *Furman*. Several of these statutes were challenged in the *Death Penalty Cases* of 1976 (see *Gregg v. Georgia* in this volume). The Court approved a number of these statutes, and use of the death penalty resumed. *SEE ALSO:* Capital Punishment; *Gregg v. Georgia*

BIBLIOGRAPHY: Robert M. Bohm, *The Death Penalty in America* (Cincinnati, OH: Anderson Publishing Company, 1991); and Bryan Vila and Cynthia Morris, eds., *Capital Punishment in the United States: A Documentary History* (Westport, CT: Greenwood Press, 1997).

MICHAEL ESLER

G

Garcia v. San Antonio Metropolitan Transit Authority   While the Tenth Amendment provides states, or the people, reserved powers not delegated to the federal government by the Constitution or prohibited by it to the states, the courts have shifted in the interpretation of this amendment over time, sometimes moving toward a strict constructionist view and protecting states' rights and at other times taking an expansive view of federal powers. However, these shifting interpretations are usually incremental and historically disparate. In *Garcia v. San Antonio Metropolitan Transit Authority* (1985), the Supreme Court made a strong redirection on federalism in interpreting the Tenth Amendment.

In a 5–4 vote in *Garcia*, the U.S. Supreme Court overruled its decision in *National League of Cities v. Usery* (1976), which had said that the individual states were not subject to wage and hour protections under the Fair Labor Standards Act as applied "in areas of traditional governmental functions." The *Garcia* Court, however, found that defining "traditional governmental functions" was a major task for the various courts. As such, it found *National League* an unworkable standard and rejected this balancing approach of determining whether an issue being regulated by Congress affected an individual state's traditional governmental functions.

In replacing the balancing approach, the *Garcia* Court determined that individual states were protected from inappropriate federal regulations against the states by their participation in the federal political process. In other words, each state has elected U.S. senators and representatives who are expected to protect the state's interests and rights. Justice Harry Blackmun wrote for the majority that these "political safeguards," and particularly that of the states' representation in the Senate, were sufficient constitutional safeguards of states' rights. It was therefore presumed by the majority that the legislative process will work properly and therefore the courts will give great deference to the actions of Congress when it is a matter of regulating both states and private entities.

The dissent in *Garcia* argued that despite the claim of the majority opinion that this ruling secured the concept of federalism, the reality was that the Tenth Amendment was effectively reduced to "meaningless rhetoric" as to issues involving the Commerce Clause. Justice Sandra Day O'Connor in dissent remarked that "the Court today surveys the battle scene of federalism, and sounds a retreat." Federalism scholar Thomas Anton remarked, "Important and thoughtful as the *Garcia* ruling may be, we should not imagine that it signifies the end to the debate [over federalism]" (Anton 1989, 16).

And John Kincaid accused the Court of abandoning "the field, abdicating its role as umpire of the federal system" (Kincaid 1993, 172). Indeed, the prediction of Justice William Rehnquist in his dissent that *Garcia* would not hold and that the respect for state sovereignty expressed in *National League* would again "in time command a majority of this Court" (*Garcia v. San Antonio Metropolitan Transit Authority* 469 U.S. 528 [1985]). was soon to be fulfilled in the enduring federalism debate. *SEE ALSO: National League of Cities v. Usery*; Tenth Amendment

BIBLIOGRAPHY: Thomas Anton, *American Federalism and Public Policy* (Philadelphia: Temple University Press, 1989); Mark R. Killenbeck, *The Tenth Amendment and State Sovereignty: Constitutional History and Contemporary Issues* (Lanham, MD: Rowman & Littlefield, 2002); John Kincaid, "Constitutional Federalisms Labor's Role in Displacing Places to Benefit Persons," *P.S. Political Science and Politics* 26, no. 2 (June 1993): 172; and Tinsley E. Yarbrough, *The Rehnquist Court and the Constitution* (New York: Oxford University Press, 2000).

J. GREGORY FRYE AND MICHAEL W. HAIL

Gender and Federalism   A federal system of government is defined as a system in which power is shared by national and constituent governments. Because the Constitution of the United States enumerates certain powers to the federal government and reserves the others to the states, policy in many areas such as abortion, education, crime and capital punishment, and domestic violence may vary greatly from state to state. Decentralization of decision making into fifty state court systems, fifty state legislatures, and fifty sets of state bureaucracy means that men and women may be treated more equally in some states than in others. This was especially true prior to the adoption of the Civil Rights Act of 1964 and other legislation as well as court decisions extending protection against sex discrimination under the Fourteenth Amendment.

The Equal Protection Clause of the Fourteenth Amendment enacted after the Civil War forbade state governments from arbitrarily treating individuals differently from one another under the law. However, the U.S. Supreme Court did not interpret the clause to protect against sex discrimination until 1971. The Supreme Court overturned a state law as a violation of the Equal Protection Clause in a sex discrimination case for the first time in *Reed v. Reed* (1971). Further protection against sex discrimination was achieved in *Craig v. Boren* (1976), a case in which the Supreme Court overturned an Oklahoma law requiring males to be older than females to purchase beer as a violation of equal protection. In the *Reed* case, the Court used the same standard it uses in scrutinizing laws that do not classify based on sex or race; the court used an increased standard in *Craig v. Boren* known as "intermediate scrutiny" for the first time. The standard makes it more difficult for a law making a gender distinction to be upheld than other laws. The Court however, did not apply the "strict scrutiny" standard, which it uses in race cases, as the National Organization for Women (NOW) and other women's groups had hoped.

One gender issue that is greatly affected by the federal system in the United States is abortion. This issue has dominated the American political scene ever since the U.S. Supreme Court decision in *Roe v. Wade* (1973). While pro-life supporters immediately began to work for a reversal of the policy at the national level, they also understood the importance for state legislatures in a federal system and began to work for state regulations on abortion. The U.S. Supreme Court strictly limited regulations in the first trimester prior to 1989. In *Webster v. Reproductive Health Services* (1989), the Court upheld a Missouri law that prohibited the use of any public facilities or public employees to perform abortions; it also required physicians to perform fetal viability testing before performing an abortion on a fetus of over twenty weeks. Again, in 1992 in *Planned Parenthood of Southeastern Pennsylvania v. Casey*, the Court upheld restrictions that had previously been rejected by the Court. The restrictions included a twenty-four-hour waiting period, informed consent, and parental consent with a judicial bypass procedure. In the years since the *Casey* ruling, many states have adopted similar restrictions. Other states, such as Maryland and New York, have few restrictions. States in the Midwest and the South generally have more restrictions than states in the Northeast. This reflects the different cultural and religious values in different regions.

Family law is very much influenced by the federal system under which we live in the United States. The U.S. Supreme Court ruled in *United States v. Morrison* in 2000 that the 1994 Domestic Violence Act was an unconstitutional infringement on the right of states to make policy in this area through the political process. The Court has long regarded family law and criminal law as areas of state policy making. Proponents of the legislation argued that the issue was one of women's rights, which are guaranteed by the federal government. But by classifying the legislation as family and criminal law, the Court has deemed this issue one that the states are free to regulate as they see fit. This means that some states will provide much more protection against domestic violence than others, depending upon the climate in the state and its history in terms of gender roles.

While women's rights under the law are protected under federal law and through federal court decisions, in areas such as family law, criminal law, and some aspects of abortion law, states can greatly influence women's lives in ways that vary greatly from state to state based on the dominant cultural and religious values of the region. *SEE ALSO:* Equal Rights Amendment; Women's Rights

> *BIBLIOGRAPHY:* Judith Resnik, "Categorical Federalism: Jurisdiction, Gender, and the Globe," *Yale Law Journal* 3 (December 2001): 619–80; and Jean Reith Schroedel, *Is the Fetus a Person? A Comparison of Policies across the Fifty States* (Ithaca, NY: Cornell University Press, 2000).

MAUREEN RAND OAKLEY

General Revenue Sharing   *See* Revenue Sharing

Gibbons v. Ogden   *Gibbons v. Ogden* (1824) gave Chief Justice John Marshall his first opportunity to expound his broad interpretation of the Commerce Clause. The complicated legal proceedings that sparked the case began in 1798, when Chancellor Robert R. Livingston obtained a monopoly grant over steam travel in state waters from the New York State Legislature. While negotiating the Louisiana Purchase in Paris, France, in 1802, Livingston formed a partnership with inventor, scientist, and artist Robert Fulton. On August 17, 1807, Fulton and Livingston successfully piloted their *North River Steam Boat* from New York City to Albany.

Fulton and Livingston's steamboat company prospered under the generous terms of the New York monopoly. Their success, however, brought public demands for cheaper steam travel and competition from rival steamboat operators. In 1814 former New Jersey Governor Aaron Ogden established a steamboat service from Elizabethtown, New Jersey, to New York City. After protracted litigation, Ogden bought a license from the Fulton-Livingston cartel in 1815.

In 1816 Ogden began a partnership with Thomas Gibbons, a wealthy Georgia businessman. After frequent squabbling, Ogden sued Gibbons in New York Chancery Court in 1818 for running an independent line of steamboats from New Jersey to New York City. In court, Gibbons produced a license granted under the Federal Coastal Licensing Act of 1793. Gibbons claimed that this permit conveyed navigation rights to the waters of any east coast state. When New York State Chancellor James Kent upheld Ogden's monopoly rights, Gibbons appealed his case to the U.S. Supreme Court.

Following a lengthy postponement, the Supreme Court finally heard arguments for *Gibbons v. Ogden* on February 4, 1824. Massachusetts Senator Daniel Webster and U.S. Attorney General William Wirt served as counsel for Gibbons. They argued that their client's coastal license rested on the Commerce Clause of the U.S. Constitution and therefore invalidated the New York steamboat monopoly. Speaking for Ogden, former New York State Attorneys General Thomas Addis Emmet and Thomas Oakley responded that New York State retained concurrent jurisdiction over commerce within its borders. The New York monopoly did not directly interfere with the federal law and therefore remained legal.

In a unanimous ruling by the Supreme Court, Chief Justice John Marshall on March 2, 1824, broadly defined interstate commerce as any form of trade conducted across state borders and maintained that the U.S. Constitution's Commerce Clause gave Congress final authority over such matters. The New York steamboat monopoly was therefore unconstitutional. Yet Marshall narrowly maintained that Gibbon's federal license trumped Ogden's state-based grant. Associate Justice William Johnson produced a concurring opinion, declaring that the authority of the Commerce Clause alone was enough to defeat the steamboat monopoly.

According to Marshall's broad view of federal authority, the commerce power "may be exercised to its utmost extent, and acknowledges no limitations." In the short run, *Gibbons v. Ogden* promoted steam travel and contributed to the rise of a national market economy. Since Marshall declined to provide specific guidelines for interstate commerce regulation in his decision, however, the Supreme Court continued to grapple with the issue. For instance, the Marshall Court upheld congressional commerce powers in *Brown v. Maryland* (1827) but reduced such authority in *Willson v. Blackbird Marsh Creek Co.* (1829). In the mid-1800s, the Taney Court used *Gibbons v. Ogden* to support state-based commercial regulation in *New York v. Miln* (1837), the *License Cases* (1847), and *Cooley v. Board of Wardens* (1852). During the Gilded Age and Progressive era, the Supreme Court cited *Gibbons v. Ogden* to augment federal commerce powers in *Wabash Railway v. Illinois* (1886) and *Swift v. United States* (1905).

In the 1930s, Supreme Court decisions such as *Schechter Poultry Corporation v. United States* (1935) and *Butler v. United States* (1936) struck down New Deal programs created by Congress under the authority of the Commerce Clause. Following President Franklin D. Roosevelt's 1937 attempted court-packing plan, Supreme Court decisions over the next half century beginning with *National Labor Relations Board v. Jones and Laughlin Steel Corporation* (1937) often accepted a broad interpretation of the Commerce Clause. As such, the *Gibbons* decision became a precedent for cases involving antisegregation laws in *Heart of Atlanta Motel, Inc. v. United States* (1964).

Yet in *United States v. Lopez* (1995) and *United States v. Morrison* (2000), the Supreme Court began providing stricter guidelines for Congress in using the Commerce Clause as a basis for federal laws in areas such as gun control and civil suit remedies for rape victims. *SEE ALSO:* Commerce among the States; Marshall, John

BIBLIOGRAPHY: Maurice G. Baxter, *The Steamboat Monopoly: Gibbons v. Ogden, 1824* (New York: Alfred A. Knopf, 1972); George Dangerfield, "The Steamboat Case," in *Quarrels That Have Shaped the Constitution*, ed. John A Garraty, 49–61 (New York: Harper and Row, 1962); R. Kent Newmyer, *John Marshall and the Heroic Age of the Supreme Court* (Baton Rouge: Louisiana State University Press, 2001); and G. Edward White, *The Marshall Court and Cultural Change, 1815–1835* (New York: MacMillan Publishing, 1988).

THOMAS H. COX

Gideon v. Wainwright   *See* Incorporation (Nationalization) of the Bill of Rights

Gitlow v. New York   *See* Incorporation (Nationalization) of the Bill of Rights

Governors and Federalism   Each American state selects its governor, the state's chief executive official, through a popular election. In the early twentieth century, most governors served two-year terms. Today, only the governors of New Hampshire and Vermont serve two-year terms; the rest serve four-year terms. This change represents a trend of the twentieth century to give governors greater authority, independence, and power. These reforms have given governors greater opportunities to participate in and influence federal issues. At first reluctant to participate in national policy issues, governors have increasingly become important players in shaping, implementing, and reforming national policies. This essay examines the rise of governors' powers, what they seek, and how reforms in the governor's office have affected their ability to influence the federal system.

Governors are elected by and serve the same citizens and population as U.S. senators. For more than a century, this was understood to represent a division of responsibilities in the federal system with the senators representing a state's interests in the federal government and the governors addressing the intrastate issues. Many people, and some governors, continue to believe in this strict separation of responsibilities. As the chief executive official bearing responsibility for the state government, however, most governors recognize that senators do not always promote what the governor thinks are the state's best interests. Former Utah Governor Scott Matheson declared, "Because most senators and members of Congress lack sufficient knowledge about the activities of the executive branch of the federal government in Washington, they cannot be relied on to protect the states' interests" (Matheson 1991, 26). Matheson was one of several governors who successfully pushed governors to become more aggressive in promoting state interests in Washington.

This shift was slow in coming. The nation's governors first met in 1908 at the behest of then-President Theodore Roosevelt (some reports suggest that President Roosevelt was trying to persuade the governors to lobby their senators to support his conservation bill, which had stalled in Congress). In 1912, the governors met again and formed the Governors' Conference (GC). While some governors wanted the GC to push the states' collective interests in national policies, New Jersey Governor Woodrow Wilson convinced the governors to use the GC to promote state-specific issues such as administration, budgeting, and uniformity of laws. It was not until the late 1930s, and largely in response to New Deal programs, that the governors began to concern themselves with federal issues. That ended with World War II, when the governors agreed to "cooperate in every possible way" to preserve freedom. By the end of the Great Depression and World War II, considerable power had been centralized in the national government and wresting it back to the states would prove very difficult.

The shift of power to the national government was accomplished, in part, because, for much of the first half of the twentieth century, states were popularly viewed as inefficient at best and horribly corrupt at worst. Governors were referred to as Goodtime Charlies—more interested in appearing in the newspaper's social pages than leading government. When President Dwight D. Eisenhower tried to return some minor responsibilities to the states, Congress failed to approve the reforms due partially to lack of state support. Those governors who tried to improve their state governments were often hampered by a lack of power that stemmed from a colonial distrust of executive power and by progressive reforms that disbursed executive power to separately elected or independently appointed officials and administrators.

As the federal government became more involved in the domestic affairs of states and individuals, governors saw the need for an organization to represent their interests before the institutions of power in Washington, D.C. The GC was the natural institution to adopt this role. In 1966, meeting at an unprecedented interim meeting, the governors voted to fund an office for federal-state relations in Washington. The office was established the next year, and the name of the GC was changed to the National Governors' Conference (NGC). The NGC accepted the role of representing the governors' interests before the federal government. Often these interests were to either increase federal funding or insure that federal funding passed through states rather than going directly to individuals or local governments. The NGC changed its name in 1977 to the National Governors' Association (NGA) as the governors worked to increase their presence in Washington and to disseminate information on good state practices, innovations, and trends (Weissert 1983).

The governors' powers to direct state government and represent it in the federal system were enhanced when states reformed their constitutions and executive branches in the 1960s, 1970s, and 1980s. These reforms enhanced the institutional powers of governors. The most important of these reforms included the following: longer terms of office, greater control over the executive branch, powers to shape the budget, and stronger veto powers to improve negotiations with legislators. In the 1960s, Joseph Schlesinger developed an index of governors' institutional powers, which has been updated by Thad Beyle (1994). That index explains the more important institutional powers of governors and shows how governors' powers have increased since the 1960s (see Table 5). Due in large part to these reforms, the governors' increased powers have attracted people to the office who were different from the Goodtime Charlies of the previous generation. The new generation of governors is energetic, bright, active, and reform oriented.

Gubernatorial power and authority also grew as a result of the federal government's expansion of powers and authority. Federal grants often required states to create an administrative agency to oversee the implementation, distribution, and enforcement of the

TABLE 5. Governors' Institutional Powers, 1960 versus 2005

Specific Power	Scores		% Change
	1960	2005	
SEP	2.3	2.9	+28
TP	3.2	4.1	+28
AP	2.9	3.1	+7
BP	3.6	3.1	−14
VP	2.8	4.5	+61
PC	3.6	3.0	−17
Total	18.4	20.7	+12.5

NOTES:

SEP—Separately elected executive branch officials: 5 = only governor or governor/lieutenant governor team elected; 4.5 = governor or governor/lieutenant governor team, with one other elected official; 4 = governor/lieutenant governor team with some process officials (attorney general, secretary of state, treasurer, and auditor) elected; 3 = governor/lieutenant governor team with process officials, and some major and minor policy officials elected; 2.5 = governor (no team) with six or fewer officials elected, but none are major policy officials; 2 = governor (no team) with six or fewer officials elected, including one major policy official; 1.5 = governor (no team) with six or fewer officials elected, but two are major policy officials; and 1 = governor (no team) with seven or more process and several major policy officials elected. *Source*: Council of State Governments, *The Book of the States, 1960–1961* (Lexington, KY: CSG, 1960), 124–25; and Council of State Governments, *The Book of the States, 2004* (Lexington, KY: CSG, 2004), 175–80.

TP—Tenure potential of governors: 5 = four-year term, no restraint on reelection; 4.5 = four-year term, only three terms permitted; 4 = four-year term, only two terms permitted; 3 = four-year term, no consecutive election permitted; 2 = two-year term, no restraint on reelection; and 1 = two-year term, only two terms permitted. *Source*: Joseph A. Schlesinger, "The Politics of the Executive," in *Politics in the American States*, ed. Herbert Jacob and Kenneth N. Vines (Boston: Little, Brown, 1965); and Council of State Governments (2004), 157–58.

AP—Governor's appointment powers in six major functional areas: corrections, K–12 education, health, highways/transportation, public utilities regulation, and welfare. The six individual office scores are totaled and then averaged and rounded to the nearest .5 for the state score. 5 = governor appoints, no other approval needed; 4 = governor appoints, a board, council, or legislature approves; 3 = someone else appoints, governor approves or shares appointment; 2 = someone else appoints, governor and others approve; and 1 = someone else appoints, no approval or confirmation needed. *Source*: Schlesinger (1965); and Council of State Governments (2004), 175–80.

BP—Governor's budget power: 5 = governor has full responsibility, legislature may not increase executive budget; 4 = governor has full responsibility, legislature can increase by special majority vote or subject to item veto; 3 = governor has full responsibility, legislature has unlimited power to change executive budget; 2 = governor shares responsibility, legislature has unlimited power to change executive budget; and 1 = governor shares responsibility with other elected official, legislature has unlimited power to change executive budget. *Source*: Schlesinger (1965); Council of State Governments (2004), 162–63, 392–93; and National Conference of State Legislatures, "Limits on Authority of Legislature to Change Budget" (Denver: National Conference of State Legislatures, 1998).

TABLE 5 (continued)

VP—Governor's veto power: 5 = has item veto and a special majority vote of the legislature is needed to override a veto; 4 = has item veto with a majority of the legislators elected needed to override; 3 = has item veto with only a majority of the legislators present needed to override; 2 = no item veto, with a special legislative majority needed to override it; and 1 = no item veto, only a simple legislative majority needed to override. *Source*: Schlesinger (1965); and Council of State Governments, (2004), 113–15, 162–63.

PC—Gubernatorial party control: 5 = has a substantial majority (75 percent or more) in both houses of the legislature; 4 = has a simple majority in both houses (less than 75 percent), or a substantial majority in one house and a simple majority in the other; 3 = split party control in the legislature or a nonpartisan legislature; 2 = has a substantial minority in both houses (25 percent or more), or a simple minority (25 percent or less) in one and a substantial minority in the other; and 1 = has a simple minority in both houses. *Source*: http://www.ncsl.org/programs/legman/elect/elect.htm.

Total—sum of the scores on the six individual indices. Score—total divided by six to keep five-point scale.

Source: Thad Beyle, "Governors," in *The Book of the States 2005* (Lexington, KY: Council of State Governments, 2005).

grant. Consequently, federal action channeled through the states increased the states' reach and services, and specifically increased the governors' power and authority, because the new agencies fell under the executive's authority. State governments were also forced to adapt to a changing economy, environmental issues, and growing public demand for less taxes and more public services. Because the nature of the executive office allows governors to adapt much quicker than the legislative branch, these changes and developments provided opportunities for thoughtful and active governors.

For example, the budget crises of the 1980s gave the governors the opportunity to stand as the head of their governments, accept greater policy responsibilities, and push for innovative policy reforms. The severe budget crises faced by the states in the 1980s resulted from many factors. First, an economic recession reduced government revenues. Second, as a result of popular antitax movements, newly adopted constitutional amendments restricted many states' authority to raise taxes. Third, the federal government, under President Ronald Reagan's direction, reduced federal funding for some social programs. Finally, rapidly rising health care costs drew enormous funds from state budgets in the form of Medicaid payments. In response, some governors successfully pushed for reforms and innovative policies to balance their budgets and provide necessary public services.

While states adopted many innovative reforms, they were prevented from reforming some policy areas due to federal mandates, preemptions, and grant program restrictions and regulations. The most energetic and creative governors chafed under the restrictions imposed on the states by the national government. After some lobbying, Congress allowed states limited "waivers" from federal social regulations in order to experiment with innovative practices. A number of governors took advantage of these waivers to create limited but innovative alternatives to welfare and Medicaid programs. States also experimented in other policy areas including banking, telecommunications, electric deregulation, and insurance reforms. Crafting and implementing these creative programs gave the governors unique policy expertise that they later used to influence federal policies.

Governors saw their power in the federal system grow significantly in 1995 after the Republican Party won a majority of seats in Congress. Congressional Republicans expected to win big in the 1994 election, but they did not expect to become the majority party. After the Republicans won control of Congress, they were forced to shift from proposing policies that would embarrass the ruling Democratic Party to approving policies that would actually govern the nation. Out of power for more than forty years, the Republicans in Congress lacked the policy expertise to craft good policy. Republican congressional leaders turned to Republican governors to help them design significant reforms to the welfare and Medicaid systems, experience that the governors had as a result of using federal waivers to reform those programs in their states. In response, Democrats in Congress turned to Democratic governors for assistance in understanding and countering the Republicans reform efforts. While this created partisan tension among the governors, they were able to overcome it and work collectively to promote a welfare reform proposal that significantly influenced the final bill that was signed into law in 1996. In many policy areas, leaders of Congress sought governors' policy expertise to help craft legislation.

Governors have many means to access and try to influence federal officials. The most common is working collaboratively through governors' associations such as the NGA or the partisan or regional governors' associations. The governors' associations' most powerful lobbying asset is the governors themselves. As the chief executive of the state, governors will almost always be granted immediate access to representatives and senators from their state. Because governors are successful politicians who have won elections and can deliver messages to the public, representatives and senators cannot ignore their opinions and requests. That does not mean they will do what the governor requests; it merely means they have to have an answer and be ready to respond if the governor appeals to the public. Governors may also work independently to promote their states' interests in Washington. Many governors establish offices in Washington, D.C., to monitor the activities of the federal government and alert the governor and his or her staff if there is a particularly detrimental or beneficial issue being considered. The staff of these officials may then lobby the federal officials or get the governor involved in lobbying.

Governors who travel to Washington face certain difficulties. Much of the public thinks governors should tend business at home and leave federal affairs to the state's elected officials in Washington. During election years, the media often report how many times the governor has been out of the state and in Washington. Governors may abstain from traveling to Washington to avoid the appearance of neglecting "home" issues and "meddling" in federal affairs. Yet, remaining home neglects opportunities only available to the governor in Washington.

Governors may use their office as a springboard to run for the Senate or the presidency. One indication of a governor seeking higher office is how often that governor visits Washington. Politically ambitious governors from medium-sized and small states often try to gain national attention by serving as leaders of the NGA. Arkansas Governor Bill Clinton used his position in the NGA to travel to Washington often to lobby for a welfare reform bill that became law in 1988. His successful efforts to pass this bill increased his national profile and his reputation in the Democratic Party. Governors of the larger states like California, Texas, and New York often receive considerable national press on their own and do not need the additional profile provided by holding an office in the NGA. The power of the governor's office as a political springboard is highlighted by the two following facts: first, between President Jimmy Carter and President George W. Bush, all but one were former governors; and second, in that same period only one presidential candidate with gubernatorial experience lost the election.

While executive office reforms have given greater institutional powers to the governors, remnants of the Progressive era's efforts to dilute the power of the executive branch remain. In many states, the governor is not the only executive official elected by the public. Some of the other elected officials in a state may include the lieutenant governor, attorney general, secretary of state, and education secretary. These executive officials, as a result of being elected by the public, have an independent base of support and may consequently ignore or work in opposition to the governor. This prevents the state executive from speaking in one voice and weakens the governors' power to influence and direct state policy.

Governors like to say that they stand where the "rubber meets the road." By that they mean they are responsible for implementing policies, and they are held accountable by the public for the policies' success or failure. Governors, consequently, are likely to see what public policies work and which ones do not before federal officials. This practical experience and public accountability give governors expertise to advise officials in Washington, and a willingness to experiment with innovative policies at home. Governors, consequently, have become some of the leading critics of existing public policies and power structures and some of the most creative and innovative reformers in the federal system. *SEE ALSO:* Banking; Council of State Governments; Deregulation; Education; Eisenhower, Dwight D.; Elections; Federal-State Relations; Insurance; Intergovernmental Relations; Medicaid; National Governors' Association; New Deal; New Federalism (Reagan); Pass through Requirements; Roosevelt, Theodore; State Government; Telecommunications; Unfunded Mandates; Welfare Policy

BIBLIOGRAPHY: Thad Beyle, "Governors: Elections, Campaign Costs, Profiles, Forced Exits and Powers," in *The Book of the States* (Lexington, KY: Council of State Governments, 1994); Scott Matheson, "Intergovernmental Relations and the New Federalism," in *Governors on Governing*, ed. Robert D. Behn (Lanham, MD: University Press of America, 1991); and Carol S. Weissert, "The National Governors' Association: 1908–1983," *State Government* 56, no. 2 (1983): 44–52.

TROY E. SMITH

Grants-in-Aid   A grant-in-aid is the transfer of money from one level of government to another for a specific purpose and subject to substantive and procedural conditions found in the authorizing legislation and administrative regulations. These requirements, or "strings," refer to both the substance of the grant (for example, eligible uses of funds, matching requirements, and maintenance of prior spending levels) and the procedures by which grant funds are to be expended (for example, opportunities for citizen participation, nondiscrimination in program activities, and consideration of environmental impacts of major projects).

Though there are many dimensions to grants-in-aid, three are of special importance. First is the extent to which recipient jurisdictions have discretion over the use of grant funds. Categorical grants allow the least amount of discretion, with spending limited to a specific category or program area (for example, construction of a senior citizens' center but not rehabilitation of an existing facility or the provision of services inside the facility). Block grants permit a broader array of services and activities, but are generally confined to a specific substantive policy area such as community development, health, or employment and training. General purpose grants provide unrestricted assistance to recipient jurisdictions.

A second key dimension of grants-in-aid is the manner in which funding is allocated. Formula grants provide funding on the basis of a prescribed formula to jurisdictions that are entitled to assistance. Project grants are awarded on a competitive basis and the amount awarded is discretionary, though often the authorizing statute or administrative regulation establishes a minimum and maximum grant award.

A third important feature of grants-in-aid is the duties and responsibilities of recipient governments. Some grant programs require recipient jurisdictions to provide matching funding, and the match rate may vary widely across programs. Some programs also require recipient jurisdictions to demonstrate maintenance of effort, that is, recipient governments must maintain spending at prior levels (or a prescribed portion of prior levels) to ensure that grant funds do not supplant previous spending by state or local governments. Administrative responsibilities also vary. Some recipient jurisdictions may decide to directly administer grant funds through existing departments and agencies, or alternatively recipients may opt to contract with subgrantees, such as nonprofit organizations, to provide some or all of the services and activities to be financed with grant funds. Programs also vary widely in terms of their application and reporting requirements.

Grants-in-aid may be used for a variety of purposes. For example, the federal government may decide it wants to encourage state and local governments to become more engaged in a specific policy area such as affordable housing or education for the disadvantaged. Grants may also be used to ensure that a minimum service level is attained for a specific service (e.g., equal grants to each state for vocational education) or to promote equalization of resources across jurisdictions (e.g., larger grants to poorer jurisdictions and smaller grants to more affluent ones). Grants are also used at times to promote economic stabilization (such as countercyclical spending on public works to stimulate the economy during times of recession) or to provide relief in response to special hardships such as natural disasters. Grants-in-aid are frequently used to demonstrate or test out new ideas for addressing important public problems and have also been used to encourage comprehensive planning and coordination at varying levels of geography ranging from neighborhoods to multistate regions.

Grants-in-aid have been the primary means through which the federal government has pursued its domestic policy objectives for the past fifty years. The 2004 edition of the *Catalog of Federal Domestic Assistance* (U.S. General Services Administration 2004) identifies nearly 1,200 federal grant programs, about half of which include grants to state and local governments. The remainder includes a variety of programs that provide direct support to nonprofit organizations or individuals for activities such as research, training, and education. Most grant-in-aid programs are relatively modest in size. A recent analysis by David Beam and Timothy Conlan (2002) reported that the twenty largest grant programs accounted for 78 percent of federal grant outlays in 1998; the share of outlays for the remaining 571 programs was only 22 percent.

In fiscal 2004, federal grant-in-aid outlays totaled $406 billion, or about 18 percent of all federal outlays and equivalent to 25 percent of total state and local government expenditures. Federal grants grew steadily during the 1960s and 1970s as many new programs were added that expanded federal involvement into a range of new policy areas such as education, employment and training, health, natural resources, and the environment. Spending slowed in the 1980s and even declined in 1982 and 1987 as the Reagan administration took aggressive actions to curtail federal spending and devolve a variety of responsibilities to state and local governments. The growth in grant outlays since 1990 has been driven primarily by increases in the Medicaid program, which have risen from $41 billion in 1990 (30 percent of grant outlays) to $176 billion in 2004 (43 percent).

Scholars and analysts who study grant-in-aid programs have tended to focus on three types of effects of grant programs: fiscal effects, for example, to what extent do increases or decreases in federal aid lead to increases or reductions in state and local spending; programmatic effects, or how do federal grants influence the amount and type of services provided by recipient jurisdictions; and institutional effects, or how do federal grants alter the organizational structure and decision-making processes of state and local governments?

Grants-in-aid have been the primary means through which intergovernmental cooperation and conflict have been played out in domestic affairs. As Richard Nathan, who has closely studied many of the largest federal grant programs for more than thirty years, has observed, "[A] grant-in-aid is the product of a political bargaining process, not just in Washington where the grant is created, but also at the state and local levels where it is executed" (Nathan 1983, 48). He adds that "the best way to think about this process is that there is a horizontal policy bargaining process, which consists of decision making about policy goals and instruments for the country as a whole, and a vertical dimension, involving the way in which a particular grant is defined and executed by individual recipient jurisdictions" (48). To heed Nathan's observations, anyone interested in learning about the dynamics of a particular policy area ought to look very closely at the major grant programs in that area. *SEE ALSO:* Block Grants; Categorical Grants; Education; Formula Grants; Housing; Local Government; Matching Requirements; Medicaid; Project Grants; Reagan, Ronald

BIBLIOGRAPHY: David R. Beam and Timothy J. Conlan, "Grants," in *The Tools of Government*, ed. Lester M. Salamon, 340–80 (New York: Oxford University Press, 2002); Richard P. Nathan, "State and Local Governments under Federal Grants: Toward a Predictive Theory," *Political Science Quarterly* 98 (Spring 1983); Paul E. Peterson, Barry G. Rabe, and Kenneth K. Wong, *When Federalism Works* (Washington, DC: Brookings Institution, 1986); Jeffrey L. Pressman and Aaron Wildavsky, *Federal Programs and City Politics* (Berkeley: University of California Press, 1975); U.S. General Services Administration, *Catalog of Federal Domestic Assistance* (Washington, DC: U.S. GSA, annually); U.S. Office of Management and Budget, "Aid to State and Local Governments," in *Budget of the United States Government: Analytical Perspectives* 47–57 (Washington, DC: U.S. OMB, issued annually); and Deil S. Wright, *Federal Grants-in-Aid: Perspectives and Alternatives* (Washington, DC: American Enterprise Institute, 1968).

Michael J. Rich

Great Society The "Great Society" is a phrase used to describe the domestic policies of President Lyndon B. Johnson (1963–69). While many of the programs had their origins in President John Kennedy's administration, while Johnson was vice president, they were not enacted until after Kennedy's assassination. In his first speech to a joint session of Congress on November 27, 1963, President Johnson said "let us continue" the work of the nation and President Kennedy by passing civil rights and tax relief legislation. Johnson worked with Congress on these and other areas of domestic policy in his hopes of crafting his great society.

Michael Harrington's book, *The Other America* (1962), brought a groundswell of public attention to the problem of poverty. In January 1964, in his first State of the Union address, President Johnson declared an "unconditional war on poverty." Later that year Congress passed the Economic Opportunity Act, which created the Office of Economic Opportunity (OEO). The OEO aimed to provide programs such as Head Start for preschoolers and vocational training under the Job Corps. The Revenue Act in 1964 also aided the poverty war by cutting taxes by more than $10 billion. Government statistics showed almost a 7 percent drop in the poverty level between 1959 and 1966.

The election of 1964 was a sweeping victory for both President Johnson and Democrats in Congress. Democrats enjoyed a comfortable 295 to 140 buffer in the House and a margin of 68 to 32 in the Senate. Social legislation under Johnson's watch moved swiftly through Congress. Aid to education was closely linked to the War on Poverty. In 1965 Congress passed more than $1 billion in funding for local schools and impoverished young students with the Elementary and Secondary Education Act. Appropriations were also made for postsecondary education under the Higher Education Act of 1965, which provided for college scholarships for needy students and subsidized interest costs on college loans.

Health benefits were another major concern for the Johnson administration. For the elderly, Congress passed a Medicare package that provided for benefits to defray medical costs to Americans over 65. For the poverty-stricken, a Medicaid package helped meet the costs of doctors' bills.

The largest of all Great Society initiatives came in the form of civil rights legislation. President Johnson and Congress followed recommendations left behind by President Kennedy and passed the Civil Rights Act of 1964. The act barred discrimination on the basis of race in all public accommodations. It also authorized the Justice Department to prosecute facilities that remained segregated. In response to violence and protest in the South, Congress moved to enact the Voting Rights Act of 1965. The act barred literacy tests or other qualifications for voting. African American voter registration in the South dramatically increased after the act was passed; Mississippi saw almost a 700 percent increase, Alabama had a jump of nearly 300 percent, and South Carolina rose 230 percent.

When President Johnson addressed commencement at the University of Michigan in May 1964, he initiated his view for a "Great Society." Poverty, education, health care, and civil rights provided the cornerstones for Johnson's vision. Since their inception, these programs continue to be the focus of great debate for historians and political scientists alike. *SEE ALSO:* Civil Rights Act of 1964; Economic Opportunity Act of 1964; Education; Elementary and Secondary Education Act of 1965; Johnson, Lyndon B.; Medicaid; Medicare; Voting Rights Act of 1965

BIBLIOGRAPHY: John A. Andrew, *Lyndon Johnson and the Great Society* (Chicago: I. R. Dee, Inc., 1998); Irving Bernstein, *Guns or Butter? The Presidency of Lyndon Johnson* (New York: Oxford University Press, 1996); Doris Kearns Goodwin, *Lyndon Johnson and the American Dream* (New York: Harper & Row, 1976); and Irwin Unger, *The Best of Intentions: The Triumph and Failures of the Great Society under Kennedy, Johnson, and Nixon* (New York: Doubleday, 1996).

D. STEVEN CRONIN

Gregg v. Georgia   In *Furman v. Georgia* (1971), the Supreme Court declared that existing state death penalty statutes were unconstitutional because they allowed too much discretion in sentencing. According to the Court, arbitrary and "freakish" implementation of the penalty was the result. Subsequently, 35 states wrote death penalty statutes that they hoped would conform to the standards that were outlined in *Furman*.

In *Gregg v. Georgia* (1976), one of the *Death Penalty Cases of 1976*, the Supreme Court approved Georgia's redrawn death penalty statute. The seven-member majority ruled that Georgia's death penalty statute did not violate the Eighth Amendment's prohibition against cruel and unusual punishment. The Court found that the statute provided sentencing standards that made imposition of the death penalty less likely to be arbitrary. It promoted individual justice by considering the particular circumstances of each case. The statute required juries to find at least one specified aggravating circumstance about the crime or the defendant, and considered against any mitigating circumstances that might be in place, before they could sentence a defendant to death. The statute also required mandatory appellate review of any death sentence. The Court concluded that a death sentence was not disproportionate to the crime of murder and that legislatures should be free to determine if the death penalty served as a deterrent to these types of crime and was supported by majority opinion.

The Court reasoned that its decision was supported by the text of the Constitution (the Fifth and Fourteenth Amendments state that *life*, liberty, or property shall not be deprived without due process of law, thus implying that life can be taken by the state as long as due process is followed), the intentions of the framers (the death penalty was commonly used during the founding era), and judicial precedents (the courts had ruled in favor of death penalty statutes in the past). The Court also considered "evolving standards of decency" and concluded that, because 35 states and Congress had passed death penalty statutes following its decision in *Furman*, majority sentiment endorsed its use. *SEE ALSO:* Capital Punishment; *Furman v. Georgia*

BIBLIOGRAPHY: Robert M. Bohm, *The Death Penalty in America* (Cincinnati, OH: Anderson Publishing Company, 1991); and Bryan Vila and Cynthia Morris, eds., *Capital Punishment in the United States: A Documentary History* (Westport, CT: Greenwood Press, 1997).

Michael Esler

Griggs v. Duke Powers Company   See Affirmative Action

Griswold v. Connecticut   *Griswold v. Connecticut* (1965) is a landmark Supreme Court decision in which the Supreme Court struck down a Connecticut statute that forbade the use of birth control drugs or devices and penalized those who advised or dispensed those materials. In a seven-to-two opinion authored by Justice William Orville Douglas, the Court held that the Connecticut statute violated a constitutionally protected right of privacy. While not specifically mentioned in the Constitution, Douglas said that the right to privacy exists within the penumbras of the First, Third, Fourth, and Fifth Amendments. In separate concurring opinions, Justice John Marshall Harlan found the right to exist within the meaning of "liberty" as that term is used in the Due Process Clause of the Fourteenth Amendment, and Arthur Goldberg placed particular reliance on the Ninth Amendment, which suggests that the listing of rights in the Bill of Rights may not be exhaustive of the rights guaranteed by the Constitution. Eight years later, in *Roe v. Wade*, the Court held that the right of privacy included a woman's right to abortion. *SEE ALSO: Roe v. Wade*

ROBERT W. LANGRAN

Guarantee Clause   In Article IV, Section 4, the Constitution declares that "[t]he United States shall guarantee to every State in this Union a Republican Form of Government, and shall protect each of them against invasion; and on Application of the Legislature, or of the Executive (when the Legislature cannot be convened) against domestic violence." Although the Supreme Court has generally held the Guarantee Clause nonjusticiable, the Rehnquist Court has intimated that the pledge of "republican government" can be a textual source of enforceable principles of federalism. Thus, while historically the clause has been invoked by the executive and legislative branches at junctures of cataclysmic national moment, the clause may have substance for the judiciary as well.

The clause can be subdivided into three separate promises, each running from the federal government to the states. In guaranteeing a "republican" government, the initial portion incorporates by reference the political theory of republicanism. Whether its meaning is restricted to the founders' conceptions or open to contemporary approaches depends on the theory of constitutional interpretation adopted. The provision's other two promises concretely describe certain types of destabilizing violence within states that the federal government pledges to prevent. The first, invasion, imposes a mandatory obligation upon the federal government. The second, the federal quelling of "domestic violence" within a state, is stated as an option available in the discretionary judgment of the state's branches that answer directly to the electorate—specifically the state's legislature or, alternatively, its governor.

> ARTICLE VI, SECTION 4
>
> *The United States shall guarantee to every State in this Union a Republican Form of Government, and shall protect each of them against Invasion; and on Application of the Legislature, or of the Executive (when the Legislature cannot be convened) against domestic Violence.*

The clause originated as the eleventh Virginia Resolution at the Constitutional Convention of 1787. Edmund Randolph stated the resolution had "two objects: first, to secure a republican government; secondly to suppress domestic commotions." Its final form can be traced primarily to James Madison and James Wilson. Although the extant writings of these men and their contemporaries during both drafting and ratification processes reveal discord as to the totality of meaning of "republican government," one universally agreed-upon principle can be clearly discerned. As understood by this revolutionary generation, the principle sine qua non of republican government is that legitimate political power rests with, and legitimate government proceeds from, the people themselves. James Madison famously wrote in *The Federalist* No. 39 that the "republican form" denotes "a government which derives all its powers directly or indirectly from . . . the people." As necessary corollaries of this principle of popular sovereignty, the founding generation broadly agreed that a republic is governed by representatives of the citizens' choosing, and that the citizens must have specific mechanisms by which they can hold their government accountable and change their representatives without having to resort to violence. Further, republican citizens' governing choices are properly inspired not by self-interest but by the "public welfare" or common good. By these essential differences, they distinguished republican government from monarchies and earlier democracies.

The Constitution offers no articulated set of requirements for "republican government." The Convention delegates not only were aware of a great diversity in the structure of existing state governments but also declined to prescribe uniform state constitutions—whether because they were politically unachievable or because they affirmatively valued maintaining a diversity of state government structures. Preceding and during the Convention, delegates criticized states for their legislative policy choices and the impediments they interposed to national interests, but they far less frequently criticized states' governmental *structures* for failing as republican. Thus, for the framers generally, a range of state government structures sufficed as republican.

Leaders of the founding generation differed sharply, however, as to which attributes other than popular sovereignty were essential to republican government. Madison argued that those vested with control over the government must be the "great body of the society" and not a privileged class. Thomas Jefferson agreed with Madison on this point, but by contrast, Alexander Hamilton advocated a life senate plus the vesting of other governing rights exclusively within an economically and socially privileged elite. As is well known, Jefferson vigorously advocated that republican government requires the protection of certain individual rights, such as freedom of religion and political association, and eventually won Madison's support. Jefferson also argued that public education, including higher education for the most talented students from throughout a state despite any economic indigency, would lay the foundation for the people's wise use of their republican freedoms and the continuation of republican government. In applying republican governing principles to the vast territory of the United States, Jefferson again contrasted sharply with Hamilton, for the Virginian considered the continuing vigor of state governments essential. Hamilton, however, envisioned the best republican government as an "entire subordination" of the states by "dividing the larger states" into administrative "districts" of the national government.

Recent scholarship critiques the founding generation's practices of republican government while offering more inclusive approaches. The framers, for instance, accepted a highly restrictive franchise under which state governments barred all women from voting, plus men of various ethnic and racial groups despite their free status. Additionally, the common prerequisite of real estate ownership ensured that only those of a certain economic status possessed political participation rights. The framers accepted chattel slavery, institutionalizing the practice constitutionally. Contemporary republican theory, while not monolithic, focuses on achieving an expansive franchise, structural reforms that would promote broader public political participation, and restrictions on the centripetal movement of regulatory power to the nation. Consistent with the framers' position, however, they emphasize that republican government must promote the "civic virtue" of citizens, specifically their active stewardship of the polity for the common good rather than use of the polity simply to further private ends.

Although rarely proffered as a basis for judicial action, the Guarantee Clause has been claimed to support federal judicial relief in some crucial cases. In the 1840s, Rhode Island's operative colonial charter restricted voter qualifications to real property owners, thereby continuing to disenfranchise large numbers of male citizens. The state legislature, elected by citizens who refused to share the franchise, rejected efforts to adopt a more democratic state constitution. A citizens' constitutional convention was held in which a new constitution was adopted, and under which a new state government was elected under exercise of a far broader franchise. In the wake of Dorr's Rebellion, with each side claiming to have been the state's legitimate "republican government," the Supreme Court held that determining which putative state government was legitimate and properly recognized federally rested not with the federal courts but exclusively with the federal political branches, that is, Congress and the president. As Congress had seated the representatives of the more restrictive state government, the Court held Congress had resolved the issue and was not to be second-guessed by the Court (*Luther v. Borden* 1849). Thus sprang the principle that "[v]iolation of the great guaranty of a republican form of government in States cannot be challenged in the courts" (*Colegrove v. Green* 1946). Continuing this approach, in landmark decisions midcentury the Supreme Court explicitly sidestepped the clause as authority for invalidating state legislatures whose structures diluted the right to vote, choosing instead to rely upon the Equal Protection Clause (*Baker v. Carr* 1962; *Reynolds v. Sims* 1964).

In *New York v. United States* (1992), however, the Court cited four cases in which "before the holding of *Luther* was elevated into a general rule of nonjusticiability," the Court had addressed the merits of claims founded on the Guarantee Clause "without any suggestion that the claims were not justiciable." *New York* did not, however, overturn the nonjusticiability of the clause but ruled rather that the state had failed to state a Guarantee Clause claim. Because the federal legislation had offered states a "legitimate choice" rather than issuing an "unavoidable command," the states retained the ability to set their legislative agendas, and state government officials remained accountable to the local electorate. The federal legislation therefore did not pose any realistic threat that it altered New York's governmental form or method of functioning.

Although largely uncharted in the federal judiciary, the Guarantee Clause has been invoked by federal political branches at critical historical junctures. In 1861, for instance, President Lincoln identified the Guarantee Clause as the authority by which he ordered military actions to force the confederate states' return to the Union. The Reconstruction Congress claimed the clause justified various legislation and prerequisites for readmission to the Union. The Court's opinion in *Texas v. White* (1869) can be read as implicitly approving the clause's invocation for unprecedented federal intrusion into state government policies. These Civil War–era legislative actions and the executive actions serve as precedents for scholars who argue that the clause properly functions as a mighty sword in the hands of the national government to force state compliance with republican political norms then current.

Since 1980, legal scholars have argued the Court should revisit its equivocal rulings that the Guarantee Clause is not a source of judicially enforceable rights. Scholarly arguments can be divided into two groups: those who advocate use of the clause as a shield protecting state governments from federal encroachments, and those who contend that the clause mandates aggressive federal action against states to force them into fuller realization of the "republican government" commitment. Scholars such as Deborah Merritt (1994) argue that the Rehnquist Court's principles protective of state governments are not well grounded in the Tenth Amendment, and would find greater textual support in the Guarantee Clause. She maintains that "the true animating principle" of established legal principles protecting states' decisional autonomy and sovereignty lies in the clause, specifically its concept of republican government. Merritt envisions four roles for a justiciable Guarantee Clause: preventing the federal government from interfering with a state's definition of the franchise for state and local elections; allowing the states to determine their own governmental structure, operations, and processes of election; protecting states' authority to set qualifications for state and local offices; and forbidding the national government from commandeering the processes for state government by compelling states to enact or administer particular laws. None of these constitutional principles is novel. Rather, Merritt seeks to position them as judicially enforceable principles tethered to the federal guarantee of republican state government.

The Supreme Court has thus far not expressly ruled the clause to be justiciable federally, but the Court has recently listed it as one of the constitutional provisions establishing the principle that national power vis-à-vis states is not unlimited (*Printz v. United States* 1997). Even justices not allied with the New Federalism movement have cited the clause as authority to restrict federal incursion into state government activities (e.g., *Bush v. Gore* 2000).

The Guarantee Clause, however, also threatens to support a nationalistic route the federal government has generally not pursued thus far. Some scholars have argued the clause provides a specific grant of affirmative federal power over state governmental structure and processes that authorizes Congress to create judicially enforceable standards for determining whether state governments are sufficiently republican. Acceptance of this principle undergirds the scholarly proposals for congressional legislative reform of state laws permitting ballot initiative lawmaking, for federally mandated campaign finance reforms for state elections (even though some of these reforms are arguably constitutionally impermissible at the national level), for legislating the abolition of state and local government patronage systems for staffing government jobs, and for aggressive federal prosecution of alleged public corruption at state and local levels of government. These changes in state government practices are advocated as essential to the contemporary realization of "republican government."

Given that the clause has historically been invoked as both a shield for state governments and a federal sword for eliminating state governmental structural choices, no assurances can be offered that the Guarantee Clause will function exclusively as an effective tool for federalism and serve as an impediment to the trajectory of greater nationalization of governmental reform. If state courts should adjudicate and apply the clause to force reforms of their own state governmental processes and structure, as has sometimes been argued, the judicial precedents might ultimately be used federally to force greater uniformity among state governments. With its dormancy period likely ending, it is too soon to know whether the Guarantee Clause will be used to justify new federal intrusions into state governments or to protect against them. *SEE ALSO: Bush v. Gore*

BIBLIOGRAPHY: Arthur Bonfield, "The Guarantee Clause of Article IV, Section 4: A Study in Constitutional Desuetude," *Minnesota Law Review* 46 (January 1962): 513–72; S. Candice Hoke, "Preemption Pathologies and Civic Republican Values," *Boston University Law Review* 71 (November 1991): 685–766; Linda Kerber, "Making Republicanism Useful," *Yale Law Journal* 97 (July 1988): 1663–72, and other articles in this symposium volume dedicated to *The Republican Civic Tradition*; Deborah Jones Merritt, "Guarantee Clause and State Autonomy: Federalism for a Third Century," *Columbia Law Review* 88 (January 1988). 1 78; Deborah Jones Merritt, "Republican Governments and

Autonomous States: A New Role for the Guarantee Clause," *Colorado Law Review* 65 (1994): 815–32, and other articles in this symposium volume focusing on *Republican Form of Government*; William M. Wiecek, *The Guarantee Clause of the Constitution* (Ithaca, NY: Cornell University Press, 1972); Gordon S. Wood, *The Radicalism of the American Revolution* (New York: Vintage Books, 1993); and Ernest Young, "*Alden v. Maine* and the Jurisprudence of Structure," *William & Mary Law Review* 41 (May 2000): 1601–76.

CANDICE HOKE

Hamilton, Alexander   Alexander Hamilton was a committed nationalist who was fearful of the promise of states' rights. As one of the authors of *The Federalist Papers*, Hamilton talked frequently about the cause of the union. Hamilton's nationalism was evident in two key areas: his authorship of most of *The Federalist Papers* and his later plans for the fiscal and monetary policy of the early United States.

THE NEW CONSTITUTION

Although they were allies in drafting *The Federalist Papers*, Hamilton and James Madison would later become political opponents over the nature of national power. This disagreement was evident even in their early defense of the new Constitution. *The Federalist* No. 17 was written by Hamilton, and in it he argued that under the new Constitution, the federal government will be able to act directly upon the citizens of the states to regulate the common concerns of the nation, which, he believed, was absolutely essential to the preservation of the union. The Articles of Confederation were far too weak to serve the nation, he argued. A stronger and more centralized system was necessary. While arguing for the necessity of the union and stronger national government, Hamilton did attempt to assuage the fears of many citizens of the states that the proposed new national government would destroy state sovereignty and subordinate the legitimate interests of the states to the national government. But he was quite firm on the necessity of a strong national government in areas of finance, national security, and domestic disorder. The *Federalist Papers* that were written by Madison were much more precise regarding specifics in the Constitution. Again, though Madison was at this time a supporter of the new Constitution, the different tone in authorship foreshadowed later, and bitter, disagreements over the nature of national versus state power.

THE NATIONAL BANK

As secretary of the treasury during the administration of George Washington, Hamilton furthered his call for a stronger national government. Thomas Jefferson, the secretary of state, emerged as Hamilton's main opponent. Jefferson tells a story of a conversation he had with John Adams and Hamilton early in Washington's tenure: Adams offered his opinion that the British system of constitutional monarchy, without the corruption, would be the best system of government in the world. Hamilton replied that the British system was already the best possible form of government. Jefferson was horrified by such comments; he believed in pure democracy and thought that men were capable of governing themselves. Hamilton and Adams, on the other hand, had a pretty bleak view of human nature: they thought that a type of benevolent dictator was necessary to keep people from destroying each other. This translated into support for a very strong national government, one shaped by strong executive power removed from popular passions.

A key component of the strong national government was the creation of a national bank in 1791. The bank was not a private entity, but a government agency that had the power to print money and make loans. It acted like most of the central banks of Europe. And as such, it was very likely the biggest point of contention between those who wanted a strong central government and those who did not: these divisions would form into incipient political parties, the Federalists and Republicans.

Hamilton was responsible for settling the issue of the debt accrued from the Revolutionary War. A major part of this task entailed finding out what each state's war debt was, how these debts were serviced, how much of the debt had been paid off, and who owned the debt. This was a fairly major task.

There were many ways of paying off the debt. Virginia had paid off almost all of its debt and was none too interested in having the national government assume the debt of other states like Massachusetts, which had paid off very little of its debt. Hamilton came up with a very promising but somewhat controversial plan for dealing with the debt: a central bank. It is not at all surprising that Hamilton would propose such a bank; it was a British idea that was created during the mid-seventeenth century by Prime Minister Robert Walpole. A central bank changed the nature of wealth by making paper money a viable form of wealth, whereas before then land had largely been the main form of wealth.

Hamilton wanted a bank because he worried that the lack of a national paper currency would restrict the development of commerce. Hamilton envisioned the United States as a national administrative republic engaged in commerce. The national bank would issue bank notes, stimulate commercial growth, provide a safe haven for federal revenues, and finance short-term loans. In the Hamiltonian vision, the national bank would foster a mercantilist economy where the central government would organize economic activity. To a great extent, the commercial states of the North, New England and New York, supported Hamilton.

Jefferson led the opposition and was supported by the plantation-based economy of the South, where land and property were the primary manufacturers of wealth. Southerners also opposed the bank because it was to be partially funded by tariffs. Hamilton wanted to put tariffs on imports that competed with indigenous manufacturing efforts. In other words, products that we could make here in the United States would have very high tariffs; those not made here would have very low tariffs. The Southerners did not favor such a system because they were free traders: they made cash crops of tobacco and cotton that they exported to Europe, and they were afraid that high tariffs might cause the Europeans to respond in kind, thus damaging the southern economy. Hamilton was able to win over Washington to his cause, and the bank was given a twenty-year charter by Congress. Slowly Washington, despite his protestations to the contrary, moved in the Federalists' direction. Hamilton's vision of a strong national government organizing economic life would become a hallmark of political and economic life in the latter part of the twentieth century. *SEE ALSO: The Federalist Papers*; Madison, James

BIBLIOGRAPHY: Richard Brookhiser, *Alexander Hamilton: American* (New York: Free Press, 1999); and Milton Cantor, ed., *Hamilton* (Englewood Cliffs, NJ: Prentice Hall, 1971).

PETER N. UBERTACCIO III

Hammer v. Dagenhart   During the early years of the 1900s, the U.S. Supreme Court sanctioned a kind of federal police power by upholding federal laws that banned the shipment of certain noxious goods in interstate commerce, thereby effectively halting their manufacture and distribution. The leading decision in this area is *Champion v. Ames* (1903) in which the Court upheld a federal ban on the shipment of lottery tickets in interstate commerce. Similar federal laws were upheld that addressed the problems of prostitution, impure drugs, and adulterated foods. In *Hammer v. Dagenhart* (1918), however, the Court brought this line of decisions to an abrupt end.

Hammer v. Dagenhart involved a challenge to the federal Keating-Owen Child Labor Act, which banned goods made by child labor from shipment in interstate commerce. In distinguishing its earlier decisions upholding federal bans on the shipment of specified goods in interstate commerce from the child labor situation, the Court held that in the former cases, the evil involved (lotteries, prostitution, unhealthy food, and so on) followed the shipment of the good in interstate commerce, while in the present case, the evil (child labor) preceded shipment of the goods. Therefore, according to the Court, the federal ban was really aimed at controlling manufacturing, which was beyond the scope of Congress's authority under the Commerce Clause. "If it were otherwise," the Court said, "all manufacture intended for interstate shipment would be brought under federal control to the practical exclusion of the authority of the States, a result . . . not contemplated by the . . . Constitution." The Court concluded that to hold otherwise would "eliminate state control over local matters, and thereby destroy the federal system." *SEE ALSO: Bailey v. Drexel Furniture Company*; *Champion v. Ames*; Commerce among the States; *Hipolite Egg Company v. United States*; Tenth Amendment

ELLIS KATZ

Harlan, John Marshall   John Marshall Harlan, the grandson of the associate justice of the Supreme Court of the same name, was born on May 20, 1899, in Chicago. A graduate of Princeton University, he studied law at Oxford University and the New York Law School. He was a successful trial lawyer in New York, served in the Air Force during World War II, and held a number of governmental positions in both New York and Washington. President Dwight D. Eisenhower appointed him to the Court of Appeals as a judge in 1954, and a year later nominated him to the Supreme Court. The Senate confirmed him by a vote of 71–11.

Harlan was a strong defender of federalism, of judicial restraint, and of the First Amendment's guarantee of free speech. His concern with federalism is manifested by his votes and opinions in criminal procedure cases. He steadfastly refused to accept the notion that the Due Process Clause incorporated all, or even some, of the Bill of Rights. Instead, he argued that the states must be given discretion in organizing their criminal justice systems so long as they did not violate fundamental fairness. For this reason, he was a dissenter in both *Mapp v. Ohio* (1961) and *Miranda v. Arizona* (1968). His

John Marshall Harlan. Library of Congress, Prints and Photographs Division.

concern with federalism also caused him to dissent in *Baker v. Carr* (1962), which held that reapportionment was a justiciable matter and could be resolved by federal courts. Generally, he believed that the states were responsible for such matters as law and order, obscenity, and elections.

Harlan was also an advocate of judicial restraint, not only warning the Court to stay out of the "political thicket" of reapportionment but also urging the Court to avoid becoming involved in controversial cases unless there was a clear requirement for it to do so. For example, he dissented in *Flast v. Cohen* (1968), which seemed to open the courtroom door to federal taxpayers' suits.

Despite his generally restraintist viewpoint, Harlan often was a strong defender of freedom of speech. In one of his first opinions, *Yates v. United States* (1957), he held that even admitted members of the Communist Party could not be convicted under the Smith Act because of their beliefs; only proof that they advocated some specific overt illegal action would permit a conviction. In a very different context, Harlan wrote the Court's opinion in *Cohen v. California* (1971), upholding Cohen's right to wear a jacket with a four-letter obscenity printed on the back in the Los Angeles County Courthouse. On the other hand, in the same year, Harlan dissented in *New York Times v. United States* (1971) when the Court lifted the lower court's injunction against the publication of the Pentagon Papers.

Harlan suffered from bad eyesight in his later years, and in 1971 was diagnosed with cancer of the spine. He retired on September 23 of that year, and died on December 29. He is not easy to classify as either a liberal or a conservative. He was, however, a staunch believer in federalism and judicial restraint. *SEE ALSO: Baker v. Carr*; Exclusionary Rule; Fourteenth Amendment; Incorporation (Nationalization) of the Bill of Rights; *Mapp v. Ohio*; *Miranda v. Arizona*; Reapportionment

BIBLIOGRAPHY: Nathan Lewin, "John Marshall Harlan," in *The Supreme Court Justices: Illustrated Biographies, 1789–1993*, ed. Clare Cushman (Washington, DC: Congressional Quarterly Inc., 1993); David L. Shapiro, ed., *The Evolution of a Judicial Philosophy: Selected Opinions and Papers of Justice John M. Harlan* (Cambridge, MA: Harvard University Press, 1969); and Tinsley E. Yarbrough, *John Marshall Harlan: Great Dissenter of the Warren Court* (New York: Oxford University Press, 1992).

ROBERT W. LANGRAN

Hartford Convention   The Hartford Convention, a gathering of New England Federalists held from December 15, 1814, to January 4, 1815, was the product of hostilities between the two political parties. It attempted to address concerns regarding fears that the federal government, controlled by a majority of southern Democratic-Republicans, was undermining states' rights, leaving the states questioning their ability to protect their individual interests and authority. These concerns were heightened by the War of 1812, which, many Federalists believed, hurt their economic interests and escalated the distress of New Englanders who feared they were vulnerable to attack by the enemy. The convention failed and the Federalists suffered irreparable damage as Federalism became known as "lacking an extensive nationwide outlook" and out of touch. Some of the convention's ideas, however, were later revived by the southern states to justify secession.

Hostilities between the two political parties, and the growth of sectionalism, were evident from the start. In the late 1790s, the Federalists controlled the government and used the Alien and Sedition Acts to restrain those who did not support the Federalist ideology. The Democratic-Republicans responded with the Kentucky and Virginia Resolutions calling the Alien and Sedition Acts unconstitutional and suggesting state nullification. The conflict escalated in 1801 when the Democratic-Republicans gained control of the federal government and began implementing economic policies that Federalists believed favored the South's economic interests. The Embargo Act of 1807 further convinced Federalists that the federal government was overlooking New England's interests. Hostilities grew with the War of 1812 as many New England states refused to turn over their militias to federal control; the national government responded by threatening conscription and enlistment of minors with no parental consent. Federalists threatened to nullify laws of this sort and some, such as John Lowell and Tim Pickering, suggested that New England states conclude a peace with Great Britain or secede from the Union. These events led Massachusetts' Federalists to call a convention of New England states.

The convention consisted of twenty-six delegates from Massachusetts, Connecticut, Rhode Island, Vermont, and New Hampshire. Moderates such as George Cabot, who presided over the delegation, and Harrison Gray Otis, considered the father of the convention, dominated the meeting and the topics discussed. After three weeks of secret deliberations, during which the idea of secession was considered and rejected, the delegates on January 4, 1815, approved a report censuring the administration of President James Madison and containing proposed amendments to the U.S. Constitution. These proposals were aimed chiefly at strengthening the political influence and securing the economic interests of the North. To counteract the success of Virginia's presidential candidates, the proposed amendments would have made future presidents ineligible for reelection, and would have prohibited the election of successive presidents from the same state. To increase the congressional influence of the North, the proposals would have abolished the constitutional provision counting slaves as three-fifths of a person for purposes of representation and direct taxation. Finally, to protect commercial interests, the amendments would have required a two-thirds vote in Congress to prohibit foreign commerce and to declare war, and would have limited the duration of any embargo to sixty days.

Though the convention dispatched a committee to deliver the report to Washington, D.C., the report was never received. Before the committee arrived, intelligence of the Treaty of Ghent, terminating the War of 1812, and of Andrew Jackson's brilliant victory against the British at New Orleans destroyed all sympathy for the convention. The Federalists were regarded as reactionary, shortsighted, and disloyal, and the failure of the Hartford Convention deprived the party of credibility and ultimately sealed its demise.

The Democratic-Republicans believed the Hartford Convention to be a treasonous ploy to organize the secession of New England states, while Federalists thought it a way to defend New England physically while protecting their perceived interests and authority. The ideas presented at the Hartford Convention ironically advanced Jeffersonian ideologies of state nullification and contradicted the Hamiltonian philosophies of American empire usually endorsed by Federalists. The Hartford Convention continued the debate over nullification begun by the Kentucky and Virginia Resolutions and promoted the idea of secession, which the southern states used in 1860 to secede from the Union. *SEE ALSO:* Alien and Sedition Acts; Federalists; Kentucky and Virginia Resolutions; Nullification; Political Parties; Secession; States' Rights

BIBLIOGRAPHY: James M. Banner, *To the Hartford Convention: The Federalists and the Origins of Party Politics in Massachusetts, 1789–1815* (New York: Alfred A. Knopf, 1970); Alfred H. Kelly and Winfred A. Harbison, *The American Constitution: Its Origins and Development*, 5th ed. (New York: W. W. Norton, 1976); Samuel Eliot Morison, *Harrison Gray Otis, 1765–1848: The Urbane Federalist* (Boston: Houghton Mifflin Company, 1969); and Garry Willis, *A Necessary Evil: A History of American Distrust of Government* (New York: Simon and Schuster, 1999).

TORY RUTLEDGE AND ANDY BARDOS

Health Care Policy   This entry examines significant health policy at the state and national levels largely since the New Deal and describes the nature of intergovernmental relations. American federalism until the New Deal has generally been characterized as constitutional federalism or dual federalism. During this period, states, local governments, and private charity took responsibility for addressing public health issues. The federal government's role was the exception, providing services to merchant marines, veterans of the armed forces, and Native Americans. States regulated physicians and other health professionals through licensure, and in the 1930s began regulating the emerging market of private insurance. With the exception of mental health, states did not provide direct services or health insurance.

The Great Depression and World War II created a shift in American federalism. By enhancing the role of the executive office, President Franklin D. Roosevelt helped create the modern American administrative state. The national government's role in health policy expanded, but goals were achieved through decentralized administration that channeled funds through the states and private sector. This period is often referred to as "cooperative federalism." Under this model, the federal government was dominant, and the states were the weaker partner lacking innovation or "particular interest in formulating policy initiatives."

During World War II, employer-provided health insurance became exempt from taxation, and this led to the rapid expansion of private insurance. Business asked for this exemption to attract workers when the demand for labor was high and wages were fixed. Blue Cross, organized by the American Hospital Association, and Blue Shield, organized by the physician societies, dominated the health insurance field. These plans were state-based, nonprofit, and community-rated (one rate for everyone in a geographic area); paid for services on a cost bases; and were regulated by the states. The McCarran-Ferguson Act of 1945 exempted insurance companies from federal antitrust regulation if they were regulated by the state. Supreme Court rulings and this statute made it clear that Congress had jurisdiction over insurance (it almost always entails interstate commerce) and delegated this responsibility to the states. McCarran-Ferguson stated explicitly that "no federal law should be interpreted as overriding state insurance regulation unless it does so explicitly."

Major federal spending for health system expansions occurred after the war, specifically for veterans' hospitals, medical research, medical education, and hospital construction. Faith in science, which became prominent in the Progressive era and was strengthened by victory in war, led to physician and hospital administrator autonomy in how federal funds were spent. This was largely a supply-side strategy, providing federal resources to hospitals and doctors as well as for medical innovation in an effort to expand access to care. These funds were not spent on providing universal insurance or direct access to care. President Harry Truman attempted to pass a national health insurance plan, but was unsuccessful. Further, this massive influx of resources was *not* accompanied by significant regulations of the industry or progressive redistribution requirements, as was the case in most of Europe.

The Hill-Burton Act of 1946 provided $3 million to states in immediate funding to survey hospital need and $75 million a year for five years in hospital construction funds. Federal administrators had no say in how much money particular hospitals received. The program was thought progressive because it provided higher funding to states with lower per capita income. However, states could only distribute resources to communities that raised two-thirds of the funds and showed "financial viability." Hill-Burton also included a federal requirement that hospitals provide care to the uninsured. However, the law merely stated that hospitals must provide "a reasonable volume of hospital services to persons unable to pay," and regulations defining what this meant were not written until twenty years later.

The Kerr-Mills proposal passed in 1960 was a means-tested, state-run program for the poor and elderly. Federal funds were provided to match state expenditures with the poorer states receiving higher reimbursements similar to the current Medicaid program. However, this program was not particularly successful or popular with the states. In 1963, five of the largest states accounted for 90 percent of program funds. Significant expansions in regulation and redistribution did not take place until Great Society efforts to expand coverage and post–Great Society efforts to control costs.

In the 1960s and 1970s, President Lyndon Johnson created a direct relationship between local communities and the national government. Community-based care for the mentally ill, established in the late 1960s, sent federal seed money directly to communities. Further, a series of neighborhood health centers providing direct services in the poorest communities developed out of the Community Action Program (CAP) administered by the Office of Economic Opportunity (OEO). The OEO made direct connections between the federal government and local communities, bypassing existing state and local governments and party structure. In 1967, Senator Edward Kennedy (D-MA) successfully sponsored an amendment to create 100 new neighborhood health centers. Neighborhood health centers were successful in providing direct care to the most vulnerable, but the program pales in comparison to the billions more that would be spent on Medicare and Medicaid.

Medicare and Medicaid, enacted in 1965, provided access to the privately developed health care infrastructure to seniors and select people with low incomes. The programs mirrored the bifurcated welfare system established during the New Deal in which the federal government administers broad-based social insurance and the states play a more direct role in implementing less popular "welfare" programs. The Medicare program provides insurance coverage for hospital, physician, and other services to senior citizens over 65. The rules are set by the federal government, which oversees the administration by private intermediaries who pay the Medicare bills. Medicaid is for low-income individuals who meet certain eligibility criteria. It is a means-tested program administered by the states. The federal government sets the rules, but there are mandatory and optional coverage groups and covered services. States choose from these options and can also seek federal waivers to develop unique programs. To reverse an old adage, "If you have seen one Medicaid program, you have [only] seen one Medicaid program."

Medicare and Medicaid were major expansions in health policy, initiated largely by the national government but administered and implemented under very different models of federalism. These programs represented a new commitment of the federal government beyond infrastructure to financing broad-based benefits directly to individuals (in 2003, these programs represented 40 percent of total health care dollars spent in the country). This redistribution strengthened existing medical institutions without regulating or modifying existing organizations and power systems. Along with expanding access to care, Medicare and Medicaid provided rich funding streams for hospitals, physicians, and other health providers. Payment systems encouraged hospitals and physicians to maximize the number of procedures they did and the charges for each procedure. This was a period of rapid economic growth. Similar reimbursement incentives in the private insurance market and the rampant inflation of the 1970s sent health care costs soaring. In response, the Nixon administration implemented a series of federally directed cost-containment strategies.

Health regulations in the 1970s were geared primarily toward controlling rampant health care costs. Federal efforts included wage and price controls, the fostering of economic competition through the encouragement of health maintenance organizations (HMOs), mandatory certificate of need programs, and mandated health planning. States were also active during this time implementing rate-setting programs designed to control hospital and nursing home costs. President Richard Nixon also introduced a national health plan that included an employer mandate and a federal Family Health Insurance program to cover those with low income. Nixon's wage and price controls in 1971 capped doctor's fees at 2.5 percent annual growth and hospital charges at 6 percent (less than half the rate they had been growing). While other wage and price controls were lifted in 1973, they were maintained for health care along with food and construction. This represented unprecedented peacetime federal control over the private sector.

The HMO Act of 1973 required businesses with over twenty-five employees that offered health insurance to contract with at least one qualified HMO being offered in their area. Prepaid group practice plans, newly termed "health maintenance organizations" (or, often, HMOs), were being used to foster competition and manage health care costs, but they were so loaded with requirements that they could not compete with traditional indemnity plans and grew at a snail's pace. The HMO Act represents federal control over an insurance product that traditionally would have been regulated by the states.

The National Health Planning and Resources Act of 1974 directed states to develop certificate of need programs to evaluate the proposed construction of health care facilities. State regulation of the provision of health insurance was further weakened by the federal Employee Retirement Income Security Act of 1974 (ERISA). ERISA prevents states from regulating the activities of employer self-funded plans. Originally, this was a minor provision that impacted only the largest corporations, but over time, the number of ERISA-protected plans expanded to cover nearly 50 percent of people with private health insurance coverage. Companies can avoid state regulation by self-insuring, but retain all the advantages of having an outside insurance company.

Beginning in the 1960s and 1970s, states also played a more direct role in efforts to control health care costs. In 1964, New York was the first state to regulate capital expenditures of hospitals and nursing homes. By 1972, 22 states had certificate of need programs prior to federal mandates. Further, by 1980, 30 states had some form of prospective rate-setting program for medical expenses. The American Hospital Association (AHA) actually supported state regulation (some of which included weak voluntary targets) as a preferred alternative to national regulation. However, AHA support for any type of rate regulation evaporated quickly as President Jimmy Carter's program for national rate regulation failed.

In the 1980s and 1990s, the number of uninsured began to rise and Medicaid became the fastest-growing state budget item. Congress inserted Medicaid expansion deep in massive end-of-the-year budget reconciliation acts to shield them from presidential veto. During this period, states also developed a number of innovative strategies to maximize federal revenue. Medicaid expansion took place through federal statute and state discretion beginning in the 1980s and continuing into the 1990s. These expansions took the form of federal mandates and state options. For example, mandatory expansions for low-income pregnant women and children at increasing income levels were included in the Consolidated Omnibus Budget Reconciliation Act of 1986, the 1988 Medicare Catastrophic Coverage Act, and the Omnibus Budget Reconciliation Act of 1989 (OBRA). OBRA 1989 extended coverage to these groups up to 133 percent of the federal poverty level. The Omnibus Budget Reconciliation Act of 1990 required coverage of children born after 1983 with family incomes under 100 percent of the poverty level. By 2002, all children with family incomes below the poverty level became eligible for Medicaid coverage.

States also took advantage of Medicaid options to increase coverage beyond federal requirements. Section 1902 (r)(2) of the Social Security Act gives states the ability to raise the coverage age and income level for children beyond federal requirements. By 1995, 41 states expanded eligibility for pregnant women and children beyond federal requirements. States took the initiative and expanded coverage and captured more federal money in the process. Simultaneously, the federal government allowed this expansion and mandated states to cover certain populations.

States could also alter their Medicaid programs and increase coverage through federal waivers. Section 1115(a) of the Social Security Act enables the secretary of health and human services to grant waivers from the act's provisions for demonstration programs. These waivers allow wholesale modification of Medicaid requirements including eligibility rules, minimum benefit requirements, freedom of choice, disenrollment requirements, federal standards for enrollment in full-risk managed care, provider reimbursement rules, and state administration requirements. These provide significant flexibility to the states, but necessitate federal approval and are subject to federal oversight. The goal of waivers is to give states an opportunity to be innovative in meeting the requirements of the act. Waivers represent an opportunity to give states flexibility to cover more people and to promote cost stabilization, predictability, and containment. Waivers started being used more widespread in the Clinton administration, with the emphasis on expanding coverage and continued under George W. Bush. On August 4, 2001, the Bush administration introduced a new approach to waivers through its Health Insurance Flexibility and Accountability (HIFA) initiative. This provides states with flexibility to modify state programs to increase efficiencies without necessarily expanding coverage. They are still subject to federal approval and oversight.

President Bill Clinton introduced comprehensive national health care reform in 1993 with the Health Security Act. Public opinion polls showed that the American people strongly supported the goals of reform—cost containment and universal coverage. No consensus developed on the specific mechanism for achieving these goals. Because of this and a number of other factors, the plan failed. The Health Security Act included a preeminent role for the states in terms of policy development and implementation under a broad national framework. States were to design and operate "health alliances," which would have been command posts for organizing and operating nearly every aspect of the proposed health care system. The Clinton Plan included flexibility for states, at their option, to implement a single-payer system similar to Canada's.

Three major pieces of health legislation have passed since the failed Clinton plan: the Health Insurance Portability and Accountability Act of 1996 (HIPAA), the State Children's Health Insurance Program of 1997 (SCHIP), and the Medicare reforms including a prescription drug benefit in 2003. Each of these programs has significant intergovernmental components.

HIPAA increased federal regulation of insurance products and privacy standards. This took place in a time characterized as devolution when Speaker of the House Newt Gingrich was advancing his Contract with America. A primary goal of HIPAA was to improve the access, portability, and renewability of private health insurance in both the group and individual market. With the private insurance sector becoming increasingly competitive, many people, particularly those with high or potentially high health care costs, were "falling through the cracks." Workers were being forced to stay in particular jobs in order to retain health insurance coverage—so-called job lock. Insurance companies were excluding coverage for preexisting conditions, including pregnancy. Insurance companies were dropping coverage completely for individuals or businesses as their health risk increased.

Many of the states had already implemented changes in the small-group market to remedy some of these problems. This legislation was necessary primarily to extend these types of protection to federally regulated self-insured plans. The scope of HIPAA insurance reforms was diminished first by the fact that health plans could, in effect, still exclude coverage of certain companies by increasing their rates, and by weak federal enforcement and oversight. States have considerable flexibility in implementation. The HIPAA privacy standards represent significant national regulation of the health care sector from top to bottom. HIPAA has elements of both centralization (new federal authority over an area traditionally regulated by the states) and devolution (state influence, leadership, and flexibility).

The Balanced Budget Act of 1997 created SCHIP, providing $20.3 billion in funding for the first five years. This act created Title XXI of the Social Security Act, which provides grants to states for the coverage of uninsured children in families with incomes below 200 percent of the federal poverty level. States that have already expanded their Medicaid programs to cover children above 150 percent of the poverty level may increase coverage by 50 percent over their current levels and be eligible for federal funds.

States may use their allotment of funds to expand Medicaid coverage, develop a new state program, or expand an existing state program. States may also use a combination of these strategies. If states choose Medicaid, they must meet all the guidelines of this program including comparability of eligibility and benefits across the state. If states choose to develop their own program, they have some flexibility to set eligibility levels, define benefit packages, and tailor programs based on age, geographic location, or disability status.

Ten percent of state funds may be used for the direct purchase of care, for outreach, or for administrative costs. SCHIP is a matching program, whereby states draw down apportioned funding of a set pool. The matching rate is based on current Medicaid matching rates that range between 50 and 79 percent based on a state's poverty level and financial capacity. The SCHIP rate is the state's Medicaid rate plus 30 percent of the difference between this rate and 100 percent. The rate is capped at 85 percent. The federal government will pay 65 percent of the program for more affluent states and up to 85 percent for less affluent states. Each state is eligible for a portion of this funding based on a formula taking into consideration the number of uninsured children with a family income below 200 percent FPL (Federal Poverty Law, $26,660 for a family of three in 1997). The formula accounts for regional differences in state health care costs and guarantees a minimum for every state.

SCHIP provides considerable flexibility to states along with enhanced funding for the coverage of children. However, the act also includes a number of federal safeguards and restrictions. Federal rules restricted state flexibility in a number of areas, including eligibility (only children meeting citizenship requirements with a certain family income not eligible for Medicaid or other insurance coverage), benefits (some variation but still had to be comprehensive), and cost sharing or payments for coverage (restricted or prohibited). In addition, states must submit detailed plans for national approval and are subject to federal audits and oversight. Because of cumulative state requirements, the program is best understood as flexibility within federally prescribed corridors.

There are also bargaining and negotiations between the federal government and the states regarding the application of federal standards to state specific circumstances. Overall the best model of federalism might be one of cooperation, but certainly not devolution. The federal government, through rules and regulations and control over how federal funds and state funds are spent, continues to play a major role in the implementation of this program.

On December 8, 2003, President Bush signed the Medicare Prescription Drug Improvement and Modernization Act of 2003 into law. This law provides a prescription drug benefit to Medicare recipients beginning January 1, 2006. Many of the states currently provide state-only programs to help seniors pay for prescription drugs and were supportive of this federal initiative. The standard benefit includes a $250 deductible, then covers 75 percent of costs up to $2,250. There is no additional coverage until a person spends $3,600. At this point, people with income below 135 percent of the poverty line have no copayments, those between 135 and 150 percent of poverty have between $2 and $5 copayments, and people with higher incomes are responsible for 5 percent coinsurance. The average premium is expected to be $35 per month. This program is means tested, providing premium support and low out-of-pocket costs to low-income seniors. This will help many states that currently have state-only programs to assist seniors with prescription drugs. *SEE ALSO:* Great Society; Medicaid; Medicare

BIBLIOGRAPHY: Robert Blendon et al., "The Beliefs and Values Shaping Today's Health Reform Debate," *Health Affairs* (Spring 1994); Sydney Milkis, *The President and the Parties: The Transformation of the American Party System since the New Deal* (New York: Oxford University Press, 1993); Len M. Nichols and Linda J. Blumberg, "A Different Kind of 'New Federalism?' The Health Insurance Portability and Accountability Act of 1996," *Health Affairs* 17, no. 3 (May–June 1998): 27; Robert F. Rich and William D. White, *Health Policy Federalism and the American States* (Washington DC: Urban Institute Press, 1996); Sara Rosenbaum and Julie Darnell, "Statewide Medicaid Managed Care Demonstrations under Section 1115 of the Social Security Act," in *The Kaiser Commission on the Future of Medicaid* (May 1997); Theda Skocpol, *Boomerang Health Care Reform and the Turn against Government* (New York: W.W. Norton, 1997); Paul Starr, *The Social Transformation of American Medicine* (New York: BasicBooks/Harper, 1982); and U.S. House of Representatives, Committee on Ways and Means, "Summary of Medicare Conference Agreement," Committee report (November 21, 2003).

MICHAEL DOONAN

Heart of Atlanta Motel v. United States   In the *Civil Rights Cases* of 1883, the Supreme Court ruled that the Fourteenth Amendment's Equal Protection Clause did not prohibit racial discrimination in public accommodations (privately owned establishments that serve a public purpose such as hotels, motels, restaurants, bars, and so on). The Court reasoned that the amendment applied only to discriminatory action by state governments, not by private organizations. For the better part of the next century, owners of public accommodations were free to discriminate. Although the Court later expanded its definition of what constitutes state action, it has never reversed the state action doctrine.

In Title II of the Civil Rights Act of 1964, Congress attempted to end racial discrimination in public accommodations. Congress justified the act as consistent with its powers under the Commerce Clause, which authorizes Congress to regulate interstate commerce; the Equal Protection Clause of the Fourteenth Amendment; and Section 5 of the Fourteenth Amendment, which empowers Congress to pass legislation to enforce provisions of the Fourteenth Amendment.

In *Heart of Atlanta Motel v. United States* (1964), the Court held unanimously that it was permissible to use the Commerce Clause to promote social policy as long as the activity in question affected interstate commerce. The Court found that Congress had provided adequate evidence to demonstrate that racial discrimination resulted in a general lack of rooms available to African Americans who were traveling interstate, and that this affected interstate commerce. Because the Commerce Clause was enough to justify Congress's action, the Court did not reach the Fourteenth Amendment issue and thus avoided having to revisit the state action doctrine that the Court articulated in the *Civil Rights Cases* of 1883. In a concurring opinion, Justice William Douglas criticized the Court for not basing its decision on the Fourteenth Amendment as well as the Commerce Clause. He argued that protections against racial discrimination under the Fourteenth Amendment were stronger than under the Commerce Clause and that such an approach would avoid a case-by-case analysis of whether a given instance of racial discrimination affected interstate commerce. *SEE ALSO:* Commerce among the States; Fourteenth Amendment

BIBLIOGRAPHY: Civil Rights Act of 1964: Title II; and Richard C. Cortner, *Civil Rights and Public Accommodations: The Heart of Atlanta and McClung Cases* (Lawrence: University of Kansas Press, 2001).

Michael Esler

Higher Education Act   The Higher Education Act of 1965 (HEA) was enacted during the Great Society. This initial legislation embodied the spirit of its times: to promote equal opportunity for underprivileged individuals. Since 1965, reauthorizations to this education legislation have occurred at least once per decade. The central focus of the HEA's programs (and its subsequent amendments) has been to increase access and persistence in higher education. These major programs fall primarily into four categories: (1) student financial aid; (2) services to help students better prepare for, access, and succeed in education beyond high school; (3) aid to higher education institutions; and (4) aid to improve teacher training efforts in colleges and universities.

There are seven titles in the HEA that are up for reauthorization each time Congress amends the HEA: (1) Title I, General Provisions; (2) Title II, Teacher Quality Enhancement Grants; (3) Title III, Institutional Aid; (4) Title IV, Student Assistance; (5) Title V, Developing Institutions; (6) Title VI, International Education Programs; and (7) Title VII, Graduate and Postsecondary Improvement Programs. The nucleus of the HEA is the student aid programs that are authorized under Title IV including grant aid, loans, and work-study assistance. The Pell Grant program is the largest Title IV student aid program and is the largest governmental appropriation for students with need who want to pursue a higher education.

Congress primarily implements incremental changes to the HEA rather than sweeping, comprehensive changes. These marginal adjustments in the administration and funding of HEA programs, however, potentially impact a large number of students and institutions. In the 1970s, for example, the federal government was urged to expand support to a broader range of students. In the 1980s, the federal government increased institution-level accountability measures for student loan default rates through the HEA. Important financial aid–related policy changes enacted in reauthorization efforts in the 1990s included, but were not limited to, higher limits on loan borrowing, expanded eligibility for student-loan programs that increased the number of middle- and upper-income borrowers, and a reduction in interest rates for borrowers.

Each policy adjustment made in HEA reauthorizations triggers policy considerations for states and higher education institutions. The specific impact of even marginal adjustments to the HEA differs across states given their unique social, political, and economic contexts. If reauthorization trends of decreased federal government investment in need-based student grant aid and increased measures of accountability continue, states and institutions may face significant policy choices associated with funding postsecondary access and opportunities for disadvantaged students. *SEE ALSO:* Education; Great Society; Johnson, Lyndon B.

BIBLIOGRAPHY: James B. Stedman, *The Higher Education Act: Reauthorization Status and Issues* (Washington, DC: Congressional Research Service, 2003); and Thomas R. Wolanin, ed., *Reauthorizing the Higher Education Act: Issues and Options* (Washington, DC: Institute for Higher Education Policy, 2003).

JANET M. HOLDSWORTH

Higher Education Compacts   *See* Regional Higher Education Compacts

Hines v. Davidowitz   In *Hines v. Davidowitz* (1941), the U.S. Supreme Court invalidated a Pennsylvania law requiring aliens to register with state authorities because the federal Alien Registration Act of 1940, which required aliens to register with federal authorities, had preempted the field. While the federal law did not explicitly preclude state regulation, the Court held that preemption was implied because of the paramount federal interest in the regulation of resident aliens. *SEE ALSO: Pennsylvania v. Nelson*; Preemption

ROBERT W. LANGRAN

Hipolite Egg Company v. United States   In *Hipolite Egg Company v. United States* (1911), the Court upheld the federal Pure Food and Drug Act of 1906, which prohibited the shipment of adulterated foods in interstate commerce. In this case, the Hipolite Egg Company was penalized for shipping fifty cans of preserved whole eggs that upon inspection contained 2 percent boric acid and were declared adulterated (impure). Relying on its 1908 precedent, *Champion v. Ames*, which had upheld a federal ban on the shipment of lottery tickets in interstate commerce, and rejecting claims that the federal law violated the Tenth Amendment, the Court commented that Congress's control over interstate commerce was "subject to no limitations except those found in the Constitution." *SEE ALSO: Champion v. Ames*; Commerce among the States; *Hammer v. Dagenhart*; Tenth Amendment

ELLIS KATZ

Holmes v. Walton   The case of *Holmes v. Walton* (1780), the first known use of the practice of judicial review, called into question a piece of legislation passed in 1778 by the New Jersey legislature. This legislation, passed to prevent trade and commerce with the enemy, made it lawful for the seizure of goods crossing enemy lines and for the prosecution of the perpetrators. The legislation further dictated that the justice, upon the request of either party involved, must allow a jury of six men to hear the case. The ruling on this case was then incapable of being appealed. On May 24, 1779, a justice of the peace of Monmouth County, New Jersey, and a jury of six men heard the case between plaintiff Elisha Walton and defendants John Holmes and Solomon Ketcham. The jury of six found Holmes and Ketcham guilty of violating the law.

However, Holmes and Ketcham appealed to the New Jersey Supreme Court on the basis that the initial legislation providing for a jury of six was unconstitutional under the provisions of the New Jersey Constitution. Arguing on why the initial ruling should be reversed, the defendants claimed that the New Jersey Constitution required a common law jury of twelve men, citing Section 22, which stated that "the inestimable right of trial by jury shall remain confirmed as part of the law of this colony without repeal forever." The final section of the same Constitution required an oath of each legislator that he will not subscribe to any law or vote that would repeal or annul Section 22. The case of *Holmes v. Walton* was decided before the New Jersey Supreme Court under the direction of Chief Justice David Brearly on September 7, 1780. Finding in favor of the plaintiffs, Holmes and Ketcham, the court ruled that common law was understood to require a jury of twelve and that the legislature, in passing the seizure law, had indeed overstepped its constitutional authority by altering the right of jury that the Constitution had previously established. Despite protestations of the decision at the time, the public later accepted the Supreme Court's verdict, as well as its authority to render it, and the legislature soon ratified the action of the judiciary by passing a law to require a jury of twelve on the demand of either party involved in the suit.

In the decision of *Holmes v. Walton*, the New Jersey Supreme Court laid the foundations for the practice that would later become known as judicial review in the famous federal case of *Marbury v. Madison*. Furthermore, the court challenged the notion of the supremacy of state legislatures held in the nation prior to the constitutional reforms. By ruling a legislative act null and void on questions of constitutionality, the New Jersey court also helped establish the republican notion of judicial independence from the popularly elected executive and legislative bodies that the founders would later adopt at the Constitutional Convention in 1787. *SEE ALSO:* Original Jurisdiction of Supreme Court

> *BIBLIOGRAPHY:* Horace Davis, "Annulment of Legislation by the Supreme Court," *American Political Science Review* 7, no. 4 (November, 1913): 541–87; and Austin Scott, "Holmes v. Walton: The New Jersey Precedent," *American Historical Review* 4, no. 3 (April 1889): 456–69.

MEREDITH BINTZ

Home Building and Loan v. Blaisdell In *Home Building and Loan Association v. Blaisdell* (1934), the U.S. Supreme Court upheld the Minnesota Mortgage Moratorium Act of 1933 over a charge that it was a violation of the Contract Clause of the Constitution. The law allowed for a time extension before mortgages could be foreclosed, but it did not cancel the debt nor did it allow the farmers to put off payment indefinitely. The Supreme Court in a five-to-four decision authored by Chief Justice Charles Evans Hughes upheld the law, saying that in times of emergency governments may do things that they cannot do in normal times. This was one of those measures, and the Contract Clause of the Constitution was not abridged because the mortgages still had to be paid. To many observers, the decision seemed to mark the end of the use of the Contract Clause as a limitation on the states' police power. *SEE ALSO:* Contract Clause; *Dartmouth College v. Woodward*; *Fletcher v. Peck*; *Stone v. Mississippi*; *United States Trust Company v. New Jersey*

ROBERT W. LANGRAN

Home Rule Also referred to as local control, community autonomy, and self-governance, home rule is the principle that local governments in the American federal system should possess a high degree of discretionary authority in serving their communities. The contrast is with strong state government control over community public affairs. Legally, there is no inherent right of self-governance for American communities, because of the constitutional status of local governments as creatures of their states. To the degree that it exists, home rule is a result of politics, voter preferences, ideology, administrative convenience, and the willingness of state governments to delegate specific powers or allow broad authority to their local governments.

The home rule movement, associated with Progressive reform in American government, originated in the later half of the nineteenth century as a response to the corruption and inefficiency involved in excessive state interference in municipal affairs. How much authority to allow local governments since that time has been the central issue in state-local relationships, marked by ongoing debate on such issues as state mandates and flexible revenue sources.

Home rule is implemented by state constitutions and legislatures in several ways— granting municipalities (and counties, to a lesser extent) the ability to adopt their own charters with variable governmental frameworks, prohibitions on "special legislation" that applies only to single communities, generic rules for municipal formation, and broad grants of regulatory and corporate powers. By applying a liberal construction to constitutional language regarding local powers, the courts in many states also maintain the local control principle.

Home rule is a relative condition that differs by state, type of local government, type of power, and policy or program area. Today about four-fifths of all states grant their local units substantial but varying degrees of home rule. It is usually confined to general purpose governments, municipalities (townships in some states), and counties, excluding narrow purpose school and special districts. Because of their role as administrative agents of state government, counties are given less discretion than municipalities. States are most generous in allowing local authority over structural or government organization choices, but also grant varying discretion over service delivery, regulatory, personnel, and fiscal matters.

The philosophical argument for home rule is grounded in the virtues of grassroots democracy. This considers local governments as not only service delivery organizations; more fundamentally they are representative institutions and thus agents of their citizens. Pluralism and local needs are served by allowing communities within the same state to adopt different governance arrangements and public policies. On the other hand, the critique is that community political systems, if left to their own devices and reflecting the vicissitudes of local prejudice, can produce governmental outcomes that are arbitrary, discriminatory, and externally negative. Thus, there are federal and state constitutional and statutory restraints on local control, as applied in First Amendment, civil rights, environmental protection, and other arenas. *SEE ALSO:* Dillon's Rule; Unfunded Mandates

ALVIN D. SOKOLOW

Homeland Security *See* USA PATRIOT Act of 2001

Homestead Act of 1862 The Homestead Act of 1862 gave a citizen, or an immigrant who intended to become a citizen, the right to buy 160 acres of government land for a modest fee after occupying it for five consecutive years.

The steady westward flow of settlers during the antebellum period helped prompt Congress to address the settlement, sale, and distribution of federally owned western lands. Legislative proposals concerning these issues frequently produced vigorous debate over both practical policy details and their wider sectional implications. In regard to policy, Congress came to consider three main approaches. Preemption, a method that became law in 1830, allowed a settler who squatted on public lands to purchase a maximum of 160 acres at prices as low as $1.25 an acre. Graduation, an approach that took the force of law in 1854, involved the steady reduction of prices on lands that did not sell after being on the market for more than a decade. The third manner of dealing with western land called for Congress to provide free or nominally "free" homesteads of 160 acres to poor and landless Americans. By the 1850s, northern and western legislators had focused their attentions on securing the passage of a homestead act of this type. By contrast, Southerners in Congress opposed such a law because they feared it would devalue their lands, produce a higher tariff, and people the West with antislavery settlers. Despite southern efforts, momentum toward a homestead act continued to build during the 1850s. After failing to pass in 1852, 1854, and 1859, a homestead bill finally passed Congress in 1860 but was vetoed by President James Buchanan.

After secession, Republican legislators, no longer hindered by southern opposition, passed the Homestead Act of 1862. It allowed a "head of a family" over the age of 21 (or younger if a veteran) who had not fought for or aided the Confederacy to pay a $10 fee for a claim of up to 160 acres. After dwelling on a homestead for five consecutive years, applicants could earn title to the land by paying fees ranging from $26 to $34. Applicants could also choose to buy the land after six months for as little as $1.25 per acre. To block speculation, the law stipulated that homestead land was solely for the use of "actual settlement and cultivation," and could not be used to benefit anyone but the settler and his or her family.

In practice, the Homestead Act did not always deliver what it seemed to promise to land-hungry settlers. Much of the land available under the Homestead Act was of limited agricultural value, and 160 acres frequently proved to be too small of a plot for profitable western farming. Yet the law's impact was significant. During the Civil War, almost 20,000 settlers claimed lands totaling 3 million acres, and in sum this law provided for the distribution of over 80 million acres of land. Perhaps most importantly, the Homestead Act of 1862 demonstrates the key role that the federal government played in the settlement of the West. *SEE ALSO:* Civil War; Public Lands

BIBLIOGRAPHY: Leonard P. Curry, *Blueprint for Modern America: Nonmilitary Legislation of the First Civil War Congress* (Nashville, TN: Vanderbilt University Press, 1968); and Roy M. Robbins, *Our Landed Heritage: The Public Domain, 1776–1936* (Princeton, NJ: Princeton University Press, 1942).

GREGORY J. RENOFF

Horizontal Federalism   *See* Interstate Relations

Housing   The housing policy arena is characterized by a highly defined division of labor across governmental jurisidictions. Funding for the largest housing programs is provided by the federal government, while local governments have responsibility for implementation of these programs. The federal government has passed laws regulating against discrimination in the housing market and regulating the operation of lending institutions. Local governments promulgate land-use and building regulations affecting housing. State government plays an intermediate role, providing lower levels of funding and program implementation that vary from state to state.

The federal government funds the largest programs of publicly subsidized housing through direct budgetary allocations as well as through tax expenditures. The Department of Housing and Urban Development (HUD) is responsible for the administration of the largest budget-based housing assistance programs, including the public housing program, the Housing Choice Voucher program, and the HOME program, the largest federal block grant designed to create affordable low-income housing. The Community Development Block Grant (CDBG), also administered by HUD, provides a large amount of funding for assisted housing. In each of these programs, HUD makes funds available to local entities that implement the program. The public housing and Housing Choice Voucher programs are operated by local public housing authorities, public agencies that are created in order to receive the federal funding from these two programs. The HOME and CDBG programs are block grants made to local governments who then use the funds for local governmental programs as well as distribute the funds locally to subgrantees (typically private or nonprofit organizations).

The federal government also authorizes tax incentives that account for large housing production programs such as the Low Income Housing Tax Credit and the Mortgage Revenue Bonds. In these programs, the federal government authorizes tax expenditures on a state-by-state basis. The implementation of these programs, like the direct budgetary programs, is done locally. Local governments allocate the tax credits and utilize the bonding authority to support specific assisted housing projects that are typically built and operated by private for-profit or nonprofit developers. The federal government also authorizes the mortgage interest deduction from personal income taxes. This is, in fact, the largest single federal subsidy program in housing. Individuals who own their homes and pay interest on a mortgage can deduct that interest on their federal income taxes.

Most state governments make direct budgetary expenditures for housing assistance. The overall amount, however, is not great. The spending of the federal government through HUD is many times greater than the aggregate of all state and local spending on housing and community development. State housing agencies typically operate their own housing assistance programs (i.e., they offer subsidies directly to families or to housing developers), and sometimes make intergovernmental transfers to localities for assisted housing.

Local governments very rarely devote any of their own revenues to subsidized housing programs, although this happens to a limited degree in some larger cities. They rely instead on the range of intergovernmental resources described above that are made available by the federal and state governments. Instead, local governments engage in housing policy in mainly two ways. First, they implement the programs funded by the federal and state governments. Local housing authorities run the public housing and housing voucher programs. Local housing and community development agencies (usually regular departments in the city government structure) implement the CDBG and HOME block grants. It is the local government that works most closely with the private and nonprofit developers who build and operate affordable housing. They do so by making loans and subsidies available to the developers.

The second manner in which local governments engage in housing policy is through the creation of land-use and building regulations. These regulations are very important in determining where and at what density housing can be built, what the materials and design alternatives are, and how the housing fits into the built environment around it. These regulations can have very large impacts on housing costs. Some suburban communities, for example, have been accused of rigging their local regulations so as to minimize the amount of affordable housing that is built. This has led a small number of states to create review processes by which local regulations and their implementation might be overturned by regional or state authorities. These programs are rare, however. In almost all states, local governments have unconstrained regulatory power in land-use and development matters. *SEE ALSO:* Land Use

BIBLIOGRAPHY: Victoria Basolo, "Passing the Housing Policy Baton in the US: Will Cities Take the Lead?" *Housing Studies* 14, no. 4 (1999): 433–52; Edward G. Goetz, *Shelter Burden: Local Politics and Progressive Housing Policy* (Philadelphia: Temple University Press, 1993); and Michael Stegman, *State and Local Affordable Housing Programs: A Rich Tapestry* (Washington, DC: Urban Land Institute, 1999).

EDWARD G. GOETZ

Implied Powers of the U.S. Constitution   The United States, unlike most other national governments, is a government of limited powers. In theory, it possess only those powers specifically granted it by the Constitution, most of which are listed ("enumerated") in Article I, Section 8. The eighteenth and last of the listed powers, however, is the power of Congress to "make all Laws which shall be necessary and proper" to the execution of its specified powers. These laws are therefore made on the basis of Congress's "implied powers," and throughout our history, a major issue has been how to define them and determine their extent.

The question of the scope of Congress's implied powers arose during President George Washington's first administration in connection with a proposal by Congress to charter a national bank. The power to charter a bank is not granted to Congress as an enumerated power, but does Congress nonetheless possess it as an implied power? In deciding whether to sign or veto the proposal, President Washington asked the advice of Secretary of State Thomas Jefferson, Secretary of the Treasury Alexander Hamilton, and Attorney General Edmund Randolph.

Jefferson and Randolph argued that additional congressional power should not be implied from an enumerated power unless it was absolutely necessary to the exercise of that power. Otherwise, implication would have no stopping point, and Congress would in effect have all power. Therefore, they advised President Washington, the law chartering the bank was unconstitutional. Hamilton argued, on the other hand, that Congress has implied power to adopt any means useful to carrying out the enumerated powers, because it was in the interest of the nation that Congress act efficiently. He said that the bank would be useful to Congress in, for example, executing its war power, which required paying troops and transferring funds from place to place in the nation. Washington accepted Hamilton's argument, and signed the bill into law.

The question of the power of Congress to charter a bank and, more generally, of the scope of Congress's implied powers came before the Supreme Court in 1819 in the famous case of *McCulloch v. Maryland*. The opinion of the Court was by Chief Justice John Marshall, who was, like Hamilton, a member of the Federalist Party and a firm believer in a strong national government. Closely following Hamilton's argument to President Washington, Marshall held that the Constitution's grant of enumerated powers to Congress carried with it a grant of the means of making their exercise effective. The Necessary and Proper Clause did not limit the implied powers, he said, to those that were absolutely necessary or indispensable to the execution of the enumerated powers; it was enough that the means chosen by Congress was convenient or useful. The law creating a national bank was within the power of Congress and constitutional, therefore, because the bank was convenient, as Hamilton had argued, for the deposit and transfer from place to place of federal funds.

The *McCulloch* decision is one of the most important in our history because it effectively settled that the scope of Congress's implied powers is very broad. Combined with the fact that some of the enumerated powers of Congress, particularly the power to tax (and spend) for the general welfare and the power to regulate interstate commerce, are also very broad, the result is that although the national government is said to be a government of limited power, as a practical matter there is very little, if anything, that is beyond its power to regulate. *SEE ALSO:* Enumerated Powers of the U.S. Constitution; Hamilton, Alexander; Commerce among the States; Jefferson, Thomas; Marshall, John; *McCulloch v. Maryland*; Necessary and Proper Clause

BIBLIOGRAPHY: Daniel J. Elazar, *American Federalism*, 3rd ed. (New York: Harper & Row, 1984); and *McCulloch v. Maryland*, 17 U.S. (4th Seat) 316 (1819).

LINO A. GRAGLIA

Incorporation (Nationalization) of the Bill of Rights   As it emerged from the Philadelphia convention in the fall of 1787, the proposed new Constitution of the United States did not contain a bill of rights. During the struggle over the Constitution's ratification, however, an almost universally voiced criticism of the new framework of government was that it lacked a bill of rights and that the national government being proposed would exercise its enhanced powers in a manner that would encroach upon the rights of individuals. The Constitution's supporters consequently promised that if it were ratified without change, the addition of a bill of rights would be proposed by the first Congress to meet after ratification. Drafted by James Madison, a bill of rights was proposed by the Congress in 1789 and was ratified by a sufficient number of the states in December 1791.

The addition of the Bill of Rights to the Constitution was therefore the political price that the supporters of the Constitution were constrained to pay for the ratification of the Constitution. And it was also clear that the almost universal demand for the addition of the Bill of Rights to the Constitution resulted from the fear that the new national government being created by the Constitution would exercise its powers in a manner inimical to the rights and liberties of the people. The founding generation thus understood that the rights guaranteed in the Bill of Rights were restrictions of the powers of the national government, and were not directed at restricting the powers of the state and local governments. This understanding of the applicability of the rights in the Bill of Rights was confirmed by the U.S. Supreme Court in *Barron v. Baltimore* in 1833. Speaking for a unanimous Court, Chief Justice John Marshall held that the rights in the Bill of Rights were not applicable to exercises of power by the state and local governments but were applicable only as restraints on the powers of the national government.

Prior to the Civil War, therefore, the Bill of Rights played an important albeit restricted role in American constitutional law, since the rights contained in the Bill of Rights could only be legitimately invoked to challenge exercises of power by the national government, but not those of state and local governments. In the wake of the Civil War, however, the Fourteenth Amendment was added to the Constitution in 1868, and unlike the Bill of Rights, the Fourteenth Amendment was directed at imposing restrictions on the powers of the state and local governments. This was particularly true of the amendment's Due Process Clause, which provided that no state shall "deprive any person of life, liberty, or property, without due process of law." During the course of interpreting the meaning of the words "liberty" and "property," and the phrase "due process of law," in the decades that followed the ratification of the Fourteenth Amendment, the Supreme Court would fundamentally alter the pre–Civil War understanding that the Bill of Rights was restrictive of the powers of the national government alone, and would incrementally through the Due Process Clause of the Fourteenth Amendment make most of the rights in the Bill of Rights applicable as restrictions of the powers of the state and local governments as well.

This nationalization of the Bill of Rights—that is, the application of most of the rights in the Bill of Rights as restrictions of the powers of state and local governments via the Due Process Clause of the Fourteenth Amendment—was nonetheless initially steadfastly resisted by the Supreme Court in its interpretation of the Due Process Clause. In a series of decisions between 1870 and 1900, for example, the Court held that the Due Process Clause did not require the states to try civil cases involving more than $20 by juries, to indict criminal defendants by grand juries, or to afford criminal defendants jury trials, although the provisions of the Fifth, Sixth, and Seventh Amendments of the Bill of Rights imposed these requirements on the national government. Such decisions provoked vigorous dissenting opinions by Justice John Marshall Harlan, who argued that the purpose of the Fourteenth Amendment had been to make all of the rights in the Bill of Rights applicable as restrictions of the powers of the state and local governments. (This contention would later be called the "total incorporation" theory or position.)

In 1897, however, a breakthrough occurred regarding the nationalization of the Bill of Rights in the decisions of the Supreme Court. In *Chicago, Burlington & Quincy Railway Co. v. Chicago* (1897), the Court held that the Due Process Clause of the Fourteenth Amendment required the state and local governments to provide just compensation when private property was taken by those governments for public purposes. Since the Just Compensation Clause in the Fifth Amendment of the Bill of Rights required just compensation for private property taken for public uses, the Court had for the first time held that a right in the Bill of Rights was also a limitation imposed on the state and local governments by the Due Process Clause of the Fourteenth Amendment.

This ruling, however, posed a theoretical problem for the Supreme Court, since it had held in *Barron v. Baltimore* in 1833 that the rights in the Bill of Rights were inapplicable to the state and local governments, yet it had now ruled that state and local governments must give just compensation for private property taken for public uses, a right also guaranteed in the Fifth Amendment of the Bill of Rights. A theoretical reconciliation of the apparently contradictory rulings in the *Barron* and *Chicago, Burlington & Quincy Railway* cases thus appeared necessary, and the Court attempted such a reconciliation in its decision in *Twining v. New Jersey* in 1908.

In the *Twining* case, the Court rejected (over another vigorous dissent by Justice Harlan) the proposition that the Due Process Clause of the Fourteenth Amendment guaranteed a right against compulsory self-incrimination in state criminal proceedings, although the Self-incrimination Clause of the Fifth Amendment of the Bill of Rights guaranteed such a right in criminal proceedings conducted by the national government. In discussing the meaning of the Due Process Clause of the Fourteenth Amendment, however, the Court conceded that the clause guaranteed fundamental rights as limitations of state and local governmental powers, and that indeed the Due Process Clause might guarantee as restrictions on state and local governments certain rights like some of those found in the Bill of Rights. If this were so, the Court added, "it is not because those rights are enumerated in the first eight Amendments [the Bill of Rights], but because they are of such a nature that they are included in the conception of due process of law."

While not free of ambiguity, the received understanding of this statement was that the Court was now saying that the rights in the Bill of Rights were not applicable to the state and local governments via the Due Process Clause of the Fourteenth Amendment (thus reaffirming the *Barron* ruling), but that the Due Process Clause might guarantee against state and local governments some rights similar to some of those in the Bill of Rights (as had been held in the *Chicago, Burlington & Quincy Railway* case). If this were so, however, the rights thus guaranteed by the Due Process Clause had as their source the Due Process Clause alone, and not the Bill of Rights, and they were consequently only similar to their counterparts in the Bill of Rights and not identical to them. It was under this *Twining* theory that the nationalization of the Bill of Rights proceeded until the 1940s with regard to First Amendment rights and until the 1960s regarding rights in the field of criminal procedure.

While the Court's discussion of the relationship between the Due Process Clause of the Fourteenth Amendment and the Bill of Rights in the *Twining* case appeared to point toward future rulings holding rights at least similar to some of those in the Bill of Rights to be protected by the Due Process Clause and thus restrictive of the state and local governments, in fact no such rulings by the Court occurred for over fifteen years following the *Twining* decision. In 1925, however, with its decision in *Gitlow v. New York*, the Court again took a major step down the road of nationalizing the Bill of Rights. Benjamin Gitlow had argued that the Due Process Clause protected freedom of speech against restrictions by state and local governments, and that his conviction in New York courts for advocating criminal anarchy thus violated the Constitution. While the Supreme Court affirmed Gitlow's conviction, it did state during the course of its opinion in the *Gitlow* case that "we may and do assume that freedom of speech and of the press—which are protected by the First Amendment from abridgment by Congress—are among the fundamental personal rights and 'liberties' protected by the due process clause of the Fourteenth Amendment from impairment by the states."

This "assumption" that the freedoms of speech and press were protected by the Due Process Clause of the Fourteenth Amendment against invasion by state and local governments was subsequently confirmed by the Court in *Near v. Minnesota* 1931. There followed a series of decisions between 1937 and 1947 starting with *DeJonge v. Oregon* (1937) in which the Court also held that the freedom of assembly and the free exercise of religion as well as the prohibition of an establishment of religion, all rights protected by the First Amendment of the Bill of Rights, were also protected by the Due Process Clause. The nationalization of the First Amendment freedoms was thus complete by 1947.

In a development that paralleled its nationalization of First Amendment freedoms, the Supreme Court began to hold that the Due Process Clause additionally protected certain rights of the criminally accused like some of those in the Bill of Rights. In

Powell v. Alabama (1932), the Court held that the states were required to appoint attorneys for indigent criminal defendants in capital cases as well as in noncapital cases in which the lack of counsel for the defendant would result in an unfair trial. In the *Powell* case, the Court thus held that the Due Process Clause guaranteed a right like that protected by the Assistance of Counsel Clause of the Sixth Amendment of the Bill of Rights. In 1936, the Court further barred the use of coerced confessions in state criminal proceedings, recognizing that the Due Process Clause protected against state abridgment a right similar to that protected by the Self-incrimination Clause of the Fifth Amendment. And in 1948 and 1949, the Court also ruled that the Due Process Clause prohibited secret criminal proceedings and unreasonable searches and seizures, rights like those protected by the Public Trial Clause of the Sixth Amendment and the prohibition found within the Fourth Amendment.

While nationalizing certain rights of the criminally accused, the Court continued to adhere to the *Twining* theory that the rights protected by the Due Process Clause had their source in the Due Process Clause alone, and were therefore only similar to their counterparts in the Bill of Rights. The right to counsel recognized by the Court in the *Powell* case in 1932 as applicable in state criminal proceedings was thus only similar to the right to counsel applicable in federal criminal proceedings via the Assistance of Counsel Clause of the Sixth Amendment. And while barring the use of coerced confessions in state criminal cases under the Due Process Clause in 1936, the Court rejected the proposition that the Self-incrimination Clause of the Fifth Amendment was applicable to the states. While continuing to adhere to the *Twining* theory, the Court also in 1937 rejected the proposition, first advanced by Justice John Marshall Harlan, that the Due Process Clause applied all of the rights in the Bill of Rights as restrictions of state and local governmental power.

In *Palko v. Connecticut* (1937), counsel for Frank Palko argued not only that the Double Jeopardy Clause of the Fifth Amendment was applicable in state criminal proceedings via the Due Process Clause but also that all of the rights in the Bill of Rights were applicable to the states. In an opinion by Justice Benjamin N. Cardozo, the Supreme Court rejected both contentions. Cardozo conceded nonetheless that certain rights, such as freedom of speech and of the press, that were guaranteed in the Bill of Rights had been "absorbed" into the Due Process Clause of the Fourteenth Amendment. Those rights that had been so absorbed, he said, were "implicit in the scheme of ordered liberty" or "of the very essence of a scheme of ordered liberty," or embodied a "principle of justice so rooted in the history and traditions of our people as to be ranked as fundamental." Additionally, Cardozo noted, the Due Process Clause also protected those rights essential to a fair trial or hearing, such as the right to appointed counsel for indigent criminal defendants, and barred the imposition in the criminal process of any hardship "so shocking that our polity will not endure it." But, Cardozo continued, the rights protected by the Due Process Clause did not include the Fifth Amendment's requirement of a grand jury indictment or the rights against self-incrimination and double jeopardy, nor the Sixth and Seventh Amendments' requirements of jury trials in criminal cases as well as civil cases involving more than $20.

The Supreme Court's opinion in the *Palko* case reflected the virtually unanimous consensus of the justices in 1937 regarding the theory guiding the nationalization process, since only Justice Pierce Butler dissented without opinion in the case. When the Court next addressed the underlying theory guiding nationalization, in *Adamson v. California* (1947), however, this virtual unanimity was shattered, and the Court was revealed to be deeply divided over the nationalization process. In the *Adamson* case, the Court was once again confronted with an argument that the Self-incrimination Clause of the Fifth Amendment should apply to the states via the Due Process Clause of the Fourteenth Amendment. And a majority of five members of the Court rejected this contention, relying on the previous decision in *Twining v. New Jersey* (1908). The Due Process Clause, the majority said, required only that the states afford criminal defendants a fair trial, and the right against compulsory self-incrimination was not essential to a fair trial.

In a dissenting opinion joined by Justices William O. Douglas, Wiley Rutledge, and Frank Murphy, Justice Hugo Black argued that the intention of the framers of the Fourteenth Amendment had been to make all of the rights in the Bill of Rights applicable to the states, including the Self-incrimination Clause of the Fifth Amendment. In addition to his support for total incorporation of the Bill of Rights into the Fourteenth Amendment, Justice Black rejected the *Twining* theory of nationalization, which was passionately defended by Justice Felix Frankfurter in a concurring opinion. The rights applicable to the states via the Fourteenth Amendment should be identical to those in the Bill of Rights, Black argued, and not just similar to their Bill of Rights counterparts, as was the case under the *Twining* theory.

The *Adamson* case was the high tide of total incorporationism, since that position would never again receive as much support on the Court as it did in 1947. And despite Justice Black's attack on the *Twining* theory, it continued to guide the Court's decisions regarding the nationalization process in the field of criminal procedure until the 1960s. Curiously, however, the *Twining* theory was abandoned without discussion by the Court in the field of First Amendment freedoms in the 1940s. At that time, the Court in case after case began to refer to the First Amendment rights applicable to the states as identical to those protected by the First Amendment and not as only similar as under the *Twining* theory. Paradoxically, however, the Court continued to adhere to the *Twining* theory in the field of criminal procedure.

By 1960, an intermediate position had emerged on the Supreme Court between the supporters of the *Twining* theory of nationalization and the total incorporation position, which continued to be supported by Justices Hugo Black and William O. Douglas. This intermediate position, supported by Chief Justice Earl Warren and Justice William Brennan, rejected total incorporation but supported the position that most but not all of the rights in the Bill of Rights should apply to the states via the Due Process Clause of the Fourteenth Amendment. This "selective incorporation" position also agreed with the total incorporation position on an important point—that is, the selective incorporationists supported the proposition that if a right in the Bill of Rights applied to the states, it should be identical to the same right in the Bill of Rights and not just similar as under the *Twining* theory. The incorporationists, whether selective or total, thus agreed that any right nationalized via the Due Process Clause had the same scope and meaning in its application to the states as it had as a limitation on the power of the national government in the Bill of Rights.

In 1961, the incorporationist approach to the nationalization process secured a breakthrough victory in *Mapp v. Ohio*. In 1949, in accordance with the *Twining* theory, the Court had ruled that the Due Process Clause protected a right against unreasonable searches and seizures similar to that in the Fourth Amendment, but that only the "core" of the prohibition in the Fourth Amendment applied to the states and not the Fourth Amendment itself. Additionally, the Court had held, the federal exclusionary rule, prohibiting the admission in criminal trials of evidence seized in violation of the Fourth Amendment, did not apply to criminal proceedings in the state courts. In the *Mapp* case, however, the Court held not only that the Fourth Amendment applied to the states via the Due Process Clause but also that evidence seized by state officers in violation of the Fourth and Fourteenth Amendments should be excluded in state criminal trials. Although the incorporationists did not command a majority on the Court in 1961, a year later the retirement of two supporters of the *Twining* theory and their replacement with supporters of the selective incorporation approach solidified an incorporationist majority on the Court, with the result that the *Twining* theory was scuttled in the field of criminal procedure as it had been in the field of First Amendment freedoms in the 1940s. Between 1962 and 1969, therefore, there occurred a series of incorporationist decisions by the Court applying most of the criminal procedure provisions of the Bill of Rights to the states in the identical form as they applied as limitations of the power of the national government. The provisions incorporated during this period included the prohibition of cruel and unusual punishments in the Eighth Amendment (1962); the full right to counsel provision of the Sixth Amendment (1963); the prohibition of compulsory self-incrimination of the Fifth Amendment (1964), reversing *Twining v. New Jersey* (1908) and *Adamson v. California* (1947); the right to confront and cross-examine witnesses in the Sixth Amendment (1965); the right to a speedy trial and to subpoena witnesses to testify for a defendant in the Sixth Amendment (1967); the right to a jury trial in state criminal cases guaranteed in the Sixth Amendment (1968), reversing the Court's earlier 1900 decision (*Maxwell v. Dow*) that jury trials were not required in state criminal cases; and finally, the prohibition of double jeopardy in the Fifth Amendment (1969), reversing *Palko v. Connecticut* (1937).

The only provisions of the Bill of Rights that were not made applicable to the states via the Due Process Clause by 1969 were the Second Amendment's provisions relating to the right to bear arms, the Third Amendment's prohibition of

---

INCORPORATION OF THE BILL OF RIGHTS

INCORPORATED

First Amendment's prohibition on the establishment of religion (Everson v. Board of Education *1947*)

First Amendment's free exercise of religion (Cantwell v. Connecticut *1940*)

First Amendment's freedom of speech (Gitlow v. New York *1925*)

First Amendment's freedom of the press (Near v. Minnesota *1931*)

First Amendment's freedom of assembly (De Jonge v. Oregon *1937*)

Fourth Amendment's ban on unreasonable searches and seizures (Wolf v. Colorado *1947*)

Fourth Amendment's exclusionary rule (Mapp v. Ohio *1961*)

Fifth Amendment's ban on compulsory self-incrimination (Malloy v. Hogan *1964*)

Fifth Amendment's ban on double jeopardy (Benton v. Maryland *1969*)

Sixth Amendment's right of notice (Cole v. Arkansas *1948*)

Sixth Amendment's right to a public trial (In re Oliver *1948*)

Sixth Amendment's right to counsel (Gideon v. Wainwright *1963*)

Continued on next page

Continued from previous page

Sixth Amendment's right to confront witnesses (Pointer v. Texas *1965)*

Sixth Amendment's right to an impartial jury (Parker v. Gladden *1966)*

Sixth Amendment's right to a speedy trial (Klopfer v. North Carolina *1967)*

Sixth Amendment's right to compulsory process (Washington v. Texas *1967)*

Sixth Amendment's right to a jury trial in criminal cases (Duncan v. Louisiana *1968)*

Eighth Amendment's ban on excessive bail (Schilb v. Kuebel *1971)*

Eighth Amendment's ban on cruel and unusual punishments (Robinson v. California *1962)*

NOT INCORPORATED

Second Amendment's right to bear arms

Third Amendment's ban on the quartering of soldiers

Fifth Amendment's right to indictment by a grand jury

Seventh Amendment's right to a jury trial in civil cases

Eighth Amendment's ban on excessive fines

quartering troops in persons' houses, the requirement of a grand jury indictment in serious criminal cases in the Fifth Amendment, the Seventh Amendment's requirement of a jury trial in all civil cases involving more than $20, and the prohibition of excessive fines and bail in the Eighth Amendment. Most, but not all, of the rights in the Bill of Rights have thus now been made applicable as restrictions of the powers of state and local governments. And the process of nationalizing the Bill of Rights has converted the Due Process Clause of the Fourteenth Amendment into a second American Bill of Rights more important than the original Bill of Rights adopted as a part of the Constitution in 1791. *SEE ALSO: Adamson v. California; Barron v. Baltimore;* Bill of Rights; Black, Hugo L.; Fourteenth Amendment; Frankfurter, Felix; Marshall, John; *Palko v. Connecticut; Slaughterhouse Cases*

BIBLIOGRAPHY: Richard C. Cortner, *The Supreme Court and the Second Bill of Rights* (Madison: University of Wisconsin Press, 1981); and William E. Leuchtenburg, *The Supreme Court Reborn* (New York: Oxford University Press, 1995).

RICHARD C. CORTNER

Insurance In his book *Couch on Insurance*, author George J. Couch defines insurance as a contract by which one party, for a consideration, which is usually paid in money either in one sum or at different times during the continuance of the risk, promises to make a certain payment of money upon the destruction or injury of something in which the other party has an interest. In fire insurance and in marine insurance the thing insured is property; in life or accident insurance it is the life or health of the person (Russ and Segalla 2002, 1, 6).

As a going concern, insurance has been defined by Kulp and Hall as "a formal social device for the substitution of certainty for uncertainty through the pooling of risks" (1968). In this vein, insurance may be conducted as either a public or private venture. Risk may be pooled, spread, and ultimately borne, either through full transference or through various kinds of cooperative ventures by which it may be shared among the risk parties themselves.

Insurance is of special note in discussions of federalism by virtue of the unique regulatory regime under which it is conducted in the United States. The regulation of most aspects of the insurance business as an aspect of commerce is carried on by the states under a very general "reverse preemption" against federal jurisdiction that is provided in the McCarran-Ferguson Act (P.L. 15, U.S.C., 1945). Jurisdictional and operational definitions of insurance therefore bear directly upon the scope and exercise of state regulatory authority.

At the level of state regulation, and therefore also in the context of establishing the scope and applicability of the reverse preemption under the McCarran-Ferguson Act, discussions of what constitutes insurance—and in a transactional sense, what constitutes the "conduct" or business of insurance—are given weight and meaning. Do, for example, the sales of auto club memberships or extended product or service warranties constitute the business of insurance? What about the terms of collision damage waivers in auto rental agreements? Regulators and state and federal courts have held variously on these and other peripheral issues over the years.

Of a less peripheral nature is the matter of regulating health insurance and managed care. There remains much continued conflict and uncertainty over the scope and meaning of the preemption clause under the federal Employee Retirement Income Security Act of 1974 (ERISA). The preemption clause is vague, and this holds major implications for state health and insurance policy makers. ERISA's preemption clause has been interpreted by courts in a piecemeal fashion and on a case-by-case basis with much inconsistency regarding the authority of the states to regulate health insurance plans. *SEE ALSO:* McCarran-Ferguson Act

BIBLIOGRAPHY: A. Kulp and John W. Hall, *Casualty Insurance*, 4th ed. (New York: Ronald Press Company, 1968); and Lee R. Russ and Thomas F. Segalla, eds. *Couch on Insurance*, 3rd ed. (St. Paul, MN: Thomson/West, 2002).

BENN PRYBUTOK

Intergovernmental Lobbying   In simple terms, intergovernmental lobbying involves governments lobbying other governments. The intergovernmental lobby is composed of state and local government officials' organizations (SLGOOs), which are similar to trade associations, and single governments, for example, a city or state. These groups lobby nationally and at state and local levels of government.

COMPOSITION OF THE INTERGOVERNMENTAL LOBBY

The intergovernmental lobby is typically thought of in terms of the "Big Seven" government officials' organizations in Washington, D.C., but it is more complex. Included in the Big Seven are the National Governors Association (NGA), United States Conference of Mayors (USCM), National League of Cities (NLC), National Association of Counties (NACo), International City County Managers Association (ICCMA), National Conference of State Legislatures (NCSL), and Council of State Governments (CSG). Each group is a policy "generalist" in that it lobbies for many programs or interests, yet there are scores of other generalist and "specialist" organizations located throughout the country that are less well known.

Policy "specialists" lobby for one or a few interrelated issues and outnumber generalists in quantity and diversity of interests. Notable specialists include the American

Association of State Highway and Transportation Officials (AASHTO), the International Association of Chiefs of Police (IACP), and the National Association of State Boards of Education (NASBE). Despite the few studies on specialists, a good resource is provided by David S. Arnold and Jeremy F. Plant in *Public Official Associations and State and Local Government: A Bridge across One Hundred Years* (1994).

The last component of the intergovernmental lobby includes individual states, cities, and special governments. All states and large municipalities have lobbying offices located in the Hall of the States located adjacent to Capitol Hill. Special governments—for example, public universities or ports—may have national, state, and (perhaps) local representation.

THE INTERESTS OF THE INTERGOVERNMENTAL LOBBY

According to Anne Marie Cammisa (1995), governments as interest groups lobby for the interests of their government, which are spatial and programmatic. Their spatial concerns, Donald Haider (1974) has argued, center on the level of government with funding control and implementation authority of programs within their geographical locale. Programmatically they are interested in flexible policies and the degree to which the federal government provides funding. While there is broad agreement among groups for increased federal funds and less federal regulation, substantial variation exists between the kinds of groups and levels of government. Generalists, for example, seek far less regulation than specialists. And specialists desire more federal provision of services while generalists want less. At the state level, Alan Rosenthal (2001) argues that county and local governments seek more state revenues, favorable tax policies, and to be left alone. Moreover, the electoral connection between national representative, state representatives, local officials, and voters makes it difficult for legislatures to act with disregard to local interests.

LOBBYING STRATEGIES AND TECHNIQUES

A useful model for understanding the decisions of where and when to lobby in our federal system is explained by the scope of conflict theory that E. E. Schattschneider (1960) presents in *Semi Sovereign People*. A requirement for effective lobbying is access, which Donald Haider (1974) argues is a result of their public official status, electoral connection, and policy expertise. The strategies and techniques employed by this lobby are similar to those used by other established lobbies; however, beyond the Big Seven operations, groups generally function under fiscal austerity.

Their most important lobbying function is monitoring bills; however, influencing officials is accomplished with an inside strategy, and outside techniques are almost never used. Most groups are classified as Internal Revenue Service 501(c)(3) organizations and prohibited from making campaign contributions. Congressional and federal agency behaviors include directly contacting national lawmakers, responding to requests for information, and joining coalitions. Lobbying the White House or the Office of Public Liaison (OPL) is infrequent, particularly for specialists. In federal courts, officials' groups, states, and cities are increasingly filing amicus curiae briefs.

In the states, Clive Thomas and Ronald Hrebenar (1996) note that public officials are some of the most powerful and active in state interest group communities. Their techniques are normally direct. Anthony Nownes (1999), in *Solicited Advice and Lobbyist*

Power: Evidence from Three American States, suggests further that public officials are often solicited for advice and gives them more opportunities to influence policy.

INTERGOVERNMENTAL LOBBYING ENVIRONMENT

The environments in which the intergovernmental groups operate are nonconflictual, as they typically do not compete for members, benefits, funding, and access to lawmakers. Where there is conflict, generalists experience greater levels both inside and outside of Washington when compared to specialists. Despite some conflict, generalists and specialists report broad consensus on policy goals. Both kinds of groups also experience low opposition from public officials and other groups. Frank Baumgartner and Beth Leech (2001) report that the intergovernmental lobby was second to business and trade groups in activity across 137 issues before the 1995 Congress. In low participatory areas (niches), state and local government lobbying accounted for 24 percent of the activity in niche issues, suggesting low conflict.

Competition and consensus vary within geographic regions and across states. Evidence suggests that government groups are present and active. Virginia Gray and David Lowery (1999) report that within interest group communities, government groups constitute 16 percent of lobbying organizations. And, more specifically, Virginia Gray and Herbert Jacob (1996) note that local governments, state departments, and local government associations are continually active as lobby organizations in at least 45 states. *SEE ALSO:* Public Officials' Associations

BIBLIOGRAPHY: David S. Arnold and Jeremy F. Plant, *Public Official Associations and State and Local Government: A Bridge across One Hundred Years* (Fairfax, VA: George Mason University Press, 1994); Frank R. Baumgartner and Beth L. Leech, "Interest Niches and Policy Bandwagons: Patterns of Interest Group Involvement in National Politics," *Journal of Politics* 63, no. 4: 1191–1213; Anne Marie Cammisa, *Governments as Interest Groups: Intergovernmental Lobbying and the Federal System* (Westport, CT: Praeger, 1995); Suzanne Farkas, *Urban Lobbying: Mayors in the Federal Arena* (New York: New York University Press, 1971); Virginia Gray and Herbert Jacob, eds., *Politics in the American States*, 6th ed. (Washington, DC: CQ Press, 1996); Donald Haider, *When Governments Come to Washington: Governors, Mayors and Intergovernmental Lobbying* (London: Free Press, 1974); David Lowery and Virginia Gray, "Interest Representation in the States," in *Change and Continuity in American State and Local Politics*, eds. Ronald E. Weber and Paul Brace (Chatham, NJ: Chatham House Press, 1999): 241–67; Anthony J. Nownes, "Solicited Advice and Lobbyist Power: Evidence from Three American States," *LegislativeStudies Quarterly* 24, no. 1 (February 1999): 113–24; E. E. Schattschneider, *The Semi-Sovereign People* (New York: Holt, Rinehart and Winston, 1960); Alan Rosenthal, *The Third House*, 2nd ed. (Washington, DC: CQ Press, 2001); and Clive S. Thomas and Ronald J. Hrebenar, "Interest Groups in the States," in *Politics in the American States*, 7th ed., eds. Virginia Gray, Russell L. Hanson, and Herbert Jacob (Washington, DC: Congressional Quarterly Press, 1999).

JACK MCGUIRE

Intergovernmental Management   Federal programs administered through the states and local governments and state programs carried out by local governments must be managed cooperatively. The process of managing programs involves officials working to solve problems that combine legal, technical, political, and project tasks.

Most domestic programs are administered through intergovernmental means in the U.S. federal system: federal-state-local, state-local, and local-local. They also employ nongovernmental organizations. The process of managing across jurisdictional boundaries is called "intergovernmental management" (IGM) by professionals and academics. IGM is the process of solving problems across the boundaries of jurisdictions that interrelate legal, political, technical, and project-related tasks in making programs work. The functions and processes of IGM are normally practiced by elected and appointed administrative officials, although on occasion legislative officials become involved in the processes of facilitating projects or clarifying policy aims.

INTERGOVERNMENTAL INSTRUMENTS

The management of programs almost always entails actions relating to the more common "action instruments" of intergovernmental relations. They are listed in Figure 1, classified by whether they are primarily economic, legal, administrative, or political in nature. Of the twenty-four actions illustrated, the most prevalent are related to grants, audits, tax policies, loans, regulation, intergovernmental agreements, basic laws, program standards, and intersectoral networks and councils.

PROGRAM MANAGEMENT

Three brief examples of managing programs illustrate the heavy involvement of administrative officials in programming within American federalism. First, a city wishes to preserve a historic three-square-block area near its central business district. It must first go through a federally required and state government–managed process of designation, which entails citizen hearings, financial feasibility studies, cost estimates for restoration, a plan of use, and ultimately a city council ordinance. If approved, the area is designated on the National Register of Historic Places. This allows building owners involved in rehabilitating their property to qualify for tax credits. After designation, the city can help developers qualify for state and federal funds and low-interest loans. There will follow numerous other contacts and negotiations to actually restore the buildings and arrange use.

Second, a county government is trying to attract a high-technology business within its borders. It will try to leverage some of its own money to gain resources from several federal and state programs. It could access U.S. Economic Development Administration funds to help with the land purchase, use Community Development Block Grants funds to pay for part of the construction, adopt an ordinance to use state-authorized/supervised tax increment financing (a program that devotes future tax increases to improvements) to pay for site improvement and infrastructure, secure state venture capital funds as a partial investment in the company, access U.S. Department of Labor funds for workforce training, and secure road improvement money from federal and state highway funding streams. Each of these efforts will require extensive work in making applications, negotiating with state/federal officials over purposes and details, seeking approvals from the county council and the potential investor, holding public hearings, and meeting a host of funding and program requirements.

Third, the Medicaid program, Title XIX of the Social Security Act, funds health care for the poor. In terms of expenditures, it is the largest single intergovernmental program in the United States. This federal state program involves the federal government setting minimum requirements for benefits, eligibility, and the reimbursement of health

FIGURE 1. Action Instruments of Intergovernmental Relations

1. **Economic Devices**

   - Grants or subventions (general revenue/unrestricted, broad/bloc, targeted/categorical)
   - Fiscal audits
   - Tax policies (reciprocal taxation schedules, tax abatements/forgiveness, tax sharing, tax transfers, tax cession)
   - Intergovernmental loans
   - Shared (with private sector and other governments) capital projects and investments, shared venture capital investments
   - Intergovernmental fiscal study/equalization commissions
   - Procurement of goods, services, and/or personnel from other governments

2. **Legal Approaches**

   - Intergovernmental regulation (program requirements, crossover rules, crosscutting requirements), executive orders, direct regulation, partial preemption, total preemption by higher level government
   - Cooperative agreements to jointly operate a program (e.g. health statistics, emergency management, and internal security)
   - Intergovernmental agreements (e.g. joint fire services, combined libraries, special education cooperatives, and mutual aid for police emergencies)
   - Interdependent legal actions (joint environmental action, joint workplace regulation, and joint income tax format agreements)
   - Basic laws on governmental structure, local taxation, local civil service, local powers

3. **Administrative Practices**

   - Program standards and requirements
   - Contracts for services/programming between governments
   - Exchange of personnel
   - Program audits (look behind reviews)
   - Regional/metropolitan governments or special authorities
   - Negotiated performance programs (in lieu of controls and requirements)

4. **Political/Government Bodies**

   - Intersectoral/intergovernmental networks and councils
   - Councils of governments (regional, metropolitan)
   - Intergovernmental associations (municipalities, counties, mayors, local councils, and local civil service unions)
   - Intergovernmental lobbying/representation
   - Elected official to elected official contacts
   - Political party channels

care providers, and establishing administrative rules that states must follow. States can then expand on the minimum requirements in regard to eligibility and services funded if they wish. Each year the states must file and then negotiate a "state plan" relating to how they intend to operate the program. The plan involves literally thousands of administrative details that are subject to interpretation, and in recent years several different kinds of "waivers" or excepted actions that permit states to fund services that would not otherwise be allowed, as well as a few dozen "assurances" that certain cross-program federal standards are met. During the plan year, state officials will engage in literally thousands of inquiries, subagreements, contracts, and informational transactions with local government and medical vendors, as well as with federal officials. Also, pages and pages of fiscal and program reporting will be collected. Finally, some two years or so after plans have been executed, the paper reporting will be audited by other federal officials. While the proportion of Medicaid spending on administration is quite small compared to its very large budget, no one has been able to estimate the cost impact of the paperwork burden or the extensive administrative time up and down the line that this program takes.

WATER QUALITY MANAGEMENT TASKS: LEGAL, TECHNICAL, POLITICAL, AND PROJECT

The multifaceted process of managing federal programs can be illustrated by examining one program that affects every citizen, that of ensuring that a healthy drinking water supply is available. The U.S. Safe Drinking Water Act (SWDA) of 1974 expanded the federal role in monitoring and standard setting to protect human health and the regulation of water suppliers. The program delegates inspection and enforcement to the states, and some states have further delegated authority to local governments. States are required to have programs that include statutory and regulatory enforcement authority adequate to ensure compliance, a system of conducting inspections of public water supply systems (sanitary surveys), a process to certify laboratories that test for contaminants, and other management provisions. The U.S. Environmental Protection Agency (EPA) pays around three-quarters of the costs of operating these programs, which includes a loan program for improvement of facilities. Most important for this illustration is the requirement in the act for the EPA to issue standards for any contaminant that may have an adverse effect on human health and that is known to occur in public drinking water supplies.

The legal issues involved are the published revisions of the Arsenic Rule in 2001 and the Drinking Water State Revolving Fund established in 1996 under amendments to SWDA. The EPA changed the Arsenic Rule from 50 parts per billion (ppb) to 10 ppb after the National Academy of Science concluded that the old level could not protect against nonfatal and fatal bladder and lung cancers and that the new level will reduce the frequency of other health effects such as diabetes, developmental problems, gastrointestinal illness, and heart disease. The rule applies to community and nontransit noncommunity water systems, 97 percent of which are small systems that serve fewer than 10,000 persons. Clearly the greatest challenge will be to help very small water systems overhaul or convert their systems at costs that will not be excessive financial burdens on their small customer bases.

Technically it means that over 3,000 community and 1,100 nontransit noncommunity systems have to overhaul their systems, the majority of which serve 500 or fewer users. Fortunately, several technologies are 90–95 percent effective, for example, modified lime softening, modified coagulation/filtration, coagulation-assisted microfiltration, oxidation filtration, and others. Some water suppliers are consolidating into larger systems or are finding new water sources. The total cost for investments in these treatment technologies is estimated to be about $900 million plus an additional $120 million in operating costs. Most states have begun to address the issue of small-system compliance with the Arsenic Rule, along with such other rules as one for uranium, by accelerating inspections and by devoting portions of their Revolving Loan Funds to upgrade small systems. In addition, other funding sources (mostly loans) are available: the U.S. Department of Agriculture/Rural Development, state-administered Community Development Block Grant funds (small cities), the Economic Development Administration, and state water resources programs. Grants or loans in some combination are available through one or more of these sources to assess water system needs, to procure an engineer's report, and to introduce new technologies.

The political process in small communities begins with finding a local official who is willing to take the lead in orchestrating the process. Most often it is the mayor, or it could be the city clerk, who may be the only full-time official. In others it might be a council member who "volunteers" to take on this administrative process. In larger cities it would be the city administrator or city manager, working along with the city engineer. Whoever leads the political process, it begins with contacting people in the state environmental agency to learn about the process and requirements, and to learn what steps need to be taken. In some states the different funding sources meet together to help smaller communities work the different sources. At this point the city will learn about the key role of hiring a consulting engineer, who will have to prepare reports and plans. The local official taking the lead will have to go back to the community and convince the city council to pass an ordinance putting the process of securing an engineering report and construction/treatment plan in motion. Normally a prior notification public hearing/meeting must also be held to seek public input on all available options, siting issues, environmental impacts, and costs. If the water system is to be consolidated with other systems either by clustering nearby communities or by establishing a new regional water system, then extensive political negotiations with other communities will ensue. After all of this processing, the local lead official can prepare applications for project funding.

The extensive project-related managerial activities then prevail over this Arsenic Rule process. The state agency receives the application that includes community financial data and the engineering consultant's report (which can be paid for by small grants). The report is reviewed for three basic concerns: feasibility of the user charge system to repay loans, city financial capability, and the environmental assessment review. The engineering report is also separately reviewed. When all reports are acceptable (and the thirty-day hearing is held), planning and design are approved. Then the process involves fee review and technical review of health effects by the state, and all federal cross-program assurances are checked. After any necessary revisions are negotiated, an approval letter for construction is issued. At this point the community must pass what is normally a routine loan authorizing resolution(s) or bond ordinance through its council if the existing revenue debt obligates the water rate. Then the loans from the various sources mentioned earlier are transacted and closed. At this point, which can take from three to six months, the community can open bids for construction. The construction phase finalizes the project, which will have a similarly involved sequence orchestrated by some manager and including the consulting engineer, city attorney, and city council/village board.

MANAGERS IN THE HORIZONTAL AND VERTICAL SYSTEM

Managers do more than talk on the phone, e-mail, or make personal contacts when they are working on programs within the federal system. Figure 2, taken from Agranoff and

FIGURE 2. Intergovernmental Management Practices

Type of Practice	Use in IGM	Purposes of Practice
Discretion-seeking (vertical)	Requesting and granting local "asymmetrical" treatment not technically or apparently within standards or regulations	Waivers Model program efforts Policy changes Funding innovation Negotiated flexibility Trading compliance for performance results
Information-seeking (vertical)	Seeking and providing program details and/or reaching operating understandings regarding program operations	Seek program availability and eligibility Seek program operation information Seek interpretation of standards Seek new funding Seek technical assistance
Project-based (horizontal)	Leverage and engagement of public and private resources to accomplish plans, projects, and other efforts	Develop managerial partnerships in projects Seek financial resources from partners Combine or leverage financial resources Build financial partnerships for projects
Structural design (horizontal)	Development and maintenance of organizations or networks for program design and implementation	Engage in joint policy making Seek policy-making assistance Consolidate policy effort Contracted planning or implementation Employ joint financial incentives Access technical resources

McGuire's *Collaborative Public Management* (2003) study of city economic development, lists twenty-one distinct type of IGM practices. They are both vertical (that is, those devices used for working with state and federal governmental officials) and horizontal (working with other local governments, NGOs, and the private sector). The vertical IGM instruments are of two types, those that try to make some form of adjustment within the system within the boundaries of the policy intent of programs and those designed to determine information or joint understandings. The horizontal instruments either serve particular investment projects or help develop or maintain networks of officials. The frequency of these actions, of course, varies from jurisdiction to jurisdiction, but all twenty-one activities are regular instruments used by managers. In sum, these are the instruments used to coordinate programs—that is, to help make programs work within a given situation.

MANAGEMENT: A KEY FEDERALISM TASK

Several forces converge to make managing within federalism a core activity of officials at all levels. First, there are high numbers of intergovernmental programs. In addition to the approximately 1,000 programs listed in the U.S. *Catalogue of Federal*

Domestic Assistance, (http://12.46.245.173/cfda/cfda.html) states offer hundreds of their own programs, which have increased in number in the past several decades. For example, the typical state has adopted up to thirty economic development programs or instruments since the 1970s. Second, the United States has a tradition of separation of governments and powers. Each level of government has different legislative and administrative branches, and at the local level many different types of government exist. Third, there is a tradition of jurisdictional autonomy in the United States. Every city or village, county government, and state government can claim some degree of independence or freedom from interference from higher levels as well as the right to pursue their own aims, even with programs that come from elsewhere. Fourth, the number of actors involved in programs has increased in recent years. In addition to governments, nongovernmental organizations such as private firms and nonprofit agencies have important implementation roles in programs. These new actors share intergovernmental administration with those who are inside governments. Fifth, many programs like the Arsenic Rule within SDWA have become very complicated, calling for legal, technical, and political skills to facilitate action. This has put a premium on administrative actors and program specialists. And sixth, there is increased concern for accountability and performance in programs. This means that there is more managerial activity involved in planning, reviewing, negotiating, and auditing. Together, these forces call attention to the less visible but important managerial aspect in American federalism. *SEE ALSO:* County Government; Economic Development; Education; Environmental Policy; Executive Orders; Federal-State Relations; Grants-in-Aid; Health Care Policy; Intergovernmental Lobbying; Intergovernmental Relations; Local Government; Medicaid; Political Parties; Preemption; Safe Drinking Water Act of 1974; Social Security Act of 1935; State Government

BIBLIOGRAPHY: Robert Agranoff and Michael McGuire, *Collaborative Public Management: New Strategies for Local Government* (Washington, DC: Georgetown University Press, 2003); Catalog of Federal Domestic Assistance, http://12.46.245.173/cfda/cfda.html; John J. Gargan, ed., *Handbook of State Government Administration* (New York: Marcel Dekker, 2000); Denise Scheberle, *Federalism and Environmental Policy* (Washington, DC: Georgetown University Press, 1997); and David B. Walker, *The Rebirth of Federalism*, 2nd ed. (New York: Chatham House, 2000).

ROBERT AGRANOFF

Intergovernmental Relations The term "intergovernmental relations" (IGR) was invented in the 1930s as a phrase unique to the United States. It was a novel concept aimed at summarizing the extensive and varied growth in relationships among the thousands of local, state, and national governing entities, as well as among the many officials holding important policy-making posts. William Anderson, widely credited with originating the concept, devoted two chapters formally titled "Intergovernmental Relations" in his comprehensive (fifty-two-chapter) *American Government* textbook (1938), with chapter subtitles labeled (1) "National-State and State-Local," and (2) "Interstate and Interlocal."

Years later, Anderson (in *Intergovernmental Relations in Review* [1960]) offered a provisional definition of IGR, stating that it "has become accepted to designate an important body of activities or interactions occurring between governmental units of all types and levels . . . it is human beings clothed with office who are the real determiners of what the relations between units of government will be, consequently the concept necessarily has to be formulated largely in terms of human relations and human behavior under the conditions that prevail when different people represent the interests of different units and different functions of government."

Anderson's initial conceptualizations and subsequent research and writings solidly established IGR in several respects. These encompassed (1) a subject for systematic study, (2) a watershed for wide-ranging policy research, (3) a topic/title for college-level courses, (4) a phrase acceptable to a broad range of public officials, and (5) a term subsequently incorporated into statutory law (P.L. 83-109; P.L. 86-380).

The first law, passed in 1953, created the temporary (1953–55) U.S. Commission on Intergovernmental Relations whose summary and multivolume reports were issued in 1955. The second legislation authorized in 1959 the presumably permanent Advisory Commission on Intergovernmental Relations (ACIR). For more than three decades this body generated regular and extensive studies and policy recommendations on IGR. An intergovernmentally representative commission, the ACIR was the premier and definitive policy research entity on IGR until political polarization around its recommendations, especially involving unfunded national mandates, caused it to lose congressional financing in 1996.

From the above early intellectual rivulets and subsequent statutory streams has come a broad river of research, analyses, and recommendations on policies and practices flowing across three-quarters of a century. These extensive efforts have produced the present features and current patterns that now characterize IGR.

We may extract from Anderson's 1960 definition the following three features to specify and elaborate the central characteristics of IGR. These are (1) governmental units of all types and levels, (2) different types of people/officials, and (3) diverse functions and financing of governments. In the process of discussing these features, the contrasts between IGR and federalism will become apparent. Likewise, a distinction between IGR and intergovernmental management will be indicated (Wright 1990; Wright and Stenberg 2005).

IGR AND FEDERALISM: DIFFERENT GOVERNMENTAL UNITS

The origin, emergence, and maturity of IGR occurred within the context of American federalism, especially as IGR was further refined by Anderson and elaborated by Elazar (1962). Both historically and institutionally, federalism placed emphasis on national-state relationships and secondarily on interstate relations. By way of contrast, IGR encompasses all the combinations and permutations of interactions among more than 87,000 units of government present within the American political system. Therefore IGR involves state-local, interlocal, national-local, interstate, and state-national interactions. Figure 3 depicts federalism as it relates to constitutional governance and electoral arrangements establishing formal institutional relationships between the nation and the states.

Figure 1 also reveals the greater inclusiveness of IGR when state-local and interlocal relationships are added. Nearly 88,000 legally constituted units of government are operating entities engaged in IGR to a greater or lesser degree. Moreover, the brackets in Figure 1 contain numbers indicating the frequency of popularly elected local, state, and national officials in the respective types of jurisdictions. (The 1992 numbers are the most recent ones available.) This massive number of popularly elected state and local

FIGURE 3. Governments in the United States: Systems and Structures

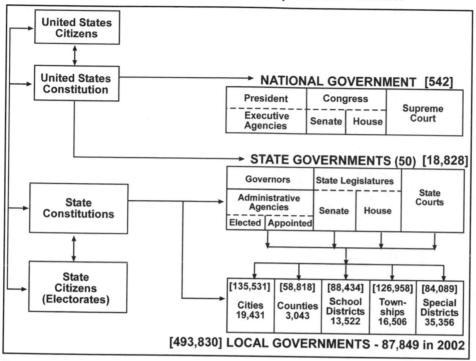

[ ] = Number of elected officials

officials emphasizes how politically diverse and decentralized IGR are in the United States. In addition, the number of full-time public employees further highlights the heavy noncentralized character of the IGR system. The 2002 employment numbers in millions are as follows: national, 2.6; state, 4.9; and local, 12.3. These arrays of elected officials and employment numbers turn attention to Anderson's emphasis on IGR as the interactions among different types of officials.

THREE TYPES OF IGR ACTORS

A second figure provides a transition toward identifying three main categories of officials prominent in IGR. Figure 4, a rectangular three-dimensional cube, displays visually several arrows showing illustrative paths of interactions among three main planes of governance—national, state, and local. (Interlocal and interstate interactions, because of their frequency and intensity, are omitted for the sake of simplicity and clarity.) Note the presence of upright planes from which interactions involving influence and authority are launched and received. These planes are not "levels" positioned in a presumed hierarchical or superior-subordinate relationship.

Two points follow from Figure 4. First, the extent of asymmetry or equality in influence across the planes is problematic, not automatic or preordained. Second, the arrows running in reciprocal directions among planes represent influence mobilized by *officials*, not units. Relevant here is my observation in *Understanding Intergovernmental Relations*: "strictly speaking, then, there are no relationships among *governments*; there are only relations among *officials* who govern different units" (Wright 1988; italics in original).

FIGURE 4. Planes of Governance in the United States: National, State, and Local Planes and Intergovernmental Interactions

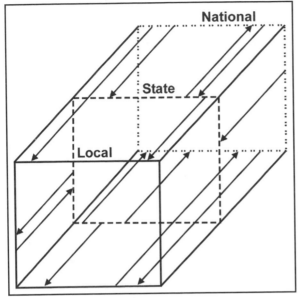

Arrows indicate intergovernmental interaction and influence—not necessarily in proportion to the number and direction of the arrows.

At the risk of oversimplification, it is useful to identify three main types of governance actors filling three important roles in IGR. These actors are the following:

1. Popularly elected generalists (PEGs): officials, both part-time and full-time, whose claim to the exercise of public authority is based upon their popular election to the position they occupy.

2. Appointed administrative generalists (AAGs): officials, almost always in full-time roles, whose status and authority derive from the direct (or proximate) appointment by the governing board/body of a governmental entity.

3. Program policy professionals (PPPs): full-time managers of programs or functions (such as departmental directors) whose access to positions of authority is chiefly through professional education and extensive experience in a career specialty, program function, or particular policy.

These three sets of officials occupy crucial and contrasting roles in the implementation of intergovernmental programs. The prominent connection between IGR and policy implementation was confirmed by Kettl (1993, 313) who noted, "Nearly 80 percent of all entries for programs and organizations in one implementation textbook are for programs and organizations that have an important intergovernmental dimension." The IGR roles of these actors can be understood better by starting with a description of the position of PPPs.

Program policy professionals are located in Figure 5 (a) at the center of the three respective planes, and (b) within the cylindrical core that penetrates and connects the national, state, and local planes. Anyone familiar with the origins and growth of federal aid across the twentieth century can readily and correctly deduce that this core figuratively contains the conduits for 700-plus grant-in-aid programs that channel money from the national to state and local governments. The PPPs are especially experienced and skilled in administering over 700 hundred categorical (and about 20 block) grant programs that move these funds across the planes of governance.

In the aggregate, the PPPs are commonly referred to as "specialists," based on their career specialization experiences. They are also the actors who are at the center of what is termed program or intergovernmental management. These specialists and the grant-in-aid conduits that they manage represent, individually and collectively, what is commonly called picket fence federalism.

Specialists are regularly contrasted with PEGs and AAGs, who are commonly grouped together as "generalists." The two types of generalists, however, operate in distinctly different settings, as can be inferred from Figure 5. The elected generalists, through their popular base, are democratically accountable and responsible officials in their respective jurisdictions. They make authoritative decisions and set policies implemented within and between planes. It falls to the AAGs to interpret, oversee, and assure that those decisions and policies are understood and followed by the PPPs, as well as the thousands (or millions) of other appointed administrators who operate within and between the multiple planes of governance. AAGs are "specialists in things in general," whose essential role is bridging the gap and coordinating the connections between PEGs and PPPs.

IGR FINANCES AND FUNCTIONS

No discussion of IGR would be complete without recognition of the scope and significance of funding the functions of government. There are, of course, two components of the intergovernmental fiscal ledger. One involves revenue sources, while the other reflects expenditure decisions.

FIGURE 5. Planes of Governance in the United States: Distinctive Positions and Roles of Three Types of Intragovernmental and Intergovernmental Actors

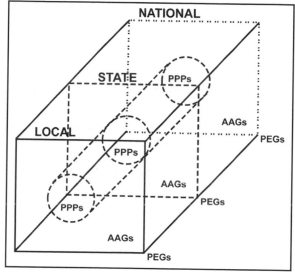

PEGs = Popular Elected Generalists
AAGs = Appointed Administrative Generalists
PPPs = Program Policy Professionals

On the revenue side, there is some specialization but considerable overlapping in the primary sources of revenues raised by national, state, and local governments. Income taxes constitute the chief revenue source of the national government, producing more than 80 percent of all collections. The states have historically relied primarily on sales/excise taxes. In recent decades, however, income taxes have become a major supplementary source so that sales and income taxes each furnish about one-third of state own-source revenues. Finally, the property tax remains a prominent if not predominant source of local revenue. Its importance over the past half century has declined as many local governments, especially cities and counties in several states, have secured statutory authority to levy sales and income taxes. These observations about the relative reliance on different revenue sources are supported by the percentages reported in Table 6.

Table 6 provides a long-term overview of the own-source revenue structures of national, state, and local governments. With one exception, the percentages for the major revenue sources from 1950 to 2000 fit the general patterns described above. The obvious departure is the consistent rise in reliance on charges/fees by local and state governments. This trend, often called "fee fever," is most obvious for local governments, who now secure nearly as much revenue from fees and charges as from the property tax. Similarly, state governments have substantially increased their reliance on this non-tax source of revenue.

The expenditure side of the fiscal ledger also reveals the diversity with which different governmental entities spend in support of nine major public functions. Table 7 dis-

TABLE 6. General Revenue from Sources by Level of Government for Selected Years: 1950–2000

Type of Revenue Source	NATIONAL *(percentages)*					
	1950	1960	1970	1980	1990	2000
Property Tax	—	—	—	—	—	—
Income Tax	65.4	70.7	75.4	73.9	86.0	88.3
Sales & excise tax	19.6	14.3	11.2	7.7	5.4	5.0
Other taxes	2.8	2.5	2.7	2.4	1.8	2.1
Charges and miscellaneous	12.1	12.5	10.7	16.0	6.9	4.6
Total	100.0	100.0	100.0	100.0	100.0	100.0
Total general own-source revenue (billions of dollars)	40.1	88.0	163.5	417.4	651.9	1,372.4

Type of Revenue Source	STATE *(percentages)*					
	1950	1960	1970	1980	1990	2000
Property Tax	3.5	2.9	1.9	1.7	1.7	1.4
Income Tax	14.8	16.5	22.5	29.8	28.9	32.2
Sales & excise tax	52.8	51.0	47.4	40.1	37.4	34.7
Other taxes	18.6	17.0	11.6	9.4	7.5	6.9
Charges and miscellaneous	10.3	12.6	16.6	19.0	24.5	24.7
Total	100.0	100.0	100.0	100.0	100.0	100.0
Total general own-source revenue (billions of dollars)	8.8	20.6	57.5	169.3	438.9	743.7

Type of Revenue Source	LOCAL *(percentages)*					
	1950	1960	1970	1980	1990	2000
Property Tax	73.5	69.0	64.1	50.5	47.9	43.7
Income Tax	.7	1.3	3.1	3.8	3.5	3.8
Sales & excise tax	5.0	5.7	6.0	9.3	9.3	10.7
Other taxes	4.1	3.0	2.3	2.9	2.6	3.0
Charges and miscellaneous	16.7	21.0	24.5	33.5	36.7	38.8
Total	100.0	100.0	100.0	100.0	100.0	100.0
Total general own-source revenue (billions of dollars)	9.6	22.9	51.5	130.0	361.1	579.5

Sources: National 1990 and 2000 data from U.S. Office of Management and Budget Historical Tables, http://www.whitehouse.gov/omb/budget/fy2006/. State and Local 1990 and 2000 data for State and Local are from U.S. Census Bureau, Statistical Abstract of the United States: 2003. Table No. 443. State and Local Governments—Revenue and Expenditures by Function.

TABLE 7. Direct General Expenditures by Function and Level of Government: 1960, 1970, 1980, 1990, and 2000

Function	Year	Level of Government (percentages)				Total Expenditures (billions of dollars)
		National	State	Local	Total	
Education	1960	4	18	78	100	19.4
	1970	5	25	70	100	55.8
	1980	7	25	68	100	143.8
	1990	5	25	70	100	305.6
	2000	3	26	71	100	539.4
Health and hospitals	1960	28	36	36	100	5.2
	1970	29	35	36	100	13.6
	1980	26	36	38	100	43.3
	1990	20	38	42	100	93.0
	2000	19	38	43	100	157.2
Public welfare	1960	1	50	49	100	4.4
	1970	16	47	37	100	17.5
	1980	30	51	19	100	64.8
	1990	24	59	17	100	140.6
	2000	26	63	11	100	317.0
Highways	1960	2	63	35	100	9.5
	1970	2	66	32	100	16.7
	1980	1	61	38	100	33.7
	1990	1	59	40	100	61.9
	2000	1	61	38	100	102.4
Police Protection	1960	9	12	79	100	2.0
	1970	8	14	78	100	4.9
	1980	11	14	75	100	15.2
	1990	15	12	73	100	35.9
	2000	17	12	71	100	71.4
Fire Protection	1960	0	0	100	100	.9
	1970	0	0	100	100	2.0
	1980	0	0	100	100	5.7
	1990	0	0	100	100	13.2
	2000	0	0	100	100	25.0
Corrections	1960	6	59	35	100	.7
	1970	5	61	34	100	1.7
	1980	6	61	33	100	6.8
	1990	6	61	33	100	26.2
	2000	6	64	30	100	56.1

TABLE 7 (continued)

Function	Year	Level of Government (percentages)				Total Expenditures (billions of dollars)
		National	State	Local	Total	
Housing and urban renewal	1960	25	1	74	100	1.1
	1970	33	1	66	100	3.2
	1980	50	3	47	100	12.1
	1990	52	5	43	100	32.4
	2000	29	8	63	100	38.2
Air transportation	1960	72	2	26	100	1.2
	1970	53	9	38	100	2.1
	1980	51	7	42	100	5.1
	1990	41	5	54	100	11.0
	2000	37	5	58	100	24.5

Sources: Bureau of the Census, *Governmental Finances in 1960*, GF60, No. 2 (Washington, DC Government Printing Office, 1960), Table 5; Bureau of the Census, *Governmental Finances in 1969–70*, GF70, No. 5 (Washington, DC: Government Printing Office, 1971), Table 6; Bureau of the Census, *Governmental Finances in 1979–80*, GF80, No. 5 (Washington, DC: Government Printing Office, 1986), Table 9; Bureau of the Census, *Governmental Finances in 1984–85*, GF85, No. 5 (Washington, DC: Government Printing Office, 1988), Table 9; Bureau of the Census, *Governmental Finances in 1989–90*, GF90, No. 5 (Washington, DC: Government Printing Office, 1991), Table 9. 2000 national data calculated from U.S. Office of Management and Budget, Historical Tables as reported by the U.S. Census Bureau in the Statistical Abstract, except for Corrections and Police, which were not reported. National data also calculated from Tables 7.2 and 7.31 in *The Book of the States*, Volume 34 (Lexington, KT: The Council of State Governments). State and Local data from *Facts and Figures on Government Finance*, Scott Moody, ed., 37th ed. (Washington DC: Tax Foundation) and U.S. Census Bureau from http://www.census.gov/govs/estimate/01s100us.html 2000 Corrections and Police data are estimated.

plays percentages showing the relative responsibilities in direct spending for those public programs from 1960 to 2000. Aggregate dollar outlays (in billions) are reported for the initial year of each decade.

Education, health/hospitals, and welfare are clearly the big three in total public expenditures. Outlays for these purposes have increased almost exponentially from 1960 to 2000. Percentages in Table 7 show that the relative roles in spending by the different governmental levels vary considerably, not only for the three major functions but also for the other six activities. Education, police, and fire protection are clearly local functions, while welfare, highways, and corrections expenditures are chiefly the operational responsibility of state governments. Only for housing/urban renewal and air transportation does the national government directly spend a substantial proportion of public outlays.

Further discussion is merited by the dominance of different planes of government in spending for various purposes. It should be emphasized that the percentages reported in Table 7 are for *direct* outlays and do not reflect intergovernmental expenditures. They do not reveal, for example, the fact that in 2000 the fifty state governments channeled over $200 billion in intergovernmental education aid to local school districts. Those funds, spent by the local units, are reflected in the 71 percent figure in Table 7. If state educational aid was counted as *state* expenditures, the 26 percent shown in Table 7 would exceed 60 percent of all public education outlays and the local percentage would drop to around 35 percent.

For public welfare, federal aid of nearly $150 billion went to the states in 2000. If counted as *national* rather than state outlays, the state percentage would drop to about 20 percent and the national figure would approach 70 percent. Similar noteworthy but varied adjustments in percentages for health/hospital and highways in Table 7 would be required if intergovernmental transfers were factored into the calculations. These revised figures reflect the fact that federal and state fiscal transfers result in different planes financing a significant share of the costs for major public programs, although they do not actually deliver the services. Fiscal complexity and interdependency are fundamental facts of IGR.

CONCLUSION

The American system of governance is really an aggregation of numerous sets of governmental systems. IGR reflects these systems within systems. The concept was invented, and emerged and matured, as a phrase intended to capture these complex realities. IGR encompasses elaborate institutional arrangements, numberless actors (officials) in diverse roles, and immensely significant fiscal and functional responsibilities. These features describe highly differentiated yet intensely interdependent patterns of relationships among thousands of governing entities. Conscious awareness and a solid understanding of IGR are necessary conditions for gaining a firm grasp on the character and content of American federalism and overall governance in the twenty-first century. *SEE ALSO:* Intergovernmental Management; Picket Fence Federalism; U.S. Advisory Commission on Intergovernmental Relations

BIBLIOGRAPHY: William Anderson, *American Government* (New York: Henry Holt, 1938); William Anderson, *Intergovernmental Relations in Review* (Minneapolis: University of Minnesota Press, 1960); Daniel J. Elazar, *The American Partnership: Intergovernmental Cooperation in the Nineteenth-Century United States* (Chicago: University of Chicago Press, 1962); Donald F. Kettl, "Public Administration: The State of the Field," in *Political Science: The State of the Field*, ed. Ada W. Finifter, 407–28 (Washington, DC: American Political Science Association, 1993); Deil S. Wright, *Understanding Intergovernmental Relations* (Pacific Grove, CA: Brooks Cole, 1988); and Deil S. Wright and Carl W. Stenberg, "Federalism Intergovernmental Relations, and Intergovernmental Management: The Origin, Emergence, and Maturity of Three Concepts across Two Centuries of Organizing Power by Area and by Function," in *Handbook of Public Administration*, 3rd ed., ed. Jack Rabin (New York: Marcel Dekker, 2005).

DEIL S. WRIGHT

Intergovernmental Tax Immunity Intergovernmental tax immunity means that the different governments in the federal system may not tax each others' agencies or operations directly, and puts limits on taxation of the employees or contractors of one government by another. It represents a constitutional check on the powers of both the federal government and state governments to levy taxes on each other. For instance, state governments may not tax land that the federal government owns, such as post offices and national parks. Likewise, the federal government may not enact a special tax on the incomes of state employees.

The U.S. Supreme Court first defined this concept in the seminal *McCulloch v. Maryland* decision in 1819. In part, this decision held that the State of Maryland could not tax the Bank of the United States. Since the U.S. Constitution made both the federal and state governments sovereign in their own proper spheres of activity, the state could not use its power of taxation to interfere with and potentially destroy the federal government's proper exercise of its power, in this case the power to create a bank.

Throughout the remainder of the nineteenth and the early part of the twentieth centuries, the courts used a very broad definition of the concept of intergovernmental tax immunity. The courts considered to be exempt from state and local taxation any activity that had a federal government component, including the salaries of federal employees. Likewise, the courts considered exempt from federal taxation state and local government activity and the salaries of state and local employees. In effect, the courts forbade any tax that would have the effect of increasing the cost of doing business for another government, or impairing its ability to make contracts.

This early broad interpretation of intergovernmental tax immunity had little practical effect on the federal government, which raised most of its revenue in the nineteenth century from import duties and used internal taxation only on an emergency basis, such as during the Civil War. State governments raised most of their revenue from the property tax until the Great Depression, and so merely had to forgo taxation of federal property. Local governments rely predominately on the property tax to this day.

This began to change in the early twentieth century when the federal government and many state governments enacted income taxes and began relying increasingly on those proceeds. With the New Deal in the 1930s, the federal government also considerably increased its expenditures on domestic projects such as roads and bridges, and states felt that they should be able to tax the contractors and their employees on these projects. The courts began to narrow their interpretation of the reach of intergovernmental tax immunity to the direct activities of governments, and allowed most taxation of government contractors. In 1938, the Supreme Court held that the federal government could tax the incomes of state employees, so long as those taxes were nondiscriminatory, that is, that state workers were not singled out but taxed like other workers.

The federal government enacted the Public Salary Tax Act in 1939, which, in addition to confirming the right of the federal government to tax state employees, allowed the states to tax federal employees in a nondiscriminatory fashion. Thereafter, courts have held that intergovernmental tax immunity barred only taxes that were placed directly on one government by another, or that discriminated against a government or its employees or contractors.

There is no similar constitutional protection in the relationship between state and local governments, since local governments are not independently sovereign from the states. Local governments share the protection that states have from federal taxes, but the courts have not granted them similar protection from state actions. However, states have generally forgone taxing local governments and exempted their activities from local taxation.

While the general interpretation of the scope of intergovernmental tax immunity has not changed since 1939, there continue to be difficulties in the application of this general interpretation to particular cases. In particular, the federal government may tax a wide range of activities and states may have some participation in these activities, so the courts must decide what is a discriminatory or a nondiscriminatory tax. For instance, the federal government may have a registration tax on civil aircraft, and a state may own a highway patrol helicopter. The courts would then have to decide if the state would have to pay the tax on the helicopter. Generally, the courts have tended to give the federal government broad powers to tax, if the tax is not specifically aimed at state or local governments.

A recent series of court cases have dealt with discrimination between the taxation of state and federal retirees. Several states had exempted all or part of the pension income of retired state employees, while not giving similar exemptions to retired federal employees. In a 1989 case, *Davis v. Michigan Department of Treasury*, the U.S. Supreme Court decided that this was discriminatory, and that since federal and state employees were similar to each other, they should be taxed similarly. However, they left it up to the states to decide whether to extend the exemptions to all retired government employees or eliminate it for the state employees. *SEE ALSO:* Crossover Sanctions; Environmental Policy; Fiscal Federalism; Pass through Requirements; Unfunded Mandates; Welfare Policy

NICHOLAS W. JENNY

Interlocal Relations   The American governmental system is extremely fragmented, with more than 87,000 units of local government including about 51,155 special districts, 19,429 cities, 16,504 townships, 13,506 school districts, and 3,034 counties. Interlocal relations include city-city, county-county, and city-county relationships, as well as relations between cities or counties and special local districts such as for schools, fire departments, water and sewer services, and economic development. Interlocal relations are studied in both their competitive nature and their cooperative nature.

A recurring theme in interlocal relations, dating to the reform movements of the early twentieth century, is city-city and city-county consolidation. Thurmaier and Wood (2002) frame cooperative relationships between local units of government in terms of four levels of interlocal agreement (communication, coordination, cooperation, and consolidation) and the type of substantive policy or service area. Wood uses a typology of service delivery arrangements that include joint initiatives, contracts, transfer of services (functional consolidation), city-county consolidation, and partnerships with regional institutions such as a council of government (2001).

Interlocal relations in the United States have largely been studied in the context of metropolitan governance. There are 324 metropolitan areas in the United States as defined by the U.S. Bureau of the Census. More than eight out of ten Americans live in one of the metropolitan areas, and nearly half live in the twenty-five largest regions. Wikstrom notes that "the average metro area contains about 100 local governments, including 40 special districts, 24 municipalities, 19 independent school districts, 16 townships, and two counties." As such, how metropolitan areas are governed is extremely important to citizens living in those regions.

Peirce, Johnson, and Hall (1993) describe the modern city-state as a closely interrelated geographic, economic, and environmental entity that defines modern civilization. They postulate that for the American city-state to survive and prosper in today's global economy, city-states must overcome urban sprawl and the deep socioeconomic gulf between poor cities and wealthy suburbs by creating effective systems of coordinated governance.

Frederickson contends the new global economy and revolution in telecommunications have altered the meaning of physical space and the importance of boundaries. The disarticulation of the state includes the declining salience of jurisdictions; the fuzziness of borders; the inability of the fragmented jurisdiction to contain and manage complex social, economic, and political issues; and the asymmetry between the governed and those who govern. Overcoming the disarticulation of the state requires local officials to practice metropolitan governance through intergovernmental communication, coordination, cooperation, and consolidation of services.

Frederickson's theory of administrative conjunction posits that intergovernmental partnerships and social networks are driven primarily by professional staff who are more inclined to think and act regionally and to build "epistemic communities" than elected officials who are more focused on electoral matters that are jurisdictional and local in nature and scope.

Savitch and Vogel (1996) analyzed patterns of intergovernmental relations in several regions (Los Angeles; New York City; Washington, D.C.; St. Louis; and Pittsburgh), and classified metropolitan governance as mutual adjustment (direct or indirect cooperation and coordination), conflict, or avoidance. Each region adopts patterns of governance that reflect their history and unique issues and problems. Using the typology, Wood found that the dominant metropolitan governance pattern in the Kansas City region was mutual adjustment. Eliciting cooperation is a slow process.

Many studies have demonstrated that cities frequently participate in intergovernmental service delivery arrangements. Pagano and others have found that intergovernmental partnerships have become the structure of choice for many jurisdictions in the delivery of urban services. Intergovernmental arrangements may be preferable to public-private partnerships in that governments share common goals and values that result in more trust, fewer agency problems, and less transaction costs.

Many scholars have found that city governments enter into intergovernmental service delivery arrangements in order to enhance economies of scale, reduce costs, improve service quality, equalize service levels, and solve common problems.

The increasing interdependence of jurisdictions, the transcendence of regional economies, and the disarticulation of the state foster the incentive and need for cooperation and coordination among local governments to finance and deliver urban services. As a result, according to Wikstrom, local governments enter into governance networks that create a spiderweb of complex relationships that are superimposed upon existing institutions. These governance networks are generally able to overcome the disarticulation of the state and reduce fiscal stress. However, metropolitan governance is not a panacea. There is little evidence that metropolitan governance is capable of overcoming fiscal disparities found between jurisdictions, solving fundamental metropolitan problems, or controlling urban sprawl. Achieving these objectives will require more intergovernmental cooperation, stronger regional institutions, and a closer partnership between local jurisdictions, states, and the federal government. *SEE ALSO:* Intergovernmental Relations; Local Government; Special Districts

BIBLIOGRAPHY: Robert Agranoff and Michael McGuire, *Collaborative Public Management: New Strategies for Local Government* (Washington, DC: Georgetown University Press, 2003); Jered Carr and Richard Feiock, *City-County Consolidation and Its*

Alternatives (Armonk, NY: M.E. Sharpe, 2004); Suzanne Leland and Kurt Thurmaier, *Case Studies of City-County Consolidation: The Changing Local Landscape* (Armonk, NY: M.E. Sharpe, 2004); Myron Orfield, *American Metro Politics: The New Suburban Reality* (Washington, DC: Brookings Institution Press, 2002); Neal R. Peirce with Curtis W. Johnson and John Stuart Hall, *Citistates: How Urban America Can Prosper in a Competitive World* (Washington, DC: Seven Locks Press, 1993); G. Ross Stephens and Nelson Wikstrom, *Metropolitan Government and Governance: Theoretical Perspectives, Empirical Analysis, and the Future* (Oxford: Oxford University Press, 2000); H. V. Savitch and Ronald K. Vogel, eds., *Regional Politics: America in a Post-City Age* (Thousand Oaks, CA: Sage, 1996); and Kurt Thurmaier and Curtis Wood, "Interlocal Agreements as Overlapping Social Networks: Picket-Fence Regionalism in Metropolitan Kansas City," *Public Administration Review* 62, no. 5 (2002): 585–98; and Curtis Wood, "Consolidated versus Fragmented Government: A Study of the Metropolitan Kansas City Region," 33rd Annual Conference of the Mid-Continental Regional Science Association, May 2002.

CURTIS H. WOOD AND KURT THURMAIER

Intermodal Surface Transportation Efficiency Act   The Intermodal Surface Transportation Efficiency Act of 1991 (ISTEA) was the first comprehensive federal surface transportation bill enacted as completion of the interstate highway system neared. Signed into law on December 18, 1991, it was one of the few innovative domestic bills passed during the administration of President George H. W. Bush. The legislation authorized spending $151 billion over six years in a variety of programs folded into the bill, and alleviated fears of transportation officials and state leaders that the federal government would significantly reduce its role in surface transportation after the interstate highway system was finished.

ISTEA represented a new approach to surface transportation programs by placing more responsibility in the hands of state and local governments and metropolitan planning organizations (MPOs) by adding flexibility to move funds from one program to another, and by encouraging decision makers at all levels of the federal system to see the relationship of surface transportation to issues of clean air, urban sprawl and congestion, and economic growth. Although the federal government retained a major role in implementing the legislation, a major impact of ISTEA was to decentralize decision making to state and local officials and MPOs, which for the first time were able to spend federal monies directly.

ISTEA provided federal funding for most programs at an 80 percent federal/20 percent state level, and provided in its different programs support for a surface transportation block grant program, a 155,000-mile National Highway System composed of the 44,000-mile Interstate Highway System and other major highways, a mass transit program, a program to build and repair bridges, and several smaller programs. Although it increased the role of state, local, and regional officials, it also included 538 demonstration projects (also called "set-asides") favored by Congress.

Experts agree that ISTEA marked a turning point in the relationship of the federal government to states, local governments, and regional organizations in transportation. ISTEA also broadened the role of planners in transportation, encouraged more interested parties to participate in transportation decisions, brought goods movement and intermodal projects more prominently into consideration for funding, and reinforced the need for state transportation departments to move from a strict highway orientation to a multimode perspective in statewide planning. The balancing of power between the levels of government made ISTEA the model for surface transportation legislation in the postinterstate era. Its basic structure was retained in the reauthorization of the succeeding six-year surface transportation bill, the Transportation Efficiency Act for the Twenty-first Century, or TEA-21, in 1998. *SEE ALSO:* Transportation Equity Act for the Twenty-first Century; Transportation Policy

BIBLIOGRAPHY: Robert J. Dilger, "ISTEA: A New Direction for Transportation Policy," *Publius: The Journal of Federalism* 22 (Summer 1992): 67–78; and Robert W. Gage and Bruce D. McDowell, "ISTEA and the Role of MPOs in the New Transportation Environment: A Midterm Assessment," *Publius: The Journal of Federalism* 25 (Summer 1995): 133–54.

JEREMY PLANT

Internal Improvements   One of the early and ongoing disputes engendered by federalism was whether the federal government has the constitutional authority to develop economic infrastructure on the state and local level. These infrastructure projects were referred to in the early republic as internal improvements. Internal improvements were always a flashpoint of federalism. From the eighteenth-century debates between the Federalists and Anti-Federalists to the twentieth-century debates between Democrats and Republicans, the role of the national government in the affairs of state and local economic development policy remains a central question.

Alexander Hamilton, whose loose interpretation of the Constitution authorized the creation of a national bank, favored internal improvements to facilitate economic growth, but he thought that the Constitution prohibited the federal government from funding internal improvements such as canals. Hamilton supported a constitutional amendment authorizing the federal government to fund and construct internal improvements.

One of the first large internal improvements, the national road, illustrates the nature of the debate. Presidents Jefferson and Madison thought internal improvements unconstitutional. Yet, they facilitated the creation of a national road that eventually stretched from Baltimore, Maryland, to the Ohio Valley by allowing the sale of federal lands in western territories to pay the states to build the road. President James Monroe believed internal improvements unconstitutional and vetoed a bill that would have allowed federal tollbooths to fund road repairs. President John Quincy Adams advocated significant federal participation in internal improvements, but his ideas faltered with the election of President Andrew Jackson who, arguing that internal improvements were a dangerous expansion of federal power, turned the national road over to the states for construction and maintenance.

The Whig Party took up the call for internal improvements, largely under the direction of President John Quincy Adams and Henry Clay of Kentucky. Clay's American System advocated internal improvements, intergovernmental grants, and nationally directed monetary policy based upon central banking. Opposition to federal participation in internal improvements declined slowly during the nineteenth century.

Internal improvements during the early republic were generally restricted to facilitating the transportation of the post—a federal responsibility—by improving roads, bridges, ports, waterways, tunnels, dams, and similar transportation and common-use infrastructure. Later, internal improvements would include education institutions, torts and military installations, the national bank, homesteading and land policy, and by the twenty-first century, internal improvements would include all areas of policy conceivably related to economic development infrastructure.

Internal improvements were an important component of the New Deal public works agenda of Franklin D. Roosevelt. And the creative federalism period of Presidents John F. Kennedy and Lyndon B. Johnson saw the establishment of new federal agencies and programs to develop internal improvements as the national government assumed responsibility for the economic welfare of all U.S. citizens.

Internal improvements have enjoyed a bipartisan endorsement for the past several decades and only in the context of limiting federal spending and reducing "pork barrel" spending have internal improvements faced any recent criticism. *SEE ALSO:* American System; Civil War; Clay, Henry; Economic Development; Jackson, Andrew; Madison, James; Rural Policy; Urban Policy

BIBLIOGRAPHY: Maurice G. Baxter, *Henry Clay and the American System* (Lexington: University Press of Kentucky, 1995); Daniel Walker Howe, *The Political Culture of the American Whigs* (Chicago: University of Chicago Press, 1979); Forrest McDonald, *Novus Ordo Seclorum* (Lawrence: University Press of Kansas, 1985), 265; and Robert Allen Rutland, *The Republicans* (Columbia: University of Missouri Press, 1996).

MICHAEL W. HAIL

International City/County Management Association The International City/County Management Association (ICMA) was founded in 1914, and its primary goal is "to create excellence in local government by developing and fostering professional local government management worldwide." ICMA is both a professional and educational organization with membership coming primarily from chief appointed managers, administrators, and assistants in cities, towns, and counties. ICMA maintains an extensive publications program in which it explores both traditional management issues and what might be considered "hot topics" for its members, who now total more than 8,000. In addition to its publications services, ICMA hosts an annual conference for its members where they can "network" with each other and explore topics of interest to local government. *SEE ALSO:* County Government; Local Government; Public Officials' Associations

DAVID R. CONNELLY

Interposition Interposition is a vital element of the theory of states' rights constitutionalism, which can be broadly defined as a doctrine seeking to protect the rights and powers of the states in relation to those of the federal government. The proponents of the theory assert that the U.S. Constitution is a compact among the states and that each state can block ("interpose") or overrule ("nullify") actions of the union adversely affecting its interests and general well-being.

The states' rights theory was first set forth in the late eighteenth century by Thomas Jefferson, then vice president of the United States, and James Madison, then a representative from Virginia. Denouncing the newly enacted 1798 Alien and Sedition Acts, Jefferson and Madison introduced resolutions respectively in the Kentucky and Virginia state legislatures, both of which insisted on a more strict constitutional interpretation of the delegated powers of the federal government. In so doing, both Jefferson and Madison asserted that a state could interpose its authority between the federal government and its citizenry, thereby forcing a constitutional test of the federal laws and actions in question. Jefferson further advanced the doctrine of interposition and contended that a state could even nullify a federal law, which the state deemed to be unconstitutional and was unwilling to recognize.

During the War of 1812, the demands for states' rights and autonomy appeared in the New England states as well in the form of the Hartford Convention of 1814. But as the implacable estrangement between the North and the South over slavery and the nature of American federalism progressed, the slogan of "states' rights" gradually became tantamount to "regional rights" in the South.

Linking a series of federal tariff policies (and particularly its Tariff of Abominations of 1828) to his region's economic decline, John C. Calhoun, a South Carolinian and vice president of the United States, elaborated the theory set forth by Jefferson and Madison. In writing the *South Carolina Exposition and Protest*, Calhoun not only argued that the states had the right of interposition, but also explained a method by which they could nullify a federal law or action. Three decades later, the eventual secession of the eleven southern states from the Union and the subsequent outbreak of the Civil War in 1861 manifested the most extreme form of states' rights ideology as well as the most acute constitutional crisis in the nation's history.

After the Civil War, any extreme assertion of states' rights theory virtually ceased for almost ninety years until the mid-twentieth century. However, when the U.S. Supreme Court outlawed legally imposed racial segregation in public schools in its 1954 *Brown v. Board of Education* ruling, white Southerners revived and reintroduced the states' rights idea of interposition. With an aura of respectability and sophistication emanating from their use of states' rights constitutionalism, southern segregationists formed and carried out the region's massive resistance to defy the Supreme Court's desegregation decree and to resist the intensifying Civil Rights movement in the South. Beginning with Virginia, eight southern state legislatures had adopted their interposition resolutions by the end of 1956 to decry the Court's encroachment on the rights reserved to their states and pledged themselves to use all lawful means to bring about a reversal of *Brown*.

The mid-twentieth-century southern segregationist use of states' rights contentions in resisting federally initiated racial desegregation ultimately rendered the doctrine of interposition morally unsavory. But as long as the institution of American federalism is perpetuated, the debate over the rights of states in the federal arrangement and the vitality of states' rights contentions—a time-honored conviction that those who are closest to a particular problem best know what ought to be done—will never desist. *SEE ALSO:* Calhoun, John C.; Jefferson, Thomas; Madison, James; Nullification

BIBLIOGRAPHY: Frederick D. Drake, and Lynn R. Nelson, eds., *States' Rights and American Federalism: A Documentary History* (Westport, CT: Greenwood, 1999); Forrest McDonald, *States' Rights and the Union: Imperium in Imperio, 1776–1876* (Lawrence: University Press of Kansas, 2000); Melvin I. Urofsky, ed., *Documents of American Constitutional and Legal History*, 2 vols. (Philadelphia: Temple University Press, 1989); and Garry Wills, *A Necessary Evil: A History of American Distrust of Government* (New York: Simon and Schuster, 1999).

YASUHIRO KATAGIRI

Interstate Commerce   The U.S. Constitution (Article I, Section 8, Clause 3) authorizes Congress "to regulate commerce . . . among the several states"; this is the so-called Commerce Clause. Since the United States was founded by combining states into a nation, this was an important step toward helping it function as a coherent economic entity. Over time, the legislature, executive, and especially the courts have interpreted the application of this clause, but generally, it has come to mean not only trade or traffic but also the promotion, protection, encouragement, restraint, and inhibition of all kinds of commercial activities that cross state borders. In some ways, interstate commerce is usefully delineated by its opposite—intrastate commerce—which is commercial activity conducted completely within a given state, of which the right to regulate is retained by the states.

In the early 1800s, the precise definition of interstate commerce was not critical, because national markets had not developed and intrastate commerce was regulated only lightly by the American state governments. Many early court interpretations focused more on limiting the export of state power over what might be defined as interstate issues. Especially after the Civil War, however, with the railroads creating the infrastructure for national markets, the precise meaning of inter-state commerce became more important. Indeed, it was necessary for the U.S. Supreme Court to entertain a series of cases attempting to specify the boundaries.

> ARTICLE I, SECTION 8, CLAUSE 3
>
> *To regulate Commerce with foreign Nations, and among the several States, and with the Indian Tribes.*

In 1887, after a decade of debates, Congress created the first regulatory agency, the Interstate Commerce Commission (ICC), specifically to address railroad safety and pricing issues across state boundaries. Railroad firms immediately challenged in court the new ICC's powers, and Congress was later forced to specify them more explicitly.

As the transportation, communications, and energy industries developed over time, and other federal regulatory agencies such as the Federal Communications Commission and Federal Power Commission were created to regulate them, the definitions of interstate commerce became more complex and controversial. These important industries were regulated on an interstate commerce basis at the federal level and on an intrastate commerce basis at the state level. But the definition of what constituted interstate commerce became more expansive, particularly as more business activities crossed state borders.

After the New Deal in the 1930s and the Great Society in the 1960s centralized greater economic regulation at the federal level, some believed that the essential rationale for retaining a category of intrastate commerce was disappearing. But, in the 1980s, the twin policies of deregulation and devolution shifted the boundaries again. Many of these industries were deregulated at the federal level, and some agencies were eliminated, including the ICC in 1995. A political movement toward the devolution of powers to the state level reinvigorated state capacity for dealing with public policy problems, and a serious conservative movement emerged to try and reverse the expansive definition of interstate commerce that had shifted greater authority to the federal level.
SEE ALSO: Commerce among the States; Interstate Commerce Act of 1887

PAUL TESKE

Interstate Commerce Act of 1887   On April 5, 1887, the Interstate Commerce Act became law. Its purpose was to stop unfair railroad practices carried out by monopolies. From the 1870s to the 1880s, momentum built to regulate the industry as the public, farm groups, business, and some railroad managers asked Congress to control the flow of commerce that crossed state lines.

Congress enacted the law after the U.S. Supreme Court reversed itself in *Wabash, St.Louis & Pacific Railroad Company v. Illinois* (1886). The court denied states the right to control interstate railroad rates and declared an Illinois law invalid since it breached congressional power found in the Commerce Clause of the U.S. Constitution. Adoption of the Interstate Commerce Act was one of the goals pursued by the Farmer's Alliance/Populists in the 1880s. It signaled a power shift away from laissez-faire policies that dominated the time and lifted the Populist cause by proving that political action led to policy change.

In 1885, the Select Committee to Investigate Commerce was established to hold hearings on transportation by rail and water between the several states. In 1886, it released the "Cullom Report," which swayed Congress to pass the act; although uncertain about its impact, Congress yielded to public sentiment, group pressure, and a need to make railroad activity uniform.

The Interstate Commerce Act prohibited rebates, drawbacks, pooling, and rate discrimination by monopolies. It mandated "reasonable and just" rates and forbade long- and short-haul clauses unless an exemption was granted. But its creation of the first regulatory agency to enforce the act was historic.

The Interstate Commerce Commission (ICC), a five-member agency appointed by the president for six-year terms and empowered to investigate complaints, call witnesses, obtain documents, and inquire into the business of all common carriers, was charged with the enforcement role.

When it was first applied, it met resistance by rail barons who used the courts, commission appointees, and political pressure to reduce the law's impact and limit the commission's authority. In the *Maximum Freight Rate Case* (1897), the Supreme Court held that the ICC did not have the power to propose detailed rate schedules. Similarly, the court ruled in the *Alabama Midland Case* (1897), that the commission's power was limited with respect to long- and short-haul discrimination. By the end of the 1890s, the ICC only monitored railroad statistics and required fee notices by companies.

However, by the turn of the century, Congress gave the ICC more power over the monopolies. The Elkins Act of 1903 ended the practice of rebates. The Hepburn Act of 1906 increased the commission size, improved rate enforcement, and expanded the jurisdiction of the agency. The Mann-Elkins Act of 1910 amended long- and short-haul language and extended the agency's bailiwick over communications.

The act changed the dynamics of American federalism. State and local governments lost some of their lawmaking authority over the railroad monopolies. The federal government exercised its "commerce power" to centralize regulation and bring consistency to a hodgepodge of state laws that slowed the flow of goods and passengers who counted on efficient rail transportation to sustain their business, employment, and safe movement from place to place. *SEE ALSO:* Commerce among the States; Interstate Commerce; Transportation Policy

BIBLIOGRAPHY: Marvin L. Fair, *Economic Considerations in the Administration of the Interstate Commerce Act* (Cambridge, MD: Cornell Maritime Press, 1972); Henry S.

Haines, *Problems in Railway Regulation* (New York: Macmillan Company, 1911); Lewis H. Haney, *Congressional History of Railways in the United States: 1850–1887*, Bulletin of the University of Wisconsin no. 342 (Madison: University of Wisconsin, 1910); and Donald V. Harper, *Transportation in America: Users, Carriers, Government* (Englewood Cliffs, NJ: Prentice Hall, 1978).

JOHN TODD YOUNG

Interstate Compacts   According to the Compact Clause (Article I, Section 10) of the U.S. Constitution, states have the authority to enter into compacts with each other for any purpose subject only to congressional approval. Interstate compacts take the form of a binding agreement that requires the parties to faithfully execute the terms outlined.

During the early years of the republic, boundary disputes were common among the states. Recognizing this, the Constitution, following procedures outlined in the Articles of Confederation, provided for a means of resolving disputes through the interstate Compact Clause. In early practice, compacts negotiated to resolve a boundary dispute never received congressional approval. In more recent times, however, the subject matter of compacts has changed and congressional assent has become the norm.

> ARTICLE I, SECTION 10, CLAUSE 3
>
> *No State shall, without the Consent of Congress, lay any Duty of Tonnage, keep Troops, or Ships of War in time of Peace, enter into any Agreement or Compact with another State, or with a foreign Power, or engage in War, unless actually invaded, or in such imminent Danger as will not admit of delay.*

Congressional approval can also be viewed as an attempt to limit the potential collective power of states to threaten the national government. Thus, the Compact Clause also prohibits states from entering into treaties with foreign nations. Chief Justice Roger B. Taney in *Holmes v. Jennison* (39 U.S. 540 [1840]) interpreted the clause broadly, arguing that the founders intended a comprehensive ban on state–foreign government interaction and that every agreement finalized by two or more states needed congressional approval. In *Virginia v. Tennessee* (148 U.S. 503 [1893]), the Supreme Court ruled that unqualified prohibitions on state agreements without congressional consent did not apply to minor agreements.

The Port of New York Authority Compact of 1921 was the first interstate compact involving regulatory power and revenue sources. This groundbreaking compact, however, did not lead to an increase in agreements among the states. Key questions remained regarding state participation. First, in creating a compact commission that has binding authority over the signatory state, to what extent can a state yield its sovereignty to such a commission? Second, are states able to commit financially over an extended period of time to the operations of the compact? In *State ex rel Dyer v. Sims* (341 U.S. 22 [1951]), the Court effectively ruled that the agency created by the compact was a state agency on par with any other state agency. Furthermore, committing to funding the commission into the future was not prohibited by the state constitution.

In the 1930s, national interest in exploring regional cooperation to extend and augment the New Deal was high. After the National Industrial Recovery Act was held invalid by the Supreme Court (*Schechter Poultry Corporation v. United States*, 295 U.S. 495 [1935]) regional attempts were considered a viable substitute for national planning. The main appeal of compacts is the flexible implementation of policies falling into the suprastate, subnational zone. For example, criminal justice is a very fruitful area of cooperation ranging from apprehension to extradition of prisoners. Still, other policy areas are amenable as well—commerce, environmental, educational, and labor legislation, among others.

Some compacts have found disfavor with Congress and/or the president. In the late 1930s, in response to a devastating flood, several of the New England states concluded a compact to establish flood control. President Franklin D. Roosevelt, however, threatened a veto so that the Federal Power Commission would not lose jurisdiction regarding the two rivers involved. This was not the only compact that threatened the authority of an agency of the federal government. For example, another proposed compact between New York and New Jersey that provided authority and immunity for state militias when aiding other states, including allowing the pursuit of anyone seeking to overthrow the government, was delayed until the FBI was assured it would not be an usurpation of its powers.

Compacts can be classified into five major policy areas: boundary or border dispute resolution compacts, river basin compacts, metropolitan services compacts, industrial compacts, and public services compacts like those pertaining to crime, education, or welfare. The administrative apparatus varies from no commission to a nonregulatory commission to a regulatory agency. Compacts can hide problems in administrative oversight and responsiveness to changing social and economic conditions. The major problem lies in the commitment because a state obligates itself to fulfilling the terms and conditions of the agreement, which over time may impair its ability to act in an independent manner.

Compacts limit state action to act independently and subject states to the actions or inactions of fellow members. Marion Ridgeway argued that by ignoring this political side to diminished state autonomy, many compact proponents fail to understand the importance of the diversion of revenues required for participation, the inevitable preoccupation with its affairs and issues, the imperfect control over planning, and the diminution in state jurisdictional authority.

Once a compact gains congressional approval, the Constitution provides for its enforcement through the Contract Clause against any breach of faith by one or more parties. By insulating compacts from political controls once they are approved, power can potentially flow into the hands of private interests. This is especially problematic in industrial compacts. Compacts negotiated to bury low-level radioactive waste, for example, have been criticized for being controlled by the nuclear power operators who have the most to gain from the successful implementation of the agreement, while the local community that would be the host for the waste facility would have less to gain outside of increased tax revenues.

Compacts are long-term commitments offering great potential for overcoming regional problems. This aspect implies the opportunity to accomplish policy goals and objectives but also the potential for diminished state autonomy. Importantly, compacts need to be monitored by elected officials and the press since in large measure many are separated from the public due to their narrow, limited scope of authority. They are, or at least can be, potentially undemocratic, unrepresentative, and unresponsive to the general public while highly responsive to the select public they supervise. Thus, the very strengths of compacts are also the sources of their weaknesses. *SEE ALSO:*

Articles of Confederation; Contract Clause; Criminal Justice; Education; Local Government; New Deal; Roosevelt, Franklin D.; Sovereignty; Taney, Roger Brooke

BIBLIOGRAPHY: Weldon V. Barton, *Interstate Compacts in the Political Process* (Chapel Hill: University of North Carolina Press, 1967); Jane Perry Clark, "Interstate Compacts and Social Legislation," *Political Science Quarterly* 50, no. 4 (1935): 502–24; Anthony L. Dodson, "Interstate Compacts to Bury Radioactive Waste: A Useful Tool for Environmental Policy?" *State and Local Government Review* 30 (1998): 118–28; Paul Hardy, *Interstate Compacts: The Ties That Bind* (Athens: Institute of Government, University of Georgia, 1982); Marion Ridgeway, *Interstate Compacts: A Question of Federalism* (Carbondale: Southern Illinois University Press, 1971); and Frederick L. Zimmermann and Mitchell Wendell, "New Experience with Interstate Compacts," *Western Political Quarterly* 5, no. 2 (1952): 258–73.

ANTHONY L. DODSON

Interstate Relations   All national constitutions establishing a federal system divide exercisable powers between the national government and state governments, provide for concurrent powers including taxation, and incorporate provisions governing relations between sister states. These later provisions are often refered to as "horizontal federalism." The U.S. Constitution contains sections pertaining to state entrance into interstate compacts, interstate disputes, full faith and credit, privileges and immunities, and rendition of fugitives from justice. The Constitution also devolves power upon Congress to regulate foreign, interstate, and Indian nation commerce to achieve a economic union of states in which products, labor, raw materials, and services move freely across boundary lines. States cooperate with each other by means of interstate compacts and administrative agreements, but also compete to attract business firms, tourists, and gamblers, and to maximize tax revenues.

INTERSTATE COMPACTS

The Constitution's framers recognized the potential of compacts to solve regional problems that otherwise would require congressional remedial actions, and they included Section 10 in Article I, authorizing states to enter into compacts with the consent of Congress. The U.S. Supreme Court in *Virginia v. Tennessee* (1893) opined that only political compacts, those encroaching "upon the full and free exercise of federal authority," require such consent.

The Constitution is silent on many subjects and does not specify the procedures by which states may enter into compacts. Until 1930, each compact was negotiated and drafted by gubernatorially appointed officers. This method continues to be utilized and has been supplemented by other negotiating bodies such as the National Association of Insurance Commissioners, which drafted the Insurance Product Regulation Compact and encourages all state legislatures and the District of Columbia city council to enact it.

Gubernatorially appointed commissioners are sensitive to the concerns of their respective governor and state legislature. A proposed compact may relate to a noncontroversial subject, such as higher education, and negotiators are able to reach an agreement within a relative short period of time. Other proposed compacts, particularly water allocation ones, involve complex issues and may require years to negotiate an acceptable draft, which will not become effective until enacted by the concerned state legislatures. State negotiators may invite representatives of federal departments and agencies to participate in the drafting of a compact, but federal participation has been limited to water compacts.

A draft compact submitted to state legislatures may generate considerable debate and political concerns and result in delayed enactment by one or both houses of the state legislature. The compact must be enacted with identical language in each party state and is subject to a gubernatorial veto.

All political and many nonpolitical compacts since 1893 have been submitted for consent to Congress, which is free to determine the duration of such consent and to grant consent in the form of permission for named states to negotiate a compact or the ratification of a compact enacted by state legislatures. Such consent is subject to a veto, and President Franklin D. Roosevelt in 1939 disallowed a bill authorizing states to negotiate and enter into Atlantic Ocean fishing compacts. In 1941, he vetoed consent for the Republican River Compact, but two years later signed a bill into law granting consent to a redrafted compact.

In 1911 Congress first granted consent-in-advance to compacts (forests and water supply), and in 1921 it included in a single statute consent for a Minnesota–South Dakota compact on criminal jurisdiction over boundary waters and consent-in-advance for other Midwestern states to enter into a similar compact.

Congress, in granting consent to most compacts, has not included a sunset provision. The Interstate Oil Compact of 1935 (now Oil and Gas) and the Atlantic States Marine Fisheries Compact of 1942 were granted consent for a specific period of time, but the sunset provisions subsequently were removed. Congress in 2001 did not act on a bill extending consent for the Northeast Dairy Compact, and its commission was forced to disband.

The grant of consent to a compact invalidates other federal statutes containing inconsistent provisions. After granting consent, however, Congress is free to enact statutes whose provisions repeal compact provisions provided that these statutes are consistent with the U.S. Constitution.

The multistate tax compact was challenged as unconstitutional by the United States Steel Corporation on the ground that the compact lacked congressional consent. The Supreme Court opined in 1978 that the compact was constitutional because it did not authorize member states to exercise powers they would be unable to exercise in the absence of the compact. Consent was granted in 1949 to the Northeastern Interstate Forest Fire Compact, the first compact to include a Canadian province. Compact members also may include the Commonwealth of Puerto Rico and the District of Columbia.

The Supreme Court in 1938 ruled that consent does not convert a compact into federal law, but reversed this decision in 1981 by opining that such consent makes a compact federal law as well as state law. This precedent reversal freed the court of the restraint of its 1874 decision holding that U.S. courts must apply the interpretation of a state law by the highest court in the concerned state, and allowed the Supreme Court to disregard the interpretation of a Pennsylvania interstate compact statute by the Pennsylvania Supreme Court.

In 1994, the Supreme Court held the Port Authority Trans-Hudson Corporation, a subsidiary of the interstate-established Port Authority of New York and New Jersey, was not shielded with immunity from suit in a U.S. court under the immunity granted to states by the Eleventh Amendment to the U.S. Constitution. The court explained that the corporation was a self-financing body and that allowing it to be sued would not impose a burden on the treasury of either state.

A state party to a compact may seek an interpretation of one or more of its provisions by filing an original suit in the Supreme Court. A dispute between Kansas and Colorado arose over the Arkansas River Compact; the former brought suit against the latter, and the Court in 1995 generally upheld the position of Kansas.

Amendment of a compact not submitted to Congress for its consent requires the approval of all party states. In 1917, the Supreme Court opined Congress possesses the authority to amend a compact in the absence of a provision reserving such authority to Congress. Only a boundary compact cannot be terminated. Other compacts contain a provision typically requiring advance notice of a proposed termination.

Compacts are describable as bilateral, multilateral, sectional, and national in terms of geographical scope. A compact-created commission or a department in each member state administers twenty-five types of compacts covering most of the alphabet ranging from agriculture to water. There has been a decline in the number of regulatory compacts since 1965, when Congress commenced more frequently to enact preemption statutes removing authority totally or partially from states in specified regulatory fields.

The first federal-interstate compact—establishing a national-state partnership—became effective in 1961 when the Delaware River Basin Compact was enacted into law by Congress and the Delaware, New Jersey, New York, and Pennsylvania state legislatures. Subsequently, Congress enacted five additional federal-interstate compacts.

Compacts have been supplemented by numerous verbal and written agreements entered into by high-level state administrative officers, particularly department heads. Many interstate administrative agreements are of great importance and include ones on the same subjects as compacts. The Connecticut River Basin Atlantic Salmon Restoration Interstate Compact was enacted by the Connecticut, Massachusetts, New Hampshire, and Vermont state legislatures. A identically worded interstate administrative agreement—the Merrimack River Anadromous Fish Restoration Administrative Agreement—was signed by Massachusetts and New Hampshire officers. Congressional consent for the compact lapsed in 2001 and was not renewed by Congress until the following year. The administrative agreement is not dependent upon congressional consent for continuation.

INTERSTATE DISPUTES

A proposal was made at the 1787 Constitutional Convention to establish a national court system, but opposition to such a national system was strong. Two arguments convinced delegates to include a provision creating the U.S. Supreme Court. First, proponents contended it was essential to have an impartial court to interpret the provisions of the Constitution. Second, they maintained that a supreme court was needed to adjudicate interstate disputes involving boundaries and other matters. Section 2 of Article III grants the Court nonexclusive original (trial) jurisdiction, which was made exclusive by Congress in 1789, over interstate suits.

The Court exercises its jurisdiction on a discretionary basis involving determinations of whether the state initiating the suit is a genuine or a nominal party representing private interests, the controversy is justiciable because the complaining state suffered a wrong, and the dispute is appropriate as determined by its seriousness, the parties to the dispute, and the availability of a alternative judicial forum. Suits most commonly involve boundaries, taxation, and water. The Court's decisions represent a blend of the English common law and international law.

FULL FAITH AND CREDIT

Section 1 of Article IV of the Constitution stipulates each state must accord full faith and credit to the public acts (statutes), records (deeds, mortgages, and wills), and judicial proceedings (final court judgments) of sister states, and authorizes Congress to determine the manner in which they "shall be proved and the effect thereof." The provision does not apply to public acts, records, or judicial proceedings of foreign nations.

Congressional statutes enacted in 1790 and 1804 prescribe the method of authenticating sister state civil acts and records. A state legislature may enact a statute containing less stringent authentication standards. Congress did not enact another full faith and credit statute until the Full Faith and Credit for Child Support Act of 1994 and the Defense of Marriage Act of 1996.

The failure of Congress to enact additional full faith and credit statutes until 1994 led to the Supreme Court issuing a series of decisions clarifying the constitutional command. Early decisions declared that a state constitution is a public act entitled to full faith and credit, the guarantee applies only to civil acts and proceedings, and the clause requires each state to recognize the decisions of sister state courts provided they have jurisdiction over the subject matter and the parties to the dispute. The Court acknowledged in 1935 that an accommodation was needed when the statutes of 2 states conflict, but in 1939 opined that a court no longer has to consider the conflicting interests of a sister state.

Historically, the clause became the basis for suits relating to the question of whether a state must recognize a divorce granted to one of its citizens by a sister state court where grounds for divorce were not limited to adultery. This question seldom is raised today because most state legislatures have broadened the grounds for the granting of a divorce, thereby removing a reason for a party seeking a divorce to travel to a state with less stringent grounds. Full faith and credit, however, increasingly has become important with respect to the interstate enforcement of child support orders issued by state courts. The National Conference of Uniform State Law Commissioners drafted in 1950 the Uniform Reciprocal Enforcement of Support Act, which was amended in 1958 and 1968, and all states have enacted a version of the act. As noted, Congress enacted a statute in 1994 facilitating the out-of-state collection of child support payments by the custodial parent.

PRIVILEGES AND IMMUNITIES

Section 2 of Article IV of the Constitution contains the Privileges and Immunities Clause designed to promote interstate citizenship by ensuring that sojourners are treated in the same manner as the state's citizens. An identically worded section in the Fourteenth Amendment forbids each state to abridge the privileges and immunities of citizens of the United States. Neither section defines the terms. In common with the full faith and credit provision, the privileges and immunities provision involves a conflict of laws. Each state legislature in defining privileges and immunities is subject to only one restraint; the definition may not reduce those guaranteed by the Fourteenth Amendment. Congress has not clarified the terms. Distinctions had been made in state law between citizens and residents, but the Supreme Court in 1975 ruled the terms are interchangeable.

The clause does not contain an absolute guarantee and has been emasculated to a large extent by Supreme Court decisions. In 1839, the Court opined in *Bank of Augusta v. Earle* that a corporation cannot migrate from the state of its creation to another state and hence is not entitled to privileges and immunities. The Court in 1928 extended this ruling to associations. A state is free to discriminate against foreign (chartered in another state) and alien (chartered in a foreign country) corporations in terms of fees and taxes, and may prohibit them from conducting business in the state without violating the Article IV Privileges and Immunities Clause. Such discrimination, however, may violate the Interstate Commerce and Due Process of Law Clauses of the Constitution.

The Court also has held that the clause is inapplicable to beneficial services—state institutions and resources—and a state legislature may charge out-of-state students at its state university a higher tuition fee compared to in-state students and may impose higher fishing and hunting fees on nonresidents. The state legislature also may exclude the latter from political and certain other privileges such as voting and admission to the state bar. In 1978, the court opined that a New York law requiring members of the state police to be U.S. citizens was constitutional.

INTERSTATE RENDITION

A person accused of committing a crime can be tried and punished only in the state in which the crime was committed. Such a person while on bail may flee the state to avoid a trial and possible confinement in a prison. Similarly, a convict on bail pending sentencing also may flee, and a convict may escape from a prison. Section 2 of Article IV of the Constitution establishes the general process by which a fugitive from justice is returned from a sister state. Only the governor of a state may demand the return a fugitive.

Congress enacted the Rendition Act of 1793, extending the process to the District of Columbia and territories and stipulating that the demand is made upon the governor of the asylum state who is responsible for arresting the fugitive and returning him or her to the demanding state. It is immaterial whether the involved crime is a crime in the asylum state, but the fugitive has the right to a hearing before the governor and an appeal to the courts if the governor orders the fugitive rendered against his or her will. The demanding state is responsible for all expenses incurred in returning the fugitive, and a state legislature may enact a rendition statute not conflicting with the congressional act. Only Mississippi has not enacted the Uniform Criminal Extradition Act (1936) drafted by the National Conference of Commissioners on Uniform Laws.

The Supreme Court in 1861 for the first time interpreted the constitutional provision and the 1793 statute in *Kentucky v. Dennison*, and ruled the governor of the asylum state has only a moral obligation to return a fugitive demanded by a sister state governor. This decision remained in effect for 126 years, during which several governors refused to return fugitives on the ground that the governor of the requesting state at an earlier date had not honored the demand to render a fugitive on various grounds, including the contention that he or she would not receive a fair trial in the requesting state. In 1987, the Court in *Puerto Rico v. Branstad* reversed its precedent, and the duty of the asylum state governor to return a fugitive became a mandatory one.

Should a fugitive from justice commit a crime in an asylum state, he or she will be subject to a trial, and if tried and convicted must serve a prison sentence prior to his or her return to the requesting state. A congressional statute makes it a federal criminal offense for a person to travel to a sister state or to a foreign nation for the purpose of avoiding prosecution or imprisonment. If apprehended for violating this statute, the person is transported to the U.S. District Court in whose jurisdiction the felony was committed and may be turned over to the control of an appropriate state officer.

The Interstate Agreement on Detainers (1970); a interstate compact enacted by 47 states and the District of Columbia, establishes a process similar to interstate rendition for prisoners in a state who have been charged with committing one or more crimes in another state (or states). Based upon the adage "Justice delayed is justice denied," the agreement provides for a speedy trial by authorizing the transportation of the prisoner to the temporary custody of a sister state for a trial and his or her return after conclusion of the trial.

INTERSTATE TRADE BARRIERS

States have engaged in economic protectionism since the adoption of the Articles of Confederation and Perpetual Union by erecting obstacles to the free flow of commerce. Such barriers were a principal reason advanced for the replacement of the Articles by the U.S. Constitution. Although the latter seeks to establish a economic union, interstate trade barriers continue to be erected.

A common barrier is based upon the police power of a state allowing it to regulate persons and property in order to promote public health, safety, welfare, morals, and convenience. This power is utilized for legitimate purposes in most instances, but occasionally has been employed to create a barrier, as illustrated by a requirement that only eggs laid within the state may be labeled fresh eggs.

A state legislature may use its licensing and taxing powers to hinder the free movement of interstate trade by refusing to issue or delaying the issuance of a license to a foreign or alien corporation, or by imposing higher taxes on them compared to domestic corporations. States as proprietors may erect barriers in the form of statutes granting preferences to their citizens and domestic corporations with respect to public employment and state contracts for goods and services.

Interstate reciprocity statutes and administrative agreements, congressional preemption statutes, and judicial decisions may be employed to remove impediments to interstate commerce. There would be less need for courts to adjudicate suits alleging that a state created a trade barrier if Congress exercised more fully its delegated powers, particularly in the area of taxation of multistate and multinational corporations.

COMPETITION FOR BUSINESS FIRMS AND TAX REVENUE

Railroads and public utility companies offered manufacturers incentives in the nineteenth century to locate new plants in areas the companies serviced. State competition for industrial firms did not become common until the immediate post–World War II period. Understandably, state and local elected leaders desire to maximize employment opportunities for their citizens and tax revenues, and offer incentives—grants, low-interest loans, tax abatements, tax credits, and so on—to encourage business firms to expand within the state or local government and to attract foreign and alien corporations to construct and operate facilities. Critics of incentives maintain they discriminate against domestic companies not planning to expand, benefit firms that in many instances would expand without incentives, deprive the governments of revenue needed for more important programs, and may fail in encouraging existing companies to expand or in attracting new companies because the state or local government suffers serious locational disadvantages.

The development of the railroad and subsequently the motor vehicle engendered interstate competition for tourists, and in the latter decades of the twentieth century a increasing number of states and local governments competed for gamblers as revenue sources. Competition for tourists has not generated a major controversy, but the attempt to attract gamblers is opposed by a number of religious and other groups fearful of the corrupting influence of gambling and the crime associated with it. A more recent development is competition for major league sports franchises and the allegation frequently is made a franchise owner may play one large city off against another in order to obtain expansion and modernization of a stadium or construction of a new one.

States export taxes to increase revenues by imposing higher rates on alien and foreign corporations operating in the state; special taxes on hotels, motels, restaurant meals, and visiting professional athletes; and severance taxes on natural resources such as coal, natural gas, oil, and timber, and by using special income tax apportionment formulas for multistate and multinational corporations.

If challenged, a court may invalidate a tax if it imposes a serious burden on interstate commerce. Congress could regulate this type of tax revenue competition, but did not enact the first such statute until 1959 and has enacted only a few additional statutes to invalidate state taxation statutes discriminating against interstate commerce.

Cooperative, conflictive, and competitive interstate relations will continue to be features of the U.S. federal system, with Congress and federal courts playing important interstate roles. *SEE ALSO:* Citizenship; Commerce among the States; Eleventh Amendment; Federal Courts; Fourteenth Amendment; Full Faith and Credit Clause: Article IV, Section 1; Governors and Federalism; Interstate Compacts; Interstate Relations; Interstate Renditions; Local Government; Political Parties; Police Power; Preemption; Privileges and Immunities Clause: Article IV; Roosevelt, Franklin D.; State Courts; State Legislatures

BIBLIOGRAPHY: Frederick L. Zimmerman and Mitchell Wendell, *The Law and Use of Interstate Compacts* (Lexington, KY: Council of State Governments, 1976); Joseph F. Zimmerman, *Interstate Cooperation: Compacts and Administrative Agreements* (Westport, CT: Praeger, 2002); Joseph F. Zimmerman, *Interstate Economic Relations* (Albany: State University of New York Press, 2004); and Joseph F. Zimmerman, *Interstate Relations: The Neglected Dimension of Federalism* (Westport, CT: Praeger, 1996).

Joseph F. Zimmerman

Interstate Rendition   This process must be distinguished from extradition, the process by which fugitives from justice are returned by one nation to another nation under the provisions of a treaty. A rendition process is essential in a confederacy where states are sovereign or in a federation where states are semisovereign. The U.S. Constitution (Article IV, Section 2) established the current interstate rendition system and based it upon a similar provision in the Articles of Confederation and Perpetual Union (Article IV, Section 2).

Although the Constitution does not specifically authorize Congress to amplify the constitutional clause, Congress enacted the Rendition Act of 1793 (1 Stat. 302) detailing the procedure. The constitutional provision refers only to states, but Congress included districts and territories in the act and made the demanding state responsible for sending an officer or officers to escort the fugitive's return and all costs associated with the arrest, incarceration, and transportation of a fugitive from justice.

The rendition procedure is as follows: (1) a fugitive from justice may be rendered for any offense made punishable by the demanding state regardless of whether the action constituting the crime is a crime in the asylum state, (2) only the governor can demand the governor of the asylum state to apprehend and return the fugitive, (3) the latter's duty to return the fugitive is mandatory and ministerial, and (4) the fugitive may exercise his or her due process of law right to appeal to the courts to secure justice.

Neither the constitutional clause nor the act refers to enforcement, although the duty imposed upon the asylum state governor appears to be mandatory. It was not until 1861, immediately prior to the outbreak of the Civil War, that the U.S. Supreme Court clarified in *Kentucky v. Dennison* (65 U.S. 66) the constitutional and statutory provisions. Kentucky sought to invoke the Court's original jurisdiction in an attempt to obtain a writ of *mandamus* requiring the Ohio governor to render Dennison, a freed slave, who had been charged with the crime of assisting a slave to escape from Kentucky. The Ohio attorney general issued an opinion to Dennison holding that the constitutional Rendition Clause pertains only to acts that are crimes under Ohio statutes.

The Court, after careful examination of the pertinent constitutional clause and the 1793 statute, rejected Ohio's contention and opined, "The act does not provide any means to complete the execution of this duty, nor inflict any punishment for neglect or refusal on the part of the Executive of the state; nor is there any clause or provision in the constitution which arms the Government of the United States with this power." While acknowledging that the constitutional duty of the asylum state governor is a mandatory one, the Court concluded that U.S. courts did not possess the authority to issue a writ of *mandamus* to compel a governor to perform a ministerial duty.

Subsequently, a governor on occasion refused to return a fugitive to the demanding state and thereby generated bad relations with it, leading in several instances to retaliation in the form of the refusal to honor the request of the governor of the state whose governor refused to return a fugitive in the past.

In 1893, the Court held in *Lascellas v. Georgia* (184 U.S. 537) that a fugitive rendered to stand trial for an offense listed in the rendition request could be tried upon return to the demanding state for all crimes committed within its jurisdiction and subsequently could be rendered to other states to stand trial for crimes committed in those states. The Court in *Pettibone v. Nichols* (203 U.S. 192) in 1906 opined there was no constitutional or statutory provision providing for the return of a fugitive from justice to the asylum state who had been returned to the demanding state by fraud, perjury, or violence.

Surprisingly, the Court did not readdress the question of the duty of the asylum state governor until 1987, when it opined in *Puerto Rico v. Branstad* (489 U.S. 219) that the governor's duty to return a fugitive from justice to the demanding state was mandatory. The Court concluded, "Considered *de novo*, there is no justification for distinguishing the duty to deliver fugitives from the many other species of constitutional duty enforceable in the federal courts."

An interstate compact, the Interstate Agreement on Detainers, contains provisions somewhat similar to those involved in the rendition of fugitives from justice. The purpose of the agreement is to ensure that prisoners in one state charged with the commission of crimes in another state (or states) are not deprived of their speedy trial right. Under the agreement, a prisoner with an untried indictment, information, or complaint must be notified and be brought to trial within 180 days after the prosecuting officer has received written notice of his or her place of imprisonment and his or her request for a final disposition of the indictment, information, or complaint. The state officer in charge of the prisoner's custody must deliver the prisoner for temporary custody in the requesting state. Upon completion of the trial, the requesting state returns the prisoner. *SEE ALSO:* Articles of Confederation; Federal Courts; Fugitive Slave Acts

BIBLIOGRAPHY: James A. Scott, *The Law of Interstate Rendition Erroneously Referred to as Interstate Extradition: A Treatise* (Chicago: Sherman Hight, 1971); Joseph F. Zimmerman, *Interstate Cooperation: Compacts and Agreements* (Westport, CT: Praeger, 2002); and Joseph F. Zimmerman, *Interstate Relations: The Neglected Dimension of Federalism* (Westport, CT: Praeger, 1996).

JOSEPH F. ZIMMERMAN

Jackson, Andrew   Andrew Jackson's (1767–1845) personality and two presidencies remain mired in controversy. Admirers saw him as embodying the democratic virtues of the West, a rough-and-tumble backwoodsman, Indian fighter, hardworking farmer, tenacious general, and defender of women—the logical culmination of the triumph of democratic values in the United States. His detractors portrayed him as uneducated, violent, and vengeful, a slaveholder and Indian hater, and the personification of the politics of mediocrity. He moved to Charleston while still a teen, where he imitated the manners of the gentry, indulging in gambling, horse racing, and cockfighting. He also studied law, and shortly after admission to the bar settled in Nashville, Tennessee, where he went to work for creditors, engaged in land speculation, and took up politics. Among the offices he held were U.S. attorney, congressman, and justice of the Tennessee Supreme Court—all before age 31. Also an army general, he became a national hero following his victory at the Battle of New Orleans in 1815.

Jackson believed that the election of 1824 was stolen from him by a deal between rivals John Quincy Adams and Henry Clay. That campaign and its 1828 successor were characterized by vicious mudslinging by both camps, reflecting a surge in popular participation in politics. Jackson's victory in 1828 was part of a democratic trend in politics inspired by the economic panic of 1819, which many blamed on the tight money policies followed by the Bank of the United States. Voter apathy gave way to renewed interest in the issues that directly affected them: monetary policy, eastern dominance, high tariffs, and public land policy. These concerns led to the abolition of property qualifications for voting, the end of the caucus system, greater numbers of elected officials, and the disestablishment of churches.

The guiding principle of the Jackson presidencies was that government intervention on behalf of the interests of the rich had to be stopped. This so-called money power was resented particularly in the West, where it was regarded as an alien force controlled by wealthy Easterners. The Jacksonian movement set its sight on annulling the marriage between big business and government, a relationship that spawned government favoritism toward the wealthy. Jackson saw his vetoes against the rechartering of the Bank of the United States, the federal purchase of stock in a Kentucky turnpike corporation, and the Marysville Road Bill as part of a broader struggle between the special privileges of the business community and the common good of the rest of society over who should control the state.

Though ideologically the Jacksonians were antistatist and paid homage to the Jeffersonian notion that the best government was one that governed least, they believed that the exercise of power on behalf of the community by a government consisting of "patriotic" people—the majority of average citizens—was permissible and necessary. Hence Jackson supported the Supreme Court's decision upholding the right of the state of Massachusetts to construct a free bridge over the Charles River at the expense of a privately owned bridge. The proper role for the state for Jackson depended on *who controlled it*. He believed that in promoting the happiness and prosperity of the community, the government never intended to curtail its power to implement those goals. Hence Jackson's position on the role of state intervention is not completely at odds with that of arch-Federalist Alexander Hamilton, who conditioned his support for wealthy entrepreneurs by using the federal government to channel their financial rapaciousness so as to benefit the nation and to speed up economic growth. To leave the business class entirely on its own, said Hamilton, "may be attended with pernicious effect." Jackson's rejection of the Federalist vision as articulated in Henry Clay's American System rested on his (mistaken) conviction that Federalist support of protective tariffs, the Bank of the United States, and internal improvements was meant solely to advance the interest of a privileged business class. Ironically, despite his antistatist credo, when Jackson left office the power of the federal government, especially its executive branch, was stronger than ever. By appealing to the people over the heads of Congress in his bank veto message and ending the legislative branch's power to select presidential candidates by "King Caucus," Jackson dramatically enhanced the powers of the presidency, leading his enemies to dub him "King Andrew."

Andrew Jackson. Library of Congress, Prints and Photographs Division.

Despite his aversion to state power, Jackson remained a staunch nationalist, dating from the American Revolution, when he was captured and mutilated by British troops at age 14, and witnessed the imprisonment and death of his two brothers and mother. Not surprisingly, then, when South Carolina claimed it could nullify the 1828 so-called Tariff of Abominations, Jackson asked Congress to authorize the federal government to use force, if necessary, to bring South Carolina back into the fold. Jackson's nationalism also played a significant part in his unwillingness to accept the Supreme Court's recognition of Cherokee sovereignty in *Worcester v. Georgia*, and in his willingness to allow state officials to override federal support for Cherokee land claims.

He eagerly signed the Indian Removal Act, forcing the Cherokee Nation to evacuate its ancestral lands and march on the Trail of Tears.

In the realms of morality and religion, Jacksonian Democrats tended to be the party of laissez-faire, and in contrast to the Federalists, were averse to government involvement in social and humanitarian reform. Jackson condemned public schooling for usurping parental responsibility, had few objections to slavery, and despised abolitionists.

While historians continue to argue over whether the main conflict in the Age of Jackson was between rich and poor (farmers and workers) or between old money and new, or was primarily a sectional dispute—West versus East—there is consensus that while loosening the hold of the Virginia dynasty, Jackson did not effect a political or social revolution. Jackson's call for rotating political offices—"in a country where offices are created solely for the benefit of the people no man has more intrinsic right to official station than any other"—was not implemented in practice. Hence, while the common man may have felt he was participating in government, for example, by being invited to Jackson's Inaugural, there was no significant redistribution of wealth under his presidencies, and despite a seeming deference to the common man, the uncommon men (of Jackson's "Kitchen Cabinet") continued to run things. *SEE ALSO:* Abolition; Adams, John; Admission of New States; *Charles River Bridge Company v. Warren Bridge Company*; Clay, Henry; Elections; Federalists; Hamilton, Alexander; Internal Improvements; Native Americans; Slavery; Sovereignty

BIBLIOGRAPHY: Richard Hofstadter, "Andrew Jackson and the Rise of the Capitalism," in *The American Political Tradition* (New York: Vintage Books, 1973); Edward Pressen, *Jacksonian America* (Urbana: University of Illinois Press, 1985); Robert Remini, *The Life of Andrew Jackson* (London: Penguin Books, 2001); Arthur Schlesinger, *The Age of Jackson* (New York: Mentor Books, 1945); Charles Sellers, *The Market Revolution: Jacksonian America* (New York: Oxford University Press, 1990); and Harry L. Watson, *Liberty and Power, The Politics of Jacksonian America* (New York: Hill and Wang, 1990).

HARVEY ASHER

Jefferson, Thomas   Thomas Jefferson, the third president of the United States, is an ironic political figure in the development of American federalism. Though Jefferson favored a stricter interpretation of the Constitution than his Federalist predecessors, his presidency dramatically expanded the powers of that office and the national government as a whole.

Jefferson was one of the chief architects of state-centered federalism, first articulated in the Virginia and Kentucky Resolutions of 1798. In resistance to the nationalist views of Alexander Hamilton and John Marshall, state-centered federalism operated from the premise that the Constitution was a product of state action because state representatives were responsible for the creation and ratification of the document. In turn, the Constitution protects state power through absolute limits on the powers of national government (Article I, Section 8, and the Tenth Amendment). As a result, a primary focus of citizens and government leaders should be to guard against any expansion of national power at the expense of the states.

Jefferson sought to impose this state-centered perspective through the Revolution of

Thomas Jefferson. Library of Congress, Prints and Photographs Division.

1800. Once in office, Jefferson reduced expenditures in all branches of government, replaced Federalists appointees with Republicans, and attempted to limit the powers of the Federalist-dominated judiciary. At the same time, each of his terms witnessed monumental expansions in the power of the national government. In 1803, the United States bought over 800,000 square miles of Louisiana territory in one of the largest land deals in American history. With no constitutional power for the national government to purchase new territory, the Louisiana Purchase directly contradicted Jefferson's governing philosophy. Faced with a unique opportunity to nearly double the country's land area and to preclude European expansion on the North American continent, Jefferson secured the deal despite his ideological predispositions.

The Napoleonic Wars further complicated Jefferson's desire for a limited national government. Although the wars created a high demand for goods, Britain, France, and United States all tried to block the others' trade. Jefferson signed the Nonimportatation Act (1806) and the Embargo Act (1807) to protect American merchants. The embargo prohibited all exports, but since foreign-bound ships were forced to depart empty, the act in effect limited imports as well. Jefferson hoped that resulting economic pressure would convince the British and French to mitigate their maritime policies. Domestically, the national government regulated foreign trade for the first time.

The Louisiana Purchase and Embargo Acts ran directly counter to Jefferson's desire for state-centered federalism. In theory, Jefferson favored the active protection of state power and the strict limitation of national power. In practice, Jefferson suspended strict constitutional construction in favor of expanding national boundaries and regulating international trade. As a result, Thomas Jefferson is remembered as an ironic figure in the development of American Federalism. *SEE ALSO:* Hamilton, Alexander; Federalists; Louisiana Purchase; Marshall, John; Presidency

BIBLIOGRAPHY: Andrew Burstein, *The Inner Jefferson: Portrait of a Grieving Optimist* (Charlottesville: University of Virginia Press, 1995); Joseph Ellis, *American Sphinx: The Character of Thomas Jefferson* (New York: Alfred Knopf, 1997); David Mayer, *The Constitutional Thought of Thomas Jefferson* (Charlottesville: University of Virginia, 1994); and Garrett Sheldon, *The Political Philosophy of Thomas Jefferson* (Baltimore: John Hopkins University Press, 1991).

LUKE PERRY

Johnson, Lyndon B. President Lyndon B. Johnson (1963–69) had a dramatic impact on federalism through a series of policy, regulatory, and fiscal initiatives broadly defined as the Great Society. During his administration, the federal government took a direct and active role in the policy problems of state and local governments. Specifically, as part of Johnson's Great Society a flurry of legislation was enacted that has permanently enhanced the role of the federal government and affected its relationship with state and local governments. Johnson's impact on federalism must be understood in terms of his commitment to fighting poverty and reducing racial injustice. Specifically, his administration was committed to finding "creative" ways to address issues of poverty and racial injustice, including encouraging state and local governments to address certain policy issues and providing federal support to do so, particularly at the local level. His landslide 1964 election, along with the election of a large Democratic majority in Congress who supported his vision, created a short-lived coalition that led to the rapid passage of an array of new intergovernmental programs to carry out his vision. These programs produced changes in every policy sphere, including health care, social welfare, transportation, the environment, housing, and crime and justice.

Several far-reaching pieces of legislation illustrate his impact on the federal system and exemplify his commitment to using the federal government to diminish differences among citizens. For example, during his administration laws such as the Voting Rights Act of 1965, the Civil Rights Act of 1964, and the Fair Housing Act were passed, which attempted to end racial discrimination by reducing state and local autonomy to pass discriminatory laws or conduct discriminatory policies. Further, Johnson and Congress created large new programs such as Medicaid, a joint state-federal program to provide health and long-term care insurance to poor citizens; the Elementary and Secondary Education Act of 1965, which provided federal financial aid to local school districts to help equalize funding differences among them; and the Model Cities program, along with large increases in aid to urban governments. In addition, Johnson created several new government agencies to support his vision of an expanded role for the federal government and assist state and local governments in addressing policy problems, including the Department of Transportation, the Department of Housing and Urban Development, and the Office of Economic Opportunity.

During Johnson's administration, federalism went through what experts have termed a "creative" phase that greatly expanded the federal government's role in state and local affairs. Specifically, three key features of federalism emerged in the creative phase: a proliferation of categori-

Lyndon B. Johnson. Library of Congress, Prints and Photographs Division.

cal project grants designed to provide financial support to states and localities in order to further national goals, enhanced program planning and a greater focus on administration, and increased citizen and interest group participation in intergovernmental affairs.

While there have been some high-profile attempts to undo some of the Great Society initiatives, such as President Ronald Reagan's New Federalism effort, many of the programs and policies of the Johnson administration continue to exist and still stimulate controversy, with critics arguing that during this period the federal government expanded its reach too far and fostered too much citizen dependence on government. Supporters argue that Johnson's more lasting programs have done much to improve the quality of life of the country's most vulnerable populations and recognize that serving these populations is a shared challenge among all levels of government. *SEE ALSO:* Civil Rights Act of 1964; Creative Federalism; Great Society; Voting Rights Acts of 1965

BIBLIOGRAPHY: David Walker, *The Rebirth of Federalism*, 2nd ed. (New York: Chatham House, 1999); and Deil S. Wright, *Understanding Intergovernmental Relations* (Pacific Grove, CA: Brooks/Cole Publishing, 1988).

THOMAS YATSCO

Judiciary Act of 1789, Section 25 After the first official U.S. Congress convened and quickly enacted legislation on the structure of the judicial branch, President George Washington signed the Judiciary Act of 1789, or "An Act to establish the Judicial Courts of the United States," into law on September 24, 1789. The federal statute elaborated on the limited language in the Constitution regarding the Supreme Court, outlined its jurisdiction, and enacted a system of lower federal courts. Within the thirty-five sections of the act was a hierarchy of federal courts. The U.S. Supreme Court, with its six justices, was at the top of this hierarchy. A two-tiered structure of inferior courts, with district courts in each state and circuit courts in each of three regional districts, composed the base of the federal judicial configuration. The Judiciary Act enabled review by the Supreme Court of lower federal court opinions and had provisions for review of state court decisions as well.

Under Section 25, the Court had jurisdiction over state supreme court decisions that passed on the validity of federal laws. This section of the Judiciary Act of 1789 provided a source of early controversy in constitutional politics. After establishing its right to judicial review in the landmark case *Marbury v. Madison* (1803), the Court used many of its initial decisions to define its authority and jurisdiction. Section 25 came into question in the Supreme Court case *Martin v. Hunter's Lessee* (1816). The state of Virginia refused to uphold a Marshall Court decision that reversed an earlier state ruling that dealt with the rights of a British subject under the Jay Treaty, which was ratified in 1975 and provided for the withdrawal of British troops from the American West and reparations for Loyalists' losses. While Virginia believed it to be bound by the Constitution, it also held to the notion that its interpretations of federal law were controlling in such matters. In *Martin*, Justice Joseph Story spoke for a unanimous Court when he reasserted the Court's jurisdiction over state court rulings contained in Section 25 of the Judiciary Act. Using the Constitution as his reasoning for upholding the statute, he stated that "the 25th section of the judiciary act . . . is supported by the letter and spirit of the constitution." Upheld by the Court in *Martin*, Section 25 of the Judiciary Act of 1789 thus established the jurisdiction of the Supreme Court over state courts on issues of federal law that is still maintained today. *SEE ALSO: Martin v. Hunter's Lessee*

BIBLIOGRAPHY: Lawrence Baum, *The Supreme Court*, 8th ed. (Washington, DC: CQ Press, 2003); Dwight F. Henderson, *Courts for a New Nation* (Washington, DC: Public Affairs Press, 1971); David M. O'Brien, *Constitutional Law and Politics, Vol. 1: Struggles for Power and Governmental Accountability* (New York: W.W. Norton, 2003); and Bernard Schwartz, *A History of the Supreme Court* (New York: Oxford University Press, 1993).

D. STEVEN CRONIN